More Advance Praise for *India Is Broken*

"This book is the most sustained, accessible, and trenchantly argued alternative account of India's political economy and democratic crisis that I have seen in many years. Engaging and well written, it tells a striking and disturbing story. A major achievement."
—Thomas Blom Hansen, author of *Melancholia of Freedom: The Social Life of an Indian Township in South Africa*

"This is a dazzling book with an ambitious arc. The juncture India stands at today is seen ever more clearly in Ashoka Mody's gripping narration. I have rarely experienced history as such a powerful tool. Compellingly written, the book coheres around a central thread that runs right through until the very last line: can India yet deliver on the hope of 1947? It is a tale tinged with sadness, a sense of loss at what might have been."
—Kavitha Iyer, author of *Landscapes of Loss: The Story of an Indian Drought*

"Mody's book traverses the entire sweep of independent India to show us how we ended up here—struggling economy, soaring unemployment, fractured society—and how to find a way out. All through, it makes a resonating connection between high-level economic and political discourse and the real lives of Indians, especially young Indians. *India Is Broken* is as absorbing as it is ambitious."
—Snigdha Poonam, author of *Dreamers: How Young Indians Are Changing Their World*

"In *India Is Broken,* Ashoka Mody writes a readable, comprehensive, though depressing history of what has gone wrong with the Indian economy. The book is a devastating take-no-prisoners indictment of the policies of successive governments. While you may not agree with the relentless criticism, and while the book is light on prescriptions, it is a must read for anyone who wants to understand India's challenges today and their roots in the past."
—Raghuram Rajan, University of Chicago and former Governor of the Reserve Bank of India.

INDIA IS BROKEN

INDIA IS BROKEN

A People Betrayed, Independence to Today

ASHOKA MODY

STANFORD UNIVERSITY PRESS
Stanford, California

STANFORD UNIVERSITY PRESS
Stanford, California

Printed in the United States of America on acid-free, archival-quality paper

Library of Congress Cataloging-in-Publication Data

Names: Mody, Ashoka, author.
Title: India is broken : a people betrayed, independence to today / Ashoka Mody.
Description: Stanford, California : Stanford University Press, 2023. | Includes bibliographical references and index.
Identifiers: LCCN 2022019311 (print) | LCCN 2022019312 (ebook) | ISBN 9781503630055 (cloth) | ISBN 9781503634220 (ebook)
Subjects: LCSH: India—Economic conditions—1947- | India—Economic policy—1947- | India—Politics and government—1947-
Classification: LCC HC435.2 .M63 2023 (print) | LCC HC435.2 (ebook) | DDC 330.954—dc23/eng/20220609
LC record available at https://lccn.loc.gov/2022019311
LC ebook record available at https://lccn.loc.gov/2022019312

Cover photos: (top) Alamy; (lower) Sujata Mody, Penn Thozhilalargal Sangam Archive

Typeset at Newgen in 11.5/15 Arno Pro

Printed and bound by CPI Group (UK) Ltd, Croydon, CR0 4YY

To

Krishnan and Lakshman

My sons, my best friends, in gratitude for their free tech support

TABLE OF CONTENTS

PART III: THE PROMISE, 1985–2004

PART IV: HUBRIS, 2005 TO THE PRESENT

PREFACE

In the decades since independence, India's achievements have fueled a narrative of a country on the rise. In awe-inspiring displays since 1951, hundreds of millions of Indians have gone to the polls every five years to select their leaders. Starting in the 1980s, India also captured the world's imagination as a potential economic superpower. Indian students excelled at top American and British universities. Indian information technology companies and customer-service agents on telephone helplines became commonplace. Soon, Indians occupied positions of great prominence at leading international companies. In 2004, U.S. presidential hopeful John Kerry tried to shock his fellow Americans by asserting that internet connectivity in the southern Indian city of Bangalore was superior to that in many American cities and towns. And although India's GDP growth began collapsing in 2018, India's image as a rapidly emerging player on the global stage persisted. Internationally recognizable and acclaimed Indians grew in number. Analyzing the COVID-19 crisis in 2020 and after, doctors of Indian origin were ubiquitous commentators on American television.

International observers and Indian pundits have long predicted that democratic India's plodding economic "tortoise" will outpace authoritarian China's cocky "hare." The world's largest democracy as an economic superpower is a tantalizing prospect—not just for Indian citizens but for the world, which would gain a crucial counterweight to the Chinese economic and geopolitical juggernaut.

The story in this book starts at the hopeful moment when India gained its independence from British colonial rule in 1947. After the horror of the bloody partition of British India into the new Indian and Pakistani states, desperately poor and largely illiterate Indians were anxious to move on. Death rates were falling because of improved management of famines and more widespread availability of medicines that had controlled disease epidemics in Europe. With lower death rates, the number of young Indians looking for jobs surged. Indian leaders and policymakers had one task above all: to create jobs for vast numbers of people. The political response to the employment-creation challenge is the central thread that holds this book together.

From the start, jobs grew slowly. By the second half of the 1960s, frustration with life's hardships provoked widespread anger. Unable to pacify that anger, Prime Minister Indira Gandhi began moving toward authoritarianism in the late 1960s, culminating in "Emergency Rule" from June 1975 to March 1977. Although the formality of democracy returned after twenty-one months, the fabric of social trust and the spirit of democracy continued to erode. Corruption lodged itself at the highest levels of government, abuse of the state's coercive power grew, and violence to advance narrow interests and win arguments became commonplace. Short-term focus on headline-grabbing policies caused a neglect—even abuse—of the public goods essential for good jobs and human welfare: education, health, vibrant cities, a fair judicial system, and a clean environment.

Even as India's poor job creation and high inflation persisted, East Asian nations, armed with heavy investments in human capital and urban development, established internationally competitive economies that generated near-full employment.

Starting in the mid-1980s, a small group of Indians amassed fabulous fortunes. Simultaneously, the direst forms of poverty began declining. But hundreds of millions of Indians continued to live precarious lives, keeping their heads just above basic sustenance levels. Persistent social anger fed criminal networks and sustained "angry Hindu" mobs. Hindu nationalism marked a further tear in the social fabric as violent mobs sought new performance arenas.

Today, as of the writing of this book, it is seventy-five years after Independence, and India's democracy and economy are broken. V-Dem, an academic think tank based in Sweden, categorizes India as an "electoral autocracy," a nation that holds elections but where the rule of law and freedom of speech have fallen to unacceptably low levels. COVID-19 revealed the fragility of the Indian economy, which crashed as the first wave of the disease struck. Of the hundred million jobs that disappeared, twenty-five million or more may never come back. More jobs disappeared in the pandemic's second wave. These losses have piled on to a large backlog of unfulfilled demand for jobs, and as new batches of young Indians enter the job pipeline, they face the specter of a precarious future. "India has an employment crisis" is a common refrain.

This book is a history to inform the present. Although I have written the book from the perspective of successive Indian leaders, my tale is one of continuous erosion of social norms and decay of political accountability. Weakened norms and accountability have made the rules and institutions of democracy a plaything of the privileged and powerful; cooperation is severely lacking in the delivery of quality education, health, and urban spaces for all; justice is no longer blind and rampant environmental damage is ferociously amplifying the damage from the ongoing climate crisis. And since restoration of norms and accountability requires accountability, India is in a classic Catch-22 situation.

It is easy, but incorrect, to lay the blame for India's troubles on its abhorrent caste system. India is in a Catch-22 because it fell victim to universal moral failures: corruption, blurring of lines between criminals and politicians, and social violence. Once key events injected these afflictions into politics and society, it became easier to keep making the wrong choice at every opportunity for change.[1]

India can emerge from this trap only by recognizing that the economy is a moral universe whose inhabitants flourish when social norms foster trust and long-term cooperation. The economy is not a machine with people as cogs and gears that respond benignly to clever shifts in policy levers by skilled engineers. Without trust and cooperation, the best policies and technologies will disappoint endlessly.

The book narrates India's story chronologically to ensure that I do not use hindsight to second-guess choices made by leaders and officials. The chronology also places a spotlight on particular moments at which events and choices critically shaped the future. While the personalities and words of leaders loom large, I often use vignettes from creative ethnographic writings to portray how Indians—especially young Indians—live. I also draw on Indian cinema for its invaluable social and cultural commentary. Statistical charts clear the fog of false narratives and discipline the analysis, an approach I learned during my quarter century as an international civil servant.

I hope anyone interested in modern Indian history or, indeed, in the history of economic development will find the book accessible and informative. When I write, I always wonder what questions my students will ask. To students everywhere, I hope you will find some of your questions answered and that you will be intrigued by new ideas. To scholars, I have tried to fairly represent your work and suggest avenues for more research.

I was born and raised in India but have lived and worked in the United States for nearly forty years. Some years ago, I had to give up my Indian citizenship to become a U.S. citizen. When I called my father to tell him of the emotional rupture I felt, he unhesitatingly reassured me, "You will always be an Indian at heart." It is that Indian-at-heart you hear in these pages.

INDIA IS BROKEN

Chapter 1
THEN AND NOW, AN INTRODUCTION

An exodus of distraught villagers, fleeing their parched farms, staggers toward Calcutta. "*Woh raha Kulkutta* [There lies Calcutta]," a haggard young farmer says, pointing with hope to the city on the horizon. The hope in his eyes quickly turns to fear of what the city may bring.

The historic city Calcutta, capital of the eastern state of Bengal, does crush the hopes of the villagers. The city offers the squalor of the footpath for a home. The specter of death continues to haunt. There are no jobs. The rich are garishly materialistic. The powerful in the city—as in the villages left behind—exploit helpless women with a cynical sense of privilege. Hence, when famine conditions ease, many who survived their trek to Calcutta and its harsh life return to their villages. For India's most vulnerable people, there is no home, no gainful work, no dignity. The reverse trek—from the city to the village—is the expression of that despair.

These scenes are from the movie *Dharti ke lal* (Children of the Earth), a 1946 portrayal of the 1943 Bengal famine. In discussing the movie, the twenty-seven-year-old emerging cinematic genius Satyajit Ray wrote, "The raw material of cinema is life itself."[1]

Touching gingerly on one of India's deepest wounds, the movie showed segregated relief kitchens for Hindus and Muslims. The partition of British-governed India into India and Pakistan was approaching.

The reality was forbidding. In August 1946, coinciding closely with the release of *Dharti ke lal,* Hindus and Muslims slaughtered each other, leaving between five thousand and ten thousand dead in the "Great Calcutta Killing." A year later, with partition now imminent, millions—Hindus toward India and Muslims toward Pakistan—crossed the eastern India-Pakistan border that ran through the state of Bengal. Mohandas Karamchand Gandhi—Mahatma Gandhi or simply the Mahatma, the great soul—prevented another episode of disastrous blood shedding. He gathered Hindu and Muslim Bengali leaders in Calcutta. Together they sat through daily prayer meetings and walked the streets in demonstration of communal solidarity. But Hindu-Muslim violence took on epic proportions on the western border running through the state of Punjab.[2]

In that moment of shame there was also political inspiration. Just before midnight on August 15, 1947, as brutalities raged in Punjab, Indian prime minister Jawaharlal Nehru spoke to the sovereign Constituent Assembly in the Indian parliament. To the new India, with 70 percent of its 360 million people depending on a fickle agriculture for their livelihoods, Nehru made a promise: India's democracy would work to honor the Mahatma's pledge, to "wipe every tear from every eye."[3]

Indian leaders quickly established a nation based on high principles. The Constituent Assembly enacted the Indian Constitution, which gave every adult a vote and established the essential institutions of a modern democracy. A determined effort brought more than five hundred previously disjointed princely kingdoms into the Indian union. India's early leaders emphasized religious tolerance. The goals of national unity and a secular democracy soaked into the national psyche and influenced the outlook and values of many Indians across generations.

Independence also brought material gains. After stagnating in the half century before the British left, average incomes of Indians increased, gradually at first and more rapidly after the mid-1980s, when millions of Indians emerged from severe poverty.

Yet the gains were tenuous. While poverty fell alongside high GDP growth rates achieved after the mid-1980s, a question mark hangs over the extent of the achievement. The difficulty arises in defining *who* is poor. Analysts had long followed the World Bank convention that a person was poor if he or she was unable to spend even $1.90 a day on consumption needs. By that definition, 22 percent of Indians in 2011 were poor. But by then India had graduated from a low- to a lower-middle-income country. And with the rise in income and life's complexities, the social benchmarks of humane existence had increased, which meant that $1.90 per day was no longer sufficient to buy minimally acceptable necessities. In 2017, the World Bank acknowledged that people living in lower-middle-income countries needed at least $3.20 a day to meet their essential needs, and it computed new poverty estimates for previous years. By that more reasonable definition, India's poverty rate was 60 percent, rather than 22 percent, in 2011.[4] I refer to the 38 percent of Indians who lived in the zone between the two poverty lines—the old $1.90/day and the new $3.20/day—as the precariously poor. Such families were typically one illness or one job loss away from falling back below the miserly $1.90/day poverty threshold. In India's precarious zone lived hundreds of millions of farmers, construction workers, and low-skilled service-sector workers. Over time, matters became worse. An official 2017–2018 survey—which the government tried to suppress—showed that even the share of those living below the dire, $1.90/day line had crept up.

By my analysis, the illusion of economic dynamism burst in August 2018, when the finance-construction bubble deflated. Soon after, Indian democracy also suffered a grievous, possibly irreversible, blow, when money, muscle, and Hindu nationalism won the vote in the 2019 election.

In January 2020, a new coronavirus entered India: SARS-CoV-2, which caused the disease known as COVID-19. On the evening of March 24, 2020, Prime Minister Narendra Modi announced that, starting at midnight, the country would be locked down for the next three weeks. Severely restricting the movement of people was necessary, he insisted, to prevent the spread of the highly contagious and lethal coronavirus. On April 14, Modi extended the lockdown. By now, the virus was unforgivingly exposing an India in 2020 that had troubling echoes from Bengal in the 1940s.[5]

As in Calcutta then, cities now were inhospitable to rural migrants. Now, the scale was much larger and made horrifying by the lockdown. Even in Delhi, one of India's richest cities, migrants from rural areas "survived in the nooks and crannies, picking up whatever [job] came their way—construction, plumbing, loading goods, pitching tents for events." They earned a wage on the days they got work. Since the lockdown began, they had yet to earn a rupee. They had no social safety net and wanted to return home to their villages and families. But the lockdown prevented travel. The "garbage- and excreta-laden banks" of the river Yamuna on the outskirts of Delhi filled up with "men who could not go home."[6]

Delhi's trapped migrants were but a small fraction of India's one hundred million "temporary" migrants, about 20 percent of the nation's workers. Such rootless Indians were mostly men who had moved from their villages to cities in the hope of beginning better lives. Often as many as seven shared a single room to sleep at night. Whenever they could, but especially at harvest time, they returned to their village families and homes. The luckier migrants, who had moved as families to places such as Mumbai's iconic slum Dharavi, congregated—commonly between five and ten of them—to live and work in one room. They queued up in long lines to use public toilets located alongside open sewers. Now, as work and incomes vanished, about 150,000 of Dharavi's one million residents joined the swelling reverse treks from hostile cities to far-flung villages.[7]

As reports of panicked migrants spread, the government turned on its media critics, accusing them of spreading "fake news." Prime Minister Modi summoned owners and editors of print media organizations and asked them to publish "positive stories" of the government's efforts to contain the crisis. The Supreme Court echoed the government's narrative that the media's "fake news" was a "menace." Most journalists followed the court's instruction to shade the dark reality with the upbeat official accounts.[8]

On April 10, 2020, the government of Uttar Pradesh ordered the police to press criminal charges against Siddharth Varadarajan, editor of the online news portal *The Wire,* for reporting fake news. *The Wire* had mistakenly attributed a statement to the chief minister Yogi Adityanath. Although Varadarajan quickly corrected the error and reposted the article, Uttar Pradesh police served him with a notice of criminal investigation. The flutter about misquotation distracted attention from Chief Minister Adityanath's COVID-related transgressions. Two weeks earlier, he had twice violated social distancing guidelines, both times in the cause of Hindu religious priorities.[9]

The Hindu-Muslim divide of yesteryear had reemerged in virulent form. Even as the Yogi (as he was commonly known) displayed an assertive Hindu religiosity, Hindu fanatics—backed by the state—targeted the Tablighi Jamaat, an Islamic evangelical organization whose members had met in various parts of the country in February and March. On March 23, the day before Modi's lockdown directive, they had convened at a seminary in Nizamuddin West in Delhi and in the following days some members of the Jamaat died from COVID-19. The police accused Jamaat members of causing a spike in COVID-19 cases and arrested some of them. The virus of hate spread. Across much of the northern belt but also in the southern state of Karnataka, attacks against Muslims surged. In the eastern state of Jharkhand, a pregnant and bleeding Muslim woman was beaten and turned away from a hospital. She lost her child. In Ahmedabad, Gujarat's largest city, a government-run hospital segregated coronavirus patients by religion.[10]

And economic inequalities now had become much wider. With exquisite timing, on April 22, four weeks into the lockdown, *Vogue India* invited its readers into another Mumbai world, the twenty-seven-story Mumbai home of Mukesh Ambani, India's reigning business tycoon and one of the world's richest people. The Ambani home, located eleven kilometers (seven miles) away from cramped Dharavi, has ceilings so high that the structure is tall as an average sixty-story building. It is equipped with three helipads, a theater that can accommodate eighty guests, a spa, and a garage for 168 vehicles. The "sun-kissed living area" offers a "breathtaking view of the sea."[11]

In the India of 2020, the Hindu-Muslim divide and egregious economic inequalities were reverberating echoes of Bengal in the 1940s. And disconcertingly, despite decades of economic progress, the echoes also sounded in the economic desperation of the reverse trek from the city to the village. The ongoing reverse trek revealed the continued risk of sudden income loss, health catastrophe, and the loss of even woeful living spaces: it revealed an India that was broken for hundreds of millions of Indians.[12]

This book is my attempt to explain why India, for so many, is broken.

Losing the Red Queen Race

In Lewis Carroll's *Through the Looking-Glass,* The Red Queen says, "It takes all the running you can do, to keep in the same place. If you want to get somewhere else, you must run at least twice as fast as that!"[13] As India's population increased, the Indian economy, far from harnessing potentially valuable young workers, could not keep up with the demand for jobs. This was the economy's essential failure.

In making the lack of sufficient jobs this book's central thread, I depart from the convention of using GDP—the sum of goods and services produced—as the measure of an economy's success. GDP is a misleading metric of a population's welfare because it skirts the all-important issue of *who* benefits and ignores the costs to future generations arising from reckless natural resource use. My emphasis on the well-being of people leads me to focus on the availability of jobs and, more broadly, on human development, livability of cities, environmental degradation, and the quality of the judicial system. The choice of well-being as the focus leads to a wholly different interpretation of modern Indian history. Recent spells of high GDP growth, although unsustainable, have engendered optimism about the future. Metrics of well-being tell a more consistently and ominously dispiriting story.

To follow the evolution of jobs, it is helpful to understand that few Indians can afford to be "unemployed" in the conventional sense of the term. Instead, they are "underemployed": they work fewer days in a year and hours in a day than they would like to. The underemployment is hidden in millions of family farms, small businesses, and casual wage laborers. On farms and in family businesses, struggling families create "make-work" to give everyone something to do. Many of these workers produce little, if anything, of value. If they stopped working, national output would barely decline. Casual wage workers work on the days they are given work to do and are idle on other days.

Unemployment as traditionally understood in advanced economies—so-called "visible," "open," or "explicit" unemployment—has mainly afflicted college graduates in India. Proliferating substandard colleges grant degrees but do not teach skills for gainful work. Such graduates are among the limited numbers who can afford spells of unemployment.

Using a methodology developed by Ajit Kumar Ghose, India's preeminent labor economist, I estimate that in 1955, India required about twenty-five million more jobs to fully employ its underemployed workers and about 1.5 million jobs for the mainly college graduates who were openly unemployed (chapter 3). Given the imprecision in such estimates, it is safe to say India was short between twenty and twenty-five million jobs. India's population then was about 360 million people. Over subsequent decades, as the population grew, this backlog of unfilled demand for jobs also grew.

The pace of job creation improved in the years of high GDP growth, which were approximately from the mid-1980s to 2011. A tiny glamorous cadre of Indians in the upwardly mobile information technology business and the financial sector did amazingly well. However, the quality of the new jobs was generally poor. The vast bulk of new employment originated in construction, with more modest additions in the low-productivity retail trade and transportation services; such jobs paid poorly and provided no social security. Construction jobs also exposed workers to serious health and safety risks. Eventually, the bubble that held up GDP growth began deflating. The overall jobs shortfall increased, especially between 2011 and 2019 when the numbers employed actually fell, such that in 2019 the Indian economy employed fewer people than in 2011.

Thus, over the longer arc of time, the jobs shortfall increased from approximately twenty-five million in 1955 to at least eighty million in 2019. The true shortfall in 2019 was almost surely much larger. Over the years, millions of rural Indian women stopped looking for work. They were neither the unemployed nor the underemployed, for they were no longer in the labor force. In 1955, 39 percent of Indian women were in the labor force—engaged in some kind of work or seeking employment.[14] By 1990, that proportion had declined to 32 percent (Figure 1.1). After 2005, the female labor force participation rate declined so steeply that the total numbers of women employed actually fell. Meanwhile, in East Asian nations, female participation rates were either high or rising. In Bangladesh, the rapid expansion of garment exports attracted women back to work.

For some scholars, India's women withdrew from the workforce because they had increased educational opportunities and their husbands

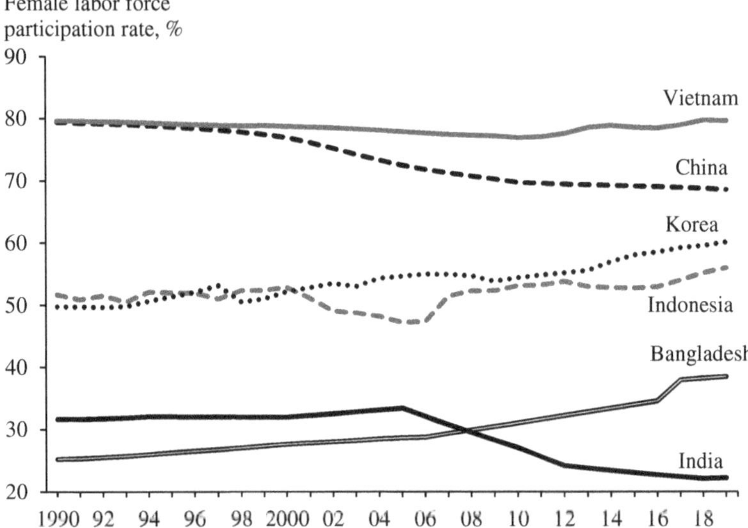

FIGURE 1.1: Growing numbers of Indian women have stopped looking for work. (Females in the labor force as percentage of the female population, ages 15–64)
Source: World Bank, World Development Indicators, estimates obtained from the International Labour Organisation, https://data.worldbank.org/indicator/SL.TLF.CACT.FE.ZS.

earned larger incomes. However, the majority of Indian women who stopped looking for work were older than twenty-five years old. They were typically from low-income families and had previously worked on family farms or in family businesses as "unpaid labor." Mechanization of agriculture had displaced them, and they had few work options once their husbands migrated to the cities to work on construction sites, in restaurants, or as street vendors. If jobs suited to their abilities had existed, jobs like the ones offered by Bangladesh's garment factories, as many as fifty million Indian women sitting on the sidelines might have taken up such work to supplement their meager and unstable family incomes. Women also faced increased violence, which deterred them from seeking work outside their homes.[15] Thus, if we add the women who had dropped out of the labor force, by 2019, India needed possibly 130 million additional jobs to fully employ its working-age men and women. I will, however, use the lower number of 80 million as the backlog of employment demand in 2019.

In addition, Ghose estimates that for the foreseeable future, India's growing population will require at least seven million more jobs per year, a number that could go up to nine million new jobs a year if the labor force participation rate (the share of workers looking for jobs) increases from its horrifyingly low level. Hence, seen from the vantage point of 2019, even if India needed only 80 million jobs to erase its backlog, adding in the new job seekers set up the nearly impossible economic challenge of generating between 150 and 170 million jobs in the decade to follow, against the reality of no addition to jobs in the immediately preceding years.[16]

COVID-19 added to that alarming outlook. About twenty-five million of the jobs lost during the two COVID-19 years may never come back, and another fifteen million new job seekers joined the queue in those two years. With that addition of forty million, at the end 2021, India needed between 190 million and 210 million jobs to fully employ its people over the next decade. This assessment of Indian job needs is likely to be an underestimate because it continues to anticipate low rates of labor force participation and does not fully factor in the jobs lost in the second and third COVID waves.

Independent India began on the wrong foot by adopting a heavy industry development strategy that could not create enough productive work for the country's rapidly growing youth population. Ever since, even in periods of high GDP growth, the composition of production has constrained the demand for workers. Despite many windows of opportunity, India has failed to emulate East Asian-style employment creation through labor-intensive manufactured exports.

The recurring inability to use exports to generate jobs represents India's most vivid failure of the Red Queen test (Figure 1.2). Strange as it may now seem, in the early 1950s, India's share of world trade in manufactured goods was slightly higher than Japan's. Although Japan had much superior industrial capabilities, it was dealing with the destruction it suffered in World War II. But despite their struggle in meeting international quality standards, Japanese producers quickly rode the postwar world trade boom, selling products such as textiles, garments, bicycles, and toys—all of which used relatively labor-intensive

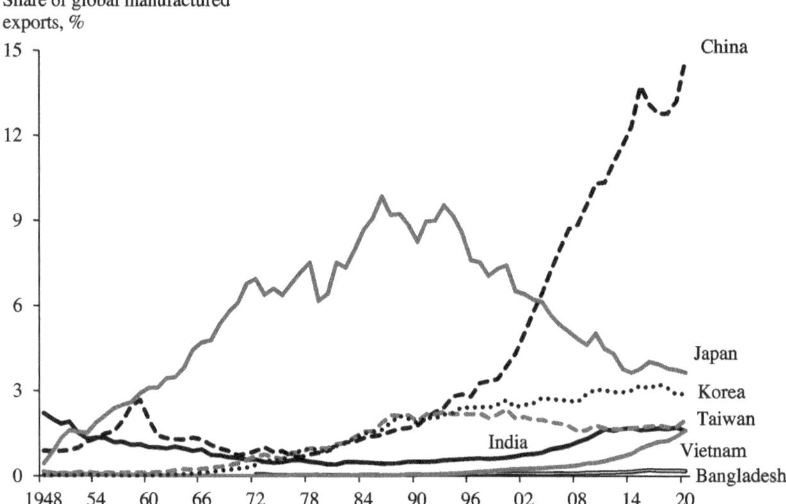

FIGURE 1.2: India has repeatedly lost the international competitiveness race. (Country exports as a percent of world manufactured exports)

Source: WTO Merchandise trade values, https://data.wto.org/, the data corresponds to UNCTAD statistics, https://unctadstat.unctad.org/wds/TableViewer/tableView.aspx?ReportId=101.

manufacturing techniques. India missed its first, admittedly narrow, window of opportunity.

In the 1960s, South Korea and Taiwan made impressive advances in the export of labor-intensive products. But perhaps India's most decisive competitive loss in international markets was to China. Chinese producers soon also quickly began selling in the Indian market, causing many Indian businesses to abandon manufacturing. In the past decade, as China ceded ground, Vietnam—a country of not even one hundred million people—has filled that space. And even though Bangladesh does not have the product range of East Asian exporters, it has been exporting a larger value of garments than India since 2006 despite having a much smaller economy.

A popularly held view of modern Indian history says that the socialist policies of the Nehru and Indira Gandhi governments stunted economic growth. The assertion also is that lingering socialism continues to damage Indian economic prospects. This simplistic view misunderstands the essence of socialism and deflects India from pursuing a more inclusive, social democratic development strategy.

Socialism means the creation of equal opportunity for all. In this sense, India never implemented socialist policies. A common mistake is to identify central planning or big government as socialism, but these are tools of economic policy, not socialism. Even if assessed narrowly by these tools, Indian planning and size of government have been similar to those in a broad range of Western capitalist economies and a far cry from the former Soviet Union.[17] Governments large and small can be distinctly anti-socialist when they promote the powerful and the elite, as was true under both Nehru and Mrs. Gandhi. Public policy did not work for the general welfare during the so-called socialist years or later. Modern India's propellant force then and ever since has been its deeply unequal development process.

The bogeyman of the alleged socialist legacy has given India's market-friendly "liberalizers" license to pursue an economic path that generates ever more inequality while continuing the neglect of public goods necessary for shared progress. Leaders and public intellectuals—irrespective of their rhetoric and professed ideologies—have always paid only lip service to public goods. Particularly worrisome, they have pursued a mythical "development" that causes possibly irreparable damage to the environment, a public good essential for current and future generations of Indians.

Public Goods: The Foundation of Fairer Growth

Economists refer to education, health, urban infrastructure, clean water, clean air, and a fair and responsive judiciary as "public goods." These public goods address human livability priorities. They make an economy more productive and create the basis for growth that benefits all. Fairer growth acts as a glue that holds societies together.

The different public goods enhance one another. In well-functioning cities, workers learn from one another in industrial and business districts; community residents enrich one another's lives. Good schools flourish in stable urban communities. Children perform better at school when clean water and air prevent the spread of illness. Well-planned urban areas and community parks keep the air clean. These are all examples of "positive externalities." In contrast, a negative externality occurs, for example, when, lacking sufficient clean water, individuals excessively deplete groundwater.

Because no individual—or indeed collection of individuals—can provide public goods on an adequate scale that accounts for positive externalities, and few individuals can be bothered about the negative externalities they generate, governments either directly provide public goods or actively regulate their provision to ensure fair availability with acceptable quality standards.

In this introductory chapter, I place the evolution and status of Indian education and cities in an international context. I defer a discussion of the other public goods to later chapters, where the main narrative unfolds.

Early achievement of universal primary education for girls was a particularly remarkable East Asian accomplishment. By now, several studies have documented that a big push to educate women is not only necessary to create an industrially literate workforce; it is essential also in reducing fertility rates and improving child health. Perhaps most important, as the historian Robin Jeffrey has so eloquently stated, an educated man typically has an educated son; an educated woman has an educated family, ensuring intergenerational transmission of learning capabilities.[18]

Japan reached universal primary education of girls by the 1920s (Figure 1.3). Taiwan achieved that goal in the mid-1950s; South Korea, a latecomer, caught up with Taiwan about a decade later, and China, which stayed at the bottom of the league with India through the mid-1940s, eventually raced ahead. Vietnam does not report school enrollment rates, but several metrics show that it has achieved education levels that are nearly the equal of most industrialized countries.

This national sequence of reaching universal primary education for girls, with emphasis everywhere on high-quality education, matches closely the sequence of global entry into the export of labor-intensive manufactured products and the durability of that global presence. East Asian female labor force work participation rates have been high, as we saw earlier in this chapter, and women have been the majority of the workers in industries such as electronics assembly, textiles, garments,

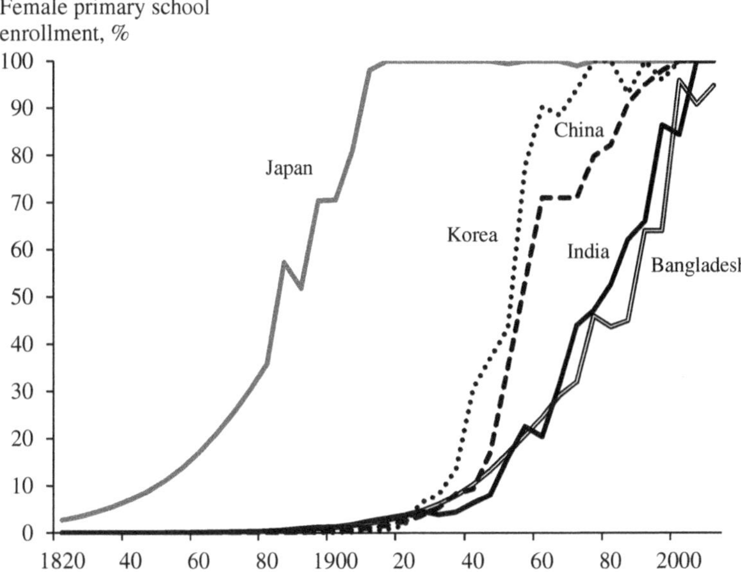

FIGURE 1.3: India fell behind in educating girls. (Female primary school enrollment, percent)

Source: Barro, Robert J. and Jong-Wha Lee. 2015. *Education Matters: Global Schooling Gains from the 19th to the 21st Century*. New York: Oxford University Press.

and footwear. As women in East Asia increased their work participation, they delayed marriage and had fewer children. And along with female education and increased work participation, son preference (measured by excessive boys at birth) disappeared in Japan after 1939 and in South Korea and Taiwan after 1990.[19]

There is reason to applaud India's recent achievement of universal female primary education enrollment. But as the Red Queen warned, you must run twice as fast as you can if you want to get someplace new. The world now demands increasingly higher education quality. The quality of school education in India remains abysmal. Indian students perform below grade level from their early years, and the gap in their performance relative to grade level increases as they go through school. Thus, they enter college largely unprepared for a university education. This characterization of schooling quality is true across the entire country, including in the more advanced states, such as Tamil Nadu. Bangladeshi women

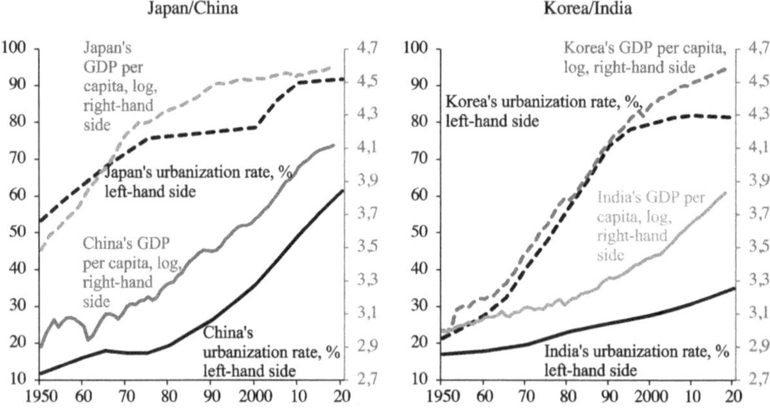

FIGURE 1.4: Indian cities never became engines of growth.

Source: Urbanization rate, Japan—The Asian Population and Development Association for 1900–1945, Table 2, p. 24, https://www.apda.jp/pdf/p04_jinkou_series/popdev_series_3_en.pdf; for 1950–2015, United Nations Department of Economic and Social Affairs, https://population.un.org/wup/Download/. GDP per capita—Angus Maddison Project Database, https://www.rug.nl/ggdc/historicaldevelopment/maddison/releases/maddison-project-database-2013.

are in a virtuous circle of increasing and improved education alongside rising work participation. Besides investing in the education and health of their own families, women in Bangladesh actively contribute to the education, health care, family planning, and other public services offered in their communities.[20]

As with education, East Asian countries offer superior city infrastructure and amenities that help manufacturers and their suppliers enhance one another's capabilities. Following an international pattern, East Asian urbanization has advanced in lockstep with economic growth (Figure 1.4).

Rather than acting as engines of productivity growth, Indian cities fell behind the rise of GDP in the late 1980s. Indian GDP growth has depended to an extraordinary degree on the financial sector, which squeezed itself into posh city areas, demanding little by way of expanded city size or amenities. Satellite images show a penumbra of urban townships and villages outside the administrative boundaries of officially designated cities. Such unplanned and unauthorized "urban" spread—rarely factored into urban design—accommodates a growing population unable to afford rising home prices and rents in cities. The spread keeps pushing further out from official city limits every year, creating stressed and unstable communities.

The simple truth is that from the Industrial Revolution in the late eighteenth century to now, no country has achieved manufacturing prowess and broad-based prosperity without continuous investment in education, health, and cities. India's attempt to make progress on the cheap by unconscionably delaying these investments has taken its toll. Indian economic growth has depended heavily on finance and construction, generating mainly low-quality jobs while hastening erosion of norms and accountability. Recurring scams have plagued the financial sector. Powerful criminal networks associated with construction have infiltrated politics.

The question arises: if public goods are so essential to achieving broadly shared economic growth, why has Indian democracy failed to respond to that need? Politicians in a democracy, even at the best of times, have short horizons. As British prime minister Harold Wilson frequently said, "A week is a long time in politics."[21] Where elected leaders work mainly for personal gain, their horizons shorten even more to severely undermine the public's long-term interest.

How India's Democracy Betrayed Its People

James Madison—constitutional scholar, American founding father, and later an American president—warned more than two centuries ago, "Men of factious tempers, of local prejudices, or of sinister designs, may, by intrigue, by corruption, or by other means, first obtain the suffrages, and then betray the interests of the people."[22]

Madison was warning that in a representative democracy, the winning political party does not always reflect—or work to fulfill—the people's views and aspirations. For this reason, I do not regard the mechanics of democracy—regular elections and the peaceful transfer of power—as sufficient indicators of democratic health. The question I pose throughout is whether Indian democracy has worked to serve the interests of the people. As with my shift in economic focus from GDP to people's well-being, the shift from the mechanics of democracy to its role in improving lives tells a much gloomier story.

One reason representative democracies do not function according to an idealized view is that the wealthy and privileged use their money and power to influence election outcomes in a manner that advances their narrow goals, thus neglecting—indeed, undermining—the interests of the majority.[23] Especially in the Nehru years, the Congress Party relied heavily on political funds and "vote banks" provided by large landlords, a dependence that made land reforms difficult if not impossible. Nehru-era controls on imports and industrial operations—triggered by the unsustainable foreign exchange demands of the ill-conceived heavy industrialization strategy—promoted an oligopolistic industrial structure within which a corrupt bureaucracy flourished.

Hence, despite high Nehru-era tax rates, Indian income and wealth inequalities remained large (and, very likely, increased). Following the tentative start of economic liberalization in 1985, inequalities ballooned. The philosophy of economic liberalization celebrated individualism, which, in practice, meant a greedy rush for access to privilege while the marketplace struggled to work its magic. As election campaign expenses mounted, wealthy businessmen such as the liquor baron Vijay Mallya became Members of Parliament, where—as members of parliamentary committees—they had an advanced preview of forthcoming policies and the ability to influence the policies.

As has been true elsewhere in the world, rising Indian inequalities hindered the provision of public goods for the general population. Rich Indians ceased to be a voice for widespread availability of public services. They hid themselves in gated communities that extended sometimes to homes in London and New York. They had little interest in urban or judicial reform, because they had what they needed. They sent their children to elite schools in India and abroad. Where they did not exit, their behavior was worse. They used their power and privilege to grab rather than create. They dug deeper wells to extract groundwater and diverted public water supply to their swimming pools and water parks. They perpetrated enormous and long-lasting damage on the environment.

A second factor that undermines a representative democracy also played a major role in India. Charismatic politicians—those who connect with voters through their words and manner—bypass normal accountability checks, allowing them to use the state's resources for their favored purposes. Jawaharlal Nehru, the first of India's charismatic politicians, was a beloved leader who won repeated election victories for the Congress Party. Nehru did not seek personal gain or prestige, but, driven by an idealism and nationalist fervor, he put all his chips on heavy industrialization, a strategy that fared poorly in employing the large numbers who wanted jobs. When Nehru lost his heavy-industry gamble and pushed the country to the edge of international bankruptcy, U.S. President John F. Kennedy—animated by his own idealism, his high regard for Nehru, and his fear that communism would take root in India—helped Nehru double down on his bet. Jobs grew anemically, high inflation rates eroded incomes, and dire poverty persisted.

Mrs. Gandhi, Nehru's daughter, who became prime minister in 1966, also benefited from a charismatic connection with Indian voters. Her task was to deal with social anger at the lack of jobs and recurring bouts of inflation she inherited from the Nehru era. She understood the anger. As she said to a journalist, post-independence idealism had given Indians a glimpse of a future they could not reach. But she had little appetite to work in a sustained manner for a better Indian future.

Instead, in that era of bitter jockeying for political power, Mrs. Gandhi established herself as a cynical, slogan-peddling politician, intent on holding on to power that she expected to pass on to her son, Sanjay. For her, the personal and the political were deeply intertwined.

She elevated corruption to the highest political level. She clamped down on the growing social anger with the heavy hand of the state, establishing a pattern of strong-arm actions for those who followed her to use and abuse. Her charisma ensured that her slogans won her elections. Even after Indian voters threw her out for the brutality of her Emergency Rule, her mystique as a champion of the poor persisted, and in 1980 she returned a triumphant victor for her last term.

And with her reliance on criminals for electoral success, Mrs. Gandhi established a new benchmark for Indian political success. Criminals, with their muscle and money, gained a foothold in Indian politics. Seduced by the rich possibilities, many politicians themselves became bosses of criminal enterprises. Criminals entered politics for quick financial gain and had little incentive to prioritize long-term investment in public goods. To the contrary, they benefited from scarcity of services, which they could then dole out as benefactors.

Mrs. Gandhi is pivotal to our story because of the intense damage she inflicted on democratic norms. For when norms break, democracy goes into a "death spiral."[24]

Norms are people's beliefs in the *right thing to do*. When those norms are anchored in a personal morality, they become a social asset because they foster the trust necessary for well-functioning markets and political institutions. When norms break down—become morally unanchored—people have license to pursue even small personal gains at the expense of others. Democratic cooperative action with long horizons becomes impossible. Education and health infrastructure suffer, cities fall into disrepair, abuse of the environment goes unchecked, and justice is no longer blind. Moral norms and trust are easy to destroy because any breach makes it uncertain that they will work in the future. Following Mrs. Gandhi's example, cheating in economic and social life became habitual because as more people began to cheat, everyone felt the need to cheat.[25]

As the norms broke down, the institutional prerequisites of a democracy frayed. The parliament and the judiciary became less effective in holding the executive accountable. In public and private life, violence to settle matters—and settle scores—became more common.

With corruption and crime in politics strengthening their hold and economic inequalities widening through the late 1980s and 1990s, Indian democracy veered into dangerous territory. The national bond born of freedom from colonial rule had disappeared in the rear-view mirror. The mutating social anger gravitated to a new focal point: Hindutva—Hindu nationalism—a powerful us-versus-them philosophy that claimed its legitimacy from a mythical Indian past. The "angry Hindu" became Hindutva's foot soldier.

Hindutva attracted a winning majoritarian movement fired by mob violence and bolstered by nationalistic zeal. Narendra Modi ascended to power in 2014, and the forces undermining democracy coalesced. "Angry Hindus," ever ready for combat with Muslims and others perceived as opponents, became agents of xenophobic nationalism. As the political theorist Robert Dahl explained, rootless mobs charged by charismatic leaders "destroy whatever stands in their way" but have no capacity to create "a stable alternative."[26]

Exponentially growing election campaign expenses increased the reliance on muscle and money in Indian politics. In Prime Minister Narendra Modi's cabinet, formed in July 2021, twenty-four of the seventy-eight ministers (31 percent) had serious criminal charges—including assault, murder, attempted murder, rape, and kidnapping—pending against them.[27]

Ever larger amounts of dark money flowed from rich Indians to politicians through shell companies and, after 2017, through the opaque device of electoral bonds, a notable innovation of the Narendra Modi government. This money flow and the influence it seeks are, by design, impossible to trace. However, election watchdogs have estimated that the aggregate sum of money spent in the Indian 2019 election exceeded that of the U.S. presidential and congressional election in 2016.

The combination of Hindutva, criminal-politicians, and dark money—in a context of broken norms and virulent social media—mounted a merciless assault on democracy.

Rather than a virtuous circle in which economic development and democracy reinforced each other, India's economy and democracy unraveled together. Disregard of public goods continued. Avenues for job creation on the scale needed seemed all but closed. Damage to the environment seemed irreparable. As India ran out of long-term sources of sustainable growth, politics became big-money business. Politicians focused on vote-buying, headline-grabbing policies, and flashy rollouts of "visible" projects and glorious monuments.[28]

The Dangerous Consequences of Focus on the Visible

Independent India quickly eliminated famines but did much less to fight chronic hunger, which kills a startlingly large number of the country's citizens. Each year, between two million and three million fewer Indians would die early deaths if nutrition (and hence life spans) rose across the country to the levels seen in the southwestern state of Kerala.

But while the media flaunts the visuals of famine deaths, which enforces political accountability, journalists rarely pay attention to the less conspicuous deaths hunger brings.[29]

Reducing hunger is a long-term and multifaceted task that does not make for easy headlines. Besides food, a hungry child needs good health (parasites and other diseases make food absorption and retention hard). Children and parents need good education to make better-informed decisions. Families need clean water and basic sanitation.[30] For these reasons, improving nutrition requires multiple players who persist with baby steps forward despite suffering repeated setbacks. But politicians see little payoff in such complex long-haul efforts.

The same logic applies to education, where politicians typically rely on "the doctrine of salvation by bricks." Inaugurating school buildings places political leaders in the limelight. Appointing teachers wins votes in the community. But buildings do not educate students. Teachers must show up to school; if they show up, they must teach; if they teach, they must address the needs of the students. Headline-grabbing solutions do not work. In the 2011 election for the state legislative assembly in Tamil Nadu, Chief Minister J. Jayalalithaa indulged in a "great laptop giveaway" to high school and college students. However, because of their financially precarious condition, many students preferred to sell their laptops and use the cash to pay urgent bills.[31]

High-quality education requires commitment of the local bureaucracy, training of teachers, cooperative teachers' unions, prestige in the community for teachers, and involvement of parents in the education of their children.[32] Schools are also creatures of their neighborhoods. As urban activist Jane Jacobs wrote, "In bad neighborhoods, schools are brought to ruination, physically and socially; while successful neighborhoods improve their schools by fighting for them."[33] Good education requires official and community coordination. Flashy individuals are no help.

For the same reason that nutrition and education standards lag, cities decay and the water and air become more polluted. They all require "dealing simultaneously with a *sizeable number of factors which are interrelated into an organic whole."*[34] Each circumstance is unique. General principles are insufficient. Knowing and acting on the particulars are essential.

The bottom line: efforts that advance economic development are doubly unforgiving. They require intense, long-term cooperation and their heroes are unsung. For politicians, headlines and slogans that enhance their brands are surer paths to electoral success.

"Business as Usual" Will Not Work

Indian and international pundits remain committed to a business-as-usual technocratic approach. They propose more economic "liberalization" and "governance" reforms. Historians, however, warn—and the narrative of this book powerfully reiterates—that political leaders disregard worthy ideas and instead are drawn to policies that serve their own financial and electoral interests. Even when India implemented bad policies, the problem was not the lack of good ideas for progress. The much deeper problem has been steadily eroding public norms and accountability. That erosion has thwarted the restoration of accountability and placed India in a Catch-22.[35]

Because achieving accountability in a democracy is hard work, the Indian discourse has perennially toyed with the temptation of an "authoritarian transition." The proposition is that India cannot afford the "luxury" of democracy: a "savior" with dictatorial powers must first establish the basis for sustained growth. The autocratic temptation, however, is fraught with grave risks. Modern-day saviors have too often done great damage—in India and elsewhere.

India needs more democracy through decentralization of authority to city and village governments. Despite its own perils, decentralized governance offers the best—possibly the only—prospect of morally anchored political accountability. Under successful decentralization, accountability arises from the blending of civic consciousnesses with formal structures of local self-governance. An individualistic "me-me-me" culture gives way to a "we" society, one that builds trust and cooperation from the ground up. Therein arises a long-term commitment to socially valuable investments in public goods.

In the fruitless business-as-usual scenario, India will stay in its trap. Indian democracy will fail to deliver the public goods necessary for economic growth that benefits all. Good jobs will remain scarce. The lack of jobs will generate more social anger, which will further increase the political incentive for the quick-fire provision of visible goods and undermine democracy's ability to work for a long-term jobs-rich future.

It all began with Nehru, although it nearly didn't.

Part I

FAKE SOCIALISM, 1947–1964

Chapter 2
AN UNCERTAIN BEGINNING

By the rules of the Indian National Congress (the Congress Party), Vallabhbhai Patel should have been the party's president at the time of independence. If that had been so, he might well have been India's first prime minister. However, in August 1947, Jawaharlal Nehru, not Patel, became prime minister.

Patel and Nehru differed greatly in their economic and social philosophies and in their approaches to the use of government authority and power. Patel, however, lived to see only the first three years of post-independence India. As deputy prime minister and home (interior) minister, he left a lasting legacy. Even during those few years, he and Nehru fought bitterly on the priorities for India's political and economic future. If Patel had become India's first prime minister or if he had lived longer as Nehru's deputy, post-independence India would have taken a very different shape.

Two Leaders—Two Worlds

Patel was born to a peasant family in October 1875 and was raised in a modest two-story home. As a young man, he observed that fame and fortune came easily to barristers educated in England. As he later explained, "I studied very earnestly" and "resolved firmly to save sufficient money for a visit to England."[1] Patel became a British-trained lawyer and, upon returning to India, established a very successful criminal law practice.

Patel made his initial mark in politics in the first half of 1928, when he led peasants in Bardoli, an administrative area in the current state of Gujarat, in their fight against the British government's onerous demands for land revenue. Despite its peaceful nature, the contest with the powerful British Raj became, in the popular imagination, the "battle of Bardoli." Patel's protest won the battle of Bardoli against British might, a victory for which Bardoli's people conferred on him the title "Sardar," chief or general. Vallabhbhai Patel has ever since been known as Sardar Patel.[2]

Nehru was born in November 1889 to one of India's most prominent families. His father, Motilal Nehru, was a wealthy lawyer and senior Congress Party leader. Anand Bhavan, the stately Nehru family home in Allahabad, now houses a historic museum and a planetarium. Jawaharlal studied at Harrow, the elite British public school, before attending the University of Cambridge. He qualified as a barrister in England, although he barely ever entered a courtroom. In August 1942, after Gandhi launched the Quit India movement, the British threw all Indian leaders in jail. Interned at the Ahmednagar Fort, Nehru grew a rose garden and played badminton with other prisoners. In a five-month period between April and September 1944, Nehru wrote his magnificent and timeless history *The Discovery of India.*

Patel was as much a man of action as Nehru was a historian and philosopher. As Gandhi pithily observed, "Jawahar is a thinker, Sardar a doer."[3]

Gandhi Chooses Nehru

In late 1945 and early 1946, India's British rulers held elections for the central and provincial assemblies in preparation for the transfer of power. The Congress Party won large majorities in these elections, aided in part by campaign funds Patel helped raise. In a gushing profile, *Time* magazine wrote that Patel had no "pretensions to saintliness." The magazine described him as, "in American terms, the Political Boss. Wealthy industrialists thrust huge campaign funds into his hands."[4]

In late April 1946, the Congress Party was ready to select its next president. Since India's freedom was imminent, the choice of the party's president was critical. The Congress Party president would lead the party, and hence India, into independence. Under the established process, twelve of the fifteen Provincial or "Pradesh" Congress Committees nominated Patel; three abstained. As the veteran Congress Party leader Jivatram Bhagwandas (Acharya) Kripalani would later write, the party favored Patel because he was a "great executive, organizer, and leader."[5] Provincial leaders also felt beholden to Patel for the campaign funds he had raised. The Pradesh Congress Committees were not necessarily endorsing Patel as India's first prime minister. They understood that Nehru was popular with the Indian public. But they recognized Patel's leadership qualities and his contributions to the Congress Party. So they placed Patel in a position of prominence from which he could well have emerged as India's first prime minister.

Gandhi, however, stood above the rules, and he made the decision on who would be the party's president. Just as he had in 1929 and 1937, when Patel and Nehru competed for the presidency of the Congress Party, Gandhi chose Nehru, knowing on this last occasion that no Pradesh Congress Committee had nominated him. Gandhi saw Nehru as "a Harrow boy, a Cambridge graduate," who would represent India in international affairs more effectively than Patel. Nehru also had a stronger connection than Patel did with India's Muslim community. Above all, Nehru was fifty-six years old and like a son to the seventy-six-year-old Gandhi. Patel, whom Gandhi thought of as a younger brother, was seventy-one and in poor health.[6]

The British viceroy, Lord Wavell, had set up an Executive Council as the midway step to India's independence. As the Congress Party's president, Nehru became vice president to the viceroy in his Executive Council and, hence, India's de facto prime minister until the country became independent. Once so established, in addition to the huge popularity he enjoyed with the Indian public, Nehru also had the incumbent's advantage to become independent India's first prime minister.

Gandhi believed that Nehru and Patel would be like "oxen yoked to the governmental cart. One will need the other and both will pull together." According to Patel's daughter, Maniben, Gandhi expected that Patel would prevent Nehru from "making mischief."[7]

The Oxen Pull Apart

Prime Minister Nehru and Deputy Prime Minister and Home Minister Sardar Patel began the post-independence years entangled in a stormy relationship. They fought about the most consequential matters that defined India back then and continue to do so today.

With Pakistan partitioned as a Muslim nation, a question on people's minds was what the role and place of Muslims in India would be. Within that broader context, an immediate issue arose as the horrors of religious hatred continued after partition in both India and Pakistan. In the Indian areas marked by Hindu-Muslim tensions, the government's machinery had collapsed or become "fiercely partisan." A rumor spread that Patel, as home minister, was protecting and aiding Hindus but not Muslims. Nehru seemed to buy into the rumor, even though it had no basis. The historian Rajmohan Gandhi, grandson of the Mahatma and Patel's biographer, writes that Patel "was unquestionably roused more by a report of 50 Hindu and Sikh deaths than by another of 50 Muslim deaths. But his hand was just."[8]

Patel, in turn, was impatient with Nehru's soft approach toward Pakistani leaders, who were making only half-hearted efforts to contain the violence against Hindus and Sikhs on their side of the border. Patel insisted that the news of this violence was triggering a "mass psychology" of resentment and anger among India's Hindus and Sikhs.[9] Nehru and Patel never resolved their differences on how best to deal with India's Hindu-Muslim issue.

They also sparred over Kashmir. On October 22, 1947, a contingent of about five thousand armed tribesmen from Pakistan drove into Kashmir. The maharaja of Kashmir, Hari Singh, was a Hindu, but the Kashmir Valley had a predominantly Muslim population. The maharaja had avoided choosing between Pakistan and India, but on October 24, he desperately appealed to the Indian government for help. On the morning of October 26, Hari Singh signed the instrument of accession to India. That evening, an Indian infantry battalion landed in Kashmir and halted the tribesmen.[10] Pakistani authorities gave the name "Azad Kashmir" (Free Kashmir) to the land west of where the Indian Army stopped the tribesmen. Indians called that area "Pakistan-occupied Kashmir."

Patel, as minister of states, directed the Kashmir operations. But in early December 1947, he found to his surprise that Nehru, as prime minister, had taken control of India's Kashmir policy. Patel complained that he had been blindsided, and the two exchanged acrimonious letters.[11]

With Nehru and Patel evidently at loggerheads, Gandhi in late December delivered an ultimatum to Patel: "Either you should run things or Jawaharlal should." Patel wearily replied, "I do not have the strength. He is younger. Let him run the show. I will help him as much as I can from the outside." Gandhi, who had kept Patel and Nehru together for so long, agreed that it was time for Patel to step aside but said that he wanted to think the matter over.[12] Fate, however, intervened. On January 31, 1948, a Hindu nationalist named Nathuram Godse shot and killed Gandhi.

After Gandhi's death, in their moment of shared grief and to quash the swirling rumors of their imminent split, Nehru and Patel came together. In a radio address, Nehru said, "We have had our differences. But India at least should know that these differences have been overshadowed by fundamental agreements about the most important aspects of our public life." On March 3, Nehru wrote to Patel that the crisis required them to work together as "friends and colleagues." He ended graciously: "this letter carries with it my friendship and affection." Patel replied with equal grace: "I am deeply touched, indeed, overwhelmed. We have been lifelong friends and comrades in a common cause." All talk of Patel's leaving was forgotten.[13] The twists of history continued, however. On March 8, 1948, while eating lunch at home with his daughter Maniben, Patel had a massive heart attack.

Patel Integrates the States

Patel returned to work quickly after his heart attack and poured his energies into a monumental task that he had begun but not finished. That task was to integrate the princely states into a unified India.

When the British left India, the Indian government in New Delhi did not have authority over the entire land area known today as India. Scattered all over the country were more than five hundred princely states ruled by hereditary princes. All together, the princes ruled over one-third of India's land area and one-fourth of its population. They had survived as princes because, after the 1857 mutiny of Indian soldiers in the British army, British authorities stopped annexing new territories. They feared that more annexation would trigger another mutiny. Instead, the British Crown established the Doctrine of Paramountcy, which granted the British authorities control over the princely states' foreign policy, defense, and communications, leaving, at least in principle, administration of the states to the princes. At independence, the British transferred to the new Indian parliament full control only over "British India," the part annexed before 1857; the British also transferred their paramountcy powers over the princely states. In independent India, therefore, the princely states could determine their political relations with the rest of India and set their own commercial policies. India risked becoming a politically and economically balkanized nation.[14]

In November 1947, an opportunity had arisen to begin merging princely states into the Indian state, the "Union of India." The prince of Nilgiri, a tiny state in Orissa, faced a domestic rebellion he could not handle, so he quickly surrendered his princely rights and powers to the Indian government. Patel took his cue from that early assimilation of a princely state into the Indian Union, and starting in mid-December, he used a vigorous combination of threats and inducements to bring other princely states into the Indian fold. He offered the princes and their heirs generous tax-free "privy purses" (pensions) and continued ownership of their personal properties if they handed over their authority quietly. If they did not, they might get nothing.[15]

The task lay incomplete when Patel had his heart attack in March 1948. But by mid-1948, the "birth and beginning of a unified India" was in sight. The last holdout was the nizam (ruler) of Hyderabad. At dawn on September 13, Indian Armed Forces began rolling toward Hyderabad. On September 18, the Hyderabadi commander surrendered.[16]

In a rare celebratory moment, on October 15, 1948, Patel wrote to the premiers of all Indian provinces (renamed chief ministers of states after India became a republic in January 1950). Patel reminded the premiers that the integration of states into the Indian Union began in earnest in December 1947 and had ended with the removal of the "Hyderabad sore." India had achieved, Patel wrote, "a measure of unity which it had never before attained in the last so many centuries."[17] That was Patel's inestimable legacy to India.

The Conflict Resumes

The conflict between Nehru and Patel resumed in early 1950, triggered by the large inflow of Hindu refugees from East Pakistan. Although not as gigantic as the migration across the Punjab border in August-September 1947, when as many as 5.5 million people crossed in each direction, "more than a million people abandoned their homes" during the great Bengal migration. Patel was again upset with Nehru for not pushing the Pakistanis to protect Hindus. He angrily called for an Indian policy of "ten eyes for an eye," expelling ten Muslims from India for every Hindu the Pakistanis pushed out. Nehru rejected this tit-for-tat strategy. India, he said, must live up to its standards of equality for its citizens and fairness of treatment.[18]

Nearly simultaneously, a controversy arose over the goals of Indian economic planning. Patel did not oppose the Planning Commission itself. But like other ministers in the Nehru cabinet, he objected to a technocratic commission that might usurp the role of the elected representatives of the people. The ideological point of conflict arose when a draft Congress Party resolution stated that the Planning Commission would seek to eliminate "the motive of private gain in economic activity." We don't know the author of these words, but they bear a striking similarity to the language Nehru used in his presidential address at the Congress Party session (convention) at Lucknow in 1936. Then, Gandhi, "without uttering a word," had ensured that Nehru's language did not filter into the party's resolutions. Now, when that language reappeared, "right-wingers" such as Patel demanded that the offending paragraph be struck out.[19]

The real tussle, however, took place on a third front: the election in 1950 of the Congress Party president. Patel backed Purshottamdas Tandon. Nehru backed Acharya Kripalani. The Tandon-Kripalani contest was a Patel-Nehru rematch.

By universal agreement, Tandon was a man of unimpeachable integrity. Such integrity was a particularly valuable virtue amid the growing corruption in Indian politics. "The spoils of power were now [being] distributed with a feverish intensity," Nehru's biographer Michael Brecher wrote. Nehru agreed that Tandon, "an old friend," was an upright man.[20]

Tandon, like Patel, was "staunchly anti-Pakistan." But he went further. He opposed changes to Hindu customs and traditions, which meant that he opposed the Hindu Code Bill that gave Hindu women rights to divorce and property inheritance. Tandon also promoted a classical (Sanskritized) version of Hindi as India's national language. He did not wear shoes of cowhide because slaughter of a cow, an animal sacred to orthodox Hindus, was a sin.[21] Tandon's prominence was a reminder that a narrow-minded Hinduism was entrenched in the Congress Party in the earliest post-independence days.

For Nehru, an important concern was Tandon's aim of subordinating the cabinet to the Congress Party's High Command.[22] Nehru was right: the Party could not micromanage the elected government.

Patel actively lobbied for Tandon, helping him win the presidency in mid-September 1950. But Tandon's election was Patel's last victory. The Sardar died on the morning of December 15. He was seventy-five years old.[23]

The Colossus Finally Rises

Without Patel to support him, Tandon resigned as Congress Party president in August 1951. Nehru held the position until 1954, after which he made sure the president he handpicked would not be overly assertive.

With Patel gone and other rivals neutralized, Nehru faced a disorderly Congress Party. It had become a "cockpit of factions," as Patel angrily said before he died, and was being pulled in many different directions. The glue, in the form of the ideals of the independence movement, had dissolved. In June 1951, just months before the first general elections in independent India, *Time* magazine commented on the party's unruly nature and the corruption that had seeped into it. The party had become a "sprawling conglomerate" that lacked "a unifying purpose." It had grown "fat and lazy." It harbored many "timeserving officeholders" and well-known "black-marketeers."[24]

Though disruptive, the factional leaders, typically large landlords and other rural notables, brought with them valuable "vote banks" that

R. K. Laxman's cartoon in *The Times of India*, 28 November 1951

FIGURE 2.1: On the eve of India's first election, Nehru towered like a colossus. Source: Gopal, Sarvepalli. 1979. *Jawaharlal Nehru: A Biography, Volume One 1889–1947*. Bombay: Oxford University Press, 163.

consisted of peasants working for them and caste affiliates. Nehru shied away from establishing structure and discipline in the Congress Party. Instead, he relied on his connection with the Indian people. He campaigned relentlessly, dispensing platitudes to crowds that idolized him.[25] In November 1951, with the balloting in progress, the cartoonist R. K. Laxman showed Nehru riding a campaign cart, towering above both party members and the Indian public (Figure 2.1).

The elections held between October 1951 and February 1952 were the first test of India's democracy. Out of 175 million registered voters, 108 million voted, amounting to a turnout of 62 percent. Although lower than the turnout rates common at the time in advanced industrial democracies, it was a remarkable performance, given that only about 17 percent of the Indian population could read and write. Even more impressive:

less than 2 percent of the votes cast were declared invalid. The gigantic election machinery worked stunningly well. On the day after polling was completed, the *Times of India* wrote, "Although there had been a few cases of impersonation and tampering with ballot-boxes, by and large, the elections were fair."[26]

The result, however, was not necessarily a victory for democracy. As Sarvepalli Gopal, Nehru's most important biographer, concluded, the Congress Party's easy victory was "a personal referendum in Nehru's favor, overriding all other issues." The affection Nehru enjoyed with the Indian people made him an uncontested national leader. He remained above the disorder in the Congress Party and ruled without a rival in any other party.[27] India's democracy was now in the hands of one person. India's problems were Nehru's problems. The conflict with Pakistan over Kashmir remained unresolved. At home, Hindu-Muslim tensions simmered. Despite Nehru's own commitment to communal harmony, pro-Hindu sentiment infused even senior Congress Party leaders. Above all, India's deep poverty and illiteracy needed immediate attention. Could Nehru the thinker also be a doer? Could he shape, as he had promised, an India that worked for all?

Chapter 3
THE PATH NOT TAKEN

On October 2, 1950, Mahatma Gandhi's birth anniversary, Nehru declared that independent India's primary goal was "to put an end to unemployment." He returned to that theme in September 1951. India's "biggest problem," he said, was "the problem of development, of removing unemployment and poverty from the country."[1]

Unemployment was, indeed, India's biggest problem. But the new nation was hopeful, a mood that filmmaker Raj Kapoor captured in his 1951 film *Awaara* (vagabond or tramp). On an anonymous city street, the lead character, Raj—dressed Charlie Chaplin–style with cocked hat and baggy trousers tied above his waist and ending above his ankles—playfully sings, "*Awaara hoon,* I am a vagabond, a tramp." Raj, played by Kapoor, has dropped out of school and is unable to find a job. So, he sharpens his skills as a pickpocket and petty thief, which regularly lands him in jail. The future is bright, however, and Raj's doting mother believes her son will one day be a lawyer, a goal for which she makes many sacrifices. As Maharajkrishna Rasgotra, one of India's most distinguished post-independence diplomats, wrote, "In 1951–52, the country's mood was one of self-discovery, and hope."[2]

Beneath the hope, economic trouble was brewing. India's exports did not pay for its imports. This shortfall created a growing balance of payments deficit—the gap between international dollar payments (for imports and other services) and receipts (from exports and other sources, such as workers' remittances). To fund that deficit, India was becoming more indebted to foreign lenders, leading to the risk of international bankruptcy.[3] India's two problems—employment shortfall and bankruptcy risk—had a common long-term solution, a competitive Indian economy, one that expanded exports to create jobs for larger numbers of people and pay for more imports.

The bankruptcy threat needed immediate attention, and Indian authorities used a quick short-term fix to diffuse it. On Monday, September 19, 1949, India devalued the rupee by 30 percent relative to the U.S. dollar—from Rs. 3.30 to Rs. 4.76 per dollar. The devaluation brought the expected relief. Indian exporters lowered their dollar prices, which helped raise exports. The rupee price of imports went up, inducing Indians to reduce their imports. India's balance of payments improved. The threat of bankruptcy diminished.[4]

It was the right step. But devaluation did not solve India's long-term problem. Devaluation is like aspirin: it reduces the pain but does not cure the sickness. As long as Indian farms and factories remained inefficient—had low productivity—prices of Indian products would remain high. India would struggle to export. Imports, however, would keep increasing to meet the food and industrial supply needs of the growing population. The balance of payments deficit would increase again. Boosting exports would require repeated devaluation—like swallowing repeated doses of aspirin. The Indian economy was in this "unhappy state," as Nehru acknowledged in parliament.[5]

To emerge from its "unhappy state," India needed higher-productivity farms and factories. More productive farms would increase the domestic supply of food and reduce the need for food imports, which accounted for between 15 and 20 percent of the dollar value of India's imports. Higher manufacturing productivity was critical to expand exports on a scale that would employ large numbers of people and pay for imported machinery and raw materials.[6]

The message in the immediate aftermath of independence was that Indians were not just greatly underemployed, they were also unproductive in their workplaces. As a new nation, India had to employ many more people and employ them in much more productive ways.

And to achieve a high-employment, high-productivity economy, India required a development strategy more closely aligned to that of Japan after the Meiji Restoration of 1868. Japan at the time of the Meiji Restoration had crucial features that made it the best economic model for India. Japan's economy was predominantly agricultural, the nature of its agriculture—small farms and hand-operated farming—was similar to India's, its youth population was growing rapidly as death rates fell faster than birth rates, and its citizens had little formal schooling. From that starting point, Japan had achieved high agricultural productivity growth and rapid expansion of primary education. Above all, Japan pioneered accelerated industrialization through aggressive pursuit of export markets. By the 1920s, Japan had bootstrapped itself into the ranks of the world's industrialized nations.

India came tantalizingly close to following Japan's development path. In an August 1949 letter to the prime ministers of Indian provinces (referred to as chief ministers of states after India became a republic in January 1950), Nehru highlighted the "relatively short period of time" within which Japan achieved "astonishing development." He even expressed admiration of the Japanese as colonial masters for industrializing Taiwan "within fifteen years or so to an amazing extent," a feat he recognized had "hardly a parallel anywhere." Russia also had lessons to offer, Nehru noted. But "Japan," he concluded, "has even more to teach us, because Russia gives us a very complicated picture."[7]

India's First Five-Year Plan (1951–1955) recognized the valuable lessons from Japan's development experience. In particular, the plan referred admiringly to the post-Meiji agricultural performance and the internationally competitive and employment-generating small and medium-sized firms. It is remarkable how quickly after independence those lessons became clear. It is also remarkable how poorly the lessons were learned.

Indian Agriculture Veers Off-Track

Indian planners knew the Japanese numbers well and saw them as achievable benchmarks for India. Grain output per farm worker in

Japan doubled over the forty-year period between 1880 and 1920. While grain output increased by 77 percent over these years, the number of agricultural workers actually *declined* and the area under cultivation increased by only 20 percent. Of special relevance to India, Japan's farmers achieved their phenomenal productivity gains on small, privately held, hand-operated land holdings, which were on average, between two and three acres in size and were typically further divided into several tiny and dispersed strips. The farmers relied on seed varieties carefully selected by local research stations and complemented these with the liberal use of fertilizers. Steadily improved water and pest control, better methods of transplanting and weed control, and more effective methods of irrigation and drainage made crop yields less sensitive to the excess or shortfall in rainfall.[8]

As farmers became more productive, labor requirements in agriculture declined and the share of Japanese workers in agriculture fell from 80 percent in 1880 to 50 percent in 1920. Japan's cities absorbed the country's rapidly increasing population. The cities provided jobs in large factories, especially in textiles; satellite townships provided jobs in small and medium-sized firms, which typically used labor-intensive techniques and either supplied specialized inputs to larger firms in the cities or made products for international sales.[9]

In the early 1950s, productivity on Indian farms was between one-fifth and a quarter of that in Japan. The best-irrigated and best-managed farms, located in the West Godavari district of Andhra Pradesh, yielded only half the rice per acre the average Japanese farm did at the time. India's First Plan's authors recognized that Japan's productivity increases occurred "mainly through better seeds, manure, and insecticides, and improved agricultural practices, none of which required large capital outlays." Indian planners believed that crop yields "comparable" to Japan's were within India's reach. With 70 percent of its workforce in agriculture, India needed Japan-style high agricultural productivity growth to feed the nation; India also needed Japan-style rapid industrialization and urbanization to employ its exponentially growing population.[10]

To accelerate agricultural productivity growth, the First Plan rightly concluded that India needed land reforms (more land to the tiller) and a community development program to provide "extension"—technical support—services to farmers. More land to the tiller would enhance fairness. It would raise incomes and nutritional levels of farming families and give them a greater incentive to raise productivity. Extension services would bring new ideas from research centers to farms. These were sensible plans. They fell victim to poor execution.[11]

The most ambitious of India's land reform initiatives was the abolition of *zamindari*. *Zamindars* were landowners and often also middlemen who collected taxes on behalf of the British government, mainly in eastern India. The *zamindar* was a hated cultural figure who loaned money to desperate cultivators at extortionary interest rates and enforced his authority with brutal financial and physical methods. In the much-acclaimed 1953 movie *Do Bigha Zamin* ("Two *bighas* of land," signifying a tiny land parcel), a memorably rapacious *zamindar* seeks to evict a tenant from two *bighas* of land using forged papers showing that the tenant owed him an insurmountable debt.[12]

Indian leaders of different ideological persuasions—Nehru with his empathy for greater equality and Sardar Patel despite his deference for private property—agreed that *zamindari* needed to go. Nehru, in a letter to the state chief ministers, wrote that if *zamindari* abolition fails, "our entire social and economic policy fails."[13]

By the early 1950s, the states had legally abolished *zamindari*. But the implementation of the legislation did little for the small Indian farmer. The main beneficiaries of the change were the former large tenant farmers, who now owned the lands they cultivated. That empowering of large peasants kick-started "capitalist" farming in India. Others gained little or nothing. The *zamindars* evicted their small tenant farmers by claiming that they had cultivated the land themselves all along, a claim that allowed them—under the law—to keep the land for themselves. Such exaggeration of personally cultivated lands was possible because the land records either did not exist or were under the control of the *zamindars*. Small independent farmers, agricultural laborers, and the landless got, at best, "tiny pieces of land." The *zamindars* received generous compensation for the revenue-collection rights they surrendered, placing a heavy fiscal burden on the state governments and reinforcing inherited inequality.[14]

Another initiative aimed to place a ceiling on the land that individual farmers held, so that land in excess of a specified limit might be distributed to small farmers and landless labor. But, as the constitutional scholar Granville Austin wrote, "The legislation that survived judicial scrutiny contained loopholes ample enough to accommodate a tractor." The implementation of the legislation dragged on for years, during which time large landholders partitioned the land they owned into many parcels. They used the common practice of *benami* transactions, which concealed the identity of the true owner by registering the parcels in the names of family members and even of farm animals, thus creating a superficially legal basis for retaining control of the land. A third initiative to protect the rights of tenant farmers in non-*zamindari* (particularly the so-called *ryotwari*) areas failed almost entirely because—as in the *zamindari* case—poor or missing land records prevented tenants from establishing their rights or because landlords claimed the land back on the grounds that they intended to cultivate it themselves. Landlords could also circumvent ceilings on land rents by charging higher interest rates on moneylending.[15]

Indian land reforms never stood a chance. Many Congress Party leaders were large landlords; they undermined the reforms to protect themselves and their friends and supporters. Nehru had little appetite to challenge the landed interests. In a letter to chief ministers, he helplessly wrote, "This result has not been what we had looked forward to."[16] However empathetic he might have been, Nehru lacked the political resolve to pursue the cause of a more equal India.

Japan's small and medium-sized farmers also did not benefit from the ineffectual Meiji land reforms. But fruitful collaboration between farmers and research centers helped boost land and labor productivity.[17] That attempted collaboration was a huge disappointment in India.

Indeed, India's extension services—under the Community Development Program—failed utterly. The World Bank diplomatically concluded that the "caliber and organization of extension work was not consistently adequate." Other commentators were brutal. One expert wrote, "The texture of operations was discouragingly shoddy." Even Indian government officials despaired about the "problems of implementation." An elaborate "web of bureaucratic routines" hindered the real work. The village-level community development workers were assigned unrelated tasks and lacked professional training and authority. Farmers refused to take their advice seriously.[18]

The University of Chicago economics professor Theodore Schultz added that a problem arose also because Indian farmers were "generally illiterate" and possessed "low levels of skill." It was a mistake, Schultz said, to think that agriculture required mainly a "strong back" and the ability to "do manual work." Japan's farmers, even with their elementary school education, could master "complex and difficult farm practices" taught by experienced extension workers.[19]

The Cost of Industrial Illiteracy

At independence, Indian manufacturing enterprises employed 10 percent of the country's workforce and produced 16 percent of the national income. These were low contributions even by the benchmark of India's low per capita income.[20]

India's low level of industrialization at independence was, in a sense, a surprise. Dynamic entrepreneurs from the highly educated Parsi community had given the Indian textile industry an early start. Cowasjee Davar founded the first mill in 1854, almost a century before independence. Maneckjee Petit followed Cowasjee but died early, and it was his brilliant son Dinshaw who blazed new trails. Others with greater name recognition today included Nowrojee Wadia, who founded the Bombay Dyeing and Century Mills, and Jamshedji Tata, who established the famous Empress Mills, a textile manufacturer, and then started India's first steel mill. India's textile factories operated machines from Lancashire, which through the early twentieth century were the best available. Non-Parsis joined the fray, slowly at first and then in greater numbers. Textile production spread from its hub in Bombay, notably to Ahmedabad (the largest city in present-day Gujarat), Kanpur (in present-day Uttar Pradesh), and Coimbatore (in the state today known as Tamil Nadu).[21]

Between 1870 and 1890, Indian textile producers earned bountiful profits. The operation of Indian railways from the mid-1850s made it easier and cheaper to transport goods across the country. Dinshaw Petit also led the spectacular charge of Indian yarn exports to China. Compared to the mills in Lancashire, Indian mills benefited from lower wages, domestic sources of cotton, and significantly lower transportation costs to China; in 1892, they sold 70 percent of their yarn in China. During these boom years, India's mill owners invested in modern spinning and dyeing innovations. In 1891, the Indian textile industry employed 150,000 workers.[22]

Signs of trouble appeared in the early 1890s. Chinese mills began increasing their efficiency. But it was the ferociously competitive Japanese mills that broke the Asian supremacy of Indian textile mills. With labor as cheap as in India, Japan's textile producers increased their productivity at an especially rapid pace. With Japan's entry, Indian mills lost their advantage of low wages and low transportation costs to the lucrative Chinese yarn market. India's textile industry did remain significantly larger than Japan's textile industry until the first decade of the twentieth century. Indian mill owners continued to use world-class machinery and adopted spinning and dyeing innovations. But they proved unable to compete with the Japanese mills.[23]

The problem through these critical years was the low productivity of Indian workers, which largely offset the advantage of their low wages. A startling calculation by the economic historian Gregory Clark showed that if Indian workers in 1910 were magically made as productive as those in New England (United States), their wages could rise fivefold, from $0.78 a week to $3.93 a week, while maintaining high profitability on scarce Indian capital.[24] The implication was sobering: Indians were poor because industrial workers—even in the country's most internationally successful industry—had such low productivity.

In the 1920s, the productivity of Japanese workers increased rapidly along with their improving education and advances in production techniques adopted by their employers. Having displaced Indian producers from the Chinese market, Japan's textile manufacturers advanced ominously into India. Some Indian companies did try to respond to that challenge but most felt overwhelmed, especially after the Japanese government allowed the yen to depreciate in the 1930s. Instead of undertaking a concerted efficiency-enhancement effort, Indian textile mills retreated behind increasingly high import tariff barriers, where they also squeezed their workers using the constant threat of job loss.[25]

In a famous research paper published in 1993, MIT economics professor Michael Kremer was struck by Gregory Clark's finding of strikingly wide variation in worker productivity across countries. Kremer reasoned that differences in education likely explained differences in productivity. Better-educated, more skilled workers made fewer errors and were typically paired with other skilled workers, who then improved each other's efficiency. The potential for efficiency gains encouraged factory managers to experiment with more innovative uses of machinery, further raising worker output.[26]

The data supports Kremer's conjecture on the importance of education. I use female primary school enrollment rates as a metric of a society's commitment to mass education. Worker productivity in 1910 was higher in countries with higher female primary school enrollment two decades earlier (Figure 3.1). The United States, having achieved 100 percent female primary enrollment by the early 1870s, had the most productive mills.

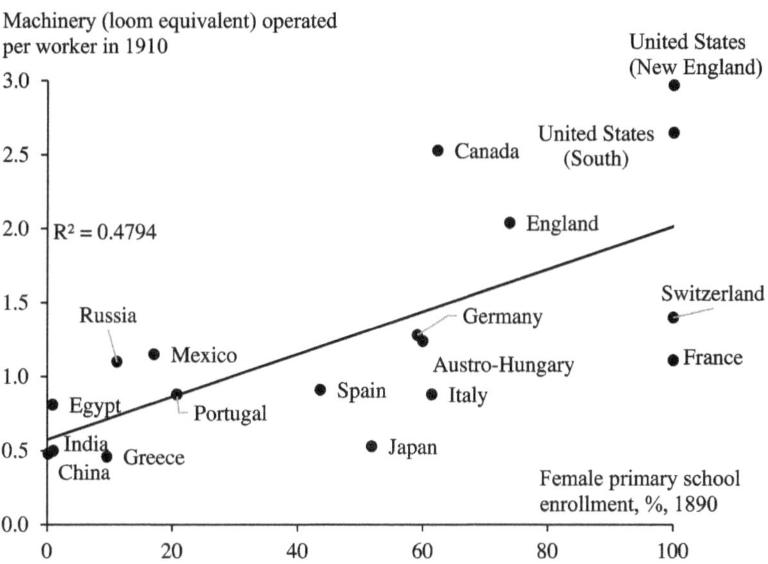

FIGURE 3.1: Textile workers were more productive in societies that made greater commitment to education.

Note: Female primary school enrollment for Austro-Hungary is the average of the now two countries.

Source: Machinery (loom equivalents) per worker from Clark, Gregory. 1987. "Why isn't the whole world developed? Lessons from the cotton mills." *The Journal of Economic History* 47.1: 141–173, Table 3; female primary school enrollment from Barro, Robert J. and Jong-Wha Lee. 2015. *Education Matters: Global Schooling Gains from the 19th to the 21st Century*. New York: Oxford University Press.

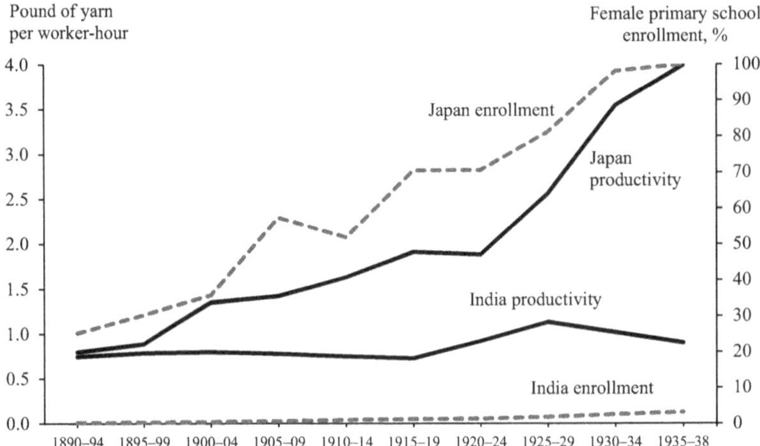

FIGURE 3.2: Japanese worker productivity soared with the spread of education.

Note: Female primary school enrollment is lagged by twenty years, that is, for 1890–1894 pounds of yarn/worker, the enrollment is in 1870.

Source: Pounds of yarn per worker from Wolcott, Susan and Gregory Clark. 1999. "Why nations fail: Managerial decisions and performance in Indian cotton textiles, 1890–1938." *The Journal of Economic History* 59 (2): 397–423, Table 1; female primary school enrollment Barro, Robert J. and Jong-Wha Lee. 2015. *Education Matters: Global Schooling Gains from the 19th to the 21st Century.* New York: Oxford University Press.

Of course, in 1910, Japan had not gained the full productivity benefits of its enormous strides in primary education since the Meiji Restoration in 1868. The message was simple: the benefits of education take time to accrue. The policy warning was clear: invest now in education or sacrifice productivity for decades.

As Japan raced toward near-universal primary education, their mills rapidly increased their productivity (Figure 3.2). That step-up in productivity in the early 1920s coincided with their entry into the Indian market.

Arno Pearse, a British historian and general secretary of the International Federation of Textile Producers' Associations, surveyed the technical operations of mills in India, China, and Japan in the late 1920s. Of Japan, he wrote that "one notices everywhere the results of a good general education; every mill girl reads and writes, and possesses a general education quite on par with that of most European countries." Japanese companies had greater incentives to run special training classes for foremen and female supervisors to help them increase the output rate of their receptive factory-floor workers. In a direct comparison with the low productivity of Indian workers, Pearse noted that the much superior education in Japan led to less "defective work" and quicker adoption of more advanced technologies.[27]

Thus, just as Japan's farmers and extension workers benefited from national mass education, mill owners and employees leveraged off their government's education drive to create learning factory floors. Indian textile producers, in contrast, fell into a "bad equilibrium." They employed largely illiterate workers whom they kept on a leash with highly insecure work. Neither the factory managers nor the workers had an incentive to invest in each other. Indian mill owners had flourished in the nineteenth century by paying low wages and selling to markets where they had little competition. But in the early twentieth century, Japan's producers exposed the weakness of India's low-wage/low-productivity strategy.[28] The stunned Indian mills quickly lost ground in the adoption of new technologies and became saddled with old machines.

Steel production was a brighter spot amid prevailing Indian industrial inefficiency. The Tata Iron and Steel Company (TISCO)—the dominant prewar producer—had produced finished steel as early as 1912 at Jamshedpur in what is now the state of Jharkhand. At first, TISCO, like the textile industry, received the protection of import tariffs, in part because India's labor force was much less efficient than in the United States and Europe. TISCO management, however, gained efficiency through improved production techniques that helped eliminate the need for tariff protection for steel by 1947. In the end, TISCO could hold its home ground against foreign competition. But a number of other Indian industrial sectors still required protection from imports.[29]

Upon achieving independence, therefore, Indian industry had only rare bright spots and was unable to compete internationally and provide employment to large numbers of Indians. That was a handicap India needed to urgently overcome.

Nehru Nixes Development of Small and Medium-Sized Firms

In principle, small and medium-scale manufacturers could generate substantial numbers of new jobs. Indian policymakers made a gesture toward small firms by promoting traditional hand spinning using a *charkha* (spinning wheel) and handloom weaving. But these traditional manufacturing operations could not compete with modern textile mills and power looms, and so served only niche markets at home and abroad. For India, hope lay in a variety of more "modern" small and medium-sized firms, which manufactured clothes, bicycles, cooking pots and pans, ceiling and table fans, and even textile machinery and parts. India's most dynamic entrepreneurs—merchants, engineers, artisans, and craftsmen—ran these businesses, typically in small-town industrial clusters.[30]

Ludhiana in Punjab was a particularly vibrant town, known for textiles, knitwear, and shoes. It was also home to a nascent bicycle industry. In 1946, the Munjal brothers set up a "workshed" for the manufacture of bicycle parts and assembly of bicycles in Ludhiana. Satyananda, one of the brothers, had previously repaired bicycles and sewing machines in Lahore and Amritsar, where he learned to take them apart and assemble them.[31] From that unheralded beginning, the brothers and their children would grow their company Hero Cycles into a major bicycle producer. India had the potential to produce many such heroes.

Another diversified cluster centered around Coimbatore, about five hundred kilometers southwest of Chennai (then Madras). Coimbatore had developed a textile industry in the pre-independence years and had also diversified into garments and light engineering products. In addition, silver thread and wire (*jari*) producers in Surat and bangles producers in Firozabad (Uttar Pradesh) formed traditional manufacturing clusters with growth potential.[32]

Small-town clusters had an honored place in the history of international industrialization. In his 1890 classic *Principles of Economics*, the great University of Cambridge economist Alfred Marshall described Staffordshire's pottery makers and Sheffield's cutlery producers as examples of industrial dynamism. Because many producers in "the same skilled trade" congregate in a cluster, their suppliers and toolmakers benefit by locating nearby. Such proximity generates tremendous productivity benefits: "If one man starts a new idea, it is taken up by others and combined with suggestions of their own; and thus, it becomes the source of further new ideas. Children learn them unconsciously."[33] Industrial clusters are intense forms of what economists call "learning-by-doing." Marshall would have recognized modern Silicon Valley as a high-tech upgrade of nineteenth-century Staffordshire and Sheffield.

In Japan, a particularly successful example of Marshall-style concentration of highly interdependent producers was the bicycle-industry cluster in Sakai, a city near Osaka. Here, manufacturers produced handlebars, wheel rims, hubs, and spokes, all destined for a final bicycle manufacturer. A similar cluster produced parts of sewing machines. Thus, Japan developed a complex system of subcontractors, who fed producers, who in turn assembled the parts and shipped the final product to the consumer.[34]

Like post-independence Indian manufacturers, Japan's small and medium-sized firms in the interwar years were "often financially unstable" and suffered from a reputation for poor quality.[35] My father, who was born in 1925, recalls that when he was a young lad in the 1930s, the Hindi word *Japani* (Japanese) was synonymous with "shoddy." He, for example, chose an English-made Hercules bicycle for thirty-five rupees over a bicycle produced in Japan that cost only twenty rupees but frequently broke down. Japanese exporters, however, didn't give up. They scoped out the Indian market to an astonishing degree, supplying plastic figures of Lord Krishna, which were used by families for decoration and by children in their religious game-playing. While Japan's exporters did not lose their low-quality reputation, they steadily upgraded to more advanced toys, such as wind-up mechanical cars and electric trams.

After the Second World War, Japan sold more sophisticated products to India, including various kinds of machinery. To the Americans, though, Japanese producers still exported low-tech, labor-intensive products such as women's blouses and men's and boy's shirts. Their reputation from the 1930s for shoddy products continued to hurt them. In 1954, a Rochester paper carried a report on "highly dangerous Japanese-made toys," which when placed near something hot would burst into intense flames and give off toxic gases."[36]

Such incidents, however, became rarer. Manufacturers in Japan subjected themselves to the supervision of American buyers and the rigor of their government's quality-control systems. They quickly leapfrogged to high-precision products. By 1957, Japanese optical instruments—cameras, binoculars, and microscopes—began to enjoy an "excellent reputation" among American consumers for their high quality and low prices.[37]

The lesson for India was once again clear. The world has a tolerance for cheap, low-quality products. Successful exporters use the period of tolerance to learn the techniques for upgrading product quality. Such learning and upgrading lies at the essence of economic development. Learning-by-doing complements and enhances domestic education capabilities. In Japan, educated workers, industrial clusters as hothouses of ideas, and the challenge of meeting the exacting standards of sophisticated foreign buyers were the multiple knowledge sources that propelled national productivity growth.

An extraordinary opportunity opened for India in the immediate postwar years. Pent-up global demand and reconstruction needs created a never-since-matched boom in world trade, especially in industrial products. With producers in Japan beginning to move upscale, India had the possibility of making headway in the less sophisticated and labor-intensive product segments of global markets.

India did not have a sensible discussion—then or later—on the potential of exports to create domestic jobs. To some analysts then, an export drive seemed out of reach. An "export pessimism" had gained ground.[38] To its credit, though, India's First Five-Year Plan ignored such pessimism, which applied mainly to Latin American countries dependent on the exports of agricultural commodities and minerals. The First Plan made a passing reference to the possibility that India could expand exports of manufactured products such as "sewing machines, batteries, bicycles, and pharmaceuticals" by increasing sales beyond the small quantities Indian producers then sold to countries of Southeast Asia.[39]

But Nehru downplayed such ideas. In July 1954, he delivered a public speech at Beawar, an industrial center in Rajasthan. The industry in Beawar included a textile mill, cotton gins, handloom weaving, and hosiery. "You will forgive me," Nehru said, "if I point out that textile mills and industries of this kind are child's play in the modern world and of no great significance. Nowadays, industries of a different kind are coming up. They are called heavy industries, which are the fountainheads of other industries." Nehru insisted that India must build industries that produce machines to make other machines. He spoke of the Sindri fertilizer plant, which he said was bigger than all the industry in Beawar. "The steel-making plants are also huge," he said.[40] He made his priority clear: big, "heavy" industry.

Thus, at the start of its post-independence journey, India neglected two essential sources of economic development: agriculture and labor-intensive manufacturing. In agriculture, powerful politicians thwarted land reforms and bureaucratic torpor weighed down extension services. And once Nehru belittled small and medium-sized manufacturing, India essentially gave up the possibility of generating job-rich manufacturing growth.

When Hope Began to Fade

In 1950, the Indian government began collecting social and economic data through sample surveys. The physicist and statistician Prasanta Chandra Mahalanobis established the method and practice for conducting these surveys under the National Sample Survey (NSS) umbrella.[41] In 1954 the NSS began a gigantic nationwide survey of employment conditions. Based on that data and additional surveys, estimates showed that only 1 percent of Indians were "openly unemployed"—they had no job. However, there was vast underemployment among the rest. Most of the "underemployed" were in agriculture; they were idle between seasons or between different phases of a crop production cycle. Most farm households did not have enough work for all family members and so they spread the work among themselves. Additionally, mom-and-pop stores, restaurants, and transport providers in the "informal" sector harbored significant numbers of underemployed workers. If some of the underemployed stopped sharing tasks in order to work full-time, 15 percent of Indians would have nothing to do. Hence, India had an effective unemployment rate of 16 percent: 1 percent "openly unemployed" and 15 percent among the underemployed.[42] Indian planners called this effective unemployment, the shortfall or "backlog" in the demand for jobs.

The numbers were large. In 1955, India's population was about 410 million people. Of these, the 250 million older than age fifteen formed the potential workforce. Many women and students chose not to work, leaving a labor force of 167.5 million. The 16 percent effective unemployment rate in a labor force of 167.5 million people implied that India had a shortfall of about twenty-six million jobs. In a 1958 research paper, Mahalanobis himself estimated the employment shortfall in 1955 to be twenty-five million.[43] Such numbers are imprecise; I believe that the shortfall was somewhere between twenty and twenty-five million jobs.

Also, India's population was growing quickly. Since the 1920s, better control of infectious diseases and modest improvements in sanitation had caused death rates—including infant mortality rates—to fall rapidly. Birth rates were declining at a more modest pace. Overall, therefore, an increasing number of babies were growing into young adults looking for jobs. If, as seemed likely, India's population were to grow at 2 percent a year for the rest of the century, the nation's population would reach a billion people by 2000. The additional workforce of hundreds of millions of people could be a blessing, a "demographic dividend" that powered savings, investment, and growth. Without productive jobs, India would be swamped by angry job seekers.

Frustration was already bubbling to the surface. In 1951, Raj Kapoor's hugely popular movie *Awaara* mirrored the nation's optimism. But as the 1950s wore on, hope turned into impatience. In 1953, twenty-eight-year-old Ritwik Ghatak, who stands today with his Bengali compatriot Satyajit Ray in the pantheon of India's greatest filmmakers, produced his first movie, *Nagarik* (Citizen). In it, Ghatak tells the story of a college graduate searching for a job. The young man views each job opening with eager anticipation. He dreams of "a pretty house" in an "idyllic setting" where a street musician strums his violin. After each setback, he wakes to a rude reality. In that reality, he and his family slip down the economic and social ladder into precarity and urban squalor.[44]

In 1955, Raj Kapoor reappeared as Raj in the movie *Shree 420,* which everyone understood as "Mr. Crook" (the number 420 was a reference to the section of the Indian Penal Code under which crimes of dishonesty and deception are punished). In the movie's opening sequence, Raj in his Charlie Chaplin garb walks along a country road, with his bag of worldly belongings tied up in a bindle and his right big toe sticking out through a hole in his shoe. He sings as he walks: "Mera joota hai Japani, yeh patloon Englistani, sar pe laal topi Rusi, phir bhi dil hai Hindustani" (My shoe is Japanese, these trousers are English, the red hat on my head is Russian, but my heart is Indian). Those words virtually became a "national anthem," writes the journalist and human rights activist Rajni Bakshi. Raj's face lights up as he passes a sign pointing toward Bombay and, soon enough, he walks onto another anonymous city street. He begins his job search right away. "Meine B.A. kiya hai" (I have completed a B.A.), he says to the first person willing to talk to him.[45]

Raj finds a home in a *basti*, a slum, above which rises a "towering mansion." To emphasize the point, the mansion's "corrupt and ruthless" owner is endowed with generous girth and multiple chins. In 1951, Raj the vagabond stuck to petty crime, remaining hopeful of better times; in 1955, Raj the crook uses his skills as a card-sharp to make a living as he moves into the orbit of a criminal gang.[46] The transition from hope to cynicism was happening quickly.

By 1954, Nehru's references to employment generation reached a new crescendo. He could see, he said, the "vastness of this unemployment problem"; he recognized that unemployment hid amid apparently employed workers. He was particularly annoyed at universities, which he said were "churning out" B.A. and M.A. degrees but imparting little education. Providing jobs for such degree holders, he said, was "very difficult."[47] Thus, Nehru shared the worry of millions of Indians, which Ghatak and Kapoor sensed. Ghatak's movie was a lament. But Kapoor in *Shree 420* warned that poor job prospects for so many college graduates would breed social pathologies.

Repeatedly—in a December 1954 speech in the Lok Sabha (the lower house of the national parliament), in the resolution he drafted for the Congress Party conference at Avadi in January 1955, and in two speeches that followed the tabling of that resolution—Nehru said that his government's goal was to eradicate unemployment over the next ten years. The government would pursue this goal, he said, in a "socialistic" society, one that gave primacy to equality in Indian society.[48]

These were worthy sentiments, but Nehru unfortunately had no strategy for a matching plan of action. As Gandhi recognized, Nehru was a thinker, not a doer. His biographer Sarvepalli Gopal wrote that Nehru had no aptitude for conducting the administration of the state. He worked tirelessly but devoted “limitless attention” to “trivial matters.” He allowed a sense of “drift” to creep into the state’s administrative machinery. An editorial in the influential Bombay-based *Economic Weekly* echoed the theme: Nehru had a “weakness for outward show” but a “lofty disregard for unpleasant necessities.”[49]

Certainly, Nehru did not have the patience to follow Japan’s development path, which required active and coordinated political and bureaucratic mobilization to raise agricultural productivity, educate the population, and create urban jobs for workers moving out of agriculture. For Nehru, it was easier to promote and open a steel plant, where he could deal with a limited number of stakeholders and moving parts.

And thus it was that, although he understood that agriculture needed revitalization and that unemployment was India’s primary economic problem, Nehru started India down an alternative path.

Chapter 4
NEHRU'S DANGEROUS GAMBLE

> NANGAL (Punjab), July 8, 1954. The foaming waters of the Sutlej gushed forth into the Nangal hydel channel and the Bhakra canals as the Prime Minister, Mr. Nehru, pressed an electric button to inaugurate the world's biggest canal network here today. An estimated 100,000 persons cheered lustily when he declared at a solemn ceremony: "I dedicate the Bhakra-Nangal works to the good of the Indian people." Thousands of balloons were released and crackers were fired by enthusiastic villages as the black sluice gates on the hydel channel rose. Flying low over the site, Indian Air Force planes dipped in salute.[1]

The Bhakra-Nangal hydroelectric project was close to Nehru's heart. For several years, while its construction was ongoing, he often went to the project area to review the progress. Once, Nehru became upset when he heard "damage had been done to one of the Bhakra canals." He wrote an agitated letter to Bhimsen Sachar, Punjab's chief minister, complaining the engineers in charge had failed to inform his office of this damage. He was especially upset by the cheeky engineer who questioned Nehru's need to know every construction detail.[2]

But on that beautiful day, after the Sutlej waters flowed into the canals and Indian air force planes saluted the achievement, Nehru said "a certain exhilaration and excitement" filled his "heart and mind." His government, he said, had given priority to "big projects" like Bhakra-Nangal (where, eventually, dams would go over the Sutlej at sites in Bhakra and Nangal) and to similar multipurpose irrigation and electricity-generation projects in the Damodar Valley (in the present states of Jharkhand and West Bengal) and at Hirakud (on the Mahanadi River in Orissa). These projects, he emphasized, would generate electricity to run "big factories." Nehru spoke of other achievements: the "magnificent" fertilizer factory at Sindri, the "big railway engines" produced at the Chittaranjan Locomotive Works located in West Bengal. He spoke of airplanes and oceangoing ships being built throughout the country. Although Bhakra-Nangal was, for him, "the greatest of these big works," they were all "the temples of today," he said. They were the new "places of worship." Honoring them was a "sacred task."[3]

Nehru's "temples" strategy was congenial to his preference for staying above complex administrative and political fray. In comparison with the business of raising agricultural productivity and stimulating labor absorbing industries in urban areas, the temples approach to development had fewer moving parts, and Nehru needed to deal mainly with science and technology experts, many of whom were his peers and friends.[4]

There was a plausible logic to using science to modernize India. India had been on the sidelines of global scientific and technological achievements. Nehru's temples used advanced science and technology to accelerate economic development. "Ours is the urgent way," Nehru said at the opening of the National Metallurgical Laboratory in Jamshedpur in November 1950. "I want to tell the scientists assembled here that the burden of today is a great burden."[5]

Science offered endless possibilities, but it also introduced great risks—particularly as the stakes grew. Contemporaries warned that large dams would silt up, upset regional ecosystems, and inflict severe costs on the villagers they displaced. Among them was Mira Ben (Madeleine Slade, born a British citizen), who had devoted her life to Gandhi and his causes. She wrote in 1949, "We have got to study Nature's balance, and develop our lives within her laws if we are to survive as a physically healthy and morally decent species."[6] She and others were particularly concerned about the displacement of tribal and other forest-based communities, who had worked the land for generations and operated within its ecological rhythms.

The warnings bore out. As India built hundreds of dams in the cause of modernization, displaced villagers then and later never received fair compensation. The dams caused great damage to the environment around them and silted up much more quickly than anticipated (on account of the accumulation of industrial wastes and deforestation). As the dams silted up, their ability to control floods declined and their lifespans shortened. Irrigation waters caused waterlogging and salination of the land, undermining potential productivity gains and leaving large tracts of the country drought prone.[7] While farmers certainly needed more irrigation waters, there was ultimately no substitute for better seeds and productivity enhancement through superior water management, soil conservation, and crop-cultivation techniques such as Japanese farmers had practiced without the irrigation waters of huge dams.

In this chapter, I describe Nehru's temples strategy as it moved to ever higher stakes, from science and technology laboratories, to developing the new city of Chandigarh, to its culmination in the promotion of heavy industry with consequences that would echo for decades after.

The Laboratories: The Small Stakes

On January 4, 1947, several months before independence, when he was still the *de facto* prime minister as vice president in the Viceroy's Executive Council, Nehru inaugurated the flagship National Physical Laboratory in Pusa, then on the outskirts of Delhi. In April 1947, when the prime minister of the state of Bombay laid the foundation stone of the National Chemical Laboratory, Nehru sent his message to be read during the formal proceedings. In his message, Nehru called on Indian scientists to weld themselves into a "band of selfless workers" dedicated to freeing millions of Indians from "material, economic, and social bondage."[8]

Nehru had taken a degree in the natural sciences from the University of Cambridge, and science fascinated him. In August 1947, ten days after India achieved independence and while the "orgy of Hindu-Muslim" violence was raging in Punjab, he squeezed in time to chair a meeting of the Council of Scientific and Industrial Research (CSIR). This was the umbrella organization under which the various research institutes fell. Nehru would remain the president of the CSIR from 1947 to 1964, his entire tenure as prime minister.[9] He traveled across the country, laying foundation stones or delivering inauguration addresses at new institutes and laboratories, including one for paleobotany (the study of fossil plants) in Lucknow, the first of its kind anywhere in the world.

The ceremony of laying foundation stones and inaugurating the institutes allowed Nehru to declare a job well done, but his hope that the institutes would harness science and technology in the service of Indians was never realistic. There was a fundamental disconnect. The institutes functioned as elitist islands of excellence. Economic development requires resolution of social conflicts and efficient administration of multifaceted and messy tasks. Nehru was comfortable in the elite world, not in the messy one.

Nehru revealed his elitist approach to development in an unguarded moment in early 1947, when he said he wanted Indian scientists to work in "the Brahminic spirit of service." He recognized quickly that singling out the Brahmin caste—sitting on top of India's caste hierarchy—might be an endorsement of inherited superiority and privilege. He then backtracked, clarifying that "the Brahminic spirit" was "something entirely apart from the Brahmins" and referred only to "service and learning." However, he kept revealing his affinity to the best and brightest. Only a few individuals could produce high-quality science, he said; larger numbers inevitably led to "mediocrity."[10] Thus, Nehru relied on Shanti Swaroop Bhatnagar, an eminent industrial chemist and first director general of the CSIR, and on Homi Bhabha, nuclear physicist and global leader in the advancing widespread use of atomic energy. Nehru was friends with the Indian physicist and Nobel laureate C. V. Raman and with the one and only Albert Einstein.

In a low-key development on May 29, 1951, an advertisement in Indian newspapers announced an "Indian Institute of Technology" (IIT) to be established in Kharagpur in the state of West Bengal. The new institute would admit all high school students who had studied mathematics, physics, and chemistry, with classes beginning in July. In its first batch, IIT

Kharagpur admitted 210 students, with a plan to grow the student body to 1,320 in five years. Four other IITs, distributed across the country, would follow in the next decade.[11]

Although the research laboratories and especially the IITs rightfully added to Nehru's aura, their benefits to India were limited. Given their elitist premise, their distance from the nation's economic and social problems remained large. In addition, their isolation from the existing educational system restricted the benefits to the chosen ones. The astrophysicist Meghnad Saha protested at the time that the new science and technology institutes might absorb the best-prepared students, attract the most distinguished teachers, and receive the bulk of the funds, leaving the broader university network to languish.[12]

As Saha had warned, an educational cocoon did emerge. Rich Indians and senior civil servants sent their children to privileged private high schools, whence they either traveled abroad for university or launched into elite liberal arts colleges, the IITs, and the best medical colleges. From there they joined the civil services, found scarce high-paying private-sector jobs, or went abroad to work.

Millions of potential Indian geniuses remained undiscovered, as even the best Indian universities—including those at Allahabad, Bombay, Calcutta, and Madras—struggled to maintain scholarship and educational standards. The most egregious example was Allahabad University, which unraveled from the "Oxford of the East" into a shambolic mess due to a severe lack of funds.

Today, Allahabad University barely educates many of its students, for whom it serves primarily as a degree certification center. Students live in the university's hostels to attend coaching centers in the city, which prepare tens of thousands like them for exams that help select handfuls for a "dream government job."[13] Put simply, for every IIT graduate who shines brightly in California's Silicon Valley, thousands of poorly educated Indians with graduation certificates stand in the tortuously long queue for government jobs.

Most seriously, adulation of the temples strategy obscured the necessity for mass primary education. The priority in Meiji Japan, strikingly, was the opposite. During the first thirty years after the Meiji Restoration, the Japanese government focused on making primary education widely available. When they approached that goal toward the end of the nineteenth century, Japan had one (yes, one) university. Only over the first two decades of the twentieth century, as Japan achieved universal primary and secondary education, did the number of Japanese universities increase.[14]

Raising the Bet: Chandigarh

In 1959, University of Chicago economist and sociologist Bert Hoselitz described Indian cities as "parasitic" rather than "generative." Most urban residents worked in dead-end jobs, commonly as "casual labor" with no certainty when they might work next, or as "self-employed" shopkeepers and vendors, idle for much of the day. Hoselitz noted that the cities were populated by an excess of young men and hence often lacked the stability of families and communities. "Ill-health, crime, prostitution, and illiteracy" were common. Writing about Calcutta a few years later, anthropologist Nirmal Kumar Bose also highlighted the excess of "lone men" who lived "without the barest minimum of housing, sanitation, comfort, and privacy." India's unanchored urban population hampered the community cohesion required for a healthy urban life.[15]

An unexpected opportunity to build a new city attracted Nehru. The Indian state of Punjab required a new capital, having lost its glamorous capital Lahore to the part of pre-partition Punjab incorporated into Pakistan. Hindu and Sikh refugees fleeing from Pakistan also needed new urban homes. For Nehru, Punjab's new capital city offered an opportunity to create a model of urban development.

The site for the new capital, Chandigarh, had fertile agricultural land "dotted with groves of mango trees, spread over seventeen villages." Its pristine setting fit perfectly with Nehru's temples strategy. As he said, "The site chosen is free from the existing encumbrances of old towns and old traditions. Let it be the first expression of our creative genius flowering on newly earned freedom."[16] That was key: "free of the existing encumbrances." Who then would deal with those encumbrances?

Nehru chose Swiss-born French architect Charles-Édouard Jeanneret (better known as Le Corbusier) to plan and design the new city. Nehru saw in Le Corbusier a "modern-day prophet of the Second Industrial Age," who could usher Indian cities into the international vanguard of urban development. He developed a close personal relationship with Le Corbusier, just as he had with the scientists Shanti Swaroop Bhatnagar and Homi Bhabha. Nehru almost always intervened in Le Corbusier's favor whenever he had to battle the Punjab government.[17]

Le Corbusier visualized Chandigarh "constructed on the principles of a garden city, with 'no heavy or obnoxious industries.'" He mixed mystical spirituality—symbolized by the open-hand monument to receive and distribute newly created wealth—with a futuristic view in the Museum of Knowledge, home to a "modern-day video arcade."[18] It was a grand vision.

Chandigarh's wide boulevards and elegant cubes and rectangles have made it one of India's more livable cities. Yet Chandigarh could not escape the social and demographic pressures that caused other Indian cities to turn parasitic. Slums appeared on the city's periphery and unauthorized commercial construction and street vendors took root in various neighborhoods. Unhygienic uses of low-income housing became common, as dwellings meant for one family often housed a family in each room.[19]

The idea that Chandigarh would provide a model for Indian urbanization proved fanciful. India urgently needed to breathe new life into its old cities, with all their encumbrances. In 1960, the World Bank wrote, in somewhat stark language: "one of the most dangerous weaknesses of [Indian planning] is the continued neglect of problems of urban development in Calcutta." Having been part of the international bureaucracy myself for a quarter century, it seems to me a miracle that the phrase "dangerous weaknesses" survived multiple rounds of internal document review, with each round designed to soften the words and blur the message. The city of Calcutta, the World Bank continued, was impeding economic growth in a crucial industrial region. As the World Bank explained, Calcutta was not serving the needs of its own population or of its economic hinterland:

> Overcrowding, degradation of housing, health hazards, primitive water supplies, lack of space for new industries, traffic bottlenecks, power shortage, a still unsolved refugee problem—all are increasing the cost

> of moving goods and providing the many services that a growing industrial region demands of its metropolis. . . . Nor is there any alternative to Calcutta as a port, financial and administrative center and major market for the heavy and light industries that should develop, and are in fact developing, on the basis of the coal/steel complex in West Bengal, Bihar, and adjoining areas of Madhya Pradesh and Orissa.[20]

This seems to be the earliest statement on the crucial importance of cities to India's economic development. In agreement with the World Bank report, the anthropologist Nirmal Kumar Bose described Calcutta as a "premature metropolis." In population and physical area, Calcutta was about the size of the world's great metropolises such as London and New York. But Calcutta served neither the social nor economic function of a metropolis.[21]

Urban development was not one single objective achieved in a single project, as Jane Jacobs explained. Indian cities needed multiple forms of infrastructure, including housing and local community amenities. Coordination of these many efforts made urban development much more complex than building standalone "temples of new India." With the passage of time, urban development became harder as local politicians staked out territories within the cities, armed with henchmen to intimidate and even "eliminate" those they viewed as competitors.[22]

Across the country, Bombay, the capital of the western state of Maharashtra, was also a premature metropolis. In 1963, the acclaimed writer-moviemaker Khwaja Ahmad Abbas, famous for portraying the Bengal famine in *Dharti ke lal*, told a story about life in Bombay. In this new film, *Shahar aur Sapna* (The city and the dream), a young couple meet when forced to take refuge in a drainpipe; once they marry, they share a dream (or rather, a nightmare) of bringing up their first child in that drainpipe. Tensions ran high in Bombay for the same reason as in Calcutta: the scarcity of essential resources and the lack of jobs.

Bombay had its unique features. The prohibition of alcohol in 1952 created a profitable illicit liquor trade. Also profitable was the smuggling of gold and watches, and Philips transistors were always in demand for piped-in film music and live cricket commentary. From small beginnings, criminal activity quickly spread. Varadarajan Muniswami Mudaliar, who started with the liquor trade, became overlord of the Dharavi slum, where he allocated land to migrants and used his clout with the local administration to get residents ration cards and illegal electricity and water connections. Haji Mastan had a flourishing smuggling business. Karim Lala specialized in the eviction of tenants and leaseholders. From the docks through the slums and streets, musclemen dotted the city. They became the *dadas*, local goons who acted as intermediaries between the people and a corrupt bureaucracy and as arbiters in private disputes.[23]

Neglect of Bombay continued. A 1971 World Bank report detailed Bombay's need for more and better transport, investment in public utilities, and better land-use and housing policies. The report emphasized that Bombay needed an administrative institution to "represent the interests of the whole region," a body with "real power" and fiscal authority.[24]

At the opposite end of large metropolises, University of Chicago economist Milton Friedman made the case for small cities that would serve as the locations of industrial clusters, in much the same way as economist Alfred Marshall had advocated in the early twentieth century. During a 1963 visit to India, Friedman was exhilarated by his tour of Ludhiana, the medium-sized town in Punjab. An entrepreneurial energy infused "the thousands of small and medium size workshops, with [their] extraordinarily detailed specialization of function." Known primarily for its knitted goods, Friedman saw in Ludhiana "a major centre for the production of machine tools, bicycles, sewing machines, and similar items."[25]

The all-hands-on-deck approach needed for energizing Indian cities and industrial clusters did not blend with Nehru's personality. He continued his passionate rhetoric while avoiding development tasks that required summoning the collective energies of Indians. He focused on new science and technology institutes, rather than strengthening existing universities or, even more important, building a strong base of mass education. He lavished attention on building a new city—Chandigarh—rather than reinvigorating the existing cities that were falling apart.[26]

That same temples strategy bet India's future on heavy industrialization.

The Big Bet: The Second Five-Year Plan

In the years of the First Five-Year Plan, 1951 to 1956, India's per capita GDP, the average income per person, grew by 1.8 percent annually. This was a performance to celebrate after near stagnation—GDP per capita growth of 0.1 percent a year—in the half century before independence.[27] Nehru, however, misjudged India's post-independence achievement, particularly in agriculture. With the exception of the drought of 1950–1951, the rain gods had cooperated. Nehru read that good luck as: "We have achieved considerable measure of success in agriculture and food production." And although the Community Development Program and the associated technical extension services, initiated in October 1952, had failed utterly, Nehru believed that the effort had been a success. He was better aware of the land reform failures, recognizing that the *zamindari* and other reforms had not achieved more equal landholding. He understood that "many loopholes" in the reform legislation and "great deal of evasion" had allowed the vast rural inequalities in income and wealth to persist. But knowing not what else to do, he gave up on the cause of agricultural development and decided it was best to move on.[28]

"The time had come," Nehru said, "to advance rapidly on the industrial front." He emphasized that the "urgent necessity for us to industrialize as rapidly as possible" meant "the development of heavy industries which would lay the foundations for future growth."[29]

What explains Nehru's fascination—indeed, obsession—with heavy industrialization? The most consistent reading of Nehru—when seen in combination with his championing of large-scale dams, scientific laboratories, advanced engineering and medical institutes, and the city of Chandigarh—is that, as Nehru himself put it, he was building the temples of modern India. Nehru could direct such activity with the help of a small number of gifted Indians while remaining distant from the rough and tumble of grassroots mobilization of people and resources.

A commonly held but lazy view says Nehru's "Fabian socialism" led him to public sector–driven heavy industrialization. Was Nehru a Fabian socialist? How, for example, did he match up with Clement Attlee who, as Britain's first postwar prime minister from 1945 to 1951, was historically the most important practitioner of Fabian socialism? Attlee nationalized coal mining, the iron and steel industries, and public services, including the railways, electric power, and gas supply. These nationalizations come closest to Nehru's reliance on the public sector to accelerate industrialization. But Nehru was his own man. His nationalization included fertilizer factories and, importantly in his own mind, electrical and non-electrical machinery. In contrast, Nehru stayed away from Attlee's true socialism, powerfully reflected in the United Kingdom's comprehensive National Health Service, free secondary education for all children, and extension of social insurance. These investments in human capital and social security, as historian Jim Tomlinson has written, "marked major changes in British society."[30]

Nehru thus discarded the socialism of Fabian socialism—healthcare, education, and social security, all of which gave people dignity and the possibility of better futures.

Some suggest that Nehru followed Soviet economic ideas, but that makes even less sense. Large parts of the Indian economy—major chunks of industry and especially agriculture—remained in private hands. And as he did with Fabian socialism, he ignored the Soviet Union's greatest achievement: world-class education and healthcare.

Nehru would have agreed that he was not a socialist. In his own words, socialism meant "equality of opportunity" and provision of basic necessities of life—"food, clothing, houses to live in, healthcare and educational facilities"—to everyone. Whether he was inspired by Fabian socialism, Soviet ideology, or his own professed commitment to equality and fairness, he practiced none of them. As Sujatha Rao, a former health secretary (the Indian government's senior-most health official) writes, "It is inexplicable why Nehru did not pay any attention to education and health."[31]

While a fuller account of Nehru's education policies must wait until chapter 6, Nehru kept up his socialist rhetoric while being self-conscious he was not living up to it. In October 1954, he said in a public speech, "I want to provide education and healthcare facilities for everyone in India as quickly as possible. But it is impossible for us to do." In another speech, this time at the foundation-laying ceremony of a women's college in Madras in January 1955, he acknowledged that education was of "basic importance" and was essential to ensure the enhanced "productive capacity of the nation." But, he added, "there are still many things of basic importance to do." And "obviously, we are struggling against the difficulties of finance."[32] Nehru espoused the cause of socialism but always had reasons for why it was not feasible.

Possibly, Nehru's commitment to heavy industry reflected the then-popular "big push" industrialization strategy advocated by the economist Paul Rosenstein Rodan. The big push strategy called for large-scale investment in core capital-intensive industrial sectors. The promise was that these critical sectors would stimulate demand for inputs from feeder industries, which would demand more of their own inputs, leading to a cascading ferment of new activity and long-term economic growth. Rosenstein Rodan understood that his big push capital-intensive production would create few jobs. But sacrificing immediate job creation, he argued, would pay off with plentiful future jobs, perhaps even "within a generation."[33] Big push was the original "trickle-down economics," well before the term was invented. The promise was that economic outcomes in a privileged sphere would eventually flow through to all.

The big push promise was backed by little evidence. Even if it worked perfectly, could India wait a generation for jobs? And what if it went wrong? V. T. Krishnamachari, vice chairman of the Planning Commission, reported a startling statistic: 50 million peasant households had more workers than they could use productively. The ranks of the educated unemployed were increasing. Population growth was adding two million new job seekers every year.[34]

Recognizing that heavy industry would not create sufficient jobs for India's needs, Nehru, in desperation, concluded that the "solution" lay in "village industries," especially those that produced "basic necessities" using raw materials easily available in rural areas. Village industries were a nod to the Gandhian vision of self-sufficient villages. The hand-spinning wheel, the *charkha,* was intimately associated with Gandhi, who used it both as a symbol of self-sufficiency and as a meditative tool. Many traditional handloom weavers produced coarse cloth; others were brilliant artisans who produced exotic textiles.[35]

Recognizing, however, the technological obsolescence of the handloom sector, Nehru also feared that reliance on traditional handicrafts might lead to "slavery and starvation for India." In any event, the highly inefficient village—or "cottage"—industries could not compensate for the overall bias toward heavy industry. Planning Minister Gulzarilal Nanda made it clear that the Second Plan would fall "substantially short" in generating job opportunities. That they nevertheless proceeded with the Second Plan tells us that Nehru and others around him were stuck in an intellectual trap.[36]

It took an outsider to highlight the policy incongruity. Milton Friedman, during his October 1955 visit to India, which occurred well before he had seen the entrepreneurial energy of Ludhiana's small firms, forcefully criticized Nehru's combination of heavy industry and handicrafts. That combination, he said, "threatens an inefficient use of capital at the one extreme by combining it with too little labor and an inefficient use of labor at the other extreme by combining it with too little capital." Friedman insisted that "the best use of capital is in general somewhere in between." India, he explained, must focus on a "a widely diversified and much expanded light industry."[37]

Just as he had given up on agricultural development, Nehru gave up on any prospect of rapid industrial employment. However, one hurdle to heavy industrialization remained. India did not have the financial resources to implement the capital-intensive strategy. A fateful conversation Nehru had on Christmas Day in 1954 proved pivotal for the Second Plan and for India's economic future.

Nehru had traveled to the Indian Statistical Institute in Calcutta to meet with the experts Mahalanobis had assembled for advice on the Second Plan. Among the experts was Ragnar Frisch, a Norwegian economist who would share the first Nobel Prize for economics in 1969 in recognition of his contributions to mathematical economics, especially as applied to long-term planning. "I have been to the Indian Statistical Institute today," Nehru wrote in notes to himself that night. "Professor Frisch was unfortunately unwell and in bed. However, I met him in his bedroom."[38] Two of Frisch's comments excited Nehru. The first proposition was: "techniques were now available for solving almost all the problems that [arise] in planning." Nehru liked the assurance. Mathematical techniques could lay out blueprints for economic progress. With the blueprints in hand, social consensus and political compromise were of secondary importance. The second proposition gave Nehru even greater comfort: planning needed to focus on physical production targets, not on financial number-crunching. In his notes, Nehru wrote that he interpreted Frisch as saying that consideration of financial resources "should come in at a later stage when the physical objectives were defined." Nehru had permission to set his production objectives and worry about their funding later.[39]

Frisch seduced Nehru. Neither was in touch with reality. Brazil had also fallen victim to the big-push seduction. In July 1954, six months before the Frisch-Nehru meeting, the World Bank wrote that in pursuing too rapid a course of industrialization, Brazil had suffered "severe crises of industrial indigestion." The "indigestion" caused chronic inflation, wasted investment, and shortage of foreign exchange reserves.[40]

Although Indian policymakers likely did not know the details of Brazil's problems, they had good reason to worry that attempting too rapid a pace of industrialization could place severe stress on the Indian economy. In December 1955, the governor of the Reserve Bank of India—India's central bank—warned the Finance Ministry that the Second Plan, by adding enormous new demand, would cause "serious inflationary pressures." In January 1956, the Reserve Bank's Board also voiced fears about "so large an investment programme."[41]

Plan implementation began in March 1956, and the World Bank's wide-ranging critique of the Second Plan arrived a few months later, in August 1956. The World Bank report agreed with India's need to expand its production of steel, cement, and fertilizers but cautioned that "the scale may be somewhat ambitious." The report frowned on premature investment in producing heavy electrical and non-electrical machinery, for which it said India lacked both capital and technical skills. Instead, the report recommended more resources for "less complex" goods produced with labor-intensive techniques. Like the Reserve Bank's Board earlier in the year, the World Bank also came to the "inescapable" conclusion that the plan was "too large." Particularly worrying were the foreign exchange needs for imports of equipment and raw materials to fulfill the

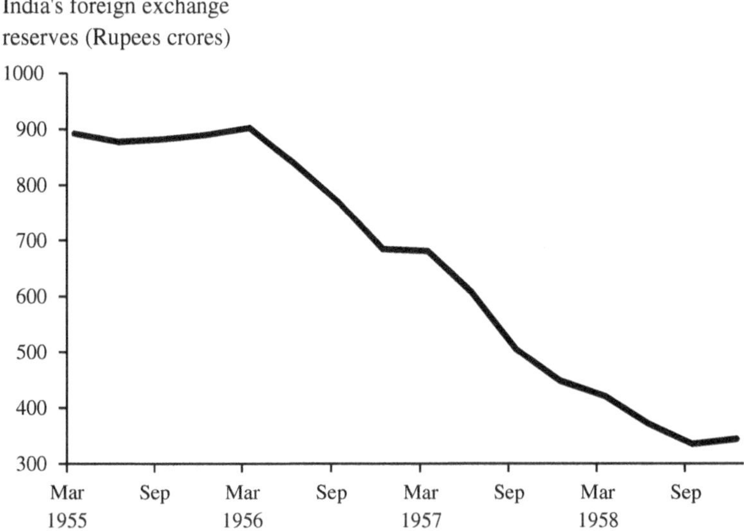

FIGURE 4.1: India's foreign exchange reserves evaporate. (Rupees crores)

Note: 1 crore equals 10 million; exchange rate: 4.76 rupees/dollar.

Source: Balachandran, Gopalan. 1998. *The Reserve Bank of India, 1951–1967*. Delhi: Oxford University Press, Table 14, 693.

plan's targets. World Bank staff added that most Indian officials privately agreed that the plan was not feasible.[42]

The outcome lived up to these warnings. The Second Plan failed almost as soon as it started. Foreign exchange reserves plummeted from 900 crore rupees ($1.90 billion) in March 1956 to 680 crores ($1.40 billion) in March 1957, a decline of $500 million in one year—with no end in sight (Figure 4.1). The sharp fall in Indian foreign exchange reserves, as the International Monetary Fund made clear, was due preponderantly to a "spurt in investment activities occasioned by the inauguration of the Second Five-Year Plan." Public-sector companies required huge imports of equipment to meet the ambitious production goals of steel and coal, and for the expansion of railways and electric power. Many public enterprises made multi-year commitments to buy equipment and materials, ensuring that a high level of imports would continue.[43]

To bolster access to foreign currency, India in early 1957 asked the IMF for $200 million. The IMF was not happy to receive the request. Its task, set out at Bretton Woods in the summer of 1944, was to help member countries tide over "temporary" balance of payments problems. Some members of the IMF's Executive Board protested that India's problems were not "temporary"; rather, they were the result of an unsustainable long-term development strategy. The Board, however, had little choice—recognizing India's urgent need, it authorized the $200 million loan.[44] Even so, the Second Plan's steep import requirements and India's stepped-up food grain imports because of a drought in 1957–1958 continued to drain foreign exchange reserves.

Those who had warned that the plan would aggravate inflation were also proved right. Prices—especially of food grains—rose rapidly. In June 1957, as a Government of India committee reported and the IMF paraphrased, "the rise in investment outlay financed by the [government's] deficit spending and credit expansion, interacting with a shortfall in food production" caused food prices to spike.[45]

The False Narrative of Socialism Persists

At the Congress Party session (convention) in January 1955, Nehru drafted a resolution calling on the party to work toward "a socialistic pattern of society." The word "socialistic" gave endless headaches to all who tried to decipher its deep meaning. The *Times of India* remarked that obscure words fit well with Nehru's "distaste for details and a penchant for soaring well above the earth, if not in the clouds." When asked how "socialistic" differed from "socialist" or "socialism," Nehru irritably responded, "As a matter of fact, there is no difference in these words." The goal, he said, was to give everyone an equal opportunity to improve their standard of living while ensuring that wealth was not heavily concentrated.[46]

The rhetoric of socialism and greater opportunity did not impress the average Indian, who was beginning to see the rot set in. Reflecting the increasing corruption and cynicism in the country, filmmaker Raj Kapoor moved further away from his idealism. His 1956 movie *Jaagte Raho* (Stay awake—stay vigilant) was set at night in a crowded apartment building. Residents aggressively chase away an anonymous peasant when he knocks on their doors, anxiously seeking a cup of water. In one apartment, an apparently legitimate businessman churns out counterfeit notes. In every apartment, residents engage in their own forms of deception. The mystified peasant shakes out of his nightmare when he hears a haunting female voice singing *Jaago Mohan Pyaare, Jaago* (Get up, dear Mohan, get up) to awaken the baby Lord Krishna. The call to wake up was a call on Indians to start again.

Although many Indians recognized Nehru's socialist rhetoric as empty, the narrative of Nehruvian socialism stuck because of the severe import controls instituted by the Indian government to stem the drain on foreign exchange reserves. Such draconian controls were new to India. Even subsequent critics of Indian economic policy, including the economists Jagadish Bhagwati and Padma Desai, recognized that India was liberalizing imports before the start of the Second Five-Year Plan. The IMF dated the events more precisely. In the second half of 1956 when foreign exchange reserves were in their initial free fall, Indian import policy was only modestly restrictive, with some controls on the import of consumer goods while allowing liberal imports of raw materials and machinery. But, by early 1957, "Severe import restrictions [had] affected supplies of raw materials and component parts."[47]

The imposition of import controls in late 1956/early 1957 was decidedly not a moment of socialist conversion, as many have since insisted. As Indraprasad Gordhanbhai ("I. G.") Patel, perhaps India's most distinguished economic policymaker in the post-independence era and one of the authors of the Second Plan, later made clear: "No one consciously initiated the policy." Import controls were based on "no theory or philosophy," Patel added emphatically. The simple truth, he explained, was that "everyone was surprised by the severity of the exchange crisis which hit us in 1956." Controls were a panicked defensive reaction to looming national bankruptcy. In Patel's words, "Necessity was the mother of invention of import controls."[48]

Once "invented," though, import controls led to the explosive spread of other controls. As Gunnar Myrdal explains in an astonishingly insightful chapter in his *Asian Drama,* when a government restricts imports it must also restrict the number of new firms as well as the expansion of existing firms. If too many companies expand production, their demand for imports could quickly exceed the limits set for certain imports. Thus, every new industrial production license soon came to require backing by import licenses for import of machinery; the industrial license also needed the green light from a "capital goods committee." Although the Second Plan was clear that the production "targets" it had set for different industries were *not* "fixed and immutable," and certainly not "ceilings," licensing authorities used the targets to deny new licenses to some businesses while also raising the targets and ceilings for those who enjoyed the favor of key decision-makers. India's production and import controls and the severity of import tariffs came to depend on the whims of the officers in charge and the ability of firms to lobby for protection.[49]

The resulting capricious import protection of domestic industry was not designed—as in many now-industrialized economies—to give chosen industries breathing space to learn and grow. Even the "leftist" economist Prabhat Patnaik concluded that the controls and their knock-on consequences "flouted all cannons of economic efficiency."[50]

The effects were distinctly anti-socialist. Large Indian businesses, especially the House of the Birlas, gained a disproportionate share of the production and import licenses. "It is well known," wrote an official inquiry into licensing practices, "Large Industrial Houses maintain liaison officers in Delhi [for] business and social contacts with senior persons in the Government and [they thus] seek to influence the exercise of discretionary power in their favour." These business houses preempted the available licenses, leaving little room for potential competitors. The top executives of big business houses sat on the boards of government-owned or -controlled financial institutions, helping them corner a disproportionate share of (especially foreign currency) lending.[51]

Nehru continued in public appearances and writings to assert his commitment to a "socialistic" path of economic development. His ministers demonstrated their allegiance to the same mystical socialism. In May 1956, at the start of the foreign exchange crisis, the brilliant political cartoonist Shankar Pillai showed Nehru looking on indulgently as his flock of reliable geese (cabinet ministers and senior Congress Party leaders) cackled, "Socialism." The rhetoric, as Myrdal noted, led many Western and South Asian pundits to the conclusion that "reliance on operational controls of an administrative discretionary type imposes a 'socialist' pattern on the economy." Myrdal placed the word "socialist" within inverted commas, as if in exasperation. Surely, he wearily added, socialism is "a misnomer for a system of policies that broadly tends to give oligopoly power and very high profits to established big business." Pakistan had very similar controls, Myrdal noted, but absent the rhetoric, no one called Pakistan "socialist."[52]

On the path Nehru set out for India, socialism was neither the intent nor the outcome. Limited job opportunities and high inflation placed greater stress on the very people Nehru professed to be helping. After the loud warning of the foreign exchange crisis in March–April 1956, Nehru had an opportunity to change course: raise productivity in agriculture and promote light industry. However, he stuck to his heavy-industry strategy. As one of Nehru's favorite poets, Robert Frost, wrote: "Oh! I kept the first for another day! Yet knowing how way leads on to way, I doubted if I should ever come back."

The Other Way Began with Rupee Devaluation

At the time, B. R. Shenoy was the only Indian economist arguing for abandoning the entire approach underlying the Second Five-Year Plan. Beginning in March 1957, in public speeches and a *Times of India* op-ed, he called for simultaneously "pruning" the Second Plan and devaluing the rupee.[53] Devaluation would make imports more expensive in rupees, thus inducing reduced imports. Bureaucrats would no longer need to decide who could import and how much. Devaluation would also encourage Indian businesses to sell their products abroad because the dollars they earned would convert to more rupees. The decline in the imports and the rise in exports would reduce the balance of payments deficit, perhaps even flipping the deficit to a surplus, as had happened after the rupee devaluation of 1949.

Nehru did not budge. Instead of using rupee devaluation to help Indian businesses sell labor-intensive, light-industrial products abroad, he continued with the original sin of heavy industrialization. Import and other controls grew like a cancer. The controls bred corruption. Private oligopoly power flourished. The inefficient Indian economy became even more inefficient. Amid surging demand for jobs, employment growth suffered.

The warning signs were flashing going into the Second Plan, and the consequences were immediate, severe, and long-lasting. Even so, an argument can be made that the Plan was not necessarily an error: it blended with globally fashionable big-push industrialization and India's postcolonial exhilaration and yearning for rapid growth. The error was continuing down that path once it was clear that it was unworkable, economically damaging, and destructive of social norms.

Nehru continued down that path because he could. One man helped him perpetuate his reflexive error: John F. Kennedy. In fact, Kennedy helped Nehru double his dangerous bet.

Chapter 5

NEHRU DOUBLES HIS BET

In October 1957, John F. Kennedy, then the junior senator from the state of Massachusetts, contended that India was strategically important for the United States. India, the forty-year-old Kennedy wrote, was uniquely positioned to "broker" the "bipolar struggle" between the superpowers. Kennedy apparently was also moved by a communist victory at the polls earlier that year in the state of Kerala. He warned that Indian communists might be poised to achieve widespread electoral victories, in which case India could fall into the clutches of the Soviets and the Chinese. Kennedy, therefore, recommended that the United States pay greater attention to India; he referenced, in particular, a recent appeal by MIT economists Max Millikan and Walt Rostow for more "durable" U.S. financial aid to India.[1]

Kennedy's essay—published in the influential *Foreign Affairs* magazine—hit the printing presses just about when the Soviet Union launched its Sputnik satellite. For America, it was a moment of grave doubt. The Soviet Union seemed to be moving ahead not just in space technology but in educational quality and in industrial and military might. Americans could also see that Soviet advances were favorably impressing unaligned and developing nations. For the United States, the communist threat became increasingly urgent.[2]

In December, responding to the Sputnik launch, Kennedy penned an op-ed in the *New York Times,* calling for a rethinking of U.S. military and foreign-policy alliances. He now paid even more attention to India. India's Second Plan was floundering, and Kennedy wrote: "Congress must pass a loan and aid program, which will prevent a failure of India's second five-year plan." India, he said, was "the showcase of the democratic experiment in Asia." It was the "most important of all uncommitted nations," and it could have, Kennedy argued, "a diversified and democratic society outside the zone of Communist influence and control, but only if we help."[3]

Having asserted that the big-push Second Plan's success was essential to preserving Indian democracy, Kennedy used his position on the Senate's Foreign Relations Committee to lobby for more financial aid to India. At a committee hearing in February 1958, Kennedy asked Walt Rostow a question, the answer to which the two of them had evidently rehearsed.

> KENNEDY: Do you think that the proposed economic assistance which the [President Dwight Eisenhower] administration has decided to give to India is sufficient to meet the minimum requirements of successful Indian development and American policy in that area?
>
> ROSTOW: I believe that the present aid program, which amounts to $290 million this year, is grossly inadequate. This [Five-Year Plan] is a great adventure for them. Here they are caught at a moment in that adventure where a lot of pressures have converged on them at once, striking at the one point we can most easily help—foreign exchange."[4]

Kennedy was positioning himself to battle the Eisenhower administration, with a possible run at the presidency already in his mind; he was also establishing his credentials as a liberal Democrat. Rostow was pursuing his own aims. He was an unwavering enemy of communism, and he viewed with great alarm the possibility that the Soviets and Chinese might woo India. Rostow also had an economic idea to sell. In his book in the making, *The Stages of Economic Growth,* he declared that just as a plane taxied on a runway, an economy taxied in preparation for "taking off" into self-sustaining capitalism. Rostow mysteriously concluded that the Indian economy, despite its near-seizure after the Second Plan began, had met the "domestic prerequisites of growth" and could take off if it received "external capital in adequate amounts and over a long enough period."[5] India was a guinea pig for his theory. Rostow needed Kennedy as much as Kennedy needed him.

In March 1958, a month after Rostow argued in the U.S. Senate for more aid to India, Kennedy joined forces with John Sherman Cooper, Republican senator from Kentucky (and formerly ambassador to India). Together, they advocated for a Senate foreign aid bill, which passed that June. The bill contained a specific reference to greatly expand aid to India. President Dwight Eisenhower, also prodded by the Communist threat, supported that aid initiative. Eisenhower followed up in August by shepherding a substantial increase in the resources available to the World Bank and IMF for supporting developing countries.[6]

The United States was then—and even more so, later—a key contributor to what came to be known as the Aid India Consortium, an international forum of major industrialized nations that helped fund India's foreign exchange needs. The World Bank, which convened and coordinated these donors, first brought them together in August 1958 to arrange emergency financing for India. Over time, the Aid India Consortium became the main source of long-term international funds for India.[7]

As donors geared up to finance Indian development, Indian authorities, having learned no lessons, prepared a hugely ambitious Third Plan that magnified the Second Plan's defects. Even Nehru's supporters were worried about the continued neglect of employment generation. In February 1959, a Congress Party committee—which included the prime minister's daughter Indira Gandhi and Planning Minister Gulzarilal Nanda—warned that the new plan did little to address India's "gigantic" employment problem. However, Nehru had won the 1957 election easily and was not accountable to anyone at home. He did have one problem, though. As the IMF noted, India's balance of payments position was under "increasing strain." Foreign exchange reserves had continued to fall.[8]

To stay on his chosen path, Nehru needed billions of aid dollars for the Third Plan. And since a large portion of that aid would come from the United States, Nehru needed, in particular, a U.S. benefactor. JFK volunteered to play that crucial role.[9]

The Seduction of "Free Money"

The moment in time allowed Nehru to have his cake and eat it too. Braj Kumar ("B. K.") Nehru—a distinguished civil servant who happened to be the prime minister's nephew—was, as commissioner general for economic affairs, the point man for amassing foreign aid. B. K. Nehru reports that the phrase "foreign aid" was "anathema" to Prime Minister Nehru, who made it clear he would not accept foreign assistance to which donors attached conditions. The prime minister was particularly attached to his policy of non-alignment to either superpower. He insisted that he would not "under any circumstances" alter his non-alignment policy as a price for the aid.[10]

And, in fact, the official assistance came with no conditions. To Indians, the funds, although they were mainly in the form of loans, seemed like "free money." This was not the case—India had to repay the debt with interest. But neither on foreign nor on domestic policy did the donors ask India to make any change. B. K. Nehru gleefully reported that the Second Plan "proved that we could get the money, that we could get it without altering any of our policies, internal or external, and that we could get it without bending the knee or bowing the head."[11]

That such "free money" would continue was a rash presumption. Non-alignment, so dear to Nehru's heart, was on shaky ground. The relationship with China had deteriorated since October 1950, when China began annexing Tibet, a friend and ally of India. Before he died, Sardar Patel suggested to Nehru that a western military alliance was the only reliable counterweight to Chinese military might. Nehru ignored the advice. After Patel's death in December 1950, the Chinese made frequent claims on Indian territory. Indo-China tensions escalated in March 1959, when the Dalai Lama, the spiritual and political head of the Tibetan Buddhists, fled Tibet for India. In 1959 and 1960, as the Third Plan took its final shape, the China threat loomed larger than ever before. Western donors could have squeezed Nehru on this non-aligned stance with little fear of a domestic communist upsurge.

India also needed to change its economic policy. B. R. Shenoy, the most consistent voice speaking out against the Nehruvian strategy, had proposed a fundamental shift: get rid of investment and production targeting and let the exchange rate depreciate. A cheaper rupee would curtail imports by making them more expensive. More important, a cheaper rupee would spur Indian businesses to export products made with labor-intensive techniques. India was well-positioned, as the August 1956 World Bank report said, to ramp up output of small engines, electric motors, pumps, bicycles, cables, lamps, and telephones. A cheaper currency would have given Indian manufacturers the boost they needed to produce and export such products.[12]

Although Indian policymakers disregarded the advice offered by Shenoy and the World Bank, Taiwanese leaders embarked on exactly that proposed route, having independently reached the same conclusions. To be clear, the Taiwanese did not make a blind commitment to free-market philosophy. K. Y. Yin, the "mastermind of Taiwanese industrialization," continued to emphasize the need for governmental investment on electric power generation and fertilizer production. However, in 1957, he put Taiwan on the path to export-led industrialization, starting with labor-intensive textiles. The Taiwanese focused on the need to catalyze—jump-start—promising areas of production. Yin had recently traveled to Japan to study Japanese industrial development in the decades following the Meiji Restoration. The lesson he learned was that "a government must lead, at least in the beginning." True to that spirit, a senior Taiwanese policymaker later said that Taiwan's strategy "was to help various parts of the economy first to start, then to walk, and then we let them go."[13] The first postwar emulation of the Japanese development model was on. However, with access to "free money"—even though donors could easily turn it off—Nehru doubled his bet on his heavy industry strategy.

Nehru Holds Firm

In late 1959, R. K. Karanjia, editor of the left-leaning Bombay-based tabloid *Blitz*, interviewed Nehru over several days. Karanjia was sympathetic to Nehruvian aspirations. Even so, he was taken aback by Nehru's vigorous but dubious justification for staying the course. Adopting the uncompromising certainty of Walt Rostow's "take-off" thesis, Nehru insisted that Indian industrialization was primed to develop its own momentum, which would become "self-feeding, self-propelling, self-developing." Even more strikingly, Nehru claimed India had chosen a "scientific approach" to economic development, adding that economic planning and development were driven by a "mathematical formula." Nehru had been hooked to the idea of mathematically driven economic development since his encounter with the Norwegian economist Ragnar Frisch in December 1954. A surprised Karanjia asked: "A mathematical formula?" "Almost, almost," Nehru responded. He conceded that the "quality of the human being" as well as "climate and other factors" did count. "But subject to these factors," Nehru asserted, "*planning and development have become a sort of mathematical formula which may be worked out scientifically*: if you do this, this is bound to follow, and this is going to be the next step and that [leads to] the third step."[14]

Nehru stripped administrative, social, and political considerations from his economic thinking. For him, economics was a set of equations, and he believed those equations were working. Indian industry had done "remarkably well," he insisted. Nehru was more realistic about India's agricultural performance. Whereas in January 1955, he had asserted "considerable progress" in agriculture, he now acknowledged that agricultural progress had been "disappointing." But greater realism did not change his policy perspective. He blamed the lack of progress on "bad harvests, bad this and that." He complained of peasants steeped in "orthodoxy and old customs."[15]

Hence, despite precarious relations with China and evidence of a failed Second Plan, the Third Plan was an unabashedly scaled-up version of the Second Plan. The total plan outlay, at $15.1 (Rs. 72.5) billion, was up from $9.7 (Rs. 46) billion spent on the Second Plan. Despite Nehru's recent recognition of disappointing progress in agriculture, the share of spending on agriculture remained unchanged. The massive industrial investment was expected to trigger an increase in imports from $10.4 to $11.9 billion. And—hold your breath—with virtually no foreign exchange reserves, the foreign aid requirement jumped from $2.2 to $5.5 billion.[16] The Second Plan document had been hazy on the plan's foreign exchange needs, and it took a mad scramble to fill the hole when the large sums needed became quickly evident. The needed foreign assistance for the Third Plan was large and boldly displayed.

Kennedy Rides to India's Aid

"One day in August 1958," writes the University of Cambridge historian David Milne, "Kennedy gave Rostow a lift to the State Department in his ostentatious convertible, with its top down. They shot the breeze about potential nominees for the 1960 primaries [to select the Democratic candidate to run against the Republican Richard Nixon in the presidential race later that year]. Kennedy casually mentioned he was planning to run."[17]

We know the rest. Nixon was viscerally anti-Indian. He found Indians "repulsive," as he once confided to a group of business executives. Kennedy won the presidency in a nail-biting election. He was committed to the liberal view of a "beneficent" government under a "powerful presidency." He also seemed to believe in India and especially in Nehru. On January 31, 1961, in his first State of the Union address to the U.S. Congress, Kennedy said he had drawn inspiration from "the soaring idealism of Mr. Nehru."[18]

On April 27 that year, John Kenneth Galbraith, Harvard University economist and American ambassador to India, wrote in his diary, "This afternoon a message came in asking me to inform the Prime Minister that the President had marked him down for a billion dollars for the next two years of the [Third] Five-Year Plan. I went over to his Parliament office to tell him. I could not be sure whether he was embarrassed or touched—he made almost no comment." Galbraith added a footnote to his observation: "Nehru's pride was closely engaged with that of India. He recognized the great role played by our help. But it also meant, I am certain, that he saw his country in some slight measure as a beneficiary of our charity, and this he did not like at all."[19]

Kennedy used his billion dollars of aid to push other countries to raise their aid commitments to India. In a message in mid-May to West German chancellor Konrad Adenauer, Kennedy attached the greatest importance to India's successful completion of the Third Plan. The Germans increased their aid contribution by $50 million to $381 million. In early June, anchored by the U.S. aid commitment, the six industrialized nations of the Aid India Consortium and the World Bank together pledged $2.25 billion to finance the first two years of the Third Plan's foreign exchange needs.[20] When Nehru visited Washington in November 1961, the State Department's briefing for President Kennedy baldly stated that Nehru's death or retirement could trigger a collapse of Indian democracy, leading perhaps to "a Hindu theocracy." The document reminded Kennedy to emphasize that the United States was upping its aid commitment to India to a billion dollars in each of 1962 and 1963.[21]

Nehru's Luck Holds, but Only Barely

Kennedy delivered the aid he promised. But the other donors were less enthusiastic about Nehru's India and his policy approach. The gap between their commitments and the actual disbursement of funds was often large. Many donors also tied their aid to projects that helped businesses in their own countries, which limited the purposes for which India could use the foreign exchange made available. In particular, the foreign aid often did not cover imports of spare parts and maintenance.[22]

Goodwill for India was also wearing thin. An early sign was a comment by Ludwig Erhard, Germany's minister of economic affairs and a key architect of Germany's postwar recovery. In late 1959, when Indian finance minister Morarji Desai asked Erhard for extending the time to repay German loans, Erhard irritably responded, "Money does not grow on trees."[23]

Both Indians and foreigners were losing confidence in India. Remittances from Indians abroad—valuable funds that reduced the current account deficit—dried up, at least through official channels. India's migrants preferred to wait before remitting funds because of the increasing likelihood that the Indian government would need to devalue the rupee. Indians at home increased purchases of gold as a hedge against inflation, which—in view of the import restrictions—led to the increased smuggling of gold into the country. Foreign private lenders to India began taking their money back. Foreign exchange reserves continued to fall. Since aid commitments made in June 1961 would take time to flow in, India turned to the IMF in July 1961 for $250 million to finance the country's immediate needs.[24]

The IMF's Executive Board had grumbled when India called to borrow in early 1957; it grumbled again. India, the Board members said, was repeatedly asking the Fund to finance a long-term development strategy and not temporary (or unanticipated) shortages of foreign currency. Indian authorities insisted that the main problem was delays in official aid flows. The Board reluctantly bought the Indian argument. But with foreign exchange reserves still falling and aid flowing in too slowly, the Indian government returned to the Fund in 1962 and like Oliver Twist asked, "Please, sir, may I have some more?" The IMF loan, this time, was for another $100 million due back in one year, but finding itself unable to repay the amount, the government renewed the borrowing in 1963 for another year.[25]

Nehru's metaphor of constructing "temples of new India" was similar to other lazy development metaphors of the time, "big-push" and "take-off." Kennedy had accepted such simplistic developmental thinking. The World Bank and the IMF, despite occasional criticism, also went along. Only the Taiwanese in 1957 boldly shifted to the more comprehensive and inclusive Japanese development approach.

By the early 1960s, the temples strategy had again brought India to the edge of international bankruptcy. Foreign aid donors (and the Reserve Bank) were worried that India might not be able to repay its international loans. The IMF's staff and Board members asked a long-overdue question: why exactly was India not devaluing the rupee? Donors and the World Bank wanted more say in Indian economic policy, especially to emphasize investment in agriculture.[26]

Nehru was losing his gamble a second time. Financial hemorrhaging aside, the true losses for India manifested as stressed agriculture, few urban jobs, and continued high levels of poverty. Neglect of human development did the greatest long-term damage. That neglect is shocking not just because Nehru was a historian who understood the central role of human development in national cohesion and economic progress, but also because Nehru had a guide he revered, the towering Rabindranath Tagore.

Chapter 6
TAGORE'S UNHEARD SONG

In 1913, Rabindranath Tagore received the Nobel Prize in literature. From the range of his magnificent writings, the Nobel Foundation singled out *Gitanjali: Song Offerings* as the "most acclaimed" collection of his poems. It was a melody of mystical union with the transcendental Lord. "Thy living touch is upon all my limbs," Tagore wrote.[1]

Though a mystic at heart, Tagore was resolutely of this world. He had a passion for education and a profound pride in India. At Santiniketan, located 150 kilometers north of Kolkata in the state of West Bengal, he practiced an educational philosophy based on communion with nature, music, and art.[2] Jawaharlal Nehru's daughter Indira, later Mrs. Gandhi, and Satyajit Ray were students at Santiniketan. But although he practiced a particular method of education, Tagore recognized the value of other approaches to achieving national educational goals. When he died in August 1941, Tagore left behind an urgent call on India's post-independence leaders to place universal education at the heart of an economic development strategy. As Tagore prayed in his poem *Gitanjali,* "Where the mind is without fear and the head is held high; Where knowledge is free; Where the clear stream of reason has not lost Its way into the dreary desert sand of dead habit; Into that heaven of freedom, my Father, let my country awake."

Tagore's Song for India

Starting in 1912, Tagore traveled across the world for nearly two decades. Everywhere he went, he interviewed educators, visited schools, and studied textbooks and educational materials. Toward the end of those travels, he wrote a letter home from Moscow in September 1930 in which he expressed his conviction that "education is the ideal path for solving all our problems."[3]

"The extraordinary vigour" of Russian education, Tagore wrote, was "amazing" to witness. "The floodgates of education" had been opened for all, whether they were resident in European Russia or in the more desolate parts of the country. Tagore emphasized that the measure of Russia's success was "not merely the numbers being educated, but the thoroughness, the intensity of education." Such thoroughness and intensity were possible only because they were "backed by the power, enthusiasm, and administrative ability of the authorities."[4] Tagore's open-mindedness with regard to Russia's educational system was remarkable. Russian rigidity in curricula and teaching methods were in direct opposition to his more flexible and "spontaneous encounters with nature" approach to education.

In a mournful passage in his September 1930 letter from Moscow, Tagore lamented: "Every day I compare conditions here with those in India: what is, and what might have been!" He added that doctor Harry Timbres, his American traveling companion, had spoken of the "astonishing excellence" of the Russian health care system. In despair, Tagore exclaimed:

> But where does that leave diseased, hungry, hapless India! A few years ago, the condition of the Russian masses was fully comparable with that of the Indian masses. Over that short period things have changed rapidly here, whereas we Indians are up to our necks in stagnation.[5]

Tagore was a mystic, but he was not a naïve romantic. He saw the "revengefulness and hatred" taking hold in Stalin's Russia. On September 25, just days before his letter lauding Russian education, he implored in an interview with the newspaper *Izvestia,* "For the sake of humanity, I hope that you may never create a vicious form of violence which will go on weaving an interminable chain of violence and cruelty." On education, though, Tagore publicly expressed gushing admiration for Russia's achievement: "I wish to let you know how deeply I have been impressed by the amazing intensity of your energy in spreading education among the masses." He lauded the "the most intelligent direction given to this noble work." He praised "the variety of channels opened out" to train the "minds and senses and limbs" of the people. He appreciated Russia's dedication "all the more keenly," he said, "because I belong to that country where millions of my fellow-countrymen are denied the light that education can bring them."[6]

On October 4, now sailing over the Atlantic, in another letter home, Tagore added Japan to his list of successes. "It is by education alone that Japan has within a short time . . . multiplied a thousand-fold her power of material production." He had a message for Indians: "In my view the imposing tower of misery which today rests on the heart of India has its sole foundation in the absence of education. Caste divisions, religious conflicts, aversion to work, precarious economic conditions—all centre on this single factor."[7]

Notice the repeated emphasis in his language: "Education is the *ideal path* for solving *all* our problems;" "It is by education *alone* that Japan has;" "all centre on this *single factor.*" For Tagore, education was not one more policy goal: it was the key to every facet of social and economic progress. Without good education, all else might come to naught.

In insisting on more and better education, Tagore was repeating for Indian ears a lesson that had previously been conveyed by the leaders of all successful industrialized nations, including by the American Founding Fathers in the late eighteenth century, the leaders of Japan's Meiji Restoration in late nineteenth century, and the communist leaders in totalitarian Soviet Union in the first half of the twentieth century. The political ideologies across time and distance could not have been more different, but the consistent and vigorous emphasis on education was always the same.

As economists Claudia Goldin and Lawrence Katz tell us, among the American Founding Fathers who signed the Declaration of Independence, John Adams, Benjamin Franklin, Thomas Jefferson, and Benjamin Rush also "wrote extensively about educational institutions." Their treatises "helped coalesce a growing sentiment in the new nation for a strong educational foundation." For them, education was fundamental for Americans "to perform their civic functions, such as voting, and to prepare them to run for office and lead the nation." Benjamin Rush, the best-known physician of his time, emphasized the importance of education for the economy. He argued that more investment in education would increase "the profits of agriculture" and would also promote manufacturing.[8]

In the decades between the American Declaration of Independence in 1776 and the U.S. Civil War in 1861, leaders at various levels of government pursued excellence and equity in education. Horace Mann, the secretary of the Massachusetts Board of Education, and his counterparts in other northeastern states wrote about the virtues of education in learned journals while they pushed the spread of education. Writing in 1840, Horace Mann reiterated the importance of education for producing efficient workers who quickly absorbed new technologies, adapted to working conditions, and added to the pool of innovation. Along with their leaders, American citizens played a crucial role by paying property taxes to finance and run free schools in local communities throughout the country. Slavery and racial discrimination remained a dark stain on America's collective consciousness, but by the early 1850s, all "free" boys and girls were enrolled in primary schools.[9]

From the very start, the Americans recognized that educational equality was the foundation of the most widely shared material progress. Educating girls was not merely a matter of gender equity, it was a recognition that educated mothers have better educated and healthier families. Through property taxes, rich community members paid to educate less fortunate neighbors, and the current generation paid for future generations. Boards of education became hubs of democratic community governance. For America's educational leaders and philosophers, equal opportunity through education was a moral obligation of the government. Robert Coram, a radical philosopher of education, said that since citizens needed knowledge to subsist, the state was "duty bound to secure to them the means of acquiring it." Noah Webster said America needed a "system of education as gives every citizen an opportunity of acquiring knowledge and fitting himself for a place of trust." Anticipating Tagore's conclusion a century later, Webster said that "education would of necessity play a central role in welding together people of diverse backgrounds and conditions, conflicting loyalties, even of strange tongues, into one nation."[10]

It was a stunning vision in the late eighteenth century and the first half of the nineteenth century: knowledge for all would foster democracy and opportunity for everyone. Just as Tagore did in the 1930s, influential Americans made the strong claim that education was not an afterthought that followed industrial development. Nor was education merely a desirable correlate that accompanied increasing national wealth. In the language of modern social science, education was a prime "cause"—a motor force—of social and economic development.

The Americans continued to build on that early momentum. As U.S. scientists and companies led the world in the science-based manufacturing and technological revolution after the Civil War, a free and universal U.S. secondary school system achieved global preeminence by the early twentieth century.[11]

The Americans had taken nearly a century for the full flowering of their primary schools and another half a century for secondary schools. The Japanese wanted the same excellence in their schools, but they wanted to do it quicker. And as would soon become a hallmark of Japan's development process, Japanese leaders decided to learn from the masters. In February 1872, four years after the Meiji Restoration, twenty-five-year-old Mori Arinori arrived in the United States as Japan's first diplomatic representative. He immediately wrote letters to "prominent Americans" asking for "advice and information" on "the educational affairs of Japan." Many of the prominent Americans wrote back to Mori. They affirmed that investment in Japan's education system would create for the country "the basis for prosperity and prestige among the nations of the world." One of the respondents, Professor David Murray of Rutgers University in New Brunswick, New Jersey, made a sweeping assertion: "Nations which have in modern times exerted the greatest influence on the world's history are those which have made education their special care."[12] Professor Murray would eventually move to Japan as an educational advisor to the Japanese government.

Mori, who became Japan's leading education reformer, took away one central lesson from the United States: above all, primary education was crucial for Japan to ascend to the front rank of industrial nations.[13] In a speech in 1885, he proclaimed:

> Our country must move from its third-class position to second-class, and from second-class to first; and ultimately to the leading position among all the countries in the world. The best way to do this is [by laying] the foundations of elementary education.[14]

The Japanese were pushing faster than the Americans, but they had work to do. At first, girls in Japanese schools faced more barriers to education than those in the United States. It was only by 1920 that Japan achieved universal primary education for girls. Then the country embarked on the goal of universal secondary education. However, discrimination against girls lingered over the following decades in limited secondary school opportunities for girls and a special curriculum that trained them to be "good wives and wise mothers."[15]

Even though the Japanese achievement in the early years of the twentieth century was limited to primary and partial success in secondary education, it was extraordinarily important in fostering economic growth and equality of opportunity. William Lockwood, the foremost Japanese economic historian in the West, explained it thus:

> The mass of people never got beyond six years' schooling. But even this helped to diffuse the more modest technical skills widely among the population, especially in the towns and cities. And education encouraged an increasing degree of geographic, occupational, and social mobility among the people which was essential to the radical restructuring of the economy. Finally, by spreading economic opportunity without legal discrimination with respect to race, religion, or class, it was the chief force at work, however ineffectively, to combat the great inequalities so deeply rooted in Japanese society. No other enterprise of the State paid handsomer dividends to the nation.[16]

And so, when Tagore made his five visits to Japan between 1916 and 1929, Japan was a nation combating its "great inequalities," a process that also placed it on the threshold of becoming a modern industrial economy.[17] While Tagore abhorred Japan's militant nationalism and its ruthless colonial expansion, he saw the importance the government accorded to creating a literate workforce. In 1930, Russia confirmed Tagore's view that education was crucial for growth and equality.

From these observations during his international travels, Tagore called on India's political leadership to push the pace of mass education, for it would accelerate economic growth and overcome the handicaps arising from the divisions of caste, religion, and language. Failure to make a big educational push could trap a nation in its historical social and economic divisions, with poorly educated people struggling in a fitfully growing economy.

Tagore had history on his side, and he was asking Indian leaders to test his proposition. Alas, they never did.

Words Race Ahead of the Actions

At the time of independence, India's population was among the most illiterate in the world, comparable to China's and Egypt's. Indian literacy rates were far below those in the Mexican and the Filipino populations. India did have a pocket of high literacy in the state of Cochin on the southwest coast, where about one-third of the population above the age of five was literate. In the Hindi-speaking heartland, less than 5 percent of the people were literate. Everywhere, but especially in the Hindi-dominated heartland, girls were less likely to be literate than boys were.[18]

Nehru, with his empathy, idealism, and historical knowledge, was, it would seem, the perfect person to energize Indian education. In 1944, he expressed dismay in his *The Discovery of India* at India's educational backwardness. Without education, he noted, millions of Indians were condemned to lives of misery, even starvation. Among those who did get education, many could look forward to nothing more than a "clerkship" on meager wages. Perhaps if "life opened its gates to them," Nehru speculated, large numbers of Indians would become scientists, educationists, artists, and industrialists, "helping build a new India and a new world."[19]

Nehru looked up to Tagore and Gandhi as the two "outstanding and dominating" Indians in the first half of the twentieth century.

Appreciatively, he noted Tagore's "constructive work in the field of education" in Santiniketan. Nehru was struck by Tagore's admiration for Russia's success in the "spread of education." In his "death-bed message" in 1941, Nehru recalled, Tagore had reminded Indians of the "unsparing energy" with which Russia had fought illiteracy and disease to reduce ignorance and poverty.[20]

Nehru knew the contemporary examples well. In Western Europe, postwar "social democrats" had focused on a people-centered strategy of social justice through universal education and good health. Even conservative politicians such as Germany's Konrad Adenauer and Ludwig Erhard subscribed to this "social democratic" approach, which underpinned the modern "welfare state."

Nehru probably read—or should have read—Milton Friedman's 1955 report to Indian finance minister C. D. Deshmukh. In that report, Friedman called for "greatly widened opportunities for education and training," which, he said, were a "basic requisite" for economic development. Friedman—the modern free-market guru—was repeating a proposition made nearly two centuries earlier by the greatest free-marketeer of all, Adam Smith. Writing in the late eighteenth century, Smith underscored that even those in the "lowest of occupations" must "acquire the essential parts of education—to read, write, and account—before they can be employed in those occupations." Smith added, "For a very small expense, the public can facilitate, can encourage, and can even impose upon the whole body of the people, the necessity of acquiring those most essential parts of education."[21]

Nehru understood the task that lay before him. As he acknowledged, political equality achieved with the right to vote was greatly diminished without economic equality. He offered soothing words: "Our effort must be to bring about equality among the people by providing equal opportunities for education and employment." Yet, for vast numbers of Indians, those sentiments remained a cruel illusion.[22]

Delivering quality education was a steep uphill climb, and Nehru's India never even tried to climb that hill. As the First Five-Year Plan noted, India began from a difficult starting point. Funding was too low for primary education and disproportionately high for universities. Making matters worse, only 40 percent of students who enrolled in first grade went on to complete fourth grade. "This wastage," the First Plan document said, "is largely due to the poor quality of teaching as well as faulty methods of education."[23]

One of the Directive Principles of the Indian Constitution set the ambitious goal of providing within a period of ten years (i.e., by 1960) free and compulsory education to all children until the age of fourteen. The First Plan had a more modest target: to raise the enrollment of children between six and eleven years old from 40 to 60 percent. For girls in that age group, the goal was even more modest: to raise enrollment from 23 to 40 percent. Although the authorities built many schools, even the modest enrollment goals slipped—and were pushed to the end of the Second Plan. Literacy rates improved sluggishly.[24]

Far from following the Red Queen's advice to run twice as fast as it could, India was moving at a leisurely pace. In contrast, Taiwan and Korea were expanding mass education at a blistering speed. Chinese primary education was quickly outpacing India's (Figure 6.1).

India went badly wrong in the Second Plan (1956–1961), which downgraded education while emphasizing heavy industry. The share of education in total plan expenditures fell to 5.9 percent from 7.9 percent in the First Plan. The share of primary education in all education spending fell to 35 percent, down from 56 percent in the First Plan. The Second Plan document noted that more than one-half of the children who joined first grade failed to complete fourth grade; children languished in the same grade for years. Poor teacher quality persisted. Yet the Second Plan did not "make even a pretense" of upgrading primary education. India was establishing a chain of national scientific laboratories while leaving large numbers of the country's growing population in virtual illiteracy. The Third Plan (1961–1966) stuck to the heavy-industry script.[25]

In 1991, political scientist Myron Weiner blamed Indian "beliefs" regarding the "social order" for India's neglect of mass education. Many have understood Weiner to be implying that India's caste system prevented the spread of education.[26]

It is true that lower-caste students suffered then—and continue to suffer—from discrimination in access to and quality of school

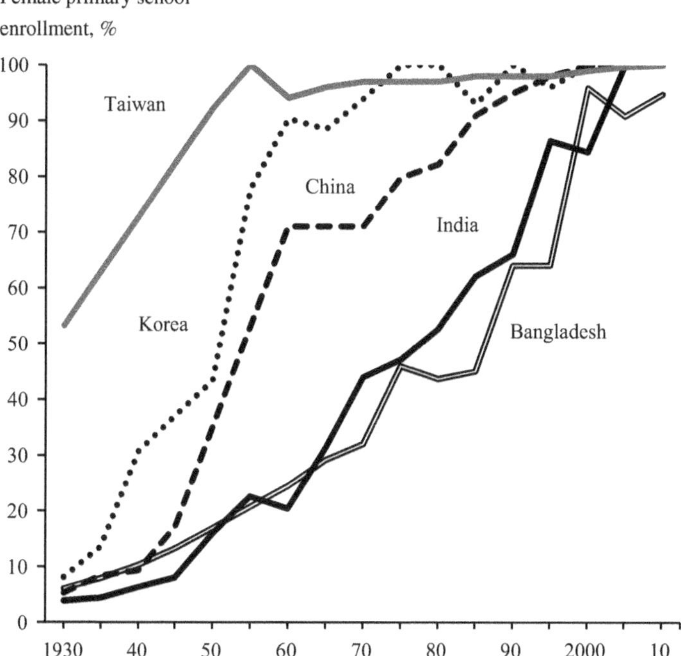

FIGURE 6.1: India loses the Red Queen race in education. (Female primary school enrollment, percent)

Source: Barro, Robert J. and Jong-Wha Lee. 2015. *Education Matters: Global Schooling Gains from the 19th to the 21st Century*. New York: Oxford University Press.

education. But the caste and economic class hierarchies overlap heavily. For this reason, Jayant Pandurang Naik, one of modern India's foremost educational experts, pointed at broader economic inequalities as a reason why India's education system served mainly the demands of the "haves" rather than of the "have-nots." Echoing Naik, Jean Drèze and Amartya Sen have concluded that "the least powerful sections of Indian society" are unable to exert "political pressure in favor of elementary education."[27]

Ultimately, however, as Tagore emphasized, a big policy-driven push to promote education was likely the only way to diminish caste- and class-induced inequalities. The big push required, in the first place, more spending on education. India in the Nehru years spent less than 2 percent of GDP on education, rather than the 4–5 percent of GDP recommended by

Indian experts through their investigations of school systems elsewhere in the world. Also as elsewhere, primary education required a great deal more resources and attention to quality. Perhaps, as importantly, Indian political and policy leaders needed to urgently clean out the corruption that had infiltrated schools and colleges.[28] In failing to root out that cancer, they let it grow.

Education Fell into a "Bad Equilibrium"

In societies with low corruption, the corrupt are easily identified and punished. People prefer to engage in productive activity. This is the "good equilibrium." But if many are corrupt, the likelihood of being caught and punished is small, not least because those who might prosecute you are also tainted by corruption. Productive activity recedes. This is the "bad equilibrium," the Catch-22. Indian education fell into that bad equilibrium.[29]

Education was a tragic victim of widespread problems. By the late 1950s, corruption was embedded in India's social and political fabric. Officials demanded kickbacks for government contracts, jobs, and the award of import and industrial licenses. In that environment, adept political entrepreneurs siphoned the limited public funds for schools and universities for their personal or partisan benefit. They appointed political hacks to plum administrative and teaching jobs and bought school supplies from businesses willing to share their spoils.[30] It is little surprise that the quality of school education remained so poor.

The system persisted in that form because the demand for education remained high. Even a worthless college-degree certificate helped employers conduct an initial screening from among multitudes of job candidates. As the scramble for jobs increased, the demand for admission to college intensified. Indian colleges filled up with ill-prepared students, appalling teachers, and shoddy libraries and laboratories.[31] The modest funds for education lined the pockets of political notables, especially in colleges and universities. The Indian education system had settled into that administratively corrupt and educationally poor-quality equilibrium.

There was a better way.

The Kerala Way

Kerala was formed as a new state in November 1956, bringing together two former princely states, Travancore and Cochin, and the Malabar and Kasargod regions that belonged to the Madras Presidency in British India. Malayalam was the principal language in all four areas, and Kerala's formation as a modern state was part of the linguistic reorganization of states under Nehru. In the mid-1960s, Kerala spent twice as much per primary school student as the northern state of Uttar Pradesh. Kerala, therefore, had more schools, which were located closer to students; it had better teachers and a tradition—unique, I believe, in India at that time—of school lunches. While most children in Kerala completed primary school, those in Uttar Pradesh dropped out quickly. The result: in 1970, Kerala had a literacy rate of 70 percent while Uttar Pradesh's literacy rate was 22 percent. Compared to Uttar Pradesh, Kerala spent *less* per student on secondary and *significantly* less on college education. At the college level, learning and job outcomes were disheartening even in Kerala; corruption and student anxiety were common. But Kerala's superior primary and secondary schools created greater consciousness of social rights and good health, to which the government responded by establishing an extensive health infrastructure. While Kerala's accessibility and quality of education and health have remained unmatched among Indian states, Uttar Pradesh has remained one of the worst-performing states throughout the post-independence decades.[32]

The historian Robin Jeffrey offers the most persuasive account of how Kerala achieved and sustained a commitment to mass education. The initial impetus came in the 1860s from the then princely state of Travancore. Guided by a "remarkable" set of administrators, the Maharaja of Travancore made widely available primary education his government's priority. The princely state of Cochin followed with its own mass education push in the 1880s. But Kerala had another reason for success. The Nayar caste in Malabar had a matrilineal tradition, which gave women substantial authority in family decisions and, in general, gave women greater freedom to live their lives. Until the early twentieth century, the Nayars were "the reference group" for many Malayalam-speaking people.

Members of other castes and religions, writes Jeffrey, "were eager to imitate matrilineal practices, which included school-going for girls." For this reason, the gap between male and female literacy rates narrowed early in Kerala and has stayed narrower than elsewhere in the country.[33]

Educated women played a vital role in helping Kerala sustain a virtuous cycle of broad-based human development. The women attached greater value to education. As Jeffrey evocatively explains: "Literate men have literate sons, literate mothers have literate families." Women also attached greater value to healthcare. They gave birth to fewer children and ensured better medical care for the children they did have. Infant mortality fell to low levels and the children grew up to be more diligent parents.

Education brought other benefits. As Tagore might have predicted, deep-rooted caste divisions weakened. Residents of Kerala were also more politically active. They elected to power the Communist Party of India (CPI) in April 1957, less than six months after the state was formed. The CPI was, in truth, not a communist party, at least insofar as it did not seek to overthrow the political order. Rather, it was a social democratic party in the Western European tradition. Whereas Kerala's CPI initiated land reforms to give greater rights to agricultural workers and tenants, elsewhere in India, the landlords won.[34]

India's Lost Opportunity

Modern scholars have echoed Tagore's belief in the power of education. "Investment in man" rather than in machines, they tell us, is central to economic progress and equality of opportunity. As an educator and witness to history in the making, Tagore also understood that there is no cookie-cutter method to promote education. Each country, each region has its historical inheritance. Moreover, a nation's educational capability does not advance without conflicts and setbacks. Japan went through periods of intense debate—on the degree of westernization of education and the appropriate balance between general schooling and vocational training. Japanese teachers were often the butt of ridicule, with one commentator describing them as "fat toads blinking their eyes after just having missed a mosquito." The privileged in Japan consistently had access to better education.[35]

However, despite multiple starting points and frictions along the way, all successful education drives have shared one feature. The top leadership's big push ensured resources and helped align various actors around an optimistic vision of a more equal and cooperative society; within that context, state and community leaders, administrators, teachers, and parents coordinated their efforts to educate children. The best moment for the big educational push typically arose when the political regime changed. In America, the vision and drive for the spread of education came from the Founding Fathers; in Japan, it came from the bureaucrats and ministers in the early Meiji era; in Kerala, the new maharajas of Travancore and Cochin were the catalysts of schooling.

Post-independence India needed a big education push. For India, Tagore was also saying that a big push to accelerate education would weaken the barriers of caste and other divisions. Kerala's experience showed the wisdom of that advice.[36]

Nehru's fascination with the temples of "modern" India kept him focused on the visible victories of steel plants and fertilizer factories and pushed him away from the administratively complex and long-haul effort of creating a world-class education system for India. Looking back, Tagore would have rightly regretted that Nehru did not hear him. Indeed, he might well have said, as he did in his *Gitanjali,* "The song that I came to sing remains unsung to this day. The blossom has not opened; only the wind is sighing by."

Chapter 7

MR. NEHRU'S TRAGEDY, DEMOCRACY'S FIRST BETRAYAL

In May 1936, Rabindranath Tagore congratulated Jawaharlal Nehru on his recently published autobiography. In a beautifully handwritten letter to Nehru, Tagore said that "a deep current of humanity" runs through the book and it "leads us to the person who is greater than his deeds and truer than his surroundings."[1]

Herein lay Nehru's tragedy. Nehru was a humane nationalist who believed in the norms of equality, tolerance, and shared progress. For him, the practice of those norms meant more democracy, secularism, and socialism, properly understood as equality of opportunity. But Nehru was a man who was greater than his deeds, as Tagore so gently put it. Gandhi was more direct: Jawahar is a thinker, Sardar (Patel) a doer. Nehru's practice set India on to a path that kept drifting away from his ideals.

As an uncontested leader after Patel's death, Nehru followed a misguided top-down economic strategy that reflected his distaste for the difficult ground-level work of economic development. The Nehruvian strategy, although wrapped in an unrelenting rhetoric of socialism, served neither the material interests of the nation nor the cause of social justice. Worse, even after the strategy patently failed in 1956, Nehru stuck to it—because he could. And as corruption took root in public and private life, he loftily dismissed concerns about its spread and ill effects as overblown. The real problem, he said, was the tendency to complain too much about corruption, which, he argued, merely "creates an atmosphere of corruption. People feel they live in a climate of corruption and they get corrupted themselves." Under Nehru, social norms and public accountability eroded, weakening the institutions of democracy he so cherished. His legacy was anemic material progress, denial of social justice, and a widening arc of moral degeneration.[2]

Democracy's Betrayal of India's People

On his way to Delhi in October 1955, Milton Friedman stopped in Tokyo. He was impressed by Tokyo's cleanliness and the beauty of objects in the stores. Nevertheless, the city's postwar poverty "depressed" him. "We really have no idea," he wrote to his wife Rose, how people can be so poor and "still live."[3]

In 1963, Friedman visited Japan on his way back from India. He wrote in his memoirs that "the change after eight years was dramatic. . . . No doubt, there was still much poverty, but the pervasive image of Japan was of growth and relative prosperity." In contrast, Friedman was "impressed with how little improvement there had been" in India since his 1955 visit.[4]

In fairness, Japan—having made huge strides since the Meiji Restoration of 1868—was in the exclusive club of "industrialized" nations as early as the 1920s. After World War II, the Japanese picked up the war's debris and embarked on a reconstruction boom, as in Western Europe, well equipped with human and physical capital. India also made progress after independence. The misguided heavy industry thrust broadened the country's industrial base. Per capita income increased over the Nehru era at about 1.5 percent a year, a big improvement over the near-stagnation of the colonial years.[5]

But India's stepped-up progress was disappointingly slow. The poor saw little or no benefit from the increase in the "average" income. The gulf between India's rich and poor was always much wider than in Western countries, and progress in the Nehru years barely touched large parts of the country, particularly those in the rural areas. Good urban jobs remained scarce. Through the seventeen-year Nehru era, 60 percent or more of the Indian population remained in severe poverty.[6] For this large fraction of Indians, the country made virtually no progress.

In November 1963, six months before he died, Nehru belatedly acknowledged that India had "drifted away from the goal of socialism." The culprit for the drift, he said, was the growth of monopoly power, which he described as "the enemy of socialism." Gunnar Myrdal elaborated on this theme, noting that the gains since independence had benefited mainly the "industrialists, big merchants, and other privileged classes," while price inflation had eroded the incomes of the poor. The limited available data indicated that India's "great inequality" had grown wider. Also, unlike in developed nations where most children could expect a better standard of living than their parents, "immobility and stagnation" characterized life in India. Rising inequality, high rates of poverty, and few opportunities for upward mobility were inherent in the "big-push" heavy industrialization strategy, as was concurrently true for Brazil. Under the top-heavy big-push industrialization, there was very little, if any, "trickle-down" development.[7]

India's poverty remained so intense because large numbers of Indians continued to work in low-productivity agriculture. The share of workers employed by agriculture remained at 70 percent between independence and 1965 because the new industries created limited job opportunities. The scarcity of good jobs reinforced caste divisions because caste groups clung on to hereditary occupations. In post-Meiji Japan between 1880 and 1920, the share of workers in agriculture fell from 80 to 50 percent. As people moved to industrial and service jobs in Japanese cities, the overlap between castes and occupations diminished.

Distracted by heavy industrialization, India missed the first (and possibly the most important) window for exporting labor-intensive products. Postwar reconstruction and pent-up consumption demand had pushed world trade growth to unprecedently high rates. Japan grabbed that trade opportunity and, in 1957, Taiwan began following in Japan's footsteps. South Korea also made "spectacular" progress, starting in the early 1960s. South Korean authorities devalued their currency, the won, in 1961 and again in 1964 under pressure from the Americans who threatened to deny financial assistance. Devaluation was only one part of the story, however.

As the World Bank pointedly said in a mid-1960s report, Korea could be "justly proud of its manpower, well-trained and well-educated." Korea's exports of cotton textiles, clothes, and footwear were increasing quickly. Exports of electrical products, such as small motors, transformers, and radios were poised to rise "rapidly." Korean exporters, already outcompeting Japanese producers in labor-intensive exports, were on track to diversify sales from their primary market in the United States to other industrialized economies.[8]

Because of the emphasis on heavy industrialization, India's major exports in 1964, as in 1949, were predominantly jute textiles, tea, and cotton yarn and textiles. Exports of some light engineering products had increased, but they were very small in quantity and value.[9]

The result: underemployment of the rural population barely changed and urban unemployment "probably increased," according to the World Bank. Official Indian documents reported the rise in underemployment and unemployment in blunt words. The draft outline of the Fourth Plan, intended to span the years 1966 to 1971, impatiently said of the previous three plans (1951–1965), "Successive plans on development are unable to find gainful employment for the net addition to the labor force and continue to add to the backlog of unemployed persons."[10] Employment surveys show that the employment backlog increased from between 20 and 25 million in 1955 to between 30 and 35 million in 1965.

The employment backlog was set to increase. By the early 1960s, India's population growth rate had quickened to 2.2 percent a year because improvements in sanitation and treatment of infectious diseases had lowered mortality rates. More children were surviving into adulthood, and the number of young adults looking for jobs was increasing faster than the total population. Because fertility rates were still high, the flood of young adults into the job market was certain to continue.[11]

The stress on livelihoods was relentless. In a poll conducted by the Indian Institute of Public Opinion in 1956, over 20 percent of respondents said that unemployment was their most acute worry. Even those who were employed expressed deep concern about making ends meet. Indeed, over half the respondents said that rising food prices were their chief source of anxiety.[12]

Food shortages and food price inflation triggered violent protests, euphemistically called "food movements." In August 1959, when crop failure and insufficient supplies from the public distribution system caused food prices to rise sharply in Bengal, between 100,000 and 300,000 demonstrators, including students, teachers, industrial workers, peasants, and impoverished refugees from Pakistani East Bengal, descended onto the streets of Calcutta. The city turned into "a scene of destruction." Police brutally fired into the throng, triggering a cycle of "violence and counterviolence" that lasted nearly a month.[13]

As journalist and civil rights activist Sumanta Banerjee described it, "Riotous destruction sprang from impotent rage and despair in the face of grinding poverty and humiliation." The overpowering sense of scarcity caused tempers to flare, and not just when food prices spiked. In 1953, Calcutta commuters had rioted when tram authorities raised fares. They attacked symbols of political authority, including police stations. In 1956, railroad strikers beat a locomotive driver unconscious and sent the locomotive on full throttle speeding into the railway station at Kharagpur, near Calcutta. In 1961, Myron Weiner, the MIT political scientist, wrote of the violent outbreaks, "Rational efforts to persuade government officials rarely succeed."[14]

In Bombay, the same sense of scarcity was hatching a new political force. In August 1960, cartoonist Bal Thackeray, then thirty-four years old, launched a weekly magazine called *Marmik* (the title denotes that which grapples with the essence). Thackeray's cartoons and satirical political commentary stoked rage against daily indignities. He used "the power of the caricature" to ignite the "anger arising out of distress and disappointment."[15]

At the macroeconomic level, in 1964 as in 1949, India was on the brink of international bankruptcy. The balance of payments deficit had increased since 1956. Imports, particularly of food and machinery, had grown sharply. Exports had barely risen. For years, there had been a crying need for rupee devaluation, but the government relied on official lenders (IMF, the World Bank, and industrialized countries) to finance its external deficits. The time to repay some of that debt was looming, and the prospects did not look good. In June 1963, lacking the $100 million owed to the IMF, Indian authorities needed a new loan to help repay the old one.[16]

Then, in November 1963, a sniper's bullet killed U.S. President John F. Kennedy as he waved to crowds from an open convertible in Dallas. Kennedy had reliably delivered aid to India without asking for anything in return. With his death, "free" foreign money (financial assistance without conditions) could not possibly continue.

Democracy's Betrayal: The Hold of Entrenched Power Structures

Despite regular elections, voters' voices didn't count for much. The traditional "power structures" maintained their hold on key policy decisions. Large landlords fought land reform legislation and implementation. In the industrial sector, the import controls and industrial licensing system—intended to curtail the bleeding of foreign exchange—became tools in the hands of big businesses to prevent the entry of competitors. Senior civil servants, working with influential politicians, allotted themselves coveted housing and gave themselves plum perks such as official cars and ultra-scarce telephones. The underprivileged protested but could not unify in demanding a better future.[17]

Corruption in public life, a quintessential privilege of the powerful, became a tool for the intimidation and harassment of those outside the power structures. In August 1962, Lal Bahadur Shastri, home minister under Jawaharlal Nehru, informed Parliament that between early 1957 and June 1962 the government had punished over twenty thousand officials on charges of corruption. The penalties were evidently not proving a sufficient deterrent. Shastri announced a committee under K. Santhanam, a Member of Parliament, to inquire into the nature and extent of corruption and to suggest more effective ways to fight the scourge.

The Santhanam Committee highlighted the well-known corruption stemming from the allocation of import and industrial licenses. But, as the committee emphasized, public corruption was pervasive. For "contracts of construction, purchases and sales," the Santhanam Committee Report noted, a "custom of percentages is prevalent and this is shared in agreed proportions amongst the concerned officials." This custom was most entrenched in the award of contracts by the Public Works Department, where the executive engineer charged between 7 and 11 percent of the cost of the contract, a sum he typically shared with junior engineers and, increasingly, with his bosses. In railway operations, bribes were common in the allocation of wagons and the booking of parcels, especially of perishables. Alarmingly, the report said it had reliably learned of corruption in the lower ranks of the judiciary and had heard similar accusations about the higher judiciary. Ministers, especially those who had long held office, had "enriched themselves illegitimately."[18]

In April 1963, the committee submitted its preliminary report. The news media greeted the report—and especially its recommendations—with a mix of outrage and despair. The *Economic Weekly* commented on the absurdity of the proposal for a "vigilance commission," a body of bureaucrats to discipline other bureaucrats. The *Times of India* wondered if it was too late to root out the "evil" of corruption, which had infiltrated "almost every level of the administration" and, indeed, "almost every sphere of the nation's life."[19]

Others were less pessimistic. To them, corruption was a largely benign cost of doing business. Bribes were "speed money" that induced bureaucrats to fast-track projects for those willing and able to pay for the service. Myrdal vehemently—and rightly—rejected this whitewash of corruption as "palpably wrong." The lure of corrupt money caused bureaucrats to invent new roadblocks to maximize their own earnings. Possible new roadblocks made the regulatory environment more arbitrary, causing firms to shy away from long-term investments that might require repeated permissions and certifications. A culture of immorality and unethical behavior dug deeper roots in public and private conduct.[20]

Democracy's Betrayal: The Dangers of a Charismatic Leader

Democracy also betrayed Indians citizens because Nehru's policies had little connection with the rights and aspirations of the majority of Indians. Nehru could pursue his policies because he faced no opposition, either from within the Congress Party and the government or from any other party. He won elections because people idolized him, often believing in his socialist rhetoric.

In June 1959, the newly formed Swatantra Party, led by C. Rajagopalachari, appeared as a prospective electoral challenger to Nehru. "Rajaji," as he was popularly known, was an unusually short man who wore thick dark glasses. Because he enjoyed wide respect for his contributions to India's independence, Nehru had selected Rajaji as governor general in June 1948, following Lord Mountbatten. Rajaji continued as governor general until January 1950, when India became a republic. He was then home minister in Nehru's cabinet from Sardar Patel's death in December 1950 until October 1951.

A scholar of ancient Hindu scriptures (generations of Indians have read his short translations of the *Bhagavad Gita* and the timeless myths *Ramayana* and *Mahabharata*), Rajaji was as secular in his public and policy outlook as Nehru, the self-professed agnostic. Rajaji's secularism came from the Hindu scriptures, which emphasize a common divinity in every human being. The imperative "we are all created equal" lies at the heart of Hinduism. Hence, although a practicing Hindu, he rejected the Hindu nationalism of the Jana Sangh as much as Nehru did.

Rajaji and Nehru differed fiercely on economic policy. For Rajaji, sensible socialism was based on "as much competition as *possible,* and as much planning as *necessary.*" He favored German social democracy. Postwar German governments, led by conservative politicians, achieved great material progress while advancing social justice through the generous provision of education and health.[21]

Rajaji and his colleagues were resolutely critical of Nehru's infeasible five-year plans, which led to persistent foreign exchange shortages and, hence, to controls on the private sector. In March 1961, in the run-up to the 1962 election, Rajaji coined the memorable phrase "permit and license raj" for the multiple permits and licenses required by India's corrupt system of bureaucratic controls. He insisted that removing these cancerous regulations—put in place since 1957 to conserve foreign exchange—required abandoning unrealistic planning goals and devaluing the rupee to eliminate the foreign exchange shortage.[22]

While Rajaji was sympathetic to Nehru's non-alignment foreign policy, he believed that Nehru was naïve in trying to build a special relationship with China, especially after Chinese leaders responded belligerently to the Dalai Lama's asylum in India in March 1959.[23]

Faced with a challenger who had name recognition and intellectual heft, Nehru reacted badly. In an interview with *Blitz* editor R. K. Karanjia, Nehru described the Swatantra Party as "a complete throwback to the past." Using uncharacteristically harsh words, he said that the Swatantra Party could give rise to "a fascist state."[24] He needn't have worried. Rajaji's challenge proved too feeble. Connections with big-money interests tainted his Swatantra Party. Nehru's charisma held and he won big in the February 1962 election just as he had in 1952 and 1957.

That was Nehru's last hurrah. On October 20, 1962, Chinese troops crossed their western border with India into Ladakh (now designated administratively as a union territory, but then a part of the Indian state of Jammu and Kashmir). Chinese troops also entered India across the eastern border, the British-drawn McMahon Line separating Tibetan territory from the northeastern region of India. Overwhelmed by Chinese force, Nehru pleaded for American help in two "midnight" letters to President Kennedy on November 19. "The situation is really desperate," Nehru wrote. He asked for twelve squadrons of supersonic fighters manned by U.S. Air Force personnel. In Nehru's proposal, American pilots would assist the Indian Air Force in countering Chinese attacks on Indian cities and communication lines. The astonished American authorities read Nehru's letter knowing they could not make the commitment he sought. The matter, however, quickly became moot. Just before midnight on November 20, the Chinese declared a ceasefire. On the western front, they kept their territorial gains in the inhospitable terrain of Aksai Chin, which they claimed as theirs, and they withdrew to a border they defined as the "Line of Actual Control." In the east, they pulled back to the McMahon Line, although areas of dispute persisted along that fuzzily defined border.[25]

The Chinese military debacle caused a setback to Nehru's health—one from which he never recovered. In reflecting on his economic legacy, it is clear that the heavy industrialization strategy cost Indians gainful employment. But Nehru's most enduring lapse was pushing education down the list of priorities. He remained satisfied that Indian school enrollment rates were increasing. But with other countries moving ahead rapidly to educate their children, especially their girls, India was simultaneously failing the aspirations of its people and, in the international arena, was failing the Red Queen competitiveness test.

While India's mass education lagged appallingly, poorly functioning colleges grew to serve those desperately seeking certificates for elusive jobs. Such colleges became magnets for politicians and their friends, who used them as personal fiefdoms. In its report on Indian corruption, the Santhanam Committee felt compelled to report with "great regret" the many "malpractices" in the "admission of students, recruitment of lecturers and professors and the general management of university funds."[26]

Nehru's mind and heart were in the scientific and technical institutes, the temples that relied on learned priests and required the prime minister to mainly inaugurate the institutes and deliver visionary lectures at scientific conferences. Nehru remained "in the clouds," as the *Times of India* unsparingly noted. Science became Nehru's excuse for distancing himself from political and social activism; it freed him of politically difficult redistribution conflicts and the administratively cumbersome apparatus of a modern welfare state.[27]

Urban development fell into the same trap as education. Like education, urban development requires multiple government and community initiatives. Initial goals and standards set by the central government create the necessary momentum for change. Yet, urban development played virtually no role in the national planning process. Without a solid base of education and cities to foster good urban jobs and humane living, India began giving up on the possibility of equitable growth.

Yet Nehru's "socialist" rhetoric became embedded in the popular imagination. In the 1961 film *Jis desh mein ganga behti hai* (The land through which the Ganga flows), Raj Kapoor reappears as Raju, a childlike villager who has strayed into a company of dacoits. The daughter of the sardar, the head dacoit, has her eye on Raju. She explains that her father took from the rich and gave the loot to the poor. "Are you folks socialists?" a wide-eyed Raju asks. "I too will work with you to make the world more equal," he offers. The film's director, Radhu Karmakar—Kapoor was the producer—later said that he did not intend any irony or sarcasm and claimed that he was just representing how Indians conceived of socialism.[28]

Nehru was a charismatic leader who, with his personal charm and socialist rhetoric, captured the popular imagination. He was the type of leader who, as political scientist Robert Dahl warned in 1961, could disregard contrary evidence and voices even when his policies ill served the people.[29]

Fractured Politics and Governance

Some observers remained optimistic that Indian democracy had taken root under Nehru and would eventually deliver material fruits. The Harvard political scientist Samuel Huntington believed that India's democracy had two crucial strengths: a dominant, highly organized Congress Party and a world-class bureaucracy imbued with the traditions of the legendary Indian Civil Service that served the country under British rule.[30]

The Indian political scientist Rajni Kothari made the further argument that the Congress Party served as a giant coalition, accommodating within it (and ensuring compromises among) multiple factions representing the country's diversity. The party's structure and processes, he said, tamed the factions by channeling their energy to orderly "built-in opposition within the party." This "Congress system," as Kothari called it, imparted political stability and resilience to Indian democracy.[31] For both Huntington and Kothari, India's stable and resilient democracy, anchored by the Congress Party, would eventually spur egalitarian growth.

Nehru spun the same story in his typically soaring language. "The Congress," he said, "has been a mighty cementing force in India, building up the real unity of India, which is something more than mere political unity. It is a unity of the heart and the mind."[32] However, far from forging unity of "heart and mind," Congress Party factions were groups of opportunistic politicians who remained within the party because joining a weak opposition meant political wilderness. Within the Congress Party, they could grab the spoils of office, which were becoming ever more plentiful as India expanded its anti-poverty and development spending. The party's leaders and members amassed fortunes by bestowing jobs (in relief works, education, and other services), lucrative contracts (for village wells, roads, and other infrastructure), and discounted loans.[33]

This fragmentation and corruption of the Congress Party was inevitable. As early as 1951, *Time* magazine bluntly described Congress Party leaders as "timeserving officeholders," many of whom were "black-marketeers." Nehru did little to counter the grabbing tendencies within the party; he merely held the system together as the country's main power broker who selected the Congress Party's electoral candidates and leaders.[34]

Eventually, even Nehru lost his grip. In the spring of 1963, the Congress Party suffered embarrassing losses in three high-profile by-elections to the Lok Sabha. All three victors—Acharya Kripalani, Minoo Masani, and Ram Mannohar Lohia—were bitter political foes of Nehru and had lost to Congress Party candidates in the general elections a year earlier. Now, as the Congress Party's garb of invincibility became tattered, rebellion brewed within the party. Members called for an assessment of the shortcomings of the party's organization. In August, the *Times of India* wrote a scathing indictment, saying that the Congress Party leadership had "reduced itself to a laughing stock." Party leaders were "a group of frightened politicians" who shrank back from addressing the country's daunting problems.[35]

The risk of a fragmented political landscape loomed. Even though the Congress Party had won an overwhelming number of seats repeatedly, these victories had depended on the Westminster "winner-take-all" (first-past-the-post) electoral system where a candidate wins a constituency if he or she receives the most votes rather than more than half the votes. Since independence, the Congress Party at the national and state levels had received just over 40 percent of the vote but nearly three-quarters of the seats in the Lok Sabha and two-thirds of the seats in state legislatures. If the non-Congress parties gained slightly greater electoral strength, they would win a lot more seats. In that case, either by themselves or in coalitions, they would begin to form governments. The Congress Party ticket would become less valuable and the factions could choose to go their own way. India was on the threshold of divisive and combative politics.[36]

The thesis of excellence in Indian bureaucracy—and its ability to maintain stability and resilience—was even easier to dismiss. The Indian

Civil Service and its successor, the Indian Administrative Service, were indeed elite bureaucracies. But after independence, the vastly expanded bureaucracy included large numbers with limited education, working under weak mechanisms of accountability. As the World Bank wrote, "The competence of higher civil servants stands comparison with that of any country in the world" but "there is too much lethargy, indifference and a lack of urgency among the lower ranks of officials who come into daily contact with the public." Corruption was the most devastating testimony to the bureaucracy's degeneration.[37]

The Ideals Crumble

In January 1964, Congress Party leaders and members assembled in Bhubaneshwar, capital of the eastern state of Orissa, to "give unequivocal allegiance to the creed of socialism." Nehru suffered a stroke, which partially paralyzed him on the left side. His ailing body lingered on, but his ideals kept crumbling. Just days after Nehru's stroke, Hindu-Muslim riots broke out in Calcutta, killing 150 people and injuring hundreds. In March, Hindus and Muslims rioted in Rourkela, a town that was home to a steel mill and its workers. The town and the mill were symbols of Nehru's "temples of new India," where he hoped people would worship at the altar of knowledge. But, as if emboldened by a weakened Nehru, Hindu nationalists chose instead to worship at the altar of division and hate. Nearly contemporaneously with Rourkela, riots also broke out in Jamshedpur, another steel town. The riots were the work of the Rashtriya Swayamsevak Sangh, the militant arm of the Hindu nationalist movement, which fueled Hindu anger and violence against Muslims in retaliation against alleged mistreatment of Bengali Hindus fleeing from Pakistani East Bengal.[38]

On the morning of May 27, Nehru's aorta burst. His doctor hurriedly gave him a blood transfusion. But he never regained consciousness. Nehru died later that afternoon. He was seventy-four years old. Veteran leader Rajaji, a comrade from his freedom-fighting days and head of the Swatantra Party that Nehru had once described as possibly fascist, paid the departed prime minister a generous tribute: "A beloved friend has gone, the most civilized among us all."[39]

The civil and idealistic Nehru had left behind the unfulfilled aspirations of a nation fearful of its future. The economic failures had grave implications for Indian democracy. Brazil's heavy industrialization and vast inequalities had just pushed it back into dictatorial rule. How long could India be different? Upon Nehru's death, obituaries in the *Financial Times* and the *Economist* foresaw quick disintegration of the Congress Party. The *New York Times* went a step further. It predicted, as the U.S. State Department had earlier done, that "India will surely be tempted by experiments in authoritarianism."[40]

Part II

VIOLENCE, 1964–1984

Chapter 8
SHASTRI MAKES A BRAVE TRANSITION

Jawaharlal Nehru died at 1:44 p.m. on May 27, 1964. All-India Radio announced his death on its regular news broadcast at 2:00 p.m. Discussion of Nehru's succession began a little after 3:00 p.m. "After Nehru, who?" had long been a parlor game, especially in Delhi and among the press corps. Now, the real game was on, and it was not a game for the faint-hearted.[1] Any successor faced a monumental task.

Congress Party President Kumaraswami Kamaraj took on the role of kingmaker. Kamaraj was a former chief minister of the state of Madras (renamed Tamil Nadu in January 1969). He headed a cabal of Congress Party bosses popularly known as the Syndicate for the power they wielded. Kamaraj spoke only Tamil and understood that his inability to communicate in either Hindi or English ruled him out as prime minister. He visualized himself part of a "collective leadership." Kamaraj fiercely opposed an active contender, Morarji Desai, who had been a finance minister in Nehru's cabinet. Desai had strong views, and as prime minister, he would not have tolerated sharing power and authority with anyone.

On June 2, 1964, five days after Nehru's death, Kamaraj announced that Lal Bahadur Shastri would be India's second prime minister. The soft-spoken Shastri appeared a perfect fit for Kamaraj's vision of collective leadership. He was sworn in as prime minister on June 9.[2]

Shastri's humble exterior appealed to the aesthetic sense of Indian pundits and the public, but he was no pushover. He had impeccable political credentials. He had been an active participant in the freedom movement. After independence, he held leadership positions in the Uttar Pradesh Congress Party and was a minister in the Uttar Pradesh government. Nehru had picked Shastri out of Uttar Pradesh politics and given him increasingly important positions in the central cabinet. Nehru said of Shastri, "He is a man of the highest integrity, with loyalty and devotion to high ideals, a man of conscience and hard work. No man can wish for a better comrade and colleague." After Nehru suffered a stroke at Bhubaneshwar in January 1964, he summoned Shastri to assign him new duties. When Shastri asked what those duties were, the nearly incapacitated Nehru answered: "Do my work." Nehru had all but pointed his finger at Shastri as his successor.

A modest upbringing and the scars of life had toughened Shastri. As a boy, whenever he had been unable to pay the fare for a boat ride to school, he swam across the river. He had watched helplessly as his daughter died of typhoid. Now, as prime minister, he consulted Kamaraj but made his own decisions, quickly revealing his resolve to emerge from the mantras of the Nehru years and move the country in new directions.[3]

Shastri Faces an Onslaught

Economic, social, and political crises came fast and furious at Shastri. He was taking over at the end of a three-year spell during which food grain output had barely increased. Food prices were rising at 20 percent a year. Drought conditions prevailed in several parts of the country, and the government's struggle to rapidly move food grains from surplus to deficit states added to the sense of crisis. Episodic rioting broke out in far-flung regions: near Poona in the west, the Bangalore area in the south, Orissa in the east, and, predictably, in Calcutta, where violent protests had erupted throughout the 1950s. Kerala felt the most acute shortage because the central government failed to supply the state with sufficient rice. A despairing schoolteacher in Kerala said, "Seventeen years ago [at the start of the Nehru years] we had our troubles but at least we had hope. Now we do not know what lies ahead; we are looking into darkness."[4] In Bombay, Bal Thackeray illustrated the year 1964 as a skeletal dying man on the cover of his widely read *Marmik* magazine's January 1, 1965, issue. To the unsuspecting "1965 baby" crawling over the horizon, the "dying 1964" says, "Only I know how I managed this past year. No food, no water, cost of living rising. Time for me to go. You take care."

Through these grim times, a ray of hope had shone through in August 1964, when M. S. Swaminathan at the Indian Agricultural Research Institute described successful experiments in growing dwarf varieties of wheat. In well-irrigated areas, dwarf varieties could absorb large quantities of fertilizers and—because of their short heights—they could yield large quantities of wheat without "lodging" (toppling over) and losing harvestable grain.[5]

The high-yielding varieties attracted Food Minister C. Subramaniam. He saw in them the potential for greater production of wheat and possibly other food grains. In January 1965, Subramaniam established the Food Corporation of India, which would buy grain from farmers at a financially attractive guaranteed price. The policy package included a subsidy to farmers for the purchase of fertilizers and a subsidy to consumers so that they could pay affordable and stable prices. Subramaniam's policy framework for promoting high-yielding varieties was in place well before the world heard of them under the label "Green Revolution" (a term coined in March 1968 by William Gaud, administrator of the U.S. Agency for International Development).[6]

The year 1965 had begun on a promising note as the new agricultural policy took shape, but multiple crises soon converged on the Shastri government. In spring 1965, Pakistani troops surprised Indians by laying claims on portions of the Rann of Kutch, a salt marsh in northern Gujarat where the Indian state bordered the province of Sindh in Pakistan. Although Indian Armed Forces pushed them back, the Pakistanis held on to some of their early gains. Emboldened by the Indian Army's limited pushback, Pakistani authorities launched a more ambitious military effort. In August, Pakistan-trained militia and then the Pakistani Armed

Forces crossed the so-called Line of Control (the de facto border between India and Pakistan) in Kashmir. To regain the initiative, India opened a new battlefront on the plains of Pakistani Punjab. The full-scale war that ensued, known as the Indo-Pakistani War of 1965, lasted from September 6 to September 22. Thousands of soldiers in both armies died.[7]

The rains failed again in the summer of 1965, causing the *kharif* (autumn) food grain production to fall precipitously. Matters got worse. On December 1, 1965, the *Times of India* wrote that the outlook was "gloomy" for the *rabi* (winter) season too. Subramaniam described the "drought conditions" as "unprecedented" and "very close to famine" in several states. Undernourishment of children and vulnerable expectant mothers was of particular concern.[8]

Even as India faced devastating food shortages, food imports became harder. To "punish" India and Pakistan for the war they fought in the spring and summer of 1965, U.S. President Lyndon B. Johnson had halted financial aid to both countries. Johnson also kept food aid on a leash, injecting uncertainty about the size and timing of food shipments from the United States. This "short-tether" policy, Johnson hoped, would induce India's leaders to support America's war in Vietnam and spur greater food grain production in India.[9]

Johnson's "short-tether" strategy came within the context of a broader change in U.S. food-aid policy. Since the early 1950s, India had imported food grains from the United States on extraordinarily generous terms under U.S. Public Law 480. The U.S. government was generous because it had a problem. To encourage production, it had guaranteed prices to farmers, who profited from selling large quantities of grain to the government. Rather than let that grain rot in warehouses, U.S. authorities "sold" part of its stocks to India for payment in rupees. Helpfully, the Americans spent the rupees they earned from P.L. 480 supplies either on U.S. programs in India or on U.S. visitors to India—such was the excess of rupees with the American government that even visiting firemen and their families received lavish treatment on visits to India. U.S. authorities had, however, recently abandoned wasteful price guarantees and started paying farmers for not planting their fields. By mid-1965, the dwindling surplus of food grains was no longer "burdensome." Food grain shipments to India did continue but their size and timing became increasingly uncertain. As B. K. Nehru, India's ambassador to the United States at that time, later wrote in his memoirs, "We lived from ship to mouth." A delay in a ship's arrival could mean "starvation."[10]

New Directions Bring New Risks and Challenges

Nehru had neglected agriculture. Now, amid recurring droughts and the changing U.S. approach to food aid, Food Minister Subramaniam—with Prime Minister Shastri's firm support—pressed ahead with his new agricultural strategy. It was clear from the start, however, that Subramaniam's policies—guaranteed food grain prices and fertilizer subsidies to farmers and food price subsidies to consumers—would place a big strain on the government's finances. Subramaniam also understood that high-yield varieties would increase inequalities: better irrigated areas would gain the most, and larger farmers, with their greater resources, would benefit more than smaller farmers. Not well understood at the time, the Green Revolution caused severe environmental damage. Heavy use of fertilizers and pesticides increased soil erosion and toxicity, the chemicals polluted the water, and intensive water use depleted groundwater. Rachel Carson, in her classic book *Silent Spring,* had warned recently that pesticides sprayed over large acreages of a single crop could "destroy us along with the insects." For the moment, though, Subramaniam's approach offered the best hope for accelerating food grain production and ending India's perpetual fear of a hunger crisis.[11]

Meanwhile, in a carefully calibrated effort, Shastri began the humongous task of dismantling Nehru's industrialization strategy. Toward that goal, he instructed officials to roll back public-sector investments in heavy industry. He downgraded the Planning Commission, which had championed heavy industrialization under India's Second and Third Five-Year Plans. Instead of the Planning Commission remaining an extension of the prime minister's economic arm, as under Nehru, Shastri turned it into more of an advisory body. He also scaled back the ambitious industrialization goals of the proposed Fourth Plan.[12]

In this vortex of history, just as hostilities with Pakistan were intensifying in August 1965, the World Bank pitched in with its ideas of an economic strategy for India. Bernard R. Bell, an external consultant to the World Bank, led that effort, and his landmark "Bell Report" called for greater emphasis on promoting agriculture. That message was, by then, uncontroversial in India.[13]

The Bell Report also called for a politically sensitive devaluation of the rupee. Tensions arose because Indian economists and politicians disagreed on this matter. Most economic policymakers understood that rupee devaluation was long overdue. As Ambassador B. K. Nehru explained in his memoirs: "Our price level at the existing exchange rate was too high; our exports were suffering and our imports had to be rigidly controlled to keep some semblance of balance in our external accounts." The economic logic was clear, but politicians associated devaluation with loss of national honor.[14]

Bell, with his abrasive style, made the Indian decision harder. He all but threatened that the World Bank and other international donors would cut off financial aid if Indian authorities did not implement his recommendations. The ubiquitous economic bureaucrat I. G. Patel would later write that Bell could turn a civilized conversation into a "slanging match." Bell's confrontational approach was a shock, especially because Indians had long been accustomed to "free money"—foreign aid without any policy conditions. The imposition of devaluation by foreigners was a painful blow to Indian pride.[15]

Shastri took the pragmatic view. India had little choice. Both the World Bank and the IMF believed India needed to devalue the rupee. Ignoring the IMF would not work. In 1963, India had borrowed $100 million from the IMF to help repay an old loan. India would need more financial assistance. But Shastri's finance minister, T. T. Krishnamachari, also known as "TTK," rejected devaluation because foreign donors were forcing it down India's throat. TTK, a favorite of Nehru's and once a member of his cabinet, enjoyed a certain political gravitas. Hence, Shastri waited for an opportune moment. That moment came in November 1965, when eleven members of parliament charged that TTK's family had "amassed enormous wealth" using his "name and prestige." Shastri decided to have the charges investigated rather than dismissing them, as TTK had demanded. On December 31, TTK resigned. On January 1, 1966, in a conversation with Ambassador Nehru, visiting home from the United States, Shastri indicated he had effectively forced TTK out. One man's "whims," Shastri said, could not hold back an important policy decision that would benefit the lives of many Indians. He would take care of the devaluation matter on return from Tashkent, where he was headed for peace talks with Pakistani President Ayub Khan.[16] Shastri left for Tashkent on January 3.

Fraying Politics

Shastri had begun moving India in a new economic policy direction. He was confident that he could devalue the rupee on his return from Tashkent. But his political position was far from secure. In the spring of 1965, Vijaya Laxmi Pandit, one of Nehru's younger sisters and a Congress Party leader with aspirations to be India's prime minister, publicly attacked Shastri in unusually harsh words. India was losing its "fine position" in the world, she said, because Shastri and his ministers were "prisoners of indecision." Such squabbling within the party had rumbled under the surface in the Nehru years. Now out in the open, the "growing irresponsibility and triviality" was "deflecting attention" from the country's many challenges.[17]

The most assertive Congress Party prima donna was Indira Gandhi, Nehru's daughter and the minister for information and broadcasting in Shastri's cabinet. She tussled at first with Shastri in the context of an ongoing controversy over the choice of an official language for India. The Indian Constitution stipulated that, starting on Republic Day, January 26, 1965, Hindi would be India's official language. Nehru had left the matter ambiguous. In 1958 he had promised southern Indians (who were linguistically farthest from Hindi) that they could use English as long as they wanted. In 1963 he said, "No nation can become great on the basis of a foreign language," to which he added, "an awakening of the people cannot take place through the English language."[18]

As the fateful day of the constitutionally required changeover to Hindi came closer, southern Indians, particularly citizens of the Tamil-speaking state of Madras, protested angrily that the imposition of Hindi would handicap them. Responding to these protests on February 11, Shastri renewed Nehru's promise: English would remain an official language, and each state would decide when it was ready for changeover to Hindi. "There is no question whatsoever of Hindi being imposed on non-Hindi-speaking states," he said. But that promise did not stem the rioting. The Tamilians wanted a statutory guarantee. The next day, without the prime minister's permission, Mrs. Gandhi flew to Madras, the state's capital city. She met with political leaders and journalists. Asked about a statutory guarantee for keeping English as the official language, she said that that would present "no difficulty at all," although she added some caveats. Shastri, who was "not amused," regarded Mrs. Gandhi's imperious behavior and statements as an effort to "jump over his head" while he was working toward a parliamentary decision to calm matters down. From Shastri's perspective, English had to remain India's official language for the sake of national unity but pro-Hindi lobbyists had to be persuaded of that rationale. As the political scientist Michael Brecher wrote, Shastri consulted broadly to give both Hindi and anti-Hindi protagonists "a greater feeling of security and dignity."[19]

Mrs. Gandhi did not believe in consultative decision-making and cabinet collegiality. Soon enough, she tried again to "upstage" Prime Minister Shastri. As before, she traveled without consulting the prime minister, this time to Kashmir in August 1965 and to Punjab a month later. Claiming that she was boosting the morale of Indian troops fighting the Pakistani foe on those battlefronts, she reveled in the press reports that lauded her as "the only man in a cabinet of old women."[20]

The journalist Inder Malhotra questioned Mrs. Gandhi on her insubordination. She defended her go-it-alone style. She was not merely minister of information and broadcasting, she said; she was one of the country's leaders. "Do you think," she asked Malhotra, "this government can survive if I resign today? Yes, I have jumped over the Prime Minister's head and I would do it again." To strengthen her political position, she was gathering around her a "coterie" of supporters who saw her as India's future.[21]

Shastri and the Congress Party also faced a threat from Hindu nationalist forces. The Hindu nationalist Jana Sangh recorded notable victories in state and national by-elections (off-cycle elections). Even within the Congress Party, as Nehru's biographer Michael Brecher wrote, "secularism was the least firmly established" of all Nehruvian principles. When Nehru was alive, members of the Congress Party paid lip service to secularism but Hindu sentiment exerted a "powerful force" among party members. After Nehru's death, "a subtle Hindu revival was in the making."[22]

Widening the lens even further, Indian democracy was under strain. In the Lok Sabha and in state legislatures, political discipline and decorum were breaking down. "Unruly scenes," including instances of throwing chairs at members of opposing parties, were becoming more common, requiring increasing resort to suspension and disciplining of members.[23]

Against this troubled background, a new crisis brewed. Shastri had been in Tashkent for a week, but the peace talks with Pakistan seemed to be going nowhere. Then, to everyone's surprise, in the evening of January 10, 1966, word of an unexpected agreement with Pakistan reached Delhi. Politicians and bureaucrats were furious at the news. Shastri had agreed to pull Indian troops from the outskirts of Lahore, the capital city of Pakistani Punjab. He had also agreed to return to the Pakistanis the prized Haji Pir Pass, a gateway to Kashmir Valley and "a symbol of the triumph of Indian arms." At the press conference that followed the signing of the agreement with Pakistan, Shastri sensed that the journalists were agitated. "Do you expect trouble back home?" one of them asked him. Shastri pleaded with journalists to set a favorable tone.[24] His fears grew when he called home that evening. "People are angry" was the message from his family.

Hours later, in the early morning hours of January 11, 1966, Shastri died of a massive heart attack. He was sixty-one years old. My mother, getting ready to take her bus to work, reported to us the news, which she had heard on All India Radio. I was still a few days shy of my tenth birthday. I began crying, surprised at myself for doing so. Shastri died a national hero with his military victory over Pakistan. He inspired admiration also because, in the growing milieu of corruption and political street fighting, Shastri was a man of high ethical principles. As B. K. Nehru later pointed out, the only asset Shastri left behind was an old motorcar, and he still needed to repay the government loan he had used to buy the car.[25] He died practically penniless.

Unfinished Business

On January 14, 1966, three days after Shastri died, the IMF presented to its Board a report on the Indian economy in 1965. Unsurprisingly, the assessment was bleak. The war with Pakistan increased the government's budget deficit. Poor rainfall in late 1965 implied a weak economic outlook, which would further increase the budget deficit and add to inflationary pressures. Food imports had increased the international payments deficit, and the prospects for foreign financial assistance were not good. IMF staff underscored the "enormity" of the task that lay ahead. They approvingly noted the shift in policy emphasis and resources toward agriculture but emphasized that much more needed to be done. On the other major policy issue, IMF managing director Pierre-Paul Schweitzer made it plain in private to Ambassador Nehru that continued financial assistance would require rupee devaluation. The IMF could not publicly call for devaluation for fear of causing foreign creditors and domestic dollar holders to flee the country in anticipation of an imminent cheapening of the rupee. But in its elliptical language, the IMF's January 1966 report all but made that call. "It was essential," the report said, "to provide an environment conducive to increased output for exportable products and bring about a more realistic pricing of imports."[26]

The previous year's report had also included a troubling stocktaking of India's employment challenge. Over the course of the Third Five-Year Plan, the Indian economy had added only about 7 million jobs as against the goal of 14 million new jobs. The backlog of unfulfilled demand for jobs had increased.[27]

In his nineteen months as prime minister, Shastri had begun changing Indian economic policy. He faced an enormous task as he stepped out of Nehru's outsized shadow and development narratives. Despite the handicap, Shastri took crucial steps to revitalize agriculture, pull back from heavy industrialization, and lay the groundwork for rupee devaluation, all measures Nehru ought to have taken in 1956–1957. Shastri had also directed Indian troops as they occupied Pakistani territory, instilling pride in Indians and restoring some of the Indian Army's standing after its humiliation at the hands of China in 1962.

But Shastri had too little time to ease the pessimism and anger in large parts of the Indian public because of poor employment prospects and high rates of inflation. Those anxieties would grow without a strong dose of employment-rich economic growth. With Shastri's death, India stood at another critical juncture, waiting for a new leader.

Chapter 9
A SAVIOR FOR INDIA'S FERMENT

When Shastri died unexpectedly in January 1966 after merely nineteen months in office, the question "After Nehru, who?" resurfaced.[1] Kamaraj and his Syndicate (the Congress Party's powerbrokers) swung into action again to keep Morarji Desai out and install a puppet prime minister. Their preferred candidate was Nehru's daughter, Indira Gandhi. She bore the last name "Gandhi" because in March 1942, she married Feroze Gandhi (no relation to the Mahatma). Feroze Gandhi was a flamboyant Parsi, a left-leaning Congress Party politician, and a feared orator in the Lok Sabha.

Feroze and Indira never formally separated, but he preferred to live on his own while she maintained her bond with the Nehru dynasty. Her grandfather, Motilal Nehru, was a prominent Congress Party leader who was the party's president twice, in 1919–1920 and 1928–1929. Her father, Jawaharlal, was not just prime minister, but also the dominant Indian of his generation. Mrs. Gandhi lived in the prime ministerial home as her father's companion and aide.

Mrs. Gandhi was no puppet, however. In 1959, when Congress Party leaders invited her to be the party's president, an ambivalent Nehru mumbled that he did not want to "encourage some sort of dynastic arrangement." But she wanted the job, and he quickly chose to disregard his high principles. As Congress Party president, Mrs. Gandhi willfully violated the democratic and secular ideals Nehru held dear. Members of the Congress Party in Kerala, having been driven out of power by the communists in 1957, were agitated. They demanded the dismissal of the elected communist government and imposition of President's Rule, an extraordinary provision in the Indian Constitution that allows the central government to rule a state in place of the state's elected representatives. Mrs. Gandhi supported the demand for President's Rule in Kerala even as Nehru repeatedly and forcefully argued against such a step. "As far as I am concerned," he said, "I do not propose, nor intend, nor look forward to, nor expect governments falling except through the democratic process." He restated that message to E. K. Ramaswami, correspondent for the Madras-based newspaper *The Hindu.* When Ramaswami asked Nehru if he was going to "fight" the communists or "throw them out," Nehru responded with a question of his own: "Throw them out? How? What do you mean? They've also been elected." But his daughter, who thought otherwise, called out, "Pappu, what are you telling them?" Turning to Ramaswami, she said, "As Congress Party president I intend to fight them and throw them out." In the following days, she persuaded Nehru to fire Kerala's communist government.[2]

During the short period under President's Rule, Mrs. Gandhi encouraged the Kerala branch of the Congress Party to form an electoral alliance with the avowedly communal Muslim League. In elections held in February 1960, the Congress Party–Muslim League coalition won fewer votes than the communists did. However, the communists won their votes by large majorities in fewer electoral districts. By the quirk of the first-past-the post, winner-take-all system, the opportunistic Congress Party–Muslim League coalition won enough seats in the legislature to form a government. The journalist and author Uma Vasudev asked Mrs. Gandhi if she had consulted her father about the Congress Party partnering with the Muslim League. "He wasn't in touch," Mrs. Gandhi dryly answered. After Nehru's death, she stuck with her aggressive brand of politics, using every opportunity to outshine the new prime minister, Lal Bahadur Shastri.[3]

Mrs. Gandhi's relentless personality made her prime ministerial tenure a pivot point in modern Indian history. As I describe in this and the following chapters, she showed little interest in economic policymaking after her initial brush with an essential rupee devaluation in 1966. She operated in slogans without articulating an economic vision, and her years as prime minister are best regarded as an enormous missed opportunity. The provision of public goods continued to lag. The Indian economy remained unable to meet the aspirations of its people. Having already lost the competitive race to Japan, Taiwan, and Korea, India began losing the race to China. When Mrs. Gandhi employed economic policy instruments, she used the garb of socialism—bank nationalization being the most notable example—to grab power.

But Mrs. Gandhi's years are even more important because of the damage she did to Indian democracy. She was different, she claimed at first; a distinctive brand. When that proved insufficient for maintaining her grip on power, she chipped away at the norms—the personal honor system—within which a democracy works. The rule of law and democratic institutions malfunctioned. India began sliding toward a Catch-22, where leaders and citizens found it advantageous to heap more abuse on norms and accountability rather than work to restore them.

The branding came easily to her. On January 19, 1966, the day the Congress Party Members of Parliament were to choose their leader, she wore a *khadi sari*—a sari made of home-spun cloth, a Gandhian symbol. She added a Kashmiri shawl and a string of large brown beads that was a talisman from her mother's spiritual guide, the Bengali saint Anandamayi Ma. Party members welcomed Mrs. Gandhi's dynastic charisma, and she easily defeated Morarji Desai to become the Congress Party's parliamentary leader. On that basis, President Sarvepalli Radhakrishnan swore her in as India's third prime minister on January 24. Rather than pledging "in the name of God," she chose to "solemnly affirm," projecting herself also as a modern, secular woman.[4] Dallying with Muslim leaders in Kerala, wearing a Hindu talisman to an all-important parliamentary vote, and showcasing secularism were all markers of her hypercompetitive political style.

The Talisman Stops Working

Shastri's year, 1965, was believed at that time to be the nastiest for the economy since independence. But 1966 was worse.

Drought from autumn of 1965 continued into the winter and spring of 1966. Food prices had risen by over 20 percent in the Indian fiscal year 1964–1965 (April 1 to March 31). Food price inflation came down to a still-high 8 percent in 1965–1966, but then jumped back up to nearly 20 percent in 1966–1967. With food such a large share of household expenses, the galloping increase in food prices was taking its toll on people's incomes—and their patience.

In late January 1966, soon after Mrs. Gandhi became prime minister, ferocious protests erupted across the country, notably in the ever-on-edge eastern state of West Bengal and in Kerala on the southwestern coast. The most violent of Bengal's food movements began on February 17, when police opened fire on students, killing a schoolboy. The violence spread throughout West Bengal, with students protesting against the scarcity of food rations and kerosene (a common cooking fuel). For a month and a half, they battled the police and then military forces. College neighborhoods became "war zones."[5]

In Kerala, food-related protests and violence occurred nearly simultaneously to those in West Bengal. Once again, students led the protests. At Varkala, about 45 kilometers north of the capital Trivandrum, they damaged the railroad station's building, set parcels in transit on fire, and stole cash and tickets from the reservation office. At Alleppey in central Kerala, students set fire to a government office responsible for collecting sales taxes. Mrs. Gandhi increased rice supplies from national stocks to Kerala, but the gesture failed to pacify the protestors.[6]

In the north, a Sikh agitation, ongoing since independence, grew more intense. Sikhs, a minority in the state of Punjab, wanted to carve out a Punjabi Suba: a state where they would be the majority of residents. Sikhs follow Guru Nanak (1469–1539), a saint who—born a Hindu—preached a religion that drew on the spiritual principles of Hinduism but frowned upon Hindu caste divisions and rituals. Sikh men do not shave their beards, they wear long hair tied in turbans, and sometimes carry a curved dagger called a *kirpan*. Sikhs speak Punjabi, a language whose vocabulary and script (Gurmukhi) differ in many ways from Hindi. Nehru resisted a separate Punjabi state because he did not want religion to define state lines. However, Sikhs maintained their demand, courting arrest and often violently confronting the police.[7]

By the time Mrs. Gandhi became prime minister in 1966, Sant Fateh Singh, leader of the Sikh political party Shiromani Akali Dal (Central Army of the Immortals), argued that Sikhs wanted a separate state not because of their religion but because they had a distinct language. The demand had a legalistic basis since the principle of linguistic states was by now well established. Fateh Singh threatened to fast for two weeks and burn himself to death unless the Indian government met the Sikh demand. The Hindi-speaking areas of Punjab wanted their own state. Hence, on March 9, the Congress Working Committee, the party's decision-making body, supported the demand for a Punjabi-speaking state where Sikhs would be in the majority. The language rationale for a separate Sikh state, although legally plausible, did not fool anyone. The religious differentiation was evident, and the Hindu nationalist party, the Jana Sangh, mounted a violent agitation against a Punjabi Suba. In Delhi, mobs burned cars and scooters and beat up press photographers, destroying their cameras. Violence spread through the towns of Punjab. There could be no winners in this tussle.[8]

Writing for the *New York Times* in the third week of March, J. Anthony Lukas expressed a sentiment widely held in India at that time. The country, he said, was going through one of its worst spells of post-independence violence. The violence was everywhere—in "the crowded streets of Calcutta's slums, the dusty towns of the Punjab, the rice paddies of Kerala and the textile mills of Maharashtra." India, Lukas wrote, had been in "almost continuous ferment" since Mrs. Gandhi became prime minister in late January. Quoting an unnamed associate of Mahatma Gandhi, Lukas added that Gandhi would have been "horrified," especially by the "young men" participating in the ferocious rioting.[9]

In late March, on the eve of her departure to Washington to meet U.S. President Lyndon Johnson, Mrs. Gandhi acknowledged the spread of violence in an interview with R. K. Karanjia, editor of the tabloid *Blitz*. "The whole situation is difficult," she said, "what with the food and economic crises." In addition, matters which "were on the shelf, like

Punjabi Suba, have also come up." The country was facing "enormous" problems that were likely to get worse, she said. When Karanjia pressed Mrs. Gandhi on "the *basic* rather than *immediate* cause of the violence sweeping the land," she answered carefully: "We have put the concept of a better future within the SIGHT of our people, but it has not yet come within their REACH."[10] It was a moment of great insight. Mrs. Gandhi was saying that unfulfilled economic aspirations from her father's years were driving people to violence. To change things around, Mrs. Gandhi had much to do. Immediately though, a sizable devaluation of the rupee was essential to begin undoing her father's distressing legacy.

Rupee Devaluation: Necessary Task, Poorly Executed

With increasing impatience, the IMF and other international donors were demanding devaluation of the rupee. On March 23, 1966, when the IMF's Board authorized a $187.5 million financial lifeline to India, several members of the Board insisted that Indian authorities "find a lasting solution to India's recurring [international] payment troubles through exchange rate adjustments [read: devaluation] and vigorous export promotion measures." The IMF's proposals made perfect sense: devaluation would increase dollar flows into India (via more exports) and reduce dollar outflows (via reduced imports). India had little choice, and its representatives did commit to devaluing the rupee by June 1966.[11]

With that promise made, Mrs. Gandhi went to Washington. Superficially, her trip went well. President Johnson was in the flush of his momentous civil rights legislation and war on poverty. Displaying Southern courtesy and warmth, Johnson broke protocol and escorted Mrs. Gandhi from the White House across the street to Blair House, where foreign dignitaries stayed. At a reception hosted by Mrs. Gandhi in his honor, Johnson stayed on well past the thirty minutes on his schedule. Seeing that president was not leaving, Fori Nehru, the Indian ambassador's wife, suggested that he stay on for dinner. He enthusiastically agreed, disrupting the seating plan for the official dinner scheduled for Washington's power elite. As a true Texan, Johnson "polished off" a spicy Indian meal.

And, in a grand flourish, he announced he intended "not to let any harm" come to Mrs. Gandhi.[12]

With the agreement that India would devalue, the all-important question was: how large would the devaluation be? The IMF's managing director Pierre-Paul Schweitzer proposed that the rupee's exchange value increase from 4.76 to 10 rupees to the dollar. But anticipating a shock in the Indian press and political circles, Indian policymakers countered with their preference for a milder devaluation to 7.5 rupees to the dollar, a pitch that the IMF waved through.[13]

Determining the "right" exchange value is difficult, as I can attest from my long years at the IMF. But any reasonable benchmark called for much greater rupee devaluation. The South Korean authorities, for example, had devalued in 1961 from 65 to 130 won/dollar, and to 255 won/dollar in 1964. That amounted to a devaluation of over 70 percent between 1961 and 1964. The Korean authorities then let the won float, setting Korea on a course to export-led growth.[14]

In contrast, after the Indian rupee's devaluation, each dollar bought an additional 2.74 (= 7.50 – 4.76) rupees, making it a 36.5 percent (= 2.74/7.50 * 100) devaluation. Moreover, the Indian government simultaneously increased taxes on exports and reduced export subsidies. Because of these offsetting factors, a typical exporter only saw a 7 percent devaluation, which was too little to overcome the large increase in the costs of production over the previous many years. At the new exchange value, Indian exporters would remain acutely uncompetitive. Instead, a more aggressive 60 percent devaluation, which brought the rupee's official exchange value close to the black-market rate of 12 rupees to the dollar, would have more accurately reflected India's severe dollar shortage. The larger exports and diminished imports would have helped alleviate the dollar shortage. The devaluation in September 1949 had indeed closed the gap between the official and black-market rates (Figure 9.1). The gap remained small for several years, allowing the devaluation to have its intended beneficial effect.[15]

Because the right exchange value keeps changing, India needed also to float the rupee. But that was a bridge too far, and Indian officials stuck to an utterly inadequate reduction in the rupee's value. Moving things

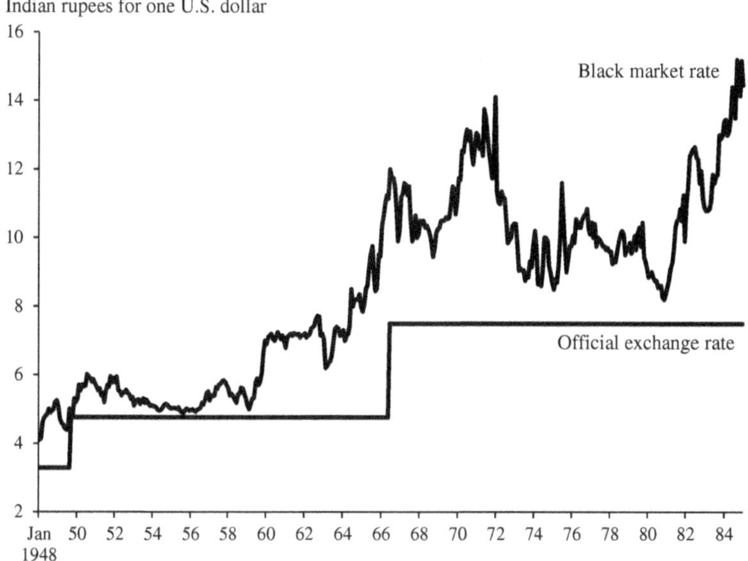

FIGURE 9.1: The 1966 devaluation was too timid: Official rate was set way below market-clearing black-market rate. (Indian rupees for one U.S. dollar)
Source: Global Financial Statistics and various IMF reports.

along in the morning on Sunday, June 5, 1966, Mrs. Gandhi told her cabinet of the impending devaluation. In the dark thus far, cabinet members erupted in fiery protest. Mrs. Gandhi quickly ended that discussion, saying simply: "If we don't devalue, we don't get aid." Taking advantage of the time difference, the IMF's Board met the same Sunday to authorize the devaluation. At 9:00 p.m. Indian time that night, Finance Minister Sachin Chaudhuri announced that the rupee's devaluation would go into effect at 2:00 a.m. on Monday, June 6.[16]

The public was understandably not informed ahead of time: if people had known that devaluation was in the works, they would have rushed to convert their rupees into dollars to later reconvert back them into more rupees. But even Kamaraj learned of the decision after it occurred. As president of the Congress Party, he had visualized himself as part of the "collective leadership." And Mrs. Gandhi had left him out in the cold. He criticized the devaluation as "a sell-out to the Americans," and engineered an official Congress Party censure. He blamed himself for helping elevate Indira Gandhi to the prime minister's position.[17]

Kamaraj's "sell-out" refrain spread quickly, even though it was a silly reaction. If your leg is fractured, you don't "sell out" by using a crutch just because someone else prescribes it. Low productivity growth had fractured India's economic leg. Hence, domestic prices—and costs of production—had increased much faster than in competitor countries. Indian exporters had lost competitiveness in international markets continuously for nearly seventeen years.[18]

Devaluation of the rupee was "inevitable," as Milton Friedman had emphasized in a 1963 lecture at the Reserve Bank of India. India had "no alternative," because no country could "indefinitely maintain an exchange rate far out of line with the rate that clears the market."[19] In June 1966, Mrs. Gandhi bowed to that inevitability.

Mrs. Gandhi—and India—suffered though because of the devaluation's timidity. With India's high inflation rate, rising domestic production costs quickly wiped out any temporary benefit from the meager devaluation. Reflecting the renewed loss of competitiveness, the black-market rate spiked soon after the devaluation.

A popular narrative emerged that the devaluation was the cause of all of India's economic ills, even though the palpable hardship felt throughout the country was predominantly because of the second consecutive year of drought. The Indian press and public also felt humiliated by President Johnson, who despite his display of gallantry to the prime minister turned off U.S. food aid. He was upset because on her return trip from Washington, Mrs. Gandhi had stopped in Moscow, where she criticized America's Vietnam policy. Johnson resumed the aid only after Ambassador Nehru visited him in a gesture of contrition.[20]

The Americans and other western industrialized nations also did not live up to their promise of more aid to finance the economic strategy laid out in the Fourth Five-Year Plan. While the financial aid promised earlier continued into 1968, the new inflows increasingly went to repay old debts rather than raise investment in India. Anticipating this turn of events, Mrs. Gandhi put the Fourth Plan on hold.[21] Postponement of the Fourth Plan caused heartache in India, but it was a blessing. The authors of the plan had learned nothing from the pitfalls of overambition in the Second and Third Plans.

The Ferment Spreads

The continuing Nehru-era problems of underemployment and inflation began to weigh on the Indian people. Students all over the country agitated and rioted. The causes for rioting were sometimes trivial, such as the expensive, poor-quality food served in hostel dining rooms. The underlying reason was that their B.A. and M.A. degrees were worthless, as Jawaharlal Nehru pointed out in the early 1950s but never did anything to correct. Throughout 1966, in every part of the country, students frustrated by the lack of jobs demanded postponement of exams and closure of universities and colleges.

In Bombay, the competition for jobs became a political flashpoint. Maharashtrian men often lost out to the better-educated South Indians in the competition for well-paying and secure clerical and administrative positions. Bal Thackeray stoked this flashpoint in *Marmik*. His message was simple: South Indians—differentiated by language, attire, and cuisine—were stealing jobs that rightfully belonged to Maharashtrians. Like German legal scholar Carl Schmitt (1888–1985), the cartoonist Thackeray saw the political arena as "combat" with an "identifiable" enemy. Like Schmitt, Thackeray viewed politics as perpetual violence, with "the real possibility of physical killing." With that dark philosophy, he jumped into the political fray.[22]

On June 19, 1966, at the auspicious hour of 8:20 in the morning, Thackeray, his father, his two brothers, and some friends broke a sanctified coconut to mark the launch of a political party, the Shiv Sena (the army of Shivaji, the seventeenth-century Maratha warrior).[23] Although he initially focused on the South Indians as the "enemy," Thackeray signaled his Hindu nationalism by naming his party after an admired Hindu warrior.

Four months later, on October 30, 1966, Thackeray held a public meeting in Bombay's Shivaji Park, the hallowed ground of lower- and middle-class Maharashtrians. To everyone's astonishment, nearly four hundred thousand people—mostly Maharashtrian men—showed up to rally behind Thackeray. The large throng formed almost 8 percent of Bombay's population of 5.3 million and as much as 25 percent of Bombay's male Maharashtrian residents. Many were young men in their teens and twenties. They were drawn to Thackeray's message that South Indians were stealing their future. Their "blood started boiling," and on their way home after the speech, they attacked several popular South Indian–owned restaurants.[24]

The Shiv Sainiks (soldiers in the Shiv Sena) operated in the style of criminal gangs. They charged protection money from local businesses to finance their party's operations. They were *dadas* (musclemen) who used intimidation to grab clerical and administrative government jobs and navigate the corrupt bureaucracy on behalf of their followers. Princeton historian Gyan Prakash writes that Bal Thackeray was an "angry young man." His Shiv Sainiks were also angry young men, who reveled in a display of hypermasculinity.[25]

Whereas the Shiv Sena was almost entirely a Bombay-based organization, this was also the moment when another deeply divisive force emerged across the broader Indian land mass. This force found its political expression in the "angry Hindu." An optimistic nationalism born of freedom from colonial rule had frayed as a unifying ideology, and attention increasingly had turned to the darker attraction of India as a Hindu state. Hindu nationalists were gaining ground by directing people's economic frustration against an "enemy," in this instance the imaginary Muslim pampered by the Indian government. Just as Thackeray in Bombay was stirring up mob anger against the "South Indian enemy," Hindu leaders across much of northern India were using the Hindu-Muslim divide to drive mob anger in the service of Hindu nationalism.[26]

On September 30, 1966, Hindu protesters demanding a ban on the slaughter of cows clashed with Muslims in a small Maharashtrian town, 450 kilometers northeast of Bombay. Hindus believe cows are sacred and that they are incarnations of the goddess Kamdhenu, who fulfills all wishes. Hindus typically do not eat beef while Muslims (and Christians) do. The protestors who were demanding a ban on cow slaughter destroyed private homes and public property. Eleven people died in the fracas.[27]

The Indian Constitution did require banning of cow slaughter, but the central government had left the matter to the states, who rarely enforced their legislated bans. Enforcing cow-slaughter bans would have required confronting Hindu farmers, who treated the cow as an economic rather than a spiritual animal. Farmers could not afford an unlimited number of cattle, and so they kept the needed draft power of bullocks (steer) and apparently killed their cows through infanticide or starvation. In the Hindu heartland states of Bihar and Uttar Pradesh, the bullock-to-cow ratio was about the same as in Muslim-dominated West Pakistan. The variation in the ratio of bullocks to cows across the districts of Uttar Pradesh bore no relationship to the religious composition of districts but rather matched the terrain (and, hence, draft power requirements) of the district. Cows featured prominently in Kerala's bovine economy because farming there required only limited draft power of bullocks.[28]

Analysts have since argued that rather than banning cow slaughter, the government should legalize the killing of cows so that peasants can make economic decisions without fear of the law or Hindu vigilantes.[29] Unfortunately, there has never been time for rational discussion on this matter. On November 7, 1966, hundreds of *sadhus* tried to storm the Indian parliament. Some *sadhus* are saints: they are trained practitioners and teachers of the scriptures. Others are charlatans and common criminals. The *sadhus* trying to storm the parliament destroyed property in the neighborhood, but police were able to stop them before they entered the Lok Sabha. Mrs. Gandhi used the occasion to dismiss her home minister Gulzarilal Nanda, whom she never liked and who was frequently suspected of sympathizing with the call for ban on cow slaughter.[30]

High in the pantheon of Hindu leaders, the holy leader Shankaracharya of Puri (also known as the *Jagadguru,* literally "universal teacher") announced on November 20 he would undertake a hunger strike unless the government banned cow slaughter. He said he was doing so to "cleanse the hearts and minds" of Indian leaders. Fearing more violence if the *Jagadguru* became a new focal point of agitation, the government tried to keep him out of sight, but he made sure that press reporters were updated constantly. After a couple of months though, he tired of his hunger strike and promptly joined the political agitation.[31]

Hindu nationalism had lurked beneath the political surface for years. Now, the Jana Sangh (formally, Akhil Bharatiya Jana Sangh, All-India People's Party), which had orchestrated the campaign for banning cow slaughter, represented a rising Hindu nationalism. When the Bengali leader Syama Prasad Mookerjee first formed the party in October 1951, Nehru promised to "crush" it, which he did electorally in the 1952 national and state assembly elections. At that time Nehru also dismissed the call for a ban on cow slaughter, pointing out that for many poor Indians beef was the only cheap form of protein. However, the recurring Hindu-Muslim riots in the Nehru years and the more open expression of Hindu sympathies among Congress Party leaders after his death were reminders of the power of Hindu nationalism. An emboldened Jana Sangh and its supporters were emerging through the social and political cracks Nehru had left behind.[32]

"Indira Amma" Becomes India's Savior

In December 1966, as Mrs. Gandhi began campaigning for the elections scheduled for two months later, she had been prime minister for less than a year. Economic and political turmoil had reigned through the year. The young and jobless were driving the turmoil. As Mrs. Gandhi well understood, economic frustration had built up during her father's years in office—and that frustration was interacting viciously with assertions of regional and religious identities.

At this pivotal moment, Mrs. Gandhi made a choice that had far-reaching effects. Unable to tame the turmoil, she sought to shake herself loose from the leadership and procedures of the Congress Party and make a direct connection with the Indian people. The first indication of her bid to serve as India's savior came on December 20. She was campaigning in her chosen parliamentary constituency Rae Bareli—from where Feroze, her now-deceased husband, had once run for the Lok Sabha. She declared, "My family consists of crores [tens of millions] of people," adding, "My family members are poverty-stricken and I have to look after them." She needed to prevent, she said, stronger family members from taking advantage of the weaker.[33] Word spread that she was "Indira Amma" (Mother Indira). She had a mother's authority and credibility.

Mrs. Gandhi broadened that theme in a Christmas Day interview with the *Times of India*. At first, she criticized the Congress Party bosses, the Syndicate. She alleged that they had selected bad candidates for parliamentary and state assembly seats. "We could have got some better candidates," she said. Then she pivoted from the criticism to enhance her own image: "You see, here is a question of whom the party wants and whom the people want. My position among the people is uncontested."[34]

She campaigned tirelessly, traveling thousands of miles and giving speeches at hundreds of meetings. On her campaign trips, as her biographer Katherine Frank later wrote, Mrs. Gandhi often spoke in the regional language. "She wore her sari as local women did and ate their food with her fingers." And even as she appeared to relate to poor Indians, she stood "lofty and awesome, copiously garlanded, immaculate in a sea of whirling dust as her prime ministerial car roared to a halt before a huge crowd." Biographer Zareer Masani also noted that Mrs. Gandhi blended "obvious aristocratic refinement" and "earthly, maternal common sense with which the average housewife could identify." The unique combination of aristocracy and empathy "made her an object of awe and veneration for large numbers of the Indian masses."[35]

But whirlwind campaigning and star power could not overcome public resentment born of years of the Congress Party's failures. When she visited Bhubaneshwar on February 8, 1967, hundreds of student demonstrators screamed "*Congress Party murdabad*" (Death to the Congress Party) and "Indira Gandhi, go back." A stone hurled by a student struck her on the nose, which bled as security guards ushered her away to safety and medical care.[36]

The election results toward the end of February reflected the sentiment at the antagonistic rally in Bhubaneshwar. The Congress Party's vote share fell from 44.5 percent in 1962 to 40.7 percent. That was a small decline in vote share. But the first-past-the-post system, which had worked in favor of the Congress Party for so long, now worked against it. The Congress Party won 283 Lok Sabha seats, 54.5 percent of all seats, down from the 72.8 percent share of 1962.[37]

The Jana Sangh made large electoral gains. The Jana Sangh's campaign for a ban on cow slaughter appealed to those drawn to Hindu nationalism. The Jana Sangh also tapped into public frustration with economic conditions and corruption. Coming third in votes received, after the Congress Party and the Swatantra Party, the Jana Sangh won 9.4 percent of the national vote and 35 seats in the Lok Sabha (up from 14 seats in 1962). In the state assembly elections, the Jana Sangh won 8.8 percent of the vote in a crowded field involving many regional parties, second only to Congress Party's 40 percent vote share.[38]

Mrs. Gandhi's bid to emerge as an Indian savior had failed for now, but she had something to cheer about—the "sweet defeats" of her foes in the Congress Party. In Tamil Nadu, voters humiliated Kamaraj, long the state's chief minister and leader of the Syndicate. Kamaraj lost his parliamentary seat to a 28-year old student leader of the Dravida Munnetra Kazhagam, the political party representing Tamil cultural interests and anti-Hindi sentiment. Some other Syndicate members also lost.[39] The Congress Party was disintegrating, but Mrs. Gandhi was still winning.

Riding on her triumph within the Congress Party's old guard, Mrs. Gandhi consolidated her authority within the party. She bought Morarji Desai's cooperation by making him deputy prime minister and finance minister. However, to make it clear that she was the boss, Mrs. Gandhi announced her list of cabinet members without consulting him. As her biographer Uma Vasudev wrote, it was time for her "to do things her way." Mrs. Gandhi also dropped from her cabinet Sanjeeva Reddy, one of the Syndicate members who had won his parliamentary seat.[40]

Mrs. Gandhi's attraction to religious props grew. At her swearing-in as prime minister by President Radhakrishnan, she again wore her talisman of holy beads. On this occasion, a mysterious man in saffron clothing accompanied her. He was Dhirendra Brahamachari, who had long choreographed her daily practice of yoga asanas. He was not yet a known commodity in political circles, and politicians and journalists referred to him as a "swami."[41] However, far from the learned ascetic that that term implies, Brahamachari was a swank charlatan, a flashy yoga teacher who liked big foreign cars, private jets, and proximity to power.

In the terminology of Harvard political scientist Samuel Huntington, India was turning into a "praetorian society," a society with the trappings of a democracy but lacking political institutions to handle social discontent. Such societies, Huntington warned, get "caught in a vicious circle." Snowballing social discontent paralyzes the very institutions whose role it is to preserve domestic peace and promote economic progress.[42]

India Becomes a Police State

On May 21, 1967, as was his custom, Bigul Kisan went to harvest the crop on the fields of a landlord in the Naxalbari district in northeastern West

Bengal. This particular day was different, however. He was to take over the land as his own, per the instructions of the Krishak Sabha (Farmer's Union), a peasant organization of the Communist Party of India (Marxist), commonly known as the CPM. As Bigul Kisan would describe the incident twenty years later, "The goons of the landlord attacked me. They nearly crushed my head. They took away my plough and oxen."[43]

That spark set off a wave of peasant attacks on landlords. On May 24, when the police tried to defend the landlords, two arrows from peasant bows killed Constable Sonam Wangdi. All the village men then went into hiding, leaving the women to form a barricade against further police force. The police stepped up its offensive, shooting and killing nine women and two children.[44]

Armed rebels continued to attack landlords. The CPM, which had unexpectedly vaulted into power as part of a United Front coalition government in the state assembly election that February, was initially sympathetic to the rebels. But by mid-June the CPM assumed its governmental role of maintaining law and order. The Chinese jumped in to counter the CPM's anti-rebel position. On June 28, Radio Peking lauded the rebels as the "front paw of a revolutionary armed struggle," adding that the peasant movement was inspired by Mao Zedong, chairman of the Chinese Communist Party.[45]

Indian authorities began repressive measures against peasant rebels on July 12. Backed by colonial-era laws, which permitted arrests without charges and trial, Indian police launched a major operation to round up the rebels and their leaders. By the end of July, about 1,500 armed policemen had established themselves in Naxalbari. Under the overwhelming force of the police, Bengal's armed peasant movement folded.[46]

In December 1967, the central government strengthened its coercive powers by passing the Unlawful Activities Prevention Act. The law gave the government and the police wide-ranging powers to make arrests without due process. Although such authority violates the International Covenant on Civil and Political Rights because it violates the principle of "innocent until proven guilty," it quickly became entrenched in the Indian governance toolkit. Police repression followed the peasant rebellion as it moved from Bengal into Andhra Pradesh and neighboring states.[47]

Police force also followed the rebellion as it turned into a student-led urban guerilla movement in Bengal. Labeled "Naxalites" because of their prior association with the peasant movement in Naxalbari, students had their own reasons to rebel. Speaking on the campus of Calcutta's prestigious Presidency College, a Naxalite leader said, "Almost everyone in this college is a sympathizer. The future's dark for most students. With unemployment what it is, they have no prospects in life unless they commit themselves to the revolutionary cause." To subdue protesting students, the police introduced draconian "fake encounters." In these episodes, policemen dispensed vigilante-style "instant justice," shooting and killing protestors on the pretext of self-defense. Ranjit Gupta, the police officer in charge of taming Bengal's urban guerillas, became a celebrity for carrying out such fake encounters. When he entered the foyer of a private club to meet the writer Dom Moraes on assignment from the *New York Times*, the elite guests "rose like a football crowd" to applaud him. "Jolly good show," they exclaimed.[48]

Two decades after independence, India's economy and democracy were in a stalemate. Agricultural productivity remained low, and urban job prospects remained bleak. The combination of underemployment and inflation was a blight on people's lives. In Bombay, many young Indians had thrown in their lot with the defiantly violent Shiv Sena; in Bengal, young Indians had participated in a failed armed rebellion.

Bedrock norms and democratic institutions were cracking. The Shiv Sena and Hindu nationalists were mobilizing mobs to peddle hatred. Amid this chaos, Mrs. Gandhi was trying to project herself as a cult figure. Democracy functioned superficially: India held elections and new governments transitioned to power in a peaceful manner. But rather than address the country's deepening problems, Mrs. Gandhi's government unleashed the police on the people. The police—shielded by unsupported claims of self-defense and celebrated by Indian elites—could act without fear of reprisal. The principles of due process and equal rights under the law were jettisoned. The judiciary looked on helplessly.

With Indian citizens and the state facing off in an antagonistic stance, what was Mrs. Gandhi's plan? What was her next move?

Chapter 10

INDIA HAS AN EMPRESS

After two years of drought, the rains were finally plentiful during the Indian fiscal year 1967–1968 (April 1 to March 31). Food production expanded, which contributed to an overall GDP growth of over 8 percent.[1] The pall over the Indian economy was starting to lift.

The gloom may have been lifting, but Indian policymakers had much work ahead of them. Shrinking foreign aid forced the government to cut back on investment in infrastructure such as the railways and electricity production and distribution. The economy's weakness over the previous two years had reduced tax revenues, and the war with Pakistan had increased defense spending. To reduce its budget deficit and rein in inflation, the government cut back its expenditures and raised taxes. As a result, manufacturing output fell.[2]

The monsoon gods were, however, delivering Mrs. Gandhi an opportunity to tackle the country's long-term economic problems. Instead, she stepped back from economic policymaking. As I. G. Patel reports in his memoirs, the 1968 budget didn't feature any significant initiatives. Mrs. Gandhi did recognize that the Indian education system was highly deficient, but she was not inclined to remedy the problem. The time to overhaul the education system was "when we became free," she said. Not having done so was "one of our mistakes," she recognized, but now it was "not easy to change it," for that would cause "tremendous dislocation." On agriculture, after two years of drought and with food aid from the United States on a leash, she had little choice but to passively continue the Green Revolution strategy initiated by Prime Minister Shastri. She increased imports of seeds for high-yield varieties, guaranteed food grain prices for farmers, and subsidized fertilizer use as well as food purchases by consumers.[3]

Lacking ambition in economic policymaking, Mrs. Gandhi continued from where she had left off in 1967 to test the guardrails of democracy. She was on her way to becoming a kind of Indian empress. And as she ascended to her throne, democratic norms and accountability fell victim to intensifying political corruption. Mrs. Gandhi's plans for maintaining her hold on power now included her son Sanjay, the prince-in-making. India was looking less and less like a democracy.

Sanjay Wants to Build a Car

In backing Sanjay, Mrs. Gandhi—more than anyone else—knew she was making a risky bet. Born on December 14, 1946, Sanjay had been a spoiled child with destructive instincts, which only increased as he grew older. In 1953, when he was seven years old, Mrs. Gandhi placed him at Welham Preparatory School in Dehradun, a small town in the beautiful foothills of the Himalayas. Upon arrival at Welham, a teacher identified Sanjay as a "problem child," an assessment he promptly lived up to. His behavior became particularly alarming when, at the age of ten, he moved to Doon School, also in Dehradun. When a student there freed a sparrow that Sanjay had trapped in a mosquito net, Sanjay destroyed the boy's new tennis racket. At the school store, he forged the signatures of other students to buy himself treats. As he grew older, he used his mother's and grandfather's visits to town to leave the school campus and steal cars that he could use for joyrides around town.[4]

Mrs. Gandhi pulled Sanjay out of Doon and enrolled him in Irish Catholic St. Columba's School in Delhi. In Delhi, he continued stealing cars and driving them recklessly through the city before abandoning them. In May 1964, the police found a stolen car with women's underwear and bottles of liquor. Though Sanjay's connection to that car was murky at best, the editor of a news magazine published the story and called on Mrs. Gandhi to deny that Sanjay was among the car thieves. When Mrs. Gandhi refused to deny her son's involvement, Sanjay was furious. But Mrs. Gandhi did not want to be sucked into the controversy, knowing that other incidents would surely come up in which Sanjay was likely guilty.[5]

After he finished high school at St. Columba's in 1964, Mrs. Gandhi sought help from the shipping tycoon Dharam Teja to place Sanjay in an exclusive apprenticeship at the Rolls-Royce factory at Crewe in England. Now, both her sons—Sanjay and his older brother Rajiv—were in England for their education. A reporter pointed out to her that many Indians believed she thought poorly of the Indian educational system; she responded that she did not care what people thought.[6]

Sanjay arrived in Crewe in September 1964 for a three-year apprenticeship, which would qualify him to be a high-quality motor mechanic. Those interested in automotive design and manufacturing needed to follow up with an advanced engineering degree. Sanjay's priority was to have a good time, as he understood it. He acquired a used Jaguar, which he often neglected to stop at red lights. On one occasion, after he had "souped up" his car to "do a ton" (i.e., drive at high speed), he lost control of the car, which flipped over. He was a continuous embarrassment to the Indian High Commission (Embassy) in London, which had to bail him out and hush up his escapades. At the end of the second year of his three-year apprenticeship, Sanjay declared he was wasting his time. His supervisors at Crewe were relieved to see him go. One of them described him as uncooperative and interested only in "booze and women." In his final escapade in England, in December 1966, a policeman fined him for driving without a license.[7]

In February 1967, on his way out of London, Sanjay spoke with *The Daily Mail*. When the journalist asked him if he was planning a career in politics, Sanjay said that he did not want to be prime minister, adding (as if he anticipated the possibility) "unless it is handed to me on a plate."[8]

Back in Delhi, Sanjay made a new friend, Arjun Das, who was also a mechanic. From the middle of 1967, the two of them banged away in "a filthy 100-square-foot truck shop surrounded by garbage dumps and overflowing sewers" in Delhi's Gulabi Bagh area. Presumably because he kept Sanjay out of trouble, Arjun gained Mrs. Gandhi's "respect and confidence." She even campaigned for him when he ran in municipal elections. "I don't have two sons, I have three," she said at the prime ministerial dining table one night.[9]

When the government announced that it was planning to license an automaker to produce a car made with wholly domestic technology and parts, Sanjay and Arjun joined the fray. The idea of India producing a car without any foreign technology or components was madness. Nehru's heavy industry ideas were misguided, but no one had ever contemplated building machinery from scratch. It was understood that India would import technology, equipment, and raw materials. And the idea of Sanjay and Arjun reinventing and assembling a car was a joke. As mechanics, they had shown no signs of budding engineering genius. In September 1968, they reportedly assembled a small car "powered by a motorcycle engine." In November, Sanjay presented a proposal to the government. He would produce a car priced at 6,000 rupees ($800) that could run 90 kilometers (56 miles) on a gallon of petrol. He pledged to make fifty thousand of those cars every year.[10]

On November 13, 1968, the Government of India announced that it had short-listed Sanjay's proposal. Others on the list included world-renowned producers, such as Renault, Toyota, and Volkswagen. In giving Sanjay entry into this elite competition, Mrs. Gandhi was unleashing a force that would have vast consequences for India.[11]

Bank Nationalization in the Arc of Indian History

Political time was not standing still. The Congress Party was continuing to lose by-elections (off-year elections) to state assemblies. Underemployment and inflation continued to trigger social and political protests. The virus of violence was spreading. In Bombay, Shiv Sena boss Bal Thackeray announced that he would not allow any central government minister to enter Bombay until the government resolved Maharashtra's claim on villages in the neighboring state of Mysore. When Morarji Desai, the deputy prime minister and finance minister, chose to enter Bombay anyway, Thackeray's Shiv Sena "turned out in force," inciting riots that injured people and damaged property for "four terrifying days."

Other *Senas* (armies), born of the same threatening premise and claiming regional rights and privileges, formed in other parts of the country.[12]

On May 3, 1969, Indian President Zakir Husain died of a heart attack. And for the third time in India's young history, following Sardar Patel and Lal Bahadur Shastri's deaths, a heart failure triggered a history-changing series of events. Mrs. Gandhi advocated for Vice President V. V. Giri as the next president, but the Syndicate dismissed her recommendation. They were determined to nominate Neelam Sanjeeva Reddy, a known political foe of Mrs. Gandhi's, whom she had pointedly kept out of her cabinet after the February 1967 election. Mrs. Gandhi evidently did not want Sanjeeva Reddy as India's president, but it was not clear why, given that Indian presidents perform mainly ceremonial functions. Possibly she feared that if, for example, Morarji Desai were to challenge her again, Reddy might use his presidential authority to invite Desai to form a government, which would leave her out in the cold.[13]

Knowing that she could not openly defy the Syndicate's decision, Mrs. Gandhi turned the political tussle for power into a superficially ideological battle. At a meeting of Congress Party leaders in Bangalore on July 9, 1969, she proposed nationalization—a state takeover—of Indian banks. Her proposal was contrary to an earlier agreement among Congress Party leaders to first employ "social control" of banks, under which the finance minister would ask banks to lend more to farmers, small firms, and other vulnerable borrowers while also trying to persuade bank owners to reduce their representation on the banks' boards. Mrs. Gandhi's bank nationalization would stop the social control experiment and place the government directly in charge of the banks and their lending decisions.

Mrs. Gandhi quickly decided to ram through the nationalization of banks. She was now in a race against time. Parliament was scheduled to return from recess on July 21, and once it did, she was not sure that she would have a parliamentary majority in favor of nationalization. Hence, she needed a presidential ordinance (decree) before Parliament reconvened. Acting President Giri planned to step down from his position at noon on July 20 to contest the presidential election as an "independent" candidate. Mrs. Gandhi needed Giri to sign the ordinance by July 19. She began on July 16 by firing Finance Minister Morarji Desai, who was sure to resist nationalization. Desai was at lunch when he received a curt letter of dismissal from the prime minister.[14]

In the late evening of July 17, Parmeshwar Narayan Haksar, Mrs. Gandhi's right-hand man, began assembling a team for drafting the ordinance. The next day, Mrs. Gandhi called in I. G. Patel, by then economic affairs secretary, the most senior economic bureaucrat. She brusquely said to Patel, "For political reasons, it has been decided to nationalize the banks." Patel's task was to complete the paperwork overnight and prepare a speech for Mrs. Gandhi to deliver to the nation after Giri signed the ordinance. Patel would later write, "It is remarkable how momentous decisions are made in the heat of a political struggle." With zero discussion regarding the economic merits of the decision—and, it seemed, zero interest—Mrs. Gandhi was unleashing an economic monstrosity. The State Bank of India, the largest Indian bank, was already under public ownership. With the additional nationalizations, the government would own virtually the entire Indian banking system, with control of 90 percent of bank deposits.[15]

The ordinance was indeed ready for Giri's signature in time. On July 19, as the world applauded Neil Armstrong's "giant leap for mankind," India's fourteen largest privately held banks fell under the ownership and control of the Indian government. The banks' shareholders accused the government in courts of expropriating private property, and the government deflected the charge by paying higher compensation than originally planned. And the deed was done.[16]

Mrs. Gandhi had made a political decision, and her political dividends poured in instantly. Millions of Indians hailed her as an "angel of the poor." She rode that sentiment, describing nationalization of the banks "as a measure for the common man and a rebuff to big business." Crowds, often arranged by her supporters, "began to stage rallies at her New Delhi bungalow, in what seemed to be spontaneous demonstrations of Mrs. Gandhi's popularity." Teachers, taxi drivers, *dhobis* (washermen/-women), rickshaw pullers, and cobblers shouted slogans "about the social benefits of nationalization." Her political opponents were "unnerved."[17]

The inevitable followed. Mrs. Gandhi "freed" Congress Party Members of Parliament (MPs) from an obligation to vote for the Congress

Party candidate, Sanjeeva Reddy. She said that they could vote as their "conscience" guided them. Many Congress Party MPs voted for Giri, who won a narrow victory for the Indian presidency in August 1969. Reddy's defeat stung the Syndicate, who threw Mrs. Gandhi out of the Congress Party on November 12. The party broke up before the end of the year. Most Congress Party MPs stayed with Mrs. Gandhi, but they were not able to secure a parliamentary majority. To remain prime minister, she had to rely on the Communist Party of India, the Dravida Munnetra Kazhagam from Tamil Nadu, and a handful of independent MPs.[18]

With the wind in her sails, Mrs. Gandhi cast herself as "more socialist than Nehru." In fact, writes biographer Uma Vasudev, she began a "virtual war of propaganda in favor of socialist ideals." In villages, towns, and cities and to all manner of audiences, she spoke nonstop of "the concepts of socialism."[19]

In the flush of her "socialist" triumph, on September 24, 1970, Mrs. Gandhi returned to Sanjay's priorities. "My son has shown enterprise and I could not say no to him. If he is not encouraged, how can I ask other young men to take risks?" Mrs. Gandhi asked in response to critics who complained about her fast-tracking of his application. Thumbing her nose at those critics, on November 30, she presided over a cabinet meeting in which Sanjay was given the official "letter of intent," the go-ahead to build prototypes of a wholly Indian car. Of the original fourteen applicants invited to submit proposals, Sanjay's was one of only two that met the criterion of using wholly domestic technology and parts. Little wonder! No reasonable car manufacturer would attempt something so unrealistic. The other applicant who offered to meet the domestic-technology criterion dropped out and disappeared into obscurity.[20] Sanjay's car would be named Maruti, the monkey god who in Hindu mythology is also the offspring of the wind god.

Sanjay's car stirred up a political whirlwind. Bansi Lal, chief minister of the state of Haryana, seeing Sanjay as a rising star, offered him prime agricultural land for setting up a factory on the road from Delhi to Gurgaon, about 25 kilometers from the prime minister's house, which was also Sanjay's residence. Sanjay "dictated" the terms of purchase, which the land acquisition officer hurriedly agreed to. About 1,500 farmers had their property possessed, and Sanjay acquired the land at a "knock-down price." Indian defense minister Vidya Charan Shukla overrode army regulations that disallowed construction close to an ammunition dump and also overrode air force regulations that disallowed construction close to an airstrip. An impressive group of industrialists formed Sanjay's Board of Directors. The board often met in the prime minister's house, a practice that, as Gyan Prakash put it, left "no doubt as to the power behind the project." Lalit Narayan Mishra, a minister in Mrs. Gandhi's cabinet, played a crucial role in raising capital, including by helping to collect large sums as advance payments from the dealers who would sell the car.[21]

Whether intended or not, Sanjay's rise as a potential car producer and the recently concluded bank nationalization came together. Two of the nationalized banks, Central Bank and Punjab National Bank, pitched in with loans to Maruti. Staff at these banks "went out of their way" to help Sanjay's Maruti affiliates. Bank staff were acutely conscious that Sanjay Gandhi was an "important" client. Sanjay, equally conscious of the clout he possessed, used that knowledge to bully bank staff into lowering the interest rate on loans to Maruti and accepting shoddy documentation, which diluted the standards of required collateral.[22]

From that unfortunate beginning, banks became hotbeds of corruption. Wealthy, politically powerful, and corrupt elites received loans on favorable terms, on which they frequently defaulted. The integrity and financial viability of the nationalized banks steadily eroded, making nonsense of the claims that the nationalized banks were serving a socialist—or indeed any economic—purpose.

The nationalized banks did rapidly increase their presence in previously "unbranched" areas. They attracted more deposits because people believed them to be safer than banks under private ownership. The government used part of the deposits to fund itself. Farmers and small urban businesses received more credit, although they learned quickly they could use political clout to get away with not repaying the loans. Customer service at nationalized banks deteriorated because bank employees had the job security enjoyed by government employees and so could not be dismissed for indifference or even hostility to customers.[23]

With the bank nationalization done, as I. G. Patel noted, the rest of economic policymaking remained "routine and cautious and on traditional lines."[24]

Policy Negligence Comes with a Cost

It was a crucial moment in the global history of economic development. India was falling behind at an alarming pace. For the fiscal year 1970–1971, the IMF reported that India's GDP had increased by 5 percent, as in the previous year. Agricultural production had held up, but industrial output and export performance had been "less favorable." Unusually for the IMF, which typically stays focused on short-term macroeconomics, the report paid special attention to India's serious long-term problem of unemployment and underemployment. The report noted that weak job creation was particularly worrisome since India's population was increasing at such a fast clip.[25]

A nearly simultaneous assessment of South Korea reported "remarkable" GDP growth of 16 percent in 1969 followed by 11 percent growth in 1970. Even the slowdown to 11 percent growth was deliberately engineered by the Korean authorities to prevent economic overheating—high inflation and a larger balance-of-payments deficit. The Fund highlighted the spurt in Korea's manufactured exports. And these exports generated plentiful jobs, ensuring nearly full employment in Korea. Korea was fulfilling its promise as a hub for labor-intensive manufactured exports, as anticipated by the World Bank in the mid-1960s.[26]

In those snapshots of India and Korea at the end of 1970, the IMF captured an India stuck in moderate economic growth that created few jobs, while the East Asian Tigers—Hong Kong, Singapore, South Korea, and Taiwan—were in the midst of explosive, job-rich economic growth. They had followed in the footsteps of Japan but were now overtaking Japan in the export of labor-intensive manufactured products.[27]

Today, the central elements of East Asia's miraculous growth are well understood. The strategy was not, as is often represented, narrow-minded "liberalization" to encourage greater play of free markets. Instead, East Asian nations placed enormous emphasis on educating their children,

FIGURE 10.1: East Asian women went to work. (Labor force participation rate by women aged 15 years or older, percent)

Source: World Bank, World Development Indicators for Korea and India, SL.TLF.CACT.FE.NE.ZS; National Statistics for Taiwan, https://eng.stat.gov.tw/ct.asp?xItem=31332&ctNode=1611&mp=5.

beginning with quality primary schooling for all. The schools produced industrially literate workers of both genders who produced manufactured products of increasing sophistication for world markets. Widespread education and employment opportunities ensured that East Asian growth came with reduced income inequality and rapid poverty reduction.[28]

A remarkable outgrowth of the East Asian strategy was increased participation of women in the workforce (Figure 10.1). East Asia was in a virtuous cycle. As educated women went to work, they had fewer children and paid closer attention to those children, especially to their health and education.[29]

East Asian governments were also attentive to sound macroeconomic management, anticipating and preventing economic overheating. Importantly, they were always open to devaluing their currencies to prevent the loss of international competitiveness whenever domestic prices increased too rapidly. While India also used austere fiscal budgets to help contain inflation, devaluation of the exchange rate was viewed as an internationally imposed humiliation; after the 1966 devaluation it became anathema. This aversion to devaluation severely constrained India's export growth.[30]

The world moved on; India remained stuck in its lane. Persisting underemployment scarcely featured in the elite policy dialogue. Mrs. Gandhi felt no compelling need to undertake ambitious economic and social policy measures. Only Sanjay and her own political survival animated her.

The Coronation of the Empress

In late 1966, Mrs. Gandhi had begun to draw attention to herself as a savior. She had asserted, "My position among the people is uncontested," and had embraced the designation of "Indira Amma." As her public charisma and mystique grew, especially after the bank nationalization, she strengthened her institutional power. She brought the crucial functions of civil service appointments and criminal investigations under her direct control in the prime minister's office. She also expanded the resources in her office for political surveillance. In December 1970, she took the next logical step. Rather than remain head of a minority government dependent on other political parties, she called for parliamentary elections in March 1971, a year ahead of schedule. When a *Newsweek* reporter asked her what the issues were in the upcoming election, Mrs. Gandhi answered quite simply, "I am the issue."[31]

In the 1971 election, Mrs. Gandhi made another determined effort to promote her brand. Congress Party workers, often students and members of the Congress Party's youth wing, inundated the country with "millions of posters and badges imprinted with Mrs. Gandhi's picture." The posters and other publicity materials "filtered down from large urban centers to small towns and into villages." As in 1966 and 1967, Mrs. Gandhi campaigned tirelessly, addressing "250 mammoth public meetings and hundreds of smaller wayside crowds." Her message was simple: "she personally, rather than the Congress Party, represented the renewed commitment to economic and social reform."[32]

The branding and messaging worked. Raj Thapar, a friend of Mrs. Gandhi's at the time, asked a Delhi taxi driver who his preferred candidate in the approaching election was. The good fellow said that the taxi drivers at his stand were all going to vote for "Indira." When Thapar probed if he meant Mrs. Gandhi's Congress Party, the cab driver responded that no political party was worth voting for; their vote was for Indira. She cared for the ordinary person. She had nationalized the banks and had shown that she could stand up to the rich. Mrs. Gandhi also received an unexpected gift from the opposition leaders. When they tried to rally voters around the slogan "Indira hatao" (remove Indira), she responded with her own slogan, "garibi hatao" (remove poverty), an opportunistic catchphrase that identified her forever as a champion of the poor.[33]

The voters gave Mrs. Gandhi a resounding victory. Her vote share rose to 44 percent, enough to net her two-thirds of the seats in the Lok Sabha.

After the election, to enhance her socialist, pro-poor image, Mrs. Gandhi immediately began the task of stripping former princes of their "privy purses." These "purses" were pensions that the government had promised the princes in return for their agreement to surrender all rights to their kingdoms. Mrs. Gandhi faced the hurdle that the justice system would view depriving the princes of their purses as taking away their private property and, hence, unconstitutional. She handpicked ministers to draft amendments to the Constitution. The amendments gave priority to the "socialist promises" in the Constitution's Directive Principles of State Policy. Parliament could now write laws that overrode constitutionally guaranteed Fundamental Rights, including the right to property. The legal trickery here was that Parliament could deny the right to private property as long it claimed it was working to achieve "socialist" objectives. To make its authority ironclad, in December 1971 Parliament further amended the Constitution to terminate privy purses.[34]

Mrs. Gandhi gained greater national and international stature when she used Indian troops to stop the genocide of East Pakistani citizens by the Pakistan Army. In the process, she acted as the midwife to Pakistan's breakup. West Pakistan remained as Pakistan, while East Pakistan turned into a new country: modern-day Bangladesh. *The Economist*, the widely read British news magazine, crowned Mrs. Gandhi "Empress of India" and indeed of South Asia. Not only had she cast the dead wood out of the Congress Party and reshaped the party "in her image," *The Economist* said, but Pakistan was a diminished country and Bangladesh would remain an

Indian "client" for the foreseeable future.[35] Not for the first nor the last time, *The Economist* was making bold forecasts that would soon prove badly mistaken.

The Rot Sets in

Four good economic years, from 1968 to 1971, had passed without a drought. High-yielding seed varieties had begun delivering on their promise in well-irrigated areas. Inflation rates were low, in part squeezed down by austere fiscal and monetary policy. Indian industry was growing quickly, helped by demand from farmers who had had a good run of years.

But although India's economy was on the move when judged by its past, it remained unable to employ the large numbers of its young job aspirants. Neither Mrs. Gandhi nor anyone else in the Indian leadership saw any reason to learn the methods of public goods provision and employment generation so successfully used by East Asian economies.

Mrs. Gandhi focused on consolidating her power. Even before the 1971 elections, she had gathered key executive authority on civil service appointments and criminal investigations in her office. She abolished democracy within the Congress Party by stopping elections for officeholders. Instead, she herself appointed party officials and chief ministers of states ruled by the Congress Party. In May 1971, two months after her electoral victory, she renewed the government's preventive detention authority. That authority had lapsed in 1969 when the Communist Party—the party that Mrs. Gandhi's minority government then depended on for support—refused to renew the government's unchecked powers under the Unlawful Activities Prevention Act of 1967. Under Mrs. Gandhi's new Maintenance of Internal Security Act, the central and state governments could detain anyone for up to a year on broadly defined charges of disturbing internal security or compromising the country's defense.[36]

As the constitutional scholar Granville Austin has emphasized, India effectively no longer had three branches of government. The legislature rubber-stamped Mrs. Gandhi's proposals. Her constitutional amendments, along with manipulation of judicial appointments, diminished the role of an independent judiciary as a check on the executive.[37]

Meanwhile, corruption swirled around Mrs. Gandhi. She had looked the other way when Sanjay used the recently nationalized banks as his personal piggy bank. Yet another, and perhaps the most corrosive, source of corruption was a parliamentary decision in May 1969 to ban companies from making contributions to political parties. Made in a moment of anti-corruption fervor some months before the Congress Party split in 1969, the decision's stated intention was to root out corporate influence in politics. More likely, though, it was a calculated effort on the part of the Congress Party to damage the fundraising prospects of pro-business parties, especially the Swatantra Party. In practice, the "banned" corporate donations continued surreptitiously. Companies used their "black money" (money that did not pass through the taxman's net) to make donations. Since companies gave their money to likely winners, Mrs. Gandhi was a major beneficiary exactly when her intensified branding efforts drove up her campaign costs.[38]

Once black money became the main currency of politics, criminals had more reason and greater ability to join the political game. They were, after all, repositories of black money, and they too wanted to exercise political influence. The coal mafia, the timber mafia, the liquor mafia—all jumped into the fray.[39]

Other forms of corruption grew. Especially after the Congress Party split in late 1969, Mrs. Gandhi's lieutenants used the power of granting licenses and regulating industry to extract increasing sums from companies. In June 1970, the government added the Monopolies and Restrictive Trade Practices Act to its array of controls. The MRTP Act has been billed as a "socialist" measure. That is an odd characterization, since every advanced capitalist nation has a system of curbing monopoly power. In India, though, the MRTP Act became an instrument of corruption almost from its inception. Bureaucrats had one more tool to delay and deny applications for industrial expansion. Some large business groups preemptively cornered the authorizations for expansion and operation, thus keeping out the competition and working in direct opposition to the MRTP Act's stated purpose.[40]

At the apex of Mrs. Gandhi's corruption machinery was L. N. Mishra. He served as a minister in Mrs. Gandhi's government—and, as the

Congress Party treasurer, he was the man in charge of squeezing businesses for funds. This was the same Mishra who helped raise capital for Sanjay's Maruti car venture. Now, the stakes were much larger. We were now in the era of "briefcase politics." Each permit or license cost a businessman a certain number of briefcases of cash. Soon, the larger sums transacted required suitcases rather than briefcases.[41]

According to the journalist and author Kuldip Nayar, it was very likely Mrs. Gandhi herself who took eventual possession of the illegal corporate money. S. K. Patil, a member of the feared and hated Syndicate, alleged in an interview with Nayar that he had given Mrs. Gandhi a large amount of cash in a suitcase. And she did not even return the suitcase, Patil complained.[42]

The more dispassionate I. G. Patel put it only somewhat more politely. Mrs. Gandhi's "hubris and delusion" grew as she strengthened her hold on power: "she could do what she liked and did not have to worry much about right and wrong." When Patel, as the economic affairs secretary, made decisions that made Indian businesses unhappy, they knew that L. N. Mishra was their man. He continuously badgered Patel "to favour some firm or another for obvious quid pro quo." And "everyone knew," wrote Patel, that Mishra had the "PM's backing."[43] The trio—Sanjay, L. N. Mishra, and the PM—were in it all together.

For four good years, Mrs. Gandhi operated in slogans and headline-grabbing decisions. Her father may have believed in his "socialism" mantra, but Mrs. Gandhi used the rhetoric with contempt for all those who could not see through it. Behind the rhetoric's facade, she injected virulent corruption into Indian politics. All the while, with little economic progress, citizens felt continuing economic anxiety. And the good economic years ended with a drought in August 1971.

Mrs. Gandhi's political success continued into the 1972 election campaign for state assemblies. She maintained her charisma. Her promise to reduce poverty still struck a chord. She had access to an unlimited supply of black money, which her party workers spent on a furious burst of "posters, films, cinema slides, leaflets, and hoardings" in multiple languages. The Congress Party swept to another easy electoral victory. Reflecting helplessly on Mrs. Gandhi's formidable political dominance, Jana

Sangh leader Atal Bihari Vajpayee remarked that while the opposition had fielded 2,700 candidates across the country, the Congress Party had simply run Mrs. Gandhi in every constituency.[44]

India was at another turning point, though. Even as Mrs. Gandhi towered over her political opponents, national discord and turmoil were gathering pace, threatening to engulf her and the country. India's politics were morally unanchored. Strong economic headwinds were approaching. And tired of the false promises and accompanying cynicism, young Indians were ready to burst forth in anger.

Chapter 11

ANGER MEETS REPRESSION

Starting in late 1971, the Indian economy took a turn for the worse. The weather gods kept their smiles turned off for much of the period from late 1971 to mid-1975. Indeed, toward the end of that spell, the gods frowned. Also, in late 1973 global oil prices spiked, adding to the inflation from rising food prices and causing a further slowdown in economic growth. These rolling crises made it harder for many Indians to find work and pay for life's necessities. The simmering clash between angry Indians and Mrs. Gandhi's repressive power boiled over.

Economic Crises Keep Coming

In August 1971, a largely unnoticed *Times of India* editorial warned of "the millstones of drought and flood" that were crushing the prospect of a good *kharif* crop. The traditionally dry areas of Maharashtra and Andhra Pradesh were particularly starved of water. Elsewhere, heavy rain was flowing down the "denuded" hills of the Himalayas, causing flood havoc in the eastern states, especially in Bihar. Indian authorities were not overly concerned. The Green Revolution seemed to be working. In the previous agricultural year, 1970–1971, Indian farms had produced 108 million tons of food grains, the highest-ever annual total. Even if production now fell short, the government's food stocks seemed enough to prevent famine and starvation.[1]

However, as the months wore on, floods and drought continued to spread. By August 1972, with another poor *kharif* crop looming, "the spectre of famine hovered over about ten states." In November, Mrs. Gandhi said that "extremely difficult days" lay ahead. Minister of State for Agriculture A. P. Shinde announced that the government was initiating a relief program to avert famine.[2]

Government relief programs were mean-spirited. In the dry areas of Maharashtra, hundreds of thousands of peasants and agricultural laborers received meager wages for "the demoralizing and strenuous task of reducing rubble with tiny hammers." The government did not pay even those meager wages on time as prices of essential commodities rose, forcing peasant and worker families to sell what few valuables they had.[3]

By January 1973, the drought had widened its reach to fourteen states, and the government's food grain stocks were down to 3 million tons, from a peak of 9 million tons. The U.S. food aid program, under which India could pay for imported food in rupees, did not exist anymore. The government used its precious foreign currency to pay for about 2 million tons of high-priced food grains, mainly from the United States, Canada, and Argentina.[4]

Mrs. Gandhi's popularity and prestige "plummeted" as food price inflation and falling demand for industrial products caused "spiraling unemployment" and industrial unrest. *The Economist,* which less than eighteen months earlier had crowned Mrs. Gandhi "Empress of South Asia," now focused on her "excessive arrogance," "misuse of privilege," and "stashing away of illegal campaign funds." *The Economist* added that Mrs. Gandhi's capacity to run the country had diminished greatly and she faced bleak prospects in the next elections.[5]

Over the next two years, India experienced extraordinary inflation. Food prices rose by about 16 percent in 1972–1973, and despite a rebound in food production in 1973–1974, food prices continued rising at a 19 percent annual rate. In October 1973, the Organization of Arab Petroleum Exporting Countries (OAPEC) placed an embargo on oil exports to the United States and other Western nations that were supporting Israel in the ongoing Arab-Israeli War. Oil prices quadrupled from $2.90 a barrel to almost $11.65 a barrel in January 1974. The sharply higher prices of imported oil and petroleum products, including fertilizers, added to Indian inflation. In mid-1974, the IMF grimly noted that India was experiencing its "highest rate of price inflation since Independence."[6]

In April 1973, Mrs. Gandhi had nationalized the wheat trade, ostensibly to counter the food inflationary spiral. The hope was that the nationalization would prevent hoarding of wheat by speculators. But as the *New York Times* wrote, "the government machinery broke down." Translation: the bureaucrats made a mess of the situation. A psychology of shortage encouraged even more hoarding. In March 1974, the government ended its misguided wheat trade adventure.[7]

Drought and floods ravaged the country again in the summer and autumn of 1974. On July 25, the *Times of India* reported that nearly three-quarters of the country was under threat of renewed drought. Among the worst affected states were Gujarat and Bihar. People sold their jewelry (a major form of savings for many Indian households), as well as their land and homes. Their cattle "perished for lack of water and fodder." Working conditions on government relief projects were once again "deplorable," and the wages were, as always, "very low." In eastern India and the southwestern state of Kerala, floods caused mayhem. Again, the *Times of India* commented, the floods were nature's "revenge" for "indiscriminate deforestation," which was destroying the "delicate" natural system of "checks and balances." Bihar, as earlier in the decade, was doubly luckless: floods in the north and drought in the south devastated crops and the livelihoods of millions.[8]

In October 1974, a brave Bangladeshi reporter asked Mrs. Gandhi if she had failed to deliver on "garibi hatao," her promise to eliminate poverty. The question annoyed her. "We never promised any miracles," she said. "We have taken steps," but "people expect much more than we can do for them."[9]

Food grain production fell again in the 1974–75 agricultural year. The additional shortfall, coming on top of the scarcity since 1972–1973, caused a heart-stopping spike of 38 percent in food grain prices. In all, over the three years from 1972 to 1975, food grain prices had risen by a cumulative 90 percent—a staggering 25 percent year-on-year average.

The Green Revolution's promise was real. Food grain output was increasing in the irrigated areas. But only about a quarter of India's cultivated land was irrigated. The rest of the land—operated with "dry farming" techniques—was highly vulnerable to rainfall deficits. In search of quick solutions, Indian officials encouraged digging more wells to extract groundwater for irrigation. That short-sighted rush merely pushed the risks into the future. Already, high-yielding varieties with large doses of fertilizers were depleting the soil.[10]

The industrial-urban economy was also troubled. Striking a note of hope in a guest column for the *Financial Times,* Indian journalist Dilip Mukerjee noted that Nehru's industrialization drive had created capability to produce technologically sophisticated products such as airplanes, diesel locomotives, and machining lathes. Surely, Mukerjee argued, with their low wage rates, Indians could soon make headway in the less technologically demanding labor-intensive products. The plausible-sounding argument was, in fact, mistaken. India's sophisticated manufacturers depended on a limited number of highly skilled workers. Mass production of labor-intensive goods required large numbers of low-skilled but productive workers. And as East Asian success stories had demonstrated, well-functioning primary and secondary schools were essential to instill the discipline and motivation for productive low-skill work. India's poor educational system was an albatross that made economic progress virtually impossible. In India, low levels of worker productivity had offset the advantage of low wages since the turn of the twentieth century.[11] To compete internationally, India needed better-educated workers and a much weaker rupee exchange rate to compensate for the inadequate devaluation in 1966 and the extraordinary rise in costs of production that followed.

Astonishingly, although the IMF called on India to tighten its fiscal belt and reduce import and industrial controls, it did not press Indian authorities for rupee devaluation in return for the large sums India borrowed to meet its surging import demand for food grains and oil/petroleum products in 1974 and 1975. And so, with no domestic source of dynamism, the Indian economy trudged on in its low-performance mode.[12]

Anger Bubbles in the Cities

The Indian economy was on its knees. In late 1974 and 1975, those most directly hurt were landowning small and medium-sized farmers and landless farm laborers. The farmers had lost much of their normal output, and the benefits of rising prices went largely to traders and speculators. But despite the dreadful hardships they suffered, farmers were in no position to voice their collective despair. In the second half of 1967, in Bengal's Naxalbari area, small peasants and landless laborers had tried to seize land from large landholders. The Bengal government had suppressed that uprising with overwhelming police force. Although most farmers had continued to struggle, those who had tasted the benefits of the Green Revolution were not inclined to protest against the state. Landless workers lacked any ability to organize themselves into a protest movement.

Hence, the anger born of relentless inflation and poor job prospects found its expression mainly in the cities. That anger, which had burst forth episodically in the 1950s, flared up in the late 1960s and rose rapidly to a crescendo in 1974 (Figure 11.1). A fearsome decay of political and bureaucratic norms aggravated the rising anger over economic hardship. Lawless officials, politicians, and policemen, acting sometimes in partnership with criminals, preyed on those who were financially vulnerable or lacked the right political connections.[13] A sense of siege gave an edge—even legitimacy—to citizens' anger and violence. Indian cities were tinderboxes ready to explode.

In his 1970 film *Pratidwandi* (The adversary), Satyajit Ray portrayed the frustration of educated young Bengalis. Dozens, if not hundreds, of applicants seek a single job. The fortunate candidates are invited to the prized (and yet dreaded) job interview. In one such encounter, the interview panel declares *Pratidwandi*'s protagonist, Siddharth, to be a communist because he praises the Vietnamese resistance, and is therefore deemed unqualified for the job. Repeated disappointments later, Siddharth is waiting with a horde of candidates for another interview. One of the candidates faints of dehydration in the sweltering heat. Siddharth has a vision that the long wait is turning them all into skeletons.

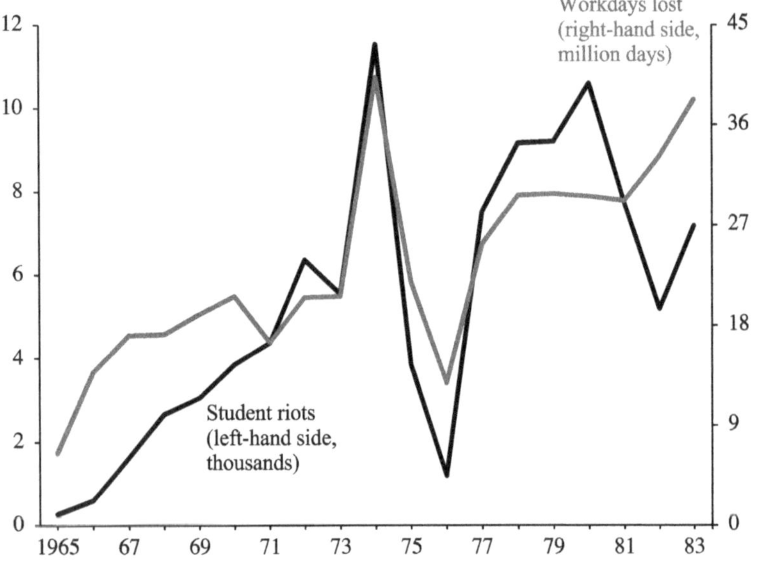

FIGURE 11.1: Urban unrest intensified in the years before the imposition of the Emergency.

Source: Rudolph, Lloyd and Susanne Rudolph. 1987. *In Pursuit of Lakshmi: The Political Economy of the Indian State*. Chicago: Chicago University Press, Table 23, 227.

In a display of his helplessness, he storms the interviewers, overturning the desk behind which they sit as ghost-like apparitions.

On the streets of Calcutta, students waged a guerrilla war in collaboration with the recently launched "Naxalite" political party, a radical breakaway from the Communist Party of India (Marxist). In mid-1971, Mrs. Gandhi used her constitutional authority (with the formal assent of the president) to suspend the elected Government of Bengal and place the state under her direct rule. Under that authority, she appointed the veteran Congress Party leader and childhood friend Siddhartha Shankar Ray as the state's governor, and he unleashed the army on students. The army arrested tens of thousands of suspected Naxalites and allegedly killed thousands of them, crushing the movement already weakened by the earlier brutal police "fake encounters."[14] India was a dictatorship on call.

That widespread urban anger found a popular escape valve in the "angry young man" Hindi films. The first of these, *Zanjeer* (Chain), was released in May 1973, just when food price inflation was gathering momentum. By January 1975, when *Deewar* (Wall) was released, high rates of inflation—driven by food and oil price hikes—had persisted for a few years. Crucial, though, was the context—the erosion of social and political norms—within which the inflation occurred. The writer Javed Akhtar, who, along with Salim Khan, scripted the first batch of "angry young man" movies later explained: "The morality of the day said that if you want justice, you had to fight for it yourself. And, if you don't fight, you will be crushed." At the heart of these movies lay the rarely reported alliance of policemen, criminals, and politicians using unchecked violence to gain power and wealth. The "angry young man" was the vigilante—also a law unto himself—who protected the victims of the lawlessness. As the political scientist Fareeduddin Kazmi wrote, the "angry young man" enacted the "innermost desires and fantasies of the audience." Urban residents most exposed to the capriciousness and unfairness of city life saw the films "again and again."[15]

Off the screen, in real life, matters reached a boil in the state of Gujarat toward the end of 1973. Riding on Mrs. Gandhi's coattails, her Congress Party had won 140 of 168 seats in the 1972 state assembly elections. The state's chief minister, Chimanbhai Patel, quickly lifted the regulatory lid on the price of groundnut (peanut) oil, commonly used in Gujarati cooking. His purpose was not to increase market efficiency. Instead, the "oil kings" made handsome profits, which they shared with Patel, who transferred a part of his loot to the Congress Party leadership in Delhi for expenses in a forthcoming election in Uttar Pradesh.[16]

For consumers, the increased price of groundnut oil came on top of rising grain prices. In late December 1973, students protested higher food bills in their college dining halls. On January 4, 1974, engineering students in Ahmedabad, the state's largest city, burned their dining hall and ransacked the rector's home. The State Reserve Police, known to be "a riot control force with a reputation for unusual brutality," beat up the students, jailed several hundred of them, and shut the college down. The rioting spread.[17]

On January 7, a coalition of mainly white-collar workers—employees of public- and private-sector enterprises—called for a *bandh* (shutdown) of Ahmedabad on January 10. A teachers' union, with its own complaints of low salaries and few opportunities for career progression, joined the call for the *bandh*. With support from Ahmedabad's beleaguered residents, the city shut down nearly completely on January 10.[18]

The students moved beyond their initial focus on dining bills and called for eliminating the cancer of corruption in Gujarat politics. United under the banner "Nav Nirman" (Rebuild), they demanded the resignation of Chief Minister Chimanbhai Patel, the most recent symbol of political corruption. In what was now becoming a customary response, on January 28, the army appeared on the streets of Ahmedabad. The people of Gujarat refused to be intimidated. They adopted the novel approach of walking up to the soldiers and offering them sweets and tea. The befuddled army packed up and left.[19]

On February 9, Chief Minister Patel resigned. The students persisted, demanding the dissolution of the state assembly. Mrs. Gandhi was reluctant to do so since her Congress Party held an overwhelming majority in the assembly. But, with nearly one hundred dead and thousands injured, she caved on March 15, granting the dissolution.[20]

Mrs. Gandhi Fights Back

On March 16, 1974, the day after the dissolution of the Gujarat State Assembly, attention shifted to student protests in Bihar. As in Gujarat, students were "protesting soaring prices, shortages of essential commodities, mounting unemployment, and outmoded education curricula." By March 18, the capital city, Patna, was a "battle zone."[21]

On March 19, the former freedom fighter Jayaprakash Narayan, popularly known as "J.P.," added his authority to the Bihar student movement. J.P. was a muddled revolutionary. Born in October 1902, he had traveled at the age of nineteen to study in the United States. There he came under the influence of Marxist scholars at the University of Wisconsin-Madison. Upon his return to India, he joined Gandhi and Nehru in the freedom struggle. But instead of following Gandhi's path of nonviolence, he "organized a guerrilla force to disrupt rails and communications and foment riots and strikes." He advocated "defensible violence," or violence to prevent greater violence and injustice.[22] Now, as he took over leadership of the violent student movement in urban Bihar, J.P. styled himself as a

Gandhian socialist who believed in Gandhi's nonviolence and vision of flourishing Indian village republics.

Bihar's troubles were profound. More so than Gujarat, Bihar had suffered grievous economic pain. Floods in the northern parts of the state and drought in the south regularly caused extensive damage to crop production. Bihar's politics, stated charitably, were chaotic. Since the 1967 election, coalition governments had changed frequently, sometimes within days, as opportunistic members of the state assembly crossed party lines for cash and lucrative ministerial positions. In the 1972 election, Mrs. Gandhi's Congress Party won a majority of the seats, just as in Gujarat. Factional infighting within the Congress Party for lucrative ministerial positions ensured that corruption continued unabated. Although J.P. was a muddled revolutionary mouthing a fuzzy Gandhian socialism, he had a real cause. His was, he said, "a struggle against the very system that has compelled almost everybody to go corrupt."[23]

As the Bihar agitation gathered steam, George Fernandes, former Catholic seminarian, Socialist Party leader, and head of a prominent railway union, called on the workers of Indian Railway to strike. By paralyzing rail transport, his goal was to cripple Indian industry's ability to source raw materials and sell its products. He saw leverage in the people who would be left to starve when stranded trains could not transport food to them. He was vocal about causing economic chaos to bring down the Indira Gandhi government. Fernandes demanded substantial increases in salaries and bonuses for the nearly two million railway workers. Mrs. Gandhi rejected the demands: they would place an unbearable burden on the government's budget at a time when country was living through an economic crisis. She refused to negotiate.[24]

When the strike began on May 8, 1974, the government's ruthless display of its strength shocked even those who opposed Fernandes's strike. Large numbers of policemen camped at the railway colonies where workers lived with their families. The policemen arrested workers who stayed home and terrorized the families of workers who were away from home and thus were presumed to be engaged in the strike. A union statement said the "wives of railway men were raped by the minions of law and order." Journalist and author Uma Vasudev also reported on the rape of a worker's wife by a policeman. Unable to withstand the pressure, workers began returning to their jobs by May 14. By the time the strike formally ended, in the early morning of May 28, the police were holding over twenty-five thousand workers without trial while a large, unknown number faced the threat of permanent job loss. Mrs. Gandhi and Railway Minister Lalit Narayan Mishra, the longtime conduit for funneling cash from private business to the Congress Party, offered conciliatory statements. They could afford to do so. They had broken the unions.[25]

On May 18, secure in the knowledge that the rail strike was effectively over, Mrs. Gandhi authorized the operation "Smiling Buddha," a test of a nuclear bomb at the Pokhran Army Base in Rajasthan. The test's success added to her prestige. The Buddha had smiled, as if to shower benediction on her. The *Economist,* in effect lauding her for her autocratic and brutal use of the state's coercive powers, declared: "Mrs. Gandhi is looking like a leader again, the kind of leader who just might save India."[26] In fact, Mrs. Gandhi was about to plunge India into a dark night.

J.P. made the first move. On June 5, 1974, addressing nearly half a million people at the Gandhi Maidan (Gandhi Park) in Patna, he declared, "Friends, this is a revolution, a total revolution [*sampurna kranti*]." He added indignantly: "Hunger, soaring prices, and corruption stalk everywhere. People are being crushed under all sorts of injustice." J.P.'s accusation that the country's leadership had failed the people was evidently correct, but as political scientist Ghanshyam Shah wrote, J.P. offered no alternative vision. His "total revolution" was a "catchy slogan" without any strategy of economic or social reform.[27]

Instead, operating by the Gujarat playbook, J.P. called for a Bihar *bandh* in early October. That luckless state was again in the midst of floods in the north and drought in the south, the third time in four years. Amid the hardship and popular anger, "opportunists and frustrated politicians" used the three-day *bandh* to cause "insensate violence" and "spread anarchy," as the *Times of India* vividly wrote.[28] This was not an auspicious start to total revolution, much less one inspired by Gandhian ideals.

A battle of attrition between J.P. and Mrs. Gandhi began. Unlike in Gujarat, she refused to concede to the demand for dismissal of the Bihar chief minister and dissolution of the state assembly. Instead, she "garrisoned" the state of Bihar with security forces. Bihar was "like an armed camp with the police and military guarding all major governmental and educational institutions."[29]

As J.P.'s total revolution dragged on, Bihar was witness to another, possibly unrelated, episode of violence on January 3, 1975. A bomb killed Railway Minister Mishra soon after he flagged off a new train from Samastipur Railway Station in northeastern Bihar. Mishra was the poster child of Indian corruption and political violence. He was the Congress Party's principal fundraiser and, alongside Mrs. Gandhi, had broken the railway workers' strike. Being from Bihar himself, Mishra "strongly backed" the state government that J.P. and his followers were trying to oust. It is fair to say that Mishra had a lot of enemies. Mrs. Gandhi said that his assassination was but a "rehearsal" to kill her.[30]

In March 1975, Mrs. Gandhi's approval rating fell to 39 percent, the lowest level recorded in an Indian Institute of Public Opinion poll. Coinciding with that low point, J.P. shifted his focus to Delhi. Lacking an anchor in any progressive ideology, he attended a conference organized by the Jana Sangh, the Hindu nationalist party. J.P. saw little irony in joining forces with the Jana Sangh, a party that rejected the fundamental Gandhian principle of equality of all religions. On March 6, J.P. led a march on the Lok Sabha. He rode in "an open jeep, followed by fifty outriders on motorcycles and scooters." Leaders of opposition parties, including the Jana Sangh, followed directly behind. Over a hundred thousand demonstrators joined the rally. J.P. presented the speaker of the Lok Sabha with a list of demands. To his followers, he promised a crusade against corruption and degeneration of Indian democracy. For him, that meant that Mrs. Gandhi could no longer be prime minister.[31]

The Shroud Descends

The fifteen months from the start of the Gujarat agitation in December 1973 to the demonstration at the Indian Parliament in March 1975 had released years of pent-up anger in a violent and unguided outburst. India was on the edge of economic, social, and political rupture.

What came next was in one sense a quirk of fate and in another sense the depraved but logical extension of trends that had led up to the moment.

Since January 1975, Mrs. Gandhi had been exploring ways of increasing her authority. On January 25, she consulted Siddhartha Shankar Ray, childhood friend, experienced barrister, and the man she had appointed as governor of West Bengal to suppress the Naxalites. On January 30, based on a source in the prime minister's office, *The Indian Express* reported that Mrs. Gandhi was planning to ban the Rashtriya Swayamsevak Sangh (RSS), the militant Hindu organization. The report added that by the end of the week Mrs. Gandhi was likely to arrest J.P. The history of those months is blurry, but sometime in the first half of 1975, D. P. Dhar, a Kashmiri politician and a dear friend of Mrs. Gandhi's, appears to have suggested to her she institute a state of internal emergency to expand her powers.[32]

Such musings stopped being speculative after June 12. On that day, Justice Jagmohan Lal Sinha of the Allahabad High Court (the high court for the state of Uttar Pradesh) ruled that Mrs. Gandhi had improperly used her prime ministerial office to contest the Rae Bareli parliamentary seat in the 1971 election. The judge highlighted two transgressions: Mrs. Gandhi's assistant, Yashpal Kapoor, had helped her campaign while still a government employee, and Mrs. Gandhi had used local officials to construct speaking platforms and provide her with high-quality loudspeakers that gave her an unfair campaigning advantage. Legally, the offenses were "corrupt practice," Justice Sinha said, and the law gave him "no choice." He invalidated Mrs. Gandhi's election as a Member of Parliament and barred her from holding public office for six years. Mrs. Gandhi's supporters urged her to fight the ruling, rather than resign, as many were suggesting. A Congress Party meeting on June 18 declared her "indispensable to the nation." Party President Dev Barooah memorably proclaimed, "India is Indira and Indira is India." The inner workings of Mrs. Gandhi's mind during that phase remain a mystery. But she did appeal to the Supreme Court, where, on June 24, Justice V. R. Krishna Iyer granted a stay of the Allahabad judgment. Her violations were not "grave electoral vices," Justice Iyer commented. She could continue as a Member of Parliament until a full bench of the Supreme Court made a final determination.[33]

J.P. chose not to wait for the Supreme Court's decision. On the evening of June 25, he announced at a rally in Delhi that he was launching nationwide demonstrations starting on June 29. Mrs. Gandhi was in no mood to wait either. Later that night of June 25, she and Siddhartha Shankar Ray visited President Fakhruddin Ali Ahmed. Asserting to the president that the country's political chaos had become unmanageable, she asked him to sign an order imposing a state of internal emergency under which she could arrest political leaders and censor the press. The president's advisor tried to dissuade him from doing so, arguing that the Constitution did not permit such an order, especially since the Council of Ministers had not approved it. President Ahmed asked his advisor to leave and signed the paper authorizing the Emergency. A pliant president and an almost certainly unconstitutional process gave Mrs. Gandhi the powers of a dictator just before midnight on June 25, 1975.[34]

The government's operation in the early morning hours of June 26 was "faultlessly efficient," wrote the *Sunday Times* of London. Just after 2 a.m., following instructions issued at 10 p.m. the previous night, a cut in electrical power stopped the printing presses at Delhi's most prominent newspapers. By 5 a.m., hundreds of opposition leaders had been "plucked from their beds and whisked into detention." J.P. and Morarji Desai, Mrs. Gandhi's longtime political rivals, were among those arrested. Sometime between 6 and 7 a.m., Mrs. Gandhi presented the "Emergency," as it would thereafter always be called, to her cabinet as a done deal, which the cabinet dutifully rubber-stamped.[35]

In her radio address to the nation that morning, Mrs. Gandhi said that malign forces were impeding her economic program for the "common man and woman," and social disorder had caused Indian democracy to break down. She promised better days ahead and implied that the Emergency was temporary, as she hoped to "dispense" with it soon. Here is a large portion of that short speech:

> I am sure you are all conscious of the deep and widespread conspiracy which has been brewing ever since I began introducing certain progressive measures of benefit to the common man and woman of India.
>
> Agitations have surcharged the atmosphere, leading to violent incidents. The whole country was shocked at the brutal murder of my Cabinet colleague, Mr. L. N. Mishra.
>
> We have been actively considering measures to strengthen the economy and relieve the hardship of various sections, including the poor and vulnerable and those with fixed incomes. I shall announce these soon.
>
> I should like to assure you that the new emergency proclamation will in no way affect the rights of law-abiding citizens. I am sure that internal conditions will speedily improve to enable us to dispense this proclamation as soon as possible.
>
> May I appeal to you for your continued cooperation and trust in the days ahead.[36]

By the afternoon of June 26, the government had issued "guidelines" for the press. A censor would consider news items "unauthorized, irresponsible or demoralizing" if they incited "hatred or contempt," "excited disaffection towards the government," or denigrated "the institution of the Prime Minister."[37]

Over the following months, Mrs. Gandhi tore up the Constitution to give herself virtually unlimited power. On July 22, 1975, Parliament passed the thirty-eighth amendment to the Constitution, which barred judicial review of the Emergency. The thirty-ninth amendment two weeks later said that no one could challenge a prime minister's election, and since that amendment applied retroactively, the Allahabad High Court judgment and the ongoing Supreme Court review were now rendered moot. The forty-second amendment gave Parliament sweeping powers. Of immediate relevance, Parliament could extend its term—which it did right away by canceling the elections due in 1976. Parliamentary laws gained greater immunity from judicial review. And the central government acquired more power over the states. In March 1976, Mrs. Gandhi triumphantly said to two visitors that state ministers were now "shaking in their shoes."

Too much devolution of powers was proving "fatal" for the country. "I have to hold India together," she said.[38]

Those jailed by Mrs. Gandhi under the Maintenance of Internal Security Act (MISA)—popularly, the "Maintenance of Indira and Sanjay Act"—protested they had the right of *habeas corpus,* the right to a trial. The Supreme Court, with one dissenting judge, denied this right under the prevailing Emergency.

Thus, with her promise of economic prosperity and return to democracy, Mrs. Gandhi set about to prove herself a benign dictator. What could go wrong?

Chapter 12

AN AUTOCRATIC GAMBLE FAILS

At least since the mid-1960s, Indian and international elites had been murmuring that India's cacophonous, slow-moving parliamentary democracy stood in the way of the nation's economic progress. While they never openly advocated a dictatorship, they proposed a shift to "a presidential form of government," under which a powerful chief executive could override dissent and quickly enforce measures for accelerating economic development. Stated as such, the view was naïve at best. The United States, with its presidential form of government, suffered from long spells of logjam and policy inaction. Thus, Indian calls for a presidential form of government were always a coded cry for autocracy, for an India ruled by a strongman—or, as it turned out, a strongwoman.[1]

On June 25, 1975, Mrs. Gandhi made the autocratic gamble for India. After acquiring dictatorial authority under the Emergency, she continued the refrain about the handicaps of democracy. "In India," she said, "democracy has given too much license to people." She insisted that newspapers and the opposition parties were misusing their freedoms and "weakening the nation's confidence." Among Mrs. Gandhi's supporters, the industrialist J. R. D. Tata said to *New York Times* correspondent J. Anthony Lukas, back in India after nine years away, "You can't imagine what we have been through here—strikes, boycotts, demonstrations.

Why, there were days I couldn't walk out of my office on to the street. The parliamentary system is not suited to our needs."[2]

Statistical studies in the years since the Emergency have shown repeatedly that while some autocracies achieve high economic performance, most perform terribly. At the time Mrs. Gandhi took office, East Asian autocracies were in the early phases of their successful run. On the other hand, Indians were well aware that Mobutu Sese Seko, president of Zaire, and Idi Amin, president of Uganda, were ruining their nations. As Ruth Ben-Ghiat, author of *Strongmen: Mussolini to the Present,* tells us, Mobutu stashed away vast sums in Swiss bank accounts while 70 percent of his country lived in dire poverty. Amin reveled in his own unpredictability, which he saw as a measure of his grandeur. Strongmen, Ben-Ghiat writes, believe they have the answers to complicated problems when, in fact, they have lost touch with reality. Violence is their calling card. Did Indians hankering after autocracy understand the risks?[3]

For India, Mrs. Gandhi's son Sanjay was part and parcel of her autocratic rule. She admired him as a "doer" in a nation of "talkers"; she stood firmly behind him and his initiatives. Now, with near-absolute power over India, what was on their agenda? It was not education, health, and social welfare, as Mrs. Gandhi had implied it would be when she announced the Emergency. The share of the central government's budget devoted to such human development and social security expenditures had fallen from 6.3 percent in 1969–1970 to just above 5 percent before the Emergency, and it remained at that low level in the post-Emergency budget announced in early 1976. Sanjay's plan for India's job crisis was to forcibly sterilize men, and his plan for urban revival was to throw slum-dwellers out of their homes and workplaces. Not surprisingly, given his history and sense of grandeur, violence was his trademark.[4]

After False Hope, a Reality Check

At first, luck smiled on Mrs. Gandhi's autocratic wager. On August 17, 1975, seven weeks after promulgation of the Emergency, a *Times of India* headline read: "Kharif production may exceed target." Monsoon rains blessed traditionally parched areas of India. Melting snows in the

Himalayas improved the prospects of hydroelectric power supply. The inflation rate had been falling before the Emergency began, helped by a July 1974 policy that "impounded" incomes or, more directly stated, forced households to save. The Reserve Bank of India kept interest rates high and restricted credit extension by banks.[5]

From a macroeconomic perspective, the first year of the Emergency went well. Helped by the summer monsoon rains, Indian farmers produced a bumper food grain crop, which reached 121 million tons and exceeded, for the first time, the level achieved in 1970–1971. The large grain output along with fiscal restraint and tight monetary policy dampened price inflation. Weak world demand kept a lid on the prices of India's imported products. The inflation rate, in fact, turned negative—prices actually fell. India's foreign exchange reserves increased, helped by remittances from Indian migrants to the Middle Eastern countries that had been hugely enriched by the recent oil price hikes.[6] The one blemish on an otherwise impressive performance was weak industrial growth: the government's anti-inflationary policies, by design, constrained domestic demand for industrial products.

The IMF was pleased. The number of strikes had fallen sharply since labor—under threat of severe reprisals—had become more "disciplined." The availability of raw materials, electric power, and transportation services had improved. With some liberalization of industrial licensing policy and increased emphasis on export promotion and population control, the IMF believed that the Indian economy's prospects were better than "at any time since the early 1960s."[7]

Many Indians echoed this bullishness. One elated businessman said to *New York Times* correspondent J. Anthony Lukas, "Ahhh, you will find things changed. We are disciplined now. The Lady has done that. Hats off to the Lady!" Another businessman said, "You can get things done these days. You can make money. That's all I care about." As Lukas made his rounds in Delhi, an official sternly added, "It is only reporters like yourself and your counterparts among the Indian upper-middle class who worry about such things as freedom of expression. What most of our people care about is filling their bellies. We are tired of being a workshop of failed democracy. The time has come to exchange some of our vaunted individual rights for some economic development."[8]

The World Bank paid India the same handsome compliments the IMF did—but added caveats. "There is no evidence," the Bank cautioned, of "a significant upward shift in long-term growth rate in food grain production in India, which, over the past 15 years, has grown only about as fast as population." Similarly, sustaining export growth would require "more far-reaching policy measures," including "a more uniform and more stable system of export incentives."[9]

The World Bank reserved its harshest comments for the government's continued neglect of the primary education and health services. With only 36 percent of children aged 11 to 14 years old in school, the small budget for primary schooling was inexcusable, while higher education remained disproportionately well funded. Health services in rural areas, meanwhile, were "extremely inadequate." The malaria eradication program had suffered "repeated set-backs": the number of positive cases had increased from 100,000 in 1965 to 2.5 million in 1974 as mosquitos developed resistance to the DDT pesticide. Leprosy was "a major health problem." Every tenth person in India had a venereal disease.[10]

In the Emergency's second year, India's luck began to run out. Drought caused food grain production to fall, and inflationary pressures reemerged. Industrial output rose in 1976–1977 because increased agricultural output in the previous year generated greater rural purchasing power for industrial products, and the number of strikes remained low. But the Ministry of Finance was disappointed by the absence of an "upsurge" in investment. The truth was that although Indian businesses were delighted by fewer strikes, they were not confident about the future and, therefore, not ready to step up investment.[11]

As a result, employment barely increased in the organized (modern) sector, where jobs provided stability, decent wages, and retirement and health benefits. In fact, private organized sector employment remained static at 6.8 million for the four years between 1973 and 1977. Public-sector employment increased over those years from 12 to 14 million workers. For perspective, India's population was increasing by *more than a million people every month*, totaling about fifty-seven million people over the four-year period. At that rate of population increase, virtually all new job aspirants ended up in agriculture or in unorganized urban employment. Large numbers fell into the underemployed swamp, remaining idle for long hours.[12]

In February 1976, eight months into the Emergency, the filmmaker Satyajit Ray pointed angrily at the dire employment conditions, especially among the ranks of the urban educated. His film's Bengali title *Jana Aranya* (Human jungle) spoke more loudly than the English title, *The Middleman*. As in his *Pratidwandi* (Adversary) in 1970, Ray set *The Middleman* in Calcutta. *New York Times* film critic Vincent Canby wrote that in Ray's portrayal, Calcutta is "clogged, figuratively and literally, with hundreds of applicants for every suitable job." Unlike in *Pratidwandi, The Middleman's* protagonist, Somnath, does not try to fight the system. Instead, in an evocative metaphor, he slips on a banana peel. That event brings him into contact with a sleazy businessman, under whose guidance Somnath becomes a "middleman," ready to buy and sell anything in a morally unanchored marketplace. The transition from innocence and idealism to fraud and vice is so rapid, it seems inevitable. Ray anticipated later research showing that young men facing poor employment prospects fall easy prey to corruption and criminality. As Canby put it, *The Middleman* was an expression of an outraged but exhausted director, "who's given up all thoughts of solutions or who fears the solutions are so radical he can't bring himself to mention them." For Canby, the film defined "hopelessness." Ray would himself say in 1982, "I felt corruption, rampant corruption everywhere. *The Middleman* is a film about that kind of corruption and I don't think there is any solution."[13]

India had two seemingly insoluble problems, each making the other worse: severe lack of employment and an overlay of corruption in all walks of life. The Emergency did nothing to deal with either problem.

The government did use its Emergency powers to redistribute land from large farmers to some small farmers and landless workers. While the land redistributed was a significant step up from past efforts, it was too little to make a material difference in land and income inequality. Of the total cultivated area of about 400 million acres, the government redistributed just 1.1 million acres of surplus land (that is, land acquired from those with holdings in excess of the ceilings set). At an annual rate, the Emergency-era redistribution was only marginally above the slow progress in the Nehru years. Mrs. Gandhi's *garibi hatao* (remove poverty) program helped the vulnerable in rural areas, but again on a scale that made little dent in national poverty trends. As the constitutional scholar Granville Austin summarized, "She denied the poor their freedom and brought them no bread."[14]

Indians remained badly educated with acute healthcare problems, facing a severe—and increasing—burden of unemployment. The superficially glossy GDP growth and inflation numbers in 1975–1976 were due to the luck of a good monsoon and the carryover of anti-inflationary policies from the year before the Emergency. Strikes fell because workers feared being thrown in jail. A government attorney, arguing before the Bombay High Court, bluntly stated, "The regime could starve prisoners or even shoot them without legal challenge."[15]

Billboards, public buses, and office walls sported photographs of Mrs. Gandhi alongside uplifting messages: "Work More—Talk Less"; "Hard Work, Clear Vision, Iron Will, Strictest Discipline"; "Courage and Clarity of Vision, Thy Name is Indira Gandhi!" With that, Mrs. Gandhi handed unchecked authority to Sanjay, the doer.[16] And what a man he was.

Failing at Cars, Sanjay Gandhi Moves on to Politics

Sanjay's breathtaking corruption was, in part, a response to his incompetence. His mother's indulgence made it all possible. And he was now India's prince.

In the pre-Emergency years, he used his mother's shadow to borrow large sums for Maruti Ltd.—his Maruti car project—from the recently nationalized Central Bank of India and Punjab National Bank. In late February 1974, with his car project obviously failing, he set up Maruti Heavy Vehicles to assemble buses, truck tractors, and road rollers. Dharam Vir Taneja, a Central Bank executive, serviced Sanjay's insatiable hunger for funds. Mrs. Gandhi rewarded Taneja in April 1974 by elevating him to the chairmanship of Central Bank, overriding the Ministry of Finance's recommendation of a highly reputed and able banker. As chairman, Taneja continued to finance the original Maruti Ltd and the new Maruti Heavy Vehicles. But eventually he began to worry. His bank had an unhealthy relationship with an obviously dubious borrower. There came a point, Taneja later said, when he "could not bear it any longer." He denied Sanjay's request for a large loan to finance an investment that Central Bank staff believed was "not viable." An upset Sanjay asked Taneja to "think it over." Later, Sanjay used an intermediary to send Taneja a message threatening him with "unforeseen and dire consequences for not helping Maruti." In April 1975, Taneja's term ended. Going against normal practice, Mrs. Gandhi instructed her finance minister to not renew his appointment because she had heard "certain complaints" about him.[17]

A month after Taneja's firing, in May 1975, Sanjay gave Mrs. Gandhi's biographer Uma Vasudev and a journalist colleague a test ride in his Maruti car. Vasudev writes that she shuddered through the drive, wondering when the car would come apart. The car was hand-stitched in a body shop that two correspondents from the *Sunday Times* of London described as "a joke." Workers hand-carried the semi-finished car from one station to another because there was no assembly line. In 1968, Sanjay had promised fifty thousand cars a year. By 1975, he had produced fewer than a dozen.[18]

Though selling no cars, Sanjay made money by selling shoddy and overpriced vehicles assembled by Maruti Heavy Vehicles to state governments and publicly owned companies. Even more of a scam was Maruti Technical Services, a firm that sold technical expertise to Maruti Ltd and to Maruti Heavy Vehicles. Besides ongoing consulting fees from the Maruti car and heavy vehicle companies, Maruti Technical Services also received at least one mysterious, interest-free loan from an untraceable individual. The whole family seemed mixed up in this sordid affair. Sanjay's older brother, Rajiv, was not directly involved but his wife, Sonia Gandhi (Sanjay's sister-in-law), was one of the owners of Maruti Technical Services, along with her two minor children, recorded as "Master" Rahul and "Miss" Priyanka, both of whom performed their duties as company board members under the "guardianship" of their father, Rajiv.[19]

Once the Emergency was in place, Sanjay also used his influence to do favors for friends. In one such instance, he confronted Raj Kumar

Talwar, chairman of State Bank of India, India's largest bank, nationalized well before Mrs. Gandhi became prime minister. As State Bank's chairman, Talwar had denied a large loan request from one of Sanjay's buddies. Sanjay was furious. He tried, at first, to intimidate Talwar through the deputy finance minister. When that failed, he ordered a probe into Talwar's activities for possible corruption charges. When that failed to unearth any dirt, Sanjay asked the finance minister to have Parliament amend the State Bank of India Act to change the provision granting the Bank's chairman security of tenure. Armed with the amended State Bank of India Act, the finance minister fired Talwar on August 4, 1976, a little over thirteen months into the Emergency.[20]

Rather than check Sanjay, Mrs. Gandhi punished those who complained about him. The best-known case was that of P. N. Haksar, her closest advisor for many years. Haksar had masterminded Mrs. Gandhi's bank nationalization strategy, the principal totem in her image as a champion of the poor. Mrs. Gandhi threw Haksar out when he complained that Sanjay's Maruti project had become a lawless enterprise. Recognizing Sanjay's clout, Cabinet ministers and chief ministers of states began to treat him as possessing something akin to Mrs. Gandhi's power. Sanjay could, and did, initiate arrests under the draconian MISA. No one was immune to his wrath.[21]

With his car-making a fiasco and money flowing in effortlessly through Maruti Heavy Vehicles and Maruti Technical Services, Sanjay became the force behind the Emergency's two signature atrocities: forced sterilizations to control population growth and brutal ejection of people from their homes and places of business to, he claimed, "beautify" India's cities. Mrs. Gandhi supported Sanjay in these Emergency-era horrors, just as she had in the Maruti-related scams.

The Indian People Pay for the Autocratic Gamble

India had a longstanding "family planning program" to slow down the country's population growth. The program was run according to internationally well-regarded practices. Voluntary male sterilizations—vasectomies—had, over the years, achieved a significant cumulative decline in national birth rates. In the first year of the Emergency, the number of sterilizations was about the same as in previously successful years.[22]

Then, in April 1976, ten months into the Emergency, the new National Population Policy created a morbid competition among states to meet and exceed Sanjay's outrageously high sterilization targets. Senior officials held back salaries and bonuses from lower-level officials who did not "submit to the surgeon's knife." Without sterilization certificates, truck drivers could not renew their licenses and displaced slum dwellers became ineligible for their resettlement plots. Under the threat of being denied salaries, allowances, and promotions, schoolteachers were tasked with preparing monthly lists of "eligible men"—those who had three or more children and were, therefore, the prime targets for sterilization. In a Maharashtrian village, police vans swooped down on those men they considered "eligible" and took them to the nearest health clinic for sterilization. Local officials and police inspectors stopped buses and shoveled men into "sterilization camps."[23]

Sanjay was attempting to compress population control goals normally achieved over several years into a few months. As Jagmohan, Sanjay's co-conspirator on slum demolitions, said, Sanjay drove only in "top gear." In the Emergency's second year, the number of sterilizations reached 8.2 million, far above the official target of 4 million and more than twice the previous peak reached in 1972–1973.[24]

Not only were compulsory sterilizations cruel, they were also based on a backward interpretation of economics and history. Fertility decline does not spur economic development. Rather, fertility falls when economic development induces women to pursue education, delay marriage, postpone the birth of children, and ultimately have fewer children. Neither Mrs. Gandhi nor Sanjay had ideas about expanding education, the health infrastructure, and employment opportunities. India, quite simply, did not have the conditions or the incentives to induce a rapid decline in birthrates.

With even greater cruelty and the same backward reasoning, Sanjay pushed his slum-clearance program. Just in Delhi, from June 1975 to March 1977, nearly 700,000 people were "resettled" and over 150,000 structures were demolished. The number of structures demolished was eight times higher than in the previous two and a half years. Sanjay's reign of terror spread across north India, and authorities in Maharashtra state also followed his lead eagerly.[25]

From the start, the evictions and demolitions were ruthless. In early August 1975, a little over a month after the clampdown of Emergency, a communist leader wrote to Mrs. Gandhi informing her that thousands of families were being arbitrarily removed from their shanty homes, and each family was being dumped on a tiny plot of land. Mrs. Gandhi disregarded the letter, and the gruesome saga continued. Biographer Uma Vasudev wrote, "Sick and pregnant women, wailing children, old men, and young stalwarts were being carried away like baggage, shown their pieces of land, and told in the midst of the monsoon, 'Here's your plot, you can build on it.'" In principle, the resettlement areas came with plans for schools, hospitals, and shopping centers. But these plans remained plans. Sanjay, the mastermind behind the heartless slum-clearance program, justified the actions. Hundreds of thousands of people lived in "sub-human conditions in any case," he said. If some were dumped on open ground in the pouring rain, the inhumanity was reasonable because it was "nothing new to them." If a newborn baby died or a family fell sick, "well, those were the hazards of making Delhi beautiful." He had a simple moral viewpoint: "People die all the time." He was clear-headed on another matter: his operation required the Emergency, for—as Vasudev paraphrased him—"people had to do what the government asked them to do."[26]

Subhadra Joshi, a veteran Congress Party member, appealed to her longtime comrade and friend, Mrs. Gandhi. "It is unbelievable," Ms. Joshi wrote, "that you might be aware of things and yet you would not take action." After an initial response, the prime minister cut off communication. Uma Vasudev summed up: Sanjay was "callous," and Mrs. Gandhi "had turned to stone."[27]

In Delhi, Sanjay's special targets were the shops and homes in the Muslim neighborhoods near Jama Masjid, the venerated seventeenth-century mosque. The first demolition in the Jama Masjid area occurred on July 19, 1975. Political worker and former freedom fighter Inder Mohan appealed to Mrs. Gandhi to pause those demolitions and first make adequate resettlement arrangements. Mrs. Gandhi sent him to Sanjay. Sanjay, who met Mohan on September 17, insisted that the time to wait was over. For his troubles, police barged into Mohan's apartment on September 19 and arrested him under MISA provisions, giving no cause for the arrest.[28]

On November 22, 1975, demolition squads, backed by police contingents, razed to the ground about four hundred shops that stuck out from the Masjid complex. Businesses in this shopping complex made their scrappy living by selling biryanis, leather goods, and woolen clothes, as well as birds, goats, and sheep. Having gotten rid of the shops, the demolition officials declared triumphantly that Jama Masjid was "clean now." An uninterrupted view of the Masjid was possible from a distance of a thousand feet. On December 10, Sanjay took a victory lap. Gathered officials cheered: "Sanjay Gandhi ki jai!" (Long live Sanjay Gandhi!). The promised new shopping complex for the displaced shopkeepers was never built, and they received no compensation.[29]

On April 13, 1976, a bulldozer "roared" in the Turkman Gate area near the Masjid. The stated purpose was to clear a transit camp, home to about forty families resettled there after their old homes were demolished. That was only the start of the vicious episode. "The dam broke on April 19," writes Gyan Prakash. This time, lustful policemen accompanied the bulldozers. They stole women's jewelry, scarred their breasts with burning cigarettes, and raped them. Area residents battled the police, leaving "a scene of carnage." Hundreds of residents gathered around the blue-domed Faiz-e-Ilahi Masjid to protest the demolitions. They pelted stones at the jail transport vans. When police fired tear gas shells, many protestors took refuge inside the mosque. The police followed them in, acting on the instructions of Sanjay's acolyte Deputy Inspector General P. S. Bhinder. In Prakash's words, "The mosque quickly turned into a scene of horror. Blood smeared the floor." The demolitions in Turkman Gate continued.[30]

Not only did Sanjay eject slum dwellers in a barbaric manner, the economic premise of his slum-clearance operation was just as absurd as his forced sterilization program. Successful "unslumming," like reduced population growth, follows the availability of work opportunities. Author and urban development visionary Jane Jacobs passionately emphasized that when residents of a slum have income-earning choices, they move out of the area and into new homes. She argued that slum residents should stay in their homes, where they are part of neighborhood support systems. The choice to relocate should be theirs, as guided by their access to work options and social networks. Jama Masjid's mainly Muslim residents had the further problem that because of widespread housing discrimination, they were not welcome in many parts of Delhi. Sanjay's approach of dumping slum dwellers in remote "resettlement" sites shrank their job options and perpetuated slum-like conditions in the new locations.[31]

India needed cleaner and more vibrant cities. But just as in the age of innocence, when Nehru's "garden city" Chandigarh did not address either the economic pressures on rural migrants or the poor infrastructure in overwhelmed urban areas, Sanjay's cruel slum clearance drive was an elitist project: It carved out spaces for privileged urban residents while perpetuating degrading urban life for the vast majority.

Mrs. Gandhi Seeks an Electoral Autocracy

In a surprise radio broadcast on January 18, 1977, Mrs. Gandhi announced that she had scheduled elections to the Lok Sabha for the third week of March. She noted she had released some political prisoners and eased curbs on the press. And she said that she had pulled the nation back from the "brink of disaster" and "nursed it back to health." She wanted people to know and believe that the economy was "vastly improved" and that the nation was "more healthy, efficient, and dynamic." Mrs. Gandhi's assertions of improvement and dynamism were simply untrue. Not surprisingly, she made no effort to support these assertions with evidence. Chillingly, in announcing the elections, Mrs. Gandhi added: "The constitution has been amended to remove impediments to policies which are designed to serve the people. Elements which wish to stir up economic trouble will be sternly dealt with."[32]

Mrs. Gandhi believed that she would return to power. Her intelligence reports predicted her party would win a majority of the Lok Sabha seats, especially since the weather trends and prospects for the food grain harvest in 1977–1978 were good. In addition, her narrative of economic progress would win her votes. Many voters had, in fact, benefited from the Emergency, and they would be beholden to her. Once back in power, she would dismiss the carping that she had destroyed Indian democracy. She would exercise authority from the prime minister's office, aided by a subservient parliament and a constitution—as she said—that could no longer restrain her. She was headed to an electoral autocracy.[33]

Mrs. Gandhi faced a ragtag group of four opposition parties: Jana Sangh, the Socialist Party, Lok Dal (formally, Bharatiya Lok Dal, People's Party), and remnants of the old Congress Party. They came together hurriedly on January 23, five days after she announced the election. Lacking a common economic or political ideology, they were united only in their goal to prevent a division of votes among themselves, a division that would help Mrs. Gandhi under the first-past-the-post electoral system. They would field only one candidate in each constituency under the label "Janata Party." Morarji Desai, Mrs. Gandhi's old rival, would be the Janata Party's leader.

Weighing against Mrs. Gandhi's prospects was the Sanjay factor. Sanjay's friends and older brother Rajiv suggested to him that he take a break from politics since he was likely to prove a magnet for opposition criticism. But Mrs. Gandhi had hitched herself to Sanjay. Despite his misdeeds, she was grateful to him for being by her side to "do what he could." He gave her a sense of "protection," she said. Perhaps, she felt, the elections would establish his political legitimacy.[34]

Sanjay, however, overstepped in a terrain where his bullying did not work. For two hundred of his volatile followers, many of whom operated in a gray legal zone, he demanded "tickets" as Congress Party candidates in contests for parliamentary seats. But if that happened, party veterans worried they would be left with few tickets for their followers. One such party veteran, Jagjivan Ram, walked out of the Congress Party on February 2. Ram had held cabinet positions since Nehru was prime minister. He was the leader of the Scheduled castes, once also known as the "untouchables," or alternatively the Harijans (children of God, the name given to them by Mahatma Gandhi). They were 80 million strong in a nation of 600 million people, constituting a crucial 15 percent of the electorate. Ram formed a new party, Congress for Democracy, and agreed to contest the election under the Janata Party's symbol. Ram's decision instantly changed the momentum.

Mrs. Gandhi's information chief told her soon after, "Madame, I am afraid you are going to lose."[35]

The first wave of election results on March 20 showed the Janata Party cruising to a big victory. The victory was overwhelming in northern India, where Sanjay had had hurt people the most. In Uttar Pradesh and Bihar, the Congress Party did not win a single parliamentary seat. Mrs. Gandhi lost her seat in the Rae Bareli constituency; Sanjay lost his contest in neighboring Amethi. In the southern states, where the pain due to forced sterilizations and slum-clearance drives was less severe, the Congress and allied parties won handily. Thus, the autocratic gamble ended. At the recommendation of Mrs. Gandhi and her cabinet, Acting President B. D. Jatti lifted India's state of internal Emergency in the early morning of March 21. Knowing that the Emergency provisions could not be used against them, she and her cabinet resigned on March 22.

Mrs. Gandhi had a story to tell. She blamed others and defended Sanjay. "I was under no compulsion to order elections and we could have continued with the Emergency for a year or two," she said. In her view, her mistake was that she relied on "some people, who ought to have known better" and who predicted she "would sweep the elections." In a television interview with David Frost of the BBC, she insisted that the charges against Sanjay were "absolutely ridiculous," for he had no role in decision-making. The future would vindicate her, she said, and those who had attacked Sanjay had in fact attacked her.[36]

The results of India's experiment with autocracy were now in. The elites who had long clamored for autocratic rule had benefited. They celebrated their higher profits achieved through repression of workers and student protests. But repression divided the economic pie rather than increased it. Indian business had no reason to invest more ambitiously or hire more workers. Mrs. Gandhi and Sanjay did not even pretend to expand public goods provision. The nation's human capital and urban infrastructure remained abysmal. Sanjay's slum evictions relied on the moral and economic premise that humiliating and killing people would solve India's urban development problems.

India had escaped all too narrowly from worse outcomes: autocracy was poised to do lasting damage. If Mrs. Gandhi had won the election, as she expected to, Sanjay could have continued with more carnage in a hollowed-out shell of democracy, within which people lacked personal freedoms and were constantly subject to his whims, cockiness, and mindless violence. Mrs. Gandhi's victory would have allowed her to assert that people endorsed the unforgiving and brutal rule, with its utterly wrongheaded economic strategies.

Now beleaguered Indians had new reasons to worry. Having escaped from autocracy, would they benefit from a new era of morally grounded social norms and political accountability? Or would democratic India merely conduct regular elections while failing to nurture a civic consciousness that encouraged trust and cooperation? If the return to democracy meant more corruption, rhetoric in place of policies, quick fixes, and a state that used the police and armed forces to subdue protest, then public goods provision would remain weak, equal opportunity for all would remain an illusion, and social anger would fester. In that case, Indian society, unable to make either moral or material progress, would remain trapped in its Catch-22.

Chapter 13

DEMOCRACY BETRAYS AGAIN, DEINDUSTRIALIZATION BEGINS

On March 24, 1977, the Indian parliament elected the Janata Party's leader Morarji Desai as the country's fourth prime minister. He had finally arrived at the position that had twice eluded him, first in June 1964 and then in January 1966. In his brief acceptance speech, Desai thanked the nation for the nonviolent return to democracy. He said the task ahead was difficult, as the nation was just coming out of a "pit." Nevertheless, he was confident that the Janata Party would fulfill the people's aspirations. Members of Parliament cheered "lustily." Desai, in an expression of gratitude, bowed his head slightly and acknowledged the applause with folded hands.[1]

The Janata government used the euphoria of its election victory to roll back the damage Mrs. Gandhi had done to the Constitution. The process, which began in December 1977, took until December 1978 to complete. Two new constitutional amendments—the forty-third and forty-fourth—made the imposition of an Emergency much more difficult, curbed the powers of the executive, and reestablished the Supreme Court's right to adjudicate on any election, including that of the prime minister. The Constitution regained the authority it had commanded before the Emergency. When the Lok Sabha passed the forty-fourth amendment on December 7, 1978, Mrs. Gandhi was back as a Member of Parliament (via an off-cycle election victory a month earlier from Chikmagalur in the southern state of Karnataka). She voted for the amendment that undid her mutilation of the Constitution.[2]

The Janata Party was clear-headed and united on the need to restore the Constitution's integrity. But the party had come together mainly to defeat Mrs. Gandhi, and it had no unifying economic or political ideology. To the contrary, the ministers represented different interest groups and had widely differing ideological preferences. In a hurry to serve their own interests and ideological goals, they self-destructed.

George Fernandes, who was leader of the railway workers' strike in May 1974 (which Mrs. Gandhi had ruthlessly crushed), was now minister of industrial development. In August 1977, in one of the Janata Party's earliest economic actions, Fernandes began pushing Coca-Cola out of the country. Fernandes demanded that the Coca-Cola company reveal the formula for the concentrate in its popular drink and transfer 60 percent of the shares of its Indian operations to Indian investors. Coke preferred to leave. In parliament, Fernandes emphasized that Coke earned very high profit margins on the sale of its concentrate to Indian bottling companies. In any case, he said, India's Central Food Technology Research Institute in Mysore had a commercially ready substitute. In October, IBM, refusing to reduce its equity holding in its Indian operations to 40 percent, also closed up shop in India.[3]

True, neither Coke nor IBM created many jobs, but they were conduits to technology, they exposed Indians to modern manufacturing methods and trends in service delivery, and they signaled to the world that India was a desirable business destination. The decision to throw them out to reduce the competition facing Indian producers was a juvenile display of nationalism.

Home (Interior) Minister Charan Singh, head of the Lok Dal, represented a powerful new interest group: "capitalist" farmers. These were large and medium-sized farmers who practiced industrial-style farming using Green Revolution technologies. They had benefited from the government's policy package of minimum support prices and fertilizer subsidies. Especially in the eastern states of Uttar Pradesh and Bihar, they had gained land and security in land rights during the reforms of the

1950s. They had become rich and greatly increased their representation in the parliament.[4]

Charan Singh, who believed he should be prime minister, had settled only grudgingly for the home minister's position. The relationship between Singh and Prime Minister Desai quickly became ugly. In the first half of 1978, Singh wrote angry letters to Desai, accusing him of favoring his son Kanti, just as Mrs. Gandhi had favored Sanjay. In June 1978, Desai dismissed Singh. However, recognizing Singh's political clout, Desai brought him back as finance minister in January 1979. As finance minister, Singh used his budgetary authority to distribute "sops" to his constituency of "capitalist" farmers in the form of increased subsidies on chemical fertilizers, mechanical tillers, motor-driven pumpsets, and the diesel used for the pumpsets. To pay for some of these sops, he raised taxes on such goods as soaps and detergents, edible oils, toothpaste and toothbrushes, pressure cookers, and motorcycles, all of which ate into the tight family budgets of those already struggling to make ends meet.[5]

The pampered and politically influential "capitalist" farmers had another demand. Many of them belonged to the "other backward castes": the Jats in Uttar Pradesh, the Kurmis and Yadavs in Bihar, the Marathas in Maharashtra, and the Vellalas in Tamil Nadu. They now also wanted urban jobs reserved for "other backward castes." The Constitution already required reservation of 15 percent of central government jobs for Scheduled Castes and 7.5 percent for Scheduled Tribes. In November 1978, Desai established a commission to recommend a "new formula" for job reservation. The commission, headed by B. P. Mandal, a former Bihar chief minister, began work in March 1979. This initiative, although intended to correct past injustices, was a losing game. Without a policy to grow the number of jobs, more Indians would rightly feel that the system was unjust and the call for more reservations would surely increase.[6]

The zero-sum attitude of Janata Party leaders proved to be their undoing. In a power grab in late July 1979, Charan Singh broke from his party and became prime minister with a "letter of support" from Mrs. Gandhi. What was he thinking? A month later, Mrs. Gandhi withdrew her support. Singh and the Janata Party collapsed. New elections were scheduled for January 1980.[7]

The Janata government had delivered on its promise to restore the Constitution. But the government had done virtually nothing to fulfill the people's economic aspirations despite Morarji Desai's promise to do so in his acceptance speech in March 1977. Instead, as the obituaries of the Janata government's brief rule were quick to point out, many of the party's leaders and functionaries engaged in an unseemly dash for the perks and spoils of power.[8]

The two-year-plus Janata government interlude revealed an old truth about democracies. To serve the people, a democracy needs more than the procedures and the checks and balances of a constitution. A democracy requires that those who command power and influence place greater value on civic welfare than on their own opportunistic profit and prestige. Only such a personal morality can ensure the social trust and cooperation necessary to serve the cause of democracy and economic progress. In failing to live by that moral code, the Janata government's leaders had not only betrayed the general public welfare but had pushed India further into a trap where politicians chased quick rewards for themselves and their followers.

The Indian economy was about to be ravaged by new shocks. The summer rains in 1979 were disappointing, causing a fall in the *kharif* harvest, and the winter rains for the *rabi* crop also fell short. In tandem, oil prices rose rapidly starting in mid-1979, as the Iranian Revolution earlier in the year disrupted the global oil supply. Indian industrial production fell, in part because the poor rainfall diminished hydroelectric power capacity. Other infrastructural bottlenecks, a sharp increase in industrial workers' strikes, and higher oil prices further decreased industrial production. GDP fell, inflation raged, and the dollar requirements to pay for imports increased sharply.[9]

Autocracy had failed under Mrs. Gandhi. Democracy under the Janata government had betrayed the people. And democracy under Indira Gandhi's triumphant new administration was about to betray Indians again.

Mrs. Gandhi Has a New Friend

Mrs. Gandhi had reason to celebrate when the votes were counted in January 1980. She won 353 (about 67 percent) of the parliamentary seats, matching her sweeping victory in 1971. During the election campaign, she had the advantage that voters blamed her opponents—the incumbent, squabbling Janata Party leaders—for the woeful state of the Indian economy. She spoke to the angst felt by the people when she promised to bring down the price of onions and restore law and order. As in previous elections, she campaigned with unbounded energy: 90 million people heard or saw her as she visited constituencies across the country. Her colored posters, a novelty for their time, urged voters to "Elect a government that works," and "Bring back Indira, save India" (*Indira lao, desh bachao*). Campaign music, set to popular film tunes, played at Congress Party rallies.[10]

The 1980 election victory emboldened Mrs. Gandhi in one unanticipated way. Up until then, as a self-styled champion of the poor, she had kept her associations with Indian business out of the public view. True, Sanjay had enriched himself through funds from Indian businesses and nationalized banks, and L. N. Mishra had ferried briefcases and suitcases of cash from businesses to Congress Party coffers. But Mrs. Gandhi's personal connection to Indian business remained invisible. That changed after the 1980 election.

One of her first public engagements was a "lavish" celebration hosted by businessman Dhirajlal Hirachand Ambani. People commonly addressed him as "Dhirubhai," as was—and is—the practice in his home state of Gujarat. Born in 1932, he had traveled in the late 1940s to the port city of Aden in Yemen, where he began work as a petrol pump attendant. Upon returning to Bombay in 1958, he became joint owner of a trading house, exporting spices and fabrics to East Africa. He diversified into buying and selling synthetic yarn and then started manufacturing textiles made of synthetic fiber. Dhirubhai diversified again, this time befriending leading Indian politicians so that he might benefit from the government's system of import and industrial licensing. Mrs. Gandhi was among those he befriended. After she lost power to the Janata Party in 1977, Dhirubhai continued to scheme on Mrs. Gandhi's behalf by offering Janata Party members financial inducements to split into self-destructive factions.[11]

Dhirubhai's loyalty did not go unrewarded. At the party after her electoral victory, Mrs. Gandhi had Dhirubhai sit next to her for nearly two hours while visitors streamed by to congratulate her. Through Mrs. Gandhi and her finance minister Pranab Mukerjee, Dhirubhai gained, in the words of his biographer Hamish McDonald, "unrivalled influence over government's policies." For example, after Dhirubhai established a plant to manufacture polyester fiber in November 1982, the government protected him from foreign competition by slapping an added duty to import such fibers. His licenses to expand capacity were approved quickly. Despite the setbacks he went on to face, his Reliance Industries became the first Indian company to make the Fortune 500 list. Upon his death in 2002, an obituary writer put it simply: "Ambani, being the favoured one, prospered beyond imagination."[12]

While Dhirubhai was important to Mrs. Gandhi, Sanjay, the crown prince, was critical to her new regime.

Sanjay Soars into the Skies

Sanjay entered parliament via a victory in the Amethi constituency in Uttar Pradesh. He also handpicked about a hundred other winning candidates who would remain fiercely loyal to him. This was a new breed of parliamentarians. As Inder Malhotra, seasoned journalist and Mrs. Gandhi's biographer, wrote, "Sanjay's acolytes looked upon their membership of Parliament and their proximity to the centre of power as a short-cut to making the maximum possible money in the shortest period of time." Jagdish Tytler, who would play a gruesome role in the not-so-distant future, was one of the new acolytes. Some of the earlier generation of politicians who had helped Sanjay with his Maruti project and aided him in the sterilization and slum demolition efforts during the Emergency also returned to parliament.[13]

Sanjay's "power," wrote Malhotra, was "practically irresistible." His star rose higher after Mrs. Gandhi dismissed nine state governments. The argument for dismissing these governments was that after the latest parliamentary contest, previously elected state assemblies no longer represented the people's will. Sanjay led the Congress Party effort in the new elections. He promoted more of his acolytes as Congress Party candidates. Among them were two young men who had hijacked a domestic Indian Airlines flight in December 1978 to protest the Janata government's week-long arrest of Mrs. Gandhi on the charge of contempt of parliament. The hijackers, along with many other Sanjay loyalists, won their electoral contests. The Congress Party scored big victories in all states other than Tamil Nadu. *India Today,* the widely read fortnightly news magazine, hailed Sanjay as the "most vital factor in Indian politics."[14] The political buzz said he might become chief minister of Uttar Pradesh or president of the Congress Party. He was riding high, figuratively and literally.[15]

In a recurring display of bravado, Sanjay frequently flew stunt aircrafts over the city of Delhi. In late May 1980, Air Marshall Jaffar Zaheer, director-general of civil aviation, charged Sanjay with violating air-safety rules and endangering his own life and that of others. Without the Emergency in effect, Sanjay could not have the air marshal arrested. But, in a fit of pique, he did have him forced into early retirement.[16]

A month later, early in the morning of June 23, Sanjay drove about a kilometer from the home he shared with his mother to Safdarjung Airport. He climbed into a Pitts-S2A, a plane designed for skilled stunt pilots, and went soaring into the sky. At one point, he took the plane into a deep dive, presumably planning to loop up at the last moment in a wild acrobatic move. Instead, he crashed. Both Sanjay and the airport instructor who had accompanied him died instantly. Sanjay was thirty-three years old.

Upon hearing of the accident, Mrs. Gandhi rushed to the crash site. She ran, at first, from her car toward the body of her fallen son but then checked herself and slowed to a walk. Her composure broke again when she saw his mutilated face. In that moment of grief only a mother knows, she sobbed inconsolably.[17]

Although Sanjay held no official position, he received a state funeral and was cremated alongside his grandfather and prime minister of India for seventeen years, Jawaharlal Nehru. After the funeral, B. K. Nehru, former ambassador to the United States and a cousin of Mrs. Gandhi's, asked Sanjay's brother Rajiv if he had found any money in Sanjay's offices. "Crores [tens of millions]," replied Rajiv, "and unaccounted crores." In his memoirs, Ambassador Nehru expressed a widely shared sentiment: had Sanjay lived, his wild policy ideas and shameless corruption could have gravely damaged India's economic and political future. His death "saved the nation from great tragedy."[18]

Within days of Sanjay's death, a public campaign gained momentum to draft his older brother Rajiv into politics. Rajiv was a pilot with Indian Airlines, the state-owned domestic airline. His wife, the Italian-born Sonia, was "dead against the idea" of her husband stepping into politics. But Rajiv said he had little choice: he had to "help mummy."[19]

Although Rajiv saved the dynasty, Mrs. Gandhi's biographers are agreed that Sanjay's death was a "cruel blow" that numbed a part of her. She turned increasingly to the charlatan Dhirendra Brahamachari for ritualistic Hindu practices and even political guidance. The economic bureaucrat I. G. Patel, by then governor of the Reserve Bank of India, would later write that Mrs. Gandhi had never shown any interest in economic policy. In this regard, she changed little upon becoming prime minister again in 1980. "What her return to power did bring," Patel added, "were a new set of actors on the political scene who were all anxious to make their mark by hook or crook." For Patel, as governor of the RBI, that meant "fending off" more people who were seeking favors.[20] Political norms were decaying rapidly.

In India's Suffering, Corruption Flourishes

The economic situation continued to worsen. In the fiscal year 1980–1981, Indian exports stagnated while the higher international oil prices pushed up the value of imports. The trade deficit (excess of imports over exports)—the dominating component of the nation's overall balance of payments deficit—increased sharply. As had repeatedly occurred since 1949, India's ability to pay for its imports was under great strain. As was typical when India faced such financial stress, migrant workers in the Middle East reduced their foreign exchange remittances home, possibly anticipating a devaluation of the rupee. To meet its urgent need for foreign exchange, in July 1980 India borrowed $345 million from the IMF (equivalent to 266 million special drawing rights, or SDR, in the IMF's unit of account). That loan came from the Compensatory Financing Facility, designed to lend at concessional interest rates amid global disruption.[21]

In September 1981, Indian authorities turned again to the IMF, this time with a request for a conventional loan of $5.7 billion (SDR 5 billion) over the following three years. Borrowing this large sum was not

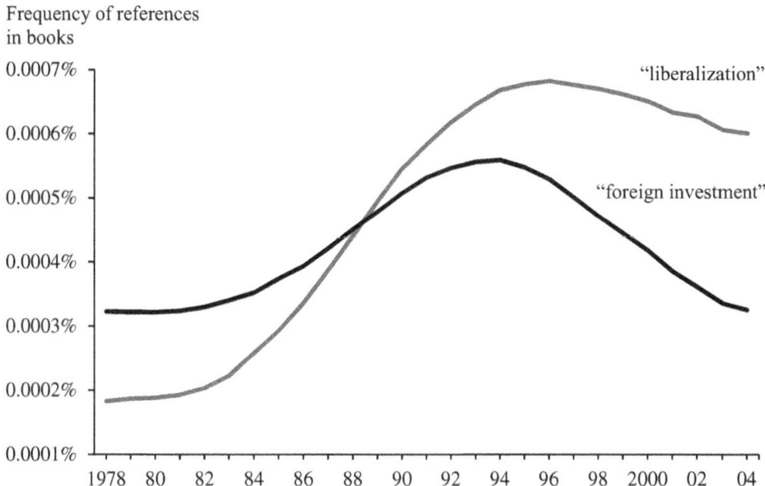

FIGURE 13.1: A new global ideology began taking shape in the early 1980s. (Frequency of reference to "liberalization" and "foreign investment" in books digitized by Google)
Source: Google NGram.

straightforward. Ronald Reagan had become U.S. president in January 1981. The mantras of "liberalization" and increasing reliance on "foreign investment" were gathering widespread acceptance (Figure 13.1). That meant a more market-oriented economy in which private investors, including international investors, played a greater role. Reagan saw little reason for the existence of the IMF or the World Bank. In his view, private banks operating internationally were perfectly capable of funding developing nations short of foreign exchange. As the IMF's largest shareholder, the United States pushed India to borrow from private banks rather than from the IMF. Indian authorities did explore alternative funding, but ultimately, the IMF came through in November 1981. The United States abstained rather than blocking the loan.[22]

Reduced controls on industry helped India make the case for an IMF loan. The policy changes were modest but were a step to break from India's past. The IMF praised India's "pragmatic industrial policy." The *Financial Times* commented India was adapting to the "Reagan age."[23]

Some scholars believe that India's turn to the Reagan Age accelerated Indian GDP growth. The proposition is that even the meager relaxation

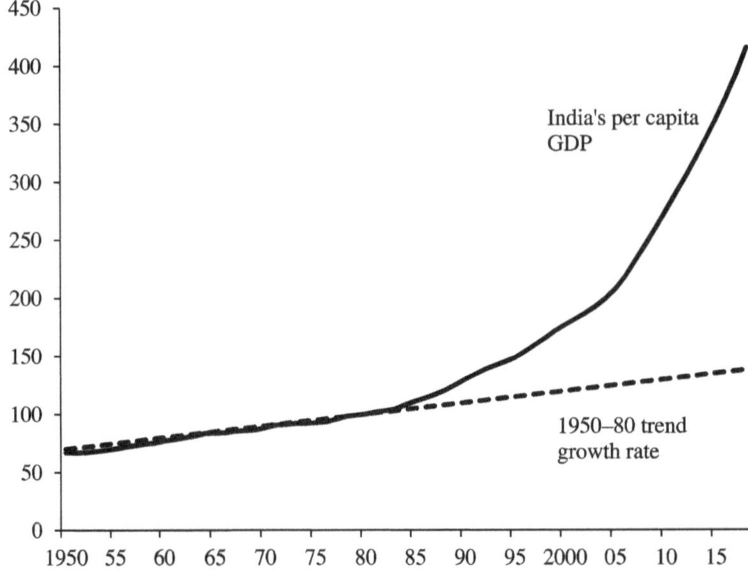

FIGURE 13.2: India's per capita GDP growth accelerated in the 1980s. (GDP per capita, 2011 prices, 1980=100, 5-year moving averages)
Source: Maddison Project Database 2020, https://www.rug.nl/ggdc/historicaldevelopment/maddison/releases/maddison-project-database-2020.

in controls signaled to Indian businesses that the government had turned "pro-business," thus inducing more investment and growth.[24] Per capita GDP growth did jump around 1980 from about 1.4 percent a year in the previous thirty years to 3.5 percent a year in the next decade (Figure 13.2). But it is a mistake to believe that the pro-business attitude caused the jump in GDP growth.

The government was not pro-business. It favored some businesses and not others, creating a personalized and capricious policy environment. Before he died, Sanjay held up a license for Nusli Wadia, a leading textile manufacturer from a nineteenth-century textile family. Wadia's crime: he had refused Sanjay a political donation. After Sanjay died, his older brother Rajiv helped Wadia get a license to manufacture petrochemical feedstock for synthetic fibers. But Indian customs detained Wadia's machinery for "inspection," causing years of delay. Upon his retirement, the customs official who engineered the delay became a generously paid employee of Dhirubhai's Reliance. Like Sanjay, Mrs. Gandhi nursed her own grudges. She held up permission for the expansion of scooter manufacturing because the owner, Kamalnayan Bajaj, had criticized her.[25]

In Maharashtra, Chief Minister Abdul Rahman Antulay, described by *India Today* as one of Mrs. Gandhi's "most loyal political retainers" and "the most faithful of the faithful," ran a corporate extortion racket. Antulay charged stiff fees for dispensing government-controlled supplies of cement, plots of land, and industrial alcohol; he charged liquor distilleries and sugar producers for the privilege of continued operations. He funneled these corporate "contributions" into slush funds, which he claimed would serve charitable activities. Mrs. Gandhi inaugurated one of Antulay's funds, the Indira Gandhi Pratibha Pratisthan ("Organization for Propagating Indira Gandhi's Splendor"). In August 1981, when the outcry against such flagrant misuse of public office grew to a crescendo, Mrs. Gandhi pulled her name from the fund. Still, Antulay retained control of the money he had raised in her name.[26]

Corruption was all-pervasive. In a justly famous 1982 article, economist and anthropologist Robert Wade described in agonizing detail the system of kickbacks in a South Indian canal irrigation system. Officials demanded bribes for access to canal water, "desirable" jobs, and construction contracts. Also, senior irrigation department engineers often had personal financial interests in construction companies, which then had an edge in receiving irrigation department contracts for construction and maintenance. These privileged companies performed overpriced, shoddy work. Farmers sometimes complained of poor irrigation services to their local politicians. But politicians earned their take from the engineers and contractors who made their money through repeated contracts, often to compensate for past shoddiness; in this environment, politicians gained stature and loyalty by securing scarce water for favored constituents. The system survived on shoddiness and scarcity. If an official refused to participate in the racket, he risked being financially and socially ostracized by colleagues. As one engineer helplessly said to Wade, he would be "crushed" if he did not play by the crooked rules.[27]

So widespread and ingrained were these practices that anthropologist Akhil Gupta, doing fieldwork in Uttar Pradesh around the same time, was struck by "how frequently the theme of corruption cropped up in the everyday conversation of villagers." Villagers regularly exchanged news on the "going price" for an electric power connection or the "terms" for a loan to buy a buffalo; they swapped stories about outwitting officials who wanted bribes and debated "the legality of actions to circumvent normal procedure."[28]

As corruption spread, filmmaker Raj Kapoor's idealism died a slow death. In 1951, Kapoor's *Awaara* had a message of hope. Ten years later, in 1961, dismayed but not yet willing to give up, Kapoor produced *Jis Desh Mein Ganga Behti Hai* (The land in which the Ganga flows). Although the film centered on a gang of dacoits, its emphasis was on the Ganga's purity. By 1985, Kapoor had lost all hope, as was manifest in *Ram Teri Ganga Maili* (Ram, your Ganga is Dirty). In the film's opening scene, an aging follower of Mahatma Gandhi inaugurates a project to clean the Ganga. He decries the embezzlement of funds from such infrastructure projects. To emphasize India's seamy trends, the movie tracks the trafficking of a young woman.[29]

Mrs. Gandhi gave legitimacy to corruption. It was a way of life, a "global phenomenon," she said to Congress Party MPs. In making this statement, Mrs. Gandhi was also asserting that it was okay to operate in a moral vacuum. As the American philosopher and revolutionary Thomas Paine had written two hundred years earlier, "a long habit of not thinking a thing *wrong*, gives it a superficial appearance of being *right*."[30]

Despite corruption being embedded in the government's functioning, Indian GDP growth picked up, in part as a bonus from the Green Revolution in agriculture. Grain production increased in the good rainfall years and fell only slightly in the poor ones, such as 1982–1983. The higher average growth rate of agricultural output directly boosted the broader economy's growth rate, and it helped indirectly by increasing the demand for industrial products. In addition, the government increased its budget deficit from an already-high 6.7 percent of GDP in 1981–1982 to 9.7 percent in 1984–1985, further boosting domestic demand. On the way to blowing its budget, India left the IMF program in May 1984, forgoing $1.1 billion of the original $5.7 billion loan. With the next general election approaching, Mrs. Gandhi's government wanted freedom from the IMF so that it could pamper influential interest groups with more subsidies.[31]

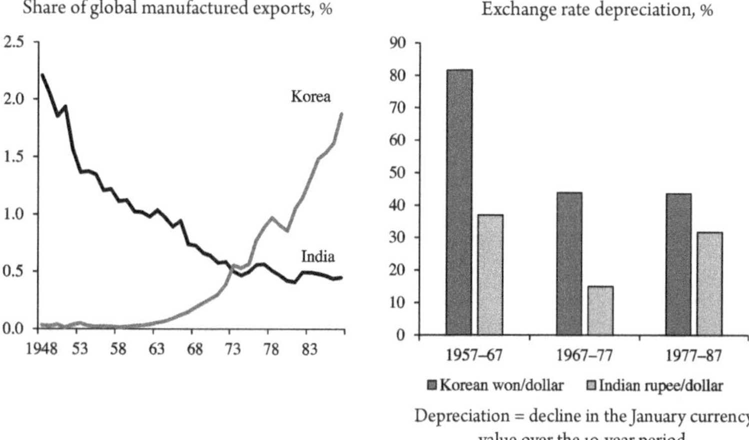

FIGURE 13.3: India lost the Red Queen race to Korea in the early 1970s, as Korea benefitted from aggressive depreciation of its currency.
Source: Left-hand panel: UNCTAD Statistics, https://unctad.org/statistics; Right-hand panel: Global Financial Data.

The Indian economy grew quickly as companies ran their production capacity harder to meet the increased demand spurred by agricultural incomes and the government's fiscal profligacy.

On the metric of true success, though, Indian economic performance remained woeful. India's share of global exports, which had fallen from 2 percent just after independence to 1 percent at the start of Mrs. Gandhi's first stint as prime minister in 1966, fell further to an abysmal 0.5 percent (Figure 13.3).

A particularly troubling consequence of losing the competitive race to the East Asian Tigers was India's poor performance in the export of labor-intensive manufactured goods. Textile exports, for example, barely grew between 1980–1981 and 1984–1985. India's exports of manufactured products were a quarter of those from Korea. The Koreans had a simple formula: a consistently cheap exchange rate to create demand for their products and widespread education to ensure quality supplies. India lacked both.[32]

From 1980 to 1984, India fell behind a new group of East Asian exporters of labor-intensive products—Malaysia, Thailand, Indonesia, and the Philippines (Figure 13.4). Repeatedly falling behind new generations of

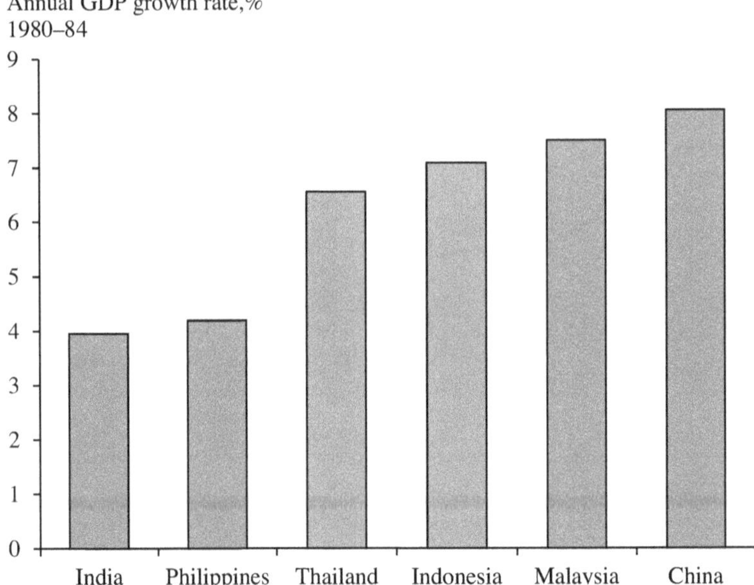

FIGURE 13.4: India began to lose the race to a new wave of East Asian economies. (Annual average GDP growth rates, 1980–84, percent)

Source: International Monetary Fund World Economic Outlook database.

global exporters perpetuated and deepened India's most serious economic problem: the lack of jobs.[33]

With India's private organized sector generating virtually no new jobs, most job seekers had no option but to squeeze themselves into the unorganized sector, where they worked only part of the time in low-productivity, often precarious tasks. India's vast "underemployment" continued to grow. By the mid-1980s, together with the more modest "open" unemployment, India's backlog of effectively unemployed—the numbers from earlier generations who needed more work—reached between 40 and 45 million workers, up from 30 to 35 million workers at the end of the Nehru era twenty years earlier. To create enough work for the unemployed and underemployed in the "backlog" and for young entrants into the job market required a staggering 9 million new jobs every year for the next ten years.[34]

India's already daunting task of creating jobs was about become harder. In early 1979, under its new leaders Hua Guofeng and Deng Xiaoping,

China had begun to pull out of the communist years of disorder. At the starting point of this "great leap in the dark," China's per capita GDP was about the same as India's. Yet Chinese dynamism would soon become evident in both agriculture and industry. In agriculture, collective farming was giving way to a "household responsibility" system that allowed farmers more authority over decision-making. In the first half of the 1980s, China's agricultural output grew at around 7 percent a year, compared to India's 4.5 percent.[35]

China's most spectacular achievement, though, was in manufacturing growth. Local authorities established township and village enterprises, an initial step toward private entrepreneurship. Special economic zones along China's eastern coast attracted a wave of foreign investment. By the early 1980s, China began establishing itself as the world's preeminent manufacturing hub. And with China set to claim a big slice of world labor-intensive exports, India faced a formidable challenge in providing manufacturing jobs for its own people.[36]

China burst onto the global economic scene because communist rule—despite the many disasters it caused—had given China distinct advantages as it began its modernizing process. In 1983, in its first major report on China, the World Bank remarked on China's "outstandingly high" life expectancy of sixty-four years, compared to India's fifty-one years. Underlying their high life expectancy, Chinese citizens had vastly superior nutritional levels compared to Indians. The Chinese also had virtually universal healthcare and high rates of primary education, including among women. And although women in China continued to battle for their rights, they had taken big strides toward emancipation. Women were active in the workforce and the Central Committee of the Chinese Communist Party. It was the supreme communist leader Mao Zedong who declared, "Women hold up half the sky." Education and workforce participation brought down the number of children women had and "contributed to improved nutrition and health practices in child-rearing."[37]

The World Bank's 1983 report made an unusually bold prediction: With its "immense wealth of human talent, effort and discipline," China stood poised "within a generation or so, to achieve a tremendous increase in the living standards of its people."[38] Institutions such as the World

Bank and the IMF do not make such strong and unqualified predictions lightly. Not for the first time and not for the last, the key message was: investment in human beings expands opportunities for citizens *and* spurs macroeconomic growth.

India Continues to Neglect Its People

During Mrs. Gandhi's last term in office, disregard for the well-being of India's people was evident in pitiful human development, severe environmental degradation, and broken cities.

Nearly simultaneous with the World Bank's report on China, Amartya Sen bemoaned the "shocking neglect" of primary education in India. India had nuclear weapons capability, Sen noted, but "only a miserable 36 percent of adult Indians are literate." As the poet Rabindranath Tagore had noted so many years before, Sen observed that "underdevelopment of elementary education seems to go hand in hand with limitation of other social services." One result, Sen highlighted, was poor medical care, which led to India's much higher infant mortality rate than in Sri Lanka, despite comparable per capita incomes in the two countries. The position of Indian women, in particular, was "scandalous," Sen lamented. The prime minister was a woman, but most women in India faced lifelong handicaps in education, medical care, and nutrition.[39]

Human development goals were not priorities for Mrs. Gandhi. Asked why Indian literacy rates remained so low, she answered: "I don't know how important literacy is. What has it done for the West? Are people happier or more alive to problems? On the contrary, I think they have become more superficial." Mrs. Gandhi had remained consistent in her neglect of human capital. When asked a similar question at the start of her years as prime minister in 1966, she replied that a big push in education was possible only immediately after independence; since then, habits and incentives had taken root, making any improvement very difficult.[40]

Now, not just human development but also a rapidly deteriorating environment and dysfunctional cities were impediments to both equitable opportunities and long-term growth. In 1982, a Delhi-based think tank, the Centre for Science and Environment, published its landmark *The First Citizens' Report,* with a follow-up in 1985. The two reports offered an unrelentingly grim view of India's environmental problems. They confirmed the long-suspected environmental damage done by the Green Revolution. Heavy irrigation had caused soil salinity and waterlogging, both of which were likely to damage longer-term cultivation possibilities. Also, with hundreds of thousands of wells dug every year, India's groundwater table was falling. The shallower wells that the poor dug were drying up. Seventy percent of India's water was polluted. In a particularly egregious instance, the number of coliform organisms (pathogens related to human feces) in the Yamuna River jumped to nearly 24 million in every 100 milliliters of water once the river entered Delhi, compared to 7,500 before entering the city. Diarrhea was a "permanent epidemic," killing 1.5 million children every year. Waterborne diseases caused a loss of millions of workdays every year. Thermal power plants and a growing number of cars and two-wheelers on the streets were polluting the air, threatening to choke increasing numbers to death. The litany of problems was unending.[41]

As Anil Agarwal, the inspiration behind these stocktaking reports on India's environment, said, "Development can take place at the cost of the environment only up to a point. Beyond that point, it will be like the foolish person who was trying to cut the very branch on which he was sitting." Agarwal reminded readers that at the 1972 United Nations Conference on the Human Environment in Stockholm, world leaders had praised Mrs. Gandhi for insisting that "poverty is the biggest polluter." Her exact statement was: "Are not poverty and need the greatest polluters?" While her full statement was not, as the world understood it then, a crude call to pursue economic development at the cost of the environment, Agarwal was right that India's pattern of economic development was causing grave damage to the environment. And economic growth that damaged the environment severely hurt the poor and benefited the rich. "Environmental damage," Agarwal wrote, "goes hand in hand with social injustice."[42]

The same disregard for equity and sustainable growth was evident in Indian cities. In a hard-hitting documentary, *Hamara Shaher* (English title: *Bombay: Our City*), Anil Patwardhan highlighted the unfairness of slum demolition in Bombay. Released in 1985, the documentary showed the rich indulging in "wasteful and flashy props of city life" while a municipal worker, backed by an abrasive policeman, hacks down a slum. A woman thrown out of her home wonders where she and her children will live and how they will find food. A disabled artist has no place to go other than the railway station. A distraught *Times of India* critic wrote in his comment on the documentary, "We feel helpless witnessing the plight of the uprooted; we wish there could be a solution, and the fact that there isn't one demoralizes us."[43]

The scale of the problem was monumental. Of Bombay's population of nearly 10 million in the early 1980s, possibly half were either homeless or lived in slums, officially defined as "buildings unfit for human habitation." Sanjay Gandhi's instinct in 1975–1976 to throw slum dwellers out of their homes ran in the bloodstream of Indian elites. In July 1981, Maharashtra Chief Minister Abdul Rahman Antulay—who sold favors for contributions to his slush funds and who described himself as friend to the poorest of the poor—launched a drive, at the height of the monsoon season, to evict slum dwellers and shoo away those living on the sidewalks. Letters from local residents to the *Times of India* praised Antulay's initiative to clean their despicably dirty neighborhoods. But witnessing the cruelty, some letter-writers asked what the game plan was: rural migrants would continue to pour into a city that lacked housing and jobs. A junior minister in Mrs. Gandhi's cabinet, on a visit to Bombay, emphasized that the city's problems could not be solved by slum demolition, which would amount only to "tinkering" on the edges. Bombay's municipal authorities needed to deal with the "fundamental flaws" in their urban planning, which had led to the city's "chaotic development."[44] Despite such pious statements, slum demolitions remained India's urban development strategy, often motivated by the profitable use of the cleared land for expensive high-rise development.

In fact, this rush for urban land was about to strike new blows on India's democracy and development prospects.

Textile Workers Strike: India's Moment of No Return

On January 18, 1982, about 250,000 workers in sixty textile mills in Bombay went on strike, demanding higher wages and better working conditions. The employers and the strike-organizing union, led by Datta Samant, began a "war of attrition," waiting to see who could bear the pain longer. The strike lasted well over a year. The end date is unclear because some textile workers, hurt by the continuing loss of wages and fearful of losing their housing, began drifting back to work in February 1983. However, at least until November 1983, yarn and cloth production remained well below 1981 levels.[45]

The strike and the crisis that accompanied it were long in the making. Even at the height of their glory in the late nineteenth and early twentieth centuries, Indian mills had very low productivity and could competitively export their products mainly to China, then a nascent textile-producing nation. From the 1930s to independence, Indian textile mills survived largely because the British colonial masters protected them with large tariffs from globally competitive producers, particularly from the hyper-competitive Japanese.[46]

The textile industry's downward spiral continued after independence. The Indian government's textile policy shackled the mills, in part by giving preference to inefficient handloom producers and (more importantly) by preventing the mills from diversifying into the production of textiles that used synthetic fibers. Because of these limitations, most Indian textile mills did not invest in new equipment. A blunt 1975 World Bank report said that while some mills were well run, "the majority can only be described as industrial slums." Factory floors were in state of "almost unimaginable squalor." Machinery was in a "bad state of repair," which, together with "appalling operating conditions" resulted in "abysmally low technical performance in terms of both quantity and quality."[47]

A decade later, India's textile mills had become "museums," even "graveyards," of machinery, wrote journalist Praful Bidwai. The mills struggled to compete with the burgeoning smaller power loom textile producers, who employed "sweated labour," stole electricity, and used cheap synthetic yarn smuggled from South Korea and Taiwan. In Bidwai's words, India's textile mills had gone from "riches to rags."[48]

The textile workers' strike was, perhaps, inevitable, but its aftereffects were so damaging because it came at a moment of deep economic and social malaise. That malaise reflected itself in Bombay as a paradox of sky-high property prices even as the city degenerated into an "urban purgatory." In the city's exclusive residential and commercial areas, property prices were above those in London, Paris, and Manhattan. Bombay's "land mafia" of colluding politicians, officials, builders, and property sharks ensured that land supply remained scarce, which generated a feverish demand for land from legitimate businesses and those seeking new homes. In that context, mill owners welcomed the textile workers' strike because they could lay off workers without severance compensation and sell the valuable land on which the mills stood. The real money no longer lay in manufacturing; it lay instead in selling land in lucrative property development deals.[49] India was at a deindustrialization moment.

As a symbol of that deindustrialization, only the workers lost at the end of the strike. Dutch scholar H. van Wersch estimated that mill owners laid off between fifty and one hundred thousand workers. A large unknown number of workers in factories making textile machinery and dyes also lost their jobs. Bombay's other manufacturing industries—chemicals and engineering—were in the Nehruvian mold: they used capital-intensive techniques and required few workers. Hence, most workers who lost their textile-related jobs never returned to work at a manufacturing facility. Some returned to their village homes, back to the grind from which they had sought escape. Now, instead of helping their families with remittances from their factory earnings, they became burdens. Among those who stayed in Bombay, some became construction workers laboring for meager daily wages. Others became hawkers, peddling wares on handcarts. Criminal activity in Bombay grew as some unemployed workers became lieutenants in the city's organized crime networks. Laid-off workers also began taking aggressive positions in Bombay's growing communal divide.[50]

The failure of the textile strike and its aftermath brought to glaring light the ongoing shift in Indian business incentives away from manufacturing toward investment in land, property, and finance. That shift was set to strengthen. A poorly educated workforce, an expensive currency, and increasing Chinese competition in world markets and soon in the Indian market reduced the payoff from manufacturing. India was approaching a point of no return.

Chapter 14

WHEN THE VIOLENCE CAME HOME

When Mrs. Gandhi became prime minister in January 1966, she inherited a dismal national legacy from her father, the former prime minister Jawaharlal Nehru. The economy created too few jobs, frequent surges of inflation caused great hardship, social upheaval was gathering momentum, the virus of corruption had infected India's bureaucracy, and the Congress Party and Indian politics were splintering. Perhaps most worryingly, Hindu nationalist forces were gathering strength.

Mrs. Gandhi accelerated the country's moral decay while doing little for its economic regeneration. Comparing herself to her more polished father, she said that he "was a saint who strayed into politics. I am a tough politician."[1] Lacking any coherent economic or political ideology and operating mainly in rhetorical soundbites, she saw preservation of her power as her main goal. After she split with the Congress Party that had won India's freedom in 1947, she created her own dominating Congress Party in 1969 with loyalists beholden to her.

Mrs. Gandhi spent almost two decades as prime minister in a cynical and self-serving socialist garb, making promises to the poor she had no intention of keeping. Having nationalized the banks to gain a political edge, she unleashed Sanjay to establish a culture of corruption in those banks. Through actions and words, she legitimized high-level political corruption. The high stakes in the political power grab drew the mafia to fund elections and use its musclemen to intimidate voters.

From the early years of her premiership, Mrs. Gandhi relied heavily on state's coercive powers to govern the country. She used preventive detention laws to hold dissenters and opponents without due process, and she made extensive use of the police and armed forces to subdue social protest well before she quashed all dissent under the Emergency. During the Emergency between June 1975 and March 1977, she let Sanjay run wild and shunned all who dared criticize him. When voters rejected her at the end of the Emergency, Sanjay and his cabal responded like lawless criminals. For her return as prime minister in January 1980, Sanjay drafted a horde of get-rich-quick MPs before he self-destructed in a characteristically arrogant stunt flight over Delhi in June 1980.

She kept her distance from the Bombay textile workers' strike, which cost tens of thousands of workers their jobs. By then, India had begun deindustrializing and the Chinese industrial machine was ascending. Jobless Indians, lacking the support of public goods to open up new opportunities, became recruits of criminal networks and Hindu nationalism.

Political and social violence were all-pervasive, which the 1983 movie *Ardha Satya* (Half-truth) captured in a memorably visceral form. In the ruling power elite of politicians, police, and mafia, the lone cop with integrity has no place. To his colleagues and superiors, he is "quaint" and therefore "dangerous." His choice is to join the power elite or face social and personal destruction.[2]

The Beginning of the End

That Mrs. Gandhi remained largely untouched by the collateral damage from her aggressive style (except for the brief political exile after the Emergency ended) is a testament to her political skills. But despite those skills, she never overcame the Sikh impasse. She conceded the long-standing demand for a separate Sikh state in 1966, thus dividing Punjab into a smaller, Sikh-dominated Punjab and a predominantly Hindu Haryana state. However, the Sikh leadership remained unhappy, in part because the new Punjab had to share its capital, Chandigarh, with Haryana. The Sikhs were also angry at the diversion of water from Punjab's rivers to less fortunate neighboring states. There were no acceptable compromises.

Into that impasse entered Sikh preacher-politician Sant Jarnail Singh Bhindranwale. He shrewdly connected the long-standing demand for a separate Punjab state with the economic anger of young, unanchored Sikh men, who became the mob—the foot-soldiers—serving his feverish purpose. In the mid-1960s, Bal Thackeray had drawn angry young Maharashtrian men to his movement against South Indians. Hindu nationalists had harnessed the same anger in inflicting violence on Muslims. As political philosopher Hannah Arendt wrote, tribal nationalism flourishes in an atmosphere of rootless anger.[3] So it was in Punjab in the early 1980s.

Bhindranwale was an imposing figure with deep-set eyes and a long flowing beard. He was the head of a Sikh seminary and his title "Sant" identified him as a preacher. He signaled his political aspirations in 1979 on the occasion of elections to the Shiromani Gurudwara Prabandhak Committee (SGPC), the Sikh religion's parliament, which is elected by all adult Sikhs. Although the SGPC mainly manages religious affairs, Sikhs regard the winning party as best representing their political interests. For years, the Akali Dal (Party of the Immortals) had won the political laurels. When Bhindranwale entered the electoral competition to challenge the Akalis in 1979, Congress Party leader Giani Zail Singh sensed an opportunity to split the Sikhs to the advantage of the Congress Party in forthcoming state and national elections. Zail Singh, with the essential support of Sanjay Gandhi, funded Bhindranwale to help him weaken the Akalis. Bhindranwale returned the favor by campaigning for Congress Party candidates in the 1980 general election, aiding Mrs. Gandhi's electoral triumph.[4]

Bhindranwale, however, was no puppet. He acquired a moral aura by hectoring Sikhs about their moral degeneration. Punjab's successful large farmers, who had played a crucial role in making India self-sufficient in food, were spending their riches on increasing quantities of alcohol, drugs, and pornography. As these habits spread to those who could least afford them, Bhindranwale sternly warned his co-religionists that they were violating the tenets of Sikhism. He grew in stature among Sikhs, many of whom were grateful for being reminded of the virtues of austere living and their spiritual roots.[5]

Bhindranwale used his celebrity to attract those whom the Green Revolution had left behind. Small farmers were under never-ending economic pressure. They borrowed unaffordable sums to buy expensive seeds, chemical fertilizers, pesticides, seed drills, tractors, insecticide sprayers, and tube wells required to successfully deploy the Green Revolution technology. In doing so, they placed themselves at risk of large losses and unrepayable debt burdens. Landless labor gained initially from higher wages, but employment prospects for workers deteriorated once the rich farmers began mechanizing their operations. As the journalist and historian Khushwant Singh has written, the "bountiful" fruits of the Green Revolution accrued mainly to large farmers. For those unable or unwilling to make a living from agriculture, college education and the hope of urban jobs also proved a disappointment. The large number of colleges that had sprung up all over Punjab, as in the rest of India, churned out thousands of unemployable graduates. A survey by Punjab University in 1984 revealed that about one-third of college graduates were unemployed. Many of them had been looking for work for over two years. With not enough work to occupy the able-bodied, a serious underemployment problem arose. That problem was an opportunity for Bhindranwale to attract rebellious young men to his cause.[6]

A Crescendo of Violence

Bhindranwale's was an old, well-tested political strategy. By defining Hindus as the designated enemy, he encouraged Sikhs to unite in a common cause. Just as the German legal philosopher Carl Schmitt had proposed in the late 1920s and Bal Thackeray was practicing contemporaneously in Bombay, Bhindranwale believed in perpetual violence against "the enemy" to gain political advantage. The preacher Bhindranwale cultivated a strongman image, wearing a bandolier laden with bullets. His young unsmiling guards carried menacing firearms and hatchets. He became the "messiah of Sikh fundamentalism."[7]

From the safe haven of the Golden Temple, the sacred Sikh shrine, where police forces were unlikely to pursue him, Bhindranwale directed killings and bank robberies on an almost daily basis. In a particularly gruesome incident, Sikh militants stopped a bus, pulled out male Hindu passengers and shot them in cold blood. Even Sikh police officers, who might try to rein him in, were seen as the enemy. A Bhindranwale hitman murdered one such Sikh officer as he departed the Golden Temple after offering his prayers.[8]

As the months dragged on and violence did not abate, Mrs. Gandhi authorized "Operation Blue Star." In the evening of June 5, 1984, army soldiers entered the Golden Temple. By then, Bhindranwale had fortified himself in the Akal Takht, the holiest shrine inside the temple. The carnage that transpired the next day took the lives of as many as a thousand Sikh militants and a few hundred Indian Army soldiers. It took several days to confirm that Bhindranwale was among the dead.[9]

Bhindranwale's death did not end Sikh extremism. Even Sikhs who abhorred his fanatical violence were aghast at the army's entry into the sacred temple and destruction of their beloved Akal Takht. Not long after the army's operation in the Golden Temple, extremists began to regroup. Rajiv Gandhi, in his incarnation as likely successor to Mrs. Gandhi, confirmed that army troops would continue to patrol Punjab. The Indian Army and Punjab's militants were once again in a standoff. Mrs. Gandhi sensed the violence coming home. On October 30, 1984, speaking to cheering supporters in Bhubaneshwar, she said, "If I die today, every drop of my blood will invigorate the nation." That night, before she went to bed in Delhi, she seemed unusually tired.[10]

Days of Shame

At about 9:30 a.m. on October 31, Amitav Ghosh, a young anthropology lecturer in Delhi University working on his first novel, was riding a bus to the university. The buzz grew that Mrs. Gandhi had been assassinated less than thirty minutes earlier. By the time he reached the university, students were whispering in huddles: Two Sikh bodyguards had shot her.[11]

The shocked whispers Ghosh heard marked the end of an era. Mrs. Gandhi, dressed in a saffron sari with a black border, had been walking through a garden that connected her private quarters to an office space. She was on her way to meet the British actor Peter Ustinov, who was on assignment in India to film a documentary. It was 9:08 that bright autumn morning when she approached the two bodyguards standing beside her path. She folded her hands and greeted them with a traditional *Namaste.* They pumped her body with bullets and then threw down their guns. One of them said to the stunned onlookers in Punjabi, "I have done what I had do. Now, you do what you want to."[12]

Later that afternoon, Ghosh was witness to surging rage in the city. His bus to a friend's home passed the hospital where Mrs. Gandhi's body lay. "Delhi was at its best," Ghosh recalled, "crisp and cool." But despite the crispness in the air, "young red-eyed men" outside the hospital were "in half-buttoned shirts." Some "were armed with steel rods and bicycle chains." Congress Party loyalists were "inciting crowds gathered there to take revenge." A few of the young men stopped Ghosh's bus and in "chilling" voices asked if there were Sikhs on board. The driver responded there were none while the passengers shielded the lone Sikh passenger who had squeezed under a seat.

In the style of a monarchy, Rajiv Gandhi was sworn in—crowned, perhaps—as India's prime minister that evening, and the violence raged on. When Ghosh woke to a bright morning, he beheld "a sight that I could never have imagined. In every direction, columns of smoke rose slowly into a limpid sky. Sikh houses and businesses were burning." Houses of Hindus and Muslims who had sheltered Sikhs were also "being looted and burned." The skyline looked like the "vault of some vast pillared hall."[13]

Over the next few days, the death toll in Delhi mounted. Around three thousand Sikhs died, some doused with kerosene and set on fire. Sanjay Gandhi's ghost was present. Victims pointed to two of his henchmen, H. K. L. Bhagat and Jagdish Tytler, as leaders of the carnage. Hundreds, maybe thousands, died in other cities. On November 19, Rajiv addressed a rally of 200,000 people at Delhi's Boat Club to honor his mother's sixty-seventh birthday. His words seemed to justify the senseless deaths of thousands of Sikhs: "When a mighty tree falls it is only natural that the earth around it does shake a little."[14]

Rajiv did not attempt to control the Sikh massacres, and he did not seek accountability for them. A commission of inquiry, constituted in April 1985 under Supreme Court Justice Ranganath Misra, dismissed the Sikh killings as the work of mysterious "satanic" forces. Although the Misra Commission and eight other commissions found evidence implicating Congress Party leaders, the justice system punished only one relatively obscure leader, Sajjan Kumar, in December 2018.[15]

With Mrs. Gandhi's assassination, an era steeped in violence ended in carnage. Her years at the helm had set India back irreparably. Social and political norms had been obliterated. The Chinese were about to take over the global jobs for labor-intensive manufacturing. No one had any idea where the jobs for tens of millions of Indians would come from. No one in the political elite cared, it seemed. The genies of religious parochialism and tribal nationalism had been unleashed. The widespread assumption was that Rajiv was entitled to the prime ministership. As Salman Rushdie later wrote, "The already tired description of India as 'the world's largest democracy' grew a good deal more exhausted."[16]

Part III

THE PROMISE, 1985–2004

Chapter 15
A PILOT FLIES INTO POLITICAL HEADWINDS

Rajiv Gandhi, born in August 1944, had stayed out of politics until his brother Sanjay died in June 1980. In fact, until that point, Rajiv had downplayed his relationship to the Nehru-Gandhi political dynasty. After the Emergency ended in 1977 and the nation's eyes turned with resentment toward Mrs. Gandhi and Sanjay, Rajiv and his Italian wife Sonia contemplated moving with their two children to Italy, but that plan fell through. As he continued flying twin-engine Avros for Indian Airlines, he shied away from the "Gandhi" name, identifying himself as "Captain Rajiv" in pre-flight announcements.[1]

Rajiv's last name thrust him into the Indian prime minister's position hours after his mother's assassination on October 31, 1984. Two weeks later, on November 13, 1984, he called for a national election. But before the polling began, a new tragedy struck the already stunned nation. In the pre-dawn hours of December 3, in the central-Indian city of Bhopal, poison gas leaked from a pesticide-production plant that was owned and operated by the American multinational firm Union Carbide. The plant was located in a densely populated area and operated under poor regulatory oversight. As the *New York Times* wrote, "A toxic cloud spread through the slums and other poor neighborhoods, killing many in their sleep and sending others running into the streets in panic." The gas ended up killing 3,500 people and severely injuring as many as two hundred thousand others.[2]

Fearing the unknown at that moment of multiple crises, the Indian public sought an anchor in Rajiv. Over three hundred million voters, a record 63.6 percent of all registered voters, turned out at the polls between December 24 and 28. The Congress Party won four-fifths of the seats in parliament, a landslide victory unmatched by either Rajiv's mother or his grandfather.[3]

Although Rajiv was prime minister because he was heir to the Nehru-Gandhi dynasty, he was also a political outsider. He was a young, reluctant entrant into politics, which meant that he was free from the web of scandal and political corruption. Many Indians saw in Rajiv the promise of a fresh start. His greatest public appeal was his "Mr. Clean" image. Shoring up that image, campaign posters showed him holding a broom to sweep away the political corruption that his mother and brother had fostered. "Sweeping away the corruption" was but a metaphor for repairing broken norms and restoring political accountability.[4]

Indians wanted to believe in Rajiv. As journalist and author Tavleen Singh wrote, "Rajiv, for a brief shining moment in Indian history, became a living symbol of hope." So great was the clamor for change, she added, that it is "hard to think of another leader who could have started with more goodwill, love and hope." Rajiv sensed the high expectations. They are "scary," he said.[5]

The Man Matches the Moment

Electronic computing and communications technologies were opening new pathways to progress, and Rajiv's youth and technical aptitude blended with the times. Montek Singh Ahluwalia, Rajiv Gandhi's economic advisor at the time and one of India's foremost economic bureaucrats in later years, tells the story of Rajiv introducing Indian government officials to the then-state-of-the-art spreadsheet Lotus 1-2-3. Rajiv had even bigger dreams. He believed that "a computer in every village school by the twenty-first century" was a goal well within India's reach.[6]

Around the globe, economic policy was opening more space for private initiative and the play of free-market forces. India began aligning itself with this global shift. Taking a page from U.S. President Ronald Reagan's playbook, Rajiv Gandhi's Finance Minister Vishwanath Pratap Singh reduced tax rates substantially in the March 1985 government budget. He brought down the personal income tax rate from 62 percent to 50 percent and also reduced the corporate tax rate to 50 percent, down from 55 percent. Singh abolished the estate tax and reduced the wealth tax. He also reduced the requirements to receive a license to start and expand a business, while lowering import tariffs and controls.[7]

Pundits (both Indian and international) welcomed the tax cuts. They were optimistic because the American economist Arthur Laffer—through his well-known "Laffer curve"—had suggested that lower tax rates could actually increase government tax revenues. With lower rates, businesses, having less incentive to dodge taxes, would invest more in growth opportunities. The global narrative predicted that a "huge" increase in the government's tax revenues would follow. A subtler view anticipated that lower tax rates would increase the incentive to allocate capital more efficiently.[8]

V. P. Singh also made it legal for businesses to finance political parties, reversing the ban in place since Mrs. Gandhi instituted it in 1969. The ban had done great political and social damage. Businesses had circumvented it by making their donations in "black" (unaccounted-for) money. Indian politics had come to depend on black money, including from criminal sources. The hope was that lifting the ban on corporate political contributions would encourage legal funding of political parties which, along with reduced incentives for tax avoidance, would gradually eliminate black money.[9]

The applause was instant. Commenting on the March 1985 budget, the *Wall Street Journal* ran a gushing editorial with the title "Rajiv Reagan." Rajiv Gandhi, the editorial said, had engineered a "minor revolution" by "slashing" taxes and cutting regulations in a manner "worthy of another famous tax cutter we know." In May, Reagan himself hailed the Indian budget. Speaking to Spanish businessmen in Madrid, he said, "Soon we may see an economic revolution in India, where Rajiv Gandhi is reducing regulations, lowering tariffs, and slashing taxes." When Rajiv visited the United States in June that year, Reagan received him on the South Lawn of the White House. In his remarks, Reagan said, "During your visit, you will find a deep well of affection and respect for India and her people."[10]

Not to be outdone by other cheerleaders, Columbia University economist Jagdish Bhagwati declared, "India has come alive." And rejecting the angst among Indian economists fearfully witnessing China race ahead, Bhagwati asserted, "Far more than China today, India is a miracle waiting to happen." And if an Indian miracle did occur, Bhagwati wrote, "the central figure will be the young Prime Minister."[11]

As if to validate such predictions, India latched on to yet another global trend. Developing nations were wooing foreign investors for capital, technology, and jobs. In an exhaustively researched essay, Nicholas Kristof of the *New York Times* wrote, "Just a decade ago, multinational companies were widely viewed as a scourge of the third world. But today, from China to Algeria, foreign multinationals are finding warm welcome everywhere."[12]

In June 1985, the American electronics firm Texas Instruments announced the opening of a research center in the southern city of Bangalore. The Indian government authorized direct satellite links from the Bangalore facility to a Texas Instruments research center in Bedford, U.K., and to the company's headquarters in Dallas, Texas. Although Texas Instruments initially invested only about $6 million and employed only about 35 engineers in Bangalore, the investment placed India in the vanguard of international outsourcing, which was an essential feature of the emerging rush to globalization (Figure 15.1).[13]

A Texas Instruments executive said that India's "large number of underemployed graduates" would help the company cut the cost of expensive engineers in Dallas and elsewhere in the developed world. A new development avenue opened up for India, which began building a reputation for software skills and low-cost "human capital" in service of world markets. Bangalore became known as India's Silicon Valley, a "boom town," the "in" city for Indian yuppies. Bangalore, an American commentator wrote, "is at the forefront of Prime Minister Rajiv Gandhi's

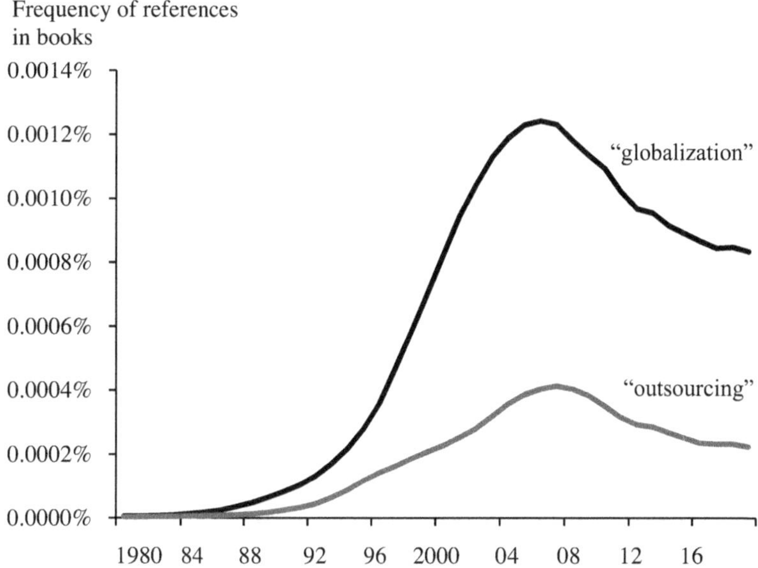

FIGURE 15.1: India caught the start of the globalization-outsourcing wave. (Frequency of reference to "globalization" and "outsourcing" in books digitized by Google)
Source: Google NGram.

ambitious plans to modernize his country with the import of Western technology."[14]

By August 1985, the *Financial Express* all-India equity index had risen by over 38 percent since the dip following Mrs. Gandhi's assassination in October 1984.[15] Rajiv the pilot had achieved a smooth takeoff. But rough weather lay ahead.

Into Economic Turbulence

Despite its cult-like following, the Laffer Curve's rosy predictions did not pan out even in the United States. Rather than stimulating economic activity and fiscal revenues, lower U.S. corporate tax rates simply put money into the pockets of rich Americans. Recent studies reaffirm that wealthy individuals and large companies worldwide avoid taxes aggressively even when rates are low. Why? Because they can![16]

In India, businesses had, for long, thrived in a black-money environment, beyond tax and regulatory oversight. Following their ingrained habits and instincts, they continued to dodge taxes and make political contributions in black money. As political scientists Milan Vaishnav and Eswaran Sridharan explained, "The system of opaque donations to parties and politicians in exchange for regulatory favors had become too deeply entrenched." Former chief election commissioner of India Navin Chawla added that donors and recipients relished being "below the radar of tax authorities." Rather than rising, as predicted, the share of direct taxes—personal plus corporate—declined from 2.9 percent to 2.4 percent of national GDP. The tax burden shifted to indirect taxes, which fall on the spending people incur for consumption. Notably, indirect taxes weigh more heavily on lower-income families, who spend larger shares of their incomes on consumption.[17] Rajiv's well-meaning policy experiments demonstrated how deeply corruption and black money were intertwined in the web of Indian life. The privileged benefited from that intertwining; the vulnerable bore the costs.

Following in his mother's footsteps, Rajiv fell into the trap of ever-increasing fiscal subsidies. The largest subsidies were a hangover of the effort to engineer the Green Revolution. The government subsidized the use of fertilizers and paid farmers minimum guaranteed prices for food grains, which it then sold at subsidized prices to consumers. India had made this bargain in the mid-1960s to stimulate higher food grain production, and now the subsidies were impossible to unwind. In addition, as economist Pranab Bardhan wrote, subsidies were implicit in the "persistent losses in Government-owned irrigation works, State Electricity Boards, Road Transport Corporations and other public enterprises." Subsidies were also implicit in "the overmanning at different levels of public bureaucracy, supporting a whole army of salaried parasites." In July 1986, the government-appointed Pay Commission recommended a large increase in salaries and benefits of Indian civil servants to compensate them for the rise in the cost of living. The government's wage bill ballooned. It was a trap: more handouts meant more inflation, which meant more handouts. As Bardhan wrote, the government needed to "placate" all who claimed they deserved more.[18]

Other demands, especially for the modernization of the Indian Armed Forces, increased the government's expenses. With tax collections as share of GDP largely unchanged, the Indian government hurtled toward a fiscal crisis. The budget deficit had already risen from 6.7 percent to 9.7 percent of GDP in the last four years of Mrs. Gandhi's final term. In his first two years in office, Rajiv pushed that deficit to over 10.9 percent of GDP, after which it declined modestly, mainly because the government cut back on its long-term investment spending. The government became more indebted as it borrowed to fund its large annual budget deficit. Increased interest payments on the debt increased the deficit further.[19]

To prevent an inflationary spiral induced by the demand pumped in by continuing fiscal deficits, India headed toward international bankruptcy. The government allowed imports to meet some part of the domestic demand, but exports did not grow fast enough to pay for those imports. India's international balance of payments turned from a small surplus to a deficit. The government used a risky strategy to finance the balance-of-payments deficit. It began depleting its foreign exchange reserves and borrowed on short-maturity contracts from foreign commercial lenders. The risk was that foreign lenders could demand their money back at any time, which—without a cushion of reserves—would push the country into bankruptcy.

The governor of the Reserve Bank of India visited Rajiv Gandhi to warn him of a looming financial crisis. The International Monetary Fund's managing director, Michel Camdessus, also raised a red flag and suggested that India consider an IMF loan. But IMF funds would come with a politically troublesome call for reducing subsidies.[20]

In principle, foreign investors with a long-term commitment to India could also have helped in financing the balance of payments deficit. But the government's welcome to Texas Instruments proved to be an exception. With Pepsi, the U.S. soft drink producer, the previous ambivalence to foreign investment reappeared. Politicians jumped in with high-minded objections. India was a poor country, they said, and did not need more soft drink producers. Also, payment for Pepsi's import of expensive equipment might require precious foreign exchange reserves.

The difference between the government's approach to Texas Instruments and Pepsi revealed how unprepared Indian businesses were to face competition. Texas Instruments slipped through because its Bangalore facility, which serviced the company's internal requirements, was not a competitive threat to any Indian company. In virtually every other line of business, foreign investors *were* a competitive threat, prompting Indian businesses to lobby aggressively against them. Ramesh Chauhan, the head of Parle Exports, a company that produced a cola named Thums Up and controlled over half the domestic name-brand market, lobbied hard against Pepsi's entry into India. Even the industrialist Rahul Bajaj, who enjoyed 70 percent market share of Indian scooter sales, rejected competition from foreign investors. "We need more time," he said. "If foreign companies come into India, we will die."[21]

Pepsi's travails revealed the difficulties foreign investors experienced in entering India. Having first approached Indian authorities in 1985, Pepsi found the Punjab government to be an ally in July 1986. To help expand Punjab's farm production and the food processing industry, Pepsi agreed to make potato chips, corn chips, sauces, and fruit and vegetable juice concentrates, the latter mainly for the export market. In February 1988, the Indian government appeared to give the go-ahead but it took until September to seal the deal. Pepsi leadership viewed the eventual deal as "harsh." The parent company was not permitted to hold more than 40 percent of the equity in its Indian operations and had to fulfill export targets from India. These conditions, the president of Pepsi-Cola International said, were tougher than those required by the Soviet Union and China. But, he added, "We're willing to go so far with India because the Indian middle-class is beginning to emerge and we see that as a big market."[22]

Foreign investment flows to India remained anemic while many other Asian countries sought and received significant sums. During Rajiv Gandhi's term from 1985 to 1989, the annual inflow of foreign direct investment into India was between $100 and $200 million. For China, foreign investment ranged from $1.7 to $3.4 billion a year. It was a "missed opportunity" for India, writes Montek Ahluwalia.[23]

Although Rajiv Gandhi had placed India on the path to a financial crisis and had done little to make the Indian economy more competitive, some commentators continued to praise his measures to "liberalize" the Indian economy. Economist Arvind Panagariya documented Rajiv Gandhi's scaling back of industrial licensing and import restrictions in great detail. Panagariya also listed the many policy incentives to encourage exports. The list of liberalization measures was long, but they only tinkered at the edges. In April 1988, the *Wall Street Journal,* full of praise for Rajiv three years earlier, lamented that the Indian bureaucracy had again bogged the country down. In its May 1990 assessment of Rajiv Gandhi's five-year term, an IMF report summarized the state of affairs:

> Industry still faces regulations that impede investment and prevent unprofitable firms from closing down; the trade regime remains complex and restrictive while tariff rates are among the highest in the world; a large number of non-performing loans [loans whose borrowers were not repaying their debts on time] weaken the health and efficiency of the banking system; and public enterprises lack commercial incentives.[24]

Thus, even in terms of its own policy objectives of spurring private initiative and market forces, Rajiv Gandhi's government had underperformed. Not surprisingly, India's economic performance was stuck in mediocrity. GDP growth was about the same as in Mrs. Gandhi's final term (about 5.5 percent a year). As in Mrs. Gandhi's final years, Rajiv's government benefited from continuing dividends from the Green Revolution, which imparted stability to agricultural output even in drought years. Severe drought in 1986–1987 and continuing poor rains in 1987–1988 caused great hardship, especially in the state of Orissa, but total national food grain production fell only slightly. Resilient incomes of large farmers generated steady demand for industrial goods. And although good jobs in the "organized" sector were scarce, subsidies and public-sector pay raises added to aggregate demand, helping industrial growth. Rich Indians (the top 15 percent of income earners but often mislabeled the middle class) also sustained the domestic demand for manufactured products.[25] But the Indian economy lacked spark or dynamism, which was clear from its persisting lack of international competitiveness. India's share of world exports remained stuck at 0.5 percent (Figure 15.2). Meanwhile, following the East Asian Tigers Taiwan and Korea in the 1960s and 1970s, China started to race ahead of India.

Reduction of the tax and regulatory burden had its place in the policy toolkit. But Indian intellectuals and policymakers looking enviously at

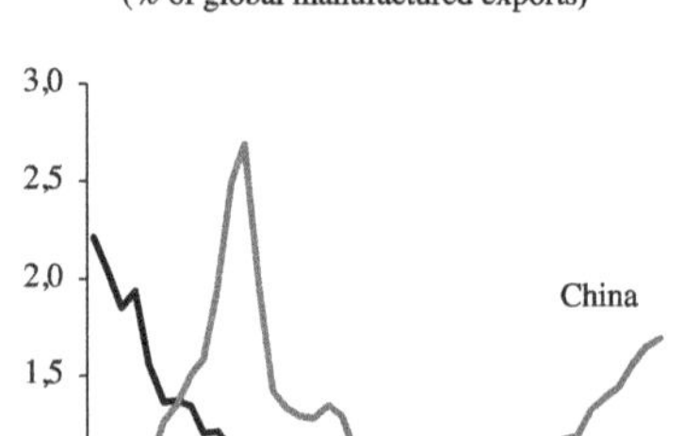

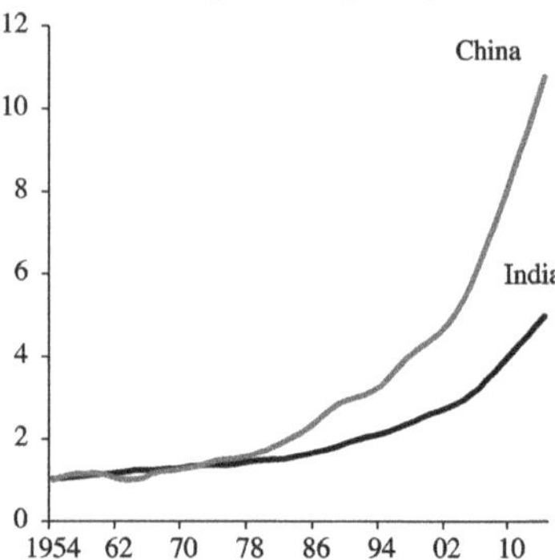

FIGURE 15.2: A newfound Chinese exporting prowess propelled it ahead of India. Source: UNCTAD Statistics, https://unctadstat.unctad.org/EN/Index.html and Maddison Project database, https://www.rug.nl/ggdc/historicaldevelopment/maddison/releases/maddison-project-database-2020.

China failed to understand what the Chinese government was doing right. China was growing rapidly not because of ambitious tax and regulatory changes, but because Chinese leaders adopted a profoundly different economic development philosophy. Hoping to replicate the success of the East Asian Tigers, China's leaders launched the country's eastern coastline as a manufacturing base for global markets. They wooed foreign investors, among them not just Pepsi but also Honda, Toyota, and Hilton Hotels. To be clear, each East Asian success story, starting with Japan, had its own specific features. But they all drew hungrily from the international pool of knowledge, and they trained their citizens to absorb that knowledge.[26]

China's widespread industrial literacy, comprehensive health delivery, and availability of critical infrastructure worked in combination with foreign ideas and investment to unleash a powerful developmental force. Naysayers dismissed East Asian, and especially Chinese, success as the product of autocratic governments. But while East Asian autocrats often inflicted grave injury on their citizens, the paradox is that East Asian regimes displayed an openness to ideas and cared about the welfare—and even the sensitivities—of their people in ways that democratic India seldom did.

Shocked by China's extraordinary growth but not recognizing the reasons for its success, commentators invoked the tortoise-hare metaphor. They said that India, the democratic tortoise, would eventually win the race against China, the totalitarian hare.[27] Such wishful thinking—just as Jagdish Bhagwati's prediction in 1985 that India would work the greater miracle—became India's intellectual refuge within which envy toward China flourished.

Rajiv had stirred hope that India could begin again. But he proved unable to make the economy more competitive. Instead, he set the economy on course to a financial crisis. Even more tragically for India, Rajiv could not halt the country's moral freefall.

Into Political Turbulence

Rajiv began his prime ministerial tenure as a "Mr. Clean" intent on breaking the back of political corruption. It was a monumental but urgent task. The question was: where should he begin? The list of his mother's moral compromises was long. But Mrs. Gandhi had chosen to make one relationship public. Dhirubhai Ambani, the rising super-industrialist, had received many regulatory and policy favors for his Reliance Industries from Mrs. Gandhi's government (especially from her finance minister Pranab Mukerjee). Rajiv began well by not including Mukerjee in his own cabinet. The arc of Rajiv's subsequent relationship with Dhirubhai describes his initial promise and his later fall from grace.

With the tainted Mukerjee gone and V. P. Singh as Rajiv Gandhi's finance minister, Dhirubhai abruptly found himself without a government benefactor. In fact, he had a relentless adversary in Singh, who as chief minister of Uttar Pradesh in the early 1980s had acquired a reputation for ruthlessness. Starting in May 1985, Singh began undermining Dhirubhai. The ministry of finance banned import of his preferred feedstock for producing polyester fiber. The ban forced Dhirubhai to buy domestically produced feedstock from his archrival, Nusli Wadia. Even though the finance ministry's import ban was introduced with little notice, Dhirubhai insisted that he had already signed contracts to import the feedstock. As proof, he had necessary loan commitments (letters of credit) from a nationalized bank and three overseas banks to finance the import. Because Dhirubhai appeared suspiciously well prepared for the ban, the government ordered a criminal investigation in October into the possibility that officials had leaked information on the impending ban to Dhirubhai. Later in October, a tax official added pressure by sending Dhirubhai a notice demanding about $22 million of unpaid taxes.[28]

In December 1985, with Singh working on Dhirubhai, Rajiv—still fired up with the zeal of "Mr. Clean"—gave his best-known speech. It was a special occasion: the one-hundredth anniversary of the Congress Party. This was the party that had brought India freedom from the British, and even though the party had morphed since his mother split with the old guard, an impassioned Rajiv believed that he carried the mantle. His speech was a biting indictment of Indian institutions for social justice. "We have government servants," he said, "who do not serve but oppress the poor and helpless, police who do not uphold the law but shield the guilty, tax collectors who do not collect taxes but connive with those who cheat the state." Rajiv vented his fury on "brokers of power and influence" and on the "battalions of law-breakers and tax evaders." The speech was a call for moral cleansing.[29]

V. P. Singh continued to come at Dhirubhai from all sides. In June 1986, Singh's ministry of finance abolished an anti-dumping duty on polyester yarn. In principle, anti-dumping duties stop foreign producers who set unreasonably low prices to steal the home market from domestic producers. In practice, these duties (in India and elsewhere) establish excessive protection from international competition. When first levied in 1982, Finance Minister Pranab Mukherjee, in one of his several gifts to Dhirubhai, had overruled ministry officials who argued that polyester yarn did not merit protection via an anti-dumping duty. Singh's removal of that duty exposed Dhirubhai's yarn production to greater import competition. Officials also began investigating the possibility Dhirubhai had illegally imported machinery to expand production capacity without necessary authorization. On another front, the finance ministry investigated his financial transactions, including borrowing from nationalized banks to improperly bid up the share prices of his companies.[30]

In August 1986, *India Today* carried a cover story with the title "Reliance Under Siege, Future Seems Peppered with Questions." The magazine noted that the "corporate juggernaut" was not just India's third-largest company but had also seemed set "to emerge on the world stage" with a place on the Fortune 500. Suddenly, that future was in doubt. While the previous government had dispensed Reliance "all manner of favours," the new government appeared almost "eager to delve into Reliance's cupboards in search of old and new skeletons." The magazine also highlighted an inquiry conducted by the Reserve Bank of India which suggested that, in May 1985, Dhirubhai had falsely claimed that he was contractually obligated to import the feedstock whose import the government had just banned. At least one letter of credit, the one from the government-owned Canara Bank, had been backdated to help Dhirubhai claim that he had tied up his imports before the government imposed the import ban.[31]

Dhirubhai was an ambitious businessman who was building a sprawling industrial empire. To achieve that goal, he had masterfully manipulated the system of import controls and industrial licenses in his favor. Now, that system had turned against him. The profitability and stock price of Reliance Industries slumped.

In parallel with his mission against Dhirubhai, Singh began to rein in tax evasion. The Indian press applauded Singh for his "tax raids." But Singh had crossed some mysterious line. Business executives, who had praised him earlier for tax cuts and easing up on regulations, began to grumble. One executive said, "Tax evasion is a universal problem. Everybody does it. Why single out the businessman?" Executives and owners complained to Rajiv that they were being given a "kangaroo court trial through the press."[32]

Singh, however, kept going. In 1985–1986, tax officials raided over six thousand businesses and homes, unearthing large sums of ill-gotten gains. As *The Economist* put it, Indian businessmen had "never been treated so roughly." In September 1986, the tax police arrested well-known industrialist Lalit Mohan Thapar and forced him to apologize for his "financial misdeeds." At this point, Rajiv asked Singh to back off. And when Singh refused to do so, he became a "marked man." In January 1987, Rajiv removed Singh from his position as finance minister and appointed him minister of defense. The official justification for the move was the need for a strong defense minister to deal with threatening maneuvers by the

Pakistan Army. In the public eye Rajiv had abandoned his Mr. Clean mission.[33]

Reliance was soon back in favor with Rajiv's government. In May 1987, the new minister of finance, Narayan Dutt Tiwari, announced changes in import duties that helped boost profitability of the Reliance companies. Tiwari allotted more foreign exchange to Reliance for import of equipment and retrospectively authorized the company's production capacity that was in excess of the originally permitted level. In celebration of renewed tax and regulatory favors, in November 1988 Dhirubhai purchased a new home, a seventeen-story building called "Sea Wind" on the plush Cuffe Parade in Bombay's Colaba district. A gym occupied its own floor, as did a swimming pool, with another set of floors reserved for parking and apartments for guests. In 1989, as Dhirubhai pursued ever grander ambitions, the various criminal investigations against him faded. Newspapers speculated that he would bankroll Rajiv's reelection campaign at the end of the year. The *Financial Times* described Dhirubhai as Rajiv's most important industrial supporter.[34]

Rajiv had returned to the familiarity of the old ways of doing things, taking his mother's place in the relationship she had with Dhirubhai. India remained firmly in its Catch-22 of broken norms and deficient accountability.

To describe the nature of Indian corruption, the anthropologist Veena Das retells a story written in 1907 by Munshi Premchand, one of the great Hindi and Urdu storytellers of the twentieth century. The story, "The Salt Inspector" (*Namak ka Daroga*), is the tale of a young man who, as salt inspector, certifies the payment of a tax levied on salt. An inspector could earn a large supplemental income by accepting bribes in return for reducing or waiving the tax. One evening, when the young inspector spots a powerful local *zamindar* hauling away salt from a salt mine, he refuses a bribe to look the other way. Instead, that early Mr. Clean arrests the *zamindar*. The next morning, the court releases the *zamindar* and reprimands the inspector for harassing innocent citizens. Going a step further, the inspector's bosses dismiss him from his job. Some days later, the *zamindar* appears at the doorstep of the despondent former inspector and offers him a job in his business. As Das remarks in her summary, "The virtue of [the former inspector's] honesty" would now serve a master "known for smuggling salt and buying up policemen and witnesses."[35]

The salt inspector metaphor does not have an exact parallel in Rajiv Gandhi's transformation. However, the message is clear: in a system infused by corruption, remaining Mr. Clean is extraordinarily challenging.

In his new position as defense minister, V. P. Singh added to Rajiv's woes. Singh had the honorable goal of cleaning up the corruption in the Indian government's arms purchases. That pursuit led him to probe into a large commission paid by a foreign arms supplier to bag an Indian defense contract. In April 1987, less than three months after Singh had become defense minister, Rajiv forced his resignation. A popular perception formed: Singh had to go because he pointed his finger at Rajiv or his friends for taking kickbacks from the Swedish arms manufacturer Bofors when it sold a field gun to India. Although there was no substantial evidence behind the accusation, the pall of corruption fell over Rajiv. The word *Bofors* entered the Hindi vocabulary to mean "rotten, broken, dirty." Rajiv the hunter had become the hunted. The Mr. Clean image transferred from him to V. P. Singh.[36]

Rajiv also fell short in his quest to resolve political conflicts simmering in Punjab and in northeastern India. In July 1985, just six months after he became prime minister, he used his outsider status and conciliatory approach to strike a deal with Sikh leader Harchand Singh Longowal. Under the agreement, Punjab would not have to share the capital city Chandigarh with the neighboring Haryana state and instead would have the entire city for itself starting the next Republic Day, January 26, 1986. In compensation, a commission would identify territory to transfer from Punjab to Haryana. Another commission would determine a fair transfer of the waters of Punjab's rivers to other states. To give political legitimacy to the deal, Rajiv called for elections to the Punjab state assembly in September. It was a worthy effort to diffuse Sikh extremism, which had claimed his mother as a victim. But the promised commissions and formulas did not pacify the extremists. On August 20, less than a month after the accord, Sikh terrorists assassinated Longowal while he was campaigning for the upcoming elections. Rajiv's effort to bring compromise and peace to Punjab effectively ended there.[37]

Punjab's economic problems continued to fuel extremists. The future appeared bleak to many young Punjabi men. They were typically children of marginal farmers whose land had undergone repeated division over generations. For them, agriculture was a dead end. Poor-quality education and the lack of urban jobs left them with few good options. Violence gave them a mistaken sense of purpose. The flower of Punjab was dying, Barbara Crossette of the *New York Times* wrote in a poignant essay in 1988.[38]

After Longowal's assassination, the newly elected Punjab government was unable to stem the rising tide of terrorism. The violence killed about six hundred people in 1986. When another three hundred had died through the end of May in 1987, Rajiv dismissed the elected Punjab government and imposed central rule. He sent five thousand paramilitary policemen to keep the peace in Punjab. Rajiv ultimately did not transfer Chandigarh to Punjab as he had promised. The official reason for this failure was the inability to reach an acceptable agreement on the land that Punjab would transfer to Haryana. But Rajiv also worried he would lose Hindu votes in Haryana if the Chandigarh transfer to Punjab went through.[39]

Forty years after independence, some of India's most severe problems—weak competitive ability of domestic industry, black money and corruption, and the demands of Punjab's extremists—seemed insoluble. Rajiv learned that same lesson in the state of Assam, where, in the second half of 1985, he tried but failed to resolve a longstanding conflict between the local Assamese and Muslim immigrants from Bangladesh. Only in the state of Mizoram, where the problem was less complex, did he manage, in June 1986, to successfully end years of separatist violence.[40]

The most diabolic of India's long-standing problems was simmering. Rajiv realized that he stood no chance of creating harmony between the Hindu and Muslim communities, who were divided by a vicious fault line. So, in this case, he tried to manipulate the divisions to his electoral advantage. He was quickly in over his head.

Chapter 16

RAJIV UNLEASHES THE GALE FORCE OF HINDU NATIONALISM

As prime minister, Rajiv inherited a fragile democracy. Even a slight disruption of that delicate state could trigger dire consequences. An effective democracy not only preserves personal freedoms, it is also essential for economic policies tethered to the general welfare. Indian democracy was fraying despite regular elections that gave voters an opportunity to throw out poorly performing governments. National and state-level politicians gained power through personal charisma, financial firepower of wealthy backers, or ideologically loyal voters. And after gaining power, the politicians worked primarily to enhance their own financial and ideological agendas rather than help improve the economic welfare of voters. Rajiv became prime minister on the threshold of a surge in Hindutva—Hindu nationalism—an authoritarian ideology animated principally by the goal of achieving Hindu supremacy.

The unraveling of Indian democracy had begun gently under Rajiv's grandfather, Jawaharlal Nehru. Deep economic anxiety born of agricultural distress, scarce urban jobs, and unending inflation triggered frequent violent social protests. Public corruption was widespread. But under Nehru, democratic institutions such as the parliament and judicial system remained largely intact. Under Rajiv's mother, Indira Gandhi, the economic anxiety and social protests grew. She greatly amplified the corruption in Indian society and politics, and she began depending on goons and criminals for holding on to electoral power. To pursue her quest for power, she gravely damaged the norms and institutions of democracy.

A recurring feature of Mrs. Gandhi's regime was the erosion of democracy in tandem with the spread of economic anxiety among young Indians. That link first appeared in her handling of the Naxalites in the late 1960s, when she responded to the Naxalite-led peasant uprising and urban guerilla movement with the ruthless use of police force. From that point on, police and armed forces, backed by "preventive detention" laws, became essential to governing the country. The police doled out instant justice by killing protestors and activists, claiming that they had acted in self-defense. Such instances, described as "fake encounters," acquired growing legitimacy among the Indian elite.[1]

In the first half of the 1970s, the "angry young man" movies were as much a window into economic and social anger as they were into the deepening politician-police-criminal nexus. Off the screen, a new wave of protests broke out. Angry students challenged the authority of elected governments in Gujarat and Bihar. Mrs. Gandhi used her coercive powers with increased ferocity, culminating in Emergency rule from June 1975 to March 1977. When she returned as prime minister in 1980, she directed the police and army in the battle against Sikh extremists, whose leader, Sant Jarnail Singh Bhindranwale, himself drew on a pool of young Punjabi men frustrated by inadequate income-earning prospects either as small farmers or as employees in urban manufacturing and services.

Bhindranwale was gone by the time Rajiv Gandhi became prime minister in December 1984, but enduring Sikh extremism still attracted those who felt they had been forgotten by Indian economic policy. When Rajiv's efforts to bring peace in Punjab did not succeed, violence spiraled. Sikh extremists killed Hindu migrants from eastern Indian states working on Punjab's farms in random acts of terror. The police and army soldiers killed Sikh extremists.[2] It was a bloodbath.

While the Emergency era's draconian controls on the press did not come back, Rajiv did attempt to limit press freedom. Police raided the offices of the widely read daily newspaper *Indian Express* after it ran a series of articles accusing Rajiv of corruption. The Editors Guild of India protested that the raids on *Indian Express* were a "deliberate attempt to intimidate one of the country's leading newspapers." Rajiv also introduced a bill in parliament that gave the government greater authority to initiate anti-defamation charges against journalists. The government ultimately withdrew the anti-defamation law, but the press was given a clear message to back off.[3]

In interpreting what came next, the hardest part is identifying what was Rajiv's role as a leader and how much was a continuation of historical trends he could do little about. Rajiv did not have the stature of Nehru or Mrs. Gandhi. Nehru dominated Indian history, towering above his contemporaries, and his policy decisions on agriculture, heavy industry, and education reverberate to this day. Mrs. Gandhi also stood above her contemporaries and shaped Indian history, although her actions were in part a response to the history her father had handed to her. Rajiv was prime minister only because he was his mother's son. He needed to "help mummy," as he once said. Rajiv had little political acumen but believed he could direct historical forces to his political advantage. He played his games at a dangerous crossroad in Indian history.

By the early 1980s the scales had begun to tip in favor of Hindu nationalists. The Nehruvian nationalist ideology, in the exhilarating aftermath of colonial rule, had failed to deliver on its promise of shared prosperity. Mrs. Gandhi's slogans brought, at best, limited improvement in people's lives, and near the end of her years as prime minister in the early 1980s, about 45 percent of Indians lived below the poverty line. Many who were technically above the poverty line (and so not counted as "the poor") worked in low-productivity, poorly paying jobs with no social safety net. They lived precariously, in fear of illness or an unexpected expense that would cause irreparable financial damage. Urban migrants in the elusive search for higher incomes all too often lacked community and social support networks. Without the celebration of newfound freedom from colonial rule or the optimism of economic promise, the consensus of India as a tolerant, secular democracy was fraying. Even those who had done well in the unforgiving economic landscape sought a more belligerent nationalism to reflect their own success. As political philosopher

Hannah Arendt might have said, Indians were experiencing an acute sense of "rootlessness," which was awakening their "tribal consciousness."[4]

Hindutva's appeal and electoral power arose from a dual advantage. Hindus formed about 82 percent of India's population in the early 1980s, holding steady from the figure of 84 percent from 1951. With the high likelihood of continued numerical dominance, a Hindu supermajority could win repeated electoral victories. Additionally, Hindu nationalism was based on a politically powerful rallying cry against the threat of a common enemy. In 1927, Carl Schmitt wrote that the "friend-enemy" distinction represents the "high points of politics." As a Schmitt commentator explains, pointing the finger at the enemy solidifies political cohesion by sharpening "one's own identity" and defining who "we" are.[5] The ruinous political attraction of this friend-enemy distinction made Schmitt himself a Nazi sympathizer.

Because it drew sustenance from social and political division, Hindutva had the potential to become a fearsome totalitarian force, even though it cloaked itself in the garb of democracy. The friend-enemy distinction ruled out "negotiation and compromise," as Schmitt noted. Hannah Arendt, with her focus on economic anxiety and social alienation, warned that "totalitarian solutions" are particularly tempting "whenever it seems impossible to alleviate political, social, or economic misery in a manner worthy of man."[6] The power of India's police state and the inclination of Indian leaders to suppress freedom of expression magnified the risks that came with Hindutva's intolerance.

Rajiv lacked the historical knowledge and the political skill to deal with such powerful tendencies. He naively tried to channel the gale force of Hindu nationalism to his political advantage. Instead, the force sucked him into its vortex.

The Long Reach of Vinayak Damodar Savarkar

In October 1905, Bal Gangadhar Tilak, the brilliant and militant Congress Party freedom fighter, supervised a bonfire of western clothes. In a nod to Hindu ritual symbolism, Tilak directed participants to walk around the fire three times and apply the ash to their foreheads. Those assembled vowed to wear clothes made only of Indian-spun fabric.[7]

The twenty-two-year-old Vinayak Damodar "Veer" Savarkar emerged from that 1905 bonfire as Hindutva's philosopher and messenger. In June 1906, he headed to London to study law on a scholarship, aided by a letter of recommendation from Tilak. He completed his degree requirements but was denied the right to practice law in Britain because he had led a band of anarchist Indian nationalists. In October 1909, Savarkar had a tense meeting with Mohandas Karamchand Gandhi, then a lawyer in South Africa who was visiting London. Gandhi frowned on Savarkar's violence but described him as a *desh bhakt,* one who worshipped his nation. Savarkar, on the fringe of India's freedom movement, was already an admired nationalist.

In July 1911, Savarkar landed in jail for seditious activities, which included plotting assassinations of British officials, circulating bomb-making pamphlets, and supplying pistols to Indian revolutionaries. He was locked up in Cellular Jail in Port Blair on the Andaman and Nicobar Islands, an archipelago in the Bay of Bengal off the coast of Myanmar. At the prison, Savarkar and other inmates were inhumanely tortured. One British politician described the facility as "hell on earth." After Savarkar repeatedly appealed for mercy, British authorities transferred him in May 1921 to a jail in Ratnagiri in the state of Maharashtra. There, he quickly completed a monograph he had worked on in Cellular Jail. His text, *Hindutva,* was published in 1923 and has remained the hallowed guidebook of Hindu nationalism.

For Savarkar, India was a nation of Hindus. Hindus were those who considered India their fatherland (*pitrubhumi*) as well as a holy land (*punyabhumi*). Referencing the four compass points, Savarkar wrote that the fatherland stretched "from Kashmir to Ceylon and from Sindh to Bengal." Hindus in this fatherland shared a "bond of common blood" that ran through a long line of ancestors. The fatherland was also holy in Savarkar's rendering because the mythological Prince of Ayodhya—the revered Indian deity "the brave Ramachandra"—had "knit" the people across this expanse into a "nation." Invocation of Ramachandra was potent because Ram, as he is more popularly known, doubles as an incarnation of the supreme transcendental lord in the Hindu philosophical system and a wise king in Hindu mythology. In his role as the wise king, the mythological Ram knit the geographical Indian space with emotional and cultural threads. That bonding "made the Nayars of Malabar weep over the sufferings of the Brahmins of Kashmir," and Hindus in Bengal empathized with the Tamil poet Kamba but not the Persian poet Hafiz. A convert to Islam or Christianity—although descended from ancestors who had lived in the fatherland—was not a Hindu and, hence, not a true Indian because he did not regard India as holy and worthy of worship.[8]

Savarkar insisted that Hindutva had nothing to do with Hinduism's religious rites and duties. He had given up a personal religious practice at the age of nine when his mother died of cholera.[9] Savarkar's assertion that Hindutva did not equal Hinduism had an ironic truth. Hindutva denigrates other religions, especially Islam and Christianity. In contrast, the philosophical Hinduism of the Upanishads, the texts known as Vedanta, teach the equality of all men and women, for everyone is animated by the same transcendental divinity.

Instead of the unity of philosophical Hinduism, Savarkar described the political arena as divided between friends and enemies even before Carl Schmitt. "The pressure of a foe," Savarkar wrote, "weld(s) peoples into a nation and nations into a state." He proclaimed that Hindus who were united at home would be strong abroad. They could "dictate their terms to the whole world."[10]

Hindutva ideology spread quickly. Keshav Baliram Hedgewar read an early hand-transcribed copy of *Hindutva*. Hedgewar was a medical doctor, an avid reader of Tilak's nationalist writings, a militant nationalist, and a member of the Congress Party. Thrilled by *Hindutva*'s message, he traveled from Nagpur in March 1925 to meet Savarkar in Ratnagiri. In September that year, on the day of the Dussehra festival celebrating the mythological victory of Lord Ram over the demon king Ravan, Hedgewar launched the Rashtriya Swayamsevak Sangh. The RSS recruited young men, often from gymnasiums. The expectation was that young recruits, equipped with training in Hindutva ideology and martial skills, would "give their uncompromising support and obedience."[11]

Twenty years after Tilak's 1905 bonfire, a Hindutva coalition was in place. Savarkar was the ideological hub, and Hedgewar was the organizer.

Despite their remarkable success as a social and cultural movement, Hindutva forces could not gain a foothold in politics. Gandhi was India's dominating leader in the fight for freedom from the British. Unlike Hindutva protagonists, who advocated violent means and promoted division between friend and foe, Gandhi—drawing on his profound reading of Hindu scriptures—preached nonviolent protest and respect for other religious beliefs.

But Gandhi could not erase Hindutva. Champions of the Hindutva cause often worked within (and with) the Congress Party. Hedgewar, for example, stayed in the Congress Party until the late 1920s, even as he built the RSS. In 1931, Hedgewar took a leave of absence from the RSS to join a Congress Party–led civil disobedience movement against the British. Until 1937, senior Congress Party members also often belonged to a less militant Hindu body, the Hindu Mahasabha. And when the formal Congress Party–Hindu Mahasabha connection ceased, the earlier leaders of the Mahasabha continued to hold important positions in the Congress Party. The RSS kept a low political profile to avoid scrutiny by British authorities, but its militant (and often militaristic) education and "character-building" activities continued. RSS membership grew steadily.[12]

On January 30, 1948, just over five months after independence, Nathuram Godse, an ideological protégé of Savarkar and a former member of the RSS, approached Gandhi as he was walking to a prayer meeting. Godse greeted Gandhi with the traditional folded-hands *namaste* gesture and then shot him dead. That evening, expressing his own and the nation's anguish and sense of void, Nehru memorably said, "The light has gone out of our lives, and there is darkness everywhere."

Reverence for Gandhi put Hindu nationalism to shame and gave Nehru the space to lead a secular India. The Indian government banned the RSS between February 1948 and July 1949, after which the RSS chose to step away from the spotlight for some years. In October 1951, the Jana Sangh emerged as the political face of Hindu nationalism. This new political party received a steady supply of members and leaders from the growing ranks of the RSS but made little electoral headway in Nehru's shadow.

In February 1966, less than two years after Nehru's death, Savarkar died a largely forgotten man. Indira Gandhi had just become prime minister. While she did not describe Savarkar as a *desh bhakt,* as Mahatma Gandhi had done, Mrs. Gandhi was nevertheless fulsome in her tribute. "Mr. Savarkar's name," she said, "has been a byword for daring and patriotism." She added: "He was cast in the mold of a classic revolutionary, and countless people drew inspiration from him. His death removes from our midst a great figure of contemporary India."[13]

The obituary in *The Times* of London carried a shrewd prediction. That newspaper, which had tracked Savarkar's anarchism in London with obsessive fascination, well understood the power of the *Hindutva* ideology. *The Times* noted that beneath "the influence of Gandhi and Nehru" and "beneath the dominance of the Congress Party," a deep-seated strain persisted "in which Indian nationalism was felt and expressed as Hindu nationalism." It went on to say that this strain of nationalism "may be in resurgence today."[14]

Hindu nationalism reemerged only fitfully. In January 1977, the Jana Sangh merged itself into the motley Janata Party to defeat Mrs. Gandhi in the election that was held at the end of her dictatorial Emergency. But Mrs. Gandhi crushed the Janata Party in the January 1980 elections. From that debris emerged, on April 6, 1980, the Bharatiya Janata Party (BJP), the Indian People's Party. The BJP, which drew its membership mainly from the old Jana Sangh, presented itself as a moderate Hindutva party. Atal Bihari Vajpayee, a man known for scribbling Hindi poetry and a longtime member of the uncompromisingly Hindu nationalist RSS, became the party's president. Lal Krishna Advani, the other senior BJP leader, made it clear the BJP would continue its close ties with the RSS.[15]

A critical phase of the Savarkar resurgence began in November 1983, seventy-eight years after Tilak's bonfire and sixty years after the publication of *Hindutva.*

Hindutva Gains Momentum

Hindu nationalists had evolved into a family of organizations, the Sangh Parivar. Of these, the Vishwa Hindu Parishad (Global Hindu Council), took a particularly assertive public posture. On November 16, 1983, the

VHP began processions (*yatras*) to affirm the Savarkar view of India as a geographically sacred Hindu unity. One of the main processions started from the banks of the holy Ganga River in Haridwar (where the Ganga comes down from its Himalayan origin on to the plains). Its goal was to make an awe-inspiring three-thousand-kilometer trip to Kanyakumari at the southern tip of peninsular India. Another major procession began from Gangasagar in the east on a journey to an iconic temple in Somnath in the west. Altogether, one hundred processions would crisscross the country. The major processions would pass through Nagpur, where the RSS had its headquarters. The VHP described the processions as the *Ekatmata yagna*, sacrificial rites to reaffirm that a single Hindu soul animated the Indian holy land.[16]

Two ceremonial "chariots"—decorated motorized vehicles—led each procession. One chariot carried copper urns filled with *Ganga jal* (sacred Ganga water), while the other chariot transported an idol of Bharat Mata (Mother India), a new addition to the pantheon of Hindu divinities. As the chariots journeyed across the country, large crowds showered them with flowers and coins. In Delhi, BJP stalwarts Atal Bihari Vajpayee and L. K. Advani addressed a huge gathering waiting to welcome the chariots into the capital city. In Bombay, when the chariots entered in the early morning hours, the city's mayor stood ready to garland the Bharat Mata idol as priests chanted ancient hymns. The Shiv Sena—the Bombay-based anti–South Indian immigrant party, now turning its vitriol on Muslims—put up a spectacular show in many parts of the city. Throughout the country, fired-up speakers emphasized that Hinduism was in "danger." They rebuked politicians for "pampering" Muslims and "lambasted" Christian missionaries.[17]

In May 1984, VHP leaders created the Bajrang Dal, a militant youth wing of underemployed Hindu men to act as a "strike force."[18] The Bajrang Dal's young recruits had their counterparts in other violent cliques: Shiv Sena cadres since the mid-1960s, the "red-eyed" Hindu men who massacred Sikhs in the days after Mrs. Gandhi's assassination, and Sikh extremists who terrorized Hindus in the 1980s and early 1990s. The Bajrang Dal, however, was India's largest collective that harnessed youth anger in the service of communal hatred and division.

In July 1984, VHP leadership raised the stakes. They established a committee to "liberate" Ram Janmabhoomi, a site located in the city of Ayodhya where Hindu leaders claimed the mythological Lord Ram was born. The site needed "liberation" because on it stood the Babri Masjid, a mosque built by Mughal Emperor Babar in 1528. For decades, Babri Masjid had been a focus of Hindu-Muslim acrimony. In December 1949, idols of Ram and his wife Sita mysteriously appeared inside the mosque. Although an administrative order wisely barricaded the site, Hindu devotees kept slipping through to worship their deities. The matter simmered until a VHP-organized march entered Ayodhya on October 7, 1984. Hindu leaders stood before a giant billboard that showed armed Hindus and Muslims staring ominously at each other. The leaders called on the thousands of assembled Hindutva activists to pledge commitment to "liberating" Ram Janmabhoomi. The prospect of liberating Lord Ram's birthplace electrified Hindus across the country. The matter had "reached a dangerously climatic state," as *India Today* reported.[19]

Savarkar's *Hindutva,* the ideology that described India as the land of citizens tied by ancestral blood and Hindu culture, appealed more in northern states and in Maharashtra than in the south. The financial backing for Hindu nationalists came from urban traders, small industrialists, and middle-level professionals. But the *yatras* and the prospect of a temple for Ram created the enticing possibility of a supermajoritarian Hindu state. This prospect pulled in poor, especially rural, voters while helping build a voter base (or at least electoral alliances) in the south.

On October 31, after two Sikh bodyguards assassinated Mrs. Gandhi, Rajiv Gandhi became prime minister. Suddenly, it was his task to deal with this gathering gale force.

Rajiv, the Modernizer, Accelerates Hindu Nationalism

Rajiv tried to please both Hindus and Muslims in his search for cheap votes. In April 1985, four months into his term as prime minister, the Supreme Court granted a plea by Shah Bano, a seventy-three-year-old Muslim woman, that her former husband pay her alimony beyond the customary three-month period specified under the Muslim *Shariat* law. The court also asked the government to legislate, as the Constitution of India promised, a uniform civil code that applied to all Indians. The modernizer in Rajiv sympathized with the Supreme Court's decision, but protests by Muslim clerics against interference with Muslim law caused him to waver. In December, Rajiv promised Muslim leaders that he would legislatively override the Supreme Court decision. By making that promise, he annoyed women's groups and progressive Muslims, who viewed the *Shariat* law's denial of alimony as retrograde. Rajiv also enraged the Hindus, because they believed he was "appeasing" Muslims to win their votes—which he was.[20]

The next series of events do not have clear fingerprints but seem curiously choreographed. On February 1, 1986, a district judge ordered the long-closed gates to the Babri Masjid property to be reopened. Thirty minutes after the judge's order, a policeman broke the lock on the gate. A camera crew from the state-owned television station Doordarshan was present to telecast the breaking of the lock live to the nation. Hindus across the country cheered. Many believe that Rajiv had sent instructions that there be no impediment to opening the Babri Masjid gate. Others suggest one of his ministers, Arun Nehru, gave the go-ahead. Either way, as a tearful Muslim elder poignantly said, "Today, it appears we have become second-class citizens."[21]

Less than a month later, on February 25, 1986, Rajiv fulfilled his promise to Muslim clerics. He introduced a bill in parliament to overturn the Supreme Court decision that awarded Shah Bano alimony. In May, he used his huge parliamentary majority to turn the bill into a law.[22]

Rajiv also had something for the Hindus. In early 1985, in the flush of his modernizer phase, he had instructed Doordarshan to commission and serially broadcast a production of the *Ramayana,* the beloved mythical tale of Lord Ram that nearly every Hindu mother tells her infant children.[23]

In January 1987, Doordarshan began broadcasting the *Ramayana* serial. It continued every Sunday for seventy-eight episodes, ending in July 1988. Indians were transfixed. All over the country, life came to a standstill during the forty-five-minute *Ramayana* time slot on Sundays. Shops closed down, nurses and doctors took time off from patients, and people scheduled social and cultural engagements for after the episode was over.

Viewers prepared for each episode with *pujas* (religious ceremonies). They even "bathed" and reverentially garlanded television sets.[24]

In 1987, Indians owned just 13 million televisions. Friends and neighbors gathered around television sets in homes and at shopfronts. In villages, hundreds of people assembled around the one available set. On average, about 80 million people (almost 10 percent of the population) watched an episode. By the time the serial ended, almost all Indians had seen multiple episodes.[25]

More so than the *Ekatmata yagna* (the series of processions in late 1983), the *Ramayana* serial fused Savarkar's view of India as the fatherland and holy land of the Hindus. In a tribute Savarkar might have savored, the *Indian Express*'s media correspondent Shailaja Bajpai commented on August 7, 1988, a week after the series ended, "From Kanyakumari to Kashmir, from Gujarat to Gorakhpur, millions have stood, sat and kneeled to watch it." Reflecting on that total absorption, she wondered: "Is there life after Ramayana?" No, she answered, there could be no life after Ramayana. Instead, echoing the void Jawaharlal Nehru sensed when Mahatma Gandhi died, Bajpai wrote: "the light has gone out of our lives and nothing will ever be the same again."

For the seventy-eight weeks that *Ramayana* ran, it presented a martially adept and angry Ram dispensing justice. The VHP projected its partisan view of the serial in its iconography of Ram. The author Pankaj Mishra described the Ram in VHP posters as an "appallingly muscle-bound Rambo in a dhoti." Theater scholar Anuradha Kapur lamented that VHP images showed Ram "far more heavily armed than in any traditional representation." In one image, Ram carried a *dhanush* (a bow), a *trishul* (trident), an axe, and a sword "in the manner of a pre-industrial warrior." In another image, Ram, the angry male crusader, marched across the skies, his dhoti flying, chest bared, his conventionally coiled hair unrolling behind him in the wind. Accompanying those images, every VHP poster pledged to build a temple in Ayodhya. The dismayed Kapur noted that Ram, the omniscient and omnipresent Lord, was everywhere. Pinning him down to Ayodhya made no sense. "Hinduism," she despairingly wrote, "is being reduced to a travesty of itself by its advocates."[26] The

Hindutva movement's heavy reliance on young hypermasculine warriors to achieve its mission only exacerbated this travesty.

In April and May 1987, when the *Ramayana* serial was in its early months, bloody Hindu-Muslim riots broke out in Meerut, a city in western Uttar Pradesh. By most accounts, Muslims provoked the riots. But then the Uttar Pradesh Provincial Armed Constabulary, infected by the Hindutva virus, killed hundreds of Muslims in cold blood.[27]

The fever spread. Bajrang Dal volunteers formed so-called suicide squads (*balidani jathas*), groups of men who professed a willingness to die for the Hindutva cause. In Maharashtra, the Shiv Sena stepped up its anti-Muslim campaign in 1987 and 1988. It rallied supporters around the slogan "Say with pride we are Hindus [*garv se kaho hum Hindu hain*]." Many of the Shiv Sena troops (*Sainiks*) were "educated" in the colleges proliferating in small Maharashtrian towns and cities. Such men with college "degrees," writes anthropologist Thomas Blom Hansen, found "their social mobility blocked by what seemed an impenetrable and complacent political establishment."[28] The Hindutva message appealed to such men.

In June 1989, the BJP concluded it would no longer ride the coattails of the Vishwa Hindu Parishad and Bajrang Dal. At a meeting of the BJP's national leadership at Palampur in Himachal Pradesh, Party President Lal Krishna Advani shepherded the "Ram Janmabhoomi resolution," which made the BJP's support of a Ram temple in Ayodhya official. Ayodhya was now an electoral issue.[29]

Rajiv continued his strategy of appeasing both Muslims and Hindus. In a nod to Muslims, he authorized the Uttar Pradesh government to adopt Urdu as the province's second official language. He approved the Hindutva protagonists' proposal to lay a foundation for the Ram temple on land next to the Masjid. Hindutva supporters around the country "consecrated" bricks (*shilas*) with Ram's name inscribed on them. These bricks traveled to Ayodhya for the foundation stone laying ceremony (the *shilanyas*) on November 9, 1989. No one, other than perhaps Rajiv, was surprised when Hindutva leaders held the foundation stone ceremony not, as they had promised, on the land *next* to the Masjid but on the disputed land itself.[30]

Rajiv began his reelection campaign from Faizabad, on the outskirts of Ayodhya, about six kilometers from the Babri Masjid. He promised he would usher in Ram Rajya, Lord Ram's golden administration. It is not clear if Rajiv understood he was making a fool of himself. He became a laughingstock for promising Ram Rajya. With his prep school and British university education, he mispronounced some Hindi words in his speech and made historically odd references. The Hindutva virus continued to rage: another gruesome Hindu-Muslim riot broke out in mid-November in Bhagalpur in Bihar.[31]

Why would Hindutva supporters vote for the Congress Party when they could have the real thing? Not surprisingly, the Congress Party was routed in the elections held in late November 1989. The BJP did not win a majority but did make a dramatic advance from two parliamentary seats in 1984 to eighty-five seats in 1989.

History had forced Rajiv to face two of India's most ferocious antidemocratic forces. He tried to confront and fight back corruption and black money, and he tried to appease Hindutva. Unfortunately for India, history's force overwhelmed him in both instances. Corruption remained entrenched in politics and society. And when he played politics with Hindu-Muslim divisions, Rajiv helped unleash virulent Hindu nationalism, an ideology imbued with the fury of an authoritarian culture but one that now showed itself capable of winning impressive parliamentary victories. Both corruption and Hindutva would continue to eat away at the country's democratic norms.

Of immediate relevance, though, was Rajiv's inability to generate economic dynamism in India. Instead, India was tumbling headlong into a financial crisis he had set in motion.

Chapter 17

AN ALL-TOO-BRIEF MOMENT OF SANITY

Starting in the late 1980s, India was gripped by heightened individualism and a growing disregard of the public interest. This change in India was part of a global movement toward individualism, prompted by the Reagan-era emphasis on economic "liberalization" and private initiative. The bumper sticker for this new era could well have read, "I me mine, I me mine," words penned years earlier by George Harrison of the Beatles.[1]

In society and politics, an increased self-centeredness weakened the sense of social responsibility essential for long-term collective progress. Pankaj Mishra captured India's emerging I-me-mine culture. In Muzaffarnagar, an Uttar Pradesh town that had benefited from the Green Revolution, the lucky ones built expensive "wedding-cake" homes. They also dumped "gigantic mounds of garbage" on the street for others to deal with. This observation pointed Mishra to a broader concern. "Far from fostering any notions of civic responsibility," he wrote, the new wealth "encouraged aggressive individualism."[2] The worry was that, even as some got ahead, the neglect of public goods provision would continue and barriers to widespread prosperity and social welfare would persist.

For most Indians, the barriers were all too evident. At a way station in Udaipur, Rajasthan, Mishra met a farmer's son named Munna Yadav who had dropped out of school after fifth grade. Munna had worked briefly on his father's farm and then as an assistant at a relative's tea shop in Delhi. He was waiting for a truck ride to Ahmedabad in search of a factory job.[3]

In Bihar, especially in the town of Gaya, Mishra writes that he encountered an anarchic Fourth World:

> The facts are too gross, the catalogue of atrocities too long. Medical colleges sell degrees and doctors pull out transfusion tubes from the veins of their patients when they go on strike. Murders and rapists become legislators through large-scale booth capturing. Rich landowners own private planes and Rolls Royces; a landless labourer owns nothing more than a scarf and has forgotten his name.

In this Fourth World, perennial job seeker Uday Prakash Singh failed the gauntlet of national and provincial civil service exams every year. These exams were the lottery tickets to financial security and prestige offered only by government jobs. Government jobs also offered sizable supplemental incomes via petty and sometimes not so petty corruption. Uday Prakash Singh and his friends, also perpetual exam takers, spoke of the allure of the Indian Police Service, which they said was "more powerful" and hence "more profitable" than the prestigious Indian Administrative Service.[4]

Those dream jobs were all but out of reach to most young men, producing yet another socially destructive tendency. Calling it the "tunnel effect," the economist Albert O. Hirschman explained that motorists stuck in a two-lane tunnel feel relieved, at first, when they see cars in the other lane beginning to move. They assume they will be next. But when their lane does not move (or moves only slowly in comparison), they "suspect foul play." That sense of grievance can make them "quite furious and ready to correct manifest injustice."[5]

Indian politicians exploited that simmering fury. Over a hundred people died during the bitter and bloody campaign for the elections held in late November 1989. Hindus battled Muslims, most furiously in Bhagalpur, Bihar, where the death toll continued to mount well after the elections. V. P. Singh's recently cobbled together Janata Dal Party fought a different fight, this one on behalf of "other backward castes" and the peasantry. Criminal gangs carrying AK-47 rifles intimidated and assaulted voters to sway votes for their candidates. Assailants shot at, but missed, Singh. A bullet ripped through the abdomen of V. P. Singh's nephew Sanjay, also a Janata Dal Party candidate. Sanjay recovered slowly from his severe wounds at a British hospital.[6]

Armed gangs also stuffed ballots at polling booths in Rajiv Gandhi's Amethi constituency in Uttar Pradesh, prompting the chief election commissioner to order repolling at several booths. In a dismayed editorial, the *Times of India* wrote that India was "fast on its way to becoming a severely flawed democracy." The editors decried the nation's moral decay, manifest both in the prime minister's unwillingness to control "hoodlums and mafia dons" working on his behalf and in the "staggering" amount of fraudulent ballots at polling booths throughout the country.[7]

A nation so unanchored and divided inevitably produced a fragmented parliament. The Hindutva wave delivered 85 parliamentary seats to the BJP, up from 2 seats in the 1984 elections. Despite its aggressive election tactics, the Congress Party won only 197 seats, down from 415 in 1984. V. P. Singh used parliamentary techniques to squeeze his way to the top. His Janata Dal won 143 seats, and his alliance with four other parties to form the National Front added minimal support. Hence, he sought and gained the tacit support ("outside" support in Indian discourse) of the BJP and Communist parties. With that motley group, representing ideologically polar extremes, and in place only to hold the reins of power, Singh won a vote of confidence on December 2, 1989, to become prime minister of a shaky government.

Aggressive individualism among political leaders was a problem for India because, as political scientist Robert Putnam observed, "the promotion of one's own interest at the expense of others" results in a "relentless zero-sum competition and a repeated failure of compromise." In the United States of the me-me-me era, Putnam explains, lack of agreement on broad social objectives "hobbled" public policy while corruption and crime in politics escalated. Physical infrastructure deteriorated, the regulation of financial markets and natural resource use suffered, and the pace of environmental damage increased. America's education system, perhaps its proudest achievement, began decaying.[8]

The trends in the United States were an ill omen for India. Indian public goods were in a dismal state even before the country transitioned to its "me-me-me" culture. In its 1990 stocktaking, the World Bank repeated its standard warning to India: long-term growth and poverty reduction could only occur when primary education, preventive medicine, and primary health care improved in quality and reached more people. The Indian government spent "far below what is required" on such vital needs, instead frittering away scarce funds on "quick fixes such as debt forgiveness" and wasteful subsidies. The World Bank rang a particularly loud alarm bell on the strikingly poor primary education and health care for women. India's failure to foster gender equality was an egregious black mark on the nation not only because the persisting inequality was reprehensible but also because educated and healthy women had fewer children and brought up better-educated and healthier families.[9]

India's water and air quality were deteriorating rapidly. Many rivers, including the holy Ganga, were "biologically dead," having become swamps of industrial waste, illegal pesticides, and untreated sewage. A special investigation found heavy metal and chemical poisoning along the banks of the Yamuna River outside Delhi. Delhi was the fourth most polluted city in the world, and the city's buses were traveling "in a shroud of their own smoke." By the late 1980s, according to the World Resources Institute, a Washington-based think tank, India had become a top-five producer of greenhouse gases.[10]

India's deplorable lag in human development and increasing environmental damage were generating long-term crises. They would impede economic development for a long time, and the greater the delay in attending to them, the harder they would be to fix. But demanding immediate attention, the me-me-me political culture was pushing the Indian economy to the edge of economic and financial disaster.

At the Cliff's Edge, Staring into an Abyss

Upon coming to power in December 1989, the V. P. Singh government needed to deal with a financial crisis it had inherited from Rajiv Gandhi's administration. Rajiv's tax cuts and subsidies doled out to various interest groups had created a large budget deficit. Increased demand from the budget deficit caused an excess of imports over exports, resulting in a current account deficit of about 3 percent of GDP. Foreign exchange reserves had dramatically fallen and could only pay for two months of imports. The imminent risk was that the reserves would evaporate, in which case foreign lenders would very likely stop lending on the reasonable premise that that India might not be able to repay its debts.[11]

"The coffers of the government are empty," V. P. Singh said to a national television audience soon after his appointment as prime minister. He promised to shrink the budget deficit and rein in inflation. But Singh's planned reduction in the fiscal deficit never happened. In fact, with its quick-fix policies, the new government made matters worse. To placate the farmers' lobby in his party, Singh honored an election pledge to waive loans of less than 10,000 rupees (about $500) owed by farmers and artisans to government-owned banks.[12]

Indians living abroad reduced their remittances to families at home because of the high likelihood of a devaluation of the rupee. By June 1990, foreign exchange reserves had fallen to just seven weeks' worth of imports. Iraqi President Saddam Hussein added to India's woes. Alleging that Kuwaitis were stealing Iraq's oil, on August 2, he sent his troops to occupy Kuwait. An anticipated reduction in Kuwaiti oil supplies and fear that Iraq might invade Saudi Arabia caused prices of crude oil and petroleum products to spike, pushing up India's inflation rate and its import bill.[13]

To regain political momentum, on August 9 Singh announced that he was pulling the Mandal Commission Report out of cold storage. Former prime minister Morarji Desai had established the Mandal Commission in November 1978 to recommend more extensive affirmative action through reservation of central government jobs. But the Commission produced its report in December 1980, well after Desai's Janata Party government had imploded. The next two prime ministers—Mrs. Gandhi and her son Rajiv—shied away from the report, anticipating that any attempt to implement it would provoke violent protests. There were only so many jobs to reserve, and someone would always be left out.

The Mandal Commission Report proposed reserving 27 percent of central government jobs for "other backward castes." The Constitution already mandated reservation of 22.5 percent of the jobs for the two most disadvantaged groups of Indians. The larger of these groups, the scheduled castes—Dalits (oppressed or broken), as they prefer to be called—occupied the lowest rung of the traditional Indian social hierarchy. Scheduled tribes (members of indigenous tribal communities) shared the 22.5 percent quota of constitutionally reserved jobs. Following the Mandal Commission's recommendation, 49.5 percent of central government jobs would be ring-fenced, just under the 50 percent limit set by the Supreme Court.[14]

India needed affirmative action to remedy past inequities. But Singh was acting opportunistically to win political followers. Without a strategy to create better work prospects, expansive reservations were certain to trigger a zero-sum struggle for jobs and deepen caste rivalries. A part of the problem was that "other backward castes" were themselves divided into several sub-castes. The sub-castes that enjoyed greater political clout would benefit more from the reserved slots, and, hence, inequities would persist. The economically weak among those excluded from reservations were particularly likely to be alarmed and angered.[15]

In mid-September, a little over a month after Singh announced the new reservations, Rajiv Goswami, the twenty-year-old son of a postal worker, attempted to burn himself to death. As a Brahmin and hence a member of a "forward" caste, his prospects had suddenly shrunk. Goswami survived but over the next two months, of the 153 who attempted self-immolation, 63 died. In Bihar, students torched a railway station, which had the effect of holding up rail traffic and disrupting lives for days. In Andhra Pradesh, students burned buses in protest. Around the country, students organized general strikes. Violent caste wars broke out in northern and western India.[16]

For the BJP, a crucial ally of the V. P. Singh government, the reservation policy and the caste wars that followed created a dual fear. The support of backward castes would strengthen Singh politically, and continued fissure among the castes would undermine the narrative of unified Hindutva.

Responding to those fears, the BJP and other Hindutva organizations intensified their demand that the Babri Masjid in the holy city of Ayodhya be torn down and a temple to Lord Ram be erected in its place. On September 25, BJP President Lal Krishna Advani began a *rath yatra* (chariot procession) starting from the temple town of Somnath in western India. The chariot, which was a dressed-up Toyota truck, would travel 10,000 kilometers across the country to Ayodhya. The Bajrang Dal, the youth cadre of Hindu nationalists, would escort the procession armed with *trishuls* (tridents).[17]

On September 30, a major Hindu-Muslim riot broke out along the path of the *rath yatra* in the Gonda district of Uttar Pradesh. Officially, forty people died, although unofficial counts placed the toll at well over one hundred people. Rioting broke out in several towns in Karnataka on October 2 and in Udaipur, Rajasthan, on October 3.[18]

On October 4, 1990, the New York–based rating agency Moody's downgraded India's credit rating by two notches, from A2 (a low-risk category) to BAA1 (warning investors of risks ahead). In its "exceptionally tough" statement, Moody's noted that the Indian government did not have the capacity to reduce its deficit and debt. Social rifts and Hindu nationalism were making a difficult economic situation worse, the agency added.[19]

The V. P. Singh government was on its last legs. Bihar chief minister Lalu Prasad Yadav, presumably acting on Singh's request, arrested Advani as he passed through Bihar in the early morning hours of October 24. However, BJP supporters marched on to Ayodhya. Amid the continuing bloodshed, the BJP leadership pulled its support of the Singh government. On November 7, 1990, at the parliamentary vote of confidence, an angry and bitter Singh asked parliamentarians, "What kind of country do you want? I am placing a mirror before you so that everyone can look himself in the face." The legislators refused to be shamed. Many of Singh's fellow party members voted against him, allegedly paid hundreds of thousands of dollars to do so by his colleague, the self-proclaimed socialist Chandra Shekhar. To become prime minister, Shekhar—with only 58 backers in a parliament of 543 members—sought and received tacit ("outside") support from Rajiv Gandhi, who led the 197-member Congress Party parliamentary contingent. Shekhar was sworn in as prime minister on November 10.[20]

Partly as a consequence of Iraq's invasion of Kuwait earlier in the year, the world economy slowed down rapidly and global inflation spiked.

Sluggish Indian exports reduced domestic GDP growth. India's already-high inflation rate crept up. Meanwhile, after the Moody's credit downgrade in October, India had lost virtually all access to private international funds to finance its current account deficit and service its debt. By December 1990, Indian foreign exchange reserves were down to a little under one month of exports. On December 28, 1990, Finance Minister Yashwant Sinha wrote to the IMF asking for a loan of about $1.8 billion. In early January 1991, the IMF approved the loan.[21]

India urgently needed more external financing, but to receive any more money, the government needed to demonstrate that it was committed to reducing its budget deficit. On February 20, 1991, Rajiv Gandhi, who—with his 197 Congress Party MPs—was crucial to the Shekhar government's survival, forced a delay in the passage of a budget. Without a new budget, the Indian government had no ability to commit to anything. As the *Financial Times* India correspondent David Housego summed up, the "twin blights of political paralysis and economic crisis" tormented India. Bajaj Auto, India's largest scooter manufacturer and bellwether of the engineering industry, had laid off 3,500 workers. With the economy hanging on by a thread, in early March 1991, the four-month-old government collapsed, and Shekhar resigned from office.[22]

Midway through the new election cycle, at a campaign stop in Tamil Nadu on May 21, 1991, a young woman approached Rajiv Gandhi, touched his feet in the Indian gesture of respect, and then detonated a belt of explosives, killing herself along with the forty-six-year-old Rajiv and fourteen others. The suicide bomber represented a Sri Lankan Tamil guerilla group. The group was aggrieved because when he was prime minister, Rajiv had "aggressively sought to crush" the Tamil rebels as they battled the Sinhalese. In the disarray that followed Rajiv's assassination, the Congress Party hurriedly appointed his forty-four-year-old Turin-born widow Sonia as party president, hoping to tug at the country's heartstrings. She declined to be sucked into the mess.[23]

The BJP—helped by its focus on a temple honoring Ram's birth—won 120 Lok Sabha seats in the 1991 elections, up from 85 in 1989. The Congress Party also improved its position to 232 seats, helped by an electorate expressing sympathy for Rajiv's shocking death. Although the Congress Party was short of an absolute majority, its new leader, the sixty-nine-year-old P. V. Narasimha Rao, became India's new prime minister on June 21, 1991.

Foreign exchange reserves were down to three weeks of imports. Remittances from Indians abroad had dried up. India was in a foreign exchange crunch, just as in 1957. Staring once again down the barrel of financial disaster, the government relied as before on severe import restrictions to prevent the further outflow of foreign exchange and international bankruptcy.[24]

The Promise of Rupee Devaluation

Narasimha Rao appointed Manmohan Singh, an Oxford-trained economist and a veteran civil servant, as his finance minister. On July 1, ten days after the new government had taken over, Singh announced a 9 percent devaluation of the rupee, from 21 to 23 rupees for a dollar. The desperately needed devaluation would allow Indian exporters to either charge lower dollar prices to sell more of their products abroad or earn larger rupee-denominated profits on their foreign sales. A devalued rupee would also make imports costlier in rupees. Increased exports and reduced imports would ease the pressure on India's international payments deficit. But, as Montek Singh Ahluwalia writes in his memoirs, a 9 percent devaluation "seemed too little" to him. He was right. The last time India officially devalued was almost exactly twenty-five years earlier, in June 1966. That devaluation was definitely too little, as I argued in chapter 9. Since 1966, India had devalued without public announcement, at first through tying the rupee to the pound sterling, which was weakening against the dollar, and then by tying the rupee to a basket of currencies. But as I. G. Patel, the former senior civil servant and governor of the Reserve Bank, noted in his memoirs, such "stratagems" were wholly inadequate to compensate for India's much larger increase in costs of production relative to costs in competing nations.[25] Another inadequate devaluation would have defeated its purpose. And so it almost did.

Narasimha Rao tried to hold back further devaluation. In India's muddled policy thinking, devaluation was associated with a loss of national honor. East Asian nations had actively used devaluation to make their exports more attractive, and they had educated their people to ensure delivery of exports that met international standards.[26] India had tied its hands on both counts.

Fortunately for India, the devaluation train had left the station. Manmohan Singh had instructed the Reserve Bank to devalue again on July 3, which the Reserve Bank did before Narasimha Rao could stop them. The new rate was approximately 26 rupees for one dollar. It had been a close call, but together, the two-step devaluation reduced the value of the rupee by about 19 percent. India had a cheaper, more reasonably valued rupee, one that better reflected the country's severe shortage of foreign exchange.[27] Although they had devalued hesitatingly, the country's leaders had displayed a collective moment of sanity and pulled back from the abyss.

The cheaper rupee did the work of export subsidies and import controls. On July 3, Manmohan Singh announced that he was largely eliminating export subsidies at midnight. On July 4, the commerce minister announced that he was removing most import controls. India had waited thirty-four yeas since the import controls had gone up in 1957 to conserve foreign exchange. Those controls had grown into the hydra-headed license-permit raj, which (as I described in chapters 4 and 5) had the impressive combination of simultaneously damaging the economy, benefiting the rich and powerful, and persisting in the name of socialism. The public chorus for dismantling this "fake socialism" had grown louder over the years, and there were few mourners when it began to topple like a house of cards.[28]

However, the foreign exchange shortage was still desperate. The government transported 25 tons of gold to London, pledging it to the Bank of England in exchange for a loan of $200 million. As with the devaluation, the notion that India needed to pawn its gold sent howls of horror throughout the country. Defending the transaction that had been set in motion by the Shekhar government, Manmohan Singh explained that the alternative was a disastrous default on payments to foreign creditors. A similar transaction was in the works with the Bank of Japan. Also, the Shekhar government had pledged twenty tons of gold to a Swiss bank for another $200 million. These ongoing gold-based transactions, however, were not enough to satisfy India's foreign exchange needs. Hence, an IMF team visited India to discuss the policy actions that would fulfil the conditions for a large IMF loan.[29]

After a tussle within the Congress Party, on July 24, 1991, parliament approved a new industrial policy. The policy abolished industrial licensing for all except eighteen industries. It limited public monopolies to eight sectors, reduced anti-monopoly restrictions, and permitted foreign companies to own 51 percent of an Indian enterprise, up from the earlier 40 percent limit.[30]

Later that afternoon, Manmohan Singh presented the budget. He reminded parliament that the government had accumulated a pile of debt to finance its deficit. Just the interest payment on the debt equaled 4 percent of GDP, which was 20 percent of the government's tax revenues. Foreign exchange reserves could pay for only a fortnight—that's right, two weeks—of imports. India's economic crisis, Singh said, was "acute" and "deep." He promised a "significant reduction" of the budget deficit, which he noted would also reduce the external payments deficit. After summarizing the government's industrial and trade policy changes, Singh ended with a flourish. Paraphrasing the author Victor Hugo, he said India as "a major economic power" was an idea whose time had come. "Let the whole world hear it loud and clear," he proclaimed, "India is now wide awake."[31]

In early October, the IMF made a loan of SDR 1.656 billion ($2.26 billion). With its liberalization package of devaluation alongside reduction of export subsidies, import controls, and industrial licensing requirements, India had taken the minimal steps to promote a market economy. Human and urban development, the essential underpinnings of long-term growth, were not even under discussion. India's market regulatory framework, especially for the financial sector and natural resources, was still rudimentary. Yet, the steps taken in July 1991 were an important beginning. Manmohan Singh, the blue-turban-wearing Sikh, was a celebrity. Several months later, as Pankaj Mishra continued his travels through India, he met a Mr. Rastogi, a train companion on a business trip, who sagely said, "I feel what Manmohan Singh is doing is good."[32]

Scam Season Begins

Manmohan Singh and his cabinet colleagues had undertaken economic liberalization measures to spur manufacturing growth. But the early action occurred in the financial sector. Over the course of seven months, from Singh's first budget on July 24, 1991, to his next one on February 28, 1992, the Sensex (the Indian stock price index) nearly doubled to 2800. The index continued to gallop higher after the second budget. The stock market frenzy was a puzzle, though. Analysts anticipated a bad monsoon and negative industrial growth. Some commentators wondered if Singh's exemption of taxes on capital gains earned on stocks and bonds was bringing a flood of money into the stock market.[33]

The events that followed are today viewed as a curiosity. In fact, they were an early demonstration of the lure of quick riches in a poorly regulated economy. They foreshadowed repeated regulatory failures in an economy heavily reliant on the financial sector for achieving high GDP growth rates, ballooning income and wealth inequalities, and veneration of the super-rich.

As the market frenzy continued, a bank executive grumbled: "Every time my phone rings, I shudder. It's my aunt. She's calling for her stock tips." The aunt knew something. In the two months following Singh's second budget, the stock index rose by about 60 percent, reaching nearly 4,500 on April 23, 1992.[34]

On April 23, *The Times of India*'s morning edition ran a story by Sucheta Dalal and R. Srinivasan reporting that the State Bank of India (SBI), the country's largest bank by far, had loaned 500 crores of rupees (about $175 million) "without due procedure and possibly without collateral" to a "big bull," who had been making "huge transactions in stock markets." The news that the big bull might now be in trouble sent the market in a tailspin. From its peak of about 4500 in late April, the Sensex fell to 3000 around early June and closed the year near 2500.[35]

The unnamed big bull in the Dalal-Srinivasan story was Harshad Mehta. The Harshad Mehta scam, as it came to be known, had its roots in the inefficient, almost entirely government-owned banking sector. Most of the banks made large losses every year, and even the more successful ones eked out small profits. Besides being poorly run, the banks were under the continuous pressure of politicians to "waive" their loans to farmers and small businesses. At the end of each such cycle, the government used its scarce budgetary resources to top up the banks' capital.[36]

Facing another profit squeeze in the early 1990s, the banks discovered that they could boost profits by trading financial securities with other banks in the interbank market. In a typical transaction, Harshad Mehta offered to buy securities for SBI, for which SBI wrote him checks. But Mehta did not always deliver (or, he took his time to deliver) the securities he claimed he had "bought." He used the free money he had received to bid up the stock market. All the banks were complicit. Some "lent" Mehta money "without due procedure," while others cashed his checks for him. When everything was added up, the free lending to Harshad Mehta and other speculators ran to the hundreds of millions of dollars. With these large sums, Mehta—the biggest of the many speculators—was an oracle. He would predict an increase in a stock's price, and it would magically rise. Mehta wanted to be, and was on his way to becoming, India's richest man. He splurged his market gains on a seafront 15,000-square-foot apartment and a fleet of cars. He was the symbol of India's "aggressive individualism," now under the cover of economic liberalization.[37]

Not surprisingly, another of Pankaj Mishra's traveling acquaintances, a Mr. Goenka, celebrated Harshad Mehta. "People consider Harshad Mehta corrupt," Mr. Goenka said. "Why is he corrupt? Because he made a lot of money? *I* think he is a genius. *I* say even if he is corrupt, he is inspiring young people."[38]

Two official inquiries absolved the financial regulator, the Reserve Bank of India, of all blame, concluding benignly that the RBI's archaic manual transactions-recording system handicapped its ability to track the "missing" money in the fast-paced interbank securities market. Both inquiry reports blamed bankers for "massive" collusion with Mehta and they blamed "brokers" like Mehta.[39]

Sadly, in the rush to absolve the RBI, its regulatory failure went unrecognized. A former RBI official noted in the *Economic Times* that a publicly revealed internal Reserve Bank memo made it clear that the RBI knew of the ongoing scam but held back from doing anything about it for nine months while the stock prices reached giddy heights. The

RBI's self-commissioned history underscored that the RBI did not follow through on compliance with directives issued to banks regarding securities transactions.[40]

The Harshad Mehta affair faded from public memory quickly, in part because of renewed vigor in economic policy. On March 1, 1993, nearly thirty years after Milton Friedman had recommended floating the rupee, the government finally did so. It abandoned any public commitment to an official exchange rate and instead allowed the market to set the rupee's value. Floating the rupee was a timely decision. The two-step 19 percent devaluation in July 1991 was already proving insufficient and the black-market rate suggested the rupee was again becoming pricey at the official exchange rate. Continuing with that rate would have slowed export growth, sped up import growth, and brought renewed pressures for import and industrial controls. The floating rupee depreciated, helping Indian exporters lift their global market share, although only to a paltry 0.85 percent. (Figure 17.1).[41] To compete internationally on a sustained basis, Indian exporters would need to raise their productivity significantly.

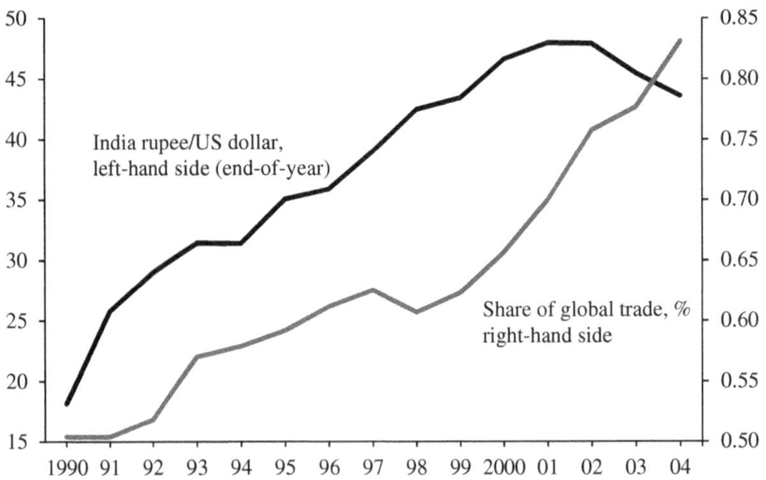

FIGURE 17.1: India gained global market share after the rupee devaluation.
Note: Indian rupee/US dollar exchange rate is the average of daily rates in the last week of December.
Source: UNCTAD Statistics, https://unctadstat.unctad.org/EN/Index.html and Global Financial Data.

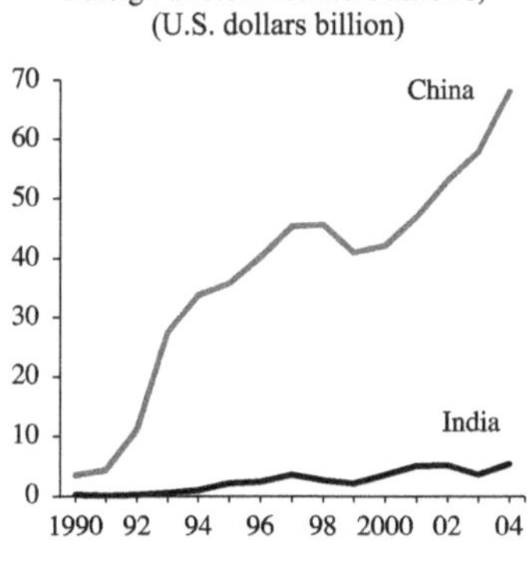

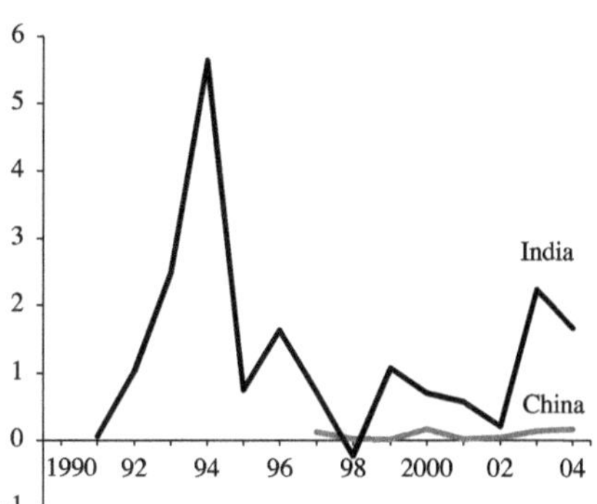

FIGURE 17.2: Foreign investment: China got the factories, India got some cash.
Source: World Bank, World Development Indicators, BX.KLT.DINV.CD.WD and BX.KLT.DINV.CD.WD.

With the rupee floating, India was back from the financial edge into safe territory. Foreign investors saw India in a more favorable light. Coca-Cola returned in October 1993, sixteen years after it had left, having then rejected the Janata government's demand to reveal the secret formula of its concentrate and refusing also to dilute its equity holdings in its Indian subsidiary. Coke reintroduced itself ostentatiously to Indians at a ceremony held at the Taj Mahal, the white-marbled monument to an emperor's love for his queen.[42]

However, most foreign funds came as investments in the Indian stock market rather than as foreign direct investment in production ventures, like Coca-Cola. The contrast with China was striking (Figure 17.2). In 1996, China received $40 billion as foreign direct investment, the type where investors built and ran factories, whereas India received only $2.5 billion of direct investment that year. India, though, received $4 billion in speculative and volatile equity flows while China received negligible such amounts. China was a global manufacturing hub. India was a risky bet.

In May 1994, in the spirit of India-as-a-financial-bet, the U.S. investment bank Morgan Stanley opened an office in India. The rumor was that Naina Lal, one of Morgan Stanley's Indian executives, would receive an annual compensation of one crore (10 million) rupees, about $300,000, which was an unheard-of sum in the Indian context. The average Indian income in 1994 was about $345. While the Harshad Mehta scam had receded in memory as a blip, the euphoria of the Narasimha Rao–Manmohan Singh liberalization continued in the financial sector, amplified by the gush of international capital seeking high returns in "emerging markets." The economic merit of a rapidly expanding financial sector was questionable.[43] As the towering Cambridge University economist Joan Robinson pithily said, finance must follow enterprise. The question for India was: would liberalization unleash enterprise?

The Limits and Dangers of "Me, Me, Me"

The overall assessment of the Rao-Singh reforms, especially of their ability to generate jobs and reduce poverty, must wait until chapter 20. But there were several cautionary messages even in the early days.

Economists who were then evaluating the experience with market reforms elsewhere in the world, notably Harvard University's Dani Rodrik, cautioned that productivity gains from such reforms were short-lived. Market reforms shifted resources to more efficient uses, but once the redirection was complete, the growth impetus ran out. Paul Krugman, a professor of economics at Stanford University at the time, emphasized Rodrik's caution. In 1995, soon after Mexico's spectacular financial crisis, Krugman pointed out that even though that country was the poster child of free market reforms, it was stuck in the limbo of pitifully low growth. Free market reforms were wildly popular, Krugman said, because important people told each other that such reforms were important. He warned that the reforms were likely to widen income and wealth inequalities and generate financial bubbles.[44] In the Indian context, the warning bells of a financial bubble had already sounded, and the widening inequalities quickly became evident (Figure 17.3).

India, having rightfully abandoned its fake socialism of controls on trade and industry, now needed a real social democratic drive to grow. Only a massive government-led investment in human capital and urban development could achieve sustained productivity growth. The World Bank kept trying to persuade Indian authorities that they needed to invest

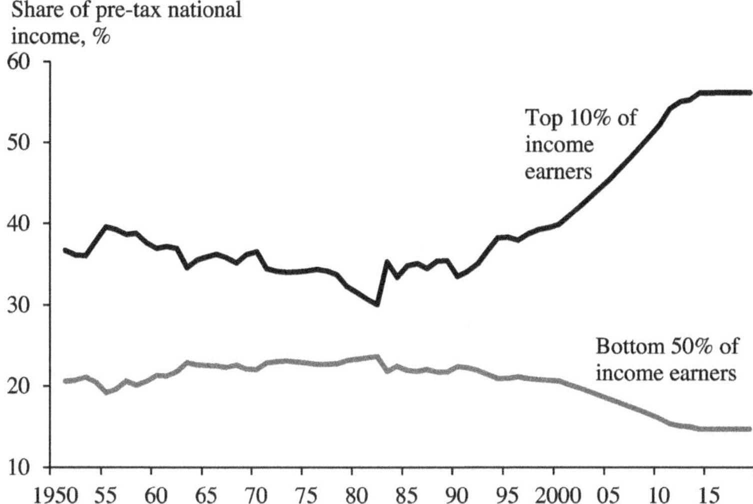

FIGURE 17.3: Income inequality in India ballooned. (Share of pre-tax national income, percent)
Source: World Inequality Database (WID), https://wid.world/country/india/.

vastly more in human capital. In its 1991 survey of India, the Bank said that adapting to "continuous changes underway in the global economy" required "constant improvements in the education and skills of the labor force." It emphasized that "even labor-intensive industries can be more competitive internationally with a better-educated labor force." In 1996, the Bank pointed Indian authorities to the East Asian example: "The benefits of primary education launched the take-off of the fast-growing economies of East Asia." The Bank praised China's "impressive" human development progress.[45] As if to validate the Bank's praise, China was becoming the world's workshop—and India was not.

In its 1996 report, the World Bank also rang the alarm bell on the state of India's cities and towns, which were "facing a crisis of serious proportions stemming from chronic underinvestment in urban areas and consequent shortages of key urban services." Put simply, Indian cities were a mess. As Pankaj Mishra continued on his travels through India, he noted that even glitzy Bangalore, India's Silicon Valley, had all the problems that plagued less glamorous Indian cities: "power and water shortages, lack of proper transport, congestion, pollution." In Shimoga, a Karnataka town of two hundred thousand people, traditional trade in arecanut was still the main business activity. Water shortages were severe. Yet the town's population kept growing, and real estate prices were comparable to those in Bangalore.[46]

India's rapidly deteriorating environment undermined future growth prospects and generated severe social conflicts over the control of land, water, fish, forests, and minerals. The most intense protest movement in the early 1990s opposed the construction of dams on the River Narmada. Villagers and tribals had learned through bitter experience in past instances of construction of dams that they almost never received the promised compensation for the land they lost, and the best new jobs went to outsiders. Equally contentious were industrial projects, which discharged effluents in the water, raised the chlorine content of drinking water, and increased soil salinity, which in turn reduced crop yields. Mining projects caused water pollution, deforestation, and erosion of hillsides. Laws existed to prevent environmental damage and limit the hardship on those who lost homes and livelihoods. But many Indian officials ignored the laws because the beneficiary businesses rewarded them for doing so. Instead, operating from an old playbook, police often brutally repressed protestors on behalf of the beneficiaries. In response to that repression, a new generation of Naxalites—who in their original mission had aided a peasant rebellion in Naxalbari in 1967—now helped mount more armed confrontations.[47]

In following this confrontational path, India's leaders and intellectuals had wedded themselves to the narrowest and most cynical economic growth strategy. It disenfranchised the weakest in society and stole the environmental inheritance of the next generation, all with an elusive promise of trickle-down prosperity. Instead of cooperation, conflict had become the driving force of Indian public policy. The problem was simple. Indians had cast an indelible taint on the word *socialism* by associating it with controls on trade and industry. Ronald Reagan's dictum that "the government is not the solution to our problem, government is the problem" became an Indian mantra. In practice, that meant the government worked for the rich and powerful.

Mirroring the disregard for the public good, politics had become a race to grab power and the riches it brought. As the 1996 elections approached, the Supreme Court denounced the ballooning campaign expenditures, virtually all of which relied on "black" (unaccounted for) funds from business donors. With the license-permit raj gone, the nexus between politicians and big business now centered on access to land, natural resources, and construction contracts. All political parties played the game. Even the BJP engaged in the flashy display of money during the elections, despite its claim of practicing principled and austere political conduct. The new money-spending toys were expensive helicopters to hop from one campaign site to another.[48]

The Rao-Singh reforms had opened up new possibilities for India. In the brief moment of sanity in 1991, a handful of politicians and officials had dismantled corrosive controls. But these steps were not nearly enough. India needed a much broader social democratic agenda. Meanwhile, a dark underbelly in politics and society—fed by Hindutva mobs, criminals in politics, and violence against women—was further stacking the odds against shared prosperity.

Chapter 18
THE PROMISE HAS A DARK UNDERBELLY

In June 1985, a new Indian promise had revealed itself when Texas Instruments announced it was opening a facility in Bangalore. India's fledgling information technology (IT) industry and its professionals got a reputational boost. And in the same way that Texas Instruments connected Bangalore via satellite links to locations abroad, young Indians who were technically adept connected to expanding global opportunities. The July 1991 "liberalization" reforms—rupee devaluation and substantial reduction in the controls on imports and industrial production—created hope of unleashing entrepreneurship across a large spectrum of economic activities. The promise of widespread economic progress appeared closer. To Indian policymakers, the path ahead seemed clear: more liberalization to work the magic of the market.

However, decaying social norms were working against that promise. Trust and cooperation were victims of the rush to personal gratification. A dark Indian underbelly nurtured surging Hindutva, a deepening relationship between criminals and politicians, and a corrosive misogyny. The question in the mid-1990s was whether the recently revealed promise would defeat the forces of darkness. Or would the dark underbelly drag the Indian promise down?

Each of the dark forces was driven by priorities other than the public good. For Hindutva leaders, in the insightful words of anthropologist

Thomas Blom Hansen, the priority was mob-fueled "permanent performance," which celebrated "ritualized violence in public spaces." Criminals were in politics to enrich themselves, not to act in the public interest. Paradoxically, the market-as-magic believers, Hindutva leaders, and criminal-politicians had one feature in common: they all had short policy horizons that encouraged quick fixes rather than the long-term perspectives necessary to create and provide public goods. And new expressions of misogyny, associated with women venturing into new workspaces and the hypermasculinity of Hindutva groups and criminal gangs, added to the violence against women, further undercutting the foundations of human development.[1]

The race was on. And the underbelly was becoming heavier and darker by the day.

"*Yes,* I Am an Angry Hindu"

In 1988, when the Hindu nationalist movement was building steam, the *Organiser*—the weekly publication of the Rashtriya Swayamsevak Sangh, the Hindutva movement's militant arm—carried an assertive essay by a self-styled "Angry Hindu." Yes, he was angry, he said. His temples had been "desecrated," and his gods were "crying." If he were not angry, he wrote, "he would be no man."[2] Hindu nationalist leaders stoked that anger and gave it a focal point: demolish the Babri Masjid, the sixteenth-century mosque built by a Muslim invader, and in its place build a rightful temple to Lord Ram.

The "angry Hindu" sentiment reached a fever pitch in the second half of 1992. The economy had not yet recovered from the financial crisis in 1991. Inflation was running at a relatively high rate around 9 percent a year. The stock market had soured since the Harshad Mehta scam became public in April.[3]

On December 6, 1992, a mass of Hindutva supporters gathered just outside the Babri Masjid. As Edward Gargan of the *New York Times* reported, "A vast carpet of saffron-festooned humanity—wearing the traditional color of Hindu holy men—listened to fiery speeches by Hindu religious and political leaders." In that crowd, one young man, presumably typical of many who had gathered, said, "I will die. There is no reason for me to live if we do not build his temple." Suddenly, around 11:00 a.m., "a wedge of young men charged through a single line of fast-retreating police officials." Once the police stepped back, first a trickle and then dozens of young men scrambled over the barbed wire fences around the mosque's property. They climbed up the sides of the mosque and demolished its three domes with pickaxes. The crowd roared in approval. By early evening, the mosque was reduced to rubble.[4]

Over the years, India's "angry young men" had taken many forms. In the 1970s, they were students protesting their poor educational opportunities and bleak futures, street goons serving ambitious politicians, and moviegoers seeking emotional release from watching vigilante justice on the screen. Two decades later, they were still poorly educated and still had bleak futures. Having given up hope in the conventional mechanisms of progress, they were easy prey for religious zealots, whether Hindu, Muslim, or Sikh. Hours after the Babri Masjid came down, Muslim and Hindu youths targeted each other with grenades in Kanpur, an industrial city 230 kilometers to the west of Ayodhya.[5]

Late-evening television on December 6 endlessly replayed Babri Masjid's demolition to a national audience. In Bombay, fifteen hundred kilometers across the country from Ayodhya, Hindus began celebrating. From the early morning hours of December 7, angry Muslims took to the street. The police, in sympathy with the Hindus, gunned down Muslim protestors. The Shiv Sena's radicalized Hindu cadres and Muslim mobs battled each other. By mid-afternoon, an unending stream of handcarts, cars, and ambulances were depositing the dead and injured on the circular driveway of Bombay's J. J. Hospital.[6]

Bombay was primed to explode. As scholars have found, adverse economic conditions deepen social conflict. In 1992, more than half of Bombay's population lived in "poverty, illiteracy, unemployment and slum-like conditions." After the collapse of the textile workers' strike in 1983, the loss of regular, permanent jobs had increased the numbers of volatile inhabitants. As India's preeminent sociologist M. N. Srinivas explained in his comments to *India Today*, degrading living and working conditions were "the richest soil for communal frenzy to build on." That proposition helped explain the shift in the Shiv Sena's behavior. In the 1960s and 1970s, when lower-middle-class Maharashtrians were competing for clerical and administrative jobs, Shiv Sena leader Bal Thackeray had directed Maharashtrian anger primarily against the better-qualified South Indians. In the 1980s, however, life had become an existential struggle for large numbers of Maharashtrians, some of whom had once had well-paying jobs as textile workers. They now competed for work as casual day laborers. In so doing, they also competed for work in economic activities that had a significant Muslim presence. In addition, job openings in the Middle East had brought prosperity to some Muslim households, making them targets for Hindu envy and hate.[7]

Thackeray poured vitriol on Muslims through his widely read daily newspaper *Saamna* (a Marathi word signifying a confrontational encounter). The newspaper's masthead proclaimed that it was the "only Marathi daily which advocates the cause of fiery, militant Hindutva."[8]

The first wave of Hindu-Muslim violence in Bombay lasted about four days, ending on December 11. Almost immediately though, the Shiv Sena organized *maha artis* (grand prayers) around city neighborhoods to stir up Hindu sentiment. Following days of simmering violence, the second wave of riots began on January 8, 1993. In a predominantly Muslim neighborhood, extremists set fire to an apartment in which a Hindu husband and wife had lived for several decades. The elderly couple perished in the fire. A front-page editorial in *Saamna* proclaimed that "the next few days will be ours." Shiv Sena activists and the Bajrang Dal, the youth wing of the Hindu nationalists, "sought out Muslims and Muslim-owned property for attack." The second wave dragged on until the third week of January. About nine hundred people died in the two waves of rioting, two-thirds of them Muslims.[9]

Fired up by the carnage, Thackeray said he intended to "kick out" India's 110 million Muslims and send them to Pakistan. "There is nothing wrong," he said, "if they are treated as Jews were in Germany."[10]

Bombay's religious fervor and economic anguish mixed explosively with the city's organized crime. Criminal gangs had a long history in Bombay. They began with bootlegging during the years of alcohol prohibition in the 1950s and quickly diversified into smuggling gold, watches, and transistor radios. Eviction of tenants, especially of those who benefited from rent control, was also an early business for organized crime. In the 1980s, criminal gangs entered the lucrative drug trade.[11]

Bombay's crime gangs scaled up their operations dramatically after the textile industry layoffs in 1983. The mass of unemployed workers added to the mob's traditional recruitment pools in the city's poor neighborhoods. At the same time, the land on which the mills stood magnetically attracted criminals. It was prime property that, after a brief correction in the early 1990s, was again experiencing a giddy price increase. The cost per square foot of land in the swanky Nariman Point business district was reportedly higher than anywhere else in the world. Prices were rising at an "absurd" pace elsewhere in the city, too. Responding to the euphoria generated by the Narasimha Rao–Manmohan Singh liberalization, multinational companies were acquiring office space and homes for their executives. Antiquated land regulations restricted the supply to meet this soaring demand for property. For mill owners, sale of their land for office towers and malls opened up the possibility of enormous riches. That pot of honey inevitably sucked in criminals and politicians.[12]

Crime and religion came together on March 12, 1993, a day since known as Black Friday. Bombs exploded in several parts of Bombay, causing vast damage, including to iconic structures such as the Bombay Stock Exchange building. Well over two hundred people died. Mob boss Dawood Ibrahim allegedly masterminded the blasts as retaliation for the massacre of Muslims a few months earlier. Since Dawood himself was hiding from Bombay police in Dubai, his associate in Bombay, the rising mobster Tiger Memon, organized the planting of the deadly explosives. The criminal world had split along the communal lines of "our" criminals and "their" criminals.[13]

By engineering the spectacular Bombay blasts, Dawood Ibrahim and Tiger Memon gave the Muslim community a sense that someone was fighting for them. "God knows that I don't approve of the killing of innocent women and children," a Muslim friend told anthropologist Thomas Blom Hansen, "but after the bomb blasts we could again live with some dignity." Hindus had their own mob bosses for protection. Shiv Sena's Thackeray was never shy about flaunting his gangland connections. He said that Muslims had Dawood, and the Hindus had Amar Naik and Arun Gawli. "These [Naik and Gawli] are *aamchi muley* [our boys]."[14]

Thackeray was not speaking lightly. Shiv Sena had started recruiting criminals early. In the 1985 Bombay municipal elections, Shiv Sena fielded a candidate who was in jail on criminal charges. Despite his charges, the man won the election. Criminals cast a spell on voters. In keeping with their Robin Hood image, criminal-politicians facilitated access to scarce public services and jobs, and they dispensed street justice. For voters, therefore, criminal-politicians were a substitute for a government that did not work. For political parties, criminals were attractive because they came with plentiful funds to contest elections and so had a high likelihood of winning their contests. The criminals themselves saw new profit opportunities and enhanced police protection in a political career. The inevitable followed. In 1990, forty candidates with criminal backgrounds took part in the Bombay municipal elections.[15]

In 1992, the movie *Angaar* (Fire) memorably depicted the influence of criminals in politics, and in October 1993, an official commission caught up with the reality. The commission, headed by the distinguished civil servant N. N. Vohra, drew on intelligence reports from throughout India to confirm the presence of a widespread criminal-politician nexus. The commission concluded that eliminating criminals from politics was nearly impossible because the courts operated at a glacial pace and the criminals enjoyed political support, which helped them beat the raps. In his final remarks, Vohra closed the circle. Tiger Memon and Dawood Ibrahim, he wrote, could not have engineered the Bombay blasts in March 1993 without assistance from those in power. It was official: India's politicians, criminals, and purveyors of religious hate were aiding and abetting each other.[16]

Thugs as Ministers

In the northern state of Uttar Pradesh, BJP leader Kalyan Singh was under criminal investigation for his role in the demolition of Babri Masjid when he was Uttar Pradesh chief minister in December 1992. Despite the investigation, he returned as Uttar Pradesh's chief minister in September 1997. He appointed an outrageously large number of ninety-three ministers to his cabinet. In a state occupying the lowest ranks among Indian states on every economic and social development indicator, each minister received a car, a furnished home, a security detail, and a generous allowance for "out-of-pocket expenses," which together cost the Uttar Pradesh government between 300,000 and 500,000 rupees (about $8,500–$14,000) every month for every minister.[17]

Nineteen of Singh's ninety-three cabinet ministers faced long lists of criminal charges. Among them was Minister for Science and Technology Hari Shankar Tiwari, who had been charged for murder, extortion, and fighting on the streets. "You name it, he was implicated in it," wrote *India Today.* Ganglord Raghuraj Pratap Singh was the minister for programme implementation. His Youth Brigade spread terror through the local community, "targeting and setting ablaze a number of houses belonging to Muslims."[18] Needless to say, a hardened criminal is not an ideal choice to be the minister for science and technology—or to be any minister, for that matter.

Criminals were also well established in the politics of Bihar and Haryana. As journalist Sunil Sethi wrote, while conditions in Uttar Pradesh were beyond redemption, they were "infinitely worse" in the "killing fields of Bihar." Throughout India, criminal-political mafia groups illegally dredged sand from riverbeds and grabbed land in urbanizing areas, thus making huge profits in the ongoing construction boom. Criminal-politicians also came from the traditional hotbeds of crime, especially the extraction of minerals ranging from diamonds to iron ore.[19]

India began its economic liberalization drive exactly when increasing numbers of criminals were merging their business with politics. A diabolical situation developed. Politicians increasingly engaged in criminal activities; they kept public services scarce to maintain their mystique and power; and they gained the favor of voters by providing them access to those scarce public services. With corrupt and criminally charged politicians in key decision-making positions, the neglect of public goods continued. Making matters worse, crime—especially against women—grew in areas that elected criminally charged politicians, further damaging the prospect of shared economic development.[20]

Precisely because shared prosperity was elusive, India could anticipate a continued plentiful supply of criminals. As research studies confirm, entry-level criminal jobs, such as those for lookouts and carriers of illegal merchandise, attract unemployed men (and sometimes women). In Mexico, for example, the numbers of criminals increased in areas that lost their U.S. export markets, and hence their jobs, to Chinese exporters. When such job-loss areas overlapped with the location of drug trade organizations, there was an especially large increase in the criminal population. In Peru, the cultivation of coca exposed children to illegal cocaine production and distribution. Such children tended to pursue criminal careers in adult life.[21] As India liberalized its economy, the prognosis was not good. Without many more jobs in legitimate occupations, crime would draw more young Indians. The pool of criminal-politicians would grow. It was another vicious circle: absence of shared progress, more crime, and continued absence of shared progress.

Criminal-politicians had merged into the fabric of governance, and their presence and role were seldom regarded as worthy of remark. But Hindutva, having put on a spectacular show recently with the demolition of Babri Masjid, was on people's minds. In late March 1993, soon after the Black Friday blasts, Alyque Padamsee, a prominent Bombay public intellectual, predicted that "a dictatorship will be imposed by Hindu radicals." In August that year, as the anniversary of independence approached, veteran journalist and historian Khushwant Singh despaired, "India may retain its secular façade but the spirit within it will be militant Hinduism. The country will no longer be the India we have known for the past 47 years."[22] Hindutva's politics of perpetual performance would further shorten political horizons and strengthen the tendency for quick-fix policymaking.

"No One Killed Jessica"

We now jump ahead in the chronology to 2 a.m. in the morning of April 30, 1999, when the pervasive culture of crime and political arrogance added a new virulence to Indian misogyny. Four male revelers asked for a drink at a Delhi bar. The bartender, Jessica Lal, refused to serve them; the bar had closed for the night, she said. When one of revelers, Manu Sharma, stepped behind the bar to help himself, Jessica tried to shoo him away. Sharma pulled out a gun and fired in the air. He then pointed his gun at Jessica Lal's temple and shot her dead.[23]

Manu Sharma was son of Haryana state politician Venod Sharma, a former liquor contractor who owned hotels and cinema halls. Venod Sharma had been friends with Indira Gandhi, and he had later been a junior minister in the Narasimha Rao government. He was the archetypal Indian politician of the 1990s who operated across the blurred boundary between business and politics. The judge acquitted his son Manu of Jessica Lal's murder because eyewitnesses changed their testimony at the trial. Astounded, the *Times of India* carried the news with the title, "No One Killed Jessica."[24] Eventually, intrepid journalists nabbed Sharma in a sting operation, bringing him to justice.

In Jessica Lal's murder, the many streams of violence in Indian society and politics coalesced in a terrifying manner. Misogyny, hypermasculinity, political power, and brazen criminality all played a role. It was no coincidence that Lal's gruesome killing was at the hands of a man from Haryana, a state with an extremely high preference for sons. It was *also* no coincidence that Manu Sharma's father was a senior politician in Haryana, which had an entrenched criminal-politician network.[25]

In addition to the handicaps arising from criminals in politics and Hindutva, misogyny weighed down the prospects of India's social and economic progress. Women disproportionately suffered from malnutrition and poor healthcare. Abortion of female fetuses was becoming more common as modern techniques made possible the identification of a child's gender while in the mother's womb. "Excess" men struggled to form stable relationships and were drawn to criminal careers. Women who lived in an environment of misogynistic violence often withdrew from the workforce because they feared unsafe neighborhoods and carried psychological scars. Withdrawal of women from the labor force reduced national output and lowered the likelihood of smaller, healthier, and better-educated families.[26]

India's Promise Hangs in Balance

In an important historical instance, economic dynamism overcame corruption and crime in politics. In the United States between 1850 and 1930, mayors and other leaders of large cities mixed corruption, crime, and governance in much the same way that politicians in India did, particularly so from the mid-1980s. The historian Rebecca Menes describes the mix of corruption and crime in American governance in words that could well be used for many parts of India:

> Municipal contracts and franchises were notoriously corrupt, regulations were applied unevenly, and access to rail and water was available only for a price. In most cities, politicians and officials accepted bribes from organized crime, and in some cities, politicians and officials organized the crime themselves—especially gambling, prostitution, and illegal sales of alcohol.

As in India, U.S. politicians had connections to construction companies, which bid for government contracts. Not surprisingly, the contracts were often overpriced.[27]

Despite such rapacious politicians, American cities prospered economically during these decades. They led the world in "the provision of clean water, sewers, paving, education, gas, electricity, public safety, public health, and mass transportation." Migrants from rural America and around the world flocked to U.S. cities for manufacturing jobs.[28]

America had several advantages, which helped inject political accountability even in its worst phases of city governance. Widespread primary education in the second half of the 1800s followed by near-universal secondary education in the early 1900s created a literate population that was receptive to the investigative reporting by an aggressive press. Also, extraordinary technological progress created jobs and optimism about the future. Indeed, America was then the global leader of technological innovation in telecommunications, electricity, drugs, medical technologies, and the internal combustion engine. Education and job opportunities gave people economic options. Especially after the invention of the motor vehicle at the turn of the twentieth century, mobility increased significantly, and people began to move away from city centers to suburbs. City leaders paid attention to the message of the ballot box because they knew people could move to areas with better public services. Also, while city leaders could misuse their financial autonomy for corrupt earnings, they also needed to heed the discipline of the bond market. And, as American businesses rode the era's economic dynamism, they too pushed back against corruption because it impeded their operations. All these factors created momentum for political reform, which steadily diminished corruption and crime in American city governance.[29]

India's economic promise in the 1980s and after could not match America's economic vigor a hundred years earlier. India's promise was also weighed down by a darker and heavier underbelly, which harbored not just corruption and crime but also violent Hindutva and deep-rooted misogyny.

The narrative of a dynamic emerging India—the "India story"—lived on because Indian leaders and Indian and global pundits repeated it often enough. Investment fund managers in Hong Kong, Singapore, and London kept their faith in the Indian market-reform-liberalization story. They bought more stocks of Indian companies for their clients. India's promise, such as it was, applied mainly to a narrow group of its citizens who were living international lifestyles. In November 1993, the Indian government approved an investment proposal by KFC, a subsidiary of PepsiCo Inc., to give Indians a taste of its "finger lickin' good" fried chicken. A British distillery announced a collaboration with an Indian company to introduce Indians to Smirnoff vodka, Malibu coconut rum, and Chelsea gin.[30]

It is unclear if the liberalization reforms imparted momentum to the Indian economy or to the policymaking process. In early 1994, with the reforms in their third year, the IMF noted that the Indian government's budget deficit had not come down. Industrial growth was slow, and inflation continued to rise. In August 1994, a photograph in *The Economist* showed a cycle-rickshaw driver snoozing. The message was unmistakable: India's reform efforts were currently in a siesta. As examples, *The Economist* noted that the Indian government did little to reduce subsidies on water and electricity to rich farmers, made minimal effort to sell highly inefficient public-sector companies, and unreasonably insisted that loss-making private companies continue operations to keep their workers employed. Unlike devaluation and lifting of import and industrial controls, which a handful of officials undertook virtually overnight through executive order, the new range of reforms required something greater and more difficult to achieve: consensus.

The test of whether Hindutva governance could do better came in early 1995. Riding on its fearsome Hindutva stand, the Shiv Sena made extravagant economic promises to voters in Maharashtra. Shiv Sena leaders said they would cap the prices of essential food items, provide 4 million houses to slum dwellers, create 2.7 million jobs, and reduce corruption. In the March 1995 state assembly elections, the Shiv Sena and BJP won a large majority, crushing the heretofore invincible Congress Party. Maharashtra's new Hindu nationalist government made a headline-grabbing change of Bombay's name to "Mumbai" in June 1995. Unfortunately, but unsurprisingly, the new government delivered on virtually none of its housing, employment, and anti-corruption promises. The government did construct flyovers (overpasses) in Bombay and a highway from Bombay to Pune. Construction was a lucrative business for politicians, after all. Prominent Shiv Sena party members became real estate developers. Party leaders displayed their new riches ostentatiously, having left behind their former low-key lifestyles.[31]

The national inflation rate remained high and employment prospects continued to be dire. The organized (modern) business sector added about two hundred thousand jobs every year during the Narasimha Rao prime ministership from 1991 to 1996. However, meeting the needs of the new entrants to the labor force and reducing the backlog of those un- or underemployed required millions of new jobs every year. Aspirants for jobs continued to pile into the unorganized sector, where they worked less than they wanted to, were paid poorly, and had no security net.[32]

India's economic promise was weak, and its heavy dark underbelly was winning. In early January 1996, a major corruption scandal erupted. A mysterious financial broker had been funneling money from businesses to politicians. The scandal implicated 115 politicians from all parties. The taint of corruption spread to Prime Minister Narasimha Rao. Three of his ministers were caught in corrupt deals; two of them had allegedly dirtied their hands in the scam through which Harshad Mehta siphoned spare cash from banks to run up the stock market. A third minister held up imports of sugar, causing sugar prices to rise and enriching sugar producers and mill owners, a powerful and corrupt political lobby. Even those who profited from Narasimha Rao's market reforms were disgusted by the corruption. "Congress is looting the country," said an auto plant worker whose salary had doubled over the Narasimha Rao years.[33]

In the extravagantly financed national elections held in late April and early May 1996, nearly 350 million of the 590 million eligible voters cast a vote. They rejected Narasimha Rao and his government. But while throwing out one set of rascals, the Indian voters brought more criminals into national politics. Forty of the 545 recently elected members of the Lok Sabha faced criminal charges ranging from theft and extortion to rape and murder. Large numbers of politicians with criminal charges entered state legislatures.[34] In the first flush of the "India story," Indians had voted in the group of politicians least likely to provide public goods and decent jobs.

The BJP, professing it had moderated its Hindutva stance, won the largest number of parliamentary seats—161 seats, which was up from 120 in 1991. The BJP had a traveled a long distance to reach this point, and the deal was not yet done. The party's leader Atal Bihari Vajpayee, unable to form a stable government, resigned after thirteen days. A series of unstable coalitions followed.

GDP growth slowed in 1996. Even in the best interpretation, India's economic reforms could give only a limited boost to growth, and the IMF wondered if the growth impetus had already "tapered off." There was some good news, however. McDonald's opened its first beef-less restaurant in the world in Delhi's upscale Vasant Vihar district. The first customer, a Hindu *sadhu* (holy man), passed on the mutton (lamb) burger, the *Maharaja Mac,* and opted for French fries and a soda. The fries needed improvement, he said.[35]

In the run-up to the new election in February 1998, BJP's senior leaders, in a bid to win coalition partners, again insisted that strident Hindutva was in their past. But virtually every one of those leaders restated the party's commitment to build a Ram Temple in Ayodhya. The BJP won 182 seats, briefly allowing Vajpayee to lead a coalition. When that too fell apart, the BJP again campaigned on a "moderation" plank, but the Hindutva family (the *Sangh Parivar*) and BJP leaders kept the Ram Temple and other divisive issues alive. The BJP's not-so-subtle message was that it would honor its commitment to the Hindutva agenda once it was in power on its own. Helped by that delicate balancing act, the BJP won 182 seats again in September-October 1999. This time, the Vajpayee-led Hindu nationalists were in power.[36]

As India stood at the threshold of a new economic promise, increasing numbers of politicians with criminal charges were becoming national legislators. In September 1999, the chief election commissioner of India said that MPs with criminal records had become a "cancer" on Indian democracy. He helplessly added, "Law breakers cannot be made law makers."[37]

Indians had also voted in the BJP, a Hindu nationalist party, to govern the nation. And all of the talk of its moderation was a smokescreen. A rising star in the BJP, Narendra Modi, was clear on this matter. In September 1990, he had coordinated the early phase of the "chariot" procession as it embarked from the Somnath temple in Gujarat on a deadly march eastward to Ayodhya. A *Times of India* reporter remarked, "The BJP's public relations machinery may have succeeded in conveying the impression it is now ready to emerge as a conventional alternative to the Congress." Yet Modi dismissed the notion brusquely. "There is no question of any dilution of our ideology," he said.

Chapter 19

NO, INDIA DOES NOT SHINE

"A lot can happen over a cup of coffee." With that promise of mysterious pleasure, Café Coffee Day opened its first cybercafé on July 11, 1996. It was glamorously located on Bangalore's posh Brigade Road, alongside boutiques selling Western designer labels. Café Coffee Day, or "CCD" as the chic people called it, was a symbol of the new aspirational India. At CCD, young, upwardly mobile Bangalore yuppies, reveling in the glow of the city's IT industry, could buy a cup of coffee and an hour on the internet for 100 rupees ($2.80).[1]

CCD outlets soon dotted the Bangalore landscape and expanded to cities across the country. Competitors rushed in to feed India's "cybernetic indulgences." Cybercafés were "the New Age alternative to the corner tea shop." They were the "cool places to hang out." Most customers were older teenagers and young adults, but "harried mommas" in search of "peace and tranquility" also dropped off their kids "for an hour or two."[2]

East and west were beginning to fuse. In Gurgaon, outside Delhi, where many multinational firms set up Indian headquarters, the U.S.-based chain Baskin-Robbins served mango-flavored ice cream.[3]

India asserted itself as an international power. On May 11, 1998, the new government formed by the BJP-led coalition, the National Democratic

Alliance, conducted nuclear tests. Although wildly popular in India, the tests attracted international criticism and U.S.-led economic sanctions. On May 24, possibly in retaliation to the Indian tests, Pakistan detonated its own nuclear devices. Prime Minister Atal Bihari Vajpayee dismissed those who blamed India for triggering a new arms race. Echoing Indian sentiment, he said that India's tests had "created a sense of pride and self-respect and enhanced the morale of the people."[4]

Starting in May 1999, India and Pakistan—now armed with nuclear weapons—fought a conventional war in Kashmir. In June, U.S. President Bill Clinton intervened in India's favor. He called Pakistan's prime minister, Nawaz Sharif, and "urged" him to pull back the Pakistan Armed Forces. Days later, as Indian troops gained a key Himalayan height in the disputed Kargil area, major world powers—the G8 nations—also asked Pakistan to withdraw its aggressors.[5] India had acquired new international stature.

These were heady days. In August 2001, the coming-of-age movie *Dil Chahta Hai* (The heart desires) expressed the self-confidence of rich Indians. At a college graduation party, one of the movie's protagonists announces that it is time to hunt for jobs. When the party revelers fall into a shocked silence, the protagonist chuckles, "Just kidding, friends." No one in that room has the slightest need to look for a job. Well-heeled parents have sewn up financially secure futures for their children, some of whom will even inherit multinational businesses. These young Indians live the "good life" in "designer spaces." They enjoy themselves in discos and "spotlessly clean" beach resorts.[6] *Dil Chahta Hai* was the acme of youthful self-indulgence, a fantasy for a new generation of Indians.

These were also the years when India's "soft power" grew. Children of Indian migrants to the United States along with growing numbers of new Indian immigrants earned prestigious places in American society. The Indian exports of yoga and meditation responded to America's emerging quest for fitness blended with eastern spiritual practices (Figure 19.1).

For Indian and international elites, the moment of India's promise had arrived. For six years—from March 1998 to May 2004—two BJP-led coalition governments under Prime Minister Atal Bihari Vajpayee governed

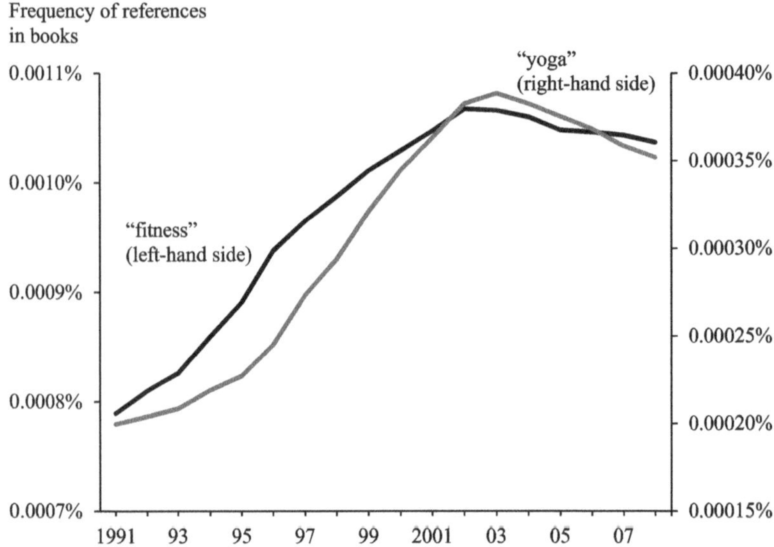

FIGURE 19.1: Yoga rode the global "fitness" wave, boosting India's soft-power image. (The frequency of the words "fitness" and "yoga" in English language books digitized by Google)
Source: Google NGram.

the country. The primary jewel, the IT industry, did shine brightly. But almost everywhere else, the shadows lengthened.

The IT Jewel

In the midst of an IT revolution, U.S. companies were investing rapidly in computers, communications, and software. Mirroring that growth, the NASDAQ Composite index, composed of the world's premier technology stocks, was spiraling up.[7]

To quote Brutus in Shakespeare's *Julius Caesar,* Indian companies took the rising tide "at the flood." India's colleges produced enough good engineering graduates to feed the global demand for software programming. On Thursday, March 11, 1999, Infosys Technologies became the first Indian-registered company to trade on the NASDAQ stock exchange. The NASDAQ Composite was at 2400, more than double the 1100 it was in August 1996. For India, it was a triumphant story. Nagavara Ramarao Narayana Murthy, the fifty-two-year-old founder and chairman of Infosys, was the son of a schoolteacher. He and six co-founders had established the company in 1981 with the princely sum, as legend had it, of $250. The NASDAQ listing placed the value of Infosys at $1.9 billion. Narayana Murthy's personal worth reached $190 million. Infosys chauffeurs and electricians with stock options in the company became millionaires in Indian rupees.[8]

Throughout 1999, the threat of the Year 2000 (Y2K) bug created huge demand for Indian programmers. The threat arose because many older computer hardware and software systems identified years by their last two digits. At the turn of the millennium, the risk was that computers calculating time differences would not distinguish the year 2000 from earlier years ending in *00,* in which case they would severely malfunction. The remedy required examining every computer program for such a threat and changing defective programs on an individual basis. Given, however, that the Y2K problem was timebound, Indian firms were also building a reputation for reliable and timely work delivery that enabled them to bag contracts after the Y2K hump.[9]

Bangalore, the capital of Karnataka state, remained India's leading city in software development. Bangalore's mystique grew as more foreign companies, including Groupe Bull, IBM, Motorola, Siemens, and Sun Microsystems followed Texas Instruments into the city. Bangalore's "lush green parks and tree-lined avenues" were reminders of its receding elegance as its population exploded and infrastructure creaked.[10]

The tech-savvy Andhra Pradesh Chief Minister Chandrababu Naidu bagged the prize of a Microsoft facility for his capital city of Hyderabad, inevitably bestowing on that city the nickname "Cyberabad." Tamil Nadu, an engineering hub, had attracted Ford, Hyundai, and Mitsubishi, and its capital city Chennai was a growing software center. The three southern states of Karnataka, Andhra Pradesh, and Tamil Nadu, along with Delhi and Bombay, accounted for the bulk of India's software production.[11]

World leaders marveled at India's progress and potential. In January 2000, U.S. Treasury Secretary Lawrence Summers visited India, at which time he also traveled to the Infosys headquarters in Bangalore. Invoking a Nehruvian analogy, Summers described the hi-tech Infosys campus as a temple of modern India. Two months later, Summers's boss, President

Bill Clinton, traveled to Hyderabad as part of his India visit. In his address to over a thousand technology officials, Clinton celebrated India's young IT millionaires. These inventive brains, he said, could employ new technologies to upgrade Indian education and healthcare systems. Clinton visualized an education revolution in the country's villages fitted with computers and educational software.[12]

"Call centers" were another IT-related phenomenon of the late 1990s. "Hi. My name is Janet, and I'm calling from G.E. Capital." She was, in fact, Pooja Atri, a twenty-three-year-old calling from G.E. Capital's facility in Gurgaon, outside Delhi. She had acquired her American accent by watching the television series *Baywatch*. In Bangalore, C. R. Suman was "Susan Sanders" and Nishara Anthony was "Naomi Morrison." They watched the TV shows *Friends* and *Ally McBeal*. Call centers were one component of the broader business process outsourcing (BPO), which also employed workers who transcribed dictated texts and performed accounting services. BPO workers earned one-fifth of their American counterparts. India had competition—from Mexico, Ireland, and, especially, the Philippines. But India led them all.[13]

The IT surge in the southern Indian states contrasted with the near complete absence of IT-related activity in the northern Hindi-speaking belt. This new technological development exacerbated a great ongoing economic divergence. The southern states had not only grown considerably richer by 1985, but their economies grew faster over the next two decades, thus increasing the income gap between the south and the north. Economic inertia was greatest in four northern states—Bihar, Madhya Pradesh, Rajasthan, and Uttar Pradesh (Figure 19.2). Known collectively as BIMARU (a pun on the Hindi word for "sickly"), they accounted for one-third of India's population; they lacked economic dynamism, and their populations were growing faster than in the south. Corruption and the politician-criminal nexus flourished in the south too, but such pathologies took a much greater toll on the BIMARU residents.

From a national perspective, the main benefit of the IT boom was welcome relief in financing India's current account deficit. Reflecting the economy's perennial lack of international competitiveness, India was

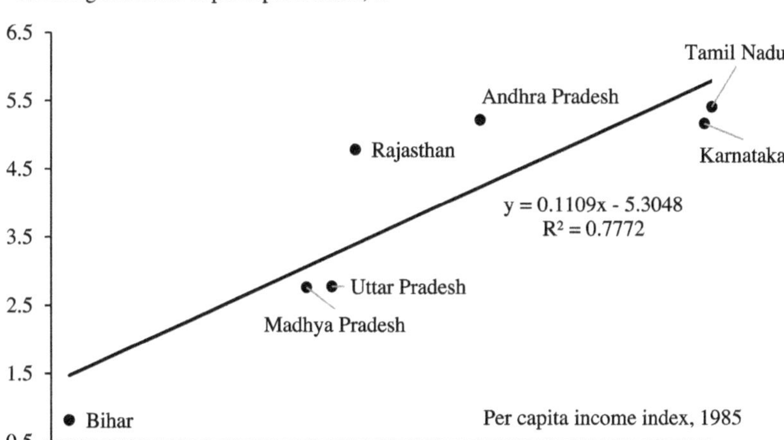

FIGURE 19.2: The southern states—richer in 1985—also grew faster over the next 20 years.

Note: In 1985, Tamil Nadu had a per capita income of 1758 rupees—the highest in this group of states—which is set equal to 100.

Source: Reserve Bank of India, Handbook of Statistics.

running large deficits in its goods trade—imports exceeded exports by big margins. In the fiscal year April 2000 to March 2001, the trade deficit was $12 billion. However, unlike on past occasions, especially in the crisis year 1990–1991, when the trade deficit nearly drained the country's foreign exchange reserves and even required India to pawn gold to pay for its imports, the situation now was more relaxed. Software and BPO exports paid for half of the trade deficit. In addition, remittances from Indians working abroad amounted to $13 billion, and equity inflows added another $2.5 billion in the Indian stock market. Although the trade deficit grew to $38 billion by the fiscal year 2004–2005, software exports also rose, reaching $17 billion. The continued inflow of remittances and foreign equity swelled the foreign exchange reserves held by the Reserve Bank.[14]

The software industry focused on international markets, with limited sales at home. One reason for this was the pathetic state of Indian telecommunications. To remedy that deficiency, the Vajpayee-led National Democratic Alliance prepared a new telecommunications policy in

March 1999. Implementation of the policy occurred over the next several months, as the government first lost its majority and then regained it in October. The policy encouraged the entry of new providers by establishing a "level playing field" between competitors operating in a new regulatory regime. Government-owned providers were on notice that they needed to get their act together.[15] Starting from among the lowest phone densities in the world, Indian phone usage began catching up with the rest of the world (Figure 19.3).

However, there was a limit though to what IT could do for the country. Even after its rapid growth in the 1990s and early 2000s, the software industry formed only 2 percent of Indian GDP in 2005. Hence its contribution to aggregate GDP growth was minimal. And because the industry employed a limited number of relatively skilled workers, its employment contribution was even smaller. In 2005, the Indian software and business services industry employed 1.3 million people out of a national labor force of 420 million.[16]

The Indian IT jewel shone brightly. But what about the India that did not shine? In that India lived the vast majority of Indians, who wondered where their jobs would come from.

"Kuch Kaam Milega?"—Is Any Work Available?

In his 1955 movie *Shree 420* (Mr. 420, which to Hindi audiences signifies "Mr. Crook"), Raj Kapoor, playing the character Raj, walks jauntily into Bombay. To the first person he meets, he says, "Kaam hi taalash me to mein aaya hoon, koi kaam batao mujhe?" (It is indeed for work that I have come, can you tell me of some work?) Forty-three years later, in Ram Gopal Varma's 1998 movie *Satya* (Truth), the lead character Satya arrives in Bombay by train. He asks his interlocutor the same question, "Kuch kaam milega?" (Is any work available?)

The word *kaam* (work) echoed eerily across the four decades. But unlike Raj in 1955, who flaunts his bachelor's degree, Satya does not bother. His education—or lack of it—is not relevant for the type of work he expects. The interlocutor understands and with a malicious gleam in his eye, asks, "Kuch bhi chalega tereko," shorthand for "Are you open to any

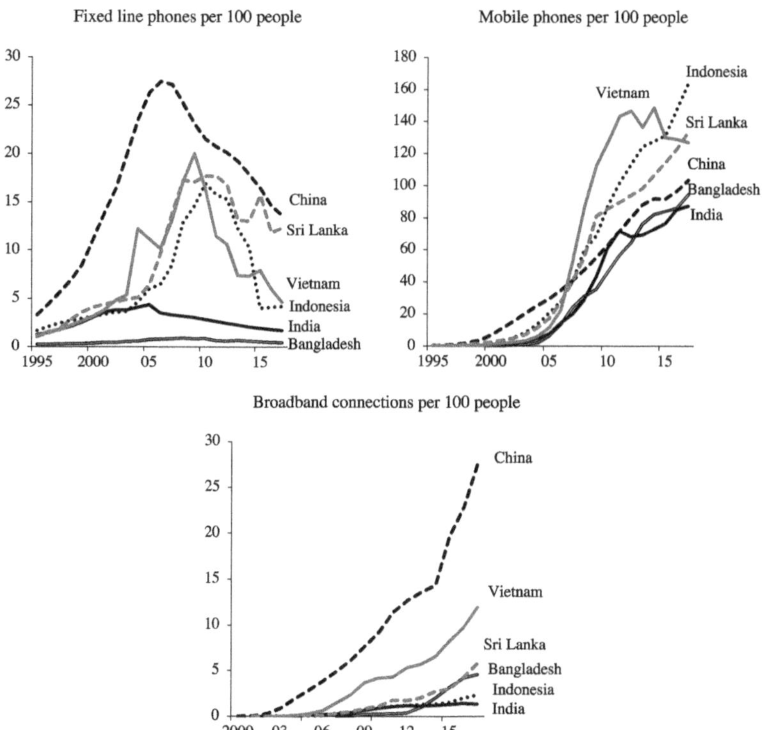

FIGURE 19.3: At long last, India began communicating in the early 2000s—although it still did so less than others.

Source: World Bank, World Development Indicators, IT.MLT.MAIN.P2, IT.CEL.SETS.P2, and IT.NET.BBND.P2.

type of work?" With that, Bombay's criminal underworld sucks Satya into its fold.

Satya, the movie, acquired cult status, winning critical acclaim and mesmerizing moviegoers. Satya, the protagonist, is no older than his contemporaries who visit Café Coffee Day for a cup of coffee and an hour of internet. Satya climbs the ladder of his criminal career, graduating in the process to a room in a crowded Bombay apartment house, having started in the city with a bed under a roof that projected from a buffalo shed. In his new abode, he makes friends with a young woman who lives across the corridor and needs help fixing a fuse. Satya's boss sends his kids to a school that instructs students in English, and he swells with pride when his daughter recites "Twinkle, Twinkle, Little Star."

Although they maintained the façade of normalcy, life was short for many in the crime business. Either they mowed each other down or police officers shot them dead in all too frequent "encounters." Such encounter killings, police officials said, were needed in self-defense or to prevent the criminals from escaping the reach of the law. Encounters had begun in the late 1960s when police snuffed out the Naxalites in Bengal. They were now standard procedure for an Indian state unable to democratically govern the nation. Encounters reached a fever pitch under Prime Minister Narasimha Rao in 1993 when the fierce police force subdued the never-ending extremists' rebellion in Punjab. In the late 1990s and early 2000s, encounters were the instrument of choice for dealing with Bombay's underworld. "Encounter specialists" among police officers racked up trophies of their killings, making them national celebrities.[17]

Satya's release in July 1998 occurred at a defining moment at which two Indian realities were unfolding. The movie's dark message of few jobs and social violence resonated in theatres around the country while Indian and international elites celebrated an upbeat "India story."

India's Growth Bubble Is No Reason to Celebrate

Indian GDP growth had slowed in the fiscal year 1997–1998, but the IMF described growth over the previous three years as "impressive." In the continuing comparison with the faster-growing Chinese economy, commentators were confident about India's prospects. India was a "genuine democracy" and committed to the rule of law, wrote the *Wall Street Journal*. On the other hand, China was a fragile authoritarian society "ruled not by laws but by the whims and anxieties of old men." An Indian columnist repeated the familiar metaphor: an "authoritarian set up" had "given the Chinese hare a jump-start." The democratic Indian "tortoise," he predicted, was "bound to produce more satisfying results."[18]

The IMF, although generally optimistic about India's potential, detected some worrying signs. Slower growth in 1997–1998 reflected domestic weakness rather than an accidental spillover of East Asia's financial crisis. Wide-ranging weaknesses afflicted the Indian economy: agricultural performance was worrisome; large parts of the population—particularly women—faced "severely constrained access to basic schooling"; and slow growth in the export of labor-intensive products hamstrung job prospects.[19] Half a century after independence, and even in the middle of an upbeat phase, India's fundamental problems persisted.

The Vajpayee government continued with market-oriented economic liberalization, which began with the Narasimha Rao–led Congress Party government. The innovation was a new emphasis on modernizing India's decrepit infrastructure. The World Economic Forum—which brought together the rich and powerful to Davos in Switzerland every year—rated Indian infrastructure as the worst among fifty-three countries surveyed in 1998. A World Bank report rated India's four largest cities as the worst in water availability and urban waste management among twenty-seven Asian cities with a population of more than one million people. The core problem was simple to understand but hard to fix politically. Infrastructure providers—particularly water and electricity suppliers—were under great pressure to subsidize Indian consumers, which led them to sell their services at below the costs they incurred. Their losses mounted also because many users stole water and electric power. To make progress in infrastructure provision, Indians needed to pay for the services so that providers could earn profits and invest in more and better services.[20]

Vajpayee was not ready to push rich Indians to pay higher municipal taxes or force payment for services. He focused on sectors where absurdly low pricing and pilferage of services were not the most important constraints. In December 1998, as part of an investment in over 13,000 kilometers of highways, he announced a plan to upgrade to four lanes the "golden quadrilateral" of roads connecting India's four metropolitan cities, Delhi, Calcutta, Mumbai, and Chennai. Also, in March 1999, as described above, Vajpayee announced a policy to upgrade telecommunications services. Some Indian states did start privatizing loss-incurring electricity distributors, which meant job losses for tenured employees and higher prices for customers, leading such beneficiaries to resist the moves and slow the process.[21]

Opening another policy front in July 2000, Vajpayee appointed the former World Bank economist and crusading investigative journalist Arun Shourie as minister for disinvestment. The word "disinvestment" in this context appears to have emerged in the early 1990s as an Indian euphemism for the privatization of public enterprises. Calling the sale of public enterprises by its rightful name was socially and politically unacceptable. The view that public enterprises served some greater purpose lingered. Those who benefited from public ownership, especially workers with lifetime jobs, protested. The biggest political opposition, though, came from the BJP's Hindu nationalist supporters. To them, public enterprises were *Swadeshi* (home-country) "crown jewels," and privatization would mean handing them over to foreigners.[22]

Shourie responded spiritedly: India's public enterprises were "bleeding ulcers," not crown jewels. He was right. Few investors were willing to buy India's publicly owned companies. Over a tortuous four years, the government sold a breadmaking enterprise, a zinc and lead producer, an aluminum producer, assorted luxury hotels, two state-trading companies, and stakes in various petroleum and telecom companies. The most noteworthy disinvestment was the sale of the government's financial stake in Maruti Udyog Limited, a joint venture established between the Indian government and Japan's Suzuki Motors in 1981. That sale ended the Maruti saga, a product of Sanjay Gandhi's technically juvenile and outrageously corrupt intent and fostered by his mother's indulgence. The biggest failure was the aborted effort to sell the international carrier Air India, the archetypal "bleeding ulcer" with a reputation for poor service and run-down aircraft that sometimes looked "held together with duct tape." Scores of public-sector companies, especially publicly owned banks, remained unsold.[23]

Vajpayee had barely scratched the surface. But he had done well by Indian standards in advancing domestic competition, infrastructure, and privatization. GDP growth, after dipping between 1999 and 2001, accelerated to 8 percent a year. In its 2004 assessment, the IMF wrote, "The recent impressive performance of the Indian economy is testimony to the benefits of the reforms undertaken since the early 1990s."[24] Such simplistic juxtaposition of reforms and GDP growth did the IMF little credit and did India no favors.

Were Indian "reforms" in the early 1990s the *cause* of the growth witnessed in the early 2000s, as the IMF and other analysts implied? If so, the manufacturing sector should have performed impressively since the main thrust of the reforms was in reducing controls on Indian manufacturing. In fact, Indian manufacturing performed indifferently at best.

The most gut-wrenching evidence of India's lackluster post-reform manufacturing performance was the widening gap between India and China in the international market for labor-intensive manufactured exports. The gap, which first emerged in the late 1970s and increased rapidly in the 1990s, blew open after December 2001 when China became a member of the World Trade Organization. China's exports grew spectacularly, and not just (or even primarily) because of the low wages paid to Chinese workers. Behind China's export success was the extraordinary growth in productivity of Chinese manufacturers and workers. Between 1993 and 2004, China's industrial total factor productivity, or efficiency in the use of all inputs, increased by 6.1 percent a year. Over those same years, India's total factor productivity grew by 1.1 percent a year. India had lived with a productivity handicap since losing the battle for international textile markets to the Japanese nearly a century earlier. As then, India's productivity failure lay in another post-reform failure: the inability to develop human capital.[25]

Durable gains in efficiency are possible only when better-educated workers reduce waste in the production process while achieving tight deadlines. Sometime in the mid-1990s, as a World Bank researcher, I visited a manufacturer of television sets in Fujian province on China's southeast coast. I managed to annoy the factory manager when I asked how far behind his production quality was relative to his Korean and Japanese competitors. He sternly walked me to his quality control room, where charts displayed the statistics on his operations. Pointing to the charts, he finally broke out into a smile. He was as good as the world's best, he said. India upped its game in the 1990s, but decisively lost the Red Queen race to China.

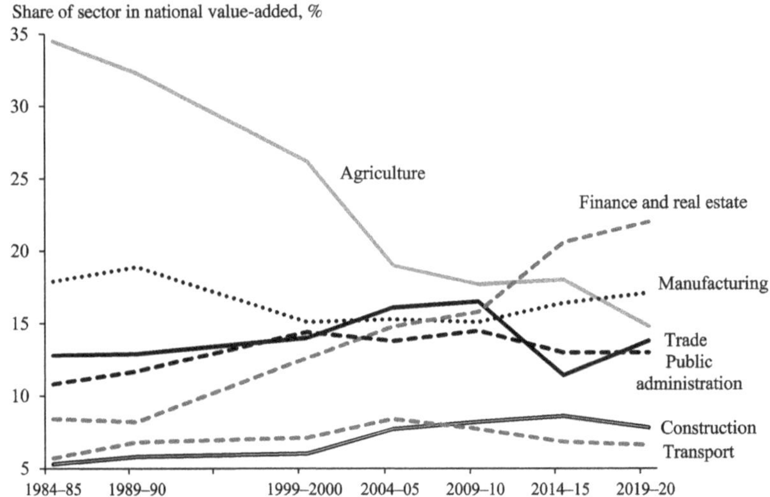

FIGURE 19.4: A finance-construction bubble inflated India's GDP growth. (Share of total gross value-added, percent)

Source: Central Statistical Office of India, http://mospi.nic.in/publication/national-accounts-statistics-2021, Statement 1.6.

For Indian businesses (and, hence, for the economy), finance and construction were the source of growth. The manufacturing sector's share in GDP fell somewhat after 1990, while the share of the financial sector grew dramatically. The construction industry's share of GDP also increased steadily (Figure 19.4). This shift toward finance and construction and away from manufacturing began with the Bombay textile industry strike in the early 1980s and kept gathering momentum. India's post-liberalization "growth story" was primarily one of a bubble in finance and construction.

Indian GDP growth was also assisted by a surging world economy bolstered at first by the remarkable U.S. tech euphoria between 1998 and 2000. After the tech bubble burst in 2001, easy finance in the United States helped maintain high rates of U.S. and world economic growth. The U.S. consumer had an inexhaustible appetite for cheap Chinese products. To meet that demand, Chinese manufacturers bought raw materials and other inputs from the rest of the world. World trade grew at its fastest pace since the post–World War II boom. In this more globalized world, the high tide of trade lifted all boats—even India's, despite its relatively limited participation in world trade.

That was a moment to worry, not to celebrate. The finance-construction bubble would burst, and world trade growth would slow. There were deeper problems. India's growth pattern was further eroding social norms and accountability while producing few good jobs.

Development with Moral Decay and Few Good Jobs

India's domestic financial boom funded commercial real estate, multistory housing, and shopping malls. The most glamorous of these developments, Phoenix, opened its doors in Mumbai in late 2002. Rising from the debris of textile mills, Phoenix was a one-million-square-foot complex of high-rise offices, apartments, and a trend-setting mall. Malls sprouted all over the country with "glitzy showrooms" of upscale stores such as Louis Vuitton, Gucci, and Mont Blanc. Catering to India's mega-rich, they were equipped with "shining granite floors and chic eateries."[26]

The construction industry became the fulcrum of a new business-crime-politics nexus, first brought to notice by the 1983 comedy *Jaane Bhi Do Yaaron* (Let it go, friends). In that movie, the criminals and politicians are bumbling amateurs. By 1998, in the movie *Satya,* the construction mafia is more organized, the humor is darker, and the violence is more grotesque.[27]

Around the world, construction is a haven for corruption and crime because much of the business is conducted in cash and several steps in the process require regulatory clearance. For this reason, the New York and Italian mafia are closely associated with the construction industry. In India, the most extensively documented construction-related crime relates to illegal riverbed sand mining, which provides sand that when mixed with cement and gravel produces concrete used in construction. According to one estimate, sand mining has grown to be India's largest criminal activity. The damage from sand mining extends well beyond the crime—riverbeds dry up, which changes the topography and stability of the land. Sand mining increases acids in the soil, which dissolve toxic metals that seep into the ground and contaminate groundwater. Sand mining destroys microorganisms and biodiversity.[28]

In 1999, employment expert Ajit Kumar Ghose rang the alarm bells on another serious problem. GDP growth, he wrote, "has failed to improve employment conditions." India "will soon," he said, "be confronted with an employment crisis." Ghose was making a crucial point: GDP growth was not synonymous with employment growth and certainly not with the quality of jobs created. The effective rate of unemployment (accounting for substantial underemployment) was around 12 percent. But, as I have noted earlier, Indians could not afford to be unemployed, and so the seriousness of the employment problem also lay in the poor quality of Indian jobs. Among those employed, only about 8 percent were in formal jobs that were well-paying and included health and pension benefits. Even the modern (organized) sector created limited numbers of formal jobs and, instead, relied increasingly on contract wage labor. The number of job seekers, Ghose emphasized, was increasing at an accelerating pace and limited opportunities would continue driving workers to low-productivity, poorly-paying informal jobs.[29]

The reasons for the lack of good jobs were straightforward. The fast-growing financial sector needed a small number of typically high-skilled workers. Low-skilled manufacturing jobs grew at an anemic rate because India had minimal presence in global labor-intensive goods trade. So the vast bulk of low-skilled workers settled into the informal economy: mainly construction and also trade, restaurants, and transportation. These jobs had long downtimes, which meant rampant underemployment. Construction jobs were also dangerous. Workers toiled in dusty, toxic environments. They often worked without helmets and harnesses and were constantly at risk of severe injury or death.[30]

Not only in "backward" Bihar but even in "advanced" Tamil Nadu, the new jobs were mainly in construction and in low-productivity, low-end services. Despite its much-acclaimed manufacturing hubs, urban Tamil Nadu saw a decline in the share of workers in manufacturing and a rise in construction (Figure 19.5). Women, unable to find decent non-farming jobs, were dropping out of the labor force.[31]

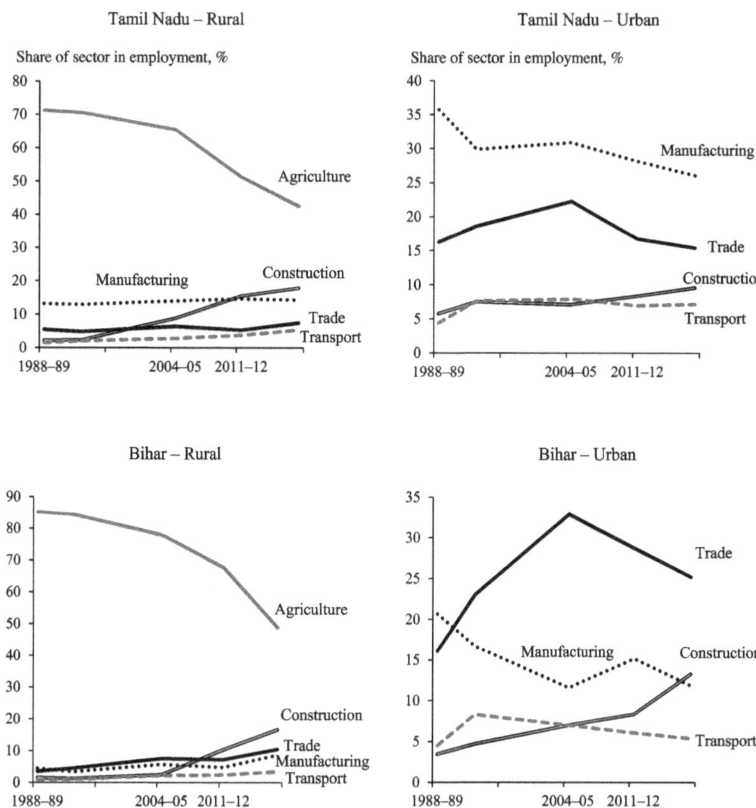

FIGURE 19.5: The employment shift from agriculture to construction occurred in "advanced" Tamil Nadu and "laggard" Bihar. (Sectoral distribution of employment, principal and subsidiary status, percent)

Source: Central Statistics Office of India, Periodic Labour Force Survey, 1987–88: Statement 36, pp. 105–108; 1993–94: Table 6.7.2, pp. 116–120; 2004–05: Statement 5.9.2, pp. 140–145; 2011–12: Statement 5.11.1, pp. 165–173; 2017–18: Table (27), pp. A-163 to A-168.

Employment was not a priority for Indian policymakers. In his review of economic policy in the 1990s and 2000s, Montek Ahluwalia addressed employment toward the end as a "medium-term" issue. Meanwhile, young men like Satya kept coming to Bombay. Knowing they had few work options, they nevertheless asked sleazy interlocutors, "Is any work available?" They had no "medium-term" plan. To them, a violent life remained a reasonable option.[32]

An even greater problem, however, lay brewing in India's vast agricultural sector.

Where the Light Does Not Shine

In 1950, not long after independence, agriculture employed 70 percent of Indian workers. Over the next half century, the share of workforce in agriculture declined by just 10 percentage points. In Japan's comparable post-Meiji half century, the share of workers on farms fell by 35 points, from 80 percent in 1880 to 45 percent in 1930. By the early 1920s, no Japanese worked on a farm, unless he or she preferred doing so.[33]

Workers moved from agriculture to the nonagricultural sector at an even faster pace in subsequent East Asian development. The share of workers in Korean agriculture declined from 55 percent in 1965 to 10 percent in 2000. In China, a poorer country (in per capita income terms) than India until the late 1970s, the share of the workforce in agriculture declined from 80 percent in 1965 to 50 percent in 2000. In both Korea and China, the

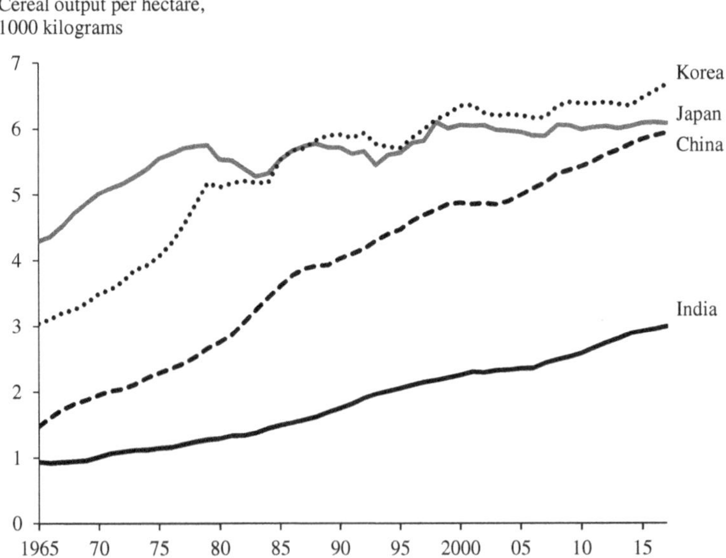

FIGURE 19.6: Indian farmland productivity is higher today than in the past, but is still far less than elsewhere. (Thousand kilograms of cereals per hectare, 5-year moving averages)
Source: World Bank World Development Indicators, AG.YLD.CREL.KG.

transition from agriculture to non-agriculture was especially rapid in the 1990s, a decade in which India stood nearly still according to this metric.[34]

In Japan, Korea, and China, the transition from agriculture occurred not just because of expanding job opportunities in manufacturing and services but also because agriculture was dynamic. In Japan, land productivity increased rapidly in the post-Meiji years and by the 1960s was among the highest in the world (Figure 19.6). In Korea, land productivity caught up with that in Japan by the early 1980s and Chinese productivity caught up in the 2000s. With the land producing more output, farm production grew at a healthy pace while young new job seekers and older farm workers found non-farm jobs.[35] Every advanced nation goes through this classical transition; only India seemed chronically unable to do so.

Even in the decade after the 1991 economic "liberalization," 35 million *more* workers piled into low-productivity agricultural tasks. From a national perspective, this was a very inefficient use of the workforce. Output (technically, value-added) per worker in Indian agriculture was less than one-quarter the output per worker in non-agricultural work.[36] But because of limited non-agricultural jobs and humiliating urban housing conditions, farmers stuck to miserable agricultural lives.

Miserable might not be a strong enough word. Starting in the late 1990s, the harsh reality of agricultural work manifested in a spate of farmer suicides, particularly in the southeastern state of Andhra Pradesh and the western state of Maharashtra. The land operated by farmers, subdivided over generations as in the rest of India, had become steadily tinier, making it harder for families to eke out a living.[37]

In Andhra Pradesh, Chief Minister Chandrababu Naidu had his gaze firmly fixed on the capital city Hyderabad, which he projected as an IT haven. Naidu loftily said that the new technological opportunities (for example, genetically modified seed varieties) would solve the farmers' problems. Technology would also permit a "leap from a rural-based society to a service-sector one."[38] Farmers awaited that bliss in vain.

Andhra Pradesh is a large state. In 2001, its population of 76 million people was comparable to Germany's 82 million in the same year. The state is blessed with the mighty Krishna and Godavari rivers and many minor ones. By Indian standards, it has had a successful agricultural sector: farmers produce rice and cash crops such as groundnuts, cotton, and sugarcane. Yet in the 1990s, as the payoff from the Green Revolution technologies diminished across India, agricultural growth rates fell. In Andhra Pradesh, the problems were widespread because even the Godavari began drying up. The state's large arid stretches, which remained utterly dependent on good rainfall, suffered grievously. Corruption-ridden canal irrigation departments spent money wastefully and neglected maintenance. Rich farmers dug deeper wells, causing an alarming decline in the water table and forcing small farmers to dig deeper to find water.[39]

Although struggling to make a living, farmers had rising expectations, as Hirschman's tunnel effect would predict: seeing others move ahead, they were anxious to make progress. Small farmers began planting cash crops and relying more on high-yielding seed varieties. Their investments in expensive inputs mounted. They needed more funds to dig water from sinking water tables. To finance these expenditures, farmers relied on expensive borrowing from moneylenders, traders, and large landlords. The risks were high. New varieties, such as the genetically modified cotton variety Bt cotton, required operational skills many small farmers lacked. Crop failure, illnesses in the family, and large expenses, such as for weddings, often combined to make debt repayment impossible. Farmer suicides increased.[40]

Despite unaffordable investment outlays with uncertain gains, Andhra Pradesh farmers and agricultural workers remained stuck. There were few urban jobs. The share of workers employed in agriculture remained almost unchanged at 62 percent in 2001 from 65 percent in 1991. With a growing population, agriculture in Andhra Pradesh employed 7 million more workers in 2001 than in 1991—a vastly greater number than the IT industry employed that decade in all of India.[41]

Andhra Pradesh's combination of large arid stretches, poor public irrigation, falling water tables, and rising input costs was common through much of India. As in Andhra Pradesh, cash cropping had spread in many regions to include fruits and vegetables. However, these crops needed plentiful water. Journalist Kavitha Iyer writes of the charred remains of sweet lime tree orchards in the dry regions of Maharashtra. Farmer suicides became depressingly common there too.[42]

To varying degrees, the Andhra Pradesh-Maharashtra stories repeated themselves all over India. After its brief, Green Revolution–induced success in the 1980s and early 1990s, Indian agriculture was in crisis again. Across India, the government invested less in irrigation and did so less efficiently. Private well irrigation was becoming more expensive. Farmer suicides jumped in the late 1990s.[43]

Then a change for the worse occurred. Perhaps induced by climate change, drought-like conditions became more frequent in the early 2000s. The *Times of India* recorded recurring droughts and severe farmer distress in large stretches of Orissa, Gujarat, Maharashtra, Madhya Pradesh, and Rajasthan. In April 2000, the editorial board wrote a searing indictment of the government's priorities. While a small number of Indians were moving into the "cyber-millennium," the other, much vaster India was trapped in "a sea of aridity." Irrigation projects, the newspaper wrote, "get completed on paper" but only "to fund a whole network of bribery and corruption." Drought in the summer of 2002 spread the pain beyond the traditionally arid areas to Punjab, Haryana, and Uttar Pradesh, where, in addition to declining water tables, intense application of fertilizers and pesticides was depleting the soil.[44]

Farmers responded by relying on Naxalites to speak for them. The Naxalites, as we saw in chapter 9, were so named because in the late 1960s they had attempted to secure greater land rights for farmers in Bengal's Naxalbari district. After the Bengal police crushed that movement and the urban guerilla activity that followed, the Naxalites lay largely underneath the radar. They reasserted themselves in the late 1970s, resuming the fight for higher wages for landless agricultural labor and greater land rights for small cultivators. In early October 2003, following a severe drought in Andhra Pradesh, a Naxalite group tried unsuccessfully to assassinate Chief Minister Chandrababu Naidu. The assassination attempt fit perfectly with the statistical finding that Naxalite activity became more commonplace after severe rainfall deficiency and became more violent where Naxalites depended on access to minerals to finance themselves, as was true in Andhra Pradesh with its rich mineral endowment. Naidu, the IT messiah, wooed Bill Gates, Bill Clinton, and the World Bank while doing little to aid the state's distressed agriculturists. Instead, as in the 1960s in Bengal, police forces and private armies commissioned by landlords forced the Naxalites to retreat, often by the method of "fake encounters." The Indian state did what it did best: inflict violence on its people.[45]

The pressure on farmers took its toll, and a wave of migration away from agricultural work began in the early 2000s. Again, headlines from the *Times of India* tell the story: "Good Intentions Pour In as Dustbowls Empty Out" (April 25, 2000); "Politics of Drought Trigger Mass Exodus from Junagadh (Gujarat)" (April 27, 2000); "Drought Is Forcing Villagers to Leave Home in M.P. (Madhya Pradesh)" (October 11, 2000); "Bonded Orissa Labourers Migrate to Other States" (April 30, 2001); "Mass Migration from Drought-Hit Villages of Latur (Maharashtra)" (February 15, 2006); "It Is Exodus Time Again: Bihar" (August 11, 2009). People left their homes in desperation, often leaving valuable livestock to die.

Validating the news reports, a research study showed that more frequent droughts rather than urban job prospects explained Indian rural-urban migration. Demographers Ram Bhagat and Kunal Keshri estimate about 77 million Indians migrated from farms to cities between 2006 and 2011. They add, however, that large numbers of farm-to-city migrants moved only temporarily, often circling back to the security of their village families and communities.[46]

Cities remained inhospitable to migrants. In 2004, Amy Waldman of the *New York Times* profiled an Andhra Pradesh peasant couple who found jobs as street sweepers in the tech city of Hyderabad. Rural migrants became construction workers. They also worked in brick making and stone quarrying to supply the construction industry. They lived in makeshift slums or in huts made of reed mats at work sites. Others worked as shoe cleaners, porters, pimps, and refuse collectors. Migration did not open doors to progress. It was a "survival strategy," write Bhagat and Keshri.[47]

Migrants had always been consigned to precarity, as first portrayed in *Dharti ke lal*, the movie depiction of the 1943 Bengal famine. A quarter century later, migrants were still on the edge of urban life. In the 1978 movie *Gaman* (Departure), a young farmer who has lost his land to a rich landlord travels to Bombay, the city of dreams. He learns to drive a taxi, spends his days looking for passengers, and lives with other cab drivers in a densely packed slum. As the movie ends, he is standing on a railway platform, knowing he does not have the money to return home to his dying mother.[48] Urban India remained just as unwelcoming to the migrant in the new millennium.

Death, in the Lord's Name

At 7:43 a.m. on February 27, 2002, the Sabarmati Express from Ayodhya pulled into the Godhra Junction railway station in eastern Gujarat. On board were *kar sevaks* (religious volunteers) returning frustrated from Ayodhya. They had been unable to begin building their much-cherished temple to Lord Ram on the site where frenzied *kar sevaks* like them had demolished the Babri Masjid in December 1992. Many *kar sevaks* belonged to the Bajrang Dal, the youth wing of the VHP, the principal instigator of the fever to build a temple in place of the masjid. These angry Hindus returning from Ayodhya had picked fights along the journey and were itching for more.[49]

At the Godhra Junction railway station platform, some of the younger *kar sevaks* refused to pay a cigarette vendor and threw tea in the face of a tea vendor. Allegedly, they also molested a girl. Godhra was a Muslim-majority town, where Muslims lived in ghetto-like conditions. After the train moved away from the station, Muslims threw bottles, stones, and burning rags at the train cars. One car caught fire, and fifty-nine *kar sevaks* perished.[50]

According to one account, rather than the angry Muslims outside, passengers on board accidentally ignited the cooking fuel they were carrying. But, in the fog of what precisely happened, a competing narrative, that the Muslims had conspired to kill the *kar sevaks,* proved powerful. Over the next several days, Hindus slaughtered Muslims throughout the state of Gujarat. Approximately two thousand people died, the vast majority of whom were Muslims. With the police standing to the side, young Hindu men, often in saffron-colored headbands that signified allegiance to Hindutva, wantonly destroyed the lives and livelihoods of Muslims. They brutally raped Muslim women. Many of the Hindutva marauders, the anthropologist Parvis Ghassem-Fachandi has written, belonged to a "generation of underprivileged and upwardly aspiring youngsters motivated toward extralegal violent acts by organizations such as the Bajrang Dal." The sociological roots of the violence in Gujarat were similar to those during the 1992–1993 riots in Mumbai. Gujarat's textile mills, once a source of good jobs as in Mumbai, had largely closed down. To young men with few options, violent Hindutva was a magnet.[51]

Some contemporary reporting blamed Narendra Modi and his government for doing little to stop the massacre of the Muslims. The "fish rots from the top," one early news report stated, adding that the lines between the government, police, and Hindutva organizations had become "totally blurred." In a nationally televised interview on March 1, Modi said that "every action inevitably produces a reaction," a statement that reinforced the sense of his government's complicity in the massacre. On April 12, at a conference of BJP leaders in Goa, Prime Minister Vajpayee repeated the theme of just retribution: "If there had been no Godhra, the tragedy in Gujarat would not have occurred." Then, in a conventional Hindutva tirade, Vajpayee added, "Wherever there are Muslims, they do not want to live with others. Instead they want to preach and propagate their religion by creating fear and terror in the minds of others."[52]

Vajpayee rejected the calls to fire Modi. Instead, he asked Modi to seek a fresh electoral mandate. Modi welcomed this instruction because he now had the Hindutva momentum behind him. When the Election Commission refused to hold early polls, citing the atmosphere of anger and hostility, Modi kept the anti-Muslim sentiment inflamed, pitching his dark message to a national print and television audience. Unable to break through that rhetoric, Congress Party leaders, including Congress Party President Sonia Gandhi, desperately attached themselves to Hindu symbols in a bid to ingratiate themselves with Hindu voters. But such "soft Hindutva"—appeal to Hindu symbolism but without the ritual violence—proved just as inadequate as similar efforts by Sonia's husband Rajiv in 1989. In December 2002, Modi won a landslide victory. Praveen Togadia, a leader of the strident Vishwa Hindu Parishad, said that the "successful experiment" in Gujarat's Hindutva "laboratory" gave reason to anticipate more such success elsewhere in the country. "Hindutva itself is development," he boldly declared. "We will colour the whole country in saffron." In March 2005, the United States denied Narendra Modi an entry visa for his role in religious persecution. Indian courts cleared him of any responsibility.[53]

International accolades of India's high GDP growth rates and its IT industry continued to pour in. In his elite echo chamber, Vajpayee was convinced that Indians shared his sense of economic good feeling. He called new elections, which the BJP contested on the "India Is Shining" slogan. Narendra Modi, who by now had become a folk hero of Hindutva, campaigned for the BJP in the final days of the drawn-out polling schedule.[54]

But with agriculture in distress and too few urban jobs, many Indians found the "shining India" language jarring. At the national level, the BJP lost to the Congress Party, which promised an employment guarantee program. In the Andhra Pradesh legislative assembly election, Chandrababu Naidu, absorbed in his cyberworld, also lost.[55]

Two decades of India's economic promise, from 1985 to 2004, came to an end. The neglect of education, health infrastructure, cities, and the environment had continued. The justice system remained sclerotic and arbitrary. Indian democracy was in peril of moral seizure. Corruption and criminals in politics were thriving. Hindutva's emphasis on a dividing line between friend and enemy was a legitimization of violence on a scale seldom before seen. Under Vajpayee's "moderate" Hindutva, his education minister had begun rewriting school textbooks with a Hindutva flavor. In 2002, Vajpayee had made no effort to stop the Hindutva cancer in Gujarat. In February 2003, he had a portrait of Vinayak Damodar Savarkar—author of the divisive and violent text *Hindutva*—hung in an alcove opposite Mahatma Gandhi's portrait in the Central Hall of the Indian Parliament. In June 2004, Vajpayee briefly wondered aloud if the Gujarat massacre of Muslims had proved the BJP's undoing in the national election. But he did not follow through.[56]

Vajpayee lost the 2004 election because he offered little economic hope to most Indians. And he could not match Narendra Modi's Hindutva fanaticism to win votes. For the sake of India's economy and democracy, the Congress Party–led coalition had much work to do. Unfortunately, hubris had set in.

Part IV

HUBRIS, 2005 TO THE PRESENT

Chapter 20
AS THE TWO INDIAS DRIFT APART, DEMOCRACY CREAKS

One evening some years ago, at a community center in Delhi, I asked my gym instructor, "Tum din mein kya karte ho?" (What do you do during the day?) He answered with a smile: "Mein timepass karta hoon." (I do timepass.) The word *timepass* has entered the Hindi language as a noun. You don't "pass your time." You "do timepass." It is an active state of filling spare time. Millions of young Indian men spend their days "doing timepass." My gym instructor watched an endless stream of cricket matches on television. However, the most poignant form of timepass occurs in the long periods of downtime amid repeated failure to find a job.

As the human geographer Craig Jeffrey narrates, Rajesh, a student at Meerut College in Uttar Pradesh, turned his job quest into a neverending acquisition of academic degrees. Over a span of thirteen years, he earned a bachelor of arts, a bachelor of education, a master's in political science, a master's in history, a master's in agriculture, and a Ph.D. "I just moved from one to the other, hoping to increase my chances," Rajesh said in 2005. Twice, he had reached the final interview for entry into the Uttar Pradesh civil service. He believed that he did not make the final cut because he refused to pay the bribes demanded from him. Instead, he had continued "taking the blows," he said, because a salaried government job remained his dream. In the meantime, he languished with others in his predicament. "Hanging out" at street corners and tea stalls was their job, which they rationalized as helpful networking.[1]

At the heart of the linguistically charming word *timepass* lie two of India's most intractable problems: substandard education and weak job creation. Together they represent the broken lower rungs on India's economic ladder, symbolizing the limits to the upward mobility of young Indians.

India replaced its early education deficit with a sprawling infrastructure within which perverse incentives stymied the cause of education. In schools, the quality of teaching remained substandard. Millions of ill-prepared school graduates harbored hope that college would be their ticket to prosperity. Indian authorities fueled that hope, allowing the proliferation of worthless educational institutions. In government-run colleges and universities, politically connected administrators lined their pockets through commissions on purchases, appointments, and admissions. In rapidly multiplying private colleges, with lax educational standards, charlatans made large, unaccounted-for fortunes through a combination of fees charged off the books and tax-exempt status as ostensibly not-for-profit organizations. A *Washington Post* investigation reported that "poorly regulated, unaccredited and often entirely fake colleges have sprung up as demand for higher education accelerates." Many had no more than a mailing address. They charged stiff prices to award certification for teaching and even for the practice of law and medicine. They preyed on desperate young Indians.[2]

The backlog in the demand for jobs increased from 35 million in 1983, near the end of the Indira Gandhi years, to 58 million in 2000. The 58 million backlog was, in fact, spread over a much larger number of aspiring workers, many of whom (like my gym instructor) had half or one-third of a job. Put another way, 10 million Indians wanted a full-time job and over 100 million wanted either half or two-thirds of a job. Every year, more than 9 million more joined the search for work. For the many who were stuck in this limbo, timepass conferred a reassuring sense of purpose.[3]

India had other urgent problems. High-yield agriculture, cities, factories, and mines were "assaulting" the rivers, the Centre for Science and

Environment warned in 1999. Polluted rivers were the "biggest threat to public health," killing children and, increasingly, adults. In the early 2000s, at the northern end of Delhi, a sewage channel, over six meters deep, carried the city's human excrement, rotting food, and plastics into the Yamuna River. The sewage water was like "fast-flowing tar" where it entered the river, wrote author Rana Dasgupta in his frightening portrait of Delhi. And while Delhi was also the global poster child for egregious urban pollution, the air in many Indian cities was toxic. The once-idyllic Dehradun in the Himalayan foothills ranked among the country's most polluted towns.[4] Such rampant damage to the environment hurt both current and future Indian generations.

In May 2004, India had a new government. The Congress Party was at the head of a left-leaning coalition, the United Progressive Alliance (UPA). In the manner of the old-style Communist Party bosses, Sonia Gandhi, widow of Rajiv Gandhi and daughter-in-law of Indira Gandhi, became chairwoman of the "National Advisory Council," a body invented to give her the authority of a super-prime minister of sorts. Manmohan Singh, an unelected technocrat, became the puppet prime minister.[5]

Indian and international elites welcomed Manmohan Singh. He was the virtuoso finance minister who had set India on the path of economic liberalization in July 1991. He had then boldly declared that India was an idea whose time had come. Now, thirteen years since he uttered those words, the assertion was, at best, a cruel joke. Farming families continued to be shattered by suicides. Millions of young men like Rajesh still spent years acquiring rubbish degrees. Women faced disturbingly public forms of violence.

The policy priority could no longer be a single-minded pursuit of private initiative and market efficiency. More so than ever, India needed to commit to a social democratic agenda, one that brought shared progress through a sturdier agriculture, better education and health, more urban jobs, and a cleaner environment. The time was right. The world was reconsidering its Reagan-era obsession with free markets, a new emphasis on social justice was ascendant globally. President Bill Clinton in the United States and Prime Minister Tony Blair in the United Kingdom had recently experimented with "third way" approaches to soften the harshness of the market by testing new ways for the government to improve social welfare. In Brazil, President Luiz Inácio Lula da Silva was pursuing economic policy with a human face. As the World Bank commented in a major report, the performance of stand-alone free-market policies in Latin America had disappointed their most ardent adherents.[6]

The new Indian government seemed to understand that the market's harshness needed softening. In August 2005, the government introduced the "right to work," providing a rural employment guarantee under the National Rural Employment Guarantee Act (NREGA). Later, with the prefix "Mahatma Gandhi," it became widely known as MGNREGA. The guarantee entitled every rural resident above the age of eighteen to employment, typically in a public works program. Each rural household could claim one hundred days of work every year.[7]

Though well intentioned, the program was miserly from the start. In some states, the MGNREGA wage was lower than the state's statutory minimum wage, which violated a Supreme Court directive. The funds allocated to the program were often insufficient to meet the demand for work, leading to delays in wage payment. The government had started well but did not appear serious about its social justice objectives.[8]

In October 2005, the government introduced the "Right to Information," which gave citizens a right to speedy access of government records. This right helped achieve greater transparency and accountability in government operations. But RTI could not live up to its promise. Almost immediately after its introduction, the authorities began restricting access and delaying their responses to information requests. Even the Supreme Court stonewalled the call for transparency. Activists and whistleblowers faced severe risks. As the *New York Times* reported, those raising "pointed inquiries at the dangerous intersection of high-stakes business and power politics have paid a heavy price." Many RTI activists were murdered.[9]

As with the employment guarantee program, meager budget allocations and paltry wages constrained the community health programs launched in April 2005 under the National Rural Health Mission. The Forest Rights Act of December 2006 benefited some forest-dwelling families and communities that were able to claim their rights under this act. However, the demands of private business took precedence over the rights of forest dwellers, who often got mired in legal loopholes and ultimately received only 3 percent of the community land to which they had claims.[10]

Hence, under the Manmohan Singh–led UPA government between 2004 and 2014, the subject of this chapter, the market mantra reigned supreme and cozy business-politics relationships prospered. The provision of public goods remained a low priority. Social norms and political accountability continued to suffer severe damage.

India Experiences a Fragile, Unequal Growth

A deceptive economic glow shone over Manmohan Singh's early years as prime minister. India's finance-construction bubble inflated GDP growth. Also, like in almost every other country in the world, as Indian exporters ramped up to meet unusually buoyant world demand, they stimulated domestic investment and consumption.[11]

Of special interest to India was the jump in the global demand for coal and iron ore. Skyrocketing coal prices triggered a rush for leases on coal mines in the four mineral-rich states of Chhattisgarh, Jharkhand, Madhya Pradesh, and Orissa. Rising international iron ore prices attracted investors to those four states plus Goa and Karnataka. Domestic demand for coal and iron ore also jumped as Indian and international companies established power plants and expanded steel production.[12]

On the land above India's rich mineral deposits grew lush forests, where the Adivasis (indigenous tribes) lived and earned their livelihoods. The Adivasis, despite constitutional protections as Scheduled Tribes, had benefited little from India's post-independence economic development. Even before the latest rush began, they had been losing their forests to mining and industrial business interests. The new mineral rush placed at increasing risk the homes and incomes of forty-one million Adivasis, about a quarter of the population in the four main mineral-rich states.[13]

"We praise the forest goddess, mother of life," the Adivasi women sing. Sumira, the village elder, points to a banyan tree and says, "We worship her and she provides us with fruit." Adivasis are the natural guardians of the land they venerate. In contrast, the mines and industrial plants, justified by the cause of development, inflict irreparable damage. They cut the trees, and pollute the air, land, rivers, and streams for miles around their locations. Their waste piles up. Compensation to Adivasis for their ancestral land is stingy, and remedial measures to protect the environment are grudging. To register their protest, angry Adivasi kill a factory owner. In Orissa, they fight to stop a Canadian-Indian aluminum venture. To protect themselves from more assault, they seek help from the Naxalites, now also widely known as Maoists.[14]

Conflict was imminent. On June 4, 2005, the venerated business house of the Tatas signed an agreement to set up a steel plant in Bastar in Chhattisgarh. Virtually on the same day, a private militia known as the Salwa Judum ("Peace March" or "Purification Hunt" in south Chhattisgarh's Gondi language), emerged in Bastar to protect the interests of the investors. Mahendra Karma, the Congress Party's leader in the Chhattisgarh Legislative Assembly, led and controlled Salwa Judum. The state's BJP government, in a bipartisan consensus with the Congress Party's Karma, supported big business over the rights of Adivasis. As more investors piled into Bastar, the new militia, backed by Indian paramilitary forces, began a bloody battle with the Adivasis and Naxalites.[15]

In April 2006, speaking to chief ministers of the thirteen states in which the Naxalites/Maoists operated, Manmohan Singh declared, "The problem of Naxalism is the single biggest internal security threat since independence." In thus framing an economic issue as a matter of internal security, Singh was taking a side. The scholar and human being in him understood and explained that the Indian state had failed "to deliver social justice to its poorest regions," which, he said, had "alienated people." The politician in Manmohan Singh worked for powerful businesses, a posture that led him to emulate Mrs. Gandhi's reliance on police and military forces to a worrisome extent.[16]

The IMF and foreign investors were bullish on Indian prospects. Foreign capital inflows increased India's foreign exchange reserves, which reached a plentiful $145 billion in the spring of 2006. "The going has never been so good," Manmohan Singh said in the customary prime minister's speech on Independence Day, August 15, 2006. "Wherever I go," Singh continued, "I see our nation on the move." He celebrated the "impressive pace of over 8 percent annual GDP growth" over the previous three years.[17]

Indian GDP was growing smartly but creating few jobs. Job growth was particularly disappointing in the manufacturing sector. In the Nehruvian heavy-industry tradition, manufacturing output grew mainly in capital- and skill-intensive industries—refined petroleum products, chemicals, automobiles, and rubber and plastics—all of which employed only handfuls of workers, often on meager wages in abysmal working conditions.[18]

Singh recognized the problem. He acknowledged that "vast segments" of the Indian population were "untouched by modernization." He acknowledged that the "crisis" in agriculture was leading many to "the desperate step of committing suicide." But he had no strategy to move people out of the desperation of agriculture into modern manufacturing.[19]

As George Orwell wrote, it is a struggle to see what lies in front of our noses. Indian policymakers refused to learn from East Asian nations, which had repeatedly demonstrated a twofold strategy of growth with equity: investment in human development and more jobs in labor-intensive manufactured exports. Following Japan and then an impressive list of smaller East Asian countries, China was now achieving that success on a scale and with a speed not previously observed. Indian leaders knew—or should have known—what they needed to do.[20]

For even as Manmohan Singh spoke, Vietnam, using the East Asian playbook, was racing ahead of India in human development, achieving much higher life expectancy and vastly superior education for its people. With its high-quality workers and an exchange rate strategy that kept its currency, the dong, competitive for exporters, Vietnam rapidly expanded international sales of clothing, footwear, wood products, and office and consumer electronics goods. In a country of about 80 million people, these labor-intensive activities generated 7 million jobs between 2000 and 2007.[21]

Bangladesh's achievement was narrower but also impressive. In 1972, the nongovernmental organization BRAC began spreading high-quality primary health services and school education. On that growing base of

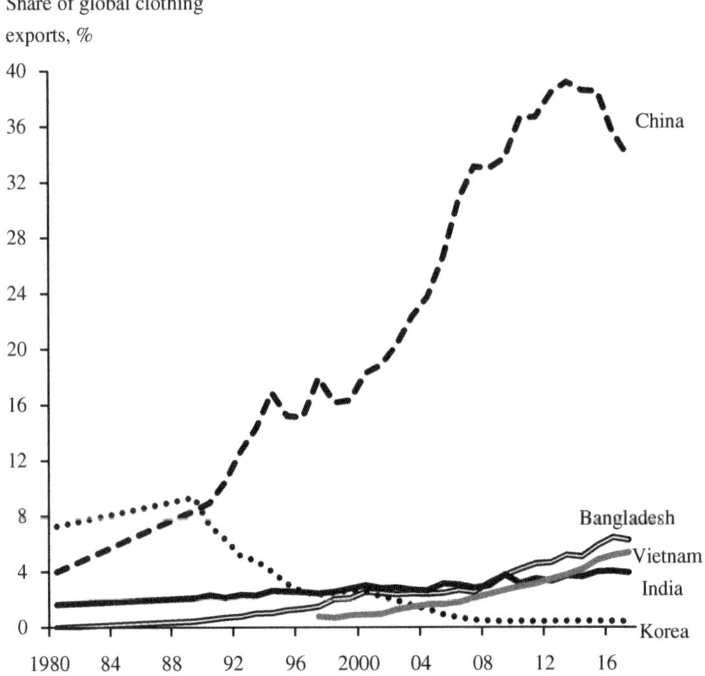

FIGURE 20.1: Clothing exports . . . first Korea, then China, and most recently Vietnam and Bangladesh have passed India by. (Share of world exports, percent)
Note: SITC code for clothing is 84.
Source: WTO, http://stat.wto.org/StatisticalProgram/WSDBViewData.aspx?Language=E.

human capital, in 1978 the Korean conglomerate Daewoo established a Bangladeshi joint venture, the Desh Garment Company. While BRAC catalyzed human development, Desh helped Bangladeshi manufacturers gain a foothold in world markets. Spurred by Desh's example and helped by skilled personnel who moved from Desh to other garment producers, by the mid-2000s Bangladesh (with a population of 141 million people in 2006) was exporting more garments than India (Figure 20.1).

In both Vietnam and Bangladesh, work opportunities opened up for women, who then followed the classic development path of having fewer children, in whose education and health they invested with greater diligence. The better-educated and healthier next generation of daughters postponed marriages and childbirth. In Bangladesh, women were prominent in schoolteaching, healthcare, and family planning services. They thus gained greater prominence and "agency" in their nation's economic progress. The delivery of public services through mainly community-based organizations also fostered social cooperation. In their different ways, Vietnam and Bangladesh were on a virtuous cycle of more employment and greater human capital.[22]

Indian policymakers ignored Vietnam and, especially, Bangladesh as competitive threats. China, though, was a country to fear. Particularly worrisome, Chinese exports to India were a growing headache for Indian producers selling even to domestic consumers. Chinese sales to India ranged from toys to electronic goods. History was repeating itself. In the 1930s, Japanese manufacturers sold toys in the Indian market. Now, more than seventy years later, low-end toys were coming from China, leaving little space for Indian producers.

For his book on Delhi, author Rana Dasgupta met Rahul, an intense and strikingly rich twenty-five-year-old man. Rahul had studied at an Ivy League college in the United States and had returned home to run the family business. As he explained to Dasgupta, "With the rise of China, we have stopped producing anything. My father closed down our production and now we only sell other people's products, German, American and Chinese." One of his aunts, Rahul said, owned the Indian monopoly for Nikon camera sales. "Money just keeps piling up without anyone doing anything."[23]

Thus, Indian businesses, terrified by China and enticed, instead, by easy money in construction and finance, shied away from labor-intensive manufacturing. For agricultural laborers and small farmers desperately seeking non-agricultural jobs, the opportunities were primarily in construction, trade, restaurants, and transportation, where workers experienced high degrees of underemployment. Construction—financially precarious and physically treacherous—still created the largest number of new jobs, setting it on a course to employ more workers than manufacturing by 2016.[24]

India's poor record in creating manufacturing jobs had two unchanging causes. The first was a strong rupee, which limited the possibility of growing manufactured exports. Briefly, after Indian authorities floated the rupee in 1993, it depreciated, and export growth picked up. But then foreign stock investors—attracted by companies supplying India's top 15-percent income earners—increased the demand for and raised the value of the rupee. Meanwhile, since Indian inflation was higher than in competitor countries, domestic production costs rose faster than prices of goods sold in international markets, making exports steadily less profitable for Indian business.

Deficiency in human capital was India's other perennial handicap, and a new policy in August 2009—the Right to Education (RTE)—did the impossible: it made matters worse. Under the new policy, schools stopped detaining or expelling students until they reached the eighth grade. The honorable intention was to prevent the loss of self-esteem among children. But such a policy could work only if teachers ensured that students did, in fact, learn grade-level skills.

That's where the RTE encountered a deep malaise in India's education system. Governments throughout India had built schools and enrolled children at a rapid speed since the early 1990s. The schools had raised salaries to attract teachers, and the education mafia had established fly-by-night colleges to award suspect or even fake degrees to certify a generation of scarcely trained teachers. Courts and official investigations decried the state of affairs, but a cozy system of shared largesse endured: small-town politicians and businessmen paid bribes to receive licenses for their so-called colleges, they charged stiff fees to certify aspiring teachers, and the teachers received increasing salaries. The RTE policy of not detaining or expelling students let the teachers off the hook, who pushed unprepared students to higher grades, where, faced with more advanced subject material, they fell further behind. "The consequences were devastating," writes Anil Swarup, a former education secretary, the most senior civil servant responsible for education. The quality of Indian school education—measured by mathematics and reading test scores—fell exactly when the global standard for education quality was rising. By one international comparison, Indian education quality got stuck at about the level of low-performing sub-Saharan African countries, such as Uganda.[25]

Instead of trying to raise worker productivity through better education, political and intellectual elites identified a culprit for anemic job growth: India's labor laws. This misguided focus fit the government's instinct to favor business interests. In November 2004, Jairam Ramesh, a member of Sonia Gandhi's National Advisory Council, said that the "labour market is too rigid to allow frequent adjustment in workforce." In August 2005, Prime Minister Manmohan Singh added his voice to this cause: "Extreme rigidities in the labor market" were not consistent with "achieving our goals," he said. These statements were code for saying that Indian laws made it too hard to fire workers. The implication was that businesses were reluctant to invest in labor-intensive production for fear they would later not be able to fire their workers if the business turned sour. Mirroring the blame on labor laws was the "missing middle" thesis, which stated that Indian producers chose to remain small—that is, below a given threshold size—so that labor laws would not apply to them and they could fire workers at will. Thus, the argument was that "rigid" labor laws were robbing India of dynamic mid-sized, export-oriented firms.[26]

The data did not support the "missing middle" thesis. A study in the prestigious *Journal of Economic Perspectives* did not find several firms bunched just below a size threshold, nor did it find very few firms just above that threshold. In any case, for decades, Indian firms had hired employees on short-term contracts and so had enormous flexibility to fire workers, further negating the accusation against labor laws.[27]

There was a bigger problem though with focusing single-mindedly on making it easier to fire workers. While threatening workers with dismissal helps employers drive down wages, that short-sighted strategy also makes workers less productive. With little or no security of tenure, both workers and their employers lose the incentive to invest in increasing operational productivity. Illustrating the principle, U.S. labor productivity growth was highest in the late 1930s and 1940s, when strong unions and minimum wages gave workers a high level of employment protection.[28]

If businesses needed more flexibility in firing workers, workers deserved legal protection against arbitrary and unfair dismissal as well as support from unemployment insurance. Unfortunately, Indian authorities could not credibly promise legal protections or safety nets for workers. So the pursuit of labor market "flexibility" continued to promote low-paid, insecure work. India remained a low-productivity economy in which the sense of unfairness simmered.[29]

Ignoring India's failings, the China fetish reemerged. In 2007, India-born Brown University political scientist Ashutosh Varshney again predicted that the democratic Indian tortoise would emerge victorious against the autocratic Chinese hare. He reasoned that Chinese autocracy would implode while India's long-term democratic stability was "a virtual certainty." Such naïveté ignored the immense strengths of the Chinese economy. True, if Chinese autocracy were to crack, its economy would face much disruption. But China's human capital and long-term relationships with foreign buyers would remain largely intact. And even if India's democracy held, the absence of the strengths China possesses would always handicap India.[30]

India did avoid being sucked into the global financial crisis that began in July 2007. Indian banks had not invested in exotic financial instruments that lay as ticking bombs in the North Atlantic countries. The Reserve Bank's large foreign exchange reserves assured foreign investors that they need not panic and flee. And the Reserve Bank's easy monetary policy and the government's sizable fiscal stimulus helped cushion the fall in GDP growth.[31]

The narrow escape from a financial crisis strengthened the hubris and instinct for quick-fix policies. Rather than address agriculture's long-term problems, the government raised minimum support prices for wheat, rice, and other crops on top of the already large increases of the previous few years. Finance Minister Pranab Mukherjee announced more subsidies for fertilizers and a hike in salaries for civil servants.[32] These "giveaways" had an obvious eye on winning voters in the upcoming April/May 2009 elections.

The fiscal profligacy had costs: government budget deficit at 10 percent of GDP, inflation rate at 10 percent a year, and current account deficit at nearly 3 percent of GDP. This was a path to a financial crisis, as in 1991. But with sizable foreign exchange reserves, Mukherjee was secure in blowing up India's public finances to win the next election.[33]

The approaching election also deepened the politician-business nexus. "Black" (unaccounted for) money from wealthy individuals and businesses financed election spending on a scale that approached the bloated dollar values seen in U.S. presidential campaigns. As before, the largest election expense was on transporting Indian leaders by helicopters and chartered flights. Advertising budgets ballooned to cover the over four hundred television channels and (of course) the new web-based media. Print media advertisements masqueraded as news. Candidates vied for voter attention with cash and other gifts. As one commentator remarked, political candidates viewed election spending as an "investment" on which they expected "a 10-fold return."[34]

With its easy access to election-spending money, the Congress Party had an advantage. The BJP was in disarray. BJP leader Lal Krishna Advani—the man who made constructing a temple in Ayodhya the BJP's central plank—was eighty-one years old. He was unsure if the Hindutva strategy was still viable. Gujarat Chief Minister Narendra Modi, although tainted by the massacre of Muslims in Gujarat in 2002, had the support of Hindutva believers as well as of leading Indian businessmen, who hoped that he would lead India into an economic renaissance. Modi crisscrossed the country delivering vigorous campaign speeches. But it was not his turn. Even with the weak employment generation and high inflation, the Congress Party won a mandate to lead another UPA coalition.[35]

The odds, though, were stacking up against India. The climate crisis increased its onslaught. Following droughts in the first half of the 2000s, poor rainfall in 2009 and 2010 caused grain output to fall for the first time since 2005. Erratic monsoons, where a drought was followed by heavy rains in the next season, were becoming more common. Rainfall was highly variable even within a season: after spells of dry weather, downpours caused additional damage. With global warming amplifying the natural variability of monsoons, India's agricultural growth remained low, generating upward pressure on prices of food grains and other essentials such as oilseeds and vegetables.[36]

Indian and international cheerleaders, however, remained upbeat. Ah, they said, Indian poverty rates have gone down! Here, then, was the puzzle. If agriculturists were struggling and new jobs were mainly in construction and other low-end informal sector work, how could poverty go down?

For India's Poor, a Precarious Living

The poverty line is the cost of goods and services needed to survive. There is no science in defining this line. The World Bank set human survival cost at a dollar a day in 1985 prices, which it then updated to $1.25 a day at 2005 prices, and $1.90 per person per day at 2011 prices. Anyone in 2011 who could spend $1.91/day was not poor; someone who could spend only $1.89/day was poor.

In 2011, $1.90/day equaled just under 30 rupees/day at India's purchasing power parity exchange rate (15.55 rupees/dollar). We use the purchasing power parity rate to convert the dollar-based poverty benchmark to rupees rather than the market exchange rate—about 50 rupees/dollar in 2011—because the purchasing power rate is based on direct price comparisons of identical goods and services in different countries. The market exchange rate is not appropriate in this context because it reflects the prices of internationally traded products such as steel and coal and hence greatly overstates the domestic costs of food and other consumption goods and services, which are typically not traded.[37]

India's poverty rate began falling at a welcome pace, starting around 1985 (Figure 20.2). The decline was a huge relief after the stubbornly high 60 percent poverty rate in the Nehru years and the extremely slow decline during Mrs. Gandhi's years.

However, we must view the much-celebrated post-1985 achievement in proper perspective. The World Bank's poverty line—its measure of the costs of goods and services needed to survive—provided for little else other than minimal nutrition: a daily diet of 400 grams of coarse rice and wheat, 200 grams of vegetables, pulses, and fruit, plus modest amounts of milk, eggs, edible oil, spices, and tea. The Indian government's poverty benchmark for 2011, which was also about 30 rupees/day, similarly made virtually no provision for education, health, and housing. These paltry sums defined the poor as those who lived in subhuman conditions. The finding that "only" 22.5 percent of Indians were below the poverty line in

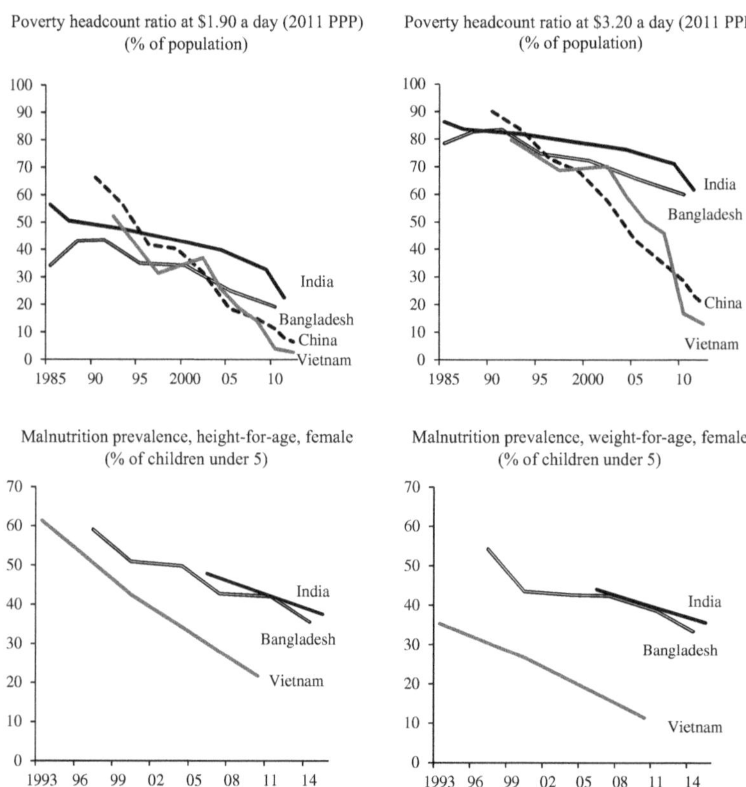

FIGURE 20.2: India's dire poverty declined, but precarious living persisted.
Source: World Bank, World Development Indicators, SI.POV.DDAY, SI.POV.LMIC, SH.STA.STNT.FE.ZS, SH.STA.MALN.FE.ZS.

2011 also hauntingly said that two decades after the liberalization reforms, more than one-fifth of Indians were living in degrading circumstances.[38]

For India, setting the poverty line at $1.90 (at 2011 prices), in effect, wished away the country's poverty. Even if that benchmark made some sense in the 1950s, the concept of *who is poor* must change over time. The Council of Economic Advisers reporting to the U.S. president noted in 1969, "Yesterday's luxuries become today's necessities." As life becomes more complex, new goods and services become necessary to ensure that a person can exist as "a participating member of society." In the India of 2011, survival needed not just minimal nutrition but also healthcare, education, and housing and often also a table fan, refrigerator, and motorcycle.[39]

Because socially necessary and acceptable consumption requires more than minimal nutrition, the World Bank recommends a higher poverty benchmark for lower-middle-income countries such as India. This higher benchmark is $3.20/day, which in 2011 was 50 rupees/day/person or 6,000 rupees/month for a family of four. When seen through that more realistic, although still frugal lens, over 60 percent of Indians were poor in 2011 (Figure 20.2).

The gap between the two poverty lines is a measure of precarity: those who can barely spend $3.20/day are at constant risk of falling below the $1.90/day threshold into severe poverty. In India, life is perilous because farming is inherently risky, construction work is physically dangerous, and workplace injuries in manufacturing employment can be debilitating. Whatever their profession, all Indians face medical emergencies. Just the costs of medicines and outpatient care can inflict lasting financial damage on families living on the margins of poverty. In 2011, about 40 percent of Indians lived in the precarious zone between $3.20 and $1.90/day, one illness away from extreme poverty. China, Vietnam, and the large Latin American middle-income countries had virtually eliminated dire poverty *and* precarity.[40]

We can now juxtapose the employment and poverty trends. As some Indians left low-earning, low-productivity agriculture, they moved into the only somewhat higher-earning informal sector. The higher earnings bumped them above the most frugal poverty line into the precarious zone. They continued living fearful lives. Elite Indians cheered this "achievement."

A high degree of malnutrition, especially among girls, was another unhappy metric of India's limited progress in improving the lives of the poor (see the bottom panel of Figure 20.2). Malnourished children get sick often and are less likely to be productive workers when they grow up. Consistent with Bangladesh's somewhat lower poverty rates, Bangladeshi girls under the age of five were slightly better nourished than Indian girls under five. Vietnam did better than India not just for the statistical reason that Bihar and Uttar Pradesh weighed down the Indian average. Vietnamese social achievements were (and still are) superior to those of Tamil Nadu, which is among the most progressive of the Indian states. In 2011, more than half the girls under five years of age in Bihar and between 40 and 50 percent of the girls in Uttar Pradesh were undernourished. In Tamil Nadu, the malnutrition rate was 30 percent, and in Vietnam it was 20 percent, even though its per capita income was about the same as Tamil Nadu's.[41]

Stolen Money

While a majority of Indians lived poor or precarious lives, financial scams flourished. The 2010 Commonwealth Games in Delhi was a simple "cash-for-contracts affair" in the hands of a Congress Party functionary, who was previously a junior minister under Prime Minister P. V. Narasimha Rao. The most memorable story is about the $62-dollar toilet paper rolls for the athletes' village. However, the value of contracts was many times greater for the construction of sports facilities and the makeover of the city. And while politicians and oligarchs became rich, they put children—as young as seven years old—to work on these construction sites.[42]

The sums of money were even larger when the government allotted the telecom spectrum and coal blocks to private companies. The government's internal auditor, the comptroller and auditor general, revealed in a 2010 report that the telecom department had awarded highly valuable licenses for second-generation (2G) telecom spectrum in 2008 in a way that favored those who had been "tipped off." The comptroller and auditor general reported again in 2012, this time on the allocation of 218 coal blocks between 2004 and 2009. Rather than auctioning the blocks to the highest bidder, the government charged throwaway prices. The Supreme Court declared the spectrum and coal awards illegal, which led to their reallocation through competitive auctions.[43]

Although neither the auditor general nor the Supreme Court found evidence of corruption, the stench was sky high. Author and business journalist T. N. Ninan expressed a widely held view: "Almost anywhere you looked, in both central and state governments, there was the reek of scandal. Heists that were so in-your-face." Underpriced sale of scarce resources, bribery in defense deals, and chicanery in negotiation of infrastructure contracts were all too common.[44]

Rich Indians drew on another pot of money: government-owned banks. Vijay Mallya understood the possibilities. Operating under the Kingfisher label, he had expanded an inherited brewery to command over half the Indian beer market. Through acquisitions, he also gained a dominant share of the whisky and rum markets.[45]

In 2002, Mallya became a member of the Rajya Sabha, the upper house of parliament. State legislatures elect Rajya Sabha members to six-year terms, and the Congress Party in Karnataka helped elect Mallya. Once in parliament, he bagged a spot on the committee for civil aviation. The government was just opening up the skies to private airlines, and Mallya's position on the civil aviation committee gave him privileged access to senior aviation officials and advance notice of policies in the pipeline. In May 2005, Mallya launched the swanky Kingfisher Airline, named after his popular beer brand. His showman instinct was now on full display. Celebrating his fiftieth birthday that year, Mallya held a six-day event at which singer Lionel Richie performed. He bought himself a yacht, a car racing team, a football club, and a cricket team. His much-awaited Kingfisher calendars featured scantily clad women. He was, as he said, the "King of Good Times."[46]

Mallya's enchanted story met the reality of the global financial crisis in 2007–2008. Airline traffic fell just when he was furiously buying more planes, in part to launch an international service. Mallya had borrowed from seventeen Indian banks, almost all of them government-owned. Now he could not pay them back. By one estimate, he owed almost 9,000 crore rupees, over $2 billion at the prevailing market exchange rate. In 2012, with his debts still unpaid, he offered a large gift of gold to a revered Hindu temple and shut down his bankrupt airline. What the gods received, the employees did not. In October that year, the wife of a Kingfisher Airline employee died by suicide allegedly because her husband had not been paid his salary for several months. In 2013, *Forbes* listed Mallya's net worth at $750 million, making him the eighty-fourth-richest Indian. In 2016, he fled to London, from where he still fights attempts by Indian authorities to extradite him.[47]

Mallya was one among many. Several businesses had borrowed from government-owned banks to finance infrastructure, mining, and steel projects, all central to India's development strategy. Defaults on such corporate loans and "waivers" (forgiveness) of loans to farmers created a hole in the capital of government-owned banks. The government stepped in to fill that hole at the expense of the Indian people, adding 58,000 crore rupees, more than $10 billion, over the four financial years from 2010–2011 to 2013–2014, with another 57,000 crore rupees injected in the three years after that. It was a never-ending drain on the exchequer. Some small farmers in distressed areas benefited from the waivers, but the big winners from forgiveness and defaults were large farmers and corporate tycoons. They played a game of "heads I win; tails you lose."[48]

The politician-business network had spread its tentacles widely. In addition to Mallya, a notable entrant to the Rajya Sabha was Parimal Nathwani. Like Mallya, Nathwani was a Congress Party–sponsored Rajya Sabha member from the state of Jharkhand. Nathwani doubled as a parliamentarian and "key troubleshooter" for Mukesh Ambani, one of the richest men in the world. Businessmen also contested and won elections to the lower house, the Lok Sabha. By 2014, the share of those who listed "business" or "trading" as their profession had risen to 26 percent of all Lok Sabha members, up from 14 percent in 1991. These businessmen were on parliamentary committees, which gave them public legitimacy and the opportunity to shape legislation and policy.[49]

Despite the privileges they enjoyed at home, many rich Indians exited the country, in both an economic and a physical sense. Between 2006 and 2008, Indian businesses invested an annual average of $17 billion a year outside the country, and the rate of outflow remained over $10 billion a year for the next several years. In principle, given its shortage of capital and technology, a less-developed nation such as India should have offered very high returns on investment. But because India lacked the necessary human capital and physical infrastructure, the returns to investment were not especially high, which prompted many businesses to invest abroad. That capital exit stripped the veneer off India's much-lauded success story. The Tatas went on an international acquisitions spree, buying coal mines, luxury hotels, and the British Jaguar and Land

Rover marquees from Ford. Having invested $16 billion in thirty-seven cross-border acquisitions, 58 percent of the Tata's business turnover came from outside India. The Tatas were not alone, adds T. N. Ninan: "One ambitious business group after the other embarked on projects abroad."[50] Put simply, India's ultra-rich only invested in India under carefully secured insider knowledge and favorable regulatory treatment; otherwise they took their money overseas.

In the category just below the ultra-rich were the mega-rich, who invested in the one Indian business sure to make money. "I have two lives," the young man Rakesh said to Rana Dasgupta. "I have an automotive business, I also have a real estate business. What you see in front of you is the wealth generated from my real estate." And his wealth on display was impressive: a massage room, a post-massage chill-out room, a beauty parlor, and a Japanese restaurant. A weary Rakesh explained, "I can't relax, man—that's the fucking problem. The only time I relax is when I have a massage."[51]

India's construction boom made the rich richer. Building contractors enjoyed large profit margins, often in collusion with politicians and the mafia. And they frequently did not pay even the minimum wage to their workers, the message to whom was, "people like you have no claims to comfort and safety . . . you are outside of this story, and you may never come in."[52]

Like the ultra-rich, the mega-rich also exited the system. Recognizing how run down the Indian education system was, many sent their children to study abroad. According to Reserve Bank of India data, funds spent by Indians to finance education abroad jumped from $237 million in the fiscal year 2003–2004 to over $2 billion in 2008–2009, after which the amount remained in the $2 billion range for the next few years. The Reserve Bank's numbers, though, were likely too low, probably by a factor of three, according to political scientists Devesh Kapur and Pratap Bhanu Mehta. The reason was that rich Indians held funds abroad, some of it in tax havens. They used those funds—which the Reserve Bank could not track—to educate their kids, among other things. Kapur and Mehta noted importantly that when rich Indians exited the Indian educational system, their "voices" went with them. With no stake in Indian education, they were content to let it rot.[53]

The exit of the rich from the water infrastructure was even more insidious. Unlike for education, the rich could not selectively travel abroad for water! Instead, in their high-rise apartments, office complexes, and luxury hotels, rich Indians competed for scarce clean water from decaying urban water systems. And the rich exercised no discipline on their water use. In Mumbai, private swimming pools and water parks used water without any check. City water departments met this demand either by diverting existing water supplies or by transporting water from nearby rivers and lakes, gradually drying them up. In the other India, women and children queued up in front of water pumps, often having walked long distances to reach a working pump. A despairing woman in a poor Mumbai neighborhood cried that she had sold her jewelry to acquire a water connection, but the police declared her connection illegal and smashed the motor she had installed to pump the water. Corrupt officials and a shadowy "water mafia" sold water at high prices to the neediest. And as was the case for education, rich voices exited. They had no stake in durable solutions. The poor, divided by regional, caste, and communal loyalties, lacked a unified democratic voice.[54]

Mumbai's water-use pattern repeated itself in other cities. Every night, hundreds of trucks brought water to Delhi's five-star hotels, for drinking water, laundry, swimming pools, and saunas. Water "entrepreneurs" pumped water from wells around the city; as one set of wells ran dry, they would move further out to deplete the land of even more water. The gated communities around Delhi in Gurgaon and Noida had their own water parks with swimming pools and water slides. In a memorable phrase, Rana Dasgupta described reckless water use as the product of "a fatally short-term marauding mentality." It was "rational" for everyone to suck the water out of the ground before others could do so.[55]

In virtually every Indian city, the new buildings closed the drains, tanks, and natural lakes. Without these water sinks, rainfall did not replenish the disappearing groundwater; instead, even mildly heavy rainfall flooded the cities. In a January 2011 judgment, Supreme Court judges directed state governments to stop encroachment on the common-property water bodies. Governments, however, were complicit in the rapacious building boom and refused to enforce the order.[56]

Only One India on the Move

In October 2012, Starbucks inaugurated its first Indian outlet in Mumbai. An excited eight-year-old girl exclaimed to her father, "Papa, this is the biggest Starbucks I have been to. It is *waaay* bigger than the one in Hong Kong or Singapore." Most Indians could not afford a cup of coffee at Starbucks, but this little world traveler had visited the coffee chain in Hong Kong and Singapore. On June 4, 2013, within minutes after Amazon.in went online, a student from the super-elite Indian Institute of Management at Ahmedabad ordered the first book from the site.[57] Millions of young Indians timepassed in shabby Indian colleges, while the high-flying management student prepared to conquer the world.

The two Indias had truly become different countries. Many Indians who had assiduously built accommodations for themselves in slums were constantly at risk of ejection in the cause of beautifying cities. Mukesh Ambani built himself a twenty-seven-story home in Mumbai. Farmers in debt committed suicide. Vijay Mallya defaulted on the $2 billion of debt he owed to government-owned banks and was fighting extradition back to India from a home in London. The winners took it all (Figure 20.3).

The two Indias confronted each other in court in 2007. The sociologist Nandini Sundar and colleagues moved the Supreme Court to declare as unconstitutional the government-promoted vigilante group Salwa Judum, which protected business interests by inflicting terror on native Adivasis in the mineral-rich forests of Chhattisgarh. In a July 2011 judgment, two Supreme Court judges offered a stinging indictment of India's development strategy. Citing a report commissioned by the Indian Planning Commission, the judges said that violence in the Adivasi areas was unending because "dominant" elites had "cornered the benefits" of Indian development at the "expense of the poor." The benefits of development projects trickled up, rather than down. The judges concluded that the government had violated the constitutional principles of equality before law and dignity of life. They ordered that the Salwa Judum be disbanded.

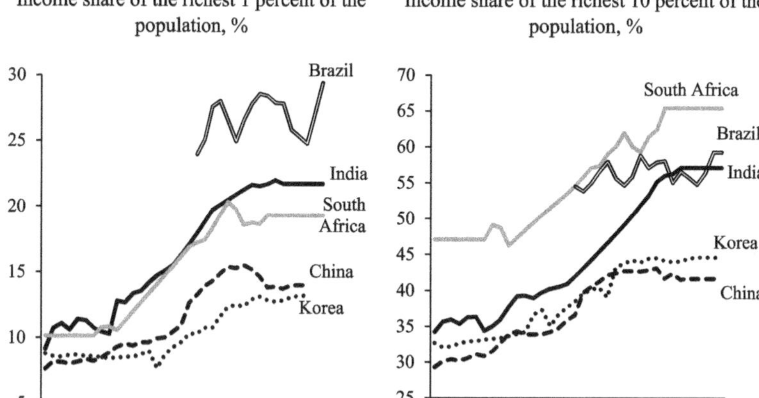

FIGURE 20.3: India grew into one of the world's most unequal societies.
Note: The share of the top one percent in Brazil is presented in 3-year moving averages since, although always high, it moves erratically from one year to another.
Source: World Inequality Database, https://wid.world/data/.

The Chhattisgarh and Indian governments ignored the decree. The name "Salwa Judum" disappeared, but state-supported vigilante forces continued under new names.[58]

In an instructive historical parallel in 1832, the U.S. Supreme Court under Chief Justice John Marshall struck down Georgia's horrifying laws that gave the state the authority to seize Cherokee territory and nullify Cherokee laws and customs. According to the folklore, U.S. President Andrew Jackson responded, "John Marshall has made his decision, now let him enforce it." Neither the State of Georgia nor Jackson enforced the Court's decision, and the removal of tens of thousands of Native Americans proceeded in one of the most shameful chapters of U.S. history.[59]

Jackson did enforce subsequent U.S. Supreme Court decisions. But in India, governments continued to ignore Supreme Court orders, especially those that sought to break the nexus between business and politicians. Miners and the mafia—the distinction was not always clear—brazenly flouted the court's ban on mining in the Aravalli hills of Rajasthan and also disregarded the ban on sand mining, which provided an essential input for the national construction boom.[60]

In his Independence Day speech in August 2006, Singh had said, "The going has never been as good. Wherever I go, I see our nation on the move." In 2014, 45 percent of Indians worked in an agricultural sector exposed to a mounting climate crisis. For agricultural workers, the main escape hatch was back-breaking construction. There was also a rich India. In a Bentley and Lamborghini showroom in Delhi, the buyers—often also owners of yachts and islands and jets—paid $600,000 for a car they only used to race on empty roads at night. That India *was* on the move. For that India, "the going had never been as good."[61]

A "fatally short-term marauding mentality" was the defining theme of India's decade under the Manmohan Singh–led UPA governments. Wealthy individuals and powerful businesses operated on the valid premise that violating rules and plundering the nation's common resources brought them substantial benefits and carried few risks. They pursued insider regulatory information, stole the taxpayer money through government-owned banks, and ran down precious mineral and water resources. The government conspired in this grand theft, leaving the Supreme Court to flail helplessly. In place of an economic policy that promoted fairness, an elitist definition of poverty wished away the poor. Public goods remained in dismal condition. Job growth was lackluster. India was losing the development race yet again, this time to Vietnam and Bangladesh.

Chapter 21

MODI PUSHES THE ECONOMY OFF THE EDGE

Narendra Damodardas Modi was born in September 1950 to a low-caste family. He grew up with six siblings in a semi-finished house in a remote Gujarat village. When he was eight years old, he joined the Rashtriya Swayamsevak Sangh, the belligerent Hindutva organization. From that early start, he rose in prominence as a leader in Gujarat's BJP. Modi jackknifed into the national and international consciousness in February 2002, when hordes of Hindus massacred Muslims under his watch as Gujarat's chief minister. He showed little compassion for those who suffered and refused to condemn the riots.[1]

Soon after the riots, though, Modi sensed political and economic trouble when business owners complained about the continuing Hindu and police violence against Muslims, civil rights activists, and journalists. Many businesses threatened to stop investing in Gujarat. In late April, an industry leader warned that not just Gujarat but India would "pay dearly" for the state's failure to protect minorities. Veteran industrialist Rahul Bajaj sustained the denunciation. "Events like the Gujarat carnage will impede our economic progress," Bajaj wrote in the *Hindustan Times*. At a conclave of industrialists in February 2003, amid a continuing chorus of criticism from businesses, Bajaj looked at Modi and asked him, "We would like to know what you believe in, what you stand for, because leadership is important."[2]

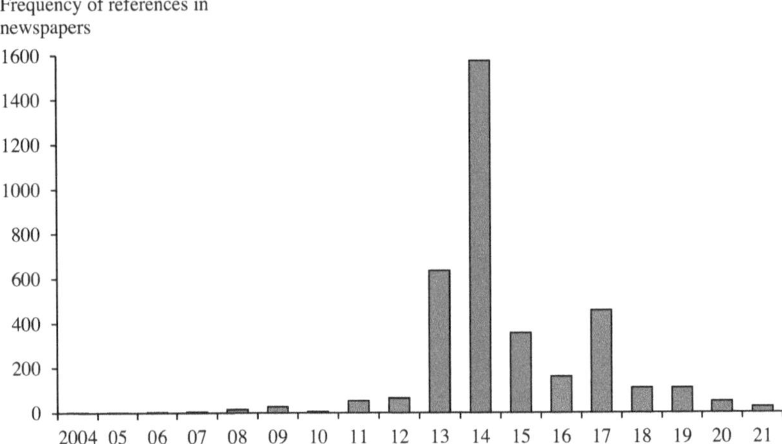

FIGURE 21.1: A new phrase emerged: "the Gujarat model of development." (Number of articles that refer to the "Gujarat model of development" in the Factiva newspaper database)

Source: Factiva database, https://www.dowjones.com/professional/factiva/.

A furious Modi dismissed his critics as "pseudo-secularists." He recast himself as a friend of business and began marketing Gujarat as a prime business location. In September 2003, with the help of the businessman Gautam Adani, Modi established *Vibrant Gujarat,* planned as a once-every-two-years gathering to sell Gujarat to Indian and foreign industrialists. Adani and other businessmen—including Mukesh Ambani—signed agreements with the Gujarat government to fund and operate large investment projects.[3]

Modi's rebranding effort went national in 2004. A new phrase— "the Gujarat model of development"—became associated with him as he campaigned that year for the BJP's Lok Sabha candidates (Figure 21.1).[4] The narrative of Modi as a development champion grew exponentially.

In late 2006, Mukesh Ambani led a delegation of Indian businessmen to the United States to market "Vibrant Gujarat." Modi, however, had set his eyes on a bigger prize: Ratan Tata, India's most respected business name. An opportunity arose in 2008 when the frustrated Tata announced he was pulling his car manufacturing investment out of West Bengal because there was no meeting of the minds with the farmers protesting against his acquisition of their land. As Modi described it, he sent a three-word text message to Tata: "Welcome to Gujarat." Tata did not disappoint. He became Narendra Modi's brand ambassador, singing his praises to a worldwide audience on Fareed Zakaria's Sunday morning program on CNN. Modi invited other Indian and foreign businessmen. He promised them that in Gujarat, instead of "red tape," a "red carpet" awaited them. The accolades for Modi descended into silliness. Anil Ambani, Mukesh's younger brother and one of India's leading businessmen, chimed in. He said that Modi was "the lord of men, a leader among leaders and the king among kings." Tata added that he had been "stupid" to have not invested more in Gujarat.[5]

The Gujarat model was marauding development on steroids. For businesses, it was bonanza time! They received virtually free land, large loans at nearly zero interest rates, generous tax breaks, and no-fuss environmental clearances. The taxpayer bore the cost. In early 2013, the Office of the Comptroller and Auditor General (the same body that highlighted improper allocation of spectrum and mining rights by Manmohan Singh's central government) rapped Modi's Gujarat government for granting approximately $120 million (750 crore rupees) in "undue" favors to big business. "The major beneficiaries of government's largesse," the *Press Trust of India* reported, were "big corporate entities like Reliance Industries, Essar Steel and Adani Power."[6]

The favored businesses invested in capital-intensive projects with large price tags well suited to flashy announcements. Petroleum (the fastest-growing industrial sector in Gujarat), steel, chemicals, and pharmaceuticals projects fit that pattern. The projects boosted GDP but created few new employment opportunities. They polluted the land and rivers flagrantly while also depleting the state's groundwater.[7]

Gautam Adani embodied the Gujarat model. Born in 1962, Adani dropped out of college in 1978 to enter the diamond trade. He soon became an export-import trader and industrialist. In the late 1990s, he embarked on infrastructure projects. The Gujarat government sold Adani land at rates that were far below the market price. He received highly underpriced natural gas from a government-owned company and paid a much lower than contractually stipulated penalty for delays in supplying electric power to the state's grid. His projects caused irreparable damage to waterways and the livelihoods of fishermen, and when he seized community pasture lands, he destroyed valuable mangroves. From 2000 until 2013, Adani's business turnover increased fourteenfold to reach $8.5 billion. His capital-intensive projects created only a limited number of jobs, and these were mainly for skilled workers.[8]

Since the state's budget prioritized giveaways for big business, expenditure on education, health, and other welfare services suffered. As University of Chicago philosopher Martha Nussbaum emphasized in a clinical dissection, Gujarat's human development indicators placed it about in the middle of the range achieved by Indian states, which was an unworthy achievement given how low the general condition of Indian human development was. Moreover, in the context of Gujarat's high GDP growth, the state's human development performance, including on such measures as life expectancy and female literacy, was "not just middling but downright bad."[9]

In early 2013, as national elections drew closer, the crescendo of the Gujarat model rose. Columbia University economist Jagdish Bhagwati lent his enormous intellectual stature to that phrase. Using a false dichotomy, Bhagwati said that the "Gujarat model" promoted "private entrepreneurship" rather than fiscally costly "redistribution." Bhagwati was among the world's most erudite economists and development experts. He must have known that much of Western Europe and East Asia became rich promoting both private entrepreneurship and a humane redistribution. Indeed, the East Asians were clear that redistribution to advance human development was essential for job-rich growth driven by private entrepreneurs. Modi, in any case, was not promoting entrepreneurship. He was subsidizing favored industrialists who created virtually no jobs and polluted the land and water.[10]

As the 2014 elections approached, the lazy "Gujarat model" narrative met a nation in search of a savior. India's GDP growth, which was the only metric by which Indians judged economic success, had started falling around 2011–2012. Even the IMF, which had cheered the marauding development pattern under Manmohan Singh, noted that India faced "a challenging macroeconomic landscape." That was IMF-speak for an economy in serious trouble. As expected, the impetus from the 1991 liberalization reform had faded. Meanwhile, world trade had slowed to a crawl and no longer provided the boost of the early 2000s. Only the finance-construction bubble lived on. Consumer price inflation ran at 10 percent a year, the budget deficit remained high, and the current account deficit had widened. India also faced formidable long-term problems: low agricultural productivity, few urban jobs, lagging human development, and widespread ecological damage.[11]

To claim credentials for broad-based development, Modi and his media experts advertised his humble beginnings. Together, they sold a national image of him as a *chaiwallah* (tea-seller) in his father's modest stall. Modi spoke stirringly of India's "immense youth capital" and its "yearning for employment." The BJP party machine touted Modi as a savior, who in solidarity with the downtrodden, would create "millions of jobs."[12]

The 2014 national election was another master class in illegal campaign financing. As one colorful account put it, "All parties are competing with one another in a decadent display of money power." Ultra-plush campaign helicopters and chartered flights were often on loan from big business houses. Black money was put to good use, buying votes with cash, fried chicken, mobile phones, home appliances, saris, and liquor (sometimes conveniently transported in milk vans).[13]

Throughout the country, politicians with communal leanings wooed ganglords for their money and their unemployed young soldiers for muscle. That darkness was intense in Uttar Pradesh, where an entrenched criminal-politician network overlapped with a fierce communalism. Hindu-Muslim riots occurred regularly, with a particularly brutal one breaking out in August 2013 in the western Uttar Pradesh town of Muzaffarnagar. A fake video, allegedly circulated by a BJP member of the Uttar Pradesh Legislative Assembly, claimed to show the lynching of two Hindu boys. As the elections approached, Uttar Pradesh's morbid flames burned furiously.[14]

Modi's trusted lieutenant Amit Shah jumped into that cauldron of hate. The *Sunday Standard* wrote that the Muzaffarnagar riots were "the glue he [Amit Shah] used to unite Hindutva forces" in a politically powerful us-versus-them mobilization. For Modi and Shah, a strong performance in Uttar Pradesh was crucial, since the state would elect 80 of India's 543 parliamentarians. Modi contested two parliamentary seats, one in his home state of Gujarat (as is conventional) and the other (which received all the public attention) in the eastern Uttar Pradesh city of Varanasi, the holiest of Hindu cities. In Varanasi, Modi made well-publicized visits to Kashi Vishwanath and Sankat Mochan, among the most sacred of Hindu temples.[15]

Indian and international commentators applauded Modi's technocratic authoritarianism in pursuit of the Gujarat model, even as they struggled with his Hindu authoritarianism. The frequently liberal *Indian Express* columnist Pratap Bhanu Mehta rose to Modi's defense. In his ornate style, Mehta wrote that Modi represented the nation's "longing for centralisation in an age of dispersion, decisiveness in a milieu of indecision, growth amidst a fear of stagnation and government in the face of raucous democracy." It was the old trope: democracy was raucous, and India needed the hand of a decisive leader. "Those worried about him," Mehta sternly said, "should first set their own house in order." In a later column, Mehta was equally stern with those who saw the specter of fascism in Modi's rise. Was their finger-pointing, he rhetorically asked, merely the "hyperbole of a crumbling elite using moral outrage as a substitute for addressing genuine political challenges?" The political scientist Ashutosh Varshney reminded the readers of his column that he was a seasoned scholar and reassured them that the institutions of Indian democracy would tame Modi's Hindutva agenda.[16]

For former Proctor & Gamble executive and author Gurcharan Das, Modi was the ideal technocrat-politician. The Modi catchphrase "minimum government, maximum governance" matched Das's well-known expression "India grows at night when the government sleeps." They both drew inspiration from Ronald Reagan's famed "government is the problem" ethic. Das favored Modi because he believed that the gains from the Modi-generated high growth would outweigh the harm from Hindutva. Das predicted—alas, with no basis—that Modi would create 8 to 10 million jobs every year. Jim O'Neill, former Goldman Sachs executive and roving global public intellectual, delivered his own quick-fire judgment. He declared that he could not judge Modi's sectarianism, but the man was "good on economics."[17]

And, in ringing words, the *Financial Times* wrote, "Part of Mr. Modi's attraction is that, by sheer force of will, he may be able to override some of the checks and balances of Indian democracy and introduce some of the clear-headedness of growth-driven China."[18] One more time, with feeling, the message was that democracy lay at the root of India's economic problems. After the disaster under a strongwoman between 1975 and 1977, the clamor was on for an Indian strongman.

Thus, Brand Modi came to represent a humble tea-seller, who would—with authoritarian force—rev up the Indian economic growth engine and whose Hindutva, ... well, don't worry about it! Another popular view was: what's the alternative? Congress Party's Manmohan Singh had not delivered anything significant, and he had decided, in any case, to retire. Rahul Gandhi—son of Sonia and Rajiv Gandhi, and thus the fourth generation of the Nehru-Gandhi family—was an obvious political lightweight, with no claim to leadership other than his last name.

The pundits wanted Modi for their imagined virtues of the Gujarat model; his Hindutva appeal won him the election. In Uttar Pradesh, the Modi-Shah focus on rousing Hindutva supporters worked impressively, winning them 71 of the state's 80 parliamentary seats, up from 10 seats in 2009. That crucial victory, as they correctly judged, put them over the top by a small national vote margin but a sizable margin in Lok Sabha seats. In mid-May 2014, Modi's BJP-led National Democratic Alliance gained power.

For Modi, the election victory erased residual international condemnation because of the Gujarat riots. In 2005, the United States had denied him a visa to enter the country, and several U.S. lawmakers and activists remained critical of Modi's polarizing personality. But President Barack Obama, ignoring the critics, was the first world leader to congratulate him on his election as India's prime minister.[19]

To take his place as India's prime minister, Modi flew from Ahmedabad to Delhi in Gautam Adani's personal plane. Embossed on the plane's right side was the Indian flag; the Adani logo was on the other side. Stock prices of Adani-held companies rose, as if with the flight's take-off path, soaring well above the broader stock market index, the Sensex (Figure 21.2).

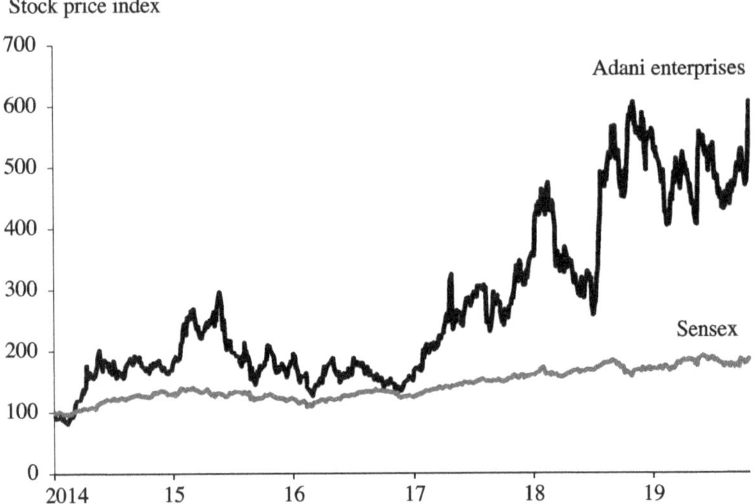

FIGURE 21.2: Gautam Adani's fortunes took off after Narendra Modi became prime minister. (January 1, 2014 = 100 to September 18, 2019)
Note: Adani Enterprises, ADEL; Sensex index, BSESN.
Source: https://www.investing.com/.

Investors in Adani's companies knew that he would profit from his connection with the prime minister, just as companies owned by friends of Indonesia's President Suharto had in the 1990s. More than ever, India was on the familiar path of backroom dealing and favoritism.[20]

India's Growth Story Fizzles

The Gujarat model quickly proved irrelevant for fixing India's vast challenges. After Modi's election as prime minister in May 2014, poor rainfall in June dimmed the prospects for the agricultural season. Industrial production lacked dynamism. The only good news was a sharp fall in global oil prices, which brought down the inflation rate and relieved the pressure on India's import bill. The fall in oil prices also helped the government reduce subsidies on petroleum products, thus providing relief to the budget. On balance, though, as the title of a Reuters report summed up on August 12, "So far, so disappointing."

Three days later, on August 15, Modi mesmerized the nation with his Independence Day speech. He wore an unconventional red, green, and gold turban. He declined the usual protection of a bulletproof glass cage and spoke for an hour, barely glancing at his notes. Modi acknowledged the continuing farmer suicides and called for a manufacturing renaissance in India. "Come make in India, ... come manufacture in India," he repeated in rhythmic cadence. India, he said, was "a country of young people" who he urged to acquire skills for manufacturing excellence. Promising social change, he decried the widespread open defecation and condemned violence against women, especially the practice of aborting female fetuses.[21]

Modi's economic promise soon wore thin. India did not become a global manufacturing hub. The modest GDP growth was debt-fueled and not sustainable. Corporate borrowing, which was typically from government-owned banks, was reaching its limits. Non-performing assets (NPAs) of banks were rising, which meant that companies were not repaying their debts on time. In November 2014, Raghuram Rajan, governor of the Reserve Bank of India, said "super" investors who had earned "fat returns" in the good times were dumping their losses on the banks. The system "protects" the super investors, Rajan brusquely said. In a memo to the prime minister in April 2015, Rajan listed thirty defaulters who owed fully one-third of the overdue loans, emphasizing that politically connected Indian businessmen were continuing to scam government-owned banks.[22]

Inevitably, the heavily indebted corporate sector slowed down its borrowing, but meanwhile—as a last gasp for growth—a consumer debt binge began in late 2014. Urban and rural consumers borrowed to buy homes amid rapidly rising property prices. They bought cars and consumer durables. Newly introduced credit cards injected a new abandon in Indian consumer spending.

Then, voilà! January 2015 brought good tidings. Indian GDP growth for the fiscal year of 2013–2014 jumped to 6.3 percent, up from the earlier estimate of 4.7 percent. This mysterious jump emerged from the previous government's initiative to review the data and methods for computing GDP. Such reviews are common but do not result in higher estimated growth rates. One market analyst said, "We are completely blind at the moment," a statement that largely holds true to this day. Other analysts noted that most indicators suggested, in fact, that growth was "sputtering" and the economy was possibly in a "mini-crisis." The new numbers, however, were convenient for maintaining the Indian growth narrative.[23]

Between June and August 2015, the rains fell short for the second year in a row. The concern arose again that rising global temperatures were causing recurring rainfall deficiency in India. As much as this was an economic problem, it was also a human problem. Forty-five percent of Indian workers were still making a meager living from agriculture. Children of once-powerful landholding communities took to the streets in protest. They were the Patidars in Gujarat, the Marathas in Maharashtra, and the Jats in Haryana and Uttar Pradesh. The spokesman for the protestors, twenty-two-year-old Hardik Patel (a Patidar) from Gujarat, said that repeated subdivision of land had whittled down the size of their landholdings. Official data confirmed that 69 percent of Indian farms were in the "marginal" category—1 hectare (2.5 acres) or less. An average farm in the marginal category was tiny, about 0.38 hectares (1 acre), and the share of such tiny farms was rapidly increasing. On these ever-smaller farms, the costs of production escalated as farmers invested in expensive wells, seeds, and fertilizers. The physical and financial stress on farmers was great—and the future only looked worse. The protestors demanded more reserved spots in educational institutions and government jobs.[24]

The clamor for reserved access to government jobs was so great because the private sector created few jobs for the teeming numbers of poorly educated young Indians. In her tormenting account of India's young "dreamers," journalist and author Snigdha Poonam describes the enormous "gap between jobs and jobseekers." Nineteen thousand people applied for 114 jobs at a municipality; thousands of college graduates, some with MBAs, competed for a sweeper's position; 1.7 million applied for 1500 jobs at a state-owned bank; and 9 million took the exam to qualify for 100,000 railway jobs. This grotesque imbalance between jobs and applicants was a reminder that India's liberalization policy had achieved so pitifully little. The private sector's plum jobs were out of reach for all but the best educated. Hence, whether as a driver or a teacher, Poonam writes, a government job offered a better salary and superior benefits than the average private-sector job.[25]

Even the once-attractive call-center jobs were under pressure. Competition from the Philippines and prison inmates in the United States had clawed away at India's lead. Struggling to survive, many in India's call center business had gravitated to scamming. The call's script is familiar: "My name is Paul Edward. I am with the Department of Legal Affairs at the United States Treasury. You are a primary suspect in a legal case with the Internal Revenue Service." Victims across the United States paid to protect themselves from the threat of doom. In another scam, victims received pop-up warnings on their computers, which led them to a call center that offered help at a price.[26]

India had become the global hub of call-center scams. For young Indians with few job opportunities, the temptation was irresistible. As nineteen-year-old Jayesh Dubey said, "Everyone was scamming around me. I thought, 'I will also become a great scammer.'" U.S. citizens reported $3.5 billion in losses to computer-related heists in 2019, up from $1.4 billion in 2017. India was the growth center of such heists. "The more you fuck them over, the better," is the motto by which the scammers operate, writes Poonam in her book *Dreamers*. Although their most lucrative targets were elderly Americans, the scammers also offered fantasy jobs to poorly educated, desperate Indians, stripping them of their meager savings and dignity. In this crucible of grinding scarcity, the lure of easy money trumped notions of morality. With an anguished cry, Poonam says: "Few young Indians I met had a clear sense of right and wrong; fewer gave a damn about it."[27]

The policy hubris continued. At 8 p.m. on November 8, 2016, Prime Minister Modi began a surprise televised address to the nation. Ten minutes into the speech, he announced that the commonly used 500- and 1000-rupee notes would not be valid after midnight. In one swoop, 86 percent of the value of cash Indians held was rendered unusable. Banks would issue new, valid notes in return for the old, unusable ones. The problem was that the government had not printed nearly enough new notes.[28]

Demonetization inflicted the biggest wounds on the most helpless Indians. Farmers and non-farming businesses in the informal sector—accounting for almost 90 percent of India's workers—operated almost entirely in cash. They went into a seizure. Families struggled to buy necessities. Replacement notes—when finally made available—were not compatible with cash machines and were in short supply until early 2017. Modi styled himself on Singapore's autocratic leader Lee Kuan Yew, known for his bold measures. But Modi proved once again that unthinking dramatic gestures end dismally.[29]

Modi's stated goal in demonetizing was to root out "black," unaccounted-for, money that circulated largely as cash. He expected that the holders of black money would not dare bring their cash for replacement for fear of being caught with illicit funds. The RBI's obligations would thus diminish by the amount of unreturned cash, creating a windfall gain that Modi could then distribute. Modi acolytes drummed up that expectation, giving him a Robin Hood persona, one who would take from the corrupt rich and give to India's poor. Unfortunately, nearly all of the money came back. Some people had advance knowledge of the impending demonetization and others found clever ways to convert illicit cash to the new notes.[30]

On July 1, 2017, with the economy barely back on its feet from the demonetization shock, the government rolled out the goods and services tax (GST). The GST was a worthy initiative. Its primary goal was to get rid of cascading taxes (taxes on taxes). Under the pre-GST system, a manufacturer would pay sales tax on inputs such as the steel he purchased from another state. He would include the taxes paid on steel and other inputs in determining the price he charged for the pots and pans he produced. His buyer would then pay sales tax on that all-inclusive pots and pans price. The GST would prevent these compounding costs. It would levy tax only on the value added by the producer of pots and pans through a system for refunding taxes paid on inputs. Importantly, the GST also sought to create a common market with uniform tax rates throughout the country, collapsing into one system the widely varying types and rates of taxes charged by different states.

The GST sought to resolve yet another problem with the earlier system. Truckers experienced long delays on state borders, where they needed to present documents on the taxes already paid on the goods they were carrying. That presentation determined the additional taxes they needed to pay. Not surprisingly, the border check points were dens of corruption. With the introduction of GST, the delays and associated corruption would, in theory, go away since the buyer would pay the tax at the point of sale (when purchasing the product or service) and an online reporting system would record all payments as well as the refunds due.

The GST was decades in the making because it required integrating the complex system of central and state indirect taxes. It also required the agreement of all states, which would not be able to set tax rates when formulating their fiscal policies. Narendra Modi as Gujarat's chief minister had long stymied the initiative.

India needed GST, but its rollout was an economic and administrative mess. States demanded that their large revenue earners—taxes and duties on petroleum, alcohol, electricity, and land transactions—be excluded from the GST net. Those exclusions undermined the objectives of reducing taxes on taxes and creating a common market with uniform rates across the country. Also, active lobbying led to arbitrary differences in tax rates on different products. Most immediately, though, onerous reporting requirements, poorly functioning online reporting and information systems, and inadequate training of tax officials made matters intolerable for businesses. Small firms were unable to cope with the new system. They went into a seizure for the second time in less than a year.[31]

The Indian GDP growth story was nearly over. In its 2018 annual report on India, the IMF confirmed that the demonetization and GST implementation shocks had taken a significant toll on the Indian economy. Non-performing loans of banks (loans that were not being repaid on time) had risen from about 4 percent of all loans in late 2014, when RBI governor Rajan first rang the alarm bells, to about 9 percent in 2017. For government-owned banks, almost 12 percent of all loans in 2017 were non-performing (Figure 21.3). The government had done little to discipline big companies for not repaying their debts. Instead, the government once again used scarce taxpayer money to refill the hole that the defaults left in the capital of the banks they owned. These bank recapitalizations added up to about $13 billion in the fiscal year 2017–2018, with similarly large amounts anticipated in each of the next two years. Choked with bad

FIGURE 21.3: Borrowers stopped repaying their loans. (Non-performing assets as a share of gross advances, percent)
Source: Reserve Bank of India, https://www.rbi.org.in/scripts/PublicationsView.aspx?id=19791; and earlier https://www.rbi.org.in/scripts/PublicationsView.aspx?id=14420.

loans, major government-owned banks drastically slowed their lending. The industrial sector, saddled with debt, virtually stopped borrowing. Although GDP growth remained mysteriously high—above a 7 percent annual rate—corporate investment was evaporating.[32]

The Indian growth bubble burst in August 2018 when the Mumbai-based Infrastructure Leasing and Financial Services (IL&FS) collapsed. IL&FS was a non-banking financial company established in 1987. It did not accept deposits except from large investors. IL&FS had a hazy relationship with the government. Legally, it was privately owned and operated to attract private investors for Indian infrastructure development; in practice, it received almost all its funding from government-owned financial entities. Its largest shareholder was the state-owned Life Insurance Corporation of India, and it had also received sovereign guarantees of repayment for borrowing from the World Bank, the Asian Development Bank, and the German development bank KfW.[33]

Ravi Parthasarathy, the pipe-smoking, fast-talking former Citibank officer, headed IL&FS. To burnish his image as a private-sector mogul,

Parthasarathy built a landmark building for the IL&FS offices in the prestigious Bandra-Kurla complex in Mumbai. Tucked away in that "swanky" building was a lavish bar, where Parthasarathy and his executives bonded with business associates, many of whom were public officials anticipating generously paid post-retirement jobs on one of his projects.[34]

IL&FS became a frequent partner with state governments, starting with road construction. But soon it diversified, winning the Gujarat International Finance Tec-City—the GIFT City—project, Modi's dream of making Ahmedabad a global financial center on the Singapore model. In the hosiery-producing town of Tirupur in Tamil Nadu, IL&FS initiated a drinking water supply and industrial effluents treatment project. As Parthasarathy "swung deals in favour of IL&FS," he grew it into a sprawling, complex, opaque, and heavily indebted financial entity.[35]

In July 2018, a few weeks after the company's transportation subsidiary missed some debt repayments, Parthasarathy resigned as chairman of IL&FS. The ship was sinking. On August 16, the Indian credit rating agency CARE noted a weakening of IL&FS's finances and downgraded its finance subsidiary from AAA to AA+. The parent company IL&FS was not publicly listed and so did not need to rate its debt. Hence, the rating of the subsidiaries provided the main clue to the parent company's financial health. On August 28 and again on August 31, IL&FS's finance subsidiary missed debt repayments due, prompting CARE on September 3 to lower its rating one more notch to A+. On September 9, CARE brought that rating down to BB and on September 17 all the way to D—default status—citing a failure to repay in full the debt due a few days earlier. The rating had fallen from AAA to default in just one month.[36]

Parthasarathy's collapse symbolized broader governmental failures. At its core, IL&FS failed because state governments refused to charge the prices for public services that would deliver the high returns Parthasarathy had promised his private-sector investors. As forensic audits after the IL&FS collapse revealed, Parthasarathy and his senior colleagues presented an inflated view of their revenues to their creditors and to the world. Under that fictional cover of flattering financial performance, they engaged in dubious transactions and financial juggling, enriching themselves and those they favored. Gamesmanship in the bidding process for infrastructure and other construction projects led to frequent and capricious renegotiation of contracts. State-owned banks, strapped for good projects, helped the financial shenanigans at IL&FS by providing it with a continuing flow of funds. All along, Parthasarathy's financial troubles grew. When directors, shareholders, and potential whistleblowers challenged him, he tried to ward them off with intimidation and litigation. Broader social goals suffered. In Tirupur, the treatment plants proved unequal to the task of cleaning effluents from the town's fabric dye producers. Pollutants kept flowing into the Noyyal River, turning it into a "frothing disaster."[37]

In principle, a paper-plan exists to salvage value from the wreckage that is IL&FS. But within the complex and opaque financial structure Parthasarathy had set up, claimants and counter-claimants to any residual value are stuck in India's labyrinthine legal system and may remain there for decades.[38]

In the absence of norms that encouraged sound business practices, the formal institutions—rating agencies, auditors, corporate boards, regulators—failed to protect the social interest and promote competitive capitalism. In that moral vacuum, easy money induced all involved to keep the financial bubble inflated. After IL&FS collapsed, the spotlight turned on other financial scamsters: Dewan Housing Finance Corporation, Yes Bank, and Reliance Capital. Like IL&FS, they all, especially Dewan Housing, had invested in unsavory real estate transactions. As these scamsters fell, a cloud descended over the entire financial sector. Sources of funding began to dry up, and panicked banks and non-bank finance companies curbed their ebullient lending for consumption finance. The liberalization era's last source of growth disappeared. And GDP growth—the metric Modi had been expected to boost—went into a downward slide. In the final quarter of 2019, GDP growth over the same period in 2018 was down to 3.3 percent. As 2020 began, GDP growth slid further down, even before the scourge of COVID-19 hit.[39]

India's Problem: No Sustainable Source of Growth

The bubble of unsustainable growth had deflated. India's long-term problems continued unabated. In the agricultural sector, millions of

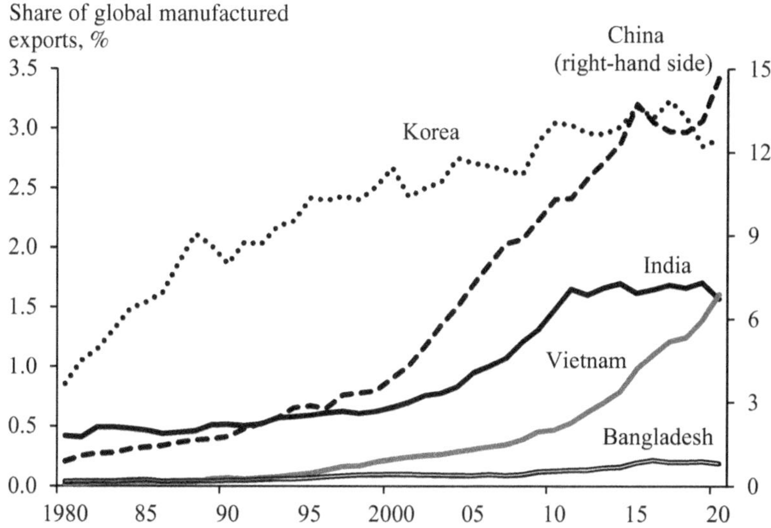

FIGURE 21.4: India remained unable to make inroads into global markets. (Country share of global manufactured goods exports, percent)

Note: China has its own scale on the right-hand side.

Sources: World Trade Organization, http://stat.wto.org/StatisticalProgram/WSDBViewData.aspx?Language=E, the data corresponds to UNCTAD statistics, https://unctadstat.unctad.org/wds/TableViewer/tableView.aspx.

cultivators and farm workers remained in distress. Modi's "Make in India" concept had failed miserably. India continued to perform dismally in international trade and its share of world exports, always small, stalled after reaching 1.5 percent in 2012 (Figure 21.4). In 2020, Vietnam—a country with a population of 97 million people—reached India's export level and was poised to race ahead. India had a large engineering industry, but Indian exporters could achieve only 0.75 percent share of the global auto trade and 1.25 percent of the global auto parts trade. At 4.5 percent and growing, India's world market share of organic chemicals reflected the preference of advanced nations for sourcing such highly polluting products from low-wage countries. There were islands of excellence: for example, India had a 2.5 percent global market share of turbojets and turbines. But they were islands.

In the early 2000s, India had gained global attention with exports of low-end, technologically sophisticated software and pharmaceutical

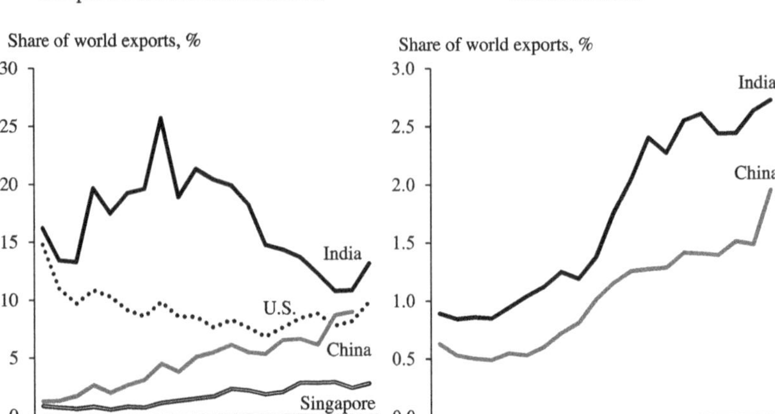

FIGURE 21.5: India's run at the low-end of technologically sophisticated products has stalled, for now. (Share of world exports, percent)

Note: Left-hand panel: 2001-2020 BPM combined revision, code for computer and information services is the sum of 9.2 Computer services and 9.3 Information services, data for China is missing for 2020; Right-hand panel: HS code for pharmaceuticals is 30.

Source: International Trade Centre, Trade Map, https://www.trademap.org.

exports. That hopeful story also stalled around in the 2010s (Figure 21.5). In computer and information services trade, America's share of global exports stopped declining, Singapore's increased, and China's galloped ahead. The world's demand for software services had become more sophisticated. America had its traditionally strong universities, and the Singaporeans and the Chinese were rapidly building universities with world-class reputations in computing and mathematics, helping them run well ahead of the Europeans. The reliability of Chinese programmers more than made up for their lack of fluency in English.

Accompanying India's software surge in the early 2000s, Indian pharmaceutical suppliers gained global market share, especially through the supply of generic drugs and active drug ingredients to the United States. U.S. authorities welcomed Indian and Chinese producers, who, with their low labor and material costs, helped reduce American drug prices. However, U.S. authorities also worried about increasing instances of substandard Indian and Chinese drugs, which either did not work or made the patient's condition worse.

Investigations starting in the mid-2000s revealed that a prominent Indian drug supplier, Ranbaxy, was producing drugs without proper safeguards and fabricating test results to meet the standards of the U.S. Food and Drug Administration. Complying with U.S. standards raised the costs of production, and since the FDA exercised limited oversight initially, the temptation was great to produce subpar drugs for exports, just as had been true for the Indian market with the connivance of Indian regulators. In May 2013, following intense FDA scrutiny over eight years, Ranbaxy pleaded guilty to U.S. federal drug safety violations and paid a fine of $500 million. The fraudulent practices at Ranbaxy and other Indian drug suppliers had proved so hard to pin down because the FDA preannounced the visits of its inspectors, allowing the suppliers time to cover up their shoddy manufacturing, quality-control, and data-documentation practices. As the investigative journalist Katherine Eban writes, "With advance notice and low-cost labor, the plants could make *anything* look like *anything*."[40]

Hence, in January 2014, the FDA initiated a pilot program of surprise inspections, which soon "exposed widespread malfeasance that had previously been hidden." Those findings required the FDA to disqualify errant suppliers, and India's global share of pharmaceutical exports declined in 2014. But loud protests from the Indian regulator, who claimed infringement of Indian sovereignty, and America's inexhaustible demand for cheap drugs caused the FDA to pull back its inspections and eventually to abandon surprise inspections in August 2015. Once the COVID-19 pandemic started, the FDA virtually stopped its inspections. Indian pharma producers continued to cut corners to increase the supply of low-cost drugs. India's global export share crept up. Despite this reprieve, however, the path ahead remains rocky for India's pharma producers. In this race to the bottom, Chinese producers, with similarly dodgy practices, are threatening to outpace Indian manufacturers and the U.S. Congress is once again pushing for surprise inspections.[41]

Unwillingness to Compete

The inability to compete had become an unwillingness to compete. As I have described, one symptom of this phenomenon was the increased resort to scamming. Young aspirants in call centers stole from unsuspecting Americans; large Indian companies stole from government-owned banks; private contractors and non-bank financial corporations stole through padded infrastructure contracts with the government; Indian pharma companies cheated both on U.S. regulations and more brazenly at home in a corrupt alliance with medical experts and the Indian regulator.[42]

Reluctance to compete became an integral feature of Modi's economic policy. From 2014–2015 until 2019–2020, the Indian government steadily raised import tariffs on a wide range of products. India was also a world leader in anti-dumping duties. In principle, these are tariffs to protect domestic producers against "surges" in imports; in practice, they shielded Indian producers from Chinese imports. Even Arvind Panagariya, a former senior advisor to Modi and a frequent cheerleader of his policies, repeatedly criticized the government for protecting Indian industry from foreign competition. In an interview with the *Times of India* in August 2017, he made the obvious point that tariff barriers induced domestic inefficiency. In July 2019, he wrote that the government's protectionist approach discouraged Indian companies from competing in the global marketplace.[43]

In November 2019, the Indian government walked out of the Asian trade agreement known as the Regional Comprehensive Economic Partnership (RCEP). The reason: RCEP would have required reducing tariffs on imports from China, and that terrified Indian producers.[44]

The opposition to RCEP in the city of Ludhiana in Punjab was a dismal confirmation of the inefficient and uncompetitive state of Indian industry. Ludhiana had charmed Milton Friedman when he observed its thriving knitwear and engineering goods industries in 1963. The city had given birth to the iconic Hero Cycles, and at one time, it seemed it could rival the great industrial clusters of Japan. But by 2019, an enfeebled Ludhiana was united in its opposition to RCEP. When India walked out of that deal, the city's "jubilant" businessmen celebrated. The cycle manufacturer's association hailed the government for its "masterstroke." The association's general secretary said, "Had this deal gone through, the micro, small, and medium enterprises of the country, especially those engaged in manufacturing of engineering goods, would have been destroyed." Even the chairman of Hero Cycles conceded that India's bicycle industry could not compete against producers in RCEP nations.[45]

Instead of the creative and aspirational town it could have been, Ludhiana was turning into a den of parasites Effluents from the knitwear and dye industries were contaminating the city's water supply and increasing the prevalence of disease in the region. Drugs and crime had taken root. As depicted in the 2016 movie *Udta Punjab* (Flying Punjab), a politician-police nexus sat atop the flourishing drug trade in Ludhiana and other parts of the state. The luxury cars plying Ludhiana's streets were often trophies of drug peddlers rather than markers of industrial success.[46]

The Economic Consequences of Mr. Modi

Modi's drummed-up reputation for leadership relied on quick handouts to businesses in Gujarat. In Delhi, that decisiveness led to the disastrous demonetization. Not surprisingly, Modi stood by cluelessly as his officials chaotically rolled out the hugely complex goods and services tax (GST). In both the demonetization and GST cases, Modi's actions (or inactivity) inflicted the maximum pain on India's most vulnerable citizens. Farmers and small businesses saw their incomes drop, and workers saw their jobs disappear.

We do not have employment data that coincides with Narendra Modi's tenure as prime minister. However, as against the promise of millions of new jobs under Modi, the Indian economy employed fewer people—yes, *fewer* people—in 2018 than in 2012. In particular, the number of informal sector jobs fell sharply as a result of the demonetization and the botched GST rollout. Manufacturing jobs, both formal and informal, continued to decline. As these dire employment trends unfolded, between seven and nine million more Indians grew old enough each year to seek employment. With the likelihood of employment decreasing, only half of working-age Indians in 2018 even bothered to look for a job. This "discouraged-worker" phenomenon had long been the case for women, whose labor force participation had fallen embarrassingly, especially since the early 2000s. This tendency was now also becoming common for men. The decline in participation was only in small part due to more time spent in education. Quite simply, there weren't enough jobs to make the hunt for paid work worthwhile.[47]

Thus, India faced a virtually insurmountable employment challenge even before COVID-19 struck. The economy needed to generate between 150 and 170 million jobs over the next decade to employ its working-age people: 80 million jobs to fully employ those who were then unemployed or underemployed and between 70 and 90 million jobs for new market entrants. Since agriculture could not possibly generate more jobs and growth of construction jobs was bound to slow down after the finance-construction bubble burst, manufacturing and services would need to produce jobs at an unprecedented pace—a task made all the more daunting by the dismal decline in manufacturing jobs since 2012.

Just as Modi's demonetization and GST rollout heightened India's job challenge, the policies likely also increased Indian poverty. On poverty, the data fog is even greater than that for GDP and employment. The only reliable estimate of those below the poverty line is from a 2011–2012 survey. An embarrassing official report for 2017–2018 appeared in late 2019, which the Modi government promptly threw out.

The data, however, leaked. Using that data, S. Subramanian, a member of the World Bank's Commission on Global Poverty, estimated the extent of Indian poverty, as defined by the Indian Planning Commission's subsistence norm of 32 rupees (at 2011–2012 prices) per person per day in rural areas. The share of rural residents living in poverty had risen from 31 percent in 2011–2012 to 35 percent in 2017–2018. In starker terms, 320 million rural Indians lived in severe poverty in 2017–2018, which was fifty million more than just six years earlier. And in 2017–2018, 160 million rural Indians lived barely above the poverty line—sixty million more than six years earlier—spending between 32 and 38 rupees a day on their consumption needs. The Modi government insisted that the survey's estimates of consumption were not credible because they were much lower than the per capita consumption implied by National Account

Statistics. This was an old and unfounded argument. National account data in all countries show higher consumption than survey data, presumably because people underreport their consumption in surveys. But the underreporting is concentrated in richer households and does not influence the poverty estimates. Additionally, India's national account statistics were suspect. Indian authorities did not directly measure the size of the informal sector; instead, they *assumed* it moved in tandem with the formal sector. After the Modi-inflicted blows to the informal sector, this procedure likely significantly overstated the income and consumption of those in the informal sector.[48]

Other evidence suggests that the incomes of poor households steadily eroded after the start of Modi's tenure as prime minister. Reflecting the disturbing increase in income inequality, one survey shows that consumption by poor households fell even as the average national consumption increased over the Modi years.[49]

Nutrition and infant mortality in the Modi years had discouraging trends. According to the Food and Agriculture Organization, the share of undernourished Indians plateaued at about 15 percent around 2013 and then rose after 2017. Stunting among children fell, but at a much slower pace than before. Anemia increased. Infant mortality rates rose in many parts of India during 2017 and 2018. Children born in these years could experience a lifetime of low economic productivity and quality of life.[50]

Although the data fog on poverty and quality-of-life indicators prevents precise conclusions, the bottom line is clear. The Gujarat "development" model and Modi were singularly unsuited to tackle India's needs. Capital intensive projects helped Mukesh Ambani and Gautam Adani—and some lesser mortals—rack up profits, but they did not create the jobs Modi and his acolytes had promised. The result: GDP growth slowed, employment levels fell, poverty and precarity very likely increased, and human development advanced barely, if at all.

Even Modi's initiatives to end open defecation and bring clean cooking fuel to poor Indian women (as I discuss in the next chapter) achieved isolated and limited gains within the broader neglect of people's health.

The share of health expenditure in GDP declined over the Modi years. This is not surprising. Hindutva's mob-driven nature reinforced shorter time horizons and fatally damaged norms and accountability in public life. Inevitably, the economy served the privileged while Indian democracy continued to unravel.

Chapter 22

MODI BREAKS INDIA'S FRACTURED DEMOCRACY

The test of a democracy is whether it supplies essential public goods, such as health, education, clean air, clean water, cities and towns, and a justice system. Provision of public goods is the bedrock of shared progress, allowing citizens to live with self-respect, participate in informed and open debate, and engage in productive work. No individual or even a small group has the resources or long-term perspective to create these collectively desirable goods on the necessary scale. For example, a successful education system needs not just buildings and equipment but also teachers who teach, sound curricula, good nutrition for children, and safe neighborhoods in which citizens can live, play, and travel. Bringing all these elements together requires that the various actors play their parts with honesty and integrity. If some start cheating and get away with it, then so does everyone else. Trust that others are acting in good faith is essential to sustain cooperation for the effective delivery of public goods.

Even before COVID-19 wreaked its havoc, India's public goods were in a dismal state because social norms and public accountability had fractured. Corruption, a criminal-politician nexus, and religious exclusion had become dominant features of Indian politics. Increasing numbers of politicians and members of society worked mainly for immediate self-gratification. The glue of a collective common vision had weakened.

In describing the state of India's public goods as dire, I am mindful that statistics on essential public services appear sporadically and with innumerable problems of interpretation. Indeed, India's failure to generate regular, high-quality data—on public services, GDP, employment, and poverty—is itself a failure of public goods provision and marks a broken political system contemptuous of transparency and accountability.

From the data that does exist, an unhappy picture emerges. India achieved nearly universal primary school enrollment in the last decade, but that was a much-delayed and hollow victory. The quality of education remained dreadful, most children fell steadily below grade-level competence, and 30 percent of children, more so girls, dropped out in high school. India ranked among the lowest in the world on child nutrition measures, below Bangladesh and Nepal. Even the modest pace of progress in nutrition slowed to a crawl after 2013.[1]

On air pollution, Indian cities stayed at the top of the world charts, relentlessly compromising the nation's health. "Air pollution is killing children and damaging their bodies beyond repair, leaving them to lead a life burdened with health issues," the Centre for Science and Environment wrote in 2020. Groundwater levels continued to fall. As the CSE noted, India was "by far, the largest and fastest growing consumer of groundwater in the world," drawing more groundwater than the United States and China put together. Even the available groundwater was increasingly polluted by chemicals and metals, a pollution potentially impossible to reverse. In place of water, which dams and barrages diverted, India's drying rivers increasingly carried waste and disease. The gathering global climate crisis exacerbated these home-spun disasters. Cyclonic activity in the Arabian Sea caused more frequent tropical storms and cyclones on India's west coast. Erratic rainfall in the Middle East triggered locust attacks on Indian farms. And, as India's average monsoon rainfall decreased, droughts became more common just when the rise in oceanic surface temperatures increased the frequency of destructive downpours.[2]

The pace of India's urbanization was pitifully slow according to official data. Satellite images showed greater spread of urban agglomerations. These images captured urban villages—previously rural areas that had grown in population size and density but had few or none of the facilities that make a city productive. Instead of helping share resources and learning, as thriving urban agglomerations do, official cities and urban villages alike were contested sites. "Water wars" between residents within a city and between states that wanted hydration for their cities were all too frequent. There was also an ongoing contest for living space. Apartment and office buildings pushed the urban poor to the outskirts of cities. The energy-intense lifestyles of the rich polluted the air for all. Urban citizens contested even the space for their junk. In Ghazipur, just outside Delhi, a landfill site (which is more of a trash mountain) grows taller. On an April afternoon in 2019, temperatures reach 45 degrees Centigrade (113 degrees Fahrenheit), and "the trash fires send acrid waves of oily, brown, superheated smoke into the already foul air."[3]

Justice died as courts dragged out the trial process (Figure 22.1). The "undertrials" often languished in jail, where they constituted three-quarters of Indian prisoners. They had virtually no pre-trial rights, despite

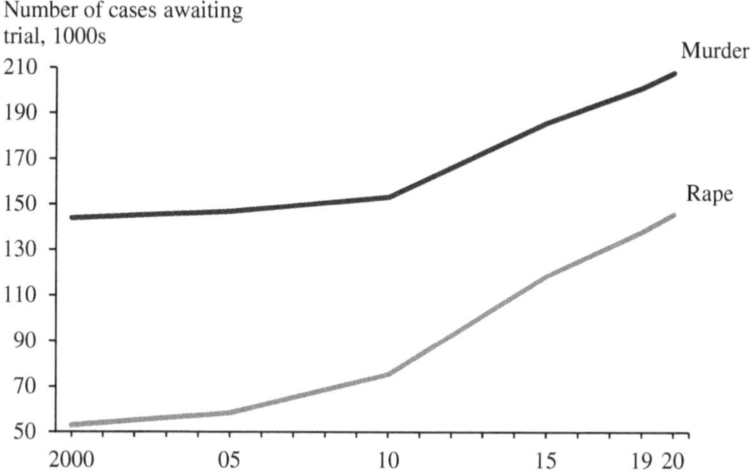

FIGURE 22.1: Justice delayed, justice denied. Indefinitely. (Number of cases under the Indian Penal Code pending trial from the previous year, in thousands)
Source: Government of India, Ministry of Home Affairs, National Crime Records Bureau, Court disposal of IPC (Indian Penal Code) crime cases (crime head-wise), https://ncrb.gov.in/en/crime-in-india-table-addtional-table-and-chapter-contents?field_date_value%5Bvalue%5D%5Byear%5D=2016&field_select_table_title_of_crim_value=4&items_per_page=50.

a 1977 Supreme Court dictum "bail, not jail." Bail applications mounted.[4] And, as the Tamil movie *Jai Bhim* showed in mind-numbing sequences, custodial torture to extract "confessions" was accepted practice.

These failures to supply quality education, good health, a clean environment, and justice for all found their focal point in women, where a new hypermasculinity emerged alongside age-old prejudices and violence. In December 2012, four men raped a physiotherapist on a bus in Delhi, leaving her at the edge of death. In May 2014, two teenage girls yearning to break out of their rural isolation instead hung lifeless from a mango tree in a Western Uttar Pradesh village. In 2016, a husband allegedly bludgeoned his wife to death (also in Western Uttar Pradesh) and nearly went unpunished until a *New York Times* report broadcast the story to the world.[5]

India shares the Asian disease of son preference and abortion of female fetuses. The "missing" Indian girls are typically among second children after an earlier daughter and among third children following two earlier daughters. If they are born, second and third daughters—especially those with older sisters—also suffer the most acute malnutrition. Unlike in other Asian countries with missing girls, Indian women also have very low work participation rates, and the work they do get is most often in occupations that pay poverty wages and place women's health at great risk. The ill health and poor life prospects of Indian women makes it hard for them to raise healthier and better-educated children. A more active role for women in the workplace and in the delivery of public services helped Bangladesh progress faster than India, in both human and economic terms.[6]

India's democracy betrayed its people from the start. Nehru's charisma won him repeated elections. He believed in and respected democratic institutions grounded in the norms of equality, tolerance, and shared progress. But his stand-alone temples strategy of development and lack of political and administrative acumen led him to neglect fostering ground-level cooperation for widespread education and health. Norms eroded rapidly under Mrs. Gandhi. Violence, endemic corruption, and a criminal-politician class were her legacy to India. The liberalization era that followed overlaid a "me-me-me" culture on persisting corruption and criminals in politics, further setting back cooperative endeavors.

India's fraying norms were hospitable to the intolerance and hostility promoted by Hindutva ideologues. Their warlike us-versus-them posture kept the mob busy while deflecting attention from economic priorities. In her book *Dreamers,* Snigdha Poonam writes that angry and frustrated un- and underemployed young Hindu men "cared little for his [Modi's] ability to create jobs or fix corruption as long as he kept their blood hot with chants of 'India will rule' and 'youth is power.'" These young men were willing to direct their "malevolent energy on one thing alone: fighting Muslims." Malevolent self-indulgence reinforced the political focus on headline-grabbing policies and—as is true in other partisan and ethnically divided societies—public goods development suffered.[7]

Contributing to the erosion of Indian democracy was India's economic path. The rich became richer and had little interest in improving the supply of public goods. Mukesh Ambani took a helicopter ride to his office in downtown Bombay, bypassing the city's chaotic traffic. The wealthy sent their children abroad for studies and laid first claim on scarce water. The buoyant construction industry fed a supply of criminal-politicians.

In 2008, Raghuram Rajan, the University of Chicago economist who would soon be governor of the Reserve Bank of India, pointed to the emergence of India's "venal politician." He observed that repeated disappointment had beaten down the underprivileged, who no longer expected better. Instead, they merely sought access to the failing services. "The venal politician," Rajan said, "does so little to reform the system simply because he is the crutch that helps the poor navigate the system." Rajan's was a powerful insight. Indian politicians practiced "access politics." They deliberately maintained scarcity of public services so that they could appear as benefactors who provided access to the scarce services.[8]

Crime and Politics: Stories from Bihar and Tamil Nadu

In early 2005, Bihar ranked lowest among Indian states on almost every development indicator. A *New York Times* report said that Bihar's people had their vote and little else. In November 2005, Bihar elected a new chief minister, Nitish Kumar. For the next five years, Bihar's economy grew rapidly, crime declined, and the state's education and health metrics improved.[9] Bihar seemed to be on an upward swing.

Especially noteworthy, in 2006 Kumar introduced the Mukhyamantri Balika Cycle Yojana, translated as "The Chief Minister's Cycle Program for Girls." Every girl graduating from ninth grade received 2,000 rupees (about $45 at 2006 exchange rate) to buy a bicycle as an inducement to finish high school. This was classic "access" politics: the program quite literally created better access to schools. With their bicycles, girls who lived farther away from school were more likely to continue to high school. But the quality of education improved only modestly. Bihar's problem, as in many parts of India, was that teachers did not show up to school, or if they did, they did not teach. And as the experience worldwide shows, merely bringing children to school does little for their learning.[10]

Even Bihar's modest progress stalled. The clue to that lay in the nature of its economic growth. An equalizing manufacturing sector grew slowly. Instead, construction—of school buildings, roads, bridges, residential homes, and shopping centers—gave the state its economic fizz. The construction mafia gained strength; illegal sand mining spawned a "sand mafia" that controlled the availability of construction-quality sand. The state's traditional coal mafia and drug dealers all wanted a piece of the new action.[11]

In an era of mounting campaign expenses, Nitish Kumar had little choice but to engage with a growing pool of criminal-politicians—for their muscle and even more so for their money. In the 2005 election that brought him to power, 22 percent of his party candidates for the state legislative assembly faced serious criminal charges. In the 2010 elections, that share had gone up to 35 percent.[12]

Kumar's valiant effort to enforce law and order helped reduce violent crime in the state. But the starting point in Patna, Bihar's capital city, was so egregious that it remained among the top three Indian metropolitan cities in the number of violent crimes per capita, competing for the highest honor with the nation's capital, Delhi. In Kumar's second five-year term, manufacturing almost literally did not grow, while construction kept growing with all the ill effects it brought. Bihar was still the poorest state in the nation when Nitish Kumar completed his second term in 2015.[13]

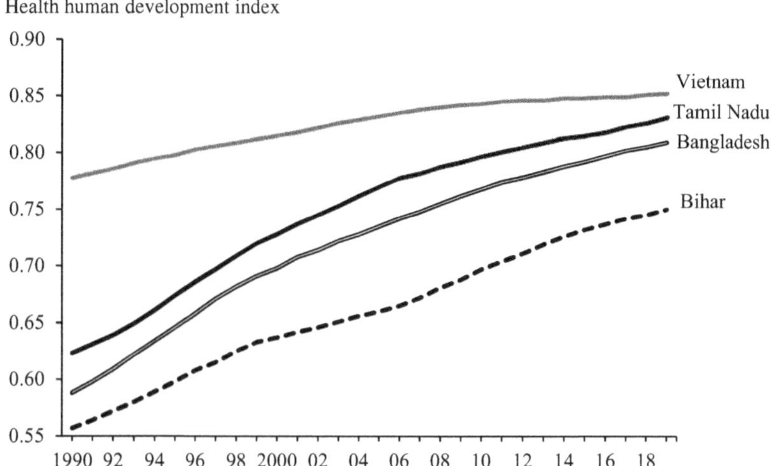

FIGURE 22.2: Tamil Nadu is ahead of Bihar, but cannot yet match Vietnam in health services. (Health component of the human development index, scale ranging from 0 to 1)
Note: The health component of the human development index is based on life-expectancy at birth.
Source: Global Data Lab, https://globaldatalab.org/shdi/download_files/.

The southern state of Tamil Nadu was a world apart from Bihar. Tamil Nadu had a per capita income almost five times that of Bihar, both at the start and the finish of Nitish Kumar's years from 2005 to 2015. Tamil Nadu was more industrialized, with 19 percent of its state product from manufacturing in 2015 compared with Bihar's 7 percent. More impressively, starting in the early 1970s, grassroots activism helped improve the quality of services to local communities. In particular, Tamil Nadu established widespread health facilities and effective healthcare delivery. By the United Nations Development Programme's Health Human Development index (which uses life expectancy at birth as a summary measure of good health), Tamil Nadu has maintained a consistent lead over Bihar (Figure 22.2). In 2015–2016, 48 percent of Bihar's children under five years old had low height for their age, while in Tamil Nadu, 27 percent of children were similarly stunted.[14]

However, Tamil Nadu appears less impressive when compared with international peers. In 2011, Tamil Nadu had a population of 72 million people, smaller than Vietnam's 89 million. In that year, Vietnam's per capita income was about the same as Tamil Nadu's. Yet Vietnam provided significantly superior health to its citizens. Twenty-eight percent of pregnant Vietnamese women were anemic in 2019 as against 48 percent of Tamil women in 2020. Tamil Nadu's pace of progress was stymied by poor housing and nutrition, especially among those who lived in the precarious income zone described earlier. Continued discrimination against women caused them to be far more undernourished than men.[15]

Vietnam's superiority in education was even more striking. Indian students, represented by Tamil Nadu and Himachal Pradesh, were at the bottom of the league in the 2009–2010 Programme for International Student Assessment conducted by the Organisation for Economic Co-operation and Development. Kyrgyzstan was the only country that ranked lower. In embarrassment, India dropped out of future assessments. In 2015, Vietnam was near the top of the world rankings (Figure 22.3). Vietnamese students matched French students in mathematics and did better in science.[16]

As multiple sources of assessment show, Tamil Nadu did no better than Bihar in the quality of rural primary education. In both states,

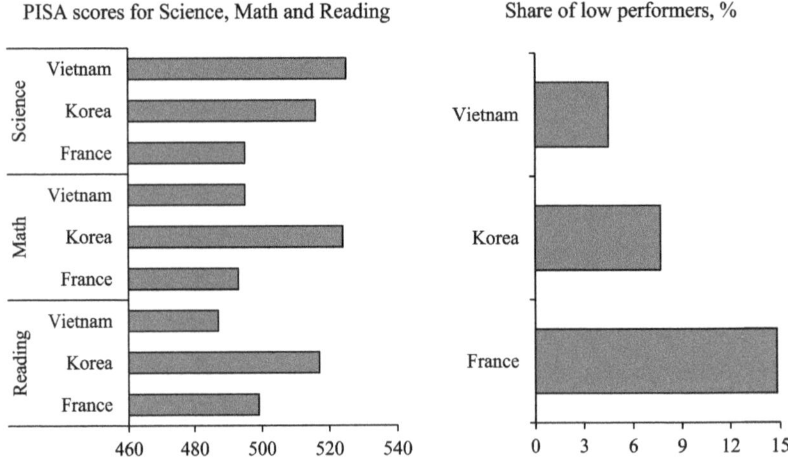

FIGURE 22.3: Vietnam provides its citizens world-class education—and does so equitably.

Note: The Programme for International Student Assessment is conducted by the Organisation for Economic Co-operation and Development to evaluate scholastic achievement of 15-year-old school students.

Source: OECD, PISA, https://www.oecd.org/pisa/pisa-2015-results-in-focus.pdf.

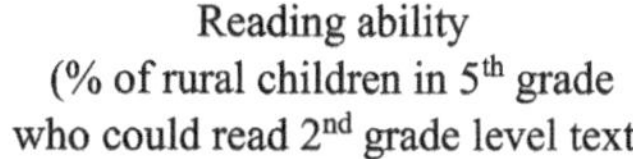

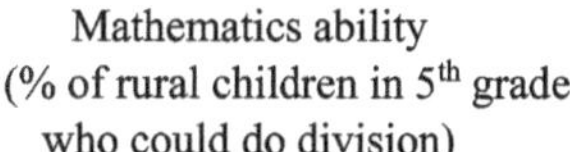

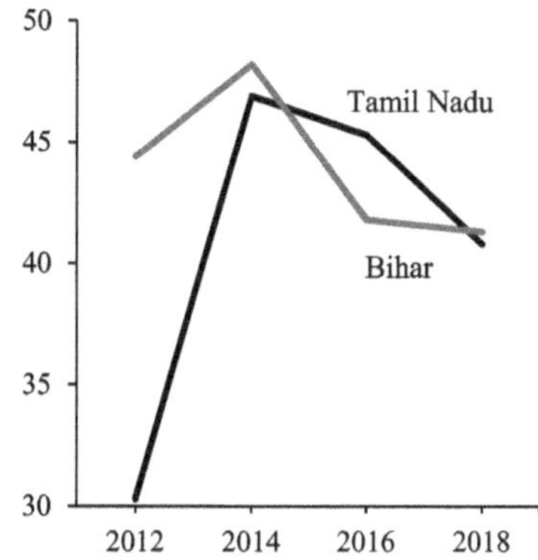

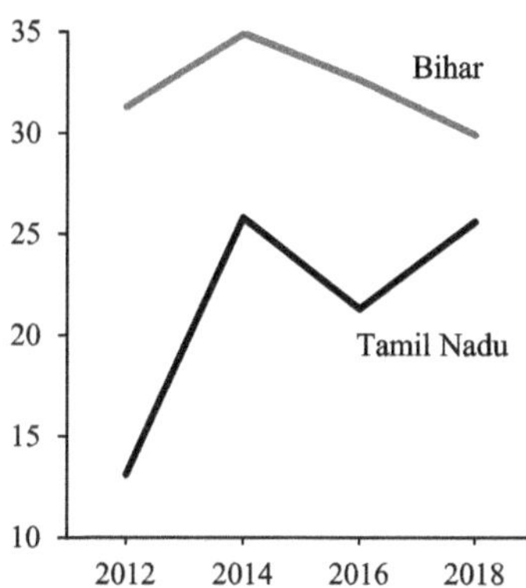

FIGURE 22.4: Most students have lacked grade-level skills. They are not getting better. Source: Annual Status of Education Report for Tamil Nadu, http://img.asercentre.org/docs/ASER%202018/Release%20Material/English%20files/tamilnadu.pdf; for Bihar, http://img.asercentre.org/docs/ASER%202018/Release%20Material/English%20files/bihar.pdf.

children in government-run schools quickly fell behind grade level competence and kept falling further behind (Figure 22.4). Teacher absenteeism was less of a problem in Tamil Nadu, with a 13 percent absenteeism rate in 2010, compared to Bihar's 28 percent. But incompetent teachers, poor teaching methods, and the difficulties of coping with students of very different abilities in the same class handicapped even Tamil Nadu's education system. Also, the growing tendency to instruct children in English, rather than in the mother tongues, compromised students' ability to learn. Private schools, which attracted an increasing fraction of children, imposed a large financial burden on low-income families. And their quality of education (measured by test scores) was not necessarily better than in government schools because they too had inadequately trained teachers and, more so than government-run schools, emphasized teaching English at the cost of math and native-language skills.[17]

The troubling question is why Tamil Nadu has not done better, despite its economic advantages, reputation for an efficient bureaucracy, and tradition of grassroots activism for better public services? When set against international peers, why are Tamil Nadu's achievements so inadequate?

The answer lies in the short-term focus of Tamil Nadu's politics, which counteracts grassroots activism.

Starting in the 1970s, electoral violence and illegal electoral practices became steadily more ingrained features of Tamil Nadu politics. Possibly more so than even in Uttar Pradesh and Bihar, Tamil Nadu developed notoriety for politicians who engaged in the large-scale buying of votes. In 2009, one political candidate allegedly distributed 5,000 rupees (over $70) to each voter in his constituency. In March 2011, campaigning for the state assembly elections, the two main rival parties "matched and bettered" each other's promises to distribute laptops, kitchen grinders, and cooling fans. Chief Minister J. Jayalalithaa promised wedding gifts—gold, cash, and land to build a home—for educated girls from families below the official poverty line.[18]

Researchers confirm that politicians who buy votes neglect the provision of public services. Voters, having received freebies, are reluctant to hold the politicians accountable. And unaccountable politicians engage in their primary objective of enriching themselves.[19]

Chief Minister Jayalalithaa had certainly amassed huge wealth. In September 2014, a special court in the neighboring state of Karnataka found her guilty of "disproportionate assets," or more simply, "wealth well beyond her known sources of income." Her assets included 880 kilograms of silver, 28 kilograms of gold, various properties, and (most notably) shell companies through which she accumulated millions of dollars. In May 2015, however, the Karnataka High Court mysteriously said, never mind. Jayalalithaa did not have disproportionate assets after all.[20] Indian courts were increasingly intimidated by electorally successful politicians.

For the people of Chennai, the incompetence and graft came to gruesome light in the early morning hours of December 2, 2015. The Adyar River flooded the city, washing away people and their homes. Large parts of the city were submerged for days. In part, it was technical failure—engineers poorly timed the release of water from a reservoir that torrential rains had filled. Bureaucracy also botched the disaster management. The most serious failure, though, arose from the prior indiscriminate construction over the city's water bodies, which might otherwise have absorbed some of the flood waters. In her heartbreaking book, Chennai-based journalist Krupa Ge quotes a beleaguered city resident with whom she toured a devastated area: "Every inch of land has been sold and buildings have come up choc-a-bloc." The city's stormwater drains were poorly maintained. Construction rubble from large buildings was dumped into canals and drains, obstructing the flow of water. Stunningly, city planners used a fake map that scrubbed out a water ecosystem to authorize construction on protected land. Even waterways spared by the construction debris were clogged with silt and frothing sewage.[21]

As in most natural catastrophes, the Chennai floods largely spared the homes and malls for the rich but destroyed the properties of hundreds of small businesses. And the flood taught no lessons. After the flood, new luxury construction resumed near water bodies. In the interest of "beautifying" the city, the poorest were shunted out to locations without schools and infrastructure, far away from their workplaces.

The construction that directly or indirectly caused the Chennai floods to inflict such havoc also fed corruption and crime in Tamil politics. More so than elsewhere in India, the Tamil Nadu construction binge was tied up with illegal sand mining. From an insignificant business in the mid-1980s, sand mining in Tamil Nadu grew into a $3 billion a year industry by the mid-2010s. Crime and politics merged, starting with district-level criminal-politicians and rising to higher levels as the stakes grew. Sand mining also caused vast environmental destruction. The mining process dried up riverbeds. And because sand acts as a "sponge," absorbing and filtering water back into the ground, sand mining hindered groundwater replenishment.[22]

The web of Tamil Nadu's corruption circled back to its pollution control board. In September 2021, an anti-corruption squad charged the chairman of the body for "criminal misconduct" and "criminal misappropriation" after finding large stashes of cash, gold, silver, and jewelry in the properties he owned. Earlier raids nabbed two other senior officials of the board. The source of their riches were "fees" that building structures and industrial plants needed to pay to pass through the several "checkpoints" at the pollution control board.[23]

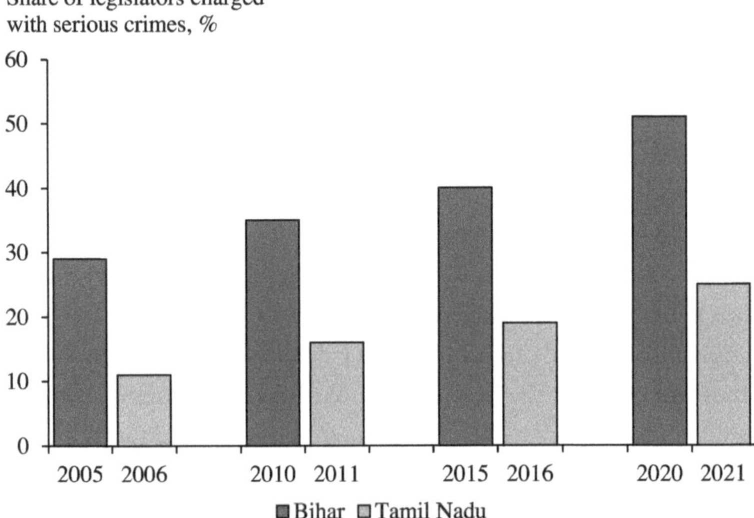

FIGURE 22.5: The share of criminally charged legislators has increased without a pause in Bihar (grey) and Tamil Nadu (black). (Percent of members of legislative assembly with serious criminal charges pending against them)

Note: Serious crimes include assault, murder, kidnapping, and rape.

Source: Association for Democratic Reforms, New Delhi, https://adrindia.org/.

By reputation, Tamil Nadu was a developmental state. But its rivers were drying, its groundwater was falling, and its water and land pollution were rising just as fast as everywhere else in the country.

The share of Tamil Nadu state legislators carrying serious criminal charges was rising quickly, on course, it seemed, to catch up with the share of criminally charged legislators in the Bihar legislature (Figure 22.5). Tamil Nadu had, however, caught up with Bihar in one important respect: in 2020, a staggering 50 percent of ministers in the Tamil Nadu government had serious criminal charges pending against them, matching Bihar's 50 percent share of ministers with similar charges. In Tamil Nadu, the bad was driving out the good. The sad truth was that Tamil Nadu was becoming more like Bihar, rather than the other way around.

The grossly unequal economic development in Tamil Nadu and other southern Indian states bred a genre of flagrantly violent cinema, starting in the 1990s and continuing to this day. The films centered around a hyper-masculine rebel who, although often a criminal himself, won the affection of the audience by battling a rigged system. That call to battle resonated in Bihar and other Hindi-speaking states, where young viewers worn out by "the lack of opportunities in their life" lapped up dubbed Tamil and other southern films. Hindi cinema had conveyed that shared frustration to the nation through its the "angry young man" movies of the 1970s and 1980s. But when Hindi films dropped this genre, southern films took up the cause.[24] Lack of economic opportunities remained a source of India's cultural homogenization.

To these trends in Indian politics and culture, Narendra Modi brought Hindutva.

Hindutva as Perpetual Performance

The violence spread quickly after Modi's installation as India's prime minister in late May 2014. In early June, a mob in Pune lynched a twenty-four-year-old Muslim technology professional, alleging (incorrectly) that the techie had posted offensive videos on Facebook. In July, Hindutva's digital soldiers stepped up activity on social media. Their trolling was designed to hurt—and it did. Arun Shourie, a once-glamorous minister in Atal Bihari Vajpayee's BJP government but now a critic of Prime Minister Narendra Modi and BJP President Amit Shah, complained that Hindutva warriors had abused his disabled son. In August 2015, M. M. Kalburgi, a scholar and Hindutva critic, was gunned down on his doorstep in Dharwad, Karnataka. In October 2015, a mob in Greater Noida outside Delhi murdered a Muslim man because, they said, he had slaughtered a cow and eaten beef.[25]

In late March 2017, a virulent Hindutva descended on Uttar Pradesh, a state with a population of 220 million people. Forty-four-year-old Yogi Adityanath—the Yogi, as he was popularly known—became Uttar Pradesh's new chief minister following the BJP's landslide victory in the state's legislative assembly elections. An elated Hindutva group described the Yogi as "a Hindu *sher*" (lion) who would unfurl "the Hindu nationalist flag across UP." Indeed, the Yogi had an unrivaled résumé for toxic Hindutva politics. In 1998, he had launched the Gau Raksha Manch, or "Cow Protection Platform." Sensing though that the cow issue did not create enough polarization, in 2002 he launched the Hindu Yuva Vahini (Hindu Youth Brigade) with a mandate on all matters "that could project minorities as enemies of Hindus." To that new enterprise, the Yogi recruited in large numbers "young and restless Hindu men." The frequency and intensity of rioting grew in his home city of Gorakhpur, a "backward" city in the "impoverished" state.[26]

In the Yogi's orbit, Hindutva always had priority over economic development. In the documentary film *Writing with Fire,* a reporter from the all-women print and online newsmagazine *Khabar Lahariya* (Waves of News) asks a sword-brandishing Hindu Yuva Vahini leader what his aspiration for India's youth was. After a reflective pause, he takes on a pensive look and says, "Young Indians should protect cows." The unperturbed reporter, with only half a smile, asks how protecting cows would help achieve economic progress. It would fulfil a Hindu religious duty, the Hindu Yuva Vahini leader replies, and economic progress would follow "automatically."

The Yogi also personified the other destructive trend in Indian politics. He continued Uttar Pradesh's tradition of criminal-politicians, a tradition that kept the state impoverished. Twenty of the Yogi's ministerial colleagues—45 percent—carried serious criminal charges. He himself faced charges of criminal intimidation, attempted murder, and rioting.[27]

Throughout the nation, Hindutva persisted in silencing its critics with fierce brutality. In July 2017, a motorcycle with two riders pulled up behind journalist and vocal Hindutva opponent Gauri Lankesh as she parked her car outside her home in Bangalore. One of the bike riders shot Lankesh three times, leaving her dead in a pool of her own blood. Hindutva trolls on Twitter celebrated. "A bitch has died a dog's death and now all the puppies are wailing in the same tune," tweeted thirty-eight-year-old Nikhil Dadhich. Dadhich was among the select 1,779 people Narendra Modi followed on Twitter. Others joined Dadhich in directing hate toward Lankesh.[28]

A glorious Hindu history emerged from the Hindutva ideology. In late October 2014, five months after he became prime minister, Modi said to a conference of doctors that ancient Indians had made scientific advances not known to contemporary scientists. In the epic mythology chronicled in the Mahābhārata, Modi explained, the warrior Karna was not born from his mother's womb, illustrating India's achievements in genetic science. Ganesh, the much-loved god with the head of an elephant on a human body, illustrated advanced plastic surgery. BJP-led state governments started rewriting the history of medieval India, exalting Hindu kings while belittling Muslim rulers. On post-independence history, Modi resorted to barbs and innuendo against Nehru. An eighth-grade textbook in BJP-governed Rajasthan state dropped all references to Nehru.[29]

The most concerted branding portrayed the freedom fighter and India's first deputy prime minister Sardar Patel as a Hindutva ideologue. Patel was a devoted disciple of Mahatma Gandhi. He practiced Gandhi's message of tolerance and nonviolence. As the country's home (interior) minister, he was scrupulously fair to Muslims. Appropriating him as an early sympathizer of Hindutva was a gross distortion of history.

Modi, though, was rewriting history. In July 2014, just over a month into his first term, he launched work on a 182-meter-high statue of Patel. It would be the world's tallest statue—called the Statue of Unity—standing at twice the height of the Statue of Liberty in New York. The Statue of Unity was completed in November 2018 at a cost of about $400 million. As Modi conducted the extravagant inauguration in Hindu ceremonial style, one awestruck visitor, at a loss for words, exclaimed, "Grand." Police rounded up activists and villagers who were protesting because the statue had displaced them from their homes without sufficient compensation.[30]

Two years later, Modi flew from the water dome at the Patel statue on the inaugural flight of India's first seaplane service to the riverfront on the Sabarmati River in Ahmedabad. The Sabarmati riverfront, completed when Modi was chief minister of Gujarat, was a glamorous 10.5-kilometer, concrete-lined structure set amid a dying river. A dam upstream had reduced the river's natural flow to a trickle by the time it reached the riverfront, which therefore was a pool of stagnant water. The last 120 kilometers of the Sabarmati River before it entered the Arabian Sea were choked with industrial effluents and sewage from Ahmedabad city.[31] The Hindutva narrative needed easy symbols to celebrate, which the Patel statue and the Sabarmati riverfront provided.

The most disturbing use of state power in the aid of Hindutva began with an event on January 1, 2018, in Bhima Koregaon, a small village in western Maharashtra. January 1 was a big date for Dalits, who fall on the lowest rung of the Indian caste hierarchy. Two hundred years earlier, on January 1, 1818, forefathers of the Dalits had won a battle at Bhima Koregaon against the Brahmin Peshwa king, a victory that symbolized for them a triumph against historical injustices inflicted by higher-caste Indians. However, the Dalit celebration was intolerable to Hindutva followers because it undercut their narrative of Hindu unity. Hindutva organizations—armed as always with cadres of unemployed youth—attacked the Dalits. In August of 2018, Maharashtra police arrested five sympathizers of the Dalit cause for being "Naxalites" (Maoists) engaged in a larger plot to assassinate Narendra Modi and overthrow his government. The arrests were under the Unlawful Activities Prevention Act, which denied the right to a speedy trial or bail.[32] A saga unfolded that continues to this day.

A Broken Economy and a Broken Democracy

In early 2019, the Indian economy was in bad shape. The GDP growth rate was falling with no end in sight. The employment condition was dire, in large part because the harebrained demonetization and poorly initiated GST had destroyed jobs. In a March 2019 survey conducted by the Washington-based Pew Research Center, 76 percent of Indians surveyed said that their biggest worry was the lack of employment opportunities.[33]

The national election was only a few months away, and the Modi government did have two notable achievements to its credit: building toilets and distributing cylinders of liquified petroleum gas for cooking. On the toilets, Modi had acted quickly after his Independence Day address in August 2014, when he expressed horror at the practice of open defecation. Six weeks later—on October 2, Mahatma Gandhi's birthday—he launched the Swachh Bharat Mission, with the goal of eliminating open defecation in five years. As the 2019 election approached, so did the five-year deadline. Modi proclaimed, "We got more than 100 million toilets built." The project undoubtedly helped to improve Indian sanitation. But, as with everything related to Modi, there was no way of judging the extent of the progress. Independent investigations showed that in the rush to build toilets, many did not have water, and many were broken and dysfunctional, with the risk that the human sewage would seep into the ground and contaminate the groundwater. The most careful study found that the backward states, including Bihar, Madhya Pradesh, Rajasthan, and Uttar Pradesh, had made significant progress. However, even in 2019, about half the households in those states continued to defecate in the open. States with better starting points made more modest gains.[34]

The Swachh Bharat Mission was a construction project that helped build more toilets. However, the lack of toilets was only the most visible part of India's vast sanitation problem, which remained largely unabated. All over the country, deadly diseases ran rampant amid increasingly polluted rivers and groundwater. Poor health services and nutrition—also invisible killers—received limited attention. A focus on visible toilets was politically attractive, as was true with the Sabarmati riverfront, a short glitzy stretch in a dying river.

Modi recognized the plight of Indian rivers. Not surprisingly, he initiated a project to clean the holy Ganga River soon after becoming prime minister. The project helped upgrade those parts of the river that are frequented by tourists. But industrial effluents and human waste continued to flow into the river and its tributaries. As one study put it, the Ganga basin continued to "drown in shit."[35]

The Ganga, in fact, stood on the verge of a crisis that was born of India's economic development strategy and made worse by Hindutva priorities. Diversion of the river's water to irrigation canals, proliferation of electric-powered wells sucking up groundwater, ecosystem degradation caused by concrete-lined riverfronts along the Gomti tributary, and sand mining reduced the water flow into the main Ganga channel, preventing the river from purifying itself. Chaotically distributed cities and towns and poorly regulated industrial plants unrelentingly pumped waste into the river. To that mess, in December 2016, Modi added the Char Dham ("Four Shrines") highway project. The $1.6 billion project began widening the 900 kilometers of highway that connect four Hindu pilgrimage sites in the upper Ganga basin, smack in the heart of the fragile Himalayan mountain range. A Supreme Court–appointed expert urged the authorities to limit the extent of the widening. Those words had no influence. The project is carving out road through the mountainside and mowing down forests on the mountain slopes. Construction debris enters the Ganga and alters its flow. Landslides destroy farming and kill residents.[36]

The clean cooking fuel initiative also focused on splashy headlines rather than sustainable development. That program, which began in May 2016, gave women highly subsidized liquefied petroleum gas cylinders with accompanying stoves. The project helped reduce the use of toxic fuels—firewood, coal, dung cakes—that cause household pollution, with particularly serious damage to women's health. This valuable initiative was another example of "access" politics: instead of development that would make life less of a struggle, just give people freebies instead. Many women who received the cylinders cannot afford to refill them. Many of the cylinders have remained unused trophies on display—and will remain unused until broader rural development increases incomes and affordability.[37]

In the run-up to the 2019 election, with jobs hard to find and toilets and gas cylinders not a sure bet to win votes, attention reverted to belligerent nationalism intertwined with Hindutva. On February 14, 2019, a Pakistan-inspired suicide bomber killed forty Indian soldiers on the Indian side of Kashmir. Modi, who described himself as the nation's *chowkidar* (watchman), responded with strikes against terrorist groups in Pakistani territory. Although journalists who visited the site found little evidence of damage inflicted by the Indian strikes, a furious nationalistic narrative unfolded over India's hyperactive social media. India had over a billion cellphone connections, with over 300 million Facebook accounts and 240 million WhatsApp users. The BJP, with 1.2 million volunteers running its social media campaign, was the 900-pound gorilla in the social media space. A widely circulated clip from a video game claimed to show a devastating aerial assault by India on an alleged terrorist camp in Pakistan.[38]

Also in February 2019, on the occasion of the holy festival Kumbh Mela, Modi—in the company of Yogi Adityanath—took a ritual dip at the sacred Sangam, the confluence of rivers Ganga, Yamuna, and the mythical Saraswati. With an accompanying video attachment, Modi tweeted, "Had the good fortune of taking a holy dip at #Kumbh. Prayed for the well-being of 130 crore [1.3 billion] Indians." Capping the symbolism, Modi visited Hindutva's holiest site, the Cellular Jail in the Andaman and Nicobar Islands, where Vinayak Damodar Savarkar, the patron saint of Hindutva, was interned by the British. Modi tweeted a photo of himself sitting in front of Savarkar's photograph in a meditative posture, his eyes closed, and his hands folded.[39]

Unlike in the 2014 elections, the promise of economic development was all but gone. The drumbeat of the "Gujarat economic model" had long since faded. Now the bond with the voter was through Modi's strongman image in dealing with Pakistani militancy and a more enduring bond through the promise of Hindutva. As a disillusioned former BJP insider who once handled the party's social media analytics said, "The 2014 elections were fought on the plank of development, but 2019 it seems is being fought on polarization."[40]

As the April/May elections approached, Facebook and WhatsApp blocked some inflammatory posts but allowed the Hindutva standard-bearer Rashtriya Swayamsevak Sangh and senior BJP politicians to continue unrestrained. Facebook-programmed recommendations spread the most vicious hate, as internal Facebook documents made public by whistleblower Frances Haugen later revealed.[41]

For the first time, Indian election campaign expenditures exceeded those of the most recent U.S. presidential and congressional cycle. And the share of Lok Sabha members with serious pending criminal charges increased to 29 percent (Figure 22.6). That's right, more than one out of four members of the Indian parliament faced charges including those for murder, kidnapping, and extortion. Matching the national trend, the share of elected BJP parliamentarians carrying serious criminal charges also rose to 29 percent. The former election commissioner Navin Chawla warns that these numbers might underestimate the criminally charged legislators since many criminals are able to use their influence to scrub past misdeeds from the judicial record. Political parties have ignored the Election Commission's repeated proposals to curb criminals in politics.

Campaign expenses for election to the Indian parliament have ballooned.
(U.S. dollars billion)

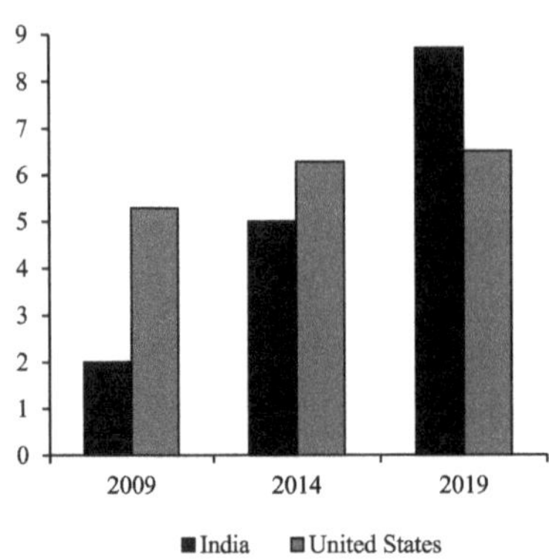

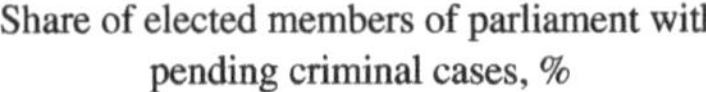

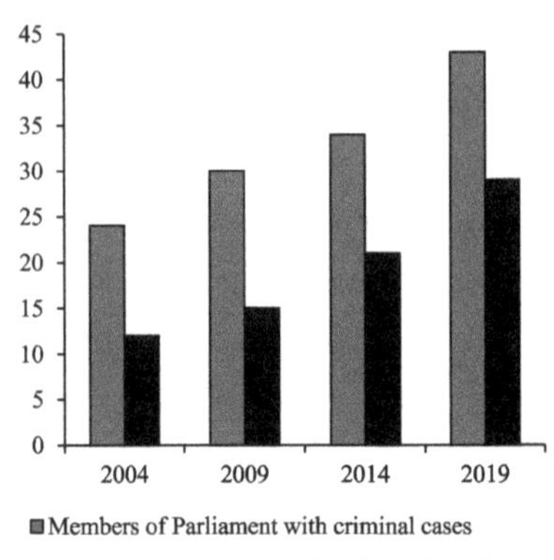

FIGURE 22.6: Money and criminally charged legislators have increased relentlessly in India's national politics.

Note: Left-hand panel: For the United States, the estimates are for the most recent previous presidential and congressional election cycle.

Sources: Left-hand panel: For India, the New Delhi-based Centre for Media Studies; U.S. estimates from https://www.opensecrets.org/overview/cost.php; Right-hand panel: Vaishnav, Milan. 2017. *When Crime Pays: Money and Muscle in Indian Politics*. New Haven, CT: Yale University Press, 9; Association for Democratic Reforms. 2019. "Lok Sabha Elections 2019: Analysis of Criminal Background, Financial, Education, Gender and other details of Winners." New Delhi, May 25.

The Indian Parliament has also ignored a September 2018 Supreme Court recommendation to enact a "strong law" that would bar politicians charged with serious crimes from contesting elections.[42]

Criminals brought their own money. But where did the rest of the election-campaign money come from? In February 2017, the Modi government had introduced "electoral bonds," a device by which an individual or corporation could donate unlimited amounts to a desired political party. Crucially, the process did not require the donor to disclose its own identity or that of the party receiving its donation. A 2017 constitutional challenge to this opaque election funding lies unresolved at the Supreme Court. The Court stayed silent even after the Election Commission opposed the electoral bonds scheme. The court's silence worked to the BJP's advantage. In 2019, the BJP received 95 percent of the funds raised through electoral bonds.[43]

Money flowed into election campaigning through another murky channel. The number of Indian so-called "shell companies" had grown exponentially since the start of liberalization in the early 1990s, with a particularly explosive increase around 2000. Many of these companies described themselves as providing business or trading services. They operated outside of the tax net, without even the oversight of audited accounts. Shell companies were perfect for transmitting untraceable funds to politicians. Although the Ministry of Corporate Affairs, including under the Modi administration, regularly shut down such shadowy entities, they kept sprouting like wild mushrooms in a rainforest.[44]

The April/May 2019 elections were a crescendo of money, muscle, and Hindutva. Modi won: the BJP increased its share of votes and seats. In the world's largest democracy, economic welfare as the bond between ruler and the ruled was broken.

Fans of the hyped-up "Gujarat economic model" did hope again. Modi's "impressive victory," economist Jagdish Bhagwati said, "was important for India's ongoing economic and social progress." The writer Gurcharan Das added that Narendra Modi, in the manner of U.K.'s "Iron Lady," Margaret Thatcher, could compress "economic reforms" into his second term.[45] What reforms would these be? The economy was in trouble, and Modi could enjoy another five years without electoral challenge. His priority was more performance to bolster Hindutva and his brand.

The Hindutva Juggernaut Keeps Moving

In August 2019, soon after his victory, Modi fulfilled a long-standing promise of Hindutva leaders to dismantle Kashmir's special constitutional status. He stripped away the small amount of autonomy that the Kashmiri government had in comparison with other state governments; he opened the possibility of non-Kashmiris buying property in the Kashmir Valley, which could change the state's demographics. Modi also split Kashmir into two parts and downgraded them both to "Union Territories," essentially placing the areas under his control. He arrested large numbers of potential Kashmiri protestors and shut down internet and mobile phone connections in Kashmir. When the human rights organization Amnesty International pointed out that cutting off communications would endanger lives, the government threatened the organization with regulatory retaliation.[46]

Meanwhile, the Supreme Court waited silently, this time on the constitutionality challenge to eliminating Kashmir's special status and splitting it into two union territories. The court's silence was again in alignment with the government's priority.[47]

In November 2019, the Supreme Court acted on the matter most dear to Hindutva hearts. The Court granted the go-ahead for building a temple for Lord Ram in Ayodhya on the site where the now-destroyed Babri Masjid once stood. In doing so, the Court acknowledged the trail of illegalities that led to the demolition of the Babri Masjid in 1992. The Court recognized also that there was little foundation for the claim that the site had always been venerated as the spot of Lord Ram's birth. But it invoked Article 142 of the Constitution, which enables the Supreme Court to take extraordinary measures when the interests of "complete justice" demand. Citing the "faith and belief" that Hindus held in the site as birthplace of Lord Ram, the justices gave the green light for constructing the temple. Hindutva's young soldiers, who lay coiled to unleash unspeakable fury if the judgment went the other way, celebrated. And by now, many Indian leaders had joined the "soft" Hindutva bandwagon. Congress Party's Rahul Gandhi flaunted his credentials as a devout Hindu Brahmin. State governments under the Congress Party's rule promised to promote the cause of the cow. Mainstream political parties and their leaders had become "hostage to the Hindutva agenda."[48]

In December, Modi shepherded the Citizenship Amendment Act through parliament, which created a path to Indian citizenship for non-Islamic refugees and immigrants from neighboring countries. The law, which excluded Muslim refugees and migrants from the possibility of Indian citizenship, was red meat for hate-filled, anti-Muslim messaging on Facebook. A protest led by women students warned that this might be a step toward a Hindu state. The police arrested protesting students all over the country and shut down mobile networks in Delhi. In the violent confrontations between Hindutva groups and protestors, a junior minister in the Modi government incited his goons to "shoot the traitors." In Karnataka, the police arrested a teacher and a mother on the charge of sedition for helping primary school students stage a play critical of the new citizenship policy. The anti-Muslim fire on Facebook continued for months. And in what was by now a recurring theme, the Supreme Court held—as it continues to hold—its silence on a constitutional challenge to the Citizenship Amendment legislation.[49]

GDP growth continued to trend down toward the dreaded 3 percent annual rate. Veteran industrialist Rahul Bajaj criticized the government for inaction on economic policy and unwillingness to hear criticism. He spoke of the violence and intimidation which Hindu nationalists encouraged. On cue, Finance Minister Nirmala Sitharaman accused Bajaj of harming the national interest.[50]

A mysterious pneumonia first identified in Wuhan, China, in December 2019 was traveling through Europe under the name "the novel coronavirus." In India, coronavirus infections appeared in the state of Kerala in January 2020, after which scattered infections were reported every day across the country. India's broken economy, decrepit health infrastructure, and broken democracy were not prepared for the imminent assault.[51]

Chapter 23

COVID-19 BARES THE MORAL DECAY

As the novel coronavirus—SARS-CoV-2—spread worldwide in early 2020, many Indians looked back to an unhappy time a century earlier. Starting in mid-1918 and continuing in waves through 1920, a ferocious influenza visited the Indian subcontinent, killing between 17 and 18 million people, which amounted to more than 5 percent of the population. Corpses clogged rivers as the firewood needed to cremate dead Hindus ran out.[1]

Experts feared that the new virus would devastate the now much larger population. By March 24, the virus had infected five hundred Indians and killed ten of them. In a televised broadcast a little after 8 p.m., Prime Minister Narendra Modi announced that India would lock down at midnight. As with demonetization in November 2016, he gave Indians no time to prepare. The lockdown would last twenty-one days, Modi said. Without it, he warned, India could slide back in time by twenty-one years.[2]

The next morning, garment and textile factories switched off operations in the Gujarati mercantile city of Surat. Mohammad Saiyub, a twenty-two-year-old Muslim, and Amrit Kumar, a twenty-four-year-old Dalit were told they had no jobs. These luckless childhood friends had fled the hopelessness of tiny family farms in Uttar Pradesh to begin new lives in Surat. Now, that city too had abandoned them. Many urban migrants like them yearned for the embrace of loved ones in the villages they had left behind. But bus and train services were rare and erratic. The numbers of those walking home swelled.

As the journalist and author Basharat Peer recounted, Saiyub and Amrit initially chose to stay on in Surat, hoping the factories would reopen. But the lockdown continued well past the scheduled twenty-one days. Their savings began to run out. Finally, on May 14—fifty-one days after the lockdown started and no end in sight—they began their journey home, first on foot and then in a truck packed with migrants. When Amrit developed a fever and his temperature began rising, passengers on the truck insisted he be dropped off. Saiyub got down too. While he waited on the side of the road for an ambulance, Saiyub "cradled Amrit in his lap, pouring handfuls of water on his lips. In that moment, somebody took a photograph of the two friends."[3]

Seventy-three years after independence, the photograph of Saiyub holding Amrit revealed how broken the Indian economy was. The photograph explained why over 40 percent of India's workers battled on in agriculture, where they barely made a living: they feared moving to cities, where the jobs were scarce and precarious. The photograph explained why, among those who did go to the cities, at least 100 million Indians were "temporary" or "circular" migrants, living on subsistence wages in cramped and unhygienic housing from which they often returned home. The fury of COVID-19, the disease caused by the new virus, revealed the scale of the precarity. Amrit, it turned out, did not have COVID-19. He died in a hospital before he could reach home because of severe dehydration in the 43-degree Centigrade (109-degree Fahrenheit) heat.[4]

The friendship that Saiyub and Amrit shared, cutting as it did across religions, was "like a gentle rain from heaven," wrote Basharat Peer. The friendship stood out in "the hate-filled public sphere." On WhatsApp, radio, and television, rumors swirled that Muslims were deliberately spreading the virus. Arrests of Muslim seminarians as alleged coronavirus spreaders gave the rumors credibility. The rumors were fabricated, the arrests typical police overreach. But Hindu mobs had a new excuse to lynch Muslims.[5]

As these early days foretold, economic opportunities vanished, and an epidemic of violence unfolded along with the spread of the coronavirus. The state either stood by or accelerated these trends. The task of restoring opportunities and social norms became more urgent, but it also became much harder.

The Mask of Official Statistics Wears Thin

To everyone's great relief, the official tracking mechanism reported far-lower-than-feared coronavirus infections (Figure 23.1). Indeed, the low numbers instilled a view that India had conquered the virus. Only in February 2021 did an official source—a national seroprevalence survey—reveal that large numbers of Indian citizens carried antibodies reflecting infection by the coronavirus. Instead of the 10 million infections recorded through the tracking mechanism by the end of December 2020, the actual number infected was over 300 million.[6]

COVID-related deaths were also vastly undercounted. Even in the past, Indian death registration systems often did not record the cause of

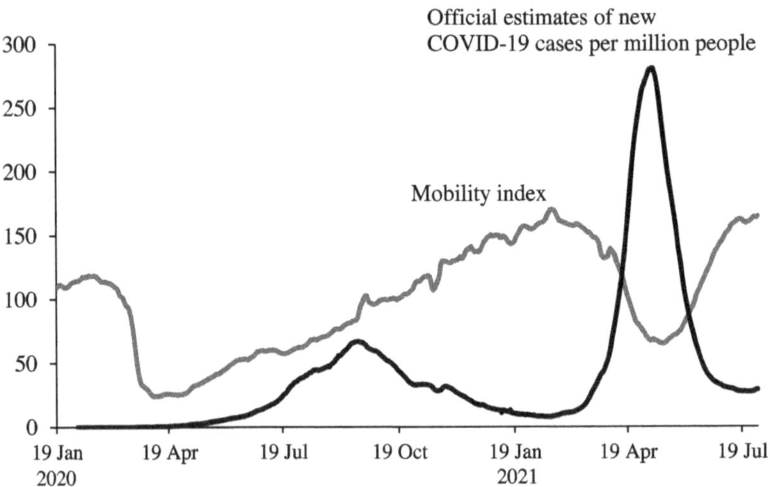

FIGURE 23.1: After the first COVID-19 wave came the tsunami. (7-day moving averages of officially reported cases and mobility January 13, 2020 = 100)
Source: Our World in Data, https://github.com/owid/covid-19-data/tree/master/public/data/; Apple mobility trends for walking (change in routing requests), https://covid19.apple.com/mobility.

death. Now officials deliberately undercounted COVID deaths. Many observers suspected from the very start that the official death counts were low, but the huge undercounting became evident only later. Following a widespread practice, mathematician Murad Banaji and demographer Aashish Gupta estimated "excess mortality": the increase in the total number of deaths when compared with the baseline of previous years. By general agreement, this excess almost entirely represented COVID-19 deaths. The metric of "excess deaths" revealed that about 900,000 Indians died of COVID-19 in the wave through December 2020, rather than the officially reported 150,000. Hence, although India was spared an even worse outcome because of its young population, which could better fight the coronavirus, the Indian COVID-19 death rate (measured relative to the national population) was about the same or higher than in advanced economies with much older citizens.[7]

Unlike the infections and deaths, whose magnitude became known only later, the economic devastation was evident immediately. Between April and June 2020, GDP fell a heart-stopping 24 percent below where it had been in the same three months in 2019, making it by far the worst fall among major international economies. What mattered more to people's lives, 100 million jobs disappeared from the approximately 500-million-people labor force in the lockdown's initial shock wave.[8]

To revive the crippled economy, the government lifted the national lockdown on June 8, 2020. But it held back from using fiscal policy to give immediate relief to those who most needed it. Echoing a widely accepted judgment, scholars and activists Jean Drèze and Anmol Somanchi write that relief in the form of cash transfers, food rations, and rural employment guarantee was "limited and unreliable" and "failed to make up for more than a small fraction of the income losses." The Reserve Bank of India reduced its policy interest rate to stimulate more private spending. That policy helped those who could borrow and spend but not necessarily those who were hurting. In addition, the RBI, following central banks worldwide, authorized the banking system's debtors to stop repaying their loans. This gave relief to borrowers who might otherwise have gone bankrupt.[9] Overall, the RBI's policy response propped up those who participated in the country's formal credit economy. Together, the government and the RBI did little for the weak, who (as always, in such situations) were hit the hardest.

Amid continuing partial lockdowns, with infections and hospitalizations still on the rise, GDP began to claw its way back. Normally, India's sharp GDP fall and higher inflation rate relative to competitor countries should have weakened the rupee's exchange value, which would have helped boost exports and achieve a quicker GDP rebound. Yet, the rupee's exchange value remained virtually unchanged at 75 rupees for a dollar through the COVID-19 crisis. The rupee remained strong because, even as the economic collapse crushed the weak and vulnerable, international investors flocked to buy stocks of select Indian companies. The winners were Mukesh Ambani, the Tatas, and especially Gautam Adani; three of their companies doubled in value over the course of the year.[10] Foreign investors made rich India richer and, by keeping the rupee strong, slowed the recovery for vulnerable Indians. Together, domestic economic policy and international market forces widened the inequality in India at warp speed.

Despite recovering from its lows, the economy employed between 15 and 20 million fewer workers in December 2020 than before the lockdown began in late March. Many workers who formerly had the privilege of receiving "regular" salaries remained without work. Teachers in private schools and those working on contracts in government schools were among the worst affected. Many of the formerly salaried workers simply dropped out of the workforce. Among those who did return, large numbers declared themselves "self-employed"; they didn't have proper jobs but reported being engaged in farming or petty trading. Time studies will show that they were unemployed much of the time. Manufacturing employment, in decline since 2011–2012, fell even more.[11]

Job losses, spread across the country, pushed large numbers into severe poverty. Poverty estimates are even dodgier than employment numbers, but the likely magnitudes are sobering. The Pew Research Center estimates that by December 2020 COVID-19 had pushed 75 million more Indians (nearly 6 percent of the population) below the most frugal poverty line of $2 a day per capita (about 6,000 rupees a month for a family of four when converted at the exchange rate that equalized purchasing power in 2020). India's huge increase in poverty contributed to 60 percent of the global COVID-19–related increase in extreme poverty. Many who had clawed their way up India's income-earning ladder, and had reason to hope for a better future, took a huge hit, falling into a severe poverty or into a state just above that abject condition. These were people who before the COVID-19 crisis had lived on between $10 and $20 dollars per head per day (families of four with monthly consumption expenditure between 30,000 and 60,000 rupees). Salil Tripathi was one such statistic. He lost a job paying him 40,000 rupees a month as a restaurant manager and became a gig worker at 10,000 rupees a month. Tripathi's case was especially tragic. He died while out to make a delivery, killed by an out-of-control police vehicle.[12] Thus, as Indians on the higher rungs of the economic ladder rose higher, everyone below fell or barely hung on.

A "nutrition crisis" unfolded. India was already among the global leaders in undernourished children, and progress had slowed down, possibly stalled, after 2013. The Modi government had cut funding for nutrition programs in its first term. After COVID-19's onset, schools closed down and stopped providing the midday meals. Health services, such as child immunizations and outpatient treatment, fell sharply, even in advanced states such as Tamil Nadu and Kerala. In the less advanced states, including Gujarat, Bihar, and Uttar Pradesh, they fell precipitously.[13] These health setbacks will leave long-term scars.

Women and young adults suffered disproportionately. Female-dominated occupations suffered heavy job destruction, and the pressure on women's time for housework and childcare increased greatly. Left with reduced work options, many women did not even bother to report themselves unemployed—they simply dropped out of the workforce. The diminished work and financial prospects for women were a continuing ill omen for the education and health of Indian children. India's young workers were placed in a vicious circle: they were easier to fire because they had weak ties to their employers, and they were the last to return to work because their lack of experience made them less employable.[14]

India's already impossible employment challenge became harder still. In 2019, India had an unfulfilled demand of over 80 million jobs, and the first COVID-19 wave added about 25 million people to that shortfall.

These included those who had lost jobs and were still looking for work (or were now underemployed among the so-called self-employed), those who had given up looking for a job, and several million from the new cohort of Indians who entered the job-scarce market that year.[15]

Modi Has Other Priorities

On June 3, 2020, in a typically surprise announcement, the government issued an ordinance (executive order) to overhaul agricultural policy. The national lockdown was still on; it would be lifted on June 8. The proposed policy had no bearing on the acute distress that Indians were experiencing and did little to address India's grave agricultural problems. Instead, its narrow focus was to reduce the government's procurement of food grains and push farmers to sell directly to private buyers.[16]

The chief minister of Punjab, India's grain basket, immediately criticized the initiative. He worried that the policy was a prelude to the government's withdrawal of its minimum support prices for food grains. If that happened, large private buyers would likely bid down grain prices. The timing was awful. Many farmers were weighed down by heavy debt burdens and had lost non-farming side jobs because of the lockdown. Farmer suicide rates were alarmingly high. Nevertheless, the Modi government barreled ahead. On September 17, with reported COVID-19 cases at a new high and unsure of support for its farm policy from alliance partners, the government used a dubious "voice vote" to rush the June orders through the Rajya Sabha. To placate farmers, Modi insisted that the generous minimum support prices would continue. That promise was not credible because if it were honored, few farmers would shift to private buyers and the new laws would be pointless.[17]

Farmers protested. On November 26, a large group marched toward Delhi. When the police stopped them at the city's borders, they set up camp there. In that sprawling camp, tens of thousands of farmers from across India braved the biting winter, serving each other in a community of kitchens and personal services. Farmers elsewhere in India protested in sympathy.[18]

It was certainly past time to greatly scale back the minimum support prices and associated subsidies for major food grains put in place by Agriculture Minister C. Subramaniam in 1965 as part of his Green Revolution policy package. Over the years, Subramaniam's policy package had greatly increased food grain production in irrigated areas, but as policymakers foresaw at the outset, minimum support prices and subsidies were a drain on the government's budget. Moreover, large quantities of wheat and rice purchased by the government rotted in warehouses.[19]

But Modi's proposed changes did not pass either the political or economic test. Politically, just as rich farmers in developed countries have continued to demand and receive large subsidies, Indian farmers (even the large ones) were unwilling to let go the government's financial crutch. Developed-country governments have gradually "decoupled" subsidies from production: instead of subsidizing to produce more, they have paid farmers to reduce land use and conserve the environment, a direction India will need to explore, especially in Punjab and Haryana where farmers' burning of rice stubble to prepare for the winter wheat crop causes heavy air pollution.[20]

The real difficulty, however, with Modi's proposal was its failure to recognize and address the agricultural sector's truly serious problems. The most intractable of these was intensifying land fragmentation. Meanwhile, groundwater tables were falling, and costs of production inputs were rising. Erosion of soil quality, rising temperatures, and higher rainfall variability induced by the climate crisis were depressing land yields. Farmers accumulated large debts and often fell into acute financial distress. Farmer suicides, which came into prominence in the 1990s, had never subsided. Farmers, already under huge stress, feared that the new farm laws would make them the easy prey of large agribusiness companies without the alternative of urban jobs to fall back on.

Indian agriculture required a huge amount of new investment to expand irrigation, replenish groundwater, and restore soil quality. Sensible pricing of water use was essential, and India likely needed a new pricing policy that paid farmers for not farming. Those were not priorities on the Modi government's agenda. Through much of 2021, negotiations between farmers and the government remained at an impasse.

Narendra Modi continued Hindutva's perpetual performance. The immediate opportunity for doing so arose in the wake of the Supreme

Court's green light in November 2019 for the construction of the Ram Temple in Ayodhya. On August 5, 2020, with COVID-19 cases still rising, Modi showcased himself as Hindutva's patron saint at a heavily publicized religious ceremony in Ayodhya to pray for the successful construction of the temple. As one reporter put it, "It was a Modi show all the way." Congress Party leaders Rahul and Priyanka Gandhi, loath to be left out of the limelight, moved from their grudging acceptance of the Ram Temple juggernaut to more actively seeking a presence on the Hindu stage. They extolled the human values Ram embodied and called for harmony in Ram's name.[21]

Further blurring the line between state and religion, in December 2020 Prime Minister Modi sat in on a televised prayer ceremony to inaugurate a new parliament building. Construction of the new building came along with a new house for the prime minister and a renovated Rajpath, the two-mile-long central axis of New Delhi from the India Gate to the president's house. Despite continuing COVID-19 infections and deaths, this $2.5 billion vanity project proceeded as an "essential service" with workers either living along the worksite or ferried from a nearby labor camp.[22]

Hubris Leaves India Unprepared for a Tsunami

For India's political leadership, the threatening phase of COVID-19 was in the past. On January 28, 2021, addressing the rich and famous (in a virtual format) at the annual Davos conclave, Modi said that India had "saved the world from disaster by bringing the [Indian] situation under control." India, Modi reported, had vaccinated 2.3 million health workers in twelve days and was "saving lives worldwide" by supplying vaccines to other countries. To his captive international audience, Modi offered Ayurveda, India's tradition-based medicinal system, which, he said, could help increase immunity to COVID-19.[23]

Indian scientists were worried. In December 2020, some weeks before Modi's upbeat assessment, they had identified a coronavirus variant circulating in India. Known eventually as the Delta variant, it transmitted the disease more rapidly from one person to another than earlier variants did and—as the evidence increasingly showed—also caused more severe illness. The new variant's ferocity was not fully recognized at the time, but in February 2021, a group of scientists warned India's National Centre for Disease Control and the health ministry that infections could spread rapidly. On March 9, the Indian Medical Association, pointing to rising infections in Maharashtra and Delhi, issued a public warning: it was premature to tout victory.[24]

Ignoring the warnings of the new threat and operating in the data fog of reassuring official statistics, on March 21 Prime Minister Modi featured in full-page newspaper advertisements extending to Hindu pilgrims "a hearty welcome" to the Kumbh Mela in Haridwar, where the Ganga descends from the Himalayas on to the plains. Starting April 11, millions of pilgrims would jostle cheek-by-jowl for three weeks, washing away their sins in the Ganga's holy waters and attending religious festivities. In neighboring Uttar Pradesh state, the government was moving ahead with another infection super-spreader: forcing the conduct of *panchayat* (village-level) elections despite the Allahabad High Court's direction to postpone the elections and impose a lockdown in the entire state, or at least in the state's major cities. Making matters worse, India, home to the world's largest vaccine producer—the Serum Institute of India—was running short of vaccine doses.[25]

The BJP and Modi had their hands in seeding another COVID-19 super-spreader event. On April 7, while campaigning for the Bengal legislative assembly, a BJP candidate had the crowds chanting, "Jai Shree Ram" (Victory to Lord Ram). Hindus needed to unite around him, he said, because Muslim appeasement endangered the practice of Hinduism. At a rally ten days later, Modi gazed at his audience in awe: "Today," he said, "I see huge crowds of people in every direction. Today, you have shown your power."[26]

The Kumbh Mela, the Uttar Pradesh *panchayat* elections, and the Bengal state election accelerated the spread of the virus in eastern India even as the COVID-19 tsunami inflicted havoc in Mumbai and other Maharashtrian cities.

The grotesquely short supply of medical-grade oxygen was a defining feature of the second wave of COVID-19. In Delhi, in late April 2021, when fifty-four-year-old Niranjan Saha complained of breathlessness, his wife told her two sons, "Find me an oxygen cylinder. Sell my gold, but

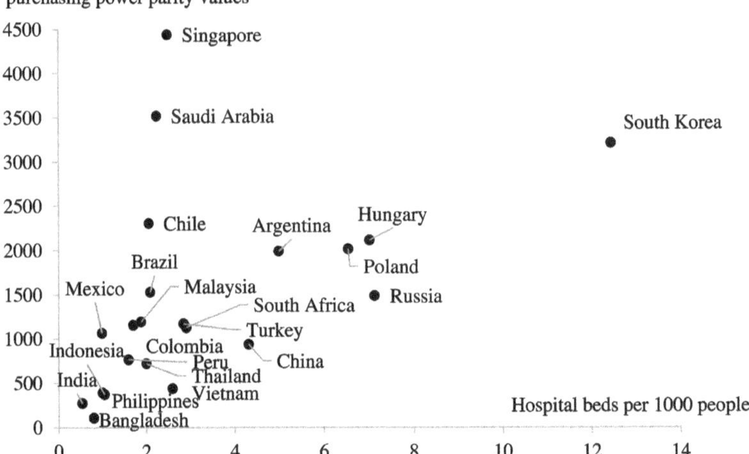

FIGURE 23.2: India's health infrastructure has suffered years of neglect.
Source: World Bank, World Development Indicators, SH.XPD.CHEX.PP.CD, SH.MED.BEDS.ZS.

get a cylinder." The boys searched for four days as their father's condition worsened. They eventually found a seller who demanded 60,000 rupees ($820) for a cylinder of oxygen, which they bought with money scraped together from friends and relatives. Their dad had the energy to take only a few breaths of the oxygen before he died. To understand the failure, notice India in the bottom left-hand corner of Figure 23.2, with its ultra-low healthcare spending and hospital beds per capita. COVID-19 rapidly overwhelmed that shameful system while charlatans preyed on the unfortunate.[27]

Compared to the first COVID-19 wave, the misery crept one rung up the economic ladder. In upscale Gurgaon, a former Indian diplomat—an avid golf player taking piano lessons in his retirement—died in his car outside a hospital, waiting for a bed.[28]

India's mega- and ultra-rich fled the country. When Britain announced its plan to stop entry from COVID-infected India, many rich Indians paid several times the price of a normal air ticket to reach London before the entry barrier came down. Those who delayed paid tens of thousands of dollars for private jets to sneak them in on time. Others hurried to the

United Arab Emirates before that country shut its doors. One air charter company spokesman said that people were willing to pay "absolutely crazy" amounts to fly on private jets. Rich Indians had long since exited the country and so ceased serving as voices for better education and other public services. Now, faster than ever, they also rushed to establish a foothold in countries offering residence in return for investment commitments.[29]

For those who could not possibly leave India, something had snapped. And it was not just the healthcare infrastructure. A Delhi High Court judge, remarking on the extortionary prices of oxygen and critical medicines, bemoaned the country's "dismembered moral fabric."[30]

At their peak, from late April to the end of May, official statistics reported over three hundred thousand COVID-19 cases and three thousand deaths every day. However, long lines of ambulances outside crematoriums were early signs of the much larger than reported number of deaths. On May 10, residents of a village in Bihar woke up to a searing image of dead bodies on the banks and in the flow of the Ganga River. Wrapped in colored sheets, bodies followed one after another along a seven-mile stretch. The scale of the horror became known over the next week when *Dainik Bhaskar*, the largest Hindi-language daily newspaper, reported over two thousand dead bodies along the Ganga, as that mighty river traveled its 1140-kilometer course through Uttar Pradesh and entered Bihar.[31]

The mobility restrictions starting early April were mainly night curfews and partial lockdowns. However, even these relatively mild restrictions on mobility forced some businesses to stop operations. In April and May 2021, over 25 million non-farm jobs disappeared—much less than the 100 million in the same months a year earlier, but still a sizable number. Many urban workers, who had trekked desperately to their village homes a year earlier and then returned to the cities to resume work, now rushed home again. As was true in the previous year, many dropped out of the labor force, not bothering to look for a job. Once again, workers and their families dipped into their savings and ran up debt to put food on the table.[32]

Two brothers with college degrees but without jobs returned to their father's farm because he could not afford to replace two bullocks (steer) that had died in an accident. The brothers plowed the land in place of the bullocks. COVID-19 kept exposing this one Indian fault line mercilessly: the lack of honorable work in cities or on farms.[33]

Many small urban businesses found themselves in a fatal squeeze. In Dharavi, the sprawling Mumbai slum, municipal authorities had controlled the fearsome flareup of infections, but workshops and factories—which normally produced leather goods, garments, and clay pots and pans—operated at much-reduced capacity, if at all. With COVID-19 restrictions, cramped workspaces prevented businesses from rehiring migrant workers who wanted to return. Logistics disrupted by COVID dealt a double blow, raising input costs and increasing the difficulties of selling products. Elsewhere, outside the iconic Taj Mahal in Agra, producers of marble inlay handicrafts for tourists now heard only the footfalls of silence. All over India, kiosks and shops—storehouses of urban underemployment—could not compete with online sales and began closing down. An entire way of life and livelihoods was disappearing.[34]

The second COVID-19 wave saved its most evil design for children. Online teaching was not a substitute for the long months of lost classroom instruction, especially for children in poor families. In August 2021, a survey of sixteen states found that half the children in grade 3, who should have been fluent readers in their mother tongues, could read but a few words. Many parents had pulled their children out of private schools, which they could no longer afford. India was facing the specter of mass illiteracy. Struggling parents put their children to work. Two brothers, ten and twelve years old, worked in a glass bangle factory in Jaipur, Rajasthan. In Rajkot, Gujarat, children fifteen to seventeen years old worked in sari processing units. The number of children at work increased threefold in Tamil Nadu, while child labor and trafficking for sex shot up in Uttar Pradesh and Bihar. Child marriages surged.[35]

Rather than helping, the government's fiscal policy continued discriminating against the defenseless. In September 2019, Finance Minister Nirmala Sitharaman had given the corporate sector a generous tax cut. Government officials described the cut in grand terms, as a "structural reform." But following the experience with earlier such tax cuts, the latest round did little to spur new activity. The government lost revenue, to compensate for which the finance minister hiked excise taxes on petroleum products in March and May 2020. The cost of fuel jumped, more so as world oil prices rose in 2021, which hurt low-income households acutely. Disrupted logistics raised prices of pulses, eggs, milk, sugar, and cooking oil, increasing the inflationary bite out of distressed incomes. In late June, the finance minister announced "fiscal relief," which mainly came in the form of guarantees to lenders on loans that borrowers did not want.[36]

Rich India continued to get richer, and fabulously so. Amid the global drought of international capital and despite India's economic woes, glamorous Indian companies attracted a sustained flow of foreign funds. The Indian benchmark stock index, the Sensex, rose at the same dramatic pace as the Standard and Poor's 500 in the buoyant U.S. economy (Figure 23.3). But even that rise paled in comparison with the stock price increase of Adani Enterprises, the flagship company of Gautam Adani, a friend of Narendra Modi's from the post–Gujarat riot period when Modi seemed to be losing friends in the business community. Adani depended heavily on government contracts, and his company's latest dramatic stock price rise came on top of the spurt since May 2014, when Modi became prime minister. Gautam Adani and Mukesh Ambani climbed the global wealth rankings during the COVID-19 months as hundreds of millions of Indians fell from the middle and lower rungs of the Indian economic ladder. As if to emphasize the point, at the height of India's COVID-19 catastrophe in late April 2021, Mukesh Ambani paid $78 million to buy the Stoke Park golf club, west of London, a private club made famous in James Bond movies. Indian sales of Lamborghinis, in the price range of $400,000 to $800,000, hit a new high while sales of low-end motorcycles languished. Stores that sold cashmere overcoats and Versace handbags flourished as never before, catering to Indians who also shopped in London and Milan. Stores that sold washing machines, electric kettles, mixers, grinders, and other staples of an Indian kitchen heard few footfalls and were on the verge of closing down. The divide between India's richest and all other Indians had never been so unsettling.[37]

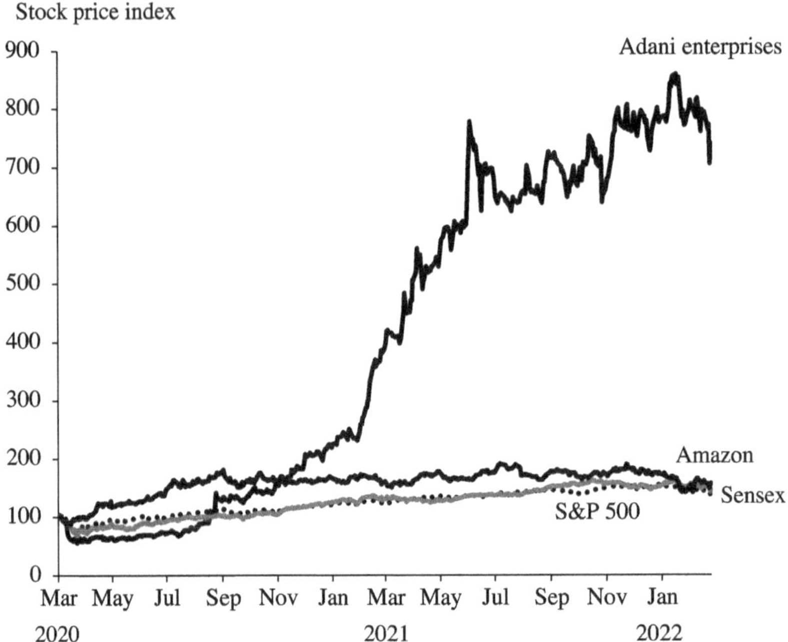

FIGURE 23.3: To whom that hath shall be given. (Stock price is normalized on March 1, 2020 = 100)

Note: Adani Enterprises, ADEL; Sensex index, BSESN; S&P 500, US500; Amazon, AMZN.

Source: https://www.investing.com.

Banaji and Gupta estimate that COVID-19 killed about another 2.9 million people in the second wave through June of 2021 (against the official count of 250,000 deaths). All told, India lost 3.8 million people to the two COVID waves, meaning there were approximately 2.8 deaths per 1000 Indians. India placed near the top in the global COVID-related death rate.[38]

Despite the moral decay all around, the good angels of many Indians worked overtime through the deepest days of distress. Volunteers helped hunt down hospital beds, oxygen, and medical supplies. Doctors offered free telecounseling. Places of worship provided free food. In one instance, a lowly rickshaw-puller equipped his vehicle with an oxygen cylinder and oximeter to ferry the sick.[39]

By mid-June 2021, as the new cases subsided, the pace of vaccinations picked up. But the Indian healthcare system was so broken that some crooked hospitals and doctors injected people with fake vaccines of saline water. A vaccination camp sent lucky individuals notifications of jabs they didn't know they had taken. Although we may never know how widespread such practices were, health workers in one survey reported strikingly high numbers of those fraudulently registered as double vaccinated.[40]

When India Lost Its Soul

Eighty-four-year-old Jesuit priest and human rights activist Father Stan Swamy had spent five decades fighting mining and steel companies as they destroyed the forests, water, and livelihoods of the Adivasis, the tribal population, in the eastern state of Jharkhand. In early October 2020, the National Investigation Agency (NIA)—India's counterterrorism task force—arrested Swamy under the Unlawful Activities Prevention Act, which denied him both bail and a speedy trial. They accused him of instigating violence after the January 2018 Dalit celebration at Bhima Koregaon near Pune in Maharashtra. The NIA described him and fifteen others similarly accused as "Maoist" terrorists. Swamy, who had advanced Parkinson's disease, was unable to hold a glass of drinking water. With COVID-19 rampant in his overcrowded jail and his frail health making him an easy victim of the deadly disease, he appealed for bail. The NIA curtly countered that he was taking "undue benefit" of the pandemic, using it merely as "a ruse." The courts repeatedly denied Swamy bail, although in late May 2021, they transferred him to a hospital. There, on July 5, he died of COVID-related complications. In truth, a ruthless state had killed "a caged bird," as he described himself.[41]

Father Swamy's callous killing was a metaphor for the state-condoned—and, in some instances, state-led—violence that overlay the COVID havoc. Swamy himself was one of many victims of a state that prioritized protection of corporate interests. As a lifelong advocate of Adivasi rights, he had recently battled a Gautam Adani project. Sudha Bharadwaj, arrested like Swamy as a Maoist for allegedly instigating the Bhima Koregaon riots, was a mathematics graduate from IIT Kanpur who became a lawyer to fight for Adivasi rights. She too had confronted an Adani investment. Bela Bhatia was a distinguished social scientist and human-rights lawyer who defended Adivasi rights; she inevitably butted heads with an Adani project. Hidme Markam, a twenty-eight-year-old former lunch cook at a school, was an Adivasi drawn to defend Adivasi rights. She also collided with Adani interests.[42]

In addition to supporting corporate interests, the state used repressive methods to suppress dissent. Arrests under national security laws, already common in the preceding Congress Party–led government, jumped after Modi became prime minister in 2014. Such arrests accelerated in early 2020 following the passage of the Citizenship Amendment Act and continued into the pandemic. Yogi Adityanath, Uttar Pradesh chief minister, was a champion in the use of repressive laws as he often felt slighted by criticism. Unfortunately, there was much to criticize the Yogi for. Large numbers of Uttar Pradesh residents died because of poor management of COVID. Of all Indian states, Uttar Pradesh constantly came in at the bottom end of governance quality measures. Its GDP growth fell after the Yogi became chief minister.[43]

The Indian state directed its special fury at journalists. In late January and early February 2021, the government arrested prominent journalists on charges of sedition for reporting on farmers' protests. The government also demanded that Twitter block accounts that carried messages on farmers' agitation, a demand Twitter briefly defied before giving in. In April 2021, as the second COVID wave killed wantonly, the international media watchdog Reporters Without Borders described India as one of the most dangerous countries in the world for journalists, ranking it 142nd out of 180 countries in its World Press Freedom Index. As if to show contempt for that ranking, in the third week of July 2021, income tax officials raided multiple offices of the Dainik Bhaskar Group, India's leading newspaper conglomerate, and the Bharat Samachar television channel, both of which had intrepidly exposed the inaccurate official count of COVID-related deaths. In particular, *Dainik Bhaskar* had highlighted the painful scenes of dead bodies along the Ganga. Om Gaur, one of the paper's editors, shamed India's leadership in a scathing *New York Times* op-ed: "The Ganges Is Returning the Dead. It Does Not Lie." *Dainik Bhaskar* had also carried several stories on the government's alleged use of Pegasus, the Israeli software, to spy on journalists and political opponents.[44]

Anurag Thakur, Modi's information and broadcasting minister, made it clear that the tax raids were meant to muzzle the Indian press. Thakur was the BJP's hatchet man who, during the January 2020 student protest against the Citizenship Amendment Act, had called on Hindu militants to "shoot the traitors." Now, as he said in mafia-speak, intimidation of *Dainik Bhaskar* and *Bharat Samachar* was a message to media outlets: "[When] agencies do their own work, we don't interfere in their functioning." In May 2022, India dropped from 142 to 150 in the World Freedom Index compiled by Reporters Without Borders.[45]

In the crevices of state violence, Hindutva vigilantes cultivated their hate. In June 2021, the targets were Muslim street vendors who plied their wares—fruits, vegetables, and comfort food—on *redhis* (carts). Hindu mobs, carrying the banner of the Bajrang Dal, Hindutva's youth wing, and chanting "Jai Shree Ram" (Victory to Lord Ram), lynched the Muslim vendors, accusing them of stealing jobs. The government had, for long, ignored the Supreme Court's 2018 directive to end the epidemic of mob violence and lynchings. Human rights lawyer Rashmi Singh protested, saying that by letting the "contemptuous government" off the hook, the Supreme Court was encouraging more lynchings.[46]

The Indian government's contempt for the Supreme Court was not new. Successive governments had ignored the Supreme Court's 1977 "bail, not jail" decree, just as they had ignored the 2011 call to disband the state-supported vigilante Salwa Judum in Chhattisgarh and the 2011 instruction to stop construction on water bodies. In several other cases, the Supreme Court chose to remain silent, giving the government the opportunity to pursue possibly unconstitutional actions. The Supreme Court inquiry on the diabolical Pegasus spying software was adrift, leaving the government just as unaccountable as when the Court failed to opine on crucial matters: constitutionality of electoral bonds, downgrading of Kashmir's autonomy, and passage of the discriminatory citizenship law.[47] The Supreme Court was no longer a check on the government.

Indeed, India was no longer a democracy, said a collective of international scholars in their 2021 V-Dem (varieties of democracy) report, the most comprehensive international assessment of democracy. The scholars classified India as an "electoral autocracy," along with Poland,

Hungary, Turkey, and Brazil. India held elections, they said, but did not ensure legislative and judicial oversight over executive power and did not protect individual liberties, the rule of law, and the freedoms of association and expression.[48]

The cost of electoral autocracy was clear. The protest against Modi's farm laws, which began on November 26, 2020, stretched over the course of nearly a year. On November 10, 2021, forty-five-year-old Gurpreet Singh, a landless farmer, hanged himself from a tree just outside New Delhi, near where thousands of farmers were still camping in protest. Gurpreet Singh, forced by circumstances to sell his four acres of land in 2000, made ends meet by renting an acre of land. The long absence from his farming duties drove him to economic despair, leaving him with no options, he concluded. COVID-19, exposure to extreme cold and heat, and suicides killed more than six hundred protesting farmers. In a gruesome incident, a BJP convoy—allegedly commanded by the son of a Modi government minister—mowed down some protestors. Then, in a televised address to the nation in the morning of November 19, Modi abruptly announced that he was repealing the farm laws.[49]

In 2014, the *Financial Times* expressed the hope that Modi's "style which brooks little opposition" would help "get things done." The newspaper anticipated that because "he may be able to override some of the checks and balances of Indian democracy," India could achieve China-like growth. Modi had indeed brooked no opposition and had overridden the checks and balances of democracy. The results were on display. After the farmers ended their protest, the *Financial Times* still did not get it. The newspaper blamed Modi for poorly planning his "bold" initiatives, such as the 2016 demonetization and the farm laws. As if it might have been otherwise! Autocrats—secure in their sense of grandeur—almost always make poor, "ill-planned" decisions.[50]

Is This How It Ends?

My task in this book, to record post-independence history, is complete. At the start of this now seventy-five-year journey, India faced three challenges: breathe new life into the agricultural sector, provide good urban jobs, and compete in the international marketplace. At the end of this journey, India faces three challenges: breathe new life into an ailing agricultural sector, provide many more jobs in an economy that seems chronically unable to create jobs, and compete in a much tougher international setting. At independence, vast illiteracy plagued India; after COVID, the risk of mass illiteracy surged.

India began as an unequal society. Inequality rose especially after the mid-1980s, and with COVID-19, the gulf between India's rich and poor increased horrifically. Indian poverty, when defined by the most frugal standards, fell for about two and a half decades starting in the late 1980s, but even at its lowest point in 2012, when defined by a more humane standard of contemporary living, about 60 percent of Indians were poor. A leaked official report suggests that poverty increased between 2012 and 2018, and COVID-19 threw even more Indians into poverty.

India started its post-independence journey as an improbable democracy relying on the wisdom of poor and illiterate citizens. The country's democracy, having betrayed the economic aspirations of millions of its citizens, no longer protects the fundamental rights and freedoms of Indians. A blanket of violence is falling over the nation. The norms of equality, tolerance, and shared progress have disappeared.

India started with hope. Can India still deliver on that hope? Or is it too late to repair the country's broken economy and democracy?

EPILOGUE: A FEASIBLE IDEALISM

In thinking of India's past, and even more so its future, we must keep our gaze unflinchingly on employment. Good jobs are the essence of economic development, indispensable for economic welfare as well as human dignity. Good jobs are also the point of contact between economics and the politics of social discontent.

In 2019, 12.5 million young Indians, virtually all of them with college degrees, applied for thirty-five thousand jobs as clerks, timekeepers, and station masters in the Indian railways. For each person who would eventually get a job, 350 would not. Over two years later, in January 2022, the job applicants set ablaze train cars and vandalized property because the railway authorities remained unable to deliver even on their miserly promise of jobs. The grim reality is that, to employ all working-age Indians, the economy needs to create 200 million jobs over the next decade, an impossible order after the past decade of declining employment numbers.[1] Right from independence, the Indian economy produced too few jobs. For more than 80 percent of Indians, the informal sector employment became the safety net, where workers idled for long stretches, earning below- or barely-above-poverty wages. Demonetization in 2016, a poorly executed goods and services tax in 2017, and COVID-19 in 2020 and 2021 struck hammer blows on the informal sector while creating no new options. Indeed, technology accelerated job destruction, especially in retail and wholesale trade. More Indians just stopped looking for work.

Set against this bleakness, many pundits and leaders look back to celebrate and draw hope from India's high GDP growth rates of the 1990s and 2000s. That celebrated growth, however, was an outcome of unusually buoyant world trade, rampant natural resource use, and a domestic finance-construction bubble. Even as wealthy Indians accumulated astonishing riches, job creation remained weak. The most severe forms of poverty came down, but still afflicted over 20 percent of Indians; another 40 percent lived precariously, ever at risk of falling back into a dire existence. The median Indian lived in that vulnerable zone—and, looking through a government-induced data fog, still lives there.

The unchanging problem through the post-independence years has been the lack of public goods for shared progress: education, health delivery, functioning cities, clean air and water, and a responsive and fair judiciary. Along with scarcity of jobs, the absence or poor quality of public goods makes the lived reality of vast numbers of Indians a struggle under constant threat of humiliation and violence.

India's problems run deep, for which reason there are no policy or technological magic bullets. Since independence in 1947, India's politics and society have been victims of cascading deterioration in norms and accountability. Politicians—with power and personal enrichment as their main goals—sought easy short-term policy fixes for economic and social problems that require complex, long-term solutions. There were opportunities for change during the spells of high—although unsustainable—growth. But even during these spells, the darker instincts held, even gathered momentum. Rather than strive to provide public goods on a scale that opened opportunities for all, political leaders presented themselves as saviors who granted access to scarce public goods, often as easy-to-advertise freebies.

Society mirrored politics. As game theorist and economist Partha Dasgupta explains, where moral norms break down, everyone expects that others will cheat and so everyone cheats to get ahead of other cheaters. In that "me-me-me" equilibrium, it makes perfect sense for citizens to indulge in scamming and marauding behavior. Financial scams thrive, pharmaceutical companies produce substandard drugs, water tables fall, and garbage landfills become mountains.[2]

Today, India is in a moral trap where norms are broken and political accountability is missing.

And grave risks to lives and livelihoods lie ahead. Dying rivers could choke not just the economy but an entire way of life. And India's climate crisis is here, threatening to compound the ravages of reckless environmental degradation.

The Looming Risks to Lives and Livelihoods

Through the post-independence years, dying rivers became a tragic symbol of India's developmental and democratic failures. Indian rivers compete with water-hungry agriculture. They struggle amid chaotically polluting urban sprawl. They are powerless against construction barons and the sand mafia, who cater to the insatiable appetite of India's newly rich for high-rise apartments, modern office blocks, flashy malls, riverfronts, and water parks. Many of these new structures close the water bodies that once absorbed excess rainfall and fed groundwater aquifers and rivers. Hence, cities experience all-too-frequent flooding. The sand mafia has become a powerful political force, and the dredging of river sands—in addition to all the other destruction it inflicts—further depletes the natural flow of rivers, making them almost impossible to clean and restore.

A loud climate crisis warning sounded in August 2021. The Intergovernmental Panel on Climate Change pointed out that as humans have dumped more carbon into the atmosphere, they have also damaged carbon-absorbing sinks, the natural cleaning systems such oceans, forests, and soil. Bottom line: the world is warming faster than earlier recognized. In November 2021, world leaders met in Glasgow for the 26th United Nations Climate Change Conference, commonly referred to as COP26, to pledge an accelerated response to global warming. But their pledges fell well short of limiting the rise in the global temperature to less than 1.5 degrees Centigrade above the level at the time of the Industrial Revolution. A rise in temperature of more than 1.5 degrees will lead the world to a potential catastrophe. India, by virtue of lying in a hot and humid zone with melting glaciers and rising Indian Ocean temperature, is particularly vulnerable to global warming. Years of rampant construction, mining, and deforestation have weakened India's defenses against extreme climate events. Catastrophe may be closer than the country's policymakers recognize.[3]

Indian policymakers furiously debate the date by when India should target reaching net-zero carbon emissions. That debate, important as it is, deflects attention from the immediate problem of protecting people from the multidimensional effects of global warming.

Over the last few decades, India has experienced more frequent extreme heat waves. High humidity and heavy air pollution have made India's heat waves especially lethal. Conveying the message of the dangers that lie ahead, India in 2022 recorded its hottest March and third hottest April since recordkeeping began 122 years ago. During these two months, relentlessly recurring heat spells coincided with deficient rainfall, leaving an as yet unknown death toll but causing an all-too-evident loss of wheat output in Punjab, Haryana, and Uttar Pradesh. That output loss triggered a spate of deaths by suicide among indebted farmers. As global temperatures rise, a severe heat wave within the next decade could make India the first major victim of the climate crisis, claiming thousands of lives and inflicting a devastating loss of income.[4]

Indian agriculture faces the triple onslaught of drier seasons, locust attacks, and extreme rainfall events. Besides reducing productivity, the drier and hotter seasons will increase malnutrition and illness, pushing more farmers and agricultural workers from arid and semiarid rural regions to seek urban refuge. But their most desirable destinations—coastal cities—will themselves struggle to survive as sea levels rise. By 2050, 80 percent of Nariman Point, Mumbai's premier business district, could be underwater. Productivity (and hence incomes) in urban industrial work will also fall as heat and humidity increase.[5]

Cyclones have traditionally featured on India's eastern coast. But by the mid-2010s, increased cyclonic activity in the Arabian sea made Mumbai a likely victim of a major cyclone. With its "filth-clogged drainage system" and unchecked construction over water bodies, a cyclone in Mumbai would cause untold devastation. That speculative scenario nearly materialized in early June 2020 when Cyclone Nisarga vented its fury just south of Mumbai.[6]

India's poor regard for environmental safeguards and the climate crisis interact explosively in the geologically fragile Himalayan mountains. Rocks left behind by melting glaciers form a debris that comes hurtling down the hillsides during episodes of heavy rainfall. Hydroelectric dams on Himalayan rivers and Prime Minister Modi's Char Dham highway-widening project in the Himalayas mow down forests and add to the debris in the mountain landslides, increasing their deadly force. As that debris rushes down the hills, it spreads havoc in the human settlements and, on reaching the plains, damages riverbanks and alters the course of rivers. Heavy rainfall-induced landslides have also become common in the Western Ghats along India's southwestern coast.

These life- and livelihood-threatening events—killer heat waves; arid agricultural seasons; episodes of extreme rainfall; rising sea levels; cyclones and melting glaciers—are all expected to increase in frequency and intensity.

Coming on top of the Indian economy's weak job creation ability, dying rivers and climate catastrophe portend social and political collapse.

In India's Catch-22, There Are No Easy Solutions

Lack of political accountability is not a bug in Indian politics, it is a feature. Skyrocketing election expenditures have increased the reliance on public corruption. Growing numbers of criminally charged individuals have infiltrated the national Parliament and state legislative assemblies. Meanwhile, Hindutva politics thrives on perpetual mob violence, and mobs, tiring of old forms of violence, keep raising the stakes, including recently calling for Muslim genocide. Government officials act in support of Hindu rioters by demolishing properties owned by Muslims, alleging the properties were illegal. Hindutva has, in effect, buried all norms and accountability. The government suppresses public dissent, intimidates journalists, and undermines the judicial system so that corruption, criminal-politicians, and Hindutva violence remain virtually unchecked.[7]

The Catch-22 arises because unaccountable politicians do not impose accountability on themselves. Why do nutrition, health, and education remain afterthoughts in the Indian policy discourse, instead of rising to the top of policy priorities? Not because we don't know what needs to be done, but because the construction of dams, riverfronts, and overpasses remains the focus of "development," as does the extension of mining franchises in rich forests. These activities provide more lucrative opportunities to politicians and businesses than does the extension of quality primary health and education. The Indian government's initiatives often have the sense conveyed in the movie *Groundhog Day*: things seem about to change, and yet they don't. Noxious gases, especially methane, generated by rotting garbage began catching fire on a landfill outside Delhi in the early 1990s, and despite innumerable "action plans" and countless rupees to clean the landfill, the garbage remains undiminished; the fires keep recurring. Where safeguards against scams and environmental damage exist, they are ignored. The rule of law works arbitrarily. The good within the system does not break through into shared prosperity.[8]

Indian policymakers and public intellectuals do not confront the Catch-22 within which welfare-enhancing policies suffer neglect and harmful policies persist. Reflecting this lack of awareness, an astonishing number of policymakers trot out easy policy solutions that they hope will propel the Indian economy forward. Many are obsessed with "labor market reforms" as the magic bullet. Such "reforms"—a euphemism for making it easier to fire workers—will not achieve the stated purpose of creating a stronger and job-rich economy. Instead, by weakening labor's bargaining power and bidding down wages, these measures would lock the economy into a low-wage/low-productivity equilibrium. In this equilibrium, social frustration and anger will only brew. Labor market reform can work only if accompanied by adequate social insurance and minimum wages that ensure decent living. As Nobel laureate Robert Solow has insisted, rather than a free-market ideology, norms of fairness and ethics must apply to the labor market. In place of beating down wages, India desperately needs a much cheaper currency, which the rich and powerful do not want.

Instead, for India, some form of universal basic income will help create a safety net, not just for the poorest but for hundreds of millions of precarious households under constant threat of tumbling down the economic ladder. As U.S. President Joseph Biden, quoting his father, rightly says, people need "a little breathing room." In India, universal basic income would importantly increase women's financial autonomy, helping them raise healthier and better-educated children. But achieving a reasonable universal basic income faces the political challenge of eliminating subsidies for the rich and influential and raising their tax rates.[9]

Many commentators, seeking to bypass the difficult long-term policy challenges, place their hope on modern technology to help India leapfrog to a brighter future. Hundreds of millions of Indians own smartphones. Many are adept at using apps that make life easier, although many are also adept at spreading fake news and hate. Smart devices and smart entrepreneurs can indeed help create new businesses. India has a slew of dazzling "unicorns," companies that have achieved a valuation of a billion dollars through offering internet-based services. Computer-based learning methods can accelerate the spread of education and help improve its quality. Indian companies have made progress in producing and installing solar cells, which when scaled up can make clean electric power widely available at low cost, stimulating new job opportunities. Global and Indian venture capitalists stand ready to fund the next generation of technologies and entrepreneurs.[10]

Technology, though, is not a substitute for fiscal resources and social action. The gains from computer-assisted teaching are modest without good human teachers. Indeed, one study finds that digitally delivered content can worsen learning outcomes "without its integration into an effective teaching practice." Smartphone apps to monitor the administration of a nutrition program, as recent experience has demonstrated, cannot replace the required funding and organization to provide nutritious food to children and their mothers. More nefariously, where norms are broken, technology itself can be misused or subverted for illegal purposes. Businesses, working in cahoots with officials, deploy technological stratagems to undermine sophisticated environmental laws and real-time monitoring techniques. The *nakal* (cheating) mafia turns away closed-circuit television cameras and silences audio recorders at examination centers. Cyber-criminals bypass two-factor authentication security measures to steal nearly $400 million for four million fake beneficiaries of PM-Kisan, a flagship government welfare program for farmers. Indian forestry officials use state-of-the-art remote-sensing software to classify urban tree-lined areas, grasslands, and desert scrub as forest. Down is up: they claim forest cover has been increasing when independent estimates show the opposite.[11]

Faced with such pathologies, Indians often call for switching off democracy and relying, instead, on an autocrat. India's two autocrats, the first a strongwoman and the second a strongman, exhibited the cruelty and violence that typically accompanies strength. Although admirers point to the economic and social progress the autocrats allegedly promoted, the Indian economy—especially the parts that serve the weak and vulnerable—suffered. The country's moral and social fabric threatened to tear apart.

It is true that India's democracy has betrayed its people. But hope for India lies only in making it a true democracy. To make Indian democracy work, we must ask ourselves a moral question: What kind of country *do* we want to be?

Needed: A New Civic Consciousness

We must move to an equilibrium in which everyone expects others to be honest, in which case most people will act honestly. That "honest equilibrium" will promote trust and cooperation to work together in the long-haul tasks of creating public goods and advancing sustainable development.

Political scientist Robert Putnam is our best guide on how to break out of the self-reinforcing "me-me-me" equilibrium. Building "civic communities" is the way forward, Putnam and his coauthors explain. In civic communities, citizens make commitments to each other through membership of sports clubs, cooperatives, mutual aid societies, and cultural associations. Such civic relationships foster norms of equality, tolerance, and shared progress. Those norms build commitment to informed and respectful participation in public life. Political leaders in civic communities tend to be well educated. They promote greater economic and political equality, and they seek compromise to resolve conflicts. Citizens in civic regions typically believe that their leaders are honest, that the rule of law prevails, and that others act in good faith. Such virtues culminate in the pursuit of public goods over purely private enrichment.[12]

Since it is an extraordinarily large transition from a me-me-me to a we-we-we society, Putnam and colleagues say the only right way is to start small. Small-scale institutions, they explain, allow people to practice working for mutual benefit, and repeated reciprocity builds the trust needed for the operation of complex institutions. Starting small also helps create a culture of reliable information and communication, thus breaking the corrosive tendency for incomplete, imperfect, and deliberately distorted information that keeps alive social anxiety, distrust, and conflict.[13]

In India, we see glimpses of civic communities in the tireless work of public-spirited individuals and nongovernmental organizations. But such activity never reaches the scale and momentum to achieve shared prosperity. Unlike in Bangladesh, where the government has used nongovernmental civil society organizations as development partners, the Indian government has treated such organizations as adversaries, curtailing their activities with increasing vigor over time.[14]

The task in India is to tie public-spirited nongovernmental work with the authority and institutional resources of governments. Decentralization of governance—the shift of authority and financial resources from the central and state governments to city and village governments—is the most plausible way of promoting vibrant civic regions. Since independence, political and policy leaders have admired decentralization. But modest advances in West Bengal and Karnataka were the exceptions until the early 1990s. In 1993, Prime Minister P. V. Narasimha Rao's Congress Party–led government shepherded through parliament two constitutional amendments to encourage decentralization. Even so, national and state capitals kept their hold on much of the power and funds.

A ray of hope shone through in 1996. Under an initiative of the Communist Party of India (Marxist) in the state of Kerala—India's leading state in education and health provision—far-reaching decentralization of authority and funds began. The results were as Putnam and his colleagues might have predicted. A survey in 2002 found that citizens' engagement in civic organizations increased after the onset of the decentralization initiative. Respondents to the survey—especially women—reported that they more proactively called on local government officials to improve the delivery of public goods. Mirroring this activism, respondents said that education, health, child care, and housing for the poor did, in fact, improve. Respondents even reported improved income-earning and employment opportunities. Political scientist James Manor finds that such a positive experience is common in decentralization experiments around the world.[15]

Commentators worry that rogue leaders of village and city councils will hijack funds for themselves and their causes, setting back economic development and continuing to widen inequalities. Such concern is greatly overstated. Throughout this book, we have seen that dysfunctional grabbing-hand politics is entrenched at the national and state levels. In contrast, local governments are much closer to the people and have the greatest likelihood of practicing accountability, as the experience in Kerala and other decentralization initiatives confirms.[16]

Kerala's decentralization experiment provides a "sense of what is possible," writes Thomas Isaac, until recently finance minister of Kerala and one of the key catalysts of the state's experiment with decentralized authority. He acknowledges that the experiment is "fragile." That fragility is most evident in the tug-of-war between successful local governments and the state government. In a recent instance of such struggle, despite furious opposition by local leaders, the Kerala state government in June 2020 waved ahead the Athirappilly hydroelectric project. The project would have accelerated deforestation and soil erosion in the Western Ghats and thus added to the havoc caused by the increasingly frequent heavy rainfall in Kerala. A vigorous grassroots movement, itself a product of the culture of local self-government, forced the state government to abandon the project. That victory notwithstanding, more obstacles lie ahead. Powerful public and private actors persist with environmentally destructive construction projects that sneer at the climate-change gods.[17]

Despite its challenges, local self-government is the most promising way to establish social norms that induce cooperative behavior and political accountability. This path is India's best and perhaps only hope for cleaning its rot in politics and giving it a fighting chance of establishing values that honor human development, environmental stewardship, and resilience against climate change. The task ahead is immensely difficult. Even in my most optimistic vision, local governments will remain unable to solve India's employment problem. However, this must not stop us from forging ahead. Local successes could stimulate a national awakening of civic consciousness. The alternative is social and political collapse, an outcome to be feared not just for India but for all humanity.

ACKNOWLEDGMENTS

This book owes an enormous debt to four people. My father, who is ninety-six years old as I write these words in July 2022, is blessed with a photographic memory and a historian's heart. Both in understanding the texture of the early post-independence decades and the details of specific events and personalities, he was an invaluable guide, correcting commonly held misconceptions to give this book a fighting chance of being an authoritative reference on those years. Alaknanda Patel helped me with both her memories and her deep empathy for the project on which I was embarked. She was a first-person witness to some of the crucial moments I describe in this book, especially in the years though the Indira Gandhi era. T. N. Ninan, perhaps the preeminent Indian business journalist of the last half-century, guided me through the hard judgments where I was trying to sort out the role of the individual and that of historical forces. And my friend and classmate from college Sukumar Muralidharan is a walking encyclopedia. His running commentary in the margins of my drafts was an education, which helped me better understand the context of what I was writing; he added detail that brought several parts of the storyline to life.

I had the benefit of friendly fire from several readers. These include Anand Anandalingam, Samantha Chai, Dan Chamby, Ajit Ghose, Anne

Krueger, Abhijit Nimgaonkar, Narendar Pani, and Robert Tombs. Paulette Altmaier, Kevin Cardiff, Scott Parris, and David Wheeler hold a special place of honor: they read multiple drafts of both this manuscript and my previous book *EuroTragedy.* Others who read parts of the manuscript and gave valuable comments include Sunit Arora, Michael Bordo, Murad Banaji, Ajai Chopra, Ravi Chopra, Venkatesh Dutta, Barry Eichengreen, Gautham, Krupa Ge, Sudipto Mundle, M. Rajshekhar, Peter Smith, Brody Viney, and Tirthankar Roy.

I could not have managed without the help of many specialists who advised me on particularly tricky questions where (as was so often the case) the data or sequence of events was cloudy. These included Rosa Abraham, Amit Basole, Ram Babu Bhagat, Mohsin Alam Bhat, Laxmi Chatterji, Diptakirti Chaudhuri, Sucheta Dalal, Biswajit Dhar, Chirag Dhara, Jean Drèze, Katherine Eban, Francisco Ferreira, Rajmohan Gandhi, Sandeep Hasurkar, Himanshu, Doug Johnson, Radhicka Kapoor, Gurinder Kaur, Anjana Kizhpadathil, Rakesh Kochhar, Ishan Kukreti, Snigdha Poonam, Vaibhav Purandare, K. S. Chalapati Rao, Martin Ravallion, Siddhartha Sahi, Rajeshwari Sengupta, Nirbhay Sharma, Sreenivasan Subramanian, Nandini Sundar, Faizal Syed, Dinesh Thakur, Milan Vaishnav, and especially R. Nagaraj, who surely is the master of Indian macroeconomic statistics.

My entire extended Indian family pitched in. I owe a special debt to my cousin Rajiv Agrawal, who, despite the adversities that life has thrown at him, maintains a cheer and sharpness of intellect that is truly inspiring. He brought to the manuscript his special perspective as a businessman. And Ravindra Chaudhary, my father's longtime driver and Man Friday, educated and entertained me with his running commentary on Indian corruption, politics, and struggles of migrant workers.

Uuriintuya Batsaikhan worked tirelessly in doing multiple iterations of the charts in this book, just as she did earlier with my *EuroTragedy*.

My family in the United States indulged me. Older brother Krishnan, his wife Andra, and younger brother Lakshman read and commented on parts of the manuscript with the precision their technical professions demand and the large hearts that their liberal arts education has endowed them with. My wife Jyothsna, who knows the English language better than I can hope to, heard me read sentences and passages aloud to her, commenting on their clarity and cadence, often many times in a day.

Princeton University librarians Bobray Bordelon and Ellen Ambrosone were an unending source of reference material and data. Simin Gul in the computing center rescued me from a near heart attack when my laptop began to die. And my assistant Lindsay Woodrick, as she always does, saved me from dealing with the administrative tasks associated with teaching.

I am grateful to my agent Peter Bernstein for not only helping manage the process but also providing very helpful suggestions on increasing the pace of the narrative. My editors, Marcela Maxfield (Stanford) and Parth Mehrotra and Nandini Mehta (Juggernaut), gave me both big-picture and detailed guidance on improving the readability of the manuscript. A big thank you also to Charlie Clark for expertly shepherding the book's production process. And, as with my previous book, my students were my hidden asset. Daniel Ju gave detailed comments on an early draft; Jack Aiello and Ishita Batra made outstanding editorial suggestions. Students in my course on modern Indian history taught me to think in new ways. Elizabeth Wahlstedt, Anna Goodman, and Caitlin Quinn gave me the most sustained editorial assistance. Anna and Caitlin had the double advantage of being neither Indian nor students of economics. As talented writers, they insisted on logical consistency and clarity in exposition. And not least, thanks to Hannah Ceja, who helped with critical last-minute proofreading.

All these fine human beings who held my hand through this process have my unending gratitude.

NOTES

Preface

1. Seymour Martin Lipset, 1960, *Political Man: The Social Bases of Politics*, Garden City, NY, Doubleday & Company, 46.

Chapter 1: Then and Now, an Introduction

1. Satyajit Ray, 1948, "Indian Films," *Statesman*, October 2.

2. Nisid Hajari, 2015, *Midnight's Furies: The Deadly Legacy of India's Partition*, Kindle edition, Houghton Mifflin Harcourt, location 147.

3. "Jawaharlal Nehru: 'Tryst with Destiny' Address to the Constituent Assembly of India in New Delhi," *American Rhetoric* website, available at www.americanrhetoric.com/speeches/jawaharlalnehrutrystwithdestiny.htm.

4. Francisco Ferreira and Carolina Sánchez-Páramo, 2017, "A Richer Array of International Poverty Lines," World Bank, Washington, DC, October 13; see also chapter 20.

5. Vidya Krishnan, 2020 "The Callousness of India's COVID-19 Response," *The Atlantic*, March 27; Niharika Sharma, 2020, "India Extends Its Nationwide Coronavirus Lockdown Till May 3," *Quartz India*, April 14.

6. Supriya Sharma and Vijayta Lalwani, 2020, "Hell on the Yamuna as Hundreds Starved for Days after Delhi Shelters Went Up in the Flames," *Scroll.in*, April 15.

7. Al Jazeera, 2020a, "Concerns after Mumbai's Dharavi Slum Reports COVID-19 Cases," April 3; Smruti Koppikar, 2020, "Dharavi's Economy Goes Down the Tubes," *Mint*, April 18.

8. *Caravan*, 2020, "Speaking Positivity to Power," March 31; Meera Emmanuel, 2020, "Coronavirus Lockdown: Fake News and Panic Driven Migration Caused Untold Misery to Migrant Labourers, Supreme Court [Read Order]," *Bar and Bench*, March 31.

9. *Business Standard,* 2020, "About 3,500 Jurists, Artists Slam FIR against Varadarajan, Call It Attack on Media Freedom," April 14; *The Wire*, 2020, "As CoV Cases Spike in Nizamuddin, Nehru Stadium Becomes Quarantine Centre," March 31; Sharat Pradhan, 2020, "Adityanath's Role in Shift of Ram Idol at Temple Site Upsets Some Ayodhya Sadhus," *The Wire*, March 20.

10. Sruthisagar Yamunan, 2020, "Tablighi Jamaat: How Did the Government Fail to Detect a Coronavirus Infection Hotspot?" *Scroll.in*, April 1; Joanna Slater and Niha Masih, 2020, "These Americans Came to India to Deepen Their Faith. They've Been Detained, Quarantined and Prosecuted," *Washington Post*, August 27; Samar Halarnkar, 2020, "Why the Slow Drip of Anti-Muslim Poison in India Is Now a Flood," *Scroll.in*, April 10; Aditya Menon, 2020, "Attacks on Muslims in the Name of COVID-19 Surge across India," *The Quint,* April 8; Abhishek Angad, 2020, "In Jharkhand, Pregnant Woman Says Told to Clean Up Blood, Loses Child," *Indian Express*, April 19; Al Jazeera, 2020b, "India Hospital Segregates Muslim and Hindu Coronavirus Patients," April 16.

11. Nitya Chablani, 2020, "29 Stunning Pictures and Videos That Take You Inside Antilia, Mukesh Ambani & Nita Ambani's Residence," *Vogue.in*, April 22.

12. See chapters 20 and 23.

13. Lewis Carroll, 1871, *Through the Looking Glass,* available at https://www.gutenberg.org/files/12/12-h/12-h.htm.

14. Ajit Kumar Ghose, 2019, *Employment,* New Delhi, Oxford University Press, 127–129, 158, Table 3.1, 43.

15. K. P. Kannan and G. Raveendran, 2012, "Counting and Profiling the Missing Labour Force," *Economic and Political Weekly* 47 (6): 77–80, 79–80; Ashwini Deshpande and Jitendra Singh, 2021, "Dropping Out, Being Pushed Out or Can't Get In? Decoding Declining Labour Force Participation of Indian Women," *Ashoka University Economics Discussion Paper* 6, July; Ajit Kumar Ghose, 2016, *India Employment Report 2016: Challenges and the Imperatives of Manufacturing-Led Growth*, New Delhi, Oxford University Press, Table 2.14, 42; Ghose 2019, 130; Tanika Chakraborty and Nafisa Lohawala, 2022, "Women, Violence, and Work: Threat of Sexual Violence and Women's Decision to Work," *GLO Discussion Paper Series* 1023, Global Labor Organization (GLO), Essen.

16. Ghose 2019, 127–129, 158.

17. John Kenneth Galbraith, 1958, "Rival Economic Theories in India," *Foreign Affairs* 36 (4): 587–596, 590, 595.

18. Robin Jeffrey, 1987, "Governments and Culture: How Women Made Kerala Literate," *Pacific Affairs* 60 (3): 447–472, 462.

19. Wataru Kureishi and Midori Wakabayashi, 2011, "Son Preference in Japan," *Journal of Population Economics* 24: 873–893; Eleanor Jawon Choi and Jisoo Hwang, 2020, "Transition of Son Preference: Evidence from South Korea," *Demography* 27: 627–652; T. C. Lin, 2009, "The Decline of Son Preference and Rise of Gender Indifference in Taiwan Since 1990," *Demographic Research* 20: 377–402.

20. Jean Drèze and Amartya Sen, 2013, *An Uncertain Glory*, Princeton, NJ, Princeton University Press, x, 8.

21. H. B. Boyne, 1966, "Labour's Mr. Fix-It Under Fire," *Daily Telegraph*, September 30.

22. Bill of Rights Institute, *Federalist Papers* No. 10 (1787), available at https://billofrightsinstitute.org/primary-sources/federalist-no-10.

23. Robert Dahl, 1961, *Who Governs? Democracy and Power in an American City*, New Haven, CT, Yale University Press, 5–6.

24. Steven Levitsky and Daniel Ziblatt, 2019, *How Democracies Die*, New York, Crown, 110–117, 148.

25. Thomas Schelling, 1984, *Choice and Consequence*. Cambridge, MA, Harvard University Press, 55; Partha Dasgupta, 2009, "Trust, Law, and Social Norms: Fundamentals of Economic Progress," https://voxeu.org/vox-talks/trust-law-and-social-norms-fundamentals-economic-progress; Francis Fukuyama, 2001, "Social Capital, Civil Society, and Development," *Third World Quarterly* 22 (1): 7–20, 8.

26. Dahl 1961, 7.

27. Association for Democratic Reforms, 2021, "Analysis of Criminal, Financial, and Other Background Details of Union Council of Ministers Post Cabinet Expansion on 7th, July, 2021," New Delhi, July 9.

28. Association for Democratic Reforms, 2021, "Analysis of Criminal, Financial, and Other Background Details of Union Council of Ministers Post Cabinet Expansion on 7th, July, 2021," New Delhi, July 9.

29. Anandi Mani and Sharun Mukand. 2007. "Democracy, Visibility, and Public Good Provision," *Journal of Development Economics* 83 (2): 506–529; Jean Drèze and Amartya Sen, 1999 (1989), *Hunger and Public Action*, in Jean Drèze and Amartya Sen, *Omnibus*, New Delhi, Oxford University Press, 261; Akhil Gupta, 2012, *Red Tape: Bureaucracy, Structural Violence, and Poverty in India*, Durham, NC, Duke University Press, 5, 296.

30. Drèze and Sen 1999 (1989), 267.

31. Agence France-Presse, 2011, "Indian State in Great Laptop Giveaway," September 15; M. C. Rajan, 2013, "Jayalalitha's Free Laptops Find Their Way to the Grey Market," *India Today*, April 10; *Indian Express*, 2018, "Students Sell Free Government Laptops to Pay College Fees in Tamil Nadu's Tiruchy," May 16.

32. Mani and Mukand 2007, 516.

33. Jane Jacobs, 1992 (1961), *The Death and Life of Great American Cities*, New York, Vintage Books, 113.

34. Jacobs 1992 (1961), 432, 441.

35. Richard Neustadt and May Ernest, 1986, *Thinking in Time: The Uses of History for Decision-Makers*. New York: Free Press.

Chapter 2: An Uncertain Beginning

1. Rajmohan Gandhi, 1999 (1991), *Patel: A Life*, Ahmedabad, Navajivan Publishing House, 3–6, 13.

2. Gandhi 1999 (1991), chapter 1, especially pages 6, 16, 30 36, and chapter 3, 149–170.

3. Michael Brecher, 1959, *Nehru: A Political Biography*, London, Oxford University Press, 392.

4. Rajmohan Gandhi, 2007, *Gandhi: The Man, His People, and The Empire*, Berkeley, University of California Press, 512; *Time*, 1947, "The Boss," January 27, 27.

5. Gandhi 2007, 521; Gandhi 1999 (1991), 370–371.

6. Gandhi 2007, 521.

7. Gandhi 2007, 521; Durga Das, 1972, *Sardar Patel's Correspondence: 1945–1950, Volume III*, Ahmedabad, Navajivan Publishing House, xxviii.

8. Gandhi 1999 (1991), 426.

9. Gandhi 1999 (1991), 427–428, 431, 458.

10. Gandhi 1999 (1991), 440–443.

11. Gandhi 1999 (1991), 446–448.

12. Gandhi 1999 (1991), 448, 458.

13. Brecher 1959, 399–400; Gandhi 1999 (1991), 470.

14. Brecher 1959, 402–404.

15. Gandhi 1999 (1991), 450–452.

16. Gandhi 1999 (1991), 458, 483.

17. Durga Das, 1973, *Sardar Patel's Correspondence: 1945–1950, Volume VI*, Ahmedabad, Navajivan Publishing House, 445.

18. Brecher 1959, 427–428; Hiren Mukerjee, 1992 (1964), *The Gentle Colossus: A Study of Jawaharlal Nehru,* Oxford: Oxford University Press, esp. 121–122.

19. Stanley Kochanek, 1968, *The Congress Party: The Dynamics of a One-Party Democracy,* Princeton, NJ, Princeton University Press, 141; and Sarvepalli Gopal, 1976, *Jawaharlal Nehru: A Biography, Volume One 1889–1947,* Bombay, Oxford University Press, 209.

20. Brecher 1959, 426, 430; Kochanek 1968, 29.

21. Brecher 1959, 430; Kochanek 1968, 15.

22. Brecher 1959, 430; Kochanek 1968, 47, 300–301.

23. Gandhi 1999 (1991), 531–533.

24. Durga Das, 1972, *Sardar Patel's Correspondence: 1945–1950, Volume II,* Ahmedabad, Navajivan Publishing House, chapter 4; Das 1972, *Volume III,* xxxv–xxxviii; *Time,* 1951, "Revolt against Nehru," June 25, 33; Ramachandra Guha, 2008 (2007), *India after Gandhi: The History of the World's Largest Democracy,* New York, Harper Perennial Edition, 137.

25. Sarvepalli Gopal, 1979, *Jawaharlal Nehru: A Biography, Volume Two 1947–1956,* Bombay, Oxford University Press, 162, 309.

26. *Times of India,* 1952, "Elections Were Fair: Mr. J. Narayan's View," February 25; Gopal 1979, 162.

27. Gopal 1979, 162.

Chapter 3: The Path Not Taken

1. *Selected Works of Jawaharlal Nehru,* edited by Sarvepalli Gopal, Series 2, 15.1: 17–18; *Selected Works,* Series 2, 16.2: 80; hereafter Nehru, *Selected Works.*

2. Maharajkrishna Rasgotra, 2019, *A Life in Diplomacy,* Gurugram, India, Penguin Books, 73.

3. International Monetary Fund, 1949a, "Report of the Mission to India," Executive Board Special No. 69, June 7, Washington, DC, 1–3.

4. International Monetary Fund, 1949b, "Memorandum from B. K. Madan to the Executive Board," Executive Board Special 85, September 17, Washington, DC; *Financial Times,* 1949, "India & U. K. Decision on Devaluation," October 6; International Monetary Fund, 1950, "Review of the Indian Economy in 1949–50," Staff Memorandum No. 505, August 4, Washington, DC, 4, 42.

5. *Financial Times* 1949.

6. International Monetary Fund 1949a, 17 (Table 10), 19.

7. Nehru, *Selected Works,* Series 2, 12: 317–318, 323.

8. Government of India (Planning Commission), 1953, "First Five Year Plan," January, New Delhi, 13; Bruce F. Johnston, 1951, "Agricultural Productivity and Economic Development in Japan," *Journal of Political Economy* 59 (6): 498–513, Table 1, 499–500.

9. William Lockwood, 1968 (1954). *Economic Development of Japan: Growth and Structural Change.* Princeton, NJ: Princeton University Press, 44, 461–465, 484.

10. World Bank (Bernard Bell Mission), 1965, "India's Economic Development Effort: Volume II, Agricultural Policy," October 1, Washington, DC, 13, 38; Government of India 1953, 13; Government of India (Planning Commission), 1956, "Second Five Year Plan," New Delhi, 12–13.

11. Government of India 1953, 88, 102–105.

12. Gunnar Myrdal, 1968, *Asian Drama: An Inquiry into the Poverty of Nations,* New York, Pantheon, 747. International studies later seemed to confirm that greater equity ensured higher productivity. See Klaus Deininger and Lyn Squire, 1998, "New Ways of Looking at Old Issues: Inequality and Growth," *Journal of Development Economics* 57 (2): 259–287; Klaus Deininger, Songqing Jin, and Hari K. Nagarajan, 2008, "Efficiency and Equity Impacts of Rural Land Rental Restrictions: Evidence from India," *European Economic Review* 52 (5): 892–918.

13. Granville Austin, 2003 (1999), *Working a Democratic Constitution: A History of the Indian Experience,* New York, Oxford University Press, 76, 82, 119.

14. Myrdal 1968, 1305–1331; Austin 2003 (1999), 119, 121; Francine R. Frankel, 1978, *India's Political Economy, 1947–1977: The Gradual Revolution,* Princeton, NJ, Princeton University Press, 191–193; see also M. L. Dantwala, 1957, "Prospects and Problems of Land Reforms in India," *Economic Development and Cultural Change* 6 (1): 3–15, 6–9.

15. Frankel 1978, 191–193; see also Dantwala 1957, 6–9; Austin 2003 (1999), 120; Myrdal 1968, 1316–1320, 1323–1325, 1327–1330.

16. Austin 2003 (1999), 118, 120, 122; Sunil Khilnani, 1999 (1997), *The Idea of India,* New York, Farrar, Straus and Giroux, 36; see also Myrdal 1968, 1330–1334.

17. Ronald Philip Dore, 1959, *Land Reform in Japan,* London, Oxford University Press, foreword, x.

18. Frankel 1978, 188–189; Dantwala 1957, 13; World Bank 1965, 12; John Lewis, 1964 (1962), *Quiet Crisis in India: Economic Development and American Policy,* Washington, DC, Brookings Institution, 133–134, 156–157.

19. Theodore Schultz, 1964, *Transforming Traditional Agriculture,* New Haven, CT, Yale University Press, 21, 190, 196.

20. Government of India, 1954, *Final Report of the National Income Committee*, New Delhi, chapter 2, 23 (Table 5), 106 (Table 28); Hollis Chenery, 1960, "Patterns of Industrial Growth," *American Economic Review* 50 (4): 648.

21. S. D. Mehta, 1954, *The Cotton Mills of India, 1854–1954*, Bombay, The Cotton Textile Association (India), 1, 13–45, 102–103; Phiroze B. Medhora, 1965, "Entrepreneurship in India," *Political Science Quarterly* 80 (4): 568–571; Ashok V. Desai, 1968, "The Origins of Parsi Enterprise," *Indian Economic and Social History Review* 5 (4): 307–317, 312–313, 316; Gregory Clark, 1987, "Why Isn't the Whole World Developed? Lessons from the Cotton Mills," *Journal of Economic History* 47 (1): 159.

22. Mehta 1954, 42, 43–48, 120.

23. Mehta 1954, 77–78, 90–92, 94–95; Clark 1987, 159; Arno Pearse, 1930, *The Cotton Industry of India: Being the Report of the Journey to India*, Manchester, U.K., Taylor Garnet Evans & Co. Ltd., 3; Lockwood 1968 (1954), 29.

24. Clark 1987, 170; see also Rajnarayan Chandavarkar, 1998, *Imperial Power and Popular Politics: Class, Resistance, and the State in India, c. 1850–1950*, Cambridge, Cambridge University Press, 59–60.

25. Lockwood 1968 (1954), 27–30; Rajnarayan Chandavarkar, 1994, *The Origins of Industrial Capitalism in India*, Cambridge, Cambridge University Press, Table 22, 255; Chandavarkar 1998, 61–62; Tirthankar Roy, 2008, "Labour Institutions, Japanese Competition, and the Crisis of Cotton Mills in Interwar Mumbai," *Economic and Political Weekly* 43 (1): 37; Dipak Mazumdar, 1984, "The Issue of Small Versus Large in the Indian Textile Industry: An Analytical and Historical Survey," *World Bank Staff Working Papers* 645, Washington, DC, 10; Chandavarkar 1994, 155–158; Chandavarkar 1998, 337–339; Mehta 1954, 119.

26. Michael Kremer, 1993, "The O-Ring Theory of Economic Development," *Quarterly Journal of Economics* 108 (3): 557.

27. Kenichi Ohno, 2013, *Learning to Industrialize: From Given Growth to Policy-Aided Value Creation*, London, Routledge, 127, 153–156, 162–165; Arno Pearse, 1929, *The Cotton Industry of Japan and China: Being the Report of the Journey to Japan and China*, Manchester, U.K., Taylor Garnet Evans & Co. Ltd., 84; Pearse 1930, 11.

28. Clark 1987, Table 1, 146; Susan Wolcott and Gregory Clark, 1999, "Why Nations Fail: Managerial Decisions and Performance in Indian Cotton Textiles, 1890–1938," *Journal of Economic History* 59 (2): Table 1, 398.

29. John Brush, 1952, "The Iron and Steel Industry in India," *Geographical Review* 42 (1): 47–48; Tirthankar Roy, 2018, *A Business History of India: Enterprise and the Emergence of Capitalism from 1600*, Cambridge, Cambridge University Press, 128–129; Medhora 1965, 559, 571.

30. Bert F. Hoselitz, 1959, "Small Industry in Underdeveloped Countries," *Journal of Economic History* 19 (4), 614; Government of India (Planning Commission), 1951, "First Five Year Plan: A Draft Outline," July, New Delhi, 162–163; 9 James Berna, 1959, "Patterns of Entrepreneurship in South India," *Economic Development and Cultural Change* 7 (April): 361.

31. Sunil Kant Munjal, 2020, *The Making of Hero: Four Brothers, Two Wheels, and a Revolution That Shaped India,* Kindle edition, HarperCollins Publishers, locations 460, 471.

32. Government of India 1951, 163; Berna 1959, 361; Fox 1960.

33. Alfred Marshall, 1930 (1890), *Principles of Economics,* Eighth edition, London, Macmillan and Co., 271.

34. Hoselitz 1959, 606–607.

35. Warren S. Hunsberger, 1957, "Japanese Exports and the American Market," *Far Eastern Survey* 26 (9): 134.

36. Hunsberger 1957, 138–139.

37. Hunsberger 1957, 138–139.

38. Surendra J. Patel, 1959, "Export Prospects and Economic Growth: India," *Economic Journal* 69 (Issue 275): 490–506; Jagdish Bhagwati, 1988, "Export-Promoting Trade Strategy: Issues and Evidence," *World Bank Research Observer* 3 (1): 27.

39. Patel 1959, 493–499; Government of India 1953, 200–201.

40. "Beawar," Britannica, available at www.britannica.com/place/Beawar; Nehru, *Selected Works,* Series 2, 26: 80.

41. "Indian Statistical System," Ministry of Statistics and Programme Implementation, available at https://mospi.gov.in/documents/213904/0/Ch+14+30.8.2001.pdf/d944ae06-bc59-ff09-9502-39d897b2edob?t=1599817175203.

42. Ghose 2019, Table 3.1, 43; Table 3.6, 79.

43. Prasanta Chandra Mahalanobis, 1958, "Science and National Planning," *Sankhya* 20 (1/2): 78.

44. Ella Datta, 1977, "Remembering Ritwik," *Times of India,* December 4.

45. Bakshi 1998, 107.

46. Bakshi 1998, 107–108.

47. Nehru, *Selected Works,* Series 2, 27: 57, 262, 539, 561.

48. Nehru, *Selected Works,* Series 2, 27: 258, 290, 309, 359.

49. Sarvepalli Gopal, 1979, *Jawaharlal Nehru: A Biography, Volume Two 1947–1956,* Bombay, Oxford University Press, 309–310; *Economic Weekly,* 1964, "Editorial: Nehru Era," July 18, 1166.

Chapter 4: Nehru's Dangerous Gamble

1. *Times of India,* 1954, "Sutlej River Waters Flow into the Bhakra Canals," July 9.

2. Nehru, *Selected Works,* Series 2, 26: 130.

3. Nehru, *Selected Works,* Series 2, 26: 131–132, 139–140, 143.

4. Nehru, *Selected Works,* Series 2, 26: 23.

5. Baldev Singh, editor, 1988, *Jawaharlal Nehru on Science and Technology: A Collection of His Writings and Speeches,* New Delhi, Nehru Memorial Museum and Library, 86.

6. Harsh Sethi, 1993, "Survival and Democracy: Ecological Struggles in India," in Poona Wignaraja, editor, *New Social Movements in the South: Empowering the People,* New Delhi, Vistaar Publications, 124; Mahesh Rangarajan, 2015, "Nature and Nation: Essays on Environmental History," Ranikhet: Permanent Black, 205–206; Smitu Kothari, 1996, "Whose Nation? The Displaced as Victims of Development," *Economic and Political Weekly* 31 (24): 1476–1485, 1479, 1481; Guha 2008 (2007), 230–231.

7. Center for Science and Environment, 1985, *State of India's Environment: The Second Citizens' Report,* 99–120; Arun Kumar Nayak, 2010, "Big Dams and Protests in India: A Study of Hirakud Dam," *Economic and Political Weekly* 45 (2): 69–73; Rangarajan 2015, 207.

8. *Times of India,* 1947, "Importance of Atomic Energy Research in India. Pandit Nehru Lays Foundation Stone of National Laboratory," January 6; *Times of India,* 1947, "Foundation Stone Laid of Chemical Laboratory," April 7.

9. Frank Moraes, 1956, *Jawaharlal Nehru: A Biography,* New York, Macmillan, 36; Gopal 1979, 306; Sarvepalli Gopal, 1985, "Nehru and Science: Aspirations and Achievements," *Interdisciplinary Science Reviews* 10 (2): 109.

10. Singh 1988, 44, 229.

11. *Times of India,* 1951a, "Classified Ad—No Title," May 29; *Times of India,* 1951b, "New Technology Institute Opened at Kharagpur," August 19.

12. Srirupa Roy, 2007, *Beyond Belief: India and the Politics of Postcolonial Nationalism,* Durham, NC, Duke University Press, 119.

13. Seema Chishti, 2022, "Prayagraj: Once Called the Oxford of the East, Now What Is the Condition of Education and Employment: Special Report," BBC New Hindi, March 1.

14. Herbert Passin, 1982 (1965), *Society and Education in Japan,* Tokyo, Kodansha International Ltd., 5.

15. Bert F. Hoselitz, 1960, "Urbanization in India," *Kyklos* 13 (3): 363, 367; Nirmal Kumar Bose, 1965, "Calcutta: A Premature Metropolis," *Scientific American* 213 (3): 90–105, 99–100; Jacobs 1992 (1961), chapter 6.

16. Ravi Kalia, 1999 (1987), *Chandigarh: The Making of an Indian City,* New Delhi, Oxford University Press, 12–13.

17. Kalia 1999 (1987), 87–88.

18. Kalia 1999 (1987), 108; 116–117.

19. *Time,* 1970, "The Jinxed Jewel," February 9; Kalia 1999 (1987), 125.

20. World Bank, 1960, "India's Third Five Year Plan: Report of Bank Mission to India, the Main Report," Report No. AS-80a, August 10, 47–48.

21. Bose 1965.

22. Bose 1965, 91–92, 102; Sumanta Banerjee, 2008 (1980), *In the Wake of Naxalbari,* Kolkata, Shishu Sahitya Samsad, 35–37.

23. S. Hussain Zaidi, 2012, *Dongri to Dubai,* Kindle edition, Lotus, locations 16, 21.

24. Ben King, 1971, *Report on Bombay,* Urban and Regional Report No. 73-6, Main Report, 37–38.

25. Milton Friedman, 2012 (1955), *Friedman on India,* New Delhi, Centre for Civil Society, 8–9.

26. *Economic Weekly* 1964, 1166.

27. Drèze and Sen 2013, Table 1.1, 4.

28. Nehru, *Selected Works,* Series 2, 27: 267; *Selected Works* Volume 27, 258, 308; Nehru, *Selected Works,* Series 2, 26: 234.

29. Nehru, *Selected Works,* Series 2, 27: 267, 375.

30. Jim Tomlinson, 1997, *Democratic Socialism and Economic Policy: The Attlee Years, 1945–1951,* Cambridge, Cambridge University Press, 96, 237.

31. Nehru, *Selected Works,* Series 2, 27: 503; K. Sujatha Rao, 2017, *Do We Care? India's Health System,* New Delhi, Oxford University Press, xviii.

32. Nehru, *Selected Works,* Series 2, 27: 437, 507.

33. Paul Rosenstein-Rodan, 1943, "Problems of Industrialisation of Eastern and South-Eastern Europe," *Economic Journal* 53 (210/211): 202–211; Paul Rosenstein-Rodan, 1961, "The Economic and Social Objectives of India's Five-Year Plans," December, Cambridge, Massachusetts Institute of Technology, 2–3.

34. Brecher 1959, 518; Myrdal 1968, 816; N. A. Sarma, 1957, "Economic Development in India: First and Second Five-Year Plans," International Monetary Fund, DM/57/34, July 30, Washington, DC.

35. Nehru, *Selected Works,* Series 2, 27: 529.

36. Mazumdar 1984, 10–11, 16–17, 70–71; Nehru, *Selected Works,* Series 2, 27: 275; *The Times,* 1955, "India Facing Economy Wave," September 3.

37. Milton Friedman, 2012 (1955), 23.

38. Nehru, *Selected Works,* Series 2, 27: 379.

39. Nehru, *Selected Works,* Series 2, 27: 380–381.

40. World Bank, 1954, "Current Economic Conditions and Prospects of Brazil," W.H. 23-b, July 8, Washington, DC, ii–iv.

41. *The Times* 1955; Gopalan Balachandran, 1998, *The Reserve Bank of India, 1951–1967,* Delhi, Oxford University Press, 14.

42. B. R. Shenoy, 1955, "A Note of Dissent on the Memorandum of the Panel of Economists," https://indiapolicy.org/debate/Notes/shenoy.PDF; Balachandran 1998, 627; David Engerman, 2018, *The Price of Aid: The Economic Cold War in India,* Cambridge, MA, Harvard University Press, 106; World Bank, 1956, "Current Economic Position and Prospects of India: Report of Bank Mission to India," Report No. AS-54a, August, Washington, DC, 6, 34, 47, 60.

43. International Monetary Fund, 1958, "1957 Consultations—India," SM/58/9, February 3, Washington, DC, 20; International Monetary Fund, 1959, "1958 Consultations—India," SM/59/9, February 9, Washington, DC, Part II, 38; I. G. Patel, 2001, "I.G. Patel," chapter 3 in V. N. Balasubramanyam, *Conversations with Indian Economists,* New Delhi, Macmillan, 45.

44. Balachandran 1998, 630–631.

45. International Monetary Fund 1958, Part II, 7.

46. Myrdal 1968, 800–801; *Times of India,* 1955, "All Too Flexible," January 19.

47. Jagdish Bhagwati and Padma Desai, 1970, *India: Planning for Industrialization: Industrialization and Trade Policies since 1951,* New York, Oxford University Press, 281–282; International Monetary Fund 1958, Part II, 39; International Monetary Fund 1959, Part II, 12.

48. Patel 2001, 45.

49. Myrdal 1968, 922–928; S. Dutt, H. K. Paranjape, and S. Mohan Kumaramangalam, 1969, *Report of the Industrial Licensing Policy Inquiry Committee,* New Delhi, Ministry of Industrial Development, 33, 38, 103–104; Government of India (Planning Commission) 1956, 406.

50. Prabhat Patnaik, 1979, "Industrial Development in India since Independence," *Social Scientist* 7 (11): 5.

51. Dutt, Paranjpe, and Kumaramangalam 1969, 63, 95, 137–138, 179–180.

52. Myrdal 1968, 933.

53. *Times of India,* 1957a, "Prune Second Plan to Match Savings," June 18; *Times of India,* 1957b, "Devaluation of Rupee: Economist's Suggestion," July 16; *Times of India,* 1957c, "Devaluation of Rupee and Pruning of Plan," December 25, 1957; *Times of India,* 1958, "Devaluation Is Essential Now," March 25; B. R. Shenoy 1958a,

"The Indian Economic Scene—Some Aspects," *Indian Economic Journal* 5 (4): 327–352, 349–350. Shenoy, 1958b, "Foreign Exchange Crisis: Devaluation Is Essential Now," *Times of India,* May 5, 1958.

Chapter 5: Nehru Doubles His Bet

1. John F. Kennedy, 1957a, "A Democrat Looks at Foreign Policy," *Foreign Affairs* 36 (1): 45, 59.

2. John Morton Blum, 1991, *Years of Discord,* New York, Norton, 4, 6–7.

3. John F. Kennedy, 1957b, "Kennedy Wants U.S. to Sacrifice," *New York Times,* December 8.

4. Kimber Charles Pearce, 2001, *Rostow, Kennedy, and the Rhetoric of Foreign Aid,* East Lansing, Michigan State University Press, 129.

5. Engerman 2018, 179; Max Millikan and Walt Whitman Rostow, 1958, "Foreign Aid: Next Phase," *Foreign Affairs* 36 (3): 429–431.

6. Engerman 2018, 184; Henry Brandon, 1958, "Senate Passes Aid Bill," *Sunday Times,* June 8; *Financial Times,* 1958, "Bigger Fund and Bank Resources," August 27.

7. Braj Kumar (B. K.) Nehru, 1997, *Nice Guys Finish Second,* New Delhi, Viking, 315, 317; Engerman 2018, 180.

8. *Times of India,* 1959, "Finding Jobs for 23,000,000: Gigantic Problem during 3rd Plan," February 25; International Monetary Fund, 1960, "1959 Consultations—India," SM/60/15, May 4, Washington, DC, 5; Balachandran 1998, 625–626.

9. Nehru 1997, 294, 335.

10. Nehru 1997, 288.

11. Nehru 1997, 294.

12. World Bank, 1956, "Current Economic Position and Prospects of India: Report of Bank Mission to India," Report No. AS-54a, August, Washington, DC, 6.

13. Binyamin Applebaum, 2019. *The Economists' Hour: False Prophets, Free Markets, and the Fracture of Society,* New York, Little, Brown and Company, 218, 414.

14. R. K. Karanjia, 1960, *The Mind of Mr. Nehru,* London, Allen and Unwin, 41, 49–50 (italics in the original); see also chapter 4.

15. Karanjia 1960, 45; Nehru, *Selected Works,* Series 2, 27: 267.

16. World Bank, 1960, "India's Third Five-Year Plan: Report of Bank Mission to India, the Main Report," Report No. AS-80a, August 10, 47–48, iii.

17. David Milne, 2008, *America's Rasputin: Walt Rostow and the Vietnam War,* New York, Hill and Wang, 59.

18. Blum 1991, 4, 392; *New York Times,* 1961, "Transcript of the President's First Report to Congress on the State of the Union," January 31.

19. John Kenneth Galbraith, 1969, *Ambassador's Journal: A Personal Account of the Kennedy Years,* Boston, Houghton Mifflin Company, 76.

20. *New York Times,* 1961a, "Bonn to Increase India Aid Offer," May 30; *New York Times,* 1961b, "$2,225,000,000 Aid Pledged for India," June 3.

21. U.S. Department of State, 1961, "Prime Minister Nehru's Visit, November 6–9: Briefing Book," Washington, DC.

22. Balachandran 1998, 651–652.

23. Nehru 1997, 324.

24. Balachandran 1998, 651–652.

25. Balachandran 1998, 655.

26. Balachandran 1998, 651, 655.

Chapter 6: Tagore's Unheard Song

1. www.sacred-texts.com/hin/tagore/gitnjali.htm. "Rabindranath Tagore—Biographical," NobelPrize.org. Nobel Prize Outreach, available at: www.nobelprize.org/prizes/literature/1913/tagore/biographical/; "Rabindranath Tagore: Gitanjali," Sacred-texts.com, www.sacred-texts.com/hin/tagore/gitnjali.htm.

2. Kathleen O'Connell, 2002, "Rabindranath Tagore: Envisioning Humanistic Education at Santiniketan (1902–1922)," *International Journal on Humanistic Ideology* 2:15–42.

3. Krishna Dutta and Andrew Robinson, editors, 1997, *Rabindranath Tagore: An Anthology,* New York, St. Martin's Press, 95, 121.

4. Dutta and Robinson 1997, 95, 121–123.

5. Dutta and Robinson 1997, 122.

6. Dutta and Robinson 1997, 123–124.

7. Rabindranath Tagore, 1960, *Letters from Russia,* Calcutta, Vishva-Bharati, 61–62; for the passage on caste divisions, I have used the more elegant translation from Amartya Sen, 1997, "Tagore and His India," *New York Review of Books,* June 26.

8. Claudia Goldin and Lawrence Katz, 2008, *The Race between Education and Technology,* Cambridge, MA, Belknap Press of the Harvard University Press, 135–136, 404.

9. Goldin and Katz 2008, 136, 138, 141, 146–147.

10. Nathaniel Wolloch, 2020, "Robert Coram and the European Sources of Radical Enlightenment in America," *Journal for Eighteenth-Century Studies* 43 (3): 376; Frederick Rudolph, 1965, *Essays on Education in the Early Republic,* Cambridge, MA, Belknap Press of Harvard University Press, xii–xiv, 65–66.

11. Goldin and Katz 2008, 130–134.

12. Passin 1982 (1965), 3, 217.

13. Passin 1982 (1965), 67–68.

14. Passin 1982 (1965), 68.

15. Kumiko Fujimura-Faneslow and Anne Imamura, 1991, "The Education of Women in Japan," in Edward Beauchamp, editor, *Windows on Japanese Education*, Westport, CT, Greenwood Press, 230–232.

16. Lockwood 1968 (1954), 512.

17. Satoshi Mizutani, 2015, "Anti-Colonialism and the Contested Politics of Comparison: Rabindranath Tagore, Rash Behari Bose, and Japanese Colonialism in Korea in the Inter-War Period," *Journal of Colonialism and Colonial History* 16 (1); Lockwood 1968 (1954), 510.

18. Kingsley Davis, 1951, *The Population of India and Pakistan*, Princeton, NJ, Princeton University Press, 150–153.

19. Jawaharlal Nehru, 1994 (1946), *Discovery of India*, sixth impression, New Delhi, Oxford University Press, 221.

20. Nehru 1994 (1946), 340, 372.

21. Milton Friedman and Rose Friedman, 1998, *Two Lucky People: Memoirs*, Chicago, University of Chicago Press, 257; Friedman 2012 (1955), 21; Adam Smith, 1937 (1776), *An Enquiry into the Nature and Causes of the Wealth of Nation*, New York, Random House, 737.

22. Nehru, *Selected Works*, Series 2, 27: 64, 503.

23. "5th Five Year Plan," India, Planning Commission, available at: https://niti.gov.in/planningcommission.gov.in/docs/plans/planrel/fiveyr/index5.html.

24. Government of India (Planning Commission), 1956, "Second Five Year Plan," New Delhi, 503.

25. Jandhyala B. G. Tilak, 2007, "The Kothari Commission and Financing of Education," *Economic and Political Weekly* 42 (10): 874–882, Figure 1 and 2, 876; Government of India (Planning Commission), 1956, 503–504; Amlan Dutta, 1961, "India," in Adamantios Pepelasis, Leon Mears, and Irma Adelman, editors, *Economic Development: Analysis and Case Studies*, New York, Harper, 411–412.

26. Myron Weiner, 1991, *The Child and the State in India: Child Labor and Education Policy in Comparative Perspective*, Princeton, NJ, Princeton University Press, 5, 175–176.

27. J. P. Naik, 1975, "Policy and Performance In Indian Education, 1947–74," Dr. K. G. Saiyidain Memorial Trust, New Delhi; Jean Drèze and Amartya Sen,

1999 (1995), *India: Economic Development and Social Opportunity,* in Jean Drèze and Amartya Sen, *Omnibus,* New Delhi, Oxford University Press, 90–91.

28. For the trend in education spending as a share of GDP, see Tilak 2007, Figure 1.

29. Kevin Murphy, Andrei Shleifer, and Robert Vishny, 1993, "Why Is Rent-Seeking So Costly to Growth?" *American Economic Review* 83 (2): 409–414.

30. Susanne Rudolph and Lloyd Rudolph, 1972, *Education and Politics in India: Studies in Organization, Society, and Politics,* Cambridge, MA, Harvard University Press, especially the essays by Harold Gould and Iqbal Narain.

31. Mark Blaug, Richard Layard, and Maureen Woodhall, 1969, *The Causes of Graduate Unemployment in India,* London, Allen Lane, 2–3, 57, 78, 82; Fredrick Harbison and Charles Myers, 1964, *Education, Manpower, and Economic Growth: Strategies of Human Resource Development,* New York, McGraw-Hill Book Company, 113, 118.

32. United Nations, 1975, *Poverty, Unemployment, and Development Policy: A Case Study of Selected Issues with Reference to Kerala,* New York, Department of Economic and Social Affairs, 124, Table 50; Weiner 1991, 175–177.

33. Robin Jeffrey, 1987, "Governments and Culture: How Women Made Kerala Literate," *Pacific Affairs* 60 (3): 449, 463–464.

34. Jeffrey 1987, 462; T. N. Krishnan, 1998, "The Route to Social Development in Kerala," in Santosh Mehrotra and Jolly Richards, editors, *Development with a Human Face,* Oxford, Clarendon Press, 200–213, 219; John Ratcliffe, 1978, "Social Justice and the Demographic Transition: Lessons from India's Kerala State," *International Journal of Health Services* 8 (1): 123–144.

35. Theodore Schultz, 1961, "Investment in Human Capital," *American Economic Review* 51 (1): 16; Richard Easterlin, 1981, "Why Isn't the Whole World Developed?" *Journal of Economic History* 41 (1): 6–9; Goldin and Katz 2008, 2; Passin 1982 (1965), 78 and, more broadly, chapters 4 and 6.

36. Jeffrey 1987, 470; Ashwini Deshpande, 2000, "Does Caste Still Define Disparity? A Look at Inequality in Kerala, India," *American Economic Review* 90 (2): 322–325.

Chapter 7: Mr. Nehru's Tragedy, Democracy's First Betrayal

1. Jawaharlal Nehru, editor, 1958, *A Bunch of Old Letters,* Bombay, Asia Publishing House, 179.

2. R. K. Karanjia, 1960, *The Mind of Mr. Nehru,* London, Allen and Unwin, 61.

3. Friedman and Friedman 1998, 258.

4. Friedman and Friedman 1998, 319.

5. Per capita income growth as cited in Figure 13.2.

6. Myrdal 1968, 570; Gaurav Datt, Martin Ravallion, Rinku Murgai, 2020, "Poverty and Growth in India over Six Decades," *American Journal of Agricultural Economics* 102 (1): 4–27, Figure 1, 7; World Bank, 1956, "Current Economic Position and Prospects of India: Report of Bank Mission to India," Report No. AS-54a, August, 3; World Bank, 1960, "India's Third Five-Year Plan: Report of Bank Mission to India, the Main Report," Report No. AS-80a, August 10, vi, 2, 15.

7. Nehru, *Selected Works,* Series2, 84: 151; Myrdal 1968, 565, 568–569, 820; Albert Fishlow, 1972, "Brazilian Size Distribution of Income," *American Economic Review* 62 (1/2): 392, 394, 400.

8. Douglas Irwin, 2021, "From Hermit Kingdom to Miracle on the Han: Policy Decisions That Transformed South Korea into an Export Powerhouse," Peterson Institute for International Economics Working Paper 21–14, September, Washington, DC, 8, 16; World Bank, 1966, "The Economy of Korea: Manufacturing," October 26, Washington, DC, 15–16, 29, 47.

9. International Monetary Fund, 1966, "India—Article XIV Consultation," SM/66/8, January 14, Washington, DC, 5, Appendix, Table XIII, 67.

10. World Bank, 1960, vi, 2, 15; Government of India (Planning Commission), 1961, "Third Five Year Plan: Summary," New Delhi, 49–50; Government of India (Planning Commission), 1966, "Fourth Five Year Plan: A Draft Outline," New Delhi, 106, 109–110.

11. Ghose 2019, 54–55, Figure 3.4.

12. Myron Weiner, 1962, *The Politics of Scarcity: Public Pressure and Political Response in India,* Chicago, University of Chicago Press, Table 3, 28.

13. Anwesha Sengupta, 2019, "Calcutta in the 1950s and 1970s: What Made It the Hotbed of Rebellion?" www.sahapedia.org/calcutta-1950s-and-1970s-what-made-it-hotbed-rebellions; Sibaji Pratim Basu, 2012, "The Chronicle of a Forgotten Movement: 1959 Food Movement Revisited," www.mcrg.ac.in/PP56.pdf, 11–13; *Times of India,* 1959, "Mob Violence Condemned," September 26.

14. Banerjee 2008 (1980), 37; Myron Weiner, 1961, "Violence and Politics in Calcutta," *Journal of Asian Studies* 20 (3): 275, 281; Siddhartha Guha Roy, 1990, "Fare Hike and Urban Protest: Calcutta Crowd in 1953," *Economic and Political Weekly* 25 (52): 2863–2867; *Time,* 1956, "Violence and Soul Force," June 11.

15. Jayant Lele, 1995, "Saffronisation of Shiv Sena: Political Economy of City, State, and Nation," *Economic and Political Weekly* 30 (25): 1520.

16. International Monetary Fund, 1963, "India—Request for Stand-By Arrangement," EBS/63/91, June 26, Washington, DC.

17. Myrdal 1968, 766–767.

18. Government of India (Santhanam Committee Report), 1964, *Report of the Committee on Prevention of Corruption,* Ministry of Home Affairs, New Delhi, https://cvc.gov.in/sites/default/files/scr_rpt_cvc.pdf, 10, 17–18, 101, 104, 108.

19. *Times of India,* 1962, "Committee to Check Corruption," August 21; *Times of India,* 1963, "Corruption," April 6; *Economic Weekly,* 1964, "Guarding the Guards," April 11.

20. Myrdal 1968, 953.

21. C. Rajagopalachari, 1961, *Satyam Eva Jayate: A Collection of Articles Contributed to Swarajya and Other Journals from 1956 to 1961,* Madras, Bharatan Publications, 498.

22. *Hindustan Times Weekly,* 1961, "Swatantra to Raise 1 Crore Election Fund," March 5.

23. Rajagopalachari 1961, 468–472.

24. Karanjia 1960, 41, 49–50.

25. Inder Malhotra, "J.N. TO JFK, 'EYES ONLY.'" *Indian Express,* November 15, 2010; Engerman 2018, 206, 209–210; R. Sukumaran, 2003, "The 1962 India-China War and Kargil 1999: Restrictions on the Use of Air Power," *Strategic Analysis* 27 (3): 332, 339–340; Bruce Riedel, 2015, *JFK's Forgotten Crisis,* Kindle edition, Brookings Institution Press, 136–140.

26. Government of India (Santhanam Committee Report), 1964, 109.

27. Randhir Singh, 1989, "'Visions for the Future': One View," *Economic and Political Weekly* 24 (14): 724; Bhikhu Parekh, 1991, "Nehru and the National Philosophy of India," *Economic and Political Weekly* 26 (1/2): 37–38; Sarvepalli Gopal, 1985, "Nehru and Science: Aspirations and Achievements," *Interdisciplinary Science Reviews* 10 (2): 107; Baldev Singh, editor, 1988, *Jawaharlal Nehru on Science and Technology: A Collection of His Writings and Speeches,* New Delhi, Nehru Memorial Museum and Library, 157–158; *Times of India,* 1955, "All Too Flexible," January 19.

28. Rajni Bakshi, 1998, "Raj Kapoor," in Ashis Nandy, editor, *The Secret Politics of Our Desires: Innocence, Culpability, and Indian Popular Cinema,* New Delhi, Oxford University Press, 112.

29. Dahl 1961, 6.

30. Samuel Huntington, 2006 (1968), *Political Order in Changing Societies,* New Haven, CT, Yale University Press, 84.

31. Kothari 1961, 81.

32. Nehru, *Selected Works*, Series 2, 26: 234.

33. Pradeep Chhibber and John R. Petrocik, "The Puzzle of Indian Politics: Social Cleavages and the Indian Party System," *British Journal of Political Science* 19 (2): 196, 208; Paul Kenny, 2017, *Populism and Patronage: Why Populists Win Elections in India, Asia, and Beyond*, Oxford, Oxford University Press, 73.

34. *Time* 1951.

35. Michael Brecher, 1976 (1966), *Nehru's Mantle: The Politics of Succession in India*," Westport, CT, Greenwood Press, 8; *Times of India*, 1963, "A Laughing Stock," August 5.

36. Singh 1971, Table 1, 68.

37. World Bank 1956, 7.

38. *Times of India*, 1964, "150 Killed in W. Bengal Riots," March 22; *Boston Globe*. 1964. "New India Riots Leave 81 Dead," March 22; Pralay Kanungo, 2003, "Hindutva's Entry into a 'Hindu Province': Early Years of RSS in Orissa," *Economic and Political Weekly* 38 (31): 3300; Srirupa Roy, 2007, *Beyond Belief: India and the Politics of Postcolonial Nationalism*, Durham, NC, Duke University Press, 151–153; Jonathan Parry and Christian Struempell, 2008, "On the Desecration of Nehru's 'Temples': Bhilai and Rourkela Compared," *Economic and Political Weekly* 43 (19): 47–57.

39. Katherine Frank, 2001, *Indira: The Life of Indira Nehru Gandhi*, London, HarperCollins, 267, 271, 274; Mukerjee 1992 (1964), 213.

40. *Financial Times*, 1964, "Death of Pandit Nehru: Now a Struggle for Succession," May 28; *The Economist*, 1964, "World without Nehru," May 30, 923; *New York Times*, 1964, "India after Nehru," May 31; see also chapter 5 on the State Department's anticipation of Hindu theocracy in India.

Chapter 8: Shastri Makes a Brave Transition

1. Brecher 1976 (1966), 33–34.

2. Katherine Frank, 2001, *Indira: The Life of Indira Nehru Gandhi*, London, HarperCollins, 269–290; Brecher 1976 (1966), 132.

3. *Times of India*, 1964, "Friend Even to His Opponents," June 3; Uma Vasudev, 1974, *Indira Gandhi: Revolution in Restraint*, New Delhi, Vikas Publishing House, 321; Brecher 1976 (1966), 132–133.

4. *Times of India*, 1964, "Warning of Food Riots in Poona," June 15; *Times of India*, 1964, "Encouraging," June 19; *Times of India*, 1964, "Food Riot in Harihar," September 16; *Times of India*, 1964, "No Police Excesses in Kerala during Food Stir," December 1; Francine Frankel, 1978, *India's Political Economy 1947–1977*, Princeton,

NJ, Princeton University Press, 249; Kathleen Gough, 1967, "Kerala Politics and the 1965 Election," *International Journal of Comparative Sociology* 8 (1): 60–61.

5. M.S. Swaminathan, 1964, "The Impact of Dwarfing Genes on Wheat Production," paper presented at All India Wheat Research Workers' Seminar, August, www.worldscientific.com/doi/abs/10.1142/9789813200074_0001, 1.

6. Brecher 1976 (1966), 145; Frankel 1978, 257–258; Engerman 2018, 237–238; William S. Gaud, 1968, "The Green Revolution: Accomplishments and Apprehensions," www.agbioworld.org/biotech-info/topics/borlaug/borlaug-green.html.

7. Guha 2008 (2007), 398–399; Engerman 2018, 221.

8. Vijay Joshi and I.M.D. Little, 1994, *India: Macroeconomics and Political Economy 1964–1991,* Washington, DC, The World Bank, Table 4.8, 82; Table 4.10, 97–98; *Times of India,* 1965, "Situation on Food Front Grim, Says Minister," December 2.

9. Engerman 2018, 221, 238–240, 246–247; *Times of India,* 1965, "U.S. Food Aid," December 11; Kristin L. Ahlberg, 2007, "Machiavelli with a Heart": The Johnson Administration's Food for Peace Program in India, 1965–1966," *Diplomatic History* 31 (4): 681.

10. *Times of India,* 1965, "Situation on Food Front Grim, Says Minister," December 2; Braj Kumar (B. K.) Nehru, 1997, *Nice Guys Finish Second,* New Delhi, Viking, 431–433.

11. *Times of India,* 1964, "Package Plan Is Being Extended," June 28; Saidur Rahman, 2015, "Green Revolution in India: Environmental Degradation and Impact on Livestock," *Asian Journal of Water, Environment, and Pollution* 12 (1): 75–80; Rachel Carson, 1997 (1962), *Silent Spring,* Boston, G. K. Hall, 22–23.

12. *Times of India,* 1964, "Shastri Urges Deferment of Some Heavy Industry Units," August 11; Frankel 1978, 248–251, 267.

13. Engerman 2018, 247–248.

14. B. K. Nehru, 1997, 446–447; Engerman 2018, 248–253; Balachandran 1998, 676.

15. I. G. Patel, 2002, *Glimpses of Indian Economic Policy: An Insider's View,* New Delhi, Oxford University Press, 104.

16. Frankel 1978, 287; International Monetary Fund 1966, 1–2; Balachandran 1998, 676, 679; *Times of India,* 1965, "Several Charges Made against TTK," November 23; *Times of India,* 1966, "TTK, Quits as Finance Minister," January 1; B. K. Nehru 1997, 446, 448–449, 452.

17. Frankel 1978, 265; Brecher 1976 (1966), 177–178, 184; B. G. Verghese, 1965, "National Scene: Poverty of Politics," *Times of India,* April 22.

18. Brecher 1976 (1966), 153–154.

19. Robert Hardgrave, 1965, "The Riots in Tamilnad: Problems and Prospects of India's Language Crisis," *Asian Survey* 5 (8): 399; Brecher 1976 (1966), 151–157, 160–167; *Times of India*, 1965a, "Centre Stands by Nehru's Assurances: P.M.," February 12; *Times of India*, 1965b, "Madras Students' Stir Ends," February 13; *Times of India*, 1965c, "Patriotism," February 14; Frank 2001, 281.

20. Inder Malhotra, 1991 (1989), *Indira Gandhi: A Personal and Political Biography*, Boston, Northeastern University Press, 84; Frank 2001, 281–282.

21. Malhotra 1991 (1989), 84, 318.

22. Brecher 1976 (1966), 184, 188.

23. Brecher 1976 (1966), 185.

24. Brecher 1976 (1966), 191–192.

25. B. K. Nehru 1997, 448.

26. International Monetary Fund, 1966, "India—1965 Article XIV Consultations," SM/66/8, January 14, Washington, DC, 21, 23.

27. International Monetary Fund, 1965, "India—1964 Article XIV Consultations," SM/65/54, June 21, Washington, DC, 9.

Chapter 9: A Savior for India's Ferment

1. Katherine Frank, 2001, *Indira: The Life of Indira Nehru Gandhi*, London, HarperCollins, 524.

2. Frank 2001, 250; Tariq Ali, 1985, *An Indian Dynasty: The Story of the Nehru-Gandhi Family*, New York, G. P. Putnam, 139–140; Uma Vasudev, 1974, *Indira Gandhi: Revolution in Restraint*, New Delhi, Vikas Publishing House, 271, 273–279.

3. Ali 1985, 140; Vasudev 1974, 274; see also chapter 8.

4. Frank 2001, 291–293.

5. Anwesha Sengupta, 2019, "Calcutta in the 1950s and 1970s: What Made It the Hotbed of Rebellion?" www.sahapedia.org/calcutta-1950s-and-1970s-what-made-it-hotbed-rebellions.

6. *New York Times*, 1966b, "Food Protest in Kerala," February 3.

7. Paul Grimes, 1960, "Embattled Sikhs," *New York Times*, November 6.

8. *New York Times*, 1966, "India Yielding to Sikh Demand for a Punjabi-Speaking State," March 10; *Times of India*, 1966, "Curfew in Parts of Delhi: Orgy of Violence on Suba Issue," March 15; J. Anthony Lukas, 1966, "Calm Returning to Punjab Area after Protests over New State," *New York Times*, March 21.

9. J. Anthony Lukas, 1966, "Violence Mounts in the Land of Gandhi: Extremists Find Gains in Ignoring Nonviolence," *New York Times*, March 22.

10. R. K. Karanjia and K. A. Abbas, 1974, *Face to Face with Indira Gandhi,* New Delhi, Chetana Publications, 13–14, emphasis in original.

11. Gopalan Balachandran, 1998, *The Reserve Bank of India, 1951–1967,* Delhi: Oxford University Press, 680–681.

12. Braj Kumar (B.K.) Nehru, 1997, *Nice Guys Finish Second,* New Delhi, Viking, 462–463; Malhotra 1991 (1989), 97.

13. B. K. Nehru 1997, 447, 452; Balachandran 1998, 683–685.

14. B. K. Nehru 1997, 452; Douglas Irwin, 2021, "From Hermit Kingdom to Miracle on the Han: Policy Decisions That Transformed South Korea into an Export Powerhouse," Peterson Institute for International Economics Working Paper, 21–14, September, Washington, DC, 8, 16.

15. Nehru 1997, 447, 452; Balachandran 1998, 683–685; B. R. Shenoy, 1966, "India's Half-Way Devaluation," *Daily Telegraph,* July 12.

16. Vasudev 1974, 370; Balachandran 1998, 684–685.

17. Balachandran 1998, 688; Malhotra 1991 (1989), 99; Engerman 2018, 263–265, 217.

18. B. K. Nehru 1997, 446.

19. Milton Friedman, 1963, *Inflation: Causes and Consequences,* New York, Asia Publishing House, Lecture 2, 36.

20. B. K. Nehru 1997, 465–467.

21. B. K. Nehru 1997, 467; I. G. Patel, 2002, *Glimpses of Indian Economic Policy,* New Delhi, Oxford University Press, 115.

22. Jayant Lele, 1995, "Saffronisation of Shiv Sena: Political Economy of City, State and Nation," *Economic and Political Weekly* 30 (25): 1520, 1522; Carl Schmitt, 2007 (1932), *The Concept of the Political,* Chicago, University of Chicago Press, 32–34.

23. V. S. Naipaul, 2011 (1990), *India: A Million Mutinies,* Kindle edition, First Vintage International Edition, location 983.

24. Gyan Prakash, 2012, "Bal Thackeray: The Original Angry Young Man," *Mint,* November 12; Vaibhav Purandare, 2012, *Bal Thackeray and the Rise of the Shiv Sena,* Kindle edition, Roli Books, locations 737–742.

25. Prakash 2012.

26. Michael Walzer, 2015, *The Paradox of Liberation: Secular Revolutions and Religious Counterrevolutions,* New Haven, CT, Yale University Press; see also chapter 8.

27. *Times of India,* 1966, "11 Killed in Akola Disturbances," October 1; J. Anthony Lukas, 1966, "11 in India Killed over in Riot over Cows," *New York Times,* October 1.

28. K. N. Raj, 1969, "Investment in Livestock in Agrarian Economies: An Analysis of Some Issues concerning 'Sacred Cows' and 'Surplus Cattle,'" *Indian Economic Review* New Series 4 (1): 80–83.

29. K. Narayanan Nair, 1981. "Studies on India's Cattle Economy," *Economic and Political Weekly* 16 (9): 321–323.

30. Joseph Lelyveld, 1966, "Riots Force Out Minister in India: Cabinet Minister Steps Down after Riots in India," *New York Times*, November 9.

31. J. Anthony Lukas, 1966, "India Acts to Head of New Riots with Arrest of Holy Man," *New York Times*, November 23; *Times of India*, multiple reports over this period.

32. J. Anthony Lukas, 1966, "The Week of the Cow," *New York Times*, November 16; *Times of India*, 1951, "Threat to Crush Jana Sangh," November 30; Malhotra 1991 (1989), 105.

33. Zareer Masani, 1975, *Indira Gandhi: A Biography*, London, Hamilton, 170–171, based on a report in *The Hindu* dated December 21, 1966.

34. *Times of India*, 1966, "Some Better Candidates Could Have Been Chosen. Influence Exerted by Party Bosses, Admits Prime Minister," December 26.

35. Frank 2001, 302; Masani 1975, 170.

36. Vasudev 1974, 400; *The Times*, 1967, "Concern in Delhi over Violence during Election Campaign," February 6; *Times of India*, 1967, "P.M. Hit by Stone at Poll Rally in Bhubaneshwar: Keeps Her Poise Even Though Injured," February 8; *Financial Times*, 1967, "Mrs. Gandhi Hit by Stone," February 9.

37. Guha 2008 (2007), 419–420; Election Commission of India, 1967, *Report on the Fourth General Elections (1967), Volume 1*, New Delhi, Table 17, 93–94.

38. Guha 2008 (2007), 419; Election Commission of India 1967, Table 18, 95.

39. Guha 2008 (2007), 420; Frank 2001, 305.

40. Vasudev 1974, 495.

41. Vasudev 1974, 495–496.

42. Huntington 2006 (1968), 63–70, 83, 237–239.

43. Nazes Afroz, 2017, "The Dream That Failed: Voices of Naxalbari across the 50 Years since the Uprising," *Caravan*, May 31.

44. Banerjee 2008 (1980), 100; Afroz 2017.

45. Banerjee 2008 (1980), 101–102.

46. Banerjee 2008 (1980), 102; Guha 2008 (2007), 423.

47. Deepali Bhandari and Deeksha Pokhriyal, 2020, "The Continuing Threat of India's Unlawful Activities Prevention Act to Free Speech," *Jurist*, June 2; A. G.

Noorani, 2009, "India: A Security State," *Economic and Political Weekly* 44 (14): 13–15.

48. Dom Moraes, 1970, "The Naxalites, Whose Extremism Knows No Extremes," *New York Times*, November 8.

Chapter 10: India Has an Empress

1. Vijay Joshi and I.M.D. Little, 1994, *India: Macroeconomics and Political Economy, 1964–1991*, Washington, DC, The World Bank, Table 4.10, 97.

2. Joshi and Little 1994, 45, 50–51, 87–89, Table 4.10, 97.

3. Karanjia and Abbas 1974, 42; Patel 2002, 125–126.

4. Ved Mehta, 2015 (1978), *The Sanjay Story*, New Delhi, HarperCollins, 34–37, 44, 46–47.

5. Mehta 2015 (1978), 51–55; Gyan Prakash, 2018, *Emergency Chronicles: Indira Gandhi and Democracy's Turning Point*, Gurgaon, India, Penguin, 207, 410.

6. Mehta 2015 (1978), 63; *The Times*, 1970, "Plea for Man India Wants Extradited," August 29; *Financial Times*, 1970, "This Week in the Courts," December 14; Vasudev 1974, 337.

7. Mehta 2015 (1978), 65–66; Prakash 2018, 207, 410; *New York Times*, 1966, "A Gandhi Fined in Britain," December 13.

8. Charles Greville, 1967, "Mrs. Gandhi's Son Took Her Advice," *Daily Mail*, February 15.

9. Mehta 2015 (1978), 66–68.

10. Prakash 2018, 225–226; Mehta 2015 (1978), 71.

11. Mehta 2015 (1978), 71; Frank 2001, 321, 400.

12. *Time*, 1969, "India: Another Setback for Indira," February 21.

13. Patel 2002, 131–132.

14. *Newsweek*, 1969, "India: Gunning for Mrs. Gandhi," July 28.

15. D. N. Ghosh, 2019 (2015), *No Regrets*, New Delhi, Rupa Publications, 7; Rahul Bajoria, 2018, *The Story of the Reserve Bank of India*, New Delhi, Rupa Publications, 74; Patel 2002, 133, 135–136; Austin 2003 (1999), 179.

16. Austin 2003 (1999), 179, 215–220.

17. Patel 2002, 136; *Time*, 1969, "India: The Lady v. the Syndicate," August 29; Vasudev 1974, 509.

18. Guha 2008 (2007), 439; *Time*, 1969, "Two Parties Face to Face," November 21; Austin 2003 (1999), 180.

19. Vasudev 1974, 505, 508.

20. Mehta 2015 (1978), 72; Frank 2001, 321.

21. Mehta 2015 (1978), 73–78; Prakash 2018, 234–236.

22. *Times of India*, 1978, "Land Hypothecated Illegally by Sanjay to Bank," November 14; Government of India, 1979, *Report of the Commission of Inquiry into Maruti Affairs*, New Delhi, 114, 116–117, 120, 124, 127.

23. C. Rangarajan, 1974, "Banking Development since Nationalization and Reduction of Disparities," in T. N. Srinivasan and P. K. Bardhan, editors, *Poverty and Income Distribution in India*, Calcutta, Statistical Publication Society, 438; Patel 2002, 139–140.

24. Patel 2002, 140.

25. Patel 2002, 140; International Monetary Fund, 1971, "India—Staff Report and Proposed Decision for the 1970 Article XIV Consultation," SM/71/39, February 17, Washington, DC, 1–4.

26. International Monetary Fund, 1970, "Korea—Staff Report and Proposed Decision for the 1970 Article XIV Consultation," SM/70/279, December 30, Washington, DC, 1–2, 4, 9; see also chapter 7.

27. World Bank, 1993, *The East Asian Miracle*, New York, Oxford University Press, Figure 1.2, 29–30, 37.

28. World Bank 1993, 24, 29–31, 37–38, 59, 106–108, 195.

29. World Bank 1993, 39–40.

30. World Bank 1993, see also chapter 3.

31. Francine Frankel, 1978, *India's Political Economy, 1947–1977*, Princeton, NJ, Princeton University Press, 450; *Newsweek*, 1971, "Mrs. Gandhi Makes Her Bid," March 1.

32. See chapter 9; *Newsweek*, 1971, "Indira's Big Gamble," January 11; Frankel 1978, 454.

33. Frankel 1978, 452; Raj Thapar, 1991, *All These Years: A Memoir*, New Delhi, Penguin Books, 322; Sydney Schanberg, 1971, "India Starts Voting in 10-Day Poll," *New York Times*, March 1; Guha 2008 (2007), 446.

34. See chapter 2; Austin 2003 (1999), 226–228, 236–240. 244, 252–253.

35. *The Economist*, 1971, "Empress of India," December 18.

36. Frankel 1978, 457, 482–484; Guha 2008 (2007), 468; Malhotra 1991 (1989), 147–148.

37. Austin 2003 (1999), 173–174; Malhotra 1991 (1989), 152–153.

38. *Times of India*, 1969, "Wide Support for Ban on Donations to Parties," May 18; Malhotra 1991 (1989), 144; Frankel 1978, 476; Stanley Kochanek, 1987, "Briefcase Politics in India: The Congress Party and the Business Elite," *Asian Survey* 27 (12): 1286.

39. Suman Sahai, 1996. "'Hawala' Politics: A Congress Legacy," *Economic and Political Weekly* 31 (5): 253; Milan Vaishnav, 2017, *When Crime Pays: Money and Muscle in Indian Politics*, New Haven, CT, Yale University Press, 97.

40. Joshi and Little 1994, 37; P. C. Mahanti, 1971, "Pressure on a Sick Economy," *Financial Times*, June 23; see also chapter 7.

41. Kochanek 1987, 1290; Malhotra 1991 (1989), 144–145.

42. Kuldip Nayar, 1971, *India: The Critical Years*. New Delhi: Vikas Publications, 3; Malhotra 1991 (1989), 145.

43. Patel 2002, 147.

44. *Times of India*, 1971, "Prone to Drought," August 21; Frankel 1978, 476; Guha 2008 (2007), 462.

Chapter 11: Anger Meets Repression

1. *Times of India*, 1971, "Ordeal by Water," August 11; *Times of India*, 1971, "Food Output Touches Record Level," August 19.

2. *Financial Times*, 1972a, "India Crops Hit by Floods and Drought," August 2; *Financial Times*, 1972b, "India Launches Program to Avert Famine," August 3; *The Economist*, 1972, "India: In Trouble Again," November 18.

3. Navroz Mody, 1972, "Famine and Famine Makers," *Times of India*, December 2.

4. *Financial Times*, 1973, "India to Import 2 Million Tons Grain," January 18; M. V. Kamath, 1972, "A Food Ship Every Three Days," *Times of India*, December 2.

5. Bertrand Weinraub, 1973, "Mrs. Gandhi's Popularity Plummets as India's Problems Continue to Worsen," *International Herald Tribune*, June 11; *The Economist*, 1973, "The Dimming Halo," May 19.

6. Joshi and Little 1994, Table 5.12, 130; Michael Corbett, 2013, "Oil Shock of 1973–74: October 1973–January 1974," *Federal Reserve History*, www.federalreservehistory.org/essays/oil-shock-of-1973-74, November 22; International Monetary Fund, 1974, "India—Use of Fund Resources," EBS/74/107, April 30, Washington, DC, 6.

7. Bernard Weinraub, 1974, "India Ending Take-Over of Distribution of Wheat," *New York Times*, March 29.

8. *Times of India*, 1974a, "Vast Areas Face Drought Threat," July 25; *Times of India*, 1975, "A Parched Land, a Desolate People," June 8; *Times of India*, 1974b, "Flood Havoc," August 5; *Times of India*, 1974c, "Drought in Flood-Hit Bihar," September 7.

9. *Times of India*, 1974d, "Indira Denies Mass Frustration," October 29.

10. Ashok Thapar, 1972, "Undoing the Green Revolution: Tinkering with Groundwater," *Times of India,* April 10; Wolf Ladejinsky, 1972, "The 'Green Revolution,'" *Financial Times*; Prem Shankar Jha, 1974, "What Next in Agriculture? I-End of Green Revolution," *Times of India,* October 7.

11. See chapter 3.

12. International Monetary Fund 1974, 1, 15, 16; International Monetary Fund, 1976, "India—Staff Report and Proposed Decision for the 1976 Article XIV Consultation," SM/76/125, June 10, Washington, DC, 17.

13. Akhil Gupta, 2012, *Red Tape: Bureaucracy, Structural Violence, and Poverty in India,* Durham, NC, Duke University Press, 19–20.

14. Frankel 1978, 457–458; on the earlier phase of police repression of Naxalites, see chapter 9.

15. Javed Akhtar quote cited in Koushik Banerjea, 2005, "'Fight Club': Aesthetics, Hybridisation, and the Construction of Rogue Masculinities in *Sholay* and *Deewar,*" in Raminder Kaur and Ajay Sinha, editors, *Bollywood: Popular Indian Cinema through a Transnational Lens,* New Delhi, Sage, 172; Fareeduddin Kazmi, 1998, "How Angry Is the Angry Young Man? 'Rebellion' in Conventional Hindi Films," in Ashis Nandy, editor, *The Secret Politics of Our Desires: Innocence, Culpability, and the Indian Popular Cinema,* New Delhi, Oxford University Press, 140, 142, 148–155.

16. Dawn Jones and Rodney Jones, 1974, "Urban Upheaval in India: The 1974 Nav Nirman Riots in Gujarat," *Asian Survey* 16 (11): 1012–1013, 1017, 1074.

17. Jones and Jones 1974, 1017, 1023.

18. Jones and Jones 1974, 1023–1024.

19. Jones and Jones 1974, 1017–1018, 1026–1027.

20. Jones and Jones 1974, 1028–1029, 1031.

21. Prakash 2018, 102–103; Frankel 1978, 528.

22. Guha 2008 (2007), 477; Vasudev 1977, 69; *Time,* 1975, "J.P.: India's Aging Revolutionary," July 14.

23. Frankel 1978, 528, 531.

24. Malhotra 1991 (1989), 158; Vasudev 1977, 71; Peter Gill, 1974, "India 'Arrests' 3000 to Keep Trains Running," *Daily Telegraph,* May 6.

25. Weinraub, Bernard. 1974. "India Strike Snarls Trains but Fails to Halt Service," *New York Times,* May 9; Ali 1985, 181–182; Vasudev 1977, 71; Bernard Weinraub, 1974, "New Delhi Widens Rail Union Curbs," *New York Times,* May 15; Bernard Weinraub, 1974, "India's Rail Strike Ends in Collapse," *New York Times,* May 28; *The Economist,* 1974, "The Empress's Bomb," May 25; *The Economist,* 1974, "Tougher Yet

and Tougher," June 8; *The Economist,* 1974, "The Woman Who Showed the Men the Way," June 22.

26. *The Economist,* 1974, "Tougher Yet and Tougher," June 8.

27. Prakash 2018, 105; Guha 2008 (2007), 478; Ghanshyam Shah, 1977, "Revolution, Reform, or Protest? A Study of the Bihar Movement: III," *Economic and Political Weekly* 12 (17): 701–702.

28. *Times of India,* 1974, "Bihar's Plight," October 4.

29. Frankel 1978, 534–535.

30. Simons Lewis, 1975, "Bomb Wounds Fatal to Indian Rail Minister," *International Herald Tribune,* January 4; *International Herald Tribune,* 1975, "Mrs. Gandhi Says She Is Assassins' Ultimate Target," January 8; *Time,* 1975, "India: Murder in Bihar," January 13.

31. Shashi Tharoor, 1982, *Reasons of State: Political Development and India's Foreign Policy Under Indira Gandhi, 1966–1977,* Delhi, Vikas Publishing House, 59 (Table 1); Prakash 2018, 108; Peter Gill, 1975, "Thousands in Delhi Protest," *Daily Telegraph,* March 7.

32. Prakash 2018, 164; Nayar 1977, 26–27; Austin 2003 (1999), 304.

33. Nayyar 1977, 3–4; Prakash 2018, 159–160; Frankel 1978, 539–540; *International Herald Tribune,* 1975, "Ruling Party Asks Mrs. Gandhi to Stay on," June 19.

34. Prakash 2018, 160, 162–163.

35. Jonathan Dimbleby and Anthony Mascarenhas, 1975, "Why Indira Gandhi Sent Democracy to Prison," *Sunday Times,* June 29; Christophe Jaffrelot and Pratinav Anil, 2020, *India's First Dictatorship: The Emergency, 1975–1977,* London, C. Hurst & Co., 1–2; Prakash 2018, 165.

36. The text of Mrs. Gandhi's speech on June 26, 1975, was reproduced in *New York Times,* 1975, "Speech and Proclamation," June 27.

37. Dimbleby and Mascarenhas 1975.

38. Guha 2008 (2007), 497–498.

Chapter 12: An Autocratic Gamble Fails

1. *Times of India,* 1967, "Asoka Mehta for Presidential Form of Government in States for Some Time," December 11; *Times of India,* 1969, "Setalvad Assails Centre's Delays," April 13.

2. William Borders, 1975, "Mrs. Gandhi Calls India Democratic Even Under Curbs," *New York Times,* July 3; Ali 1985, 187; J. Anthony Lukas, 1976, "India Is as Indira Does," *New York Times,* April 4.

3. Raaj Sah, 1991, "Fallibility in Human Organizations and Political Systems," *Journal of Economic Perspectives* 5 (2): 71; Carl Henrik Knutsen, 2018, "Autocracy and Variation in Economic Development Outcomes," Working Paper Series 2018:80, The Varieties of Democracy Institute, Gothenburg, Sweden, 17; Fabio Monteforte and Jonathan R. W. Temple, 2020, "The Autocratic Gamble: Evidence from Robust Variance Tests," *Economics of Governance* 21: 363–384; Daron Acemoglu et al., 2019, "Democracy Does Cause Growth," *Journal of Political Economy* 127 (1): 47–100; Ruth Ben-Ghiat, 2021, *Strongmen: Mussolini to the Present,* Kindle edition, W. W. Norton & Company, locations 11, 14, 143, 167.

4. *Times of India,* 1980, "Sanjay Gandhi," June 24; M. R. Nair, 1976, "Loose Ends in the Budget," *Economic and Political Weekly* 11 (16): 599.

5. International Monetary Fund, 1976, "India—Staff Report and Proposed Decision for the 1976 Article XIV Consultation," SM/76/125, June 10, Washington, DC, 3.

6. World Bank, 1977, "Economic Situation and Prospects of India," Report No. 1529-IN, April 25, Washington, DC, Tables 7.1 and 7.4; International Monetary Fund 1976, 5; Joshi and Little 1994, Table 5.12, 130.

7. International Monetary Fund 1976, 2, 7, 9, 14.

8. Lukas 1976.

9. World Bank, 1976, "Economic Situation and Prospects of India," Report No. 1073-IN, March 29, Washington, DC, i, iii.

10. World Bank 1976, 24.

11. Government of India, 1977, *Economic Survey 1976–1977,* chapter 3, 13.

12. Government of India, 1977, *Economic Survey 1976–1977,* chapter 8, Tables 3.1–3.2, 80–81.

13. Vincent Canby, 1976, "Ray's Film, 'The Middleman' Seen as His Most Sorrowful Work," *New York Times,* October 12; Udayan Gupta, 1982, "The Politics of Humanism: An Interview with Satyajit Ray," *Cinéaste* 12 (1): 26.

14. Frankel 1978, 507, 552; Jaffrelot and Anil 2020, 73–74; Granville 2003 (1999), 658.

15. Lukas 1976.

16. Lukas 1976; David Selbourne, 1977, *An Eye to India: The Unmasking of a Tyranny,* New York, Penguin, 263.

17. See chapter 10; Government of India, 1979, Report of the Commission of Inquiry into Maruti Affairs, New Delhi, 114, 124, 127–128.

18. Uma Vasudev, 1977, *Two Faces of Indira Gandhi,* New Delhi, Vikas Publishing House, 106–107; Anthony Mascarenhas and Graham Searjeant, 1977, "How Sanjay's Car Crashed," *Sunday Times,* April 24; Prakash 2018, 240.

19. Prakash 2018, 243; Government of India 1979, 14–15; 63–64; 139–140.

20. *Pioneer,* 2017, "Talwar Was a Sabre Who Could Slay Any Enemy," November 23.

21. Vasudev 1977, 182–186; Mehta 2015, 82; Guha 2008 (2007), 469; Prakash 2018, 144–145, 151.

22. World Bank, 1980, "Economic Situation and Prospects of India," Report Number 2933-IN, May 1, Washington, DC, 119.

23. World Bank 1980, 120; Guha 2008 (2007), 512–513; Vasudev 1977, 162.

24. Prakash 2018, 303; Guha 2008 (2007), 512; World Bank 1980, 119–120; World Bank. 1981. "Economic Situation and Prospects of India," Report No. 3401-IN, April 15, Table 1.5.

25. Vasudev 1977, 145; Patrick Clibbens, 2014, "'The Destiny of This City Is to Be the Spiritual Workshop of the Nation': Clearing Cities and Making Citizens during the Indian Emergency, 1975–1977," *Contemporary South Asia* 22 (1): 51–66; Prakash 2018, 282; Christophe Jaffrelot and Pratinav Anil, 2021, *India's First Dictatorship: The Emergency, 1975–77,* London, C. Hurst and Co., 165; Frankel 1978, 564; Government of India, 1978, *Shah Commission of Inquiry,* Interim Report II, April 28, New Delhi, 78.

26. Jaffrelot and Anil 2021, 175; Vasudev 1977, 134–137.

27. Government of India (*Shah Commission,* Volume 2), 1978, 80–81; Prakash 2018, 290–291; Vasudev 1977, 134–137.

28. Government of India (*Shah Commission,* Volume 2), 1978, 82; Vasudev 1977, 123–125.

29. Ajoy Bose and John Dayal, 2018, *For Reasons of State,* Kindle edition, Penguin Random House India, locations 282, 291, 1445; Jaffrelot and Anil 2021, 167–169.

30. Dayal and Bose 2018, location 781; Vasudev 1977, 161, 165; Prakash 2018, 255–257, 296–298; Jaffrelot and Anil 2021, 172–173.

31. Jacobs 1992 (1961), chapter 15; on Chandigarh, see chapter 4.

32. *New York Times,* 1977, "Mrs. Gandhi, Easing Crisis Rule, Decides on March Election," January 19; Devadas S. Pillai, editor, 1977, *The Incredible Election, 1977: A Blow-by-Blow Account as Reported in the Indian Express,* Bombay, Popular Prakashan, 19–21.

33. Vasudev 1977, 188–189; Kuldip Nayyar, 1977, *The Judgement: Inside Story of the Emergency in India,* New Delhi, Vikas Publishing House, 157–158, 162–163.

34. Vasudev 1977, 188–191; William Borders, 1975, "India's Crown Prince: Sanjay," *New York Times,* February 13.

35. Vasudev 1977, 190–191; Frankel 1978, 563, 571; Guha 2008 (2007), 519–520.

36. *Times of India,* 1977, "Generals Refused to Aid Congress, Says Star," April 18; *Times of India,* 1977, "Indira Strongly Defends Son," July 23.

Chapter 13: Democracy Betrays Again, Deindustrialization Begins

1. *Times of India,* 1977, "Unanimous Choice by Janata," March 25.

2. Guha 2008 (2007), 538.

3. *New York Times,* 1977, "India Stands Firm against Coca-Cola," September 5; *Times of India,* 1977, "Soft Drink Formula Available," August 9; *Financial Times,* 1977, "Curbs on Multinational Groups 'This Winter,'" October 11.

4. Frankel 1978, 573–574; Guha 2008 (2007), 521–523, 534.

5. Guha 2008 (2007), 528–529, 535–536; Girilal Jain, 1979, "Janata Party's New Face: Populism Replaces Liberalism," *Times of India,* March 7; *Times of India,* 1979, "Budget to Fleece Urban Taxpayer," March 1.

6. Guha 2008 (2007), 528–529; *Time of India,* 1978, "Backward Classes Panel Named," November 16; *Times of India,* 1979, "PM Inaugurates Backward Classes Commission," March 22.

7. Guha 2008 (2007), 535–536.

8. Guha 2008 (2007), 535–536.

9. World Bank, 1980, "Economic Situation and Prospects of India," Report Number 2933-IN, May 1, Washington, DC, 43, 48, 56, 60, 64, 80; International Monetary Fund, 1980a, "India—Staff Report for the 1980 Article IV Consultation," SM/80/151, Washington, DC, June 23, 2–7.

10. *India Today,* 1980, "Indira Gandhi's Win Aided by Well-Conceived, Neatly Executed Plan," January 31.

11. Gita Piramal, 1996, *Business Maharajas,* Kindle edition, Penguin Random House India, location 751; Hamish McDonald, 2010, *Ambani and Sons: The Making of the World's Richest Brothers and Their Feud,* New Delhi, Roli, 25, 33–36, 54–58, 63–64.

12. McDonald 2010, 63–64, 75, 106; Piramal 1996, location 751; Kuldip Singh, 2002, "Dhirubhai Ambani," *Independent,* July 18.

13. Malhotra 1991 (1989), 214–215; *India Today,* 1980, "Sanjay Gandhi and His Young Loyalists Sweep Lok Sabha Elections," January 31; *India Today,* 1980, "Emergency Was a Non-Issue in the 1980 Election," January 31.

14. Malhotra 1991 (1989), 215; *India Today,* 1980, "Assembly Elections: Sanjay Re-Emerges as the Most Vital Factor in Indian Politics," May 31; *India Today,* 1980, "Assembly Elections: Sanjay Gandhi Emerges as the Unquestioned Leader of New

Legislators," June 30; Stuart Auerbach, 1980, "Sanjay Gandhi Was India's 'Crown Prince'; His Death Leaves a Vacuum," *Washington Post*, June 24; Sidney Weintraub, 1980, "Parliament Expels Gandhi, Orders Her to Delhi Jail Cell," *Washington Post*, December 20.

15. *India Today*. 1980. "Assembly Elections: Sanjay Re-Emerges as the Most Vital Factor in Indian Politics," May 31.

16. *Times of India*. 1980. "Sanjay Plane Crash: No Judicial Probe," June 28; Malhotra 1991 (1989), 222.

17. *India Today*, 1980, "Pitts S-2A Is Considered to Be the Most Sturdy, Reliable Aerobatic Biplane," July 15; Frank 2001, 445; *India Today*, 1980, "Sanjay Gandhi Dies in a Dramatic Plane Crash, His Passing Leaves a Political Vacuum," July 15.

18. Nehru 1997, 582; Malhotra 1991 (1989), 224; Frank 2001, 450.

19. *India Today*, 1980, "Sonia Is Dead Against the Idea of My Getting into Politics: Rajiv Gandhi," August 31; *India Today*, 1980, "After Sanjay Gandhi's Death, Congressmen Look to the Gandhi Family to Fill the Void," August 31.

20. Ali 1985, 213; Frank 2001, 447–448; Patel 2002, 164.

21. International Monetary Fund, 1980b, "India: Use of Fund Resources—Compensatory Financing Facility," EBS/80/171, Washington, DC, July 30; International Monetary Fund, 1986, "India: Staff Report for the 1986 Article IV Consultation," SM/86/54, Washington, DC, March 6, Table 4, 29 for the U.S. dollar/SDR conversion rate.

22. International Monetary Fund, 1981, "India: Use of Fund Resources—Extended Fund Facility," EBS81/198, Washington, DC, October 7, 1, 53; Patel 2002, 168.

23. International Monetary Fund 1981, 19–21, 46. *Financial Times*, 1981, "India to Taste the Market Medicine," October 27.

24. Arvind Panagariya, 2004, "Growth and Reforms during the 1980s and 1990s," *Economic and Political Weekly* 39 (25): 2581–2594; Ashok Kotwal, Bharat Ramaswami, and Wilima Wadhwa, 2011, "Economic Liberalization and Indian Economic Growth: What's the Evidence?" *Journal of Economic Literature* 49 (4): 1172; Dani Rodrik and Arvind Subramanian, 2004, "Why India Can Grow at 7 Percent a Year or More: Projections and Reflections," *Economic and Political Weekly* 39 (16): 1519–26.

25. McDonald 2010, 106; Piramal 1996, locations 1579–1585.

26. *India Today*, 1981, "I Honestly Believe the Nehru Family Is Giving Continuity: Abdul Rahman Antulay," August 31; Arun Shourie, 1983, *Mrs. Gandhi's Second Reign*, New Delhi, Vikas, 107–117.

27. Robert Wade, 1982, "The System of Administrative and Political Corruption: Canal Irrigation in South India," *Journal of Development Studies* 18 (3): 309, 318–319.

28. Akhil Gupta, 1995, "Blurred Boundaries: The Discourse of Corruption, the Culture of Politics, and the Imagined State," *American Ethnologist* 22 (2): 375.

29. Bakshi 1998, 113, 115–116, 131–133.

30. *Times of India,* 1981, "It's the Corrupt Who Protest Too Much," September 19; Thomas Paine, 1918 [1776], *Common Sense,* New York: Peter Eckler Publishing Co., ix.

31. International Monetary Fund, 1986, "India—Staff Report for the 1986 Article IV Consultation," SM/86/54, March 6, Washington, DC, 2, 5, 24, 42; Joshi and Little 1994, 163–164, 174 (Table 6.13).

32. International Monetary Fund 1986, Table 4, 14; World Bank, 1986, "India Economic Situation and Development Prospects," Report No. 6090-IN, May 9, Washington, DC, 143, 146 (Table 5.4); C. P. Chandrashekhar, 1984, "Growth and Technical Change in Indian Cotton-Mill Industry," *Economic and Political Weekly* 19 (4): PE-35; Joshi and Little 1994, 15.

33. International Monetary Fund 1980a, 6; World Bank 1980, 88; Oli Havrylyshyn and Iradj Alikhani, 1982, "Is There Cause for Export Optimism? An Inquiry into the Existence of a Second Generation of Successful Exporters," *Weltwirtschaftliches Archiv* 118 (4): 653 (Table 1); Frankel 1978, 580.

34. Government of India, 1987, *Economic Survey 1987–1988,* Ministry of Finance, New Delhi, S-37–38. 1980s' backlog estimated from Ajit Kumar Ghose, 2019, *Employment in India,* New Delhi, Oxford University Press, 43, 79; backlog at the end of Nehru years from chapter 7; World Bank, 1978, "Economic Situation and Prospects of India," Report No. 2008-IN, April 17, Washington, DC, 76.

35. David Housego, 1979, "China's Great Leap in the Dark," *Financial Times,* January 19; Pranab Bardhan, 2010, *Awakening Giants, Feet of Clay: Assessing the Economic Rise of China and India,* Princeton, NJ, Princeton University Press, 19; World Bank 1986, Table 1.1, 3.

36. Bardhan 2010, 20.

37. World Bank 1983, "China: Socialist Economic Development, Volume 1," Washington, DC, August, 11, 69, 96 (Table 3.22), 98 (Table 3.23), 99; Adam Tooze, 2021, "Adam Tooze's Chartbook #28: China in 1983, a Miracle Waiting to Happen?" https://adamtooze.substack.com/p/adam-toozes-chartbook-28-china-in; Nicholas Kristof and Sheryl WuDunn, 2009, *Half the Sky,* Kindle edition, Knopf Doubleday Publishing Group, location 229.

38. World Bank 1983, 29.

39. Amartya Sen, 1982, "How Is India Doing?" *New York Review of Books,* December 16.

40. Frank 2001, 294, 432–433 and chapter 9.

41. Centre for Science and Environment, 1982, *State of India's Environment: The First Citizen's Report,* New Delhi, 3, 126; Centre for Science and Environment, 1985, *State of India's Environment: The Second Citizen's Report,* New Delhi, 27, 121.

42. Centre for Science and Environment 1985, 362–364, 367; Jairam Ramesh, *Indira Gandhi: A Life in Nature,* Kindle edition, S&S India, locations 151, 156.

43. *Times of India,* 1985, "Excellent Documentary on Sunday," April 20.

44. See chapter 12; Madhura Swaminathan, 1995, "Aspects of Urban Poverty in Bombay," *Environment and Urbanization* 7: 133, 136; *Times of India,* 1981, "Hut Demolition," August 1; *Times of India,* 1982, "'Slum Demolition Not the Answer to the City's Problems,'" March 27.

45. Hubert W. M. van Wersch, 1992, *The Bombay Textile Strike, 1982–83,* New York, Oxford University Press, 129–130.

46. See chapter 3.

47. See chapter 3; World Bank, 1975, "India: Survey of the Textile Machinery Industry (With a Note on the Indian Cotton Textile Industry)," Report No. 9 76-IN, December, Washington, DC, Annex 1, 16.

48. Praful Bidwai, 1983, "Hard Times: The Imperatives of Modernisation," in Factsheet Collective. *The 10th Month: Bombay's Historic Textile Strike,* Mumbai: Centre for Education and Documentation, 81; Praful Bidwai, 1984, "From Rags to Riches," *Times of India,* March 19.

49. Praful Bidwai, 1983, "Metropolises in Decay: I—Perverse Urban Policies," *Times of India,* April 27; *Times of India,* 1984, "Bombay's Land Mafia," July 16.

50. See chapter 1; van Wersch 1992, chapters 4 and 5, section 5.1; K. C. Zachariah, 1968, *Migrants in Greater Bombay,* Bombay, Asia Publishing House, 337; Kalpana Sharma, 2000, *Rediscovering Dharavi: Stories from Asia's Largest Slum,* Kindle edition, Penguin, location 873; Rajni Bakshi, 1986, *The Long Haul: The Bombay Textile Workers Strike of 1982–83,* Bombay, Build Documentation, 104; R. N. Sharma, 2000, "Politics of Urban Space," *Seminar.* www.india-seminar.com/2000/491/491%20r.n.%20sharma.htm; *Times of India,* 1983, "Law Limits Power of the Police," July 24; Liza Weinstein, 2008, "Mumbai's Development Mafias: Globalization, Organized Crime and Land Development," *International Journal of Urban and Regional Research* 32 (1): 28; Gyan Prakash, 2010, *Mumbai Fables: A History of an Enchanted City,* Princeton, NJ, Princeton University Press, 205–206.

Chapter 14: When the Violence Came Home

1. Nayantara Sahgal, 1982, *Indira Gandhi: Her Road to Power,* New York, Ungar, 53.

2. A. S. Abraham, 1988, "Police Revolt in Gujarat: Makings of an Ominous Trend," *Times of India,* August 1.

3. Arendt, 1985 (1951), 106, 232.

4. Khushwant Singh, 2012 (2004), "Prosperity and Religious Fundamentalism," in *A History of the Sikhs: Volume 2: 1839–2004,* Oxford Scholarship Online, 1, 8, 15; Ayesha Kagal, 1982, "Armed Coup in Golden Temple," *Times of India,* December 19.

5. Singh 2012 (2004), 6; Vandana Shiva, 2016, *The Violence of the Green Revolution,* Kindle edition, University Press of Kentucky, locations 178–179; Surindar Suri, 1982, "Identity Crisis amidst Change: Background of Akali Agitation," *Times of India,* December 23.

6. Singh 2012 (2004), 4, 6; George J. Bryjak, 1985, "The Economics of Assassination: The Punjab Crisis and the Death of Indira Gandhi," *Asian Affairs: An American Review* 12 (1): 29, 38.

7. On Schmitt and Thackeray, see chapter 9; Singh 2012 (2004), 1, 8.

8. Singh 2012 (2004), 12–13.

9. Frank 2001, 478.

10. Richard Weintraub, 1984, "Gandhi and the Sikhs: A Policy Gone Awry," *Washington Post,* November 2; *Times of India,* 1984, "Army Not to Pull Out of Punjab Now: Rajiv," September 16; *Time,* 1984, "Indira Gandhi: Death in a Garden," November 12; P. C. Alexander, 2018 [1991], *My Years with Indira Gandhi,* New Delhi, Vision Books, 147.

11. Amitav Ghosh, 1995, "The Ghosts of Mrs. Gandhi," *The New Yorker,* July 17, 35–41.

12. Frank 2001, 491–493; *Time,* 1984, "Death in a Garden," November 12

13. Ghosh 1995.

14. Hartosh Singh Bal, 2014, "Sins of Commission," *Caravan,* September 30; *Times of India,* 1984, "Rajiv Call for Unity," November 20; William Claiborne, 1984, "Gandhi Sees Conspiracy in Death of His Mother," *International Herald Tribune,* November 20; Manoj Mitta and H. S. Phoolka, 2007, *When a Tree Shook Delhi,* Kindle edition, Roli Books, locations 196, 1123.

15. Bal 2014.

16. Salman Rushdie, 1985, foreword to Tariq Ali, 1985, *The Nehrus and the Gandhis: An Indian Dynasty,* London, Picador, xi.

Chapter 15: A Pilot Flies into Political Headwinds

1. Aarthi Ramachandran, 2012, *Decoding Rahul Gandhi*, Kindle edition, Westland Publishing, locations 26, 28; *Washington Post*, 1980, "Gandhi's Other Son Shies Away from Role in Public Life," August 15.

2. Sanjoy Hazarika, 1989, "Bhopal Payments by Union Carbide Set at $470 Million," *New York Times*, February 15.

3. International Idea, "India," available at: www.idea.int/data-tools/country-view/146/40; John Elliot, "Mr. Gandhi Sets the Pace: Indian Election Called," *Financial Times*, November 14.

4. Mehta 1994, 61; William Stevens, 1984, "Gandhi, Slain, Is Succeeded by Son," *New York Times*, November 1;

5. Tavleen Singh, 2013, *Durbar*, New Delhi, Hatchette, 197, 200; Steven Weisman, 1988, "Gandhi Is Finding Out How Much He Has to Lose," *New York Times*, July 3.

6. Montek Singh Ahluwalia, 2020, *Backstage: The Story behind India's High Growth Years*, New Delhi, Rupa Publications, 73–74; Ved Mehta, 1994, *Rajiv Gandhi and Rama's Kingdom*, New Haven, CT, Yale University Press, 81.

7. International Monetary Fund, 1986, "India: Staff Report for the 1986 Article IV Consultation," SM/86/54, March 6, Washington, DC, 11; Ahluwalia 2020, 79.

8. Robert J. Shiller, 2017, "Narrative Economics," *American Economic Review* 107 (4): 981; Martin Feldstein, 1994, "American Economic Policy in the 1980s: A Personal View," in Martin Feldstein, editor, *American Economic Policy in the 1980s*, Chicago, University of Chicago Press, 1994, Section 1.2, "Tax Policy in the 1980s," 13–14.

9. *Times of India*, 1985, "Firms' Donations to Parties to Be Allowed," March 17; International Monetary Fund 1986; Ahluwalia 2020, 79; Joshi and Little 1994, 180.

10. *Wall Street Journal*, 1985, "Review and Outlook (Editorial): Rajiv Reagan," March 21; *Times of India*, 1985, "Reagan Hails PM's Policies," May 9; *Times of India*, 1985, "U.S. All for United India: Reagan," June 13.

11. Jagdish Bhagwati, 1985, "Is India's Economic Miracle at Hand?" *New York Times*, June 9.

12. Nicholas Kristof, 1985, "Curbs Give Way to Welcome for Multinational Companies," *New York Times*, May 11.

13. *Times of India*, 1985a, "Concession Aimed at Software Export," March 18; *Times of India*, 1985b, "Indo-U.S. Satellite Link to Be Set Up," June 24; Harihar Krishnan, 1985, "Business Today: TI Gains Strategic Presence," United Press International, August 19; John Elliot, 1985, "Showing the Way for Developing

Countries," *Financial Times*, October 4; Marc Beauchamp, 1986, "Planet Computer," *Forbes*, February 24.

14. Sheila Tefft, 1987, "Welcome to Silicon Valley, India-Style," *Journal of Commerce*, May 18.

15. Gangadhar Gadgil, 1985, "The Bulls Have Run Amok," *Times of India*, August 18.

16. Olivier Blanchard, 1987, "Reaganomics," *Economic Policy* 2 (5): 15–56; Austan Goolsbee, Robert E. Hall, and Lawrence F. Katz, 1999, "Evidence on the High-Income Laffer Curve from Six Decades of Tax Reform," *Brookings Papers on Economic Activity* 2: 1–64, 44, 52–53; Annette Alstadsæter, Niels Johannesen, and Gabriel Zucman, 2019, "Tax Evasion and Inequality," *American Economic Review* 109 (6): 2073–2103; Thomas R. Tørsløv, Ludvig S. Wier, and Gabriel Zucman, 2020, "The Missing Profits of Nations," NBER Working Paper No. 24701, June 2018, revised April 2020.

17. Eswaran Sridharan and Milan Vaishnav, 2018, "Political Finance in a Developing Democracy: The Case of India," in Devesh Kapur and Milan Vaishnav, editors, *Costs of Democracy: Political Finance in India*, New York, Oxford University Press, 21; Vaishnav 2017, 97; Navin Chawla, 2019, *Every Vote Counts: The Story of India's Elections*, New Delhi, HarperCollins, 123; Joshi and Little 1994, 180, 226 (Table 9.1).

18. Pranab Bardhan, 1998, *The Political Economy of Development in India*, Oxford, Oxford University Press, 62; Government of India, 1986, *Fourth Central Pay Commission: Report*, New Delhi, July; *Times of India*, 1986, "A Necessary Correction," July 3.

19. Joshi and Little 1994, 168 (Table 6.8), 180–182, 193 (Table 7.5).

20. Joshi and Little 1994, 186; Ahluwalia 2020, 92–94.

21. Anthony Spaeth, 1988, "India's 'Rajiv Revolution' Bogged Down by the Bureaucracy It Tried to Overcome," *Wall Street Journal*, April 12.

22. *Times of India*, 1986, "Barnala Espouses Pepsi's Cause," July 29; John Elliot, 1988, "PepsiCo Clears Indian Hurdles," February 4; Anthony Spaeth and Amal Kumar, 1988, "PepsiCo Accepts Tough Conditions for the Right to Sell in India," *Wall Street Journal*, September 20.

23. Foreign investment data is net inflow (which nets an investor's debits and credits) obtained from the World Bank's World Development Indicators, BX.KLT.DINV.CD.WD; Ahluwalia 2020, 91.

24. Arvind Panagariya, 2004, "Growth and Reforms during 1980s and 1990s," *Economic and Political Weekly* 39 (2): 2581–94; Spaeth 1988; Prem Shankar Jha,

1989, "The Age of Technology: India Dangerously Out of Step," *Times of India,* March 20; International Monetary Fund, 1990, "India—Staff Report for the 1990 Article IV Consultation," SM/90/92, May 16, Washington, DC, 18.

25. Nicholas Rada, 2016, "India's Post-Green-Revolution Agricultural Performance: What Is Driving Growth?" *Agricultural Economics* 47 (3): 341–350, 343 (Table 1); Ahluwalia 2020, 82.

26. Jha 1989; Ahluwalia 2020, 94–97; Daniel Southerland, 1988, "China Plans Export-Led Economy; New Course Could Expand Foreign Investment Opportunities," *Washington Post,* January 24.

27. Peter Passel, 1987, "India as Tortoise, China as Hare: Which Stirring Giant Will Set the Pace for the Third World?" *New York Times,* April 28.

28. Prem Shankar Jha, 1993, *In the Eye of the Cyclone: The Crisis in Indian Democracy,* New Delhi, Viking, 69–70; Steven Weisman, 1987, "Gandhi in Dispute over Hiring of U.S. Detectives," *New York Times,* April 5; McDonald 2010, 111–112, 115.

29. Rajiv Gandhi, "Full Text of Rajiv Gandhi's Famous Speech," available at: www.indiatoday.in/india/story/full-text-of-rajiv-gandhis-famous-1985-speech-152145-2013-01-21.

30. McDonald 2010, 136–137, 140–142.

31. *India Today,* 1986, "Reliance Industries under Siege, Future Seems Peppered with Question Marks," August 15; T. N. Ninan and Prabhu Chawla, 1986, "There Was No Breach of Faith with Reliance: Singh," *India Today,* August 15.

32. Jha 1993, 71–72; Steven R. Weisman, 1985, "India Cracks Down on Its Huge 'Black Economy.'" *International Herald Tribune,* December 26.

33. Jha 1993, 71–72; *The Economist,* 1987, "India's Economy," January 31.

34. McDonald 2010, 179–182, 188–191; Matt Miller, 1987, "One of India's Leading Firms Is Beset by Investigations—Reliance Industries Rose Rapidly with the Help of Government Favors," *Wall Street Journal,* July 3; Moses Manoharan, 1989, "Indian Tycoon with Common Touch Turns to World Market," *Reuters News,* July 6; David Housego, 1989, "Survey of Bombay (I): A Wayward Trendsetter," *Financial Times,* September 11.

35. Veena Das, 2015, "Corruption and the Possibility of Life," *Contributions to Indian Sociology* 49 (3): 324–328.

36. Steven Weisman, 1987, "Aide's Resignation Creates Political Crisis for Gandhi," *New York Times,* April 14; Inder Malhotra, 1987, "Political Commentary: After the Bofors Gun-Fire," *Times of India,* April 23; David Housego, 1989, "The Uncertain Road Ahead: Controversies surrounding the Forthcoming Indian Elections," *Financial Times,* October 27.

37. Mehta 1994, 66–67; Tavleen Singh 2013, 215.

38. Barbara Crossette, 1988, "A Flower of North India, the Punjab, Slowly Dies," *New York Times,* October 25.

39. Khushwant Singh, 2004, *History of the Sikhs: Volume 2,* Chapter 23; Steven Weisman, 1987, "Gandhi Bolsters Forces in Punjab," *New York Times,* May 13.

40. Steven Weisman, 1985, "Gandhi Signs Pact to End Conflict on Assam Settlers," *International Herald Tribune,* August 16; Steven Weisman, 1985, "Assam Moslems Haunted by Fear of New Violence," *International Herald Tribune,* December 7–8; Sanjoy Hazarika, 1987, "India's Assam State Demanding Ban on Migration," *New York Times,* September 13; Guha 2008 (2007), 572

Chapter 16: Rajiv Unleashes the Gale Force of Hindu Nationalism

1. See chapters 9 and 10; Huntington 2006 (1968), 3–5, 359.

2. Sanjoy Hazarika, 1988a, "Sikhs Surrender to Troops at Temple: The Blockade Is Seen as a Victory for Gandhi," *New York Times,* May 19; Sanjoy Hazarika, 1988b, "45 Killed and 100 Wounded in Attacks in Punjab," *New York Times,* May 21; Sanjoy Hazarika, 1988c, "India Sending More Troops to Punjab as Toll Rises," *New York Times,* May 22; Sanjoy Hazarika, 1988d, "Thousands of Hindu Workers Flee Punjab as Sikhs Step Up Violence," *New York Times,* May 24; *New York Times,* 1988, "Sikh Terrorists Kill 10 Men after Pulling Them off a Bus," November 4.

3. Moses Manoharan, 1987, "Demonstrators, Police, Converge on Raided Newspaper Office," *Reuters News,* September 1; Richard Weintraub, 1987, "Authorities Raid Offices of Major Paper in India," *Washington Post,* September 2; Derek Brown, 1988, "Gandhi Drops Defamation Bill," *Sydney Morning Herald,* September 24.

4. Gaurav Datt, Martin Ravallion, Rinku Murgai, 2020, "Poverty and Growth in India over Six Decades," *American Journal of Agricultural Economics* 102 (1): 4–27, Figure 1, 7; Arendt 1985 (1951), 232.

5. Stanford Encyclopedia of Philosophy, "Carl Schmitt," available at: https://plato.stanford.edu/entries/schmitt/; Schmitt 2007 (1927), 67; Tracy Strong, 2007, "Foreword: Dimensions of the New Debate around Carl Schmitt," in Schmitt 2007 (1927), xx–xxi.

6. Strong 2007, xxi–xxii; Arendt 1985 (1951), 460.

7. The details in this passage are from Vaibhav Purandare, 2019, *Savarkar: The True Story of the Father of Hindutva,* New Delhi, Juggernaut Books, 22, 28, 31, 44–47, 57–60, 76, 163–165.

8. Vinayak Damodar Savarkar, 2009 (1923), *Hindutva: Who Is a Hindu?* New Delhi, Hindi Sahitya Sadan, 11–12, 45–6, 84, 96.

9. Purandare 2019, 26.

10. Savarkar 2009 (1923), 43, 141.

11. Walter Andersen and Sridhar Damle, 2019 (1987), *The Brotherhood in Saffron: The Rashtriya Swayamsevak Sangh and Hindu Revivalism,* New Delhi, Penguin Random House India, xiii, xvii–xviii, 24–26, 29–31; Christophe Jaffrelot, 1996, *The Hindu Nationalist Movement and Indian Politics, 1925 to the 1990s,* London, C. Hurst and Co., 34–36.

12. Andersen and Damle 2019, 34–46; Jaffrelot 1996, 32–35.

13. *New York Times,* 1966, "V. D. Savarkar Is Dead at 83; A Nationalist Leader," February 27.

14. *The Times,* 1966, "Mr. V. D. Savarkar," February 28.

15. *Times of India,* 1980a, "Vajpayee Chief of Bharatiya Janata Party," April 7; *Times of India,* 1980b, "B.J.P. Will Never Sever RSS Link," April 21.

16. *Times of India,* 1983a, "VHP Yagna Launched," November 15; Jaffrelot 1996, 360–362.

17. *Times of India,* 1983b, "VHP Chariots Start Journey," November 16; *Times of India,* 1983c, "Huge Delhi Crowds Hail Yatra," November 19; *Times of India,* 1983d, "Yatra Draws Big Crowds in City," December 8; *India Today,* 1983, "VHP-Organised Ekatmata Yagna to Roll across India," November 30.

18. Jaffrelot 1996, 363; Thomas Blom Hansen, 1999, *The Saffron Wave,* Princeton, NJ, Princeton University Press, 155; Prem Shankar Jha, 1993, *In the Eye of the Cyclone,* New Delhi, Penguin Books, 187.

19. Jaffrelot 1996, 363; S. P. Udayakumar, 1997, "Historicizing Myth and Mythologizing History," *Social Scientist* 25 (7/8): 13; *India Today,* 1984, "Ram Janmbhumi: Ayodhya Becomes Rallying Point for Start of Yet Another Communal Skirmish," October 31.

20. Jaffrelot 1996, 334–335; Inder Malhotra, 2014, "Rear View: The Era of the Politics of Appeasement," *Indian Express,* December 8.

21. *Times of India,* 1986, "Arif Quits over "Talaaq" Bill," February 27; Francine Frankel, 2005, *India's Political Economy, 1947–2004,* second edition, New Delhi: Oxford University Press, 684; Wajahat Habibullah, 2020, *My Years with Rajiv: Triumph and Tragedy,* Kindle edition, Westland Publications, location 104; Krishna Pokharel and Paul Beckett, 2012, "WSJ BLOG/India Real Time: Ayodhya, the Battle for India's Soul: Chapter Three," *Dow Jones Global Equities News,* December 5.

22. Malhotra 2014; Udayakumar 1997, 14.

23. Bhaskar Ghosh, 2005, *Doordarshan Days,* New Delhi, Penguin Books, 38.

24. Soutik Biswas, 2011, "Ramayana: An 'Epic' Controversy," BBC News, October 19; William Darlymple, 2008, "An Indian Life Is Here," *Guardian,* August 22; Associated Press, "Televised Hindu Epic Mesmerizes India," January 27; Rahul Verma, 2019, "The TV Show That Transformed Hinduism," BBC Culture, October 22.

25. Arvind Rajagopal, 2001, *Politics after Television: Religious Nationalism and the Reshaping of the Indian Public,* Cambridge, Cambridge University Press, 77, 84.

26. Pankaj Mishra, 2013 (1995), *Butter Chicken in Ludhiana: Travels in Small Town India,* Gurgaon, India, Penguin, 80; Anuradha Kapur, 1991, "Militant Images of a Tranquil God," *Times of India,* January 10.

27. M. J. Akbar, 1988, *Riot after Riot: Report on Caste and Communal Violence in India,* New Delhi, Penguin Books, 126, 151, 168; Ajay Kumar, 1987, "Factors behind December riots," *Times of India,* December 9; Seema Sirohi, 1987, "Anatomy of a Riot: Hindu-Moslem Incident Explodes into Bloodbath," Associated Press, June 5; Rajendra Bajpai, 1987, "Amnesty Accuses Indian Police of Killing Moslems," *Reuters News,* November 19; Manira Chaudhury, 1987, "30 Years after UP's Hashimpura Massacre, Survivors Recount Night of 'Bloodbath,' Rue Lack of Justice," *Hindustan Times,* May 22.

28. Thomas Blom Hansen, 2001, *Wages of Violence,* Princeton, NJ, Princeton University Press, 74, 76–77, 83; Jayant Lele, 1995, "Saffronisation of Shiv Sena: Political Economy of City, State, and Nation," *Economic and Political Weekly* 30 (25): 1526.

29. *Times of India,* 1989, "Return to the Slot," June 13.

30. David Housego, 1989a, "Mosque May Become Storm Centre of Election: A Communal Flare-Up Is Likely to Favour the Congress Party," *Financial Times,* October 19; David Housego, 1989b, "Gandhi Yields to Hindu Militants in Dispute over Temple," *Financial Times,* November 10; Habibullah 2020, 125; Frankel 2005, 685.

31. Chandan Mitra, 1989, "Anti-Rajiv Backlash: The Price of Modernism," *Times of India,* November 17; *Times of India,* 1989, "Arson Spree in Bhagalpur," November 15.

Chapter 17: An All-Too-Brief Moment of Sanity

1. Putnam 2020, 303–306.

2. Mishra 2013 (1995), xii–xvii.

3. Mishra 2013 (1995), 88–91,

4. Mishra 2013 (1995), 243–250.

5. Francine Frankel, 2005, *India's Political Economy, 1947–2004,"* second edition, New Delhi, Oxford University Press, 686–687; Albert Hirschman and Michael Rothschild, 1973, "The Changing Tolerance for Income Inequality in the Course of Economic Development: With a Mathematical Appendix," *Quarterly Journal of Economics* 87 (4): 545.

6. Barbara Crossette, 1989, "Ayodhya Journal; Among Marigolds, a Holy Place and Unholy Fury," *New York Times,* October 27; Francine Frankel, 2005, *India's Political Economy, 1947–2004,* 2nd edition, New Delhi, Oxford University Press, 686–687; Sanjoy Hazarika, 1989, "Shots Miss India's Opposition Leader," *New York Times,* November 25.

7. John Pomfret, 1989, "New Balloting Order in Gandhi's District; Vote Fraud Cited," Associated Press; *Times of India,* 1989, "Poll Perversion," November 25.

8. Robert Putnam, 2020, *The Upswing: How America Came Together a Century Ago and How We Can Do It Again,* Kindle edition, Simon & Schuster, locations 4, 6, 41–48.

9. *Times of India,* 1990, "Open Industry to Competition," June 19; World Bank, 1990, "India: Trends, Issues, and Options," Report No. 8360-IN, May 1, Washington, DC, ii, 33–34; World Bank, 1991, "Gender and Poverty in India: Issues and Opportunities concerning Women in the Indian Economy," Report No. 8072-IN, June 14, Washington, DC.

10. Barbara Crossette, 1990, "A Gandhi Crusades against a Befouled India," *New York Times,* June 7; *The Times,* 1990, "Mrs. Maneka Gandhi Starts Green Campaign to Clean Up Delhi," May 11; World Resources Institute, 1990, *World Resources 1990–91: A Guide to the Global Environment,* Oxford, Oxford University Press, 3 (Figure 1.4).

11. See chapter 15; macro data for 1990 from the International Monetary Fund's *World Economic Outlook* database; International Monetary Fund, 1990, "India: Staff Report for the 1990 Article IV Consultation," SM/90/92, Washington, DC, May 16, 4.

12. Bill Tarrant, 1989, "New Indian Prime Minister Pledges More Help for Poor," December 3; David Housego, 1989, "Man in the News: Time of Trial for a Shy Man's Political Skills," *Financial Times,* December 2; International Monetary Fund, 1991, "India: Article IV Consultation and Request for Stand-By Arrangement," EBS/91/176, Washington, DC, October 9, 5; World Bank, 1991, "India: 1991 Country Economic Memorandum," Report No. 9412-IN, August 23, Washington, DC, ii, 13, 17, 43.

13. International Monetary Fund, 1992, "India—Staff Report for the 1992 Article IV Consultation and Second Review under Stand-By Arrangement," EBS/92/175, November 6, Washington, DC, 4a (Chart 1).

14. Christophe Jaffrelot, 2003, *India's Silent Revolution: The Rise of the Lower Castes in North India,* New York, Columbia University Press, 337; see also chapter 12; *Times of India,* 1981, "Backward Class Report on, December 31," December 23; Ashwini Deshpande, 2013, *Affirmative Action in India,* New Delhi, Oxford University Press, 67, 73; Deshpande 2013, 75.

15. Sanjay Ruparelia, 2015, *Divided We Govern: Coalition Politics in Modern India,* New Delhi, Oxford University Press, chapters 5 and 6.

16. Jaffrelot 2003, 347; *Times of India* news reports, August 1990; Paul Flather, 1990, "When Caste Becomes a Burning Issue," *The Times Higher Education Supplement,* November 9.

17. *Times of India,* 1990a, "... and Accent on Harmony," September 25; *Times of India,* 1990b, "Keep Out, BJP, Tells Police," September 25; Prasun Sonwalkar, 1990, "Can Advani Ape Sardar?" *Times of India,* September 27.

18. Violette Galonnier, 2013, "Hindu-Muslim Riots in India II (1986–2011). www.sciencespo.fr/mass-violence-war-massacre-resistance/en/document/hindu-muslim-communal-riots-india-ii-1986-2011.html.

19. Reuters, 1990, "India Ratings Lowered: Cut Will Mean Costlier Credit," *International Herald Tribune,* October 5; World Bank 1991, 13, 43; Tim McGirk, 1990a, "India Urged to Seek Funds from IMF," *The Independent,* October 14.

20. Tim McGirk, 1990b, "Prime Minister Resigns amid Shouts and Fisticuffs," *The Independent,* November 8; Barbara Crossette, 1990a, "India's Cabinet Falls as Premier Loses Confidence Vote by 142–346," *New York Times,* November 8; Barbara Crossette, 1990b, "A Question Unanswered: Where Is India Headed?" *New York Times,* November 11.

21. International Monetary Fund, 1991, "India—Use of Fund Resources; Request for Stand-By Arrangement and for a Purchase under the Compensatory and Contingency Financing Facility," EBS/91/4, January 7, Washington, DC, 3–4, 25.

22. David Housego, 1991, "A Passage to Paralysis," *Financial Times,* February 22; Associated Press, 1991, "Gandhi Asks for Elections," March 9.

23. Barbara Crossette, 1991, "Sonia Declines Presidency of Party," *New York Times,* May 23.

24. International Monetary Fund, 1991, "India: Staff Report for the 1991 Article IV Consultation and Request for Stand-By Arrangement," EBS/91/176, Washington, DC, October 9, 18; and chapters 4 and 5.

25. Montek Singh Ahluwalia, 2020, *Backstage: The Story behind India's High Growth Years,* New Delhi, Rupa Publications, 130; Agence France-Presse, 1991, "India's Finance Minister Denies IMF Pressure to Devalue Rupee," July 1; I. G. Patel, 2002, *Glimpses of Indian Economic Policy: An Insider's View,* New Delhi, Oxford University Press, 170–171.

26. Ahluwalia 2020, 131.

27. Agence France-Presse, 1991b, "Rupee Cut Further; Devaluation Not at IMF Behest, Indian Premier Says," July 3; Ahluwalia 2020, 132.

28. See chapter 5; I. G. Patel, 1990, "Economic Policy: II Indian Scene," *Economic Times,* April 26; Bimal Jalan, 1991, "India's Economic Crisis: The Way Ahead," New Delhi, Oxford University Press, 222–223; Ahluwalia 2020, 136.

29. *Times of India,* 1991, "Gold Deposited Not Sold, Says RBI," July 9; K. K. Sharma and R. C. Murthy, 1991, "India Sends 25 Tonnes of Gold to London as Loan Security," *Financial Times,* July 9.

30. Vinay Sitapati, 2018, *The Man Who Remade India: A Biography of P. V. Narasimha Rao,* Kindle edition, Oxford University Press, locations 129–130.

31. Manmohan Singh, 1991, "Budget 1991–92 Speech of Shri Manmohan Singh," July 24, www.indiabudget.gov.in/doc/bspeech/bs199192.pdf.

32. International Monetary Fund 1991, 32–35; Mishra 2013 (1995), 126.

33. Agence France-Presse, 1992, "Eco News Indian Stock Prices Sky-Rocket in Unprecedented Bull Rampage," March 24; David Housego and R. C. Murthy, 1992, "India Gets a Big Bout of Asian Stock Market Fever," *Financial Times,* March 6.

34. A. Banerjee, 1992, "The Many Joys of Insider Trading," *Times of India,* April 12.

35. Sucheta Dalal and R. Srinivasan, 1992, "SBI Asks Broker to Square Up," *Times of India,* April 23.

36. K.B.L. Mathur, 2002, "Public Sector Banks: Should They Be Privatized?" *Economic and Political Weekly* 37 (23): 2245–2256, Table 1.

37. Joshi and Little 1996, 119–121; D. N. Ghosh, 2015, *No Regret,* New Delhi, Rupa Publications, 183–184; Rajendra Bajpai, 1992, "Details of US$1 billion Bombay Scam Unveiled," *Business Times Singapore,* June 4; Suman Dubey, 1992, "Bank Shortfalls Mount in Probe of India Scandal—Criminal Complaint Expected to Be Filed in Securities Affair," *Asian Wall Street Journal,* May 26; Debashis Basu and Sucheta Dalal, 2014 (1993), *Scam: From Harshad Mehta to Ketan Parekh,* Kindle edition, Kensource Information Services, location 17.

38. Mishra 2013 (1995), 126.

39. Singh 2020, 157; Richard Waters and R. C. Murthy, 1992, "Top Banker Casualty of Share Scandal," *Financial Times,* June 4; Agence France-Presse, 1993,

"Managing Director of Top Indian Bank Sacked," June 25; Suman Dubey, 1993, "India's Political, Economic Stability Faces Threat from Payoff Allegations," *Wall Street Journal*, June 17.

40. R. C. Mody, 1992, "Stocks Scandal: Where the RBI Went Wrong," *Economic Times*, June 17; Bimal Jalan, editor, 2013, *The Reserve Bank of India, Volume 4, 1981–1997*, Bombay, Reserve Bank of India, 846.

41. Vijay Joshi and Ian Little, 1996, *India's Economic Reforms 1991–2001*, Oxford, Oxford University Press, 149; Ahluwalia 2020, 161.

42. Madhav Reddy, 1993, "Coke Returns to India in Launch near Taj Mahal," *Reuters News*, October 25.

43. *Reuters News*, 1994, "India Allows Morgan Stanley to Start Investment Bank," May 30; N. Vidyasagar, 2001, "3 Indians in Fortune-50 List of Powerful Women," *Times of India*, October 7; per capita income in current U.S. dollars from https://data.worldbank.org/indicator/NY.GDP.PCAP.CD?locations=IN.

44. Dani Rodrik, 1992, "The Limits of Trade Policy Reform in Developing Countries," *Journal of Economic Perspectives* (Winter): 90, 102; Paul Krugman, 1995, "Dutch Tulips and Emerging Markets," *Foreign Affairs* 74:(4): 28–44.

45. World Bank 1992, 25, 84. World Bank 1991, viii; World Bank, 1996a, "China: Social Sector Expenditure Review," Report No. 17348 CHA, February, Washington, DC, i; World Bank, 1996b, "India Country Economic Memorandum—Five Years of Stabilization and Reform: The Challenges Ahead," Report No. 15882-IN, August 8, Washington, DC, iv; World Bank 1996c, "India: Primary Education Achievement and Challenges," Report No. 15756-IN, September 1, Washington DC, xi.

46. World Bank 1996b, xvii; Mishra 2013 (1995), 143, 189–190.

47. Madhav Gadgil and Ramachandra Guha, 1995, *Ecology and Equity: The Use and Abuse of Nature in Contemporary India*, New York, Routledge, 68–96.

48. Shiraz Sidhva, 1996, "Court Crackdown on Dubious Campaign Funds," *Financial Times*, April 6; Vinay Sitapati, 2020, *Jugalbandi: The BJP before Modi*, Penguin, Gurgaon (India), 193.

Chapter 18: The Promise Has a Dark Underbelly

1. Thomas Blom Hansen, 2001, *Wages of Violence: Naming and Identity in Postcolonial Bombay*, Princeton, NJ, Princeton University Press, 227–235.

2. *Organiser*, 1988, "Angry Hindu! Yes, Why Not?," February 14.

3. I have used the numbers in the International Monetary Fund's *World Economic Outlook* database. The IMF regularly updates these numbers, which

therefore differ somewhat from those presented at the time by the IMF itself and by the Government of India.

4. Edward Gargan, 1992, "A Religious Zeal Turns into Abuse," *New York Times*, December 7; Christophe Jaffrelot, 1996, *The Hindu Nationalist Movement and Indian Politics, 1925 to the 1990s: Strategies of Identity-Building, Implantation, and Mobilisation*, London, Hurst and Company, 455.

5. *Reuters News*, 1992, "Death Toll Crosses 200 in Indian Riots," December 7.

6. Clarence Fernandez and Naresh Fernandes, 1993, "The Winter of Discontent," in Dileep Padgaonkar, editor, *When Bombay Burned; Reportage and Comments on the Riots and Blasts from the Times of India*, New Delhi, UBS Publishers' Distributors Ltd., 13–14.

7. Edward Miguel and Shanker Satyanath, 2011, "Re-examining Economic Shocks and Civil Conflict," *American Economic Journal: Applied Economics* 3 (October): 228–232; Ramesh Menon and Raj Chengappa, 1993, "Explosive Factors Like Unemployment and Ghettos Turn Cities into Communal Tinder-Boxes," *India Today*, January 31; Darryl D'Monte, 1993, "What Bombay Teaches Us," in Dileep Padgaonkar, editor, 296.

8. Vaibhav Purandare, 2012, *Bal Thackeray and the Rise of Shiv Sena*, Kindle edition, Roli Books, location 3154.

9. Clarence Fernandez and Naresh Fernandes, 1993, "A City at War with Itself," in Dileep Padgaonkar, editor, 13–14; Rajdeep Sardesai, 1993, "The Great Betrayal," in Dileep Padgaonkar, editor, 199; Jaffrelot 1996, 458–460; Kalpana Sharma, 1995, "Chronicle of a Riot Foretold," in Sujata Patel and Alice Thorner, editors, *Bombay: Metaphor for Modern India*, Bombay, Oxford University Press, 276–282; Hansen 2001, 125–126; Prakash 2010, 229–300.

10. William Darlymple, 1993, "Major Will Feel the Heat in Bombay," *Sunday Telegraph*, January 24.

11. See chapter 7; Sharma 1995, 274.

12. Jan Nijman, 2000, "Mumbai's Real Estate Market in the 1990s: Deregulation, Global Money, and Casino Capitalism," *Economic and Political Weekly*, February 12–16, 35 (7): 575–582; R. Sridhar, 1994, "Why the Price Rise?" *Times of India*, October 29; Molly Moore, 1995, "As Bombay Real Estate Soars, Yuppies Go Slumming," *International Herald Tribune*, February 6; Prakash 2010, 295–298.

13. Gyan Prakash, 2010, *Mumbai Fables: A History of an Enchanted City*, Princeton, NJ, Princeton University Press, 300–301; Sharma 1995, 285.

14. Curtis Milhaupt and Mark West, 2000, "The Dark Side of Private Ordering: An Institutional and Empirical Analysis of Organized Crime," *University of Chicago*

Law Review 67 (1): 41–98; Sharma 1995, 274; Hansen 2001, 125; Zaidi, S. Hussain, 2014, *Byculla to Bangkok,* Noida, India: Harper Collins, 90.

15. Sharma 1995, 274; Vaishnav 2017, xi, 77; Navin Chawla, 2019, *Every Vote Counts: The Story of India's Elections,* New Delhi, HarperCollins, 136–137; Sardesai 1993, 185.

16. "Vohra Committee Report," Ministry of Home Affairs, India, https://adrindia.org/sites/default/files/VOHRA%20COMMITTEE%20REPORT_0.pdf.

17. M. L. Sharma, 1999, "Organized Crime in India: Problems and Perspectives," *Resource Material Series* No. 54, The United Nations Asia and Far East Institute for the Prevention of Crime and the Treatment of Offenders (UNAFEI), Tokyo; Nicholas Martin and Lucia Michelutti, 2017, "Protection Rackets and Party Machines," *Asian Journal of Social Science* 45 (6): 704; Sam Asher and Paul Novosad, 2020, "Digging for Dirt: Rent-Seeking among Elected Politicians in India's Mineral Belt," voxdev.org, November 16; *Business Standard,* 1997, "Cong Flays Installation of Kalyan as CM," September 22; *India Today,* 1997a, "Uttar Pradesh: Stooping to Conquer," November 10.

18. *India Today,* 1997b, "Rule of Flaw," November 24.

19. M. L. Sharma 1999; Sunil Sethi, 1998, "Criminal Virus in Body Politic," *Times of India,* February 13; Agence France-Presse, 1997, "Indian Minister Wants Parties to Keep Criminals out of Elections," August 31; Agence France-Presse, 1998, "Hindu Nationalist Leader among Indian 'Blacklisted' Candidates," February 12; Nicholas Martin and Lucia Michelutti, 2017, "Protection Rackets and Party Machines," *Asian Journal of Social Science* 45 (6): 704; Sam Asher and Paul Novosad, 2020, "Digging for Dirt: Rent-Seeking among Elected Politicians in India's Mineral Belt," voxdev.org, November 16.

20. Nishith Prakash, Marc Rockmore, and Yogesh Uppal, 2019, "Do Criminally Accused Politicians Affect Economic Outcomes? Evidence from India," *Journal of Development Economics* 141: 102370; Nishith Prakash, Soham Sahoo, Deepak Saraswat, and Reetika Sindhi, 2022, "When Criminality Begets Crime: The Role of Elected Politicians in India," *IZA DP 15259*, April.

21. Melissa Dell, Benjamin Feigenberg, and Kensuke Teshima, 2019, "The Violent Consequences of Trade-Induced Worker Displacement in Mexico," *American Economic Review: Insights* 1 (1): 43–58; Maria Micaela Sviatschi, 2019, "Making a *Narco*: Childhood Exposure to Illegal Labor Markets and Criminal Life Paths," Princeton University, February 18, www.micaelasviatschi.com/wp-content/uploads/2019/02/jmp37.pdf.

22. Coll 1993; Khushwant Singh, 1993, "India, the Hindu State," *New York Times,* August 3, 7.

23. *Hindustan Times,* 1999, "Quartet Was at Party for Long," May 6.

24. Surinder Awasthi, 1999, "Venod Sharma Was in Line for Cong Ticket," *Times of India,* May 5; *Times of India,* 2006, "No One Killed Jessica," February 22, https://timesofindia.indiatimes.com/city/delhi/no-one-killed-jessica/articleshow/1423393.cms.

25. Seema Jayachandran, 2017, "Fertility Decline and Missing Women," *American Economic Journal: Applied Economics* 9 (1): 120; Milan Vaishnav, 2017, *When Crime Pays,* New Haven, CT, Yale University Press, 65, 90, 109.

26. Sen 1982; Nishith Prakash and Krishna Chaitanya Vadlamannati, 2019, "Girls for Sale? Child Sex Ratio and Girl Trafficking in India," *Feminist Economics* 25 (4): 267–308; Scott South, Katherine Trent, and Sunita Bose, 2014, "Skewed Sex Ratios and Criminal Victimization in India," *Demography* 51: 1019–1040; Lena Edlund, Hongbin Li, Junjian Yi, and Junsen Zhang, 2013, "Sex Ratios and Crime: Evidence from China," *Review of Economics and Statistics* 95 (5): 1520–1534; Joseph Sabia, Angela Dills, and Jeffrey DeSimone, 2013, "Sexual Violence against Women and Labor Market Outcomes," *American Economic Review* 103 (3): 274–278; Zahra Siddique, 2018, "Violence and Female Labor Supply," IZA Discussion Paper No. 11874.

27. Rebecca Menes, 2006, "Limiting the Reach of the Grabbing Hand: Graft and Growth in American Cities, 1880 to 1930," in Edward L. Glaeser and Claudia Goldin, editors, *Corruption and Reform: Lessons from America's Economic History,* Chicago, University of Chicago Press, 63–64, 81–82, 87, 90; Edward L. Glaeser and Claudia Goldin, 2006, "Introduction," In Glaeser and Goldin, editors, 7.

28. Menes 2006, 63.

29. Robert Gordon, 2016, *The Rise and Fall of American Growth: The U.S. Standard of Living since the Civil War,* Princeton, NJ, Princeton University Press, 1–18, 535–538, 562–565; Menes 2006, 67; Glaeser and Goldin 2006, 19–20.

30. Hamish McDonald, *Ambani and Sons,* New Delhi, Roli Books, 234, 243; *Strait Times,* 1993, "Colonel Sanders to Head for India, More Foreign Brands to Follow," November 20.

31. Purandare 2014, locations 3286, 3862, 3836, 3898, 3900, 3913, 3926; *Times of India,* 1995, "City Renamed as Mumbai," June 29.

32. Government of India, 2000, *Economic Survey,* New Delhi, 192 and Tables 3.1–3.2.

33. John Zubrzycki, 1996, "India's Corruption Scandal Casts a Shadow Over Elections," *Christian Science Monitor,* March 26; *Reuters News,* 1994, "Details of Charges against Fired Ministers," December 23; Miriam Jordan, 1996, "India's Reforms Excite Growth, Not Voters," *Wall Street Journal,* April 26.

34. Agence France-Presse, 1997, "Indian Poll Panel Wants Criminals out of Politics," August 25; Agence France-Presse, 1998, "Hindu Nationalist Leader among Indian 'Blacklisted' Candidates," February 12.

35. International Monetary Fund, 1997, "India—Staff Report for the 1997 Article IV Consultation," June 11, Washington, DC, 11–14; Tony Lawrence, 1996, "Untitled," Agence France-Presse, October 13.

36. *Hindustan Times,* 1998, "Discordant Voices," February 2; Neena Vyas, 1999, "BJP Seeks to Reap Twin Advantage," *The Hindu,* August 25.

37. Agence France-Presse, 1999, "No Place for Criminals in Indian Parliament: Election Commissioner," September 28; Vidya Subrahmaniam, 1995, "Why the BJP Cannot Have a Secular Face," *Times of India,* April 18.

Chapter 19: No, India Does Not Shine

1. Sandhya Soman, 2016. "How a Thirst for a Good Coffee Has Transformed Bengaluru's Cafes," *Times of India,* July 12; Apoorva Puranik, 2019, "A Lot Still Happening over Coffee: How VG Siddhartha's Café Coffee Day Transformed the Simple Brew into a Lifestyle," *Economic Times,* August 3; *Financial Times,* 1997, "Bargain Brains Are a High-Power Force," June 24.

2. *Times of India,* 1998, "Cybernetic Indulgences," September 20.

3. Miriam Jordan, 1996, "Irony in India: Will Voters Bite the Hand That Fed Them?" *Wall Street Journal,* May 6.

4. Ahluwalia 2020, 198–200; Agence France-Presse, 1998, "Indian PM Defends Bold Nuclear Tests," December 31.

5. *Financial Times,* 1999, "Asia-Pacific: Full-Scale War Stalks Kashmir's Line of Control," June 17; Amir Zia, 1999, "Clinton Urges Pakistan to Withdraw Guerrilla Forces from Kashmir," Associated Press, June 16; Narayanan Madhavan, 1999, "WRAP-UP: India Takes Kashmir Height, Gets G8 Support," *Reuters News,* June 20.

6. Amit Baishya, 2016, "What Do We Know… . What Have We Learnt?" *South Asian Review* 37 (3): 113.

7. Mary Daly and Robert Valletta, 2004, "Performance of Urban Information Technology Centers: The Boom, the Bust, and the Future," *Federal Reserve Board of San Francisco Economic Review,* April, 1.

8. Associated Press Newswires, "First Indian-Registered Direct Listing on a U.S. Market," March 11; Saritha Rai, 2004, "Infosys Sales Show the Power of Outsourcing," *International Herald Tribune,* April 14; *Business Standard,* 1999, "Options Flourish at Infosys," March 11.

9. Agence France-Presse, 1999, "Indian Software Firms Digging Y2K Goldmine," February 14; Abhijit Banerjee and Esther Duflo, 2000, "Reputation Effects and the Limits of Contracting: A Study of the Indian Software Industry," *Quarterly Journal of Economics,* August, 989–1017.

10. *The Economist,* 1996, "Software in India: Bangalore Bytes," March 23; *Financial Times* 1997.

11. *The Economist,* 1999, "Booting up Andhra Pradesh," September 11; *Business Line,* 1999, "Inviting Investments," January 24; *The Hindu,* 1999, "A Tale of Three Cities," January 10.

12. *Business Times Singapore,* 2000, "East Asia Should Tap India's Software Boom," January 31; Jane Perez, 2000, "Clinton Lauds Technology as Key to India's Economy," *New York Times,* March 25; Charles Babington, 2000, "Clinton Urges Indian High-Tech Leaders to Help Poor," *Washington Post,* March 25.

13. Sadananda Dhume and Pramit Mitra, 1999, "Indian Service Sector as Engine for Econ Growth," *Dow Jones International News,* August 25; Mark Landler, 2001, "Hi, I'm in Bangalore (But I Can't Say So)," *New York Times,* March 21.

14. Reserve Bank of India, "Handbook of Statistics on Indian Economy" (hereafter Reserve Bank Handbook), www.rbi.org.in/scripts/PublicationsView.aspx?id=7704.

15. Ahluwalia 2020, 214–216.

16. Employment in the IT sector from Ministry of Electronics and Information Technology, "Software and Services Sector," available at: www.meity.gov.in/content/software-and-services-sector; national labor force data from Ghose 2019, 6, Table 3.1, 44; see also T. S. Papola and Partha Pratim Sahu, 2012, "Growth and Structure of Employment in India: Long-Term and Post-Reform Performance and Emerging Challenge," Institute for Studies in Industrial Development, Delhi, March.

17. Hamish McDonald, 1993, "India—Punjab Pacified: Terrorism Wanes but Police Methods Come under Fire," *Far Eastern Economic Review,* April 1.

18. International Monetary Fund, 1998, "India—Staff Report for the 1998 Article IV Consultation," SM/98/197, July 29, Washington, DC, 6, 10; Karen Elliott House, 1995, "Two Asian Giants Growing Apart," *Wall Street Journal,* February 24; B. Raman, 1997, "Race to the New Millennium," *Business Line* (*The Hindu*), April 8.

19. International Monetary Fund 1998, 8, 10.

20. Ahluwalia 2020, chapters 9 and 10; David Gardner, 2000a, "Indian Infrastructure: Populist Polices Undermine New Investment," *Financial Times,* March 29.

21. *Business Line,* 1999, "Integrated Highway Project Gets off the Mark," January 2; Shefali Rekhi, 1999, "Roads: Work in Progress," *India Today,* January 11.

22. David Gardner, 2000b, "Sell-offs to Favour Indian Investors," *Financial Times,* August 22.

23. Hugo Restall, 2001, "Examining Asia: Press Ahead with Privatization," *Asian Wall Street Journal,* July 11; Agence France-Presse, 2000a, "India to Sell Stakes in Oil Firm, Trading Companies," October 6; Agence France-Presse, 2000b, "Indian Cabinet Sets in Motion Privatization Plan for Leading Carmaker," November 18; *Business Today,* 2001, "Divestment's Daring Duo," December 9; P. Manoj, 2018, "Golden Period of Privatisation," *Business Line* (*The Hindu*), August 17.

24. International Monetary Fund, 2004, "India—Staff Report for the 2004 Article IV Consultation," SM/04/431, December 23, Washington, DC, 3.

25. Barry Bosworth and Susan Collins, 2008, "Accounting for Growth: Comparing China and India," *Journal of Economic Perspectives* 22 (2): 45–66, Table 3, 54; see also chapter 3.

26. Shalini Singh, 2001, "Mill to Mall—Phoenix Comes of Age," *Economic Times,* November 14; Neha Deewan, 2007, "Check Out the Most Expensive Malls in the Country," *Economic Times,* December 3.

27. Jonathan Lehne, Jacob Shapiro, and Oliver Vanden Eynde, 2018, "Building Connections: Political Corruption and Road Construction," *Journal of Development Economics* 131: 62–78.

28. Casey Ichniowski and Anne Preston, 1989, "The Persistence of Organized Crime in New York City Construction: An Economic Perspective," *ILR Review* 42 (4): 549–565; Giuseppe De Feo and Giacomo Davide De Luca, 2017, "Mafia in the Ballot Box," *American Economic Journal: Economic Policy* 9 (3): 134–167; David Roos, "Sand Is in Such High Demand, People Are Stealing Tons of It," available at: https://science.howstuffworks.com/environmental/conservation/issues/sand-is-such-high-demand-people-are-stealing-tons-it.htm; M. Naveen Saviour, 2012, "Environmental Impact of Soil and Sand Mining: A Review," *International Journal of Science, Environment, and Technology* 1 (3): 127, 130, 132.

29. Ajit K. Ghose, 1999, "Current Issues of Employment Policy in India," *Economic and Political Weekly* 34 (36): 2592, 2594, 2599; Ghose 2019, Figure 3.6, 60–62.

30. Rana Dasgupta, 2015 (2014), *Capital: The Eruption of Delhi,* London, Canongate, 276.

31. Smriti Rao and Vamsi Vakulabharanam, 2018, "Migration Crises and Social Transformations in India since the 1990s," *Political Economy Research Institute: Working Paper Series* 450, 7; Jan Breman, 1996, *Footloose Labour: Working in India's Informal Economy,* Cambridge, Cambridge University Press, 45–46, 51, 55–56, 73–79; Ghose 1999, 2592; Ghose 2019, 60 (Figure 3.6), 134.

32. Ahluwalia 2020, 399–403.

33. Government of India, 1951, "The First Five Year Plan: A Draft Outline," Planning Commission, New Delhi, July, 14; Lockwood 1968 (1954), 462 and Table 40, 465.

34. World Bank, 1992, *Trends in Developing Countries 1992,* Washington, DC, 119, 301; World Bank's *World Development Indicators* database.

35. Kenneth Kang and Vijaya Ramachandran, 1999, "Economic Transformation in Korea: Rapid Growth without an Agricultural Revolution?" *Economic Development and Cultural Change* 47 (4): 790; Kang Hua Cao and Javier Birchenall, 2013, "Agricultural Productivity, Structural Change, and Economic Growth in Post-Reform China," *Journal of Development Economics* 104: 177; Bosworth and Collins 2008, 54.

36. Census of India 1991 and 2001, Economic Tables on distribution of main and marginal workers; Ghose 1999, Table 8, 2599.

37. Government of Andhra Pradesh, 2012, "Statistical Abstract of Andhra Pradesh 2011," Table 1.1, 12; Table 4.27, 190; Guillaume Gruère and Debdatta Sengupta, 2011, "Bt Cotton and Farmer Suicides in India: An Evidence-Based Assessment," *Journal of Development Studies* 47 (2): 326–328.

38. Randeep Ramesh, 2004, "Prophets of Cyberabad Face Rural Backlash: Farmers in India's Most IT-Friendly State Set to Vote Chief Minister out of Office," *Guardian,* May 10.

39. World Bank, 1997, "India Andhra Pradesh: Agenda for Economic Reforms," Report No. 15901-IN, Washington, DC, January 16, 1–4; Gruère and Sengupta 2011, 318.

40. B. B. Mohanty, 2005, "We Are Like the Living Dead: Farmer Suicides in Maharashtra, Western India," *Journal of Peasant Studies* 32 (2): 243–276; Gruère and Sengupta 2011, 318; Ramesh 2004.

41. Government of Andhra Pradesh, 2012, "Statistical Abstract of Andhra Pradesh 2011," Table 1.1, 12; Table 4.27, 190.

42. Kavitha Iyer, 2021, *Landscapes of Loss,* Kindle edition, HarperCollins India, esp. chapter 3.

43. Ramesh Chand, S. S. Raju, and L. M. Pandey, 2007, "Growth Crisis in Agriculture: Severity and Options at National and State Levels," *Economic and Political Weekly* 42 (26): Tables 1 and 2, 2529–2531; Akhil Gupta, 2016, "Farming as a Speculative Activity: The Ecological Basis of Farmers' Suicides in India," University of California, Los Angeles, February, 12–15; Scott Jasechko and Debra Peronne, 2021, "Global Groundwater Wells at Risk of Running Dry," *Science* 372, 418–421, 419.

44. Felix Kogan and Wei Guo, 2016, "Early Twenty-First-Century Droughts during the Warmest Climate," *Geomatics, Natural Hazards, and Risk* 7 (1): 133; *Times of India,* 2000, "Famines as Photo Ops," April 20; *Times of India,* 2002, "Grain Output, May Decline to 90.8 mt," September 24.

45. Ashok Das, 2003, "Naidu Back, Writes to PM on Drought," *Hindustan Times,* October 6; K. Balagopal, 2006, "Maoist Movement in Andhra Pradesh," *Economic and Political Weekly* 41 (29): 3183–3187; P. V. Ramana, 2006, "The Maoist Movement in India," *Defense and Security Analysis* 22 (4): 435–449; Maitreesh Ghatak and Oliver Vanden Eynde, 2017, "Economic Determinants of Maoist Conflict in India," *Economic and Political Weekly* 52 (39): 69–76, Figure 1 and Table 1, 70; Oliver Vanden Eynde, 2018, "Targets of Violence: Evidence from India's Naxalite Violence," *Economic Journal* 128 (March): 887–916.

46. Ingrid Dallmann and Katrin Millock, 2017, "Climate Variability and Inter-State Migration in India," *CESifo Economic Studies,* 583–584; Ram B. Bhagat and Kunal Keshri, 2020, "Internal Migration in India," in Martin Bell, Aude Bernard, Elin Charles-Edwards, and Yu Zhu, editors, *Internal Migration in the Countries of Asia,* Cham, Switzerland, Springer, 211–212.

47. Amy Waldman, 2004, "Low-Tech or High, Jobs Are Scarce in India's Boom," *New York Times,* May 6; Kunal Keshri and Ram B. Bhagat, 2013, "Socioeconomic Determinants of Temporary Labour Migration in India," *Asian Population Studies* 9 (2): 175, 180–182.

48. Uttaran Das Gupta, 2020, "Frames per Second: The Long Walk Home," *Business Standard,* April 10.

49. Martha C. Nussbaum, 2007, *The Clash Within: Democracy, Religious Violence, and India's Future,* Kindle edition, Harvard University Press, location 339; Parvis Ghassem-Fachandi, 2012, *Pogrom in Gujarat,* Kindle edition, Princeton University Press, locations 31–32; Ashish Khetan, 2020, *Undercover: My Journey into the Darkness of Hindutva,* Kindle edition, Context, locations 197, 211.

50. Nussbaum 2007, locations 340–349, 369; Ghassem-Fachandi 2012, 32; Khetan 2020, 214.

51. Nussbaum 2007, locations 356–363, 379–380; Rajesh Joshi, 2011, "11 Death Sentences in India's Gujarat Riots Case," *Agence France-Presse,* March 1; Ghassem-Fachandi 2012, 1, 21, 37–43, 64, 74, 92, 190, 283, 283; Achyut Yagnik, 2005, *Shaping of Modern Gujarat,* Kindle edition, Penguin Books, locations 256, 286.

52. *Times of India,* 2002, "'Newton' Modi Has a Lot to Answer," March 3; Siddharth Varadarajan, 2002, "Carnage in Gujarat: Telling Silence, Mr. Vajpayee," *Times of India,* March 6. Modi later said he could not recall the words he used, he was a man of peace. See *Tehelka,* 2011, "The Truth about the Godhra SIT Report," February 12; *Times of India,* 2002, "Unmasked Truth," April 15.

53. *Press Trust of India,* 2002, "Election Commission Says No to Early Polls in Gujarat," August 16; Vinay Sitapati, 2020, *Jugalbandi: The BJP before Modi,* Penguin, New Delhi, 275–281; Myra MacDonald and Thomas Kutty Abraham, 2002, "Update 4—India's BJP in Landside Win in Gujarat," *Reuters News,* December 15; *Hindustan Times,* 2002, "We'll Repeat Gujarat—Togadia," December 16; Nussbaum 2007, locations 771–777.

54. Agence France-Presse, 2004, "India's Ruling Party Brings out Right-Wing Firebrand for Close Election," May 2.

55. Sunil Khilnani, 2004, "Reality Strips Off India's Veneer," *Financial Times,* May 14.

56. Kumkum Chadha, 1998, "History with Blinkers on...," *Hindustan Times,* June 28; Nandini Sundar, 2004, "Teaching to Hate: RSS' Pedagogical Programme," *Economic and Political Weekly* 39 (16): 1605–1612; Alex Traub, 2018, "India's Dangerous New Curriculum," *New York Review of Books,* December 6; Agence France-Presse, 2003, "India's President Boycotted over Portrait of Hindu Rights Leader," February 26; *The Hindu,* 2003, "Savarkar Portrait Unveiled," February 27; *Times of India,* 2004, "Modi Out of the Manali Woods, for Now," June 21.

Chapter 20: As the Two Indias Drift Apart, Democracy Creaks

1. Craig Jeffrey, 2010, *Timepass: Youth, Class, and the Politics of Waiting in India,* Stanford, Stanford University Press, 82–83, 96.

2. Devesh Kapur and Pratap Bhanu Mehta, 2008, "Mortgaging the Future? Indian Higher Education," *India Policy Forum 2007–2008* 4: 126, 131–135; Rama Lakshmi, 2012, "India's University System in 'Deep Crisis,'" *Washington Post,* March 28.

3. Ghose 1999, Tables 3.1 and 3.6.

4. World Bank, 2014, "Republic of India: Accelerating Agricultural Productivity Growth," Washington, DC, May 21, 43, 46 (Figure 30); Centre for Science and Environment, 1999, "The Citizen's Fifth Report: Part I," New Delhi, 58, 168; Dasgupta 2015 (2014).

5. *BBC Monitoring South Asia*, 2014, "Indian Prime Minister-Designate Says 'Sonia Gandhi Is My Leader,'" May 19; Agence France-Presse, 2004, "Manmohan Singh Named as Indian PM," May 19; Prabhu Chawla, Bhavdeep Kang, and Lakshmi Iyer, 2005, "Couple at Odds," *India Today*, May 16.

6. World Bank, 2005, "Economic Growth in the 1990s: Learning from a Decade of Reform," Washington, DC.

7. Drèze and Sen 2013, 132.

8. Sowmya Sivakumar, 2022, "Undermining the Legal Guarantee of MGNREGA: Right, Left, And Centre," *The India Forum*, March 11.

9. Sevanti Ninan, 2019, "Defanging RTI, Step by Step," *The India Forum*, August 23; *The Hindu*, 2012, "Exercise of Right to Information Runs into Hurdles," March 9; *The Statesman*, 2011, "Supreme Court Cannot Deny Info under RTI Act, Says CIC," May 16; Lydia Polgreen, 2011, "Indians Use Information Law, at a Deadly Risk," *New York Times*, January 23.

10. K. Sujatha Rao, 2017, *Do We Care: India's Health System*, New Delhi, Oxford University Press, 303–316, 328, 340–348; Kundan Kumar, Neera Singh, and Y. Giri Rao, 2017, "Promise and Performance of the Forest Rights Act: A Ten-Year Review," *Economic and Political Weekly* 52 (25–26): 40–43; Geetanjoy Sahu, Tushar Dash, and Sanghamitra Dubey, 2017, "Political Economy of Community Forest Rights," *Economic and Political Weekly* 52 (25–26): 44–47.

11. International Monetary Fund, 2004, *World Economic Outlook—Prospects and Policy Issues*, Washington, DC, April, 1, 3 (Table 1.1); International Monetary Fund, 2005, *World Economic Outlook—Prospects and Policy Issues*, Washington, DC, April, 2 (Table 1.1).

12. Federal Reserve Bank of St. Louis (hereafter FRED), https://fred.stlouisfed.org/series/PCOALAUUSDM; T. N. Ninan, 2017 (2015), *Turn of the Tortoise*, Kindle edition, Oxford University Press, locations 54–55; FRED, https://fred.stlouisfed.org/series/PIORECRUSDM.

13. Government of Maharashtra, "Statewise Total and Tribal Population," available at: https://trti.maharashtra.gov.in/index.php/en/statewise-total-tribal-population; Ram Ranjan, 2019, "Assessing the Impact of Mining on Deforestation in India," *Resources Policy* 60 (March): 23–35.

14. *Guardian,* 2009, "They Call This Progress?," November 23; Amit Sengupta, 2004, "Guns vs Flowers," *Tehelka,* February 14.

15. Suresh Nair, 2005, "Iron and Steel Cos Make a Beeline for Chhattisgarh," *Economic Times,* January 10; *Business Line,* 2005, "Tata Steel Signs MoU to Set Up Plant in Chhattisgarh," June 6 (reproduced by *Indian Business Insight*); Nandini Sundar, 2020, *The Burning Forest,* Kindle edition, Juggernaut Books, location 1262; *Hindustan Times,* 2005, "After Tata, Essar Plans Plant in Bastar," July 4, Ramachandra Guha et al. 2006, "Salwa Judum: War in the Heart of India: Excerpts from the Report by Independent Citizens Initiative," *Social Scientist* 34 (7/8): 48; Randeep Ramesh, 2006, "Inside India's Hidden War," *Guardian,* May 8.

16. Simon Denyer, 2006, "Indian PM Says Maoist Rebellion Gravest Threat," *Reuters News,* April 13.

17. International Monetary Fund, 2006, *World Economic Outlook—Prospects and Policy Issues,* Washington, DC, April, 8, 35 (Table 1.6); foreign investment and private equity data from the World Bank's *World Development Indicators* database; foreign exchange reserves are from the Reserve Bank of India, https://rbi.org.in/Scripts/PublicationsView.aspx?id=19882; *Hindustan Times,* 2006, "Text of Prime Minister's Independence Day Address," August 15.

18. K. P. Kannan and G. Raveendran, 2009, "Growth sans Employment: A Quarter Century of Jobless Growth in India's Organized Manufacturing," *Economic and Political Weekly* 44 (10): 80; Jayan Jose Thomas, 2013, "Explaining the 'Jobless' Growth in Indian Manufacturing," *Journal of the Asia Pacific Economy* 18 (4): 677–679 and Table 5; Kalpana Kochhar et al., 2006, "India's Pattern of Development: What Happened, What Follows?" *Journal of Monetary Economics* 53: 981–983, 1006–1007.

19. *Hindustan Times,* 2006, "Text of Prime Minister's Independence Day Address," August 15.

20. George Orwell, 1946, "In Front of Your Nose," in Sonia Orwell and Ian Angus, editors, 1968, *The Collected Essays, Journalism, and Letters of George Orwell: In Front of Your Nose, 1945–1950,* New York, Harcourt Brace Jovanovich, 122–125.

21. Our World in Data, "Human Development Index," available at: https://ourworldindata.org/human-development-index; United Nations Development Programme, 2006, *Human Development Report 2006,* New York, Table 2, 288–291; Alison Warner, 1998, "Economy Still in Danger," *Banker,* June 1; *Economist Intelligence Unit,* 2004, "Vietnam: Country Outlook," December 3; Trung Kien Nguyen,

2015, "Manufacturing Exports and Employment Generation in Vietnam," *Southeast Asian Journal of Economics* 3 (2): 1–21.

22. A. Chowdhury, R. Mushtaque, and Abbas Bhuiya, 2004, "The Wider Impacts of BRAC Poverty Alleviation Programme in Bangladesh," *Journal of International Development* 16, 371; Yung Whee Rhee, 1990, "The Catalyst Model of Development: Lessons from Bangladesh's Success with Garment Exports," *World Development* 18 (2): 336; Amartya Sen, 2013, "What's Happening in Bangladesh?" *Lancet* 382, December 14, 1966–1967.

23. Dasgupta 2015 (2014), 219.

24. Ghose 2019, 71.

25. Chaitanya Kalbag, 2017, "Near Total Enrollment, Improved Infra; So, What's the Problem with our Education System?" *Economic Times,* October 27; Soumen Datta, 2013, "Private B.Ed. Colleges Fleecing Students, Govt Mute Spectator," *Hindustan Times,* December 26; Azim Premji University, 2021, *Issues in Education; Volume 1: Teachers and Teacher Education,* Bangalore, chapter 2; Manisha Shah and Bryce Steinberg, 2019, "The Right to Education Act: Trends in Enrollment, Test Scores, and School Quality," *AEA Papers and Proceedings* 109: 232–38; Anil Swarup, 2020, *Ethical Dilemmas of a Civil Servant,* Kindle edition, Unique Publishers India Private Limited, location 267; Noam Angrist, Simeon Djankov, Pinelopi K. Goldberg, and Harry A. Patrinos, 2021, "Measuring Human Capital Using Global Learning Data," *Nature* 592: 404.

26. *India Today,* 2004, "A Bloom, Not Yet a Boom," November 1; *Press Trust of India,* 2005, "Limitations of Coalition Hampering Labour Reforms: Indian PM," August 25; Kochhar et al. 2006, 1016.

27. Chang-tai Hsieh and Benjamin Olken, 2014, "The Missing Middle," *Journal of Economic Perspectives* 28 (3): 90; Thomas 2013, 684, 690–691; Ghose 2019, 63.

28. Federico Lucidi and Alfred Kleinknecht, 2010, "Little Innovation, Many Jobs: An Econometric Analysis of Italian Labor Productivity Crisis," *Cambridge Journal of Economics* 34: 526, 539; Robert Gordon, 2016, *The Rise and Fall of American Growth: The U.S. Standard of Living Since the Civil War.* Princeton, NJ, Princeton University Press, 18, 563.

29. Raghuram Rajan, 2008, "Is There a Threat of Oligarchy in India?," speech to the Bombay Chamber of Commerce on its Founders Day celebration, September 10, 2008, https://faculty.chicagobooth.edu/-/media/faculty/raghuram-rajan/research/papers/is-there-a-threat-of-oligarchy-in-india.pdf.

30. Ashutosh Varshney, 2007, "India's Democratic Challenge," *Foreign Affairs* 86 (2): 105.

31. International Monetary Fund, 2009, "India—Staff Report for the 2008 Article IV Consultation," SM/09/22, Washington, DC, January 23, 3–6.

32. Reserve Bank Handbook, https://rbi.org.in/Scripts/PublicationsView.aspx?id=19758; *Press Trust of India*, 2009, "Farmers Real Heroes of India, Says Pranab," February 16; *Wall Street Journal*, 2009, "Delhi's Deficit Disorder; India Digs Itself into a Budget Hole—for Nothing," February 19.

33. International Monetary Fund, 2011, "India—Staff Report for the 2010 Article IV Consultation," IMF Country Report 11/50, Washington, DC, February, Table 2, 38.

34. Pratap Chakravarty, 2009, "No Recession for Indian Election Spending," Agence France-Presse, March 24.

35. *Economic Times*, 2009, "BJP Red-Faced as Kulkarni Holds Mirror," June 9; Alistair Scrutton, 2009, "Analysis—Hindu Nationalist Becomes India Inc Poster Boy," *Reuters News*, January 15.

36. Reserve Bank Handbook, https://rbi.org.in/Scripts/PublicationsView.aspx?id=19750; Sunita Narain, 2009, "Rain and Still No Rain," *Business Standard*, September 11.

37. Angus Deaton, 2013, *The Great Escape: Health, Wealth, and the Origins of Inequality*, Princeton, NJ, Princeton University Press, 183, 221–223; Shaohua Chen and Martin Ravallion, 2010, "The Developing World Is Poorer Than We Thought But No Less Successful in the Fight against Poverty," *Quarterly Journal of Economics* 125 (4): 1580; data for purchasing power parity exchange rates is from the International Monetary Fund's *World Economic Outlook* database.

38. Chen and Ravallion 2010, 1585; Jean Drèze, 2019 (2017), *Sense and Solidarity: Jholawala Economics for Everyone*, New Delhi, Oxford University Press, 50.

39. Allen Matusow, 1984, *The Unraveling of America: A History of Liberalism in the 1960s*, New York, Harper and Row, 219.

40. Renu Shahrawat and Krishna Rao, 2012, "Insured Yet Vulnerable: Out-of-Pocket Payments and India's Poor," *Health Policy and Planning* 27: 213–221.

41. Angus Deaton and Jean Drèze, 2009, "Food and Nutrition in India: Facts and Interpretations," *Economic and Political Weekly* 44 (7): 42–65; Malnutrition data for Vietnam is in Figure 20.3; data for Indian states comes from Drèze and Sen 2013, Table A.2.

42. James Crabtree, 2018, *The Billionaire Raj: A Journey through India's New Gilded Age*, Noida, India, Harper Collins, 112–114; Phil Han, 2010, "Hard Evidence of Child Labor at 2010 Commonwealth Games," CNN, September 26, www.cnn.com/2010/WORLD/asiapcf/09/23/commonwealth.games.child.labor/index.html.

43. Crabtree 2018, 112–114, 125.

44. Ninan 2017 (2015), 128–129.

45. Kushan Mitra, 2005, "Indian Aviation's Take Off," *Business Today,* February 13; Vivek Kaul, 2020, *Bad Money: Inside the NPA Mess and How It Threatens the Indian Banking System*, Kindle edition, HarperCollins Publishers India, locations 166, 169.

46. A. Jayaram, 2002, "Mallya, Cong. Nominees Win RS Polls," *The Hindu,* March 2002; Kaul 2020, 164, 169; Josy Joseph, 2016, *A Feast of Vultures: The Hidden Business of Democracy in India,* New Delhi, HarperCollins, 173.

47. *India Today,* 2013, "King of Bad Times," January 7; Joseph 2016, 171; Forbes, "India's Richest (2013)," www.forbes.com/profile/vijay-mallya/?sh=47d8fed278e4.

48. Credit Suisse, 2012, "India Financial Sector," Bombay, August 2, Table 2; Government of India, 2017, "Report of the Comptroller and Auditor General of India on Recapitalisation of Public Sector Banks," New Delhi, Table 1.6.

49. Joseph 2016, 173; Aseema Sinha, 2019, "How Business and Politics Intersect in India's Porous State," *Wire,* January 17.

50. Ninan 2017 (2015), 44–45.

51. Dasgupta 2015 (2014), 13.

52. Ghose 2019, 17; Dasgupta 2015 (2014), 276.

53. Reserve Bank of India, "RBI Bulletin," www.rbi.org.in/scripts/BS_View-Bulletin.aspx?Id=11029; Mint, "More Indians Going Abroad for Studies, But Foreign Students aren't coming in," www.livemint.com/Education/qVtlWO1E9D923fiDD2069I/More-Indians-going-abroad-for-studies-but-foreign-students.html; Kapur and Mehta 2008, 127–128.

54. Stephen Graham, Renu Desai, and Colin McFarlane, 2013, "Water Wars in Mumbai," *Public Culture* 25 (1): 118, 121–122, 131, 136.

55. Dasgupta 2015 (2014), 430–433.

56. Supreme Court of India, "Jagpal Singh and Ors vs State of Punjab and Ors," https://indiankanoon.org/doc/1692607/.

57. T. V. Mahalingam, 2012, "ET Review: India's 1st Starbucks Outlet," *Economic Times,* October 22; Sudipto Dey, 2013, "We Are Just Focusing on Providing a Great Customer Experience," *Business Standard,* June 6.

58. Supreme Court of India, "Nandini Sundar and Ors vs State of Chhattisgarh," https://indiankanoon.org/doc/920448/; Nandini Sundar, 2020, locations 301–310, 4534.

59. Jeffrey Rosen, 2006, *The Supreme Court,* Kindle edition Henry Holt and Co., locations 66–67.

60. *TerraGreen*, 2012, "The Mined Aravalli Hills," November 30; Laiqh Khan, 2014, "Building Bengaluru, Plundering Cauvery," *The Hindu*, November 12.

61. Dasgupta 2015 (2014), 374.

Chapter 21: Modi Pushes the Economy off the Edge

1. Crabtree 2018, 86–87; BJP, "Election Manifesto 2014," www.thehinducentre.com/multimedia/archive/03226/full_manifesto_eng_3226788a.pdf, 3, 29.

2. Nirmal Ghosh, 2002, "Gujarat's Dream of Prosperity Shatters," *Straits Times*, April 23; Agence France-Presse, 2002, "Sectarian Riots Will Impede India's Economic Progress: Industrialist," April 28; Vinod Jose, 2012, "The Emperor Uncrowned: The Rise of Narendra Modi," *Caravan*, February 29.

3. Ghosh 2002; Dinesh Narayanan, 2014, "Billion-Dollar Loan to Adani Cements Modi's Friendship with Corporate India," *Scroll*, November 18; *Business Standard*, 2003, "Adanis, Malaysian Firm Sign Port Upgrade Alliance," September 29.

4. *The Hindu*, 2004, "EC Urged to Ensure Free, Fair Polls," April 26.

5. Partha Ghosh, 2006, "Mukesh Push for Vibrant Gujarat," *Economic Times*, August 14; Narayanan 2014; Ellen Barry, 2014, "Local Policies Help an Indian Candidate Trying to Go National," *New York Times*, May 7; Fareed Zakaria, Candy Crowley, and Diana Magnay, 2013, "India at the Cross-Roads," *Fareed Zakaria GPS*, CNN, December 29; *Indian Express*, 2013, "Anil Ambani Lifts Modi to the League of 'King of Kings'", January 12; Mahesh Langa, 2013, "All Hail Modi, 'A Leader of Grand Vision.'" *Hindustan Times*, January 11.

6. Christophe Jaffrelot, 2019, "Business-Friendly Gujarat under Narendra Modi the Implications of a New Political Economy," in Christophe Jaffrelot, Atul Kohli, and Kanta Murali, *Business and Politics in India*, Kindle edition, Oxford University Press. locations 215, 217–218; *Press Trust of India*, 2013, "CAG Slams Modi Govt for 'Undue' Favours to Corporates," April 3.

7. Sumesh Dudani et al., 2017, "Heavy Metal Accumulation in the Mangrove Ecosystem of South Gujarat Coast, India," *Turkish Journal of Fisheries and Aquatic Sciences* 17: 755–766; Centre of Science and Environment, 2012, *State of India's Environment: A Citizen's Report 7—Excreta Matters*. Volume 2, New Delhi, 282, 290, 426.

8. Jim Yardley and Vikas Bajaj, 2011, "Skirting the State on the Road to Riches," *International Herald Tribune*, July 27; M. Rajshekhar, 2013, "Gautam Adani: Meet the Man Who Built Rs 47,000 Crore Infrastructure Empire," *Economic Times*, September 5; *Tehelka*, 2011, "Vibrant Gujarat? Your Coast Is Not Clear, Mr. Adani," February 26.

9. Martha Nussbaum, 2014, "Development Is More Than Growth," www.thehinducentre.com/verdict/commentary/article5985379.ece.

10. N. P. Ullekh, 2013. "Gujarat Promises Continued, Accelerated an All-Round Progress: Jagdish Bhagwati and Arvind Panagariya," *Economic Times*, January 3.

11. International Monetary Fund, 2014, "India—Staff Report for the 2014 Article IV consultation," SM/14/10, January 10, Washington, DC, 19, 38 (Table 2), 51.

12. Crabtree 2018, 86–87; *Statesman*, 2015, "So Much for Promise," August 4; BJP "Election Manifesto 2014," www.thehinducentre.com/multimedia/archive/03226/full_manifesto_eng_3226788a.pdf, 3, 29.

13. Prabhu Chawla, 2013, "Muscled with Dosh from India Inc, Poll Industry Yields Richest Dividends in the Game," *Sunday Standard*, November 23; *The Economist*, 2014, "Campaign Finance in India; Black Money Oower," May 4.

14. Zeeshan Shaikh, 2013, "Dhule, a Town Divided," *Indian Express*, January 13; Seema Kamdar, 2013, "Economics at Heart of Dhule Riots," *DNA*, January 22; Manmohan Rai, 2013, "Narendra Modi to Debut in Uttar Pradesh in September, Campaign to be Rolled from Vrindavan," *Economic Times*, September 4; Sreenivasan Jain, 2013, "Muzaffarnagar Riots: Warrants against Politicians, Still No Arrests," NDTV, September 18; Prabhu Chawla, 2014, "Bread and Butter Have Expiry Dates, But Divide and Rule is Forever," *Sunday Standard*, April 13.

15. Chawla 2014; Christophe Jaffrelot, 2015, "The Modi-centric BJP 2014 Election Campaign: New Techniques and Old Tactics," *Contemporary South Asia* 23 (2): 160.

16. Pratap Bhanu Mehta, 2012, "A Modi-fied Politics," *Indian Express*, December 21; Pratap Bhanu Mehta, 2014, "Regarding Fascism," *Indian Express*, April 11; Ashutosh Varshney, 2014, "Modi, on Balance," *Indian Express*, April 29.

17. Gurcharan Das, 2014, "Secularism or Growth? The Choice Is Yours," *Times of India*, April 6; The Ronald Reagan Presidential Foundation and Institute, "Inaugural Address, 1981," www.reaganfoundation.org/media/128614/inaguration.pdf; Jim O'Neill, 2013, "A 10-Step Programme to Tap into India's Potential," *Independent*, June 25.

18. David Pilling, 2014, "A Vote for Modi Could Make India More Chinese," *Financial Times*, March 19.

19. Shaun Tandon, 2014, "US Lawmakers Press India on Minorities Before Vote," Agence France Presse, April 4; *New York Times*, 2014, "Live-Blogging the Vote Count in India," May 15.

20. Jaffrelot 2019, 224; Raymond Fisman, 2001, "Estimating the Value of Political Connections," *American Economic Review* 9 (4): 1095–1102.

21. *Indo-Asian News Service,* 2014, "Text of Narendra Modi's I-Day Address," August 15; Victor Mallet, 2014, "Modi Prioritises Factories and Toilets in Independence Day Speech," *Financial Times,* August 15.

22. Third Dr. Verghese Kurien Memorial Lecture, Institute of Rural Management Anand (IRMA), Anand, November 24, 2014, www.bis.org/review/r141126b.htm; Sanjib Baruah, 2015, "RBI Chief Wants PMO to Act against Bank Frauds Worth Rs 17,500 Crore," *Hindustan Times,* April 24.

23. Joshi 2017, Table 8.1, 140; Anant Vijay Kala, 2015, "Indian Economists' Embarrassing Confession: They Don't Know What GDP Is," *Dow Jones Institutional News,* February 6; Arvind Subramanian, 2019, "Validating India's GDP Growth Estimates," CID Faculty Working Paper 357, Harvard University, July, 2; Raymond Zhong and Anant Vijay Kala, 2015, "World News: India's Growth Trumps China's," *Wall Street Journal Asia,* June 1.

24. World Bank, 2014, "Accelerating Agricultural Productivity Growth: Overview," Washington, DC, May 21; Akshat Kaushal and Mayank Mishra, 2015, "What Is Causing Distress among Erstwhile Dominant Castes?" *Business Standard,* November 1; Government of India, 2019, *Agricultural Statistics at a Glance 2018,* New Delhi, Ministry of Agriculture and Farmers Welfare, Directorate of Economics and Statistics, Table 15.1, 364.

25. Snigdha Poonam, 2018, *Dreamers: How Young Indians Are Changing Their World,* New Delhi, Penguin, 225–227, 232–233.

26. Victoria Barret, 2010, "Silicon Valley's Prison Call Center," *Forbes,* June 10; Yudhijit Bhattacharjee, 2021, "Who's Making All Those Scam Calls?" *New York Times Magazine,* January 27.

27. Ellen Barry, 2017, "India's Call-Center Talents Put to a Criminal Use: Swindling Americans," *New York Times,* January 3; Yudhijit Bhattacharjee, 2021, "Who's Making All Those Scam Calls?" *New York Times,* April 21; Poonam 2018, 225–228, 239, 241, 243–245, 249.

28. Dev Goswami, 2017, "*Mitron* [Friends] .... It Has Been a Year Since That Speech," *India Today,* November 8.

29. Ravi Velloor, 2015, "'Lion among Leaders' and 'Inspiration' to Asians," *Straits Times,* March 24; Pranab Bardhan, 2019, "Merchants of Hype and Hate: A Political-Economic Evaluation of the Modi Regime," in Chatterji, Hansen, and Jaffrelot, 179–180.

30. T. N. Ninan, 2017, "At the Two-Thirds Mark," *Business Standard,* September 1.

31. Parthasarathy Shome, 2017, "Goods and Services Tax (GST)," *Madras Institute of Development Studies Working Paper* 227, Chennai, October; Prasanna

Mohanty, 2020, "Rebooting Economy XXIV: 7 Critical GST Flaws Govt Needs to Address at the Earliest," *Business Today*, September 3.

32. Swati Chaturvedi, 2018, "Raghuram Rajan Gave PMO a List of 'High Profile NPA Fraud Cases' But No Action Was Taken," *Wire*, September 12; International Monetary Fund, 2017, "India: 2017 Article IV Consultation—Press Release; Staff Report; and Statement by the Executive Director for India," IMF Country Report No. 17/54, Washington, DC, February, 4, 7; International Monetary Fund, 2018, "India: 2018 Article IV Consultation—Press Release; Staff Report; and Statement by the Executive Director for India," IMF Country Report No. 18/254, Washington, DC, August, 7, 26; International Monetary Fund, 2019, "India: 2019 Article IV Consultation—Press Release; Staff Report; and Statement by the Executive Director for India," IMF Country Report No. 19/385, Washington, DC, December, 49 and Table 1; Raghuram Rajan, 2018, "Note to the Parliamentary Estimates Committee on NPAs," September 6.

33. David Housego, 1992, "Survey of India (15): Pioneer for the Private Sector—Profile: IL&FS," *Financial Times*, June 26; Andy Mukherjee, 2018a, "India Rues Its Own Belt-and-Road Debt Fiasco," *Bloomberg Opinion*, September 18; World Bank, 1996, "Guarantee Agreement (Private Infrastructure Finance (IL&FS Project) between India and the International Bank for Reconstruction and Development," Loan Number 3992 IN, Washington, DC, July 10; Sandeep Hasurkar, 2020, *Never Too Big to Fail: The Collapse of IL&FS and its Ten Trillion-Rupee Maze*, Kindle edition, Rupa Publications, location 49.

34. Sugata Ghosh, 2019, "Lessons for India from the IL&FS Fiasco," *Economic Times*, September 2; Mukherjee 2018a; Hasurkar 2020, 50, 70, 179.

35. Mukherjee 2018a; Hasurkar 2020, 36–39; Abhijit Madhav Lele and Jyoti Mukul, 2018, "Three Decades of Parthasarathy Led to IL&FS's Lateral Growth," *Business Standard*, July 25.

36. Lele and Mukul 2018; CARE Rating, 2018, "IL&FS Financial Services Ltd," Press Releases.

37. Sucheta Dalal, 2018, "IL&FS Scandal: When a Director Was Threatened with Jail and Slapped with Criminal Defamation for Raising Questions," *Moneylife*, October 31; Sucheta Dalal, 2018, "IL&FS's Tirupur Project: Destructive Impact of RBI's Failure to Act," *Moneylife*, December 2018; Dalal 2019; Hasurkar 2020, 38; M. Rajshekhar, 2016, "Can the Courts Save India's Rivers from Pollution? Tirupur Shows the Answer Is No," *Scroll*, August 30; Shalini Lobo, 2018, "Coimbatore's Noyyal River Transforms into Frothing Disaster," *India Today*, July 12.

38. Sucheta Dalal, 2022, "IL&FS Resolution: Little Hope for Creditors and Pensioners, While Lawyers and Consultants Collect Fat Fees," *Moneylife,* March 24.

39. Andy Mukherjee, 2018b, "India Needs to Stop the IL&FS Rot from Spreading," *Bloomberg Opinion,* September 24; *Moneylife,* 2019, "Reliance Capital Companies of Anil Ambani Group Headed for Default?" April 27; Andy Mukherjee, 2018c, "India Misses Wake-Up Call from Shadow-Bank Bust," *Bloomberg Opinion,* November 11.; FRED, https://fred.stlouisfed.org/series/INDGDPRQPSMEI/.

40. Katherine Eban, 2019, "Ranbaxy and the Culture of Jugaad: What Brought a Leading Company Down," *Outlook India,* October 10; Katherine Eban, 2019, *Bottle of Lies: Ranbaxy and the Dark Side of Indian Pharma,* New Delhi, Juggernaut, 366.

41. Katie Thomas, 2013, "Generic Drug Maker Pleads Guilty in Federal Case," *New York Times,* May 14; *Adverse Event Reporting,* 2014, "FDA Takes Aim at Yet Another Indian API Maker," April 1; Eban 2019, 364–366, 372; Gardner Harris, 2014, "Medicines Made in India Set Off Safety Worries," *New York Times,* February 15; Katherine Eban and Sony Salzman, 2019, "In Generic Drug Plants in China and India, Data Falsification Is Still a Problem," *Stat,* October 29; Government Accountability Office, 2022, "Drug Safety: FDA Should Take Additional Steps to Improve Its Foreign Inspection Program," Washington, DC, January, 27.

42. Samiran Nundy, Keshav Desiraju, and Sanjay Nagral, 2018, *Healers or Predators? Healthcare Corruption in India,* Kindle edition, Oxford University Press, locations 318, 320.

43. World Trade Organisation, 2020, "Trade Policy Review," WT/TPR/S/403, November 25, 9; *Times of India,* 2017, "India Must Lower, Not Raise, Tariff Walls," August 12; Arvind Panagariya, 2019, "The Caravan of Reforms Keeps Moving in Full Pace," *Economic Times,* July 6.

44. Mike Bird, 2015, "Asia's Huge Trade Pact Is a Paper Tiger in the Making," *Wall Street Journal Online,* November 5.

45. *Times of India,* 2019, "City Inc Jubilant after RCEP Deal Falls Through," November 7; *Press Trust of India,* 2019, "Ludhiana's Bicycle Industry against Inclusion in RCEP Trade Pact," October 9.

46. Deepika Bhatia et al., 2018, "Physicochemical Assessment of Industrial Textile Effluents of Punjab (India)," *Applied Water Science* 8, Article 83; I. P. Singh, 2019, "Ludhiana: Drug Menace Fueled by Politician-Police-Drug-Mafia Nexus," *Times of India,* August 30; *Indian Express,* 2020, "Ludhiana: STF Arrests Four with

5.39 Kg Heroin, Rs 21 Lakh Drug Money," November 7; *Indian Express,* 2021, "Drug Smuggler in STF Net Makes Startling Allegations against Senior Punjab Cops," March 15.

47. Ghose 2019, Epilogue; Mahesh Vyas, 2018, "Using Fast Frequency Household Survey Data to Estimate the Impact of Demonetisation on Employment," *Review of Market Integration* 10 (3): 159–183.

48. S. Subramanian, 2019, "What Is Happening to Rural Welfare, Poverty, and Inequality in India?" *The India Forum,* December 12, Table 4; Deaton and Kozel 2005, 179–182.

49. Himanshu, 2019, "What Happened to Poverty during the First Term of Modi?" *Mint,* August 15; World Bank, 2020, *Poverty and Shared Prosperity 2020: Reversals of Fortune,* Washington, DC, October, Box 1.2, 31.

50. Dipa Sinha, 2022, "Persistence of Food Insecurity and Malnutrition," *The India Forum,* March 11, Figure 2; Jean Drèze, Aashish Gupta, Sai Ankit Parashar, and Kanika Sharma, 2020, "Pauses and Reversals of Infant Mortality Decline in India in 2017 and 2018," November 8, available at SSRN: https://ssrn.com/abstract=3727001.

Chapter 22: Modi Breaks India's Fractured Democracy

1. Karthik Muralidharan, Abhijeet Singh, and Alejandro J. Ganimian, 2019, "Disrupting Education? Experimental Evidence on Technology-Aided Instruction in India," *American Economic Review* 109 (4): 1437 and Figure 1; David Autor, Claudia Goldin, and Lawrence F. Katz, 2020, "Extending the Race between Education and Technology," *National Bureau of Economic Research Working Paper* 26705, Cambridge, MA; Dipa Sinha, 2022, "Persistence of Food Insecurity and Malnutrition," *The India Forum,* March 11, Figure 2; Jean Drèze, 2020, "New Evidence on Child Nutrition Calls for Radical Expansion of Child Development Services," *Indian Express,* December 17.

2. Centre for Science and Environment, 2020, *State of India's Environment 2020,* New Delhi, 197, 243, 281; Centre for Science and Environment, 2019, *State of India's Environment 2019,* New Delhi, 18–23; Amitav Ghosh, 2016, *The Great Derangement: Climate Change and the Unthinkable,* Chicago, University of Chicago Press; Mohana Basu, 2020, "Climate Change to Blame for 'Plague-Like' Locust Attacks in Rajasthan, Gujarat, Say Experts," *Print.in,* February 10; Chirag Dhara and Roxy Mathew Koll, 2021, "How and Why India's Climate Will Change in the Coming Decades," *The India Forum,* August 20.

3. Amy Kazmin, 2018, "India's Dried-Out Rivers Feed Spate of Water Wars," *Financial Times,* May 7; Nilanjana Roy, 2019, "A Ferocious Heat in Delhi," *New York Review of Books,* July 8; Center for Science and Environment 2019, 238–239.

4. "State of Rajasthan, Jaipur vs Balchand @ Baliay," https://indiankanoon.org/doc/8258/; Supreme Court of India, "Arnab Manoranjan Goswami vs The State of Maharashtra," https://indiankanoon.org/doc/84792457/.

5. Julie McCarthy, 2012, "Rape Case in India Provokes Widespread Outrage," *All Things Considered,* NPR, December 18; Sonia Faleiro, 2021, *The Good Girls: An Ordinary Killing,* New York, Grove Press; Ellen Barry, 2017, "How to Get Away with Murder in Small-Town India," *New York Times, August* 19; on Modi's Independence Day speech, see chapter 21.

6. Nandita Saikia et al., 2021, "Trends in Missing Females at Birth in India from 1981 to 2016: Analyses of 2.1 Million Birth Histories in Nationally Representative Surveys," *Lancet Global Health* 9: e813–e821; Seema Jayachandran and Rohini Pande, 2017, "Why Are Indian Children So Short? The Role of Birth Order and Son Preference," *American Economic Review* 107 (9): 2600–2629; Sujata Mody and Meghna Sukumar, 2013, "Women Workers in Tamil Nadu: Working in Poverty," Chennai, Penn Thozhilalargal Sangam; Amartya Sen, 2013, "What's Happening in Bangladesh?" *Lancet* 382, December 14, 1966–1967.

7. Poonam 2018, 113–115, 127; Dahl 1961, 7–8; Hansen 2001, 230; Tommaso Colussi, Ingo E. Isphording, and Nico Pestel, 2021, "Minority Salience and Political Extremism," *American Economic Journal: Applied Economics* 13 (3): 237–271; Alberto Alesina, Reza Baqir, and William Easterly, 1999, "Public Goods and Ethnic Divisions," *Quarterly Journal of Economics* 114 (4): 1243–1284.

8. Raghuram Rajan, 2008, "Speech to the Bombay Chamber of Commerce on its Founders Day celebration, September 10, 2008," https://faculty.chicagobooth.edu/-/media/faculty/raghuram-rajan/research/papers/is-there-a-threat-of-oligarchy-in-india.pdf.

9. Somini Sengupta, 2005, "In a Corner of India, They Have the Vote, But Little Else," *New York Times,* February 23.

10. Karthik Muralidharan and Nishith Prakash, 2017, "Cycling to School: Increasing Secondary School Enrollment for Girls in India," *American Economic Journal: Applied Economics* 9 (3): 327, 348–349; Christel Vermeersch and Michael Kremer, 2005, "School Meals, Educational Achievement and School Competition: Evidence from a Randomized Evaluation," *Policy Research Working Paper* 3523, Washington, DC, World Bank, 43.

11. Lisa Björkman and Jeffrey Witsoe, 2018, "Money and Votes: Following Flows through Mumbai and Bihar," in Devesh Kapur and Milan Vaishnav, editors, 2018, *Costs of Democracy: Political Finance in India,* New Delhi, Oxford University Press, 170–171.

12. Björkman and Witsoe 2018, 199; Milan Vaishnav, 2017, *When Crime Pays: Money and Muscle in Indian Politics,* New Haven, CT, Yale University Press, 181.

13. National Crime Records Bureau, "Violent Crimes in Metropolitan Cities—2016," https://ncrb.gov.in/sites/default/files/crime_in_india_table_additional_table_chapter_reports/Table%202.3B.pdf. Reserve Bank Handbook, www.rbi.org.in/scripts/PublicationsView.aspx?id=15797.

14. Vivek Srinivasan, 2015, *Delivering Public Services Effectively: Tamil Nadu and Beyond,* New Delhi, Oxford University Press, 40; International Institute for Population Sciences, 2017, National Family Health Survey (NFHS-4), 2015–16, India, Mumbai, https://dhsprogram.com/pubs/pdf/FR339/FR339.pdf, 294.

15. M. Rajshekhar, 2016, "Tamil Nadu's Healthcare Numbers Look Good—But Its People Aren't Getting Healthier," *Scroll.in,* December 12.

16. Maurice Walker, 2011, "PISA 2009 Plus Results: Performance of 15-Year-Olds in Reading, Mathematics, and Science for 10 Additional Participants," Melbourne, ACER Press, Tables 2.1 and 3.1.

17. Karthik Muralidharan et al., 2017, "The Fiscal Cost of Weak Governance: Evidence from Teacher Absence in India," *Journal of Public Economics* 145 (January): Table A4, 131; Karthik Muralidharan, 2019, "The State and the Market in Education Provision: Evidence and the Way Ahead," *Columbia University SIPA Working Paper* 2019-06, October 29. The official assessment is in the National Achievement Survey for 2017, conducted by the National Council for Educational Research and Training, New Delhi, and is also discussed in M. Rajshekhar, 2016, "Tamil Nadu's Schools Are in Crisis (But Nobody Is Talking about It)," *Scroll.in,* November 24; Anjali Mody, 2018, "Viral Photo of Students Weeping at TN Teacher's Transfer Shows What's Wrong With Education in India," *Scroll.in,* June 23; Anjali Mody, 2019, "The False Allure of English-Medium Schooling," *Hindu,* November 18.

18. Vaishnav 2017, 91, 140–141, 278, 365; *The Hindu,* 2011, "Tamil Nadu Ranks High in Poll Irregularities," February 27; Sarah Hiddleston, 2011, "Cash for Votes a Way of Political Life in South India," *The Hindu,* March 16; *Hindustan Times,* 2011, "Populism Powers TN Battle," March 24.

19. Jessica Leight et al., 2020, "Value for Money? Vote-Buying and Politician Accountability," *Journal of Public Economics* 190 (October).

20. Vibhuti Agarwal, 2014, "India's Powerful Regional Party Leader Jayalalithaa Jailed for Corruption," *Wall Street Journal Online,* September 28; Victor Mallet, 2014, "Indian Politician Jailed for Lavish Corruption," *Financial Times,* September 28; Nida Najar, 2015. "Court Clears an Ex-Chief Minister in India of Graft on Appeal," *New York Times,* May 12.

21. References in this paragraph and the next two are from Krupa Ge, *Rivers Remember: #CHENNAIRAINS and the Shocking Truth of a Manmade Flood,* Chennai, Context, 30–36, 73–81; 105–106.

22. M. Rajshekhar, 2016a, "Politicians Aren't Only Messing with Tamil Nadu's Water—They're Making Rs 20,000 Crore from Sand," *Scroll.in,* September 19; M. Rajshekhar, 2016b, "Think Sand Mining Damages the Ecology? It Ruins Politics as Well," *Scroll.in,* September 20.

23. *New Indian Express,* 2021, "Venkatachalam Just a Tip of an Iceberg at TNPCB?" September 25.

24. M. Rajshekhar, 2020, *Despite the State: Why India Lets Its People Down and How They Cope,* Kindle edition, Westland Publications, location 170; Sowmya Rajendran, 2020, "The Rise of the Violent Hero in South Cinema: What Explains It?" *News Minute,* December 8; Abhimanyu Mathur, 2022, "Decoding the Success of KGF Chapter 2 and Pushpa The Rise: How They Brought Back Bollywood's Own Angry Young Man Formula," *Hindustan Times,* April 17.

25. Prateek Goyal, 2014, "Over FB Post, Hindutva Rioters Lynch Innocent Techie to Death," *Bangalore Mirror,* June 4; *Telegraph,* 2014, "Modi Cyber Army Eyes Early Ambush—Social Media Warriors Meet to Plan for 2016," July 2; Sreenivasan Jain, 2015, "'Modi Supporters on Social Media Abused My Disabled Son': Arun Shourie," NDTV.com, November 9; Amy Kazim, 2017, "Journalist's Killing Sends Shockwaves across India," *Financial Times,* September 6; Purusharth Aradhak, 2015, "Beef Murder Bid to Stir Hatred Ahead of Polls?" *Times of India,* October 1.

26. Rahul Bedi, 2017, "Controversial Priest to Lead India's Biggest State; Adityanath Accused of Attempted Murder and Inciting Violence against Muslims," *Irish Times,* March 20; Snigdha Poonam, 2017a, "Yogi Adityanath Takes Charge as CM: UP's Hindutva Fringe Feels Empowered," *Hindustan Times,* March 24; Snigdha Poonam, 2017b, "The Rise and Rise of Yogi Adityanath," *Hindustan Times,* March 25; Dhirendra K. Jha, 2017, *Shadow Armies,* Kindle edition, Juggernaut Books, location 409; Amy Kazmin, 2017, "Elevation of Hindu Firebrand Casts Doubt on Modi's Avowed Agenda," *Financial Times,* March 20.

27. Association for Democratic Reform: https://adrindia.org/content/analysis-criminal-background-financial-education-gender-and-other-details-ministers-uttar.

28. Agence France-Presse, 2017, "Outspoken Journalist's Murder Sparks Outcry in India," September 6; Rollo Romig, 2019, "Railing against India's Right-Wing Nationalism Was a Calling. It Was Also a Death Sentence," *New York Times,* May 14; Snigdha Poonam, 2017c, "Nikhil Dadhich, Ashish Mishra Accused of Hate Tweets against Gauri Lankesh, Unrepentant," *Hindustan Times,* September 9; Siddhartha Deb, 2018, "The Killing of Gauri Lankesh," *Columbia Business Review,* Winter.

29. Maseeh Rahman, 2014, "Indian Prime Minister Claims Genetic Science Existed in Ancient Times," *Guardian,* October 28; *Times of India,* 2013, "Sonia Hits Out at Modi over Nehru Barb"; Christophe Jaffrelot and Pradyumna Jairam, 2019, "BJP Has Been Effective in Transmitting Its Version of Indian History to Next Generation of Learners," *Indian Express,* November 16; see also chapter 2.

30. *Reuters News,* 2014, "India's Modi Budgets $33 Million to Help Build World's Tallest Statue," July 10; Snigdha Poonam, 2018, "One Statue, Two Visitors, Different Views," *Hindustan Times,* November 2.

31. *Times of India,* 2020, "PM Makes Splash with First Seaplane Flight from Kevadia," November 1; Manoj Mishra, 2013, "Mirage of a River," *Down to Earth,* May 31; Rajiv Khanna, 2019, "The Dark Side of Sabarmati River Development," *Down to Earth,* March 27.

32. Prabodhan Pol, 2018, "Understanding Bhima Koregaon," *The Hindu,* January 4; Ajeet Mahale, 2018, "Police Ploy to Gain More Time: Gonsalves' Wife," *The Hindu,* August 29; *Scroll.in,* 2018, "Bhima Koregaon Case: Maharashtra Moves SC against Delhi HC Order Releasing Activist Gautam Navlakha," October 3.

33. FRED, https://fred.stlouisfed.org/series/INDGDPRQPSMEI; Kat Devlin, 2019, "A Sampling of Public Opinion in India," Pew Research Center, Washington, DC, March 25.

34. Sachin Ravikumar and Munsif Vengattil, 2019, "Modi Proclaims a Cleaner India, But the Reality May Be More Murky," *Reuters News,* May 16; Aarefa Johari, 2019, "The Modi Years: How Successful Is the Swachh Bharat Mission or Clean India Campaign?" *Scroll.in,* February 4; Diane Coffey and Dean Spears, 2017, "Why Doesn't Anybody Know If Swachh Bharat Mission Is Succeeding?" *Ideas for India,* July 10; Centre of Science and Environment, 2019, *State of India's Environment 2019,* New Delhi, 40–41; Diane Coffey, Nathan Franz, and Dean Spears, 2021, "What Can We Learn about Swachh Bharat Mission from NFHS-5 Factsheets?" February 2.

35. Bhitush Luthra and Harsh Yadava, 2019, "Is the Ganga Basin Drowning in Shit?" *Down to Earth,* October 4.

36. Tushaar Shah and Abhishek Rajan, 2019. "Cleaning the Ganga: Rethinking Irrigation Is Key," *Economic and Political Weekly* 54 (39): 57–66; Centre of Science and Environment, 2019, *State of India's Environment 2021,* New Delhi, 302–304; Venkatesh Dutta et al., 2018, "Impact of River Channelization and Riverfront Development on Fluvial Habitat: Evidence from Gomti River, a Tributary of Ganges, India," *Environmental Sustainability* 1 (2): 167–184; M. Rajshekhar, 2019, "Three Ways in Which the Modi Government Is Ruining the Ganga," *Scroll.in,* January 19.

37. Ranjana Mall and Sangeeta Rani, 2020, "Women's Satisfaction with Pradhan Mantri Ujjwala Yojana (PMUY)," *International Journal of Home Science* 6 (1): 363–368; Sunil Mani, Abhishek Jain, Saurabh Tripathi, and Carlos F. Gould, 2020, "The Drivers of Sustained Use of Liquified Petroleum Gas in India," *Nature Energy* 5 (June): 450–457.

38. Simon Sturdee, 2019, "India's Modi on Course for Big Election Win," Agence France-Presse, May 23; Dexter Filkins, 2019, "Blood and Soil in India," *The New Yorker,* December 9; Rishabh R. Jain, 2019, "In India's Election, Voters Feed on 'Fake News' from Social Media, But Take It Seriously," *USA Today Online,* April 9; Swati Chaturvedi, 2019 (2016), *I Am a Troll,* Kindle edition, Juggernaut Books, location 1031; Snigdha Poonam and Samarth Bansal, 2019, "Misinformation Is Endangering India's Election," *The Atlantic,* April 1; Vindu Goel, Sheera Frenkel, and Suhasini Raj, 2019, "Flood of Fake Posts Tests Facebook as India Votes," *New York Times,* April 2.

39. Kiran Tare, 2019, "Maharashtra: Maoists Strike Back," *India Today,* February 9; *India Today,* 2018, "Modi Renames 3 Islands of Andaman and Nicobar: Other Projects Announced by the PM," December 31.

40. Chaturvedi 2019 (2016), Location 903.

41. Poonam and Bansal 2019; Sheera Frenkel and Davey Alba, 2021, "In India, the Ugliness on Facebook Is Amplified," *New York Times,* October 25.

42. Navin Chawla, 2019, *Every Vote Counts: The Story of India's Elections,* New Delhi, HarperCollins, 138–139; Supreme Court of India, 2018, "Public Interest Foundation vs Union Of India," https://indiankanoon.org/doc/146283621/.

43. Gautam Bhatia, 2021, "A Docket Full of Unresolved Constitutional Cases," *The Hindu,* December 7.

44. R. Nagaraj, 2015, "Size and Structure of India's Private Corporate Sector Implications for the New GDP Series," *Economic and Political Weekly* 50 (45): 45; Ministry of Corporate Affairs, *Annual Reports,* various years, Statements IX and

X available at https://mca.gov.in/content/mca/global/en/data-and-reports/reports/annual-reports/companies-2013.html; Alwyn Furtado, 2018, "Direct Tax Audit of Shell Companies," *Journal of Government Audit and Accounts,* January 2.

45. Deutsche Welle, 2019, "India Elections: Narendra Modi's BJP Set to Sweep Back to Power," May 23; Gurcharan Das, 2019, "Strong State, Strong Society: The Reforms India Needs Prime Minister Narendra Modi to Courageously Undertake," *Economic Times,* May 31.

46. Agence France-Presse, 2019, "Amnesty Chief Vows to Defy India Bid to 'Crush' Criticism," September 16.

47. Bhatia 2021.

48. *Statesman,* 2020, "India's Secular Construct-II," February 14; Supreme Court decision available at www.sci.gov.in/pdf/JUD_2.pdf; Bharat Bhushan, 2019, "How Will Modi's New India Look?" *Business Standard,* August 26.

49. Anup Sharma, 2019, "India Deploys Troops as Protestors Defy Curfew over Citizen Bill," Agence France-Presse, December 12; Benjamin Parkin, 2019, "Modi Defiant as Citizenship Bill Riots Escalate," December 19; Stephanie Findlay and Benjamin Parkin, 2019, "India Shuts Down Mobile Networks as Protests Spread," *Financial Times,* December 19; Namita Bhandare, 2019, "Anti-CAA Protests Have Shown Women Can Lead," *Hindustan Times,* December 27; Newley Purnell and Jeff Horwitz, 2021, "Facebook Services Are Used to Spread Religious Hatred in India, Internal Documents Show," *Wall Street Journal Online,* October 23; BBC .com, 2020, "Shaheen Bagh: Anurag Thakur, Parvesh Varma Penalised for Comments," January 29; Bhatia 2021.

50. Shivam Vij, 2019, "Why Haven't Others in India Inc Questioned the Modi Government, Like Rahul Bajaj Did?" *Quartz India,* December 2; Dev Chatterjee, 2019, "Rahul Bajaj Criticism Can Hurt National Interest: FM," *Business Standard,* December 2.

51. *Eurosurveillance,* 2020, "First Cases of Coronavirus Disease 2019 (COVID-19) in the WHO European Region, 24, January to 21, February 2020," 25 (9), March 5.

Chapter 23: COVID-19 Bares the Moral Decay

1. I. D. Mills, 1986, "The 1918–1919 Influenza Pandemic—the Indian Experience." *Indian Economic and Social History Review* 23 (1): 10, 22, 32, 34–36.

2. Ramanan Laxminarayan, 2020, "Covid-19: A Response Now Will Help Mitigate Impact," *Hindustan Times,* March 9; Jeffrey Gettleman and Kai Schultz, 2020, "Modi Orders 3-Week Total Lockdown for All 1.3 Billion Indians," *New York Times,*

March 24. The data on the spread of the virus comes from *Our World in Data*, available at https://github.com/owid/covid-19-data/tree/master/public/data/.

3. Basharat Peer, 2020, "A Friendship, a Pandemic, and a Death beside the Highway," *New York Times*, July 31.

4. Government of India, 2017, *Economic Survey 2016–17*, Ministry of Finance, New Delhi, January, 267.

5. Peer 2020; Snigdha Poonam, 2020, "Virus and the Village: A Covid Chronicle," *Hindustan Times*, April 20; Billy Perrigo, 2020, "It Was Already Dangerous to Be Muslim in India. Then Came the Coronavirus," *Time*, April 3; Amit Agnihotri, 2021, "SC Flags Fake News, Slander on Social Media," *Tehelka*, September 28; *India Today*, 2020, "Tablighi Jamaat Case: Delhi Court Acquits 36 Foreigners Accused of Violating Covid Guidelines, Visa Norms," December 16.

6. On seroprevalence studies, see https://twitter.com/PIB_India/status/1417443252404297728; *Down to Earth*, 2021, "ICMR Sero Survey Finds Antibodies in only 21.5% Indians," February 4.

7. Murad Banaji and Aashish Gupta, 2021, "Lessons from India's All-Cause Mortality Data," *The Hindu*, August 20; Murad Banaji, 2021, "The COVID-19 Pandemic in India: Data, Stories, and Myths," Kerala Council of Historical Research, July 23, available at https://youtu.be/YVAssVJbHpk.

8. Azim Premji University, 2021, "State of Working India 2021," Bengaluru, 20.

9. FRED, https://fred.stlouisfed.org/series/INDGDPRQPSMEI; Agence France-Presse, 2020, "India Re-Opens despite Record Virus Infections," June 8; Banaji 2021; Jean Drèze and Anmol Somanchi, 2021, "The Covid-19 Crisis and People's Right to Food," *SocArXiv*, June 1, doi:10.31235/osf.io/ybrmg, 1–2, 8; Rakesh Mohan, 2021, "The Response of the Reserve Bank of India to Covid-19: Do Whatever It Takes," Centre for Social and Economic Progress Working Paper No. 8, June 17, 6, 8–9, 11.

10. United Nations Conference on Trade and Development, "Investment Trends Monitor," https://unctad.org/system/files/official-document/diaeiainf2021d1_en.pdf; Reserve Bank Handbook, https://rbi.org.in/scripts/BS_ViewBulletin.aspx?Id=20357; Biswajit Dhar and K. S. Chalapati, 2021. "'Record' FDI Inflows, Yes, Cause for Celebration, No," *The Hindu*, June 17; Deepak Korgaonkar, 2020, "Markets in 2020," *Business Standard*, December 31.

11. FRED, https://fred.stlouisfed.org/series/NAEXKP01INQ652S; Government of India, 2021, "Press Note: Second Advance Estimates of National Income, 2020–21," Ministry of Statistics and Programme Implementation, New Delhi, February 26, Statement 5, 8; Azim Premji University 2021, 26, 33, 45, 56, 59, 85, 102;

Mrinalini Jha and Rosa Abraham, 2021, "Reading between Pandemic's Economic Shockwaves: Among Worst Hit Are Our Teachers and Small Business Owners," *Times of India.*

12. Rakesh Kochhar, 2021, "In the Pandemic, India's Middle Class Shrinks and Poverty Spreads While China Sees Smaller Changes," Pew Research Center, Washington, DC, March 18; S. Subramanian, 2021, "Pandemic-Induced Poverty in India after the First Wave of COVID-19: An Elaboration of Two Earlier Estimates," The Hindu Centre for Politics and Public Policy, August 19; Rohit Azad and Shouvik Chakraborty, 2022, "A Tale of Two Indias," *The India Forum,* January 28.

13. Drèze and Somanchi 2021, 1, 2, 8; Jean Drèze and Vipul Kumar Paikra, 2020, "The Uneven Decline of Health Services Across States During Lockdown," *Wire,* October 5.

14. Azim Premji University 2021, 21–22, 68; Pinelopi Koujianou Goldberg, 2020, "What COVID Is Costing Women," *Project Syndicate,* November 19.

15. Ghose 2019, Table 5.2.

16. *United News of India,* 2020, "Cabinet OKs Farmers (Empowerment and Protection) Agreement on Price Assurance, Farm Services Ordinance," June 3.

17. *Press Trust of India,* 2020, "Ordinance on Allowing Farmers to Sell Outside Mandis as Violative of Federal Structure," June 5; Karan Deep Singh, 2020, "'The Lockdown Killed My Father': Farmer Suicides Add to India's Virus Misery," *New York Times,* September 8; *Reuters News,* 2020, "India's Modi Defends New Law as Critics Warn of Risks to Farmers," September 17; David Pilling, 2014, "A Vote for Modi Could Make India More Chinese," *Financial Times,* March 19.

18. *Reuters News.* 2020. "Indian Farmers Intensify Protests over New Grain Bills," September 24; Aarefa Johari, 2021, "Beyond Punjab-Haryana: Meet Farmers Protesting against New Farm Laws across India from Rajasthan and Bihar to Maharashtra and Kerala, Opposition to the Three Agricultural Laws Passed in, September Is Intensifying," *Scroll.in,* January 11; Harsh Mander, 2021, "Harsh Mander: Six Months On, India's Protesting Farmers Are Creating History," *Scroll.in,* May 30; Richard Mahapatra, 2021, "An Agrarian Biopsy," *Down To Earth,* February 16–28, 25.

19. See chapter 8.

20. World Bank, 2007, *World Development Report 2008: Agriculture and Economic Development,* Washington, DC, 97.

21. Sharat Pradhan, 2020, "At Ayodhya Bhoomi Pujan, Modi Became All-In-One; Proper Rituals Not Followed, Allege Pundits," *Wire,* August 17; *Indian Express,* 2020, "Congress Breaks Silence on Ayodhya Event, Priyanka Gandhi Says

Lord Ram Belongs to Everybody," August 4; Sandeep Phukan, 2020, "Ram Temple Bhoomi Pujan; Congress Walks a Tightrope," *The Hindu,* August 5.

22. Siddharth Varadarajan, 2020, "India's Priest King and His Shivering Gods," *The India Cable,* December 15; Vijayta Lalwani, 2021, "As Covid-19 Devastates Delhi, Central Vista Project Declared an Essential Service, Work Continues," *Scroll.in,* April 27.

23. *United News of India,* 2021, "India Beat All Odds to Fight Corona Virus: PM Modi," January 28; *Press Trust of India,* 2021, "We Are in the Endgame of COVID-19 Pandemic in India: Vardhan," March 7.

24. Devjyot Ghoshal and Krishna Das, 2021, "EXCLUSIVE Scientists Say India Government Ignored Warnings amid Coronavirus Surge," *Reuters News,* April 30; Vidya Krishna, 2022, "Modi's Doctors: How Four Men Botched India's COVID Response," *Caravan,* March 1. On the Delta variant, see www.cdc.gov/coronavirus/2019-ncov/variants/delta-variant.html; *Pioneer,* 2021, "Don't Evoke False Sense of Security over Covid: IMA," March 9.

25. *Wire,* 2021, "BJP Makes a Delayed U-Turn, Modi Says Kumbh Attendance Should Now Be 'Symbolic,'" April 17; Jatin Anand and Omar Rashid, 2021, "Delhi Imposes Six-Day Lockdown; U.P. Declines Allahabad HC Directive on Shutdown," *The Hindu Online,* April 19; Stephanie Findlay, Michael Peel, and Donato Paolo Mancini, 2021, "India Blocks Vaccine Exports in Blow to Dozens of Nations," *Financial Times,* March 25.

26. Romita Datta, 2021, "Bengal Assembly Polls: The Last Leg," *India Today,* April 5; Mujib Mashal, 2021, "A Fierce Election Tests Modi's Campaign to Remake India," *New York Times,* April 7; *Times Now,* 2021, "Huge Turnout at PM Modi's Bengal Rally amid COVID Spike Draws Flak from Rahul Gandhi," April 18.

27. Sameer Yasir, 2021, "Their Father Was Dying, So Two Brothers in India Went on a Desperate Hunt for Oxygen," *New York Times,* May 4.

28. Aniruddha Ghosal, Aijaz Hussain, and Tim Sullivan, 2021, "The Poor, the Rich: In a Sick India, All Are on Their Own," Associated Press, May 23.

29. Martin Robinson, 2021, "First Passengers to Arrive in the UK after India Was Put on the 'Red List.'" *Mail Online,* April 23; Agence France-Presse, 2021, "Airfares Soar, Private Jets in Demand as Rich Indians Flee Covid," April 23; Nikhil Inamdar, 2021, "Covid Accelerates India's Millionaire Exodus," BBC News, April 13.

30. *Hindustan Times,* 2021, "'Moral Fabric Dismembered': HC on Hoarding, Black Marketing amid Covid-19 Surge," May 6.

31. Hannah Ellis-Petersen and Aakash Hassan, 2021, "Kumbh Mela: How a Superspreader Festival Seeded Covid across India," *Guardian,* May 29; *Hindustan*

Times, 2021, "Covid Quietly Ravages Rural UP," May 7; Jeffrey Gettleman and Suhasini Raj, 2021, "Covid Desperation Is Spreading Across India," *New York Times,* May 11, updated May 31; *Free Press Journal,* 2021, "Horrifying! Over 2,000 Bodies Found within 1,140 kms on Banks of River Ganga in Uttar Pradesh," May 15.

32. *Hindustan Times,* 2021, "BMC Announces Fresh Covid-19 Restrictions for Mumbai, in Addition to Maharashtra Govt Curbs," April 6; *Hindustan Times,* 2021, "Night curfew in Delhi But UP Rules It Out for Now," April 7; *Times Now,* 2021, "Curfews, Curbs Spark Fear of Another Mass Exodus as Migrants Flee Cities to Return Home," April 9; Mahesh Vyas, 2021, "Employment Rate Continues to Fall," *Business Standard,* June 7; Shreehari Paliath, 2021, "Second Wave of Covid-19 Has Left Migrant Workers in India with No Savings and Few Job Opportunities," *Scroll.in,* June 2; Shubham Kaushal, 2021, "India Failed Its Migrant Workers Yet Again during the Second Wave of Covid-19," *Scroll.in,* June 26.

33. *Times of India,* 2021, "Telangana: Bullocks Dead, Siblings Put Yoke on Shoulders, Plough Field to Survive," July 7.

34. Dipti Singh, 2021, "Budget Fails to Provide Hope to Dharavi's Leather Market," *Free Press Journal,* February 2; Emily Schmall and Karan Deep Singh, 2021, "'Don't Sacrifice Your Life to Visit the Taj Mahal': India Reopens but Fear Pervades," *New York Times,* July 6; Vivek Kaul, 2021, "In Post-Covid-India, Big Business Is Getting Bigger and Smaller Businesses Are Being Destroyed," *Mint,* June 17.

35. Mitali Mukherjee, 2021, "Education in India Has Plunged into a Crisis. Just Reopening Schools Isn't Enough," *The Wire,* October 1; Namita Bhandare, 2021, "Why the Pandemic Is a Child Rights Emergency in India," *Article-14.com,* June 18; Kumar Divyanshu, 2021, "The New Child Brides of India's Covid-19 Pandemic," *Article-14.com,* June 16.

36. C. P. Chandrasekhar, 2021, "Few Reasons to Hope Union Budget 2021 Will Be One 'Like Never Before' as Claimed by Finance Minister," *Frontline,* January 24; Government of India, 2021, *Economic Survey 2020–21,* Ministry of Finance, New Delhi, January, Volume 2, 56, 70; Roshan Kishore, 2021, "Recovering Economy Faces Inflation Threat," *Hindustan Times,* June 15; Roshan Kishore and Vineet Sachdev, 2021, "India's Tax Burden Shifted from Boardrooms to Petrol Pumps during Covid-19," *Hindustan Times,* June 1; *Reuters News,* 2021, "Economists Doubt India's New Loan Guarantees Will Boost Growth," June 28; Reserve Bank of India Bulletin, July 2021, 20.

37. For equity inflows, see: www.fpi.nsdl.co.in/web/Reports/Yearwise.aspx?RptType=6; Benjamin Parkin, 2021, "Surging Fortunes of India Inc Contrast

with Covid Trauma," *Financial Times,* June 22; *India Cable,* 2021, "'India Takes Political Prisoners'; Pegasus Is State Attack on Democracy," July 19; Karan Deep Singh, 2021, "Weak Recovery Leaves India's Middle Class Anxious and Frugal," *New York Times,* November 30.

38. Murad Banaji and Aashish Gupta, 2021, "Estimates of Pandemic Excess Mortality in India Based on Civil Registration Data," www.medrxiv.org/content/10.1101/2021.09.30.21264376v1, September 30.

39. Chitrangada Choudhury, 2021, "Modi Is Worsening the Suffering from India's Pandemic: An Authoritarian Apparatus Is Being Turned on Wider Society with Lethal Consequences," *Scientific American,* May 24.

40. *Hindustan Times,* 2021, "1055 of Andheri Firm Given Fake Vax Shots," July 3; *Hindustan Times,* 2021, "Madhya Pradesh Govt Brushes Aside Allegation of Vaccination Irregularities," July 1; Aakash Hassan and Hannah Ellis-Petersen, 2022, "Indian Health Workers Allege Widespread Vaccine Certificate Fraud," *Guardian,* February 1.

41. Hannah Ellis-Petersen, 2021, "Fury in India over Death of 84-Year-Old Political Prisoner Stan Swamy," *Guardian,* July 5; Sadaf Modak, 2021, "Stan Swamy Dead," *Indian Express,* July 6.

42. Harsh Mander, 2021, "The Song of a Caged Bird: A Tribute to Fr Stan Swamy," *Scroll.in,* July 7; Deepak Tiwari, 2018, "Sudha Bharadwaj: Arrested Activist Who Led Legal Fight against Adani's Mines," *The Week,* September 7; Malini Subramaniam, 2019, "Dantewada Goes to Polls in the Shadow of Alleged Fake Encounters in Villages Protesting Adani Mine," *Scroll.in,* September 23; Chitrangada Choudhry, 2021, "Why Hidme Markam, a Voice for Adivasis, Is in Prison," *Article-14.com,* March 19.

43. Kunal Purohit, 2021, "Our New Database Reveals Rise in Sedition Cases in the Modi Era," *Article-14.com,* February 2, updated May 23; Emily Schmall and Sameer Yasir, 2021, "'Are We Human?' Modi's Use of Antiterror Law Draws Scrutiny from Courts," *New York Times,* October 12; Murad Banaji, 2021, "Why the IIT Kanpur Report on UP's COVID-19 Crisis Was Dishonest," *Wire,* October 20; Gurucharan Gollerkeri et al., 2020, "Public Affairs Index (2020): Governance in the States of India," Bangalore, Public Affairs Centre.

44. Zeba Siddiqui, 2021, "Indian Journalists Accused of Sedition over Protest Reporting," *Reuters News,* February 1; Benjamin Parkin and Amy Kazmin, 2021, "Twitter Blocks Accounts after Indian Government Demands," *Financial Times,* February 10; *Hindustan Times,* 2021, "India Stays at 142nd Position in World Press

Freedom Index," April 21; Reporters Without Borders, "World Press Freedom Index 2021," https://rsf.org/en/ranking; *The Wire*, 2021, "IT Department Raids Multiple Premises of Dainik Bhaskar Group, Bharat Samachar Channel," July 21.

45. *The Wire* 2021 [July 21]; Reporters Without Borders, "World Press Freedom Index 2022," https://rsf.org/en/country/india.

46. Alishan Jafri, 2021, "The 'Hindutva Ecosystem' Has a New Anti-Muslim Narrative. This Time Street Vendors Are the Target," *The Wire*, June 28; Rashmi Singh, 2021, "The Supreme Court Needs to Step In to Stop Mob Lynchings," *The India Forum*, June 19.

47. See chapters 20 and 22.

48. V-Dem Institute, 2021, *Autocratization Turns Viral: DEMOCRACY REPORT 2021*, March, www.v-dem.net/files/25/DR%202021.pdf; Anna Lührmann, Marcus Tannenberg, and Staffan I. Lindberg, 2018, "Regimes of the World (RoW): Opening New Avenues for the Comparative Study of Political Regimes," *Politics and Governance* 6 (1): 61.

49. Jaswal Srishti, 2021, "The Human Cost of India's Yearlong Farmers' Protest," Al Jazeera, November 30.

50. Pilling 2014; *Financial Times*, 2021, "Narendra Modi Is Humbled by India's Farmers," November 23.

Epilogue: A Feasible Idealism

1. Aarefa Johari, 2022, "Inside Patna's Exam Bub, Where a Million Hopes Die Every Year," *Scroll.in*, March 16.

2. Partha Dasgupta, 1988, "Trust as a Commodity," in Diego Gambetta, ed., *Trust: Making and Breaking Cooperative Relations*, Oxford, Blackwell.

3. Sunita Narain, 2021, "No Time to Lose, Says Sunita Narain on the New IPCC Report," www.cseindia.org/no-time-to-lose-says-sunita-narain-on-the-new-ipcc-report-10934; Chirag Dhara and Mathew Roxy Koll, 2021, "How and Why India's Climate Will Change in the Coming Decades," *The India Forum*, August 6; United States National Intelligence Council, 2021, "Climate Change and International Responses Increasing Challenges to US National Security through 2040," Washington, DC, October.

4. Omid Mazdiyasni et al., 2017, "Increasing Probability of Mortality During Indian Heat Waves," *Science Advances* 3 (6): DOI: 10.1126/sciadv.1700066; Bill McKibben, 2021, *Falter: Has the Human Game Begun to Play Itself Out?* New York, Henry Holt and Company, 60; Kapil Kajal, "Heatwave Takes a Toll on North

India's Wheat Yield," *India.mongbay.com*, June 8, 2022; Kim Stanley Robinson, 2021 (2020), *The Ministry for the Future*, Kindle edition, Orbit, locations 16, 19, 23; *The Economist*, 2021, "A Tale of Two Cities: What If a Deadly Heatwave Hit India?," July 3.

5. McKibben 2021, 38–39, 41; Ram Bhagat, 2018, "Climate Change, Vulnerability and Migration in India: Overlapping Hotspots," in S. Irudaya Rajan and Ram Bhagat, eds., *Climate Change, Vulnerability, and Migration*, London, Routledge, 20, 31–35; see also chapters 20 and 22; Poulomi Ghosh, 2021, "Mumbai's Nariman Point Will Be Under Water by 2050, Says Civic Body Chief; Explains Why," *Hindustan Times*, August 28; E. Somanathan, Rohini Somanathan, Anant Sudarshan, and Meenu Tewari, 2021, "The Impact of Temperature on Productivity and Labor Supply: Evidence from Indian Manufacturing," *Journal of Political Economy* 129 (6): 1797–1827.

6. Ghosh 2016, 16–17, 40–50.

7. *The Wire*, 2021, "Hindutva Leaders at Haridwar Event Call for Muslim Genocide," December 21; Umang Poddar, 2022, "Explainer: How the Jahangirpuri Demolitions Continued Despite the Supreme Court Stay," *Scroll.in*, April 20.

8. See chapters 20 and 22.

9. Pranab Bardhan, 2018, "Universal Basic Income—Its Special Case for India," *Indian Journal of Human Development*, January 11.

10. M. G. Arun, 2021, "India's Unicorn Boom," *India Today*, July 12; Aroon Purie, 2021, "From the Editor-in-Chief," *India Today*, July 12; *Financial Times*, 2021, "The New 'Venture Capitalists' Riding the Unicorn Boom," July 9.

11. Karthik Muralidharan et al., 2019, "Disrupting Education? Experimental Evidence on Technology-Aided Instruction in India," *American Economic Review* 109 (4): 1430; Sabrin Beg, Waqas Halim, Adrienne M. Lucas, and Umar Saif, 2022, "Engaging Teachers with Technology Increased Achievement, Bypassing Teachers Did Not," *American Economic Journal: Economic Policy* 14 (2): 86; Arefa Johri, 2021, "A New App Is Failing India's Fight against Child Malnutrition," *Scroll.in*, October 13; Tiwari, Umesh. 2022. "UP Board Paper Leak Nakal Mafia Overshadows Hi-Tech Arrangements to Stop Copying in up Board Exam," *Dainik Jagran*, March 30; Monika Mondal, 2021, "Investigation: Hidden Water Crisis behind India's Sugar Dominance," *The Third Pole*, July 8; Sadiq Naqvi and Snigdha Poonam, 2022, "The Untold Story of India's Rs 3,000-Crore Farmer Scheme Scam," *Scroll.in*, May 11; M. D. Madhusudan, 2020, "Missing the Forest for the Trees," January, https://mdmadhusudan.medium.com/missing-the-forest-for-the-trees-37a94c13ab8c.

12. Robert Putnam, Robert Leonardi, and Raffaella Nanetti, 1993, *Making Democracy Work,* Kindle edition, Princeton University Press, locations 91, 105, 109, 110, 116, 181.

13. Putnam et al. 1993, 173, 178.

14. See chapters 20 and 22; Suparna Chaudhry, 2022, "The Assault on Civil Society: Explaining State Crackdown On NGOs," *International Organization,* February: 1–42; Gautam Bhatia, 2022, "Comforting the Comfortable and Afflicting the Afflicted: The Supreme Court's FCRA Judgment," *Indian Constitutional Law and Philosophy,* April 12, https://indconlawphil.wordpress.com/2022/04/12/comforting-the-comfortable-and-afflicting-the-afflicted-the-supreme-courts-fcra-judgment/.

15. Patrick Heller, K. N. Harilal, and Shubham Chaudhuri, 2007, "Building Local Democracy: Evaluating the Impact of Decentralization in Kerala, India," *World Development* 35 (4): 626–627, Table 1 (p. 362), Table 6 (640), Tables 7 and 8a (641–642); James Manor, 2010, "Local Government," in Niraja Gopal Jayal and Pratap Bhanu Mehta, eds., *The Oxford Companion to Politics in India,* New Delhi, Oxford University Press, 64–67.

16. Esther Duflo, Greg Fischer, and Raghabendra Chattopadhyay, 2005, "Efficiency and Rent Seeking in Local Government: Evidence from Randomized Policy Experiments in India," working paper, MIT, February 28; Pranab Bardhan and Dilip Mookherjee, "Pro-Poor Targeting and Accountability of Local Governments in West Bengal," *Journal of Development Economics* 79: 303–327.

17. Madhav Gadgil, 2020, "Ecology Is for the People," *The India Forum,* January 10; K. A. Shaji, 2020, "Kerala Government Gives Go-Ahead to Athirappally Hydel Power Project: Decision Elicits Angry Response from a Cross-Section of Society," *Down to Earth,* June 10; K. A. Shaji, 2021, "Kerala Government Abandons Controversial Athirappilly Hydroelectric Project amid Widespread Protests," *Down to Earth,* October 7; T. M. Thomas Isaac and Richard Franke, 2001, *Local Democracy and Development,* New Delhi, LeftWord, 255–256; *Hindustan Times,* 2021, "'Destructive Activities Are Carried Out in the Name of Development': Madhav Gadgil," October 10.

INDEX

f denotes figure.